PRENTICE HALL

GENERAL SCIENCE

A Voyage of Adventure

PRENTICE HALL

GENERAL SCIENCE

A Voyage of Adventure

Dean Hurd
Physical Science Instructor
Carlsbad High School
Carlsbad, California

George F. Matthias
Earth Science Instructor
Croton-Harmon High School
Croton-on-Hudson, New York

Susan M. Johnson
Associate Professor of Biology
Ball State University
Muncie, Indiana

Edward Benjamin Snyder
Earth Science Instructor
Yorktown High School
Yorktown Heights, New York

Jill D. Wright
Professor of Science Education
University of Tennessee
Knoxville, Tennessee

PRENTICE HALL
Englewood Cliffs, New Jersey
Needham, Massachusetts

Prentice Hall General Science Program: Third Edition

Student Text and Annotated Teacher's Edition

Laboratory Manual and Annotated Teacher's Edition

Teacher's Resource Book

General Science Color Transparencies

General Science Courseware

Computer Test Bank with DIAL-A-TEST™ Service

Other programs in this series

Prentice Hall General Science *A Voyage of Discovery* © 1992

Prentice Hall General Science *A Voyage of Exploration* © 1992

General Science Reviewers

John K. Bennett
Science Specialist
State Department of Tennessee
Cookeville, Tennessee

Sue Teachey Bowden
Department of Science Education
East Carolina University
Greenville, North Carolina

Edith H. Gladden
Curriculum Specialist
Division of Science Education
Philadelphia, Pennsylvania

Gordon Neal Hopp
Carmel Junior High School
Carmel, Indiana

Stanley Mulak
Science Supervisor
Springfield School District
Springfield, Massachusetts

Richard Myers
Science Instructor
Cleveland High School
Portland, Oregon

Reading Consultant

Patricia N. Schwab
Chairman, Department of Education
Guilford College
Greensboro, North Carolina

ISBN 0-13-717869-7

10 9 8 7 6

Prentice-Hall of Australia, Pty. Ltd., Sydney
Prentice-Hall Canada Inc., Toronto
Prentice-Hall Hispanoamericana, S.A., Mexico
Prentice-Hall of India Private Ltd., New Delhi
Prentice-Hall International (UK) Limited, London
Prentice-Hall of Japan, Inc., Tokyo
Prentice-Hall of Southeast Asia Pte. Ltd., Singapore
Editora Prentice Hall do Brasil Ltda., Rio de Janeiro

Photograph credits begin on page 573

Cover Photographs

The three main branches of science studied in a General Science course are illustrated on the cover. The Green frog on the leaf represents Life Science. *(Michel Tcherevkoff, Image Bank)* The launch of *Apollo 15* from the Kennedy Space Center represents Physical Science. *(Photri, The Stock Market)* The stream running through a winter woodland represents Earth Science. *(Sorensen/Bohmer Olse, Tony Stone Worldwide)*

Back Cover Photographs

Top center, Bryon Crader/*Tom Stack & Associates;* Top right, O.S. Pettingill, Jr./*Photo Researchers;* Bottom left, Center for Astrophysics; Bottom center, Breck P. Kent/*Earth Scenes;* Bottom right, Nicholas Devore/*dpi*

Staff Credits

Editorial	Harry Bakalian, Pamela E. Hirschfeld, Maureen Grassi, Robert P. Letendre, Elisa Mui Eiger, Christine A. Portante
Art Direction	Arthur F. Soares, Susan Walrath, Laura Jane Bird
Production	Suse Cioffi, Christina Burghard, Lisa Meyerhoff, Cleasta Wilburn
Photo Research	Libby Forsyth
Marketing	Paul P. Scopa, Victoria Willows
Manufacturing	Loretta Moe, Denise Herkenrath
Consultant	Linda Grant

Prentice Hall
A Division of Simon & Schuster
Englewood Cliffs, New Jersey

Contents

UNIT ONE
Characteristics of Living Things 10–127

CHAPTER 1
Exploring Living Things 12–33
1-1 What Is Science? 14
1-2 Scientific Measurements 20
1-3 Tools of a Scientist 24
1-4 Safety in the Science Laboratory 28

CHAPTER 2
The Nature of Life 34–55
2-1 Characteristics of Living Things 36
2-2 Needs of Living Things 44
2-3 Chemistry of Living Things. 48

CHAPTER 3
Cells 56–77
3-1 Cell Structure and Function 58
3-2 Cell Activities 67

CHAPTER 4
Tissues, Organs, and Organ Systems 78–91
4-1 A Division of Labor 80
4-2 Organization of Living Things 81

CHAPTER 5
Interactions Among Living Things 92–119
5-1 Living Things and Their Environment 94
5-2 Food and Energy in the Environment 100
5-3 Relationships in an Ecosystem 107

SCIENCE GAZETTE 120–127
Katharine Payne and the "Language" of Elephants 120
Pests or Pesticides: Which Will It Be? 122
The Computer That Lives! 125

5

UNIT TWO
Classification of Living Things   128–309

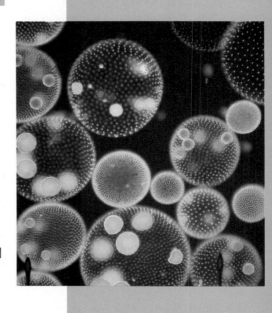

CHAPTER 6

Classification   130–145

6-1 History of Classification   132
6-2 Modern Classification Systems   135
6-3 The Five Kingdoms   140

CHAPTER 7

Viruses, Bacteria, and Protists   146–167

7-1 Viruses   148
7-2 Bacteria   152
7-3 Protozoans   158

CHAPTER 8

Nonvascular Plants and Plantlike Organisms   168–191

8-1 Algae   170
8-2 Fungi   178
8-3 Lichens and Slime Molds   184
8-4 Mosses and Liverworts   186

CHAPTER 9

Vascular Plants   192–215

9-1 Ferns   194
9-2 Seed Plants   196
9-3 Gymnosperms   204
9-4 Angiosperms   206

CHAPTER 10

Animals: Invertebrates   216–251

10-1 Characteristics of Invertebrates   218
10-2 Sponges   219
10-3 Coelenterates   221
10-4 Worms   225
10-5 Mollusks   229
10-6 Spiny-Skinned Animals   234
10-7 Arthropods   236
10-8 Insects   241

CHAPTER 11

Animals: Vertebrates   252–279

11-1 Fish   254
11-2 Amphibians   260
11-3 Reptiles   264
11-4 Birds   271

CHAPTER 12

Mammals 280–301

12-1 Characteristics of Mammals 282
12-2 Egg-Laying Mammals 284
12-3 Pouched Mammals 285
12-4 Placental Mammals 287

SCIENCE GAZETTE 302–307

Jane Goodall and the Chimps of Gombe Stream 302
Conservationists to the Rescue? 304
The Corn Is as High as a Satellite's Eye 307

UNIT THREE
Matter 310–357

CHAPTER 13

General Properties of Matter 312–327

13-1 Matter 314
13-2 Mass 315
13-3 Weight 317
13-4 Volume 319
13-5 Density 320

CHAPTER 14

Physical and Chemical Changes 328–349

14-1 Physical Properties and Changes 330
14-2 The Phases of Matter 331
14-3 Phase Changes 337
14-4 Chemical Properties and Changes 342

SCIENCE GAZETTE 350–357

W. Lincoln Hawkins—He Solved the Puzzle of the Aging Wires 350
Can the Energy of Volcanoes Be Harnessed? 352
Wired to the Sun 355

UNIT FOUR
Structure of Matter 358–411

CHAPTER 15

Atoms and Molecules 360–375

15-1 An Atomic Model of Matter 362
15-2 Structure of the Atom 365
15-3 The Molecule 370

CHAPTER 16
Elements and Compounds   376–389
16-1   Elements   378
16-2   Compounds   382

CHAPTER 17
Mixtures and Solutions   390–403
17-1   Properties of Mixtures   392
17-2   Types of Mixtures   395
17-3   Solutions   397

SCIENCE GAZETTE   404–411
Shirley Ann Jackson: Helping Others Through Science   404
Wasting Time: The Nuclear Clock Ticks Down   406
The Right Stuff—Plastics   409

UNIT FIVE
Composition of the Earth   412–475

CHAPTER 18
Minerals   414–431
18-1   What Is a Mineral?   416
18-2   Uses of Minerals   424

CHAPTER 19
Rocks   432–449
19-1   Rocks of Liquid and Fire: Igneous Rocks   434
19-2   Rocks in Layers: Sedimentary Rocks   437
19-3   Rocks That Change: Metamorphic Rocks   441
19-4   The Rock Cycle   444

CHAPTER 20
Soils   450–467
20-1   Soil   452
20-2   Tropical Rain Forest Soil   455
20-3   Temperate Forest Soil   457
20-4   Prairie Grassland Soil   460
20-5   Desert Soil   461
20-6   Tundra Soil   462

SCIENCE GAZETTE   468–475
Maria Reiche—Solving the Mysteries of the Nazca Lines   468
Diving for Natural Treasures: A Risky Business?   470
Wanted! Space Pioneers   473

UNIT SIX
Structure of the Earth 476–549

CHAPTER 21
Internal Structure of the Earth 478–499
21-1 The Earth's Core and Earthquake Waves 480
21-2 Exploring the Earth's Mantle 486
21-3 The Earth's Crust and Floating Continents 492

CHAPTER 22
Surface Features of the Earth 500–521
22-1 The Earth's Surface: Landmasses 502
22-2 The Earth's Surface: Water 511

CHAPTER 23
Structure of the Atmosphere 522–541
23-1 The Layers of the Atmosphere 524
23-2 The Magnetosphere 535

SCIENCE GAZETTE 542–549
William Haxby Maps the Invisible Ocean Floor 542
Should People Build Lakes? 544
The Longest Winter 547

For Further Reading 550

Appendix A The Metric System 552

Appendix B The Laboratory Balance 553

Appendix C The Microscope 556

Glossary 559

Index 565

Amazing life forms of the ocean bottom

Characteristics of Living Things

The tiny submarine slips deeper and deeper into the ocean. Inside, three scientists prepare for their arrival on the sea floor. Outside the submarine, there is nothing but darkness. With a soft bump, the submarine touches bottom. The depth gauge shows 2590 meters. The water pressure is a crushing 264 kilograms per square centimeter. Lava oozes from cracks in the ocean floor. The lava heats the water to a blistering 371° C, hot enough to melt lead.

Suddenly the floodlights of the submarine flash on. The view is astounding. Giant clams and pale yellow mussels lie on the sand. A white crab walks by. The scientists wonder how living things can exist in such a harsh place. And they realize with excitement that finding out will be a great adventure. This is an adventure made possible by thousands of years of curiosity and learning about the nature of living things.

CHAPTERS

1 Exploring Living Things

2 The Nature of Life

3 Cells

4 Tissues, Organs, and Organ Systems

5 Interactions Among Living Things

1 Exploring Living Things

CHAPTER SECTIONS

1-1 What Is Science?

1-2 Scientific Measurements

1-3 Tools of a Scientist

1-4 Science Safety in the Laboratory

CHAPTER OBJECTIVES

After completing this chapter, you will be able to:

1-1 Describe the various steps of a scientific method.

1-2 Make and understand metric measurements.

1-3 Describe several tools used by scientists.

1-3 Compare different types of microscopes.

1-4 Apply safety procedures in the classroom laboratory.

A howling wind shook the walls of the wooden temporary building at Rocky Hill, Connecticut. Torrents of rain swept over the building's roof. With a groan, the building suddenly fell apart.

Unknown to the scientists at Rocky Hill, where the Connecticut State Dinosaur Park is located, the collapse of the building was soon to lead to an unexpected discovery. For later, when the earth was moved to make room for the new building, strange scratches were found on the exposed rock. An expert on dinosaurs, Dr. W. P. Coombs, Jr., of Western New England College in Massachusetts, was contacted.

Dr. Coombs took one look at the mysterious scratches and immediately knew what they were—dinosaur footprints. But there was more to the story. The scratches appeared in groups of three. Dr. Coombs concluded the scratches were made by an animal having three toes with sharp claws. They were clearly the marks of a meat-eating dinosaur.

Carefully, the scientist measured the distance between the footprints—130 centimeters. Dr. Coombs reasoned that only a very large animal, perhaps the 7-meter-long *Megalosaurus,* could take such long strides. There was something very peculiar about the footprints, however. Only the tips of the dinosaur's toes seemed to have touched the rock. But *Megalosaurus* did not run on its toes, at least not on land.

Dr. Coombs could draw only one conclusion. The prints were made under water, which kept most of the animal's weight off the rock. Dr. Coombs had discovered the first evidence of swimming, meat-eating dinosaurs. A simple accident, a sharp eye, and some smart detective work had led to a scientific discovery.

Megalosaurus—the first swimming, meat-eating dinosaur

1-1   What Is Science?

The universe around you and inside of you is really a collection of countless mysteries. It is the job of scientists to solve those mysteries. And, like any good detective, a scientist uses special methods to find truths about nature.

These truths are called facts. An example of a fact is that the earth is populated with millions of different kinds of living things. But science is more than a list of facts. Jules Henri Poincaré, a famous nineteenth-century French scientist, put it this way: "Science is built up with facts, as a house is with stones. But a collection of facts is no more a science than a heap of stones is a house."

So scientists go further than simply discovering facts. Scientists try to use facts to solve larger mysteries of nature. In this sense, you might think of facts as clues to scientific mysteries. An example of one of these larger mysteries is how the relatively few and simple organisms of three billion years ago gave rise to the many complex organisms that inhabit the earth today.

Figure 1-1 *It is a fact that this red diamondback rattlesnake injects poison into its prey. It is a hypothesis that the rattler locates its injured victim by following the smell of its own venom.*

Scientific Methods

To uncover scientific facts and solve scientific mysteries, scientists can use any one of a number of **scientific methods.** There are various basic steps in these methods. But these steps need not be followed in any particular order, although some orders make more sense than others. Sometimes the order in which a scientist tries to solve a mystery depends on the nature of the mystery. **The basic parts of any scientific method are the following:**

Stating the problem

Gathering information

Suggesting an answer for the problem

Performing an experiment to see whether the suggested answer makes sense

Recording and analyzing the results of experiments or other observations

Stating conclusions

The following example shows how a scientific method was used to solve an actual problem. As you will see, the basic steps of a scientific method often overlap.

Stating the Problem

Most people know enough to walk the other way if they should run into a rattlesnake. However, if you could safely observe a rattler, you would discover a rather curious kind of behavior.

With fangs flashing and body arching, the deadly rattler strikes. The snake's fangs quickly inject poisonous venom into its victim. Then, in a surprise move, the rattler allows the wounded animal to run away! But the rattlesnake will not miss its intended meal. After waiting for its poison to take effect, the rattler follows the trail of the injured animal.

Although the rattler cannot see well, somehow it manages to find its victim on the dense, dark, forest floor. Clearly, something leads the snake to its prey. What invisible trail does the snake follow in tracking down its bitten prey? This is a *problem* that scientists recently tried to solve.

Figure 1-2 *The rattler does not have an especially keen sense of sight. Its pit organs detect the body heat given off by this field mouse.*

Gathering Information on the Problem

The first step in solving a scientific problem is to find out or review everything important related to it. For example, the scientists trying to solve the rattlesnake mystery knew that a rattlesnake's eyes are only sensitive to visible light. However, they also knew that a pair of organs located under the animal's eyes detects invisible light in the form of heat. These heat-sensing pits pick up signals from warmblooded animals. The signals help the snake to locate its intended prey. But the heat-sensing pits cannot help the snake find a wounded victim that has run many meters away. Some other process must be responsible for that.

The scientists knew that a rattler's tongue "smells" certain odors in the air. The rattler's tongue picks up these odors on an outward flick. The odors enter the snake's mouth on an inward flick. The scientists also knew that the sight or smell of an unbitten animal did not trigger the rattler's tracking action. Using all this information, the scientists were able to suggest a solution to the problem.

Forming a Hypothesis

A suggested solution is called a **hypothesis** (high-PAH-thuh-sis). A hypothesis is almost always formed after the information related to the problem is carefully studied. But sometimes a hypothesis is the result of creative thinking that often involves bold, original guesses about the problem. In this regard, forming a hypothesis is like good detective work, which involves not only logic, but hunches, intuition, and the taking of chances.

To the problem, "What invisible trail does a rattler follow in tracking down its prey?" the scientists suggested a hypothesis. The scientists suggested that *after the snake wounds its victim, the snake follows the smell of its own venom to locate the animal.*

Experimenting

The scientists next had to test their hypothesis by performing certain activities and recording the results. These activities are called experiments. Whenever scientists test a hypothesis using an experiment, they must make sure that the results of the experiment clearly support or do not support the hypothesis. That is, they must make sure that one, and only one, factor affects the results of the experiment. The factor being tested in an experiment is called the **variable.** In any experiment, only one variable is tested at a time. Otherwise it would not be clear which variable had caused the results of the experiment.

Figure 1-3 *Sinking its fangs into its victim, the rattler injects the mouse with deadly poison.*

In the rattlesnake experiments, the scientists tested whether the snake's venom formed an invisible trail that the snake followed. The venom was the variable, or single factor, that the scientists wanted to test. The scientists performed the experiment to test this variable.

First, the scientists dragged a dead mouse that had been struck and poisoned by a rattlesnake along a curving path on the bottom of the snake's empty cage. When the snake was placed in its cage, its tongue flicked rapidly, its head moved slowly from side to side, and it followed the exact trail the scientists had laid out. The results seemed clear, but the scientists had one more experiment to perform.

To be sure it was the scent of the venom and no other odor that the snake followed, the scientists ran a **control** experiment. A control experiment is run in exactly the same way as the experiment with the variable, but the variable is left out. So the scientists dragged an unbitten dead mouse along a path in the cage. The experiment was exactly the same, except this mouse had not been poisoned. This time the snake seemed disinterested. Its tongue flicked very slowly and it did not follow the path.

Recording and Analyzing Data

The rattlesnake experiments were repeated many times, and the scientists carefully recorded the **data** from the experiments. Data include observations such as measurements.

Stating a Conclusion

After analyzing the recorded data, the scientists concluded that the scent of venom was the only factor that could cause a rattlesnake to follow its bitten victim. Rattlesnake venom is made up of many different substances. Exactly which ones are responsible for the snake's behavior are as yet unknown. As is often the case in science, a solution to one mystery brings to light another mystery. Using scientific methods similar to those described here, scientists hope to follow a path that leads to the solution to this new mystery.

Branches of Science

Science is divided into many branches according to subject matter. Each branch is made up of a small or large topic in science. There are three main branches of science.

Life science   Life science deals with living things and their parts and actions. Smaller branches of life science include **zoology,** the study of animals, and **botany,** the study of plants.

Earth science   Earth science is the study of the earth and its rocks, oceans, volcanoes, earthquakes, atmosphere, and other features. Usually, the earth sciences also include **astronomy.** Astronomers explore nature beyond the earth. They study such objects as stars, planets, and moons.

Physical science   Physical science is the study of matter and energy. For example, some physical scientists explore what substances are made of and how they change and combine. This branch of physical science is called **chemistry.** Other physical scientists study forms of energy such as heat and light. This is the science of **physics.**

Figure 1-4   *Life science includes the study of animals such as these penguins who nest in Antarctica.*

Figure 1-5   *The earth-orbiting Space Shuttle (left) helps gather important information about the nature of the earth and the universe beyond. The laws of motion, a part of the science of physics, explain how Olympic cyclists speed along their circular track (right).*

1. What is a hypothesis?
2. Why does an experiment have only one variable?
3. What are the three main branches of science?

1-2 Scientific Measurements

As part of the process of experimenting and gathering information, scientists must make accurate measurements. They must also be able to share their information with other scientists. To do this, scientists must speak the same measurement "language." **The common language of measurement in science used all over the world is the metric system.** Scientists often refer to the **metric system** as the International System of Units, or SI.

The metric system is a decimal system, or a system based on ten. That is, each unit in the metric system is ten times larger or ten times smaller than the next unit. Metric calculations are easy to do because they involve multiplying or dividing by ten. Some frequently used metric units and their abbreviations are listed in Figure 1-6.

Figure 1-6 *The metric system is easy to use because it is based on units of ten. What is the basic unit of length in the metric system?*

COMMONLY USED METRIC UNITS

Length

Length is the distance from one point to another.

A meter is slightly longer than a yard.

1 meter (m) = 100 centimeters (cm)

1 meter = 1000 millimeters (mm)

1 meter = 1,000,000 micrometers (μm)

1 meter = 1,000,000,000 nanometers (nm)

1 meter = 10,000,000,000 angstroms (Å)

1000 meters = 1 kilometer (km)

Mass

Mass is the amount of matter in an object.

A gram has a mass equal to about one paper clip.

1 kilogram (kg) = 1000 grams (g)

1 gram = 1000 milligrams (mg)

1000 kilograms = 1 metric ton (t)

Volume

Volume is the amount of space an object takes up.

A liter is slightly larger than a quart.

1 liter (L) = 1000 milliliters (mL) or 1000 cubic centimeters (cm^3)

Temperature

Temperature is the measure of hotness or coldness in degrees Celsius (°C).

0°C = freezing point of water

100°C = boiling point of water

Length

The **meter** is the basic unit of length in the metric system. One meter is equal to 39.4 inches. Sometimes scientists must measure distances much longer than a meter, such as the distance a bird may fly across a continent. To do this, scientists use a unit called a kilometer. The prefix *kilo-* means 1000. So a kilometer is 1000 meters, or about the length of five city blocks.

A hummingbird, on the other hand, is too small to be measured in meters or kilometers. So scientists use the centimeter. The prefix *centi-* means that 100 of these units make a meter. Thus there are 100 centimeters in a meter. The hummingbird is only about 5 centimeters long. For objects even smaller, another division of the meter is used. The millimeter is one thousandth of a meter. The prefix *milli-* means ¹⁄₁₀₀₀. One meter equals 1000 millimeters. In

Figure 1-7 *Scientists use many tools to study their world. A metric ruler (top, left) measures length. A graduated cylinder (top, right) helps measure the volume of liquids. A triple-beam balance (bottom, left) may be used to measure mass. And a Celsius thermometer is used to measure temperature.*

Practicing Metric Measurements

Using a meterstick, measure the length of the following objects. Choose the proper metric prefixes for the measurements.

height of a door

diameter of a dime

length of your foot

thickness of a slice of bread

Look around your home for products whose volume is measured in liters or whose mass is measured in grams. Make a list of at least ten items. For each example, give the product and the measurement.

Figure 1-8 *In the metric system, height or length is measured in units called meters. As you can see from this photograph, height varies from one person to another.*

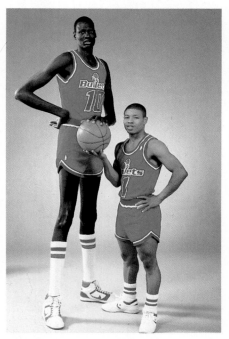

bright light, the diameter of the pupil of your eye is about 1 millimeter. Even this unit is too large to use when describing the sizes of the smallest germs, such as the bacteria that cause sore throats. These germs are measured in micrometers, or millionths of a meter, and nanometers, or billionths of a meter.

Volume

The amount of space an object takes up is called its volume. The **liter** is the basic unit of volume in the metric system. The liter is slightly larger than the quart. Here again scientists use divisions of the liter to measure smaller volumes. The milliliter, or cubic centimeter, is $\frac{1}{1000}$ of a liter. There are 1000 milliliters, or cubic centimeters, in a liter. The volumes of both liquids and gases are measured in liters and milliliters. For example, a scientist may remove a few milliliters of blood from an animal in order to study the types of substances the blood contains.

Mass and Weight

The **kilogram** is the basic unit of mass in the metric system. **Mass** is a measure of the amount of matter in an object. Your experience tells you that there is more matter in a tree trunk than in a leaf. Therefore, a tree trunk has more mass than a leaf.

One kilogram is slightly more than two pounds. For smaller units of mass, the gram is used. Remember that the prefix *kilo-* means 1000. There are 1000 grams in a kilogram. One milligram measures an even smaller mass, $\frac{1}{1000}$ of a gram. How many milligrams are there in one kilogram?

Mass is not the same as **weight.** Weight is a measure of the force of attraction between objects due to **gravity.** All objects exert a force of gravity on other objects. The strength of the force depends on the mass of the objects and the distance between them. You may not be aware of it, but the gravity of your body pulls the earth toward you. At the same time, the gravity of the earth pulls you toward its center. The mass of the earth is, however, much greater than your mass. As a result, the force of gravity you exert is very small compared to that of the earth. You remain on the surface of the earth because of

Figure 1-9 *Astronaut Bruce McCandless, weightless in space, uses his jet-powered backpack and foot restraint to maneuver around the Space Shuttle.*

the force of the earth's gravity. And it is the size of this force that is measured by your weight. As the distance between objects decreases, the force of gravity between them increases. Therefore, you would weigh a little more at sea level than on the top of a mountain. At sea level, you are closer to the center of the earth.

It may be apparent to you now that mass is a constant and weight is not. Because weight can change, it is not a constant. For example, a person who weighs a certain amount on Earth would weigh much less on the moon. Can you explain this? The force of gravity of the moon is about one sixth that of the earth. Therefore, a person's weight on the moon would be one sixth that on the earth. The mass of the person, however, does not change. It is the same on the moon or the earth because the amount of matter in the person does not change.

DENSITY The measurement of how much mass is contained in a given volume of an object is called its **density.** Density can be defined as the mass per unit volume of a substance. The following formula shows the relationship between density, mass, and volume.

$$\text{density} = \frac{\text{mass}}{\text{volume}}$$

Activity

Metric Conversion

Complete the following metric conversions.

a. 21,537 millimeters = _____ meters

b. 425 kilometers = _____ centimeters

c. 6.87 grams = _____ kilograms

d. 96.3 milliliters = _____ liters

e. 11 milliliters = _____ cubic centimeters

Figure 1-10 *Scientists measure temperature in degrees Celsius. Temperature affects all living things. This chameleon must step lightly as it walks across a hot road.*

Density is an important concept because it allows scientists to identify and compare substances. Each substance has its own characteristic density. For example, the density of water is $1g/cm^3$ while that of butterfat is $0.91g/cm^3$. Based on this data, will butterfat sink or float in water?

Temperature

Scientists measure temperature according to the **Celsius** scale, in degrees Celsius. The fixed points on the scale are the freezing point of water at sea level, 0° C, and the boiling point of water, 100° C. The range between these points is 100 degrees, and each degree is $1/100$ of the difference between the freezing point and boiling point of water. Normal human body temperature is 37° C, while some birds maintain a body temperature of 41° C.

SECTION REVIEW

1. What are the basic units of length, volume, and mass in the metric system?
2. What is the difference between mass and weight?
3. If a scientist wanted to identify an unknown substance, would it be more helpful for her to measure its mass or its density? Explain.

Activity

Using Metric Measurements

Use the appropriate scientific tools and the metric system to measure the following. Construct a chart of your results.

 length of the textbook
 length of your arm
 temperature indoors
 temperature outdoors
 volume of a glass of water
 volume of a bucket of water

1-3   Tools of a Scientist

Scientists use a wide variety of tools, ranging from simple microscopes to complex computers. The scientist chooses the tools most useful for solving a specific problem.

Microscopes

Have you ever looked through a magnifying glass to examine a leaf or the body of an insect more closely? If so, you used a simple **microscope.** A microscope is an instrument that produces an enlarged image of an object. A magnifying glass is a simple

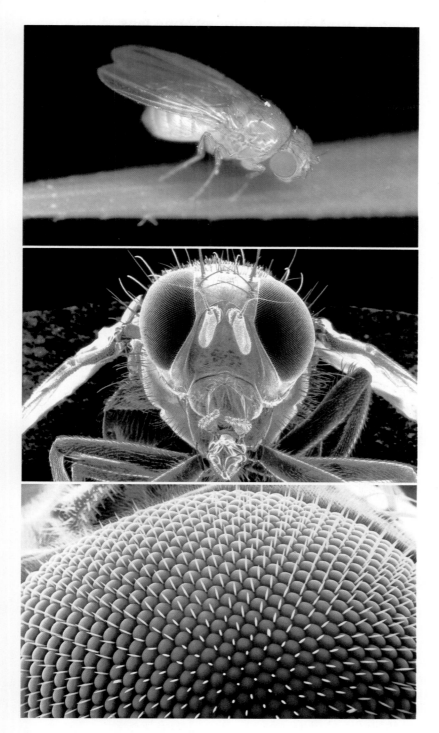

Figure 1-11 *On this unmagnified fruitfly* (top), *notice the two large, red structures, which are the eyes. Then look at the head of the fruitfly, which is magnified 60 times* (center). *The two rounded structures on each side of the head are the eyes. A scanning electron microscope produced this detailed, three-dimensional image of the eye of the fruitfly* (bottom).

microscope because it has only one **lens.** A lens is a curved piece of glass that bends light rays as they pass through it. In certain lenses, this bending increases the size of an object's image.

THE COMPOUND LIGHT MICROSCOPE   Optical, or light, microscopes that have more than one lens are called **compound light microscopes.** These microscopes use light to make an object look up to 2000 times larger than it really is. Compound light microscopes can be used to examine the cells in your body.

ELECTRON MICROSCOPES   An **electron microscope** does not use light to magnify the image of an object. Instead, it uses a beam of tiny particles called electrons. Pictures produced by this beam are focused on a television screen or photographic film. Electron microscopes can magnify objects hundreds of thousands of times. One type, the scanning electron microscope, or SEM, produces a three-dimensional

Career: *Electron Microscopist*

HELP WANTED: ELECTRON MICROSCOPIST Bachelor's degree in histotechnology preferred. Training in the operation of the electron microscope and the interpretation of electron micrographs required.

Until the invention of the electron microscope in the 1930s, scientists examined the inner structures of living things by viewing slices of plant and animal tissues through light microscopes. Light microscopes magnify only large cell structures, not tiny structures. The tiny cell structures can be seen only when viewed through an electron microscope. Users of electron microscopes need special training and extensive practice before they become **electron microscopists.** Once their skill is developed, they can use the electron microscope to bring objects as small as bacteria, viruses, or even atoms into focus.

Electron micrographs are photographs of specimens seen through the electron micro-scope. By studying these photographs, research scientists learn more about the normal activities of cells. Human tissue micrographs help doctors diagnose patients.

Electron microscopists work in hospitals, universities, and research laboratories. If you wish to know more about a career in electron microscopy, write to the National Society for Histotechnology, P.O. Box 36, Lanham, MD 20706.

image. Biologists use electron microscopes to study such things as viruses and parts of cells.

Lasers

A simple microscope uses light and lenses to magnify an image. The laser uses light in an entirely different way than a microscope does. A laser produces a narrow, intense beam of light. Lasers have many biological uses. A laser beam can be a surgeon's "light scalpel," cutting and sealing off blood vessels. Lasers can also be used to destroy clumps of cancer cells.

Computers

Computers are electronic devices that collect, analyze, display, and store data. They have a wide range of uses in the biological sciences. In medicine, for example, computers help doctors diagnose diseases and prescribe treatments. Computers also help researchers gather information about the structure and function of cells and the activities of all living things.

Seeing Through Barriers

In order for scientists to learn more about living things, they must be able to view the inside of organisms *from the outside*. Certain tools make this investigation possible.

X-RAYS Invisible radiations known as X-rays have been used by scientists for almost one hundred years. X-rays easily pass through barriers such as skin and muscle but tend to be blocked by more dense materials such as bone. The result is a picture of the interior of an object. X-rays are most useful for taking pictures of bones inside an organism.

CAT A relatively new technique, Computerized Axial Tomography scanning, or CAT scan, provides a two-dimensional picture of an object. A beam of radiation may take as many as 720 separate exposures of the object. A computer then constructs a picture by combining and analyzing each exposure. CAT scans are used to produce pictures of the head and other body parts.

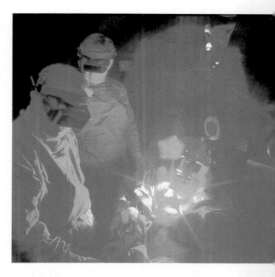

Figure 1-12 *Lasers produce a narrow, concentrated beam of light that can be used in medicine to cut through, destroy, or repair damaged tissue.*

Figure 1-13 *Top view of a computer-generated image of a DNA molecule.*

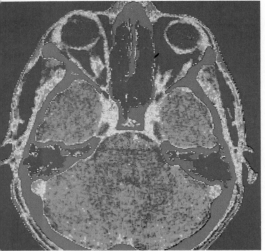

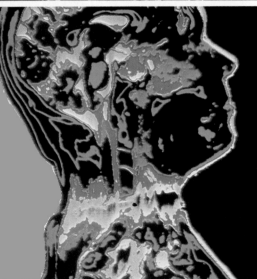

Figure 1-14 *This image of a person's head* (top) *was produced by CAT scanning. NMR images* (bottom) *help scientists study the internal structure of body parts.*

NMR Another tool for seeing and studying the inside of objects is Nuclear Magnetic Resonance, or NMR. This tool uses magnetism and radio waves to produce images. With no apparent harmful effects on living tissue, NMR promises to be a valuable tool for studying the structure of body cells and how they function.

SECTION REVIEW

1. Explain the difference between the compound light microscope and the electron microscope.
2. Name three other tools of the scientist and briefly explain their uses.

1-4 Safety in the Science Laboratory

The scientific laboratory is a place of adventure and discovery. Some of the most exciting events in scientific history have happened in laboratories. For example, the structure of DNA, the blueprint of life, was discovered by scientists in laboratories.

To better understand the facts and concepts you will read about in science, you may work in the laboratory this year. If you follow instructions and are as careful as a scientist would be, the laboratory will turn out to be an exciting experience for you.

Scientists know that when working in the laboratory, it is very important to follow safety procedures. **The most important safety rule is to always follow your teacher's directions or the directions in your textbook exactly as stated.** You should never try anything on your own without asking your teacher first. And when you are not sure what you should do, always ask first.

As you read the laboratory investigations in the textbook, you will see safety alert symbols. Look at Figure 1-15 to learn the meanings of the safety symbols and all the important safety precautions you should take. If you do not understand a rule, ask your teacher about it. You may even want to suggest further safety rules that apply to your classroom.

LABORATORY SAFETY: RULES AND SYMBOLS

Glassware Safety

1. Whenever you see this symbol, you will know that you are working with glassware that can be easily broken. Take particular care to handle such glassware safely. And never use broken glassware.
2. Never heat glassware that is not thoroughly dry. Never pick up any glassware unless you are sure it is not hot. If it is hot, use heat-resistant gloves.
3. Always clean glassware thoroughly before putting it away.

Fire Safety

1. Whenever you see this symbol, you will know that you are working with fire. Never use any source of fire without wearing safety goggles.
2. Never heat anything—particularly chemicals—unless instructed to do so.
3. Never heat anything in a closed container.
4. Never reach across a flame.
5. Always use a clamp, tongs, or heat-resistant gloves to handle hot objects.
6. Always maintain a clean work area, particularly when using a flame.

Heat Safety

Whenever you see this symbol, you will know that you should put on heat-resistant gloves to avoid burning your hands.

Chemical Safety

1. Whenever you see this symbol, you will know that you are working with chemicals that could be hazardous.
2. Never smell any chemical directly from its container. Always use your hand to waft some of the odors from the top of the container towards your nose—and only when instructed to do so.
3. Never mix chemicals unless instructed to do so.
4. Never touch or taste any chemical unless instructed to do so.
5. Keep all lids closed when chemicals are not in use. Dispose of all chemicals as instructed by your teacher.

6. Rinse any chemicals, particularly acids, off your skin and clothes with water immediately. Then notify your teacher.

Eye and Face Safety

1. Whenever you see this symbol, you will know that you are performing an experiment in which you must take precautions to protect your eyes and face by wearing safety goggles.
2. Always point a test tube or bottle that is being heated away from you and others. Chemicals can splash or boil out of the heated test tube.

Sharp Instrument Safety

1. Whenever you see this symbol, you will know that you are working with a sharp instrument.
2. Always use single-edged razors; double-edged razors are too dangerous.
3. Handle any sharp instrument with extreme care. Never cut any material towards you; always cut away from you.
4. Notify your teacher immediately if you are cut in the lab.

Electrical Safety

1. Whenever you see this symbol, you will know that you are using electricity in the laboratory.
2. Never use long extension cords to plug in an electrical device. Do not plug too many different appliances into one socket or you may overload the socket and cause a fire.
3. Never touch an electrical appliance or outlet with wet hands.

Animal Safety

1. Whenever you see this symbol, you will know that you are working with live animals.
2. Do not cause pain, discomfort, or injury to an animal.
3. Follow your teacher's directions when handling animals. Wash your hands thoroughly after handling animals or their cages.

SECTION REVIEW

1. What is the most important general rule to keep in mind when working in the laboratory this school year?
2. Explain why the laboratory is important in scientific research.
3. Suppose your teacher asked you to boil some water in a test tube. What precautions would you take so that this activity would be done safely?

Figure 1-15 *You should become familiar with these safety symbols because you will see them in the laboratory investigations in the textbook. What is the symbol for special safety precautions with heat?*

LABORATORY ACTIVITY

A Moldy Question

Purpose

In this activity, you will investigate variables that may affect the growth of bread mold.

Materials *(per group)*

2 jars with lids
2 slices of bread
1 medicine dropper

Procedure

1. Put half a slice of bread into each of two jars. Moisten each half slice with ten drops of water. Cap the jars tightly. Keep one jar in sunlight and place the other in a dark closet.

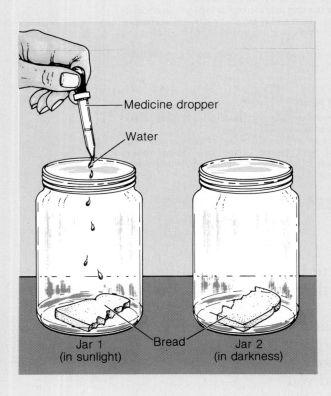

Jar 1
(in sunlight)

Jar 2
(in darkness)

Medicine dropper

Water

Bread

2. Observe the jars every few days for about two weeks. Record your observations. Does light seem to influence mold growth?
3. Ask your teacher what scientists know about the effect of light on mold growth. Was your conclusion correct? Think again. What other conditions might have affected mold growth?
4. Did you think of temperature? How about moisture? Light, temperature, and moisture are all possible variables in this activity. Design a second experiment to retest the effect of light on mold growth—or to test one of the other variables. Test only one variable at a time. Other groups of students will test the other two variables. Then you can pool your results and draw your conclusions together.

Observations and Conclusions

1. In your second experiment, what variable were you testing? Did you have a control for your experiment? If so, describe it.
2. Study the class data for this experiment. What variables seem to affect mold growth?
3. Cathy set up the following experiment: She placed a piece of orange peel in each of two jars. She added 3 milliliters of water to jar 1 and placed it in the refrigerator. She added no water to jar 2 and placed it on a windowsill in the kitchen. At the end of a week, she noticed more mold growth in jar 2. Cathy concluded that light, a warm temperature, and no moisture are ideal conditions for mold growth. Discuss the accuracy of Cathy's conclusion.

CHAPTER REVIEW

1-1 What Is Science?

■ A scientific method is a process scientists use to discover facts and truths about nature.

■ The basic steps of any scientific method are stating the problem, gathering information, forming a hypothesis, experimenting, recording and analyzing data, and stating a conclusion.

■ A suggested solution to a problem is called a hypothesis.

■ An experiment should have only one variable, or factor being tested.

■ Every experiment should have a control. A control experiment is run in exactly the same way as the experiment with the variable, but the variable is left out.

■ The three main branches of science are life science, earth science, and physical science.

1-2 Scientific Measurements

■ The metric system is the system of measurement used in science. It is a decimal system, or a system based on ten.

■ The meter is the basic unit of length in the metric system.

■ The liter is the basic unit of volume in the metric system.

■ The kilogram is the basic unit of mass in the metric system.

■ Mass is a measure of the amount of matter in an object. Weight is a measure of the attraction between objects due to the force of gravity.

■ Density is the measurement of the amount of mass that is contained in a given volume of an object.

■ The Celsius temperature scale has 100 degrees between the freezing and boiling points of water.

1-3 Tools of a Scientist

■ The compound light microscope and the electron microscope magnify small objects and produce enlarged images of them.

■ Lasers and computers have important applications in biology.

■ X-rays, CAT, and NMR can provide pictures of internal body structures.

1-4 Science Safety in the Laboratory

■ When you are working in the science laboratory, it is important for you to follow correct safety procedures at all times and to be familiar with your safety symbols.

■ The most important safety rule is to always follow your teacher's directions or the directions of your textbook exactly as stated.

Define each term in a complete sentence.

astronomy	data	lens	physics
botany	density	liter	scientific
Celsius	electron microscope	mass	method
chemistry	gravity	meter	variable
compound light	hypothesis	metric system	weight
microscope	kilogram	microscope	zoology
control			

CONTENT REVIEW: MULTIPLE CHOICE

Choose the letter of the answer that best completes each statement.

1. The branch of physical science that deals with the composition of substances, their changes and combinations is
   a. astronomy.   b. chemistry.   c. physics.   d. botany.
2. The basic unit of length is the
   a. liter.   b. gram.   c. meter.   d. kilogram.
3. One kilometer is equal to
   a. 1000 meters.   b. 1/1000 meter.   c. 100 meters.   d. 10 meters.
4. One centimeter is equal to
   a. 100 meters.   b. 1/100 meter.   c. 10 meters.   d. 1000 meters.
5. The liter is the basic unit of
   a. volume.   b. mass.   c. weight.   d. density.
6. The basic unit of mass is the
   a. liter.   b. gram.   c. kilogram.   d. meter.
7. The amount of mass contained in a given volume of an object is called
   a. gravity.   b. temperature.   c. area.   d. density.
8. The freezing point of water is
   a. 32° C.   b. 0° C.   c. 100° C.   d. 212° C.
9. A device doctors can use to perform surgery is the
   a. X-ray.   b. CAT scan.   c. NMR.   d. laser.
10. The most important laboratory safety rule is to
    a. wear a lab coat.   b. have a partner.
    c. follow directions.   d. use the metric system.

CONTENT REVIEW: COMPLETION

Fill in the word or words that best complete each statement.

1. A(n) _____ is a suggested solution to a problem.
2. The factor being tested in an experiment is the _____.
3. _____ is the study of plants.
4. The _____ system is the system of measurement used in science.
5. One meter is equal to _____ centimeters.
6. A millimeter is _____ of a meter.
7. _____ is a measure of the amount of matter in an object.
8. Water boils at _____° C.
9. A(n) _____ magnifies and produces an enlarged image of an object.
10. A narrow beam of intense light is produced by a(n) _____.

CONTENT REVIEW: TRUE OR FALSE

Determine whether each statement is true or false. If it is true, write "true." If it is false, change the underlined word or words to make the statement true.

1. The process used by scientists to discover facts and truths about nature is called a <u>scientific method</u>.
2. Recorded observations that often involve measurements are called <u>conclusions</u>.

3. The <u>control</u> experiment is the experiment without the variable.

4. <u>Botany</u> is the study of animals.

5. The prefix <u>kilo-</u> means 1000.

6. The basic unit of volume is the <u>meter</u>.

7. The force of attraction between objects is called <u>gravity</u>.

8. Your <u>weight</u> on the moon would be the same <u>as it is</u> on the earth.

9. A <u>mirror</u> is a curved piece of glass that bends light rays as they pass through it.

10. In the laboratory, never heat anything in an <u>open</u> container.

CONCEPT REVIEW: SKILL BUILDING

Use the skills you have developed in the chapter to complete each activity.

1. Classifying metric units Which metric units would you use to measure each of the following?

a. the length of your classroom
b. the amount of milk you had for breakfast
c. the temperature outside
d. the distance from school to your home
e. the mass of a grasshopper
f. the length of your big toe
g. the mass of a great white shark
h. the amount of water in a swimming pool

2. Making calculations Complete the following metric conversions.

a. 13 L = _____ mL
b. 476 g = _____ kg
c. 52 mL = _____ cm^3
d. 74 cm = _____ mm
e. 12,891 mg = _____ g
f. 65 km = _____ m

3. Following safety rules Explain the potential danger involved in each of the following situations. Describe the safety precautions that should be used to avoid injury to you or your classmates.

a. reaching across a flame
b. pointing a test tube that is being heated toward yourself or others
c. heating a substance in a closed container
d. tasting an unknown chemical in order to identify it

4. Applying concepts Explain why every substance has a characteristic density, but no substance has a characteristic mass.

5. Making calculations The density of water is 1 g/cm^3. Therefore, objects with densities less than 1 g/cm^3 float in water.

a. Is the density of air greater or less than 1g/cm^3?
b. Will an object with a mass of 49 g and a volume of 21 cm^3 float in water?
c. Sample X sinks in water. Would a 25 cm^3 sample of X have a mass of 20 g or a mass of 40 g?

CONCEPT REVIEW: ESSAY

Discuss each of the following in a brief paragraph.

1. Briefly describe the basic steps of a scientific method.

2. Compare an experimental setup with a control setup.

3. Explain the difference between mass and weight.

4. Compare a simple, a compound, and an electron microscope.

5. Describe how lasers and computers are being used in medicine.

6. Explain how chance sometimes plays a role in scientific discoveries.

2 The Nature of Life

CHAPTER SECTIONS

2-1 Characteristics of Living Things

2-2 Needs of Living Things

2-3 Chemistry of Living Things

CHAPTER OBJECTIVES

After completing this chapter, you will be able to:

2-1 Discuss the basic characteristics of all living things.

2-1 Describe metabolism and the activities involved in metabolism.

2-2 Identify the basic needs of all living things.

2-3 Distinguish between elements and compounds.

2-3 Describe the organic compounds that are the building blocks of life.

Slowly, the scientist fills the clear glass flask. First he pours in three colorless gases. The odor is awful—a combination of rotten eggs and swamp gas that stings the scientist's nose and brings tears to his eyes. Now the scientist adds two more gases. Nothing seems to happen. The flask looks empty. But the gases it contains may be changed into something very special, if everything goes right!

The mixture needs a spark to produce the necessary change. The scientist sends a surge of electricity through the flask again and again. Suddenly, a sticky brown coating begins to form on the walls of the flask. The mixture of gases inside is changing—turning into substances that scientists believe may help them solve a key mystery of life.

Magic? It may seem to be, and at times the scientist may seem to be a magician. But this exciting experiment was actually performed, and its results are being used by scientists today as they attempt to study the "stuff of life."

In 1952, the American scientist Stanley Miller mixed together three foul-smelling gases: hydrogen sulfide, methane, and ammonia. To this mixture he added hydrogen, a colorless, odorless gas, and gaseous water. Then he passed an electric current through the colorless mixture. Soon a brown tarlike substance streaked the sides of the container. Dr. Miller analyzed the tarlike substance and found that it contained several of the same substances that make up all living things. From nonliving chemicals, Stanley Miller had made some of the building blocks of life.

Primitive Earth, on which life evolved

Figure 2-1 *A great variety of animals and plants inhabit the earth. The llama* (top, left) *may not be as familiar to you as the lovely crocus* (bottom, left). *The baobab tree* (top, right) *and the aardvark* (bottom, right) *may also be unfamiliar. Yet all are made up of the same basic elements.*

2-1 Characteristics of Living Things

Take a short walk in the city or the country and you will see an enormous variety of living things. In fact, scientists estimate that there are over five million different types of organisms on the earth, ranging from one-celled bacteria to huge blue whales. Yet all living things are composed mainly of the same basic elements: carbon, hydrogen, nitrogen, and oxygen. These elements make up the gases Miller placed in his flask. These four elements along with iron, calcium, phosphorus, and sulfur all link together to form the stuff of life.

Well-known chemical rules govern the way these elements combine and interact. But less well understood is what gives this collection of chemicals a very special property—the property of life.

But what are the characteristics that make living things special? That is, what distinguishes even the smallest organism from a lifeless streak of brown tar on a laboratory flask? **Living things are able to move, grow, reproduce, respond to a stimulus, and perform certain chemical activities.**

Life from Life

People did not always understand that living matter is so special. Until the 1600s, many people believed in the theory of **spontaneous generation.** According to this theory, life could spring from nonliving matter. For example, people believed that mice came from straw and frogs and turtles developed from rotting wood and mud at the bottom of a pond.

In 1668, an Italian doctor named Francesco Redi disproved this theory. In those days, maggots, a wormlike stage in the life cycle of a fly, often appeared on decaying meat. People believed that the rotten meat had actually turned into maggots, and that flies formed from dead animals. In a series of experiments, Redi proved that the maggots hatched from eggs laid by flies. Today there is no doubt that living things can arise *only* from other living things.

Activity

Disproving Spontaneous Generation

Redi's conclusions were not well accepted. The controversy over the theory of spontaneous generation continued for many years. Each of the men listed below was involved in either proving or disproving the theory. Using books and reference materials in the library, find out what contribution each man made to a better understanding of living things.

John Needham

Lazzaro Spallanzani

Louis Pasteur

Figure 2-2 *Redi's experiment helped disprove spontaneous generation. No maggots were found on the meat in jars covered with netting or tightly sealed. Maggots appeared on the meat only when flies were able to enter the jars and lay eggs.*

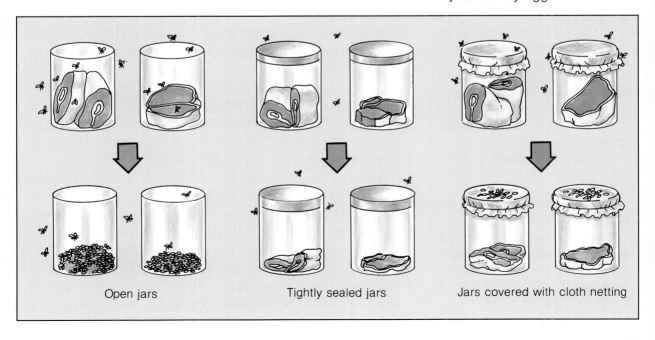

Open jars   Tightly sealed jars   Jars covered with cloth netting

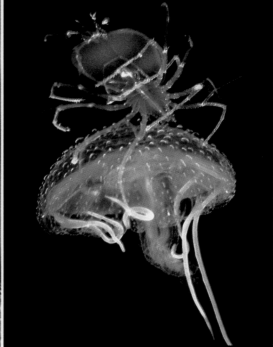

Figure 2-3 *The arctic tern* (left) *survives by commuting between the Arctic and the Antarctic. The larval crab* (right) *gets around by hitching a ride on a jellyfish.*

Activity

Catch Those Rays

1. Obtain two coleus plants of equal size.

2. Place one of the plants on a table or windowsill directly in front of a window.

3. Place the other plant on a table of the same height. Move this table so that it is about 70 cm to the left or the right of the same window.

4. Water both plants once or twice a week or whenever the soil feels dry.

5. Observe the growth of the plants for three weeks.

Write down your observations and the date on which you make them. What conclusion can you draw about the movement of plants in response to light?

Movement

The arctic tern is a small, gull-like bird that at first glance may not appear to be a record breaker. See Figure 2-3. Yet for seven months of every year, the arctic tern is in flight, covering a distance of nearly 32,000 kilometers. The tern begins its journey near the Arctic, travels south to its winter quarters in the Antarctic, and then flies back north again. Its yearly trip gives the tern the "long-distance record" for birds in flight. An ability to move through the environment is an important characteristic of many living things.

Animals must be able to move in order to find food and shelter. In times of danger, swift movement can be the difference between safety and death. Of course, animals move in a great many ways. Fins enable fish such as salmon to swim hundreds of kilometers in search of a place to mate. The kangaroo uses its entire body as a giant pogo stick to bounce along the Australian plains looking for scarce patches of grass upon which to graze.

Most plants do not move in the same way animals do. Only parts of the plants move. The stems of the common houseplant *Pothos* bend toward the sunlight coming through windows. Its leaves turn to catch the sun's rays.

Metabolism

Building up and breaking down is a good way to describe the chemical activities that are essential to life. During some of these activities, simple substances combine to form complex substances. These substances are needed for growth, to store energy, and to repair or to replace living materials. During other activities, complex substances are broken down, releasing energy and usable food substances. Together, these chemical activities in an organism are called **metabolism** (muh-TA-buh-li-zuhm). Metabolism, then, is another characteristic of living things.

Metabolism includes many chemical reactions that go on in the body of a living thing. However, metabolism usually begins with eating.

INGESTION   All living things must either take in food or produce their own food. For most animals, **ingestion,** or eating, is as simple as putting food into their mouths. But some organisms, such as worms that live inside animals, absorb food directly through their skin.

Green plants do not have to ingest food because they make it. Using their roots, green plants absorb water and minerals from the soil. Tiny openings in the underside of their leaves allow carbon dioxide to enter. The green plants use the water and carbon dioxide, along with energy from the sun, to make food.

DIGESTION   Getting food into the body is the first step in metabolism, but there is a lot more to metabolism than just eating. The food must be digested in order to be used. **Digestion** is the process by which food is broken down into simpler substances. Later, some of these simpler substances are reassembled into more complex materials for use in the growth and repair of the living thing. Other simple substances store energy that the organism will use for its many activities.

RESPIRATION   Organisms combine oxygen with the products of digestion to produce energy. The energy is used to do all the work of the organism. The process by which living things take in oxygen and use it to produce energy is called **respiration.**

Figure 2-4   *Until baby thrushes are old enough to fly, they must rely on their mother for food.*

Figure 2-5 *A cougar* (left) *could not run very fast without the energy produced during respiration. Dolphins* (right) *also need oxygen for respiration, so they continually surface for breaths of air.*

Land animals like yourself have lungs that remove oxygen from the air. Most sea animals have gills that absorb oxygen dissolved in water. Some sea animals, however, come to the surface to breathe with their lungs. Whales, porpoises, and dolphins are examples of air-breathing sea animals. Some of these animals can remain under water for as long as 120 minutes!

Plants, too, need oxygen to stay alive. Most plants absorb oxygen through tiny pores in their leaves. Plants use oxygen for respiration, as do almost all living things. For respiration is the main process that provides energy necessary to living things. You get this energy by combining the foods you eat with the oxygen you breathe. The amount of energy a food can supply is measured in units called Calories.

EXCRETION Not all the products of digestion and respiration can be used by the organism. Some products are waste materials that must be released. The process of getting rid of waste materials is called **excretion.** If waste products are not removed, they will eventually poison the organism.

Growth and Development

Standing under a giant oak tree, you might marvel at the fact that it grew from a tiny acorn. Within that acorn, metabolic activity produced a supply of energy from stored food. The acorn used this energy to begin to grow into a tree. Without the energy of metabolism, no living thing can grow. And growth is one of the characteristics of living things.

Activity

Counting Calories

The amount of energy a food can supply is measured in Calories. In general, people gain weight when they take in more Calories than they use up. Often the extra Calories come from snacks. Ten average-sized potato chips, for example, contain about 110 Calories.

Make a chart listing ten of your favorite snack foods and the number of Calories contained in each. This information may be obtained from food packages or reference materials.

Figure 2-6 *A tiger swallowtail caterpillar* (left) *will grow and develop into an adult butterfly* (right).

But growing things do more than just increase in size. They also develop and become more complex. Sometimes this development results in dramatic changes. A tadpole, for example, swims for weeks in a summer pond. However, one day that tadpole becomes the frog that sits near the water's edge. And surely the caterpillar creeping through a garden gives little hint of the beautiful butterfly it will soon become. Certainly development must be added to your list of the characteristics of living things.

Different organisms grow at different rates. A person will grow from a newborn baby to an adult in about 18 years. But puppies become adult dogs in only a few years. And a lima bean seed becomes a bean plant in just a few weeks. Some living things, such as certain insects, can change from an egg to an adult within a few days.

Life Span

One of the important characteristics of living things is **life span,** or the maximum length of time a particular organism can be expected to live. Life span varies greatly from one type of organism to another. For example, an elephant lives for about 60 or 70 years. A bristlecone pine tree may live to be 5500 years old!

In certain organisms, growth and development take up most of the life span. The mayfly, for example, spends two years in lakes or ponds growing and

Figure 2-7 *According to this chart, what is the maximum life span of a tortoise?*

MAXIMUM LIFE SPANS

Organism		Life Span
Adult mayfly		1 day
Marigold		8 months
Mouse		1–2 years
Dog		13 years
Horse		20–30 years
Alligator		56 years
Asiatic elephant		78 years
Blue whale		100 years
Human		117 years
Tortoise		152 years
Bristlecone pine		5500 years

Figure 2-8 *The adult mayfly* (left) *lives for only about one day. The bristlecone pine* (right) *has a life span of about 5500 years.*

developing into an adult. However, the adult lives for only about one day. It finds a mate and starts a new family of mayflies. Then it dies.

Response

When the alarm clock rings in the morning, you wake up. The smell of eggs and toast makes your mouth water as you hurry to breakfast. On your way to school, you stop at a red light. In just a matter of several hours, you have reacted to signals in your surroundings that determine much of your behavior.

Scientists call each of the signals to which an organism reacts a **stimulus.** A stimulus is any change in the environment, or surroundings, of an organism that produces a **response.** A response is some action or movement of the organism.

Some stimuli come from outside the organism's body. For example, smells and noises are stimuli to which you respond. So is tickling. Light and water are stimuli to which plants respond. Other stimuli come from inside an organism's body. A lack of oxygen in your body is a stimulus that often causes you to yawn.

Figure 2-9 *Even if they must swim thousands of kilometers, most salmon return to the same stream in which they were hatched to lay their eggs.*

Some plants have special responses that protect them. For example, when a gypsy moth caterpillar chews on the leaf of an oak tree, the tree responds by producing bad-tasting chemicals in its other leaves. The chemicals discourage all but the hungriest caterpillars from eating these leaves. Can you think of responses that help you protect yourself?

Reproduction

You probably know that dinosaurs that lived 230 million years ago are now extinct. Yet crocodiles, which appeared before dinosaurs, are still living today. An organism becomes extinct when it no longer produces other organisms of the same kind. In other words, all living things of a given kind would become extinct if they did not reproduce.

The process by which living things give rise to the same type of living thing is **reproduction.** Crocodiles, for example, do not produce dinosaurs. Crocodiles only produce more crocodiles. You are a human, and not a water buffalo, a duck, or a tomato plant, because your parents are human. An easy way to remember this is *like produces like.*

There are two different types of reproduction: **sexual reproduction** and **asexual reproduction.** Sexual reproduction usually requires two parents. Most higher forms of plants and animals reproduce sexually.

Some living things reproduce from only one parent. This is asexual reproduction. This type of reproduction can be as simple as an organism dividing into two parts. Bacteria reproduce this way. Yeast form growths called buds, which break off and then form new yeast plants. Geraniums and African violets can grow new plants from part of a stem, root, or leaf of the parent plant. All of these examples demonstrate asexual reproduction.

Sexual and asexual reproduction have an important function in common. In each case, the offspring receive a set of very special chemical "blueprints," or plans. These blueprints determine the characteristics of that type of living thing and are passed from one generation to the next.

Figure 2-10 *Strawberries reproduce asexually when their stems produce bundles of roots, each of which forms a new plant.*

SECTION REVIEW

1. What is the theory of spontaneous generation, and what did Redi's experiments reveal about the theory?
2. What is metabolism? What are some processes that are part of metabolism?
3. What are the six basic characteristics of living things?

Figure 2-11 *This empty shell is home to a hermit crab, as well as to the sea anemones growing on the shell.*

2-2 Needs of Living Things

Living things interact with one another and with their environment. These interactions are as varied as the living things themselves. Birds, for example, use dead twigs to build nests, but they eat live worms and insects. Crayfish build their homes in the sand or mud of streams and swamps. They absorb a chemical called lime from these waters to build a hard body covering. Crayfish rely, however, on living snails and tadpoles for their food. And some people rely on crayfish for a tasty meal!

It seems clear, then, that living things depend on both the living and nonliving parts of their environment. **In order for a living organism to survive, it needs energy, food, water, oxygen, living space, and the ability to maintain a fairly constant body temperature.**

Energy

All living things need energy. The energy can be used in different ways. A lion uses energy to chase and capture its prey. The electric eel defends itself by shocking its attackers with electric energy.

What is the source of this energy so necessary to living things? The primary source of energy for most living things is the sun. Plants use the sun's light energy to make food. Some animals feed on plants and in that way obtain the energy stored in the plants. Other animals may then eat the plant eaters. In this way, the energy from the sun is passed on from one living thing to another.

Figure 2-12 *These glowworm larvae* (left) *use energy to produce light. The original source of energy for all living things, worms as well as grasses, is the sun* (right).

Figure 2-13 *Many animals and plants have unusual ways of obtaining food. The woodpecker finch (left) uses a twig to get at insects in the bark of trees. The Venus' flytrap snares a grasshopper with special leaves (right).*

Food and Water

Have you ever heard the saying "You are what you eat"? Certainly this saying does not mean you will become a carrot or a hamburger if you eat these foods. But it does tell you that what you eat is very important. Food is a need of living things.

FOOD The kind of food organisms eat varies considerably. You would probably not want to eat eucalyptus leaves, yet that is the only food a koala eats. A diet of wood may not seem tempting, but for the termite it is a source of energy and necessary chemical substances. And surely a green plant's diet of simple sugar would not suit your taste.

Although all plants and animals must obtain food to live, some do it in very unusual ways. For example, the Venus' flytrap has special leaves that attract insects. When an insect lands on these leaves, they immediately close and trap the insect. Then the plant slowly digests the insect.

WATER Although you would probably not enjoy it, you could live a week or more without food. But you would die in a few days without water. It may surprise you to learn that 65 percent or more of your body is water. Other living things are also made up mainly of water.

Aside from making up much of your body, water serves many other purposes. Most substances dissolve in water. In this way, important chemicals can be transported easily throughout an organism. The blood of animals and the sap of trees, for example, are mainly water.

Activity

You're All Wet

About 65% of your body mass is water.

1. Find your mass in kilograms.

2. Use that number to determine how many kilograms of water you contain.

Breathe Easy

The air you inhale contains oxygen. But what is in the air you exhale? Is there carbon dioxide in this air?

1. Use the following facts to devise an experiment that will determine whether carbon dioxide is present in exhaled air:
- The indicator bromthymol blue turns blue when an acid is present.
- Carbon dioxide, when added to water, forms carbonic acid.

2. After you have devised your experiment, show it to your teacher. With your teacher's approval, try the experiment. What were your results? What conclusions can you draw?

Most chemical reactions in living things cannot take place without water. Metabolism would come to a grinding halt without water. And it is water that carries away many of the metabolic waste products produced by living things. For green plants, water is also a raw material needed to make food.

Air

You already know that oxygen is necessary for the process of respiration. Most living things get oxygen directly from the air or from air that has dissolved in water. When you breathe out, you release the waste gas called carbon dioxide. However, this gas is not wasted. The green plants around you use carbon dioxide in the air to make food.

Living Space

Do you enjoy hearing the chirping of birds on a lovely spring morning? Surprisingly, the birds are not simply singing. Rather, they are staking out their territory and warning intruders to stay away.

Often there is only a limited amount of food, water, and energy in an environment. As a result, only a limited number of the same kind of living thing can survive there. That is why many animals defend a certain area that they consider to be their living

Figure 2-14 *Here two bighorn sheep are engaged in battle.*

space. The male sunfish, for example, defends its territory in ponds by flashing its colorful fins at other sunfish and darting toward any sunfish that comes too close. You might think of this behavior as a kind of **competition** for living space.

Competition is the struggle among living things to get the proper amount of food, water, and energy. Animals are not the only competitors. Plants compete for sunlight and water. Smaller, weaker plants often die in the shadow of larger plants.

Proper Temperature

During the summer, temperatures as high as 58°C have been recorded on the earth. Winter temperatures can dip as low as −89°C. Most organisms cannot survive at such temperature extremes because many metabolic activities cannot occur at these temperatures. Without metabolism, an organism dies.

Actually, most organisms would quickly die at far less severe temperature extremes if it were not for **homeostasis** (ho-mee-o-STAY-sis). Homeostasis is the ability of an organism to keep conditions inside its body the same even though conditions in its external environment change. Maintaining a constant body temperature, no matter what the temperature of the surroundings, is part of homeostasis. Birds and certain other animals, such as dogs and horses, produce enough heat to keep themselves warm at low temperatures. Trapped air in the feathers of birds keeps

Figure 2-15 *Coldblooded turtles* (left) *must absorb the sun's heat to keep warm. Flowers such as these coltsfoots* (right) *can grow in extremely cold conditions.*

them cool when temperatures get too high. Panting and sweating do the same for dogs and horses. Animals that maintain a constant body temperature are called **warmblooded** animals. Warmblooded animals can be active during both day and night, in hot weather and in cold.

Animals such as reptiles and fish have body temperatures that can change somewhat with changes in the temperature of the environment. These animals are called **coldblooded** animals. To keep warm, a coldblooded reptile, such as a crocodile, must spend part of each day lying in the sun. At night, when the air temperature drops, so does the crocodile's body temperature. The crocodile becomes lazy and inactive. Coldblooded animals do not move around much at relatively high or low temperatures.

SECTION REVIEW

1. Name five basic needs of living things.
2. What is the relationship between the sun and the energy needed by all living things?
3. What is the difference between warmblooded organisms and coldblooded organisms?

2-3 Chemistry of Living Things

What do a diamond, foil wrap, and a light bulb filament have in common? These objects look very different and certainly have very different uses, but all are examples of **elements.** An element is a pure substance that cannot be broken down into any simpler substances by ordinary means. A diamond is the element carbon. Foil wrap is the element aluminum. And the light bulb filament is the element tungsten. Carbon, oxygen, hydrogen, nitrogen, copper, gold, and sulfur are elements.

When two or more elements are chemically joined together, **compounds** are formed. Water is a compound made up of the elements hydrogen and oxygen. Table salt, which you probably use to flavor your food, is a compound made up of sodium and chlorine. Sand and glass are compounds composed of the elements silicon and oxygen. There are thousands of different compounds all around you. In fact, you are made up of many compounds. Scientists classify compounds in two groups.

Inorganic Compounds

Compounds that may or may not contain the element carbon are called **inorganic compounds.** Most inorganic compounds do not contain carbon. However, carbon dioxide is an exception. Table salt, ammonia, rust, and water are examples of inorganic compounds.

Organic Compounds

Many compounds contain carbon, which is usually combined with other elements such as hydrogen and oxygen. These compounds are called **organic compounds.** There are more than three million different organic compounds. Some of these compounds are the basic building blocks of life. **Organic compounds that are basic to life include carbohydrates, fats and oils, proteins, enzymes, and nucleic acids.**

CARBOHYDRATES The main source of energy for living things is **carbohydrates.** Carbohydrates are made up of the elements carbon, hydrogen, and oxygen. Sugar and starch are two important carbohydrates. Fruit and candy contain sugar. Potatoes, rice, noodles, and bread are sources of starch. What are some foods that you eat that contain sugar and starch?

All carbohydrates are broken down inside the body into a simple sugar called **glucose.** The body then uses glucose to produce the energy needed for life activities. If an organism has more sugar than it needs for its energy requirements, it will store the sugar for later use. The sugar is stored as starch. Starch is a stored form of energy.

FATS AND OILS Energy-rich organic compounds made up of carbon, hydrogen, and oxygen are **fats** and **oils.** Fats are solid at room temperature; oils are liquid at room temperature.

Figure 2-16 *The active element sodium* (top) *combines chemically with poisonous chlorine gas* (center) *to form crystals of ordinary table salt* (bottom).

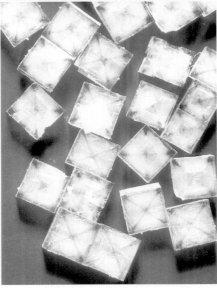

Fats can provide twice as much energy as carbohydrates. Foods high in fat, such as butter, cheese, milk, nuts, and some meats, should be included in your diet, but not to excess. Fats are stored by the body as body fat. And although this stored fat helps keep you warm, protects your internal organs from injury, and gives you energy, it can make you overweight.

Figure 2-17 *The foods on this picnic table provide the organic compounds that are the basic building blocks of life.*

PROTEINS Like carbohydrates and fats, **proteins** are organic compounds made up of carbon, hydrogen, and oxygen. But proteins also contain the element nitrogen and sometimes the elements sulfur and phosphorus. Some important sources of proteins are eggs, meat, fish, beans, nuts, and poultry.

The building blocks of proteins are **amino acids.** There are about 20 different types of amino acids. But because amino acids combine in many ways, they form thousands of different proteins.

Career: *Enzymologist*

HELP WANTED: ENZYMOLOGIST Requires Ph.D. in biochemistry and experience in this field. Needed for research project. Will investigate the action of various poisons on enzymes found in living things.

Two young children enter the hospital emergency room sweating and complaining of headaches and nausea. They have eaten the pits of some purple berries they found growing in a field. Although the berries themselves were harmless, the pits contained poisonous chemicals called cyanides. Scientists know that in the body cyanides quickly combine with an important respiratory enzyme. When this enzyme is bonded with cyanide, the enzyme can no longer perform its normal, vital job. As a result, cells cannot use oxygen in the process of metabolism.

Scientists who do research into the action of enzymes are called **enzymologists.** They isolate, analyze, and identify enzymes. They determine the enzyme's effects on body functions. The human body contains more than one thousand different enzymes. Enzymologists know much about these enzymes.

Enzymes are now being used in the manufacture of detergents, bread, cheese, and coffee. Physicians use enzymes for cleaning wounds, dissolving blood clots, and treating certain diseases. Enzymologists are learning how enzymes can be helpful in cleaning up the environment.

Enzymologists can use their knowledge and skill in industry, in public and private research institutes, and in colleges and universities. To learn more about this career, write to the American Society of Biological Chemists, 9650 Rockville Pike, Bethesda, MD 20014.

Proteins perform many jobs for an organism. They are necessary for the growth and repair of body structures. Proteins are used to build body hair and muscle. Proteins provide energy. Some proteins, such as those in blood, carry oxygen throughout the body. Other proteins fight germs that invade the body. Still other proteins make chemical substances that start, stop, and regulate many important body activities.

ENZYMES   A special type of protein that regulates chemical activities within the body is called an **enzyme.** Enzymes act as **catalysts.** A catalyst is a substance that speeds up or slows down chemical reactions, but is not itself changed by the reaction. Without enzymes, the chemical reactions of metabolism could not take place.

NUCLEIC ACIDS   Do you remember the "blueprints" of life discussed earlier? These blueprints are organic chemicals called **nucleic acids.** Nucleic acids are very large compounds that store information that helps the body make the proteins it needs. The nucleic acids control the way the amino acids are put together so that the correct protein is formed. This process is similar to the way a carpenter uses a blueprint to build a house. Now you understand why nucleic acids are called the blueprints of life.

One nucleic acid is **DNA,** deoxyribonucleic acid. DNA stores the information needed to build a protein. DNA also carries "messages" about an organism that are passed from parent to offspring. Another nucleic acid, **RNA,** ribonucleic acid, "reads" the DNA messages and guides the protein-making process. Together, these two nucleic acids contain the information and carry out the steps that make each organism what it is.

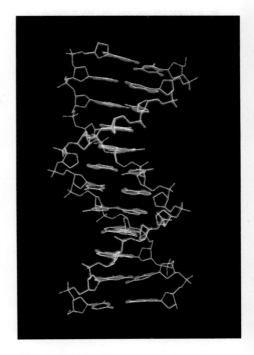

Figure 2-18   *This computer-generated image shows the structure of the nucleic acid DNA. DNA stores information needed to build proteins and carries "messages" from one generation to the next.*

SECTION REVIEW

1. What is the basic difference between inorganic and organic compounds?
2. Of what importance are carbohydrates, fats and oils, and proteins to living things?
3. What are two nucleic acids? What is the function of each of these nucleic acids?

LABORATORY ACTIVITY

You Are What You Eat

Purpose

In this activity, you will study your school's lunch menus for one week.

Materials *(per group)*

School lunch menus for the current week
Pencil
Paper
Reference book or textbook on foods
and nutrition

Procedure

1. Obtain a copy of your school's lunch menus for one week.
2. Make a table listing the four basic food groups: meat group, vegetable-fruit group, milk group, bread-cereal group. For each day of the week, place the items from the menu in the appropriate food group.

Meat Group	Vegetable-Fruit Group	Milk Group	Bread-Cereal Group
Hamburger			Roll

Carbohydrates	Fats	Proteins
Roll		Hamburger

3. Make a second table listing the three major nutrients: carbohydrates, fats, and proteins. List those foods containing large amounts of these nutrients under the proper heading.
4. On a third table, identify those foods that are plants or plant products and those that are animals or animal products.

Plants or Plant Products	Animals or Animal Products
Roll	Hamburger

Observations and Conclusions

1. Study the data you have collected and organized. What conclusions can you draw regarding your school's lunch program?
2. According to your data, do the foods represent a balanced diet? Do foods in certain categories appear much more often than foods in some other categories?
3. What changes, if any, would you make in the menus?

SUMMARY

2-1 Characteristics of Living Things

■ The elements most abundant in living things are carbon, hydrogen, nitrogen, and oxygen.

■ Metabolism is the sum of all chemical activities essential to life. Ingestion, digestion, respiration, and excretion are metabolic activities that occur in all organisms.

■ Life span is the maximum length of time a particular organism can be expected to live.

■ A living thing reacts to a stimulus, which is a change in the environment, by producing a response.

■ Reproduction is the process by which organisms produce offspring.

2-2 Needs of Living Things

■ Living things need energy for metabolism. The primary source of energy for all living things is the sun.

■ All living things need food and water.

■ Oxygen in the air or dissolved in water is used by all organisms during respiration. Carbon dioxide is used by plants to make food.

■ Competition is a struggle for food, water, and energy.

■ Homeostasis is the ability of an organism to keep conditions constant inside its body when the outside environment changes.

■ Warmblooded animals maintain a constant body temperature. Coldblooded animals have body temperatures that change with changes in the external temperature.

2-3 Chemistry of Living Things

■ Elements are pure substances that cannot be broken down by ordinary chemical means. Compounds are formed when two or more elements are chemically joined.

■ Most inorganic compounds do not contain the element carbon. Organic compounds do contain carbon. The organic compounds important to living things are carbohydrates, fats and oils, proteins, enzymes, and nucleic acids.

■ DNA and RNA are two important nucleic acids. They carry the information for and control the building of proteins that make each organism what it is.

VOCABULARY

Define each term in a complete sentence.

amino acid	element	metabolism	sexual
asexual	enzyme	nucleic acid	reproduction
reproduction	excretion	oil	spontaneous
carbohydrate	fat	organic	generation
catalyst	glucose	compound	stimulus
coldblooded	homeostasis	protein	warmblooded
competition	ingestion	reproduction	
compound	inorganic	respiration	
digestion	compound	response	
DNA	life span	RNA	

CONTENT REVIEW: MULTIPLE CHOICE

Choose the letter of the answer that best completes each statement.

1. The theory that life could spring from nonliving matter is called
   a. spontaneous respiration.   b. spontaneous generation.
   c. asexual reproduction.   d. homeostasis.
2. The building up and breaking down of chemical substances necessary for life is called
   a. reproduction.   b. excretion.   c. competition.   d. metabolism.
3. The process of combining oxygen with the products of digestion to produce energy is called
   a. reproduction.   b. ingestion.   c. excretion.   d. respiration.
4. Which organism cannot produce offspring by asexual reproduction?
   a. yeast   b. bacterium   c. human being   d. geranium plant
5. The gas in air used by plants to make food is
   a. oxygen.   b. nitrogen.   c. carbon dioxide.   d. hydrogen.
6. The struggle among living things to obtain the resources needed to live is called
   a. competition.   b. homeostasis.
   c. metabolism.   d. spontaneous generation.
7. Which of these is a warmblooded animal?
   a. fish   b. bird   c. reptile   d. crocodile
8. Which of these is a substance made entirely of a single element?
   a. diamond   b. table salt   c. water   d. glass
9. Carbohydrate is to glucose as
   a. fat is to oil.   b. protein is to amino acid.
   c. DNA is to RNA.   d. hydrogen is to oxygen.
10. The complex compound that carries the information needed to make protein from amino acids is
   a. carbohydrate.   b. homeostasis.   c. glucose.   d. DNA.

CONTENT REVIEW: COMPLETION

Fill in the word or words that best complete each statement.

1. _____ is the sum of all the chemical activities essential to life.
2. The process by which food is broken down into simpler substances is known as _____.
3. The process by which living things produce offspring is called _____.
4. A response is the reaction of an organism to a(n) _____.
5. All organisms directly or indirectly receive energy from the _____.
6. About 65 percent of your body mass is composed of _____.
7. Animals that maintain a constant body temperature are _____.
8. Two or more elements joined together form a(n) _____.
9. Most inorganic compounds do not contain the element _____.
10. Because it can influence the rate of chemical reactions without itself changing, an enzyme is a(n) _____.

Determine whether each statement is true or false. If it is true, write "true." If it is false, change the underlined word or words to make the statement true.

1. Most forms of life are composed almost entirely of <u>carbon</u>, hydrogen, nitrogen, and oxygen.
2. The theory of <u>spontaneous combustion</u> states that life can spring from nonliving matter.
3. The process by which an organism puts food into its body is <u>digestion</u>.
4. Green plants use <u>water</u> and carbon dioxide to make food.
5. The process of getting rid of waste material is called <u>reproduction</u>.
6. The maximum length of time a particular organism can be expected to live is called its <u>life span</u>.
7. Animals that maintain a constant body temperature are <u>coldblooded</u> animals.
8. Ammonia, carbon dioxide, and water are examples of <u>inorganic compounds</u>.
9. Stored <u>fat</u> helps keep you warm and protects your internal organs from injury.
10. <u>DNA and RNA</u> guide the protein-making process in living things.

CONCEPT REVIEW: SKILL BUILDING

Use the skills you have developed in the chapter to complete each activity.

1. **Making inferences**   Is a peach pit living or nonliving? Explain.
2. **Identifying relationships** Figure 2-2 shows three sets of jars that illustrate Redi's experiments. Explain why the second set of jars did not provide enough evidence to disprove the theory of spontaneous generation.
3. **Making comparisons**   How is the growth of a sand dune different from the growth of a living organism?
4. **Relating concepts**   Why is the study of chemistry important to the understanding of life science?
5. **Drawing conclusions**   Which life function is necessary for the survival of a species but not necessary for the survival of an individual?
6. **Applying concepts**   Which is more likely to result in increased variety among organisms, sexual reproduction or asexual reproduction?
7. **Relating cause and effect**   During the time people believed in spontaneous generation, a scientist developed this recipe for producing mice: Place a few wheat grains and a dirty shirt in an open pot; wait three weeks. Suggest a reason why this recipe may have worked. How could you prove that the appearance of mice was not due to spontaneous generation?

CONCEPT REVIEW: ESSAY

Discuss each of the following in a brief paragraph.

1. List five characteristics of living things.
2. Your friend believes that because they do not move, plants cannot be alive. Use specific examples to explain why your friend is wrong.
3. Describe four metabolic processes.
4. Describe four organic compounds that are the building blocks of life.
5. Explain this statement: The primary source of energy for all organisms is the sun.

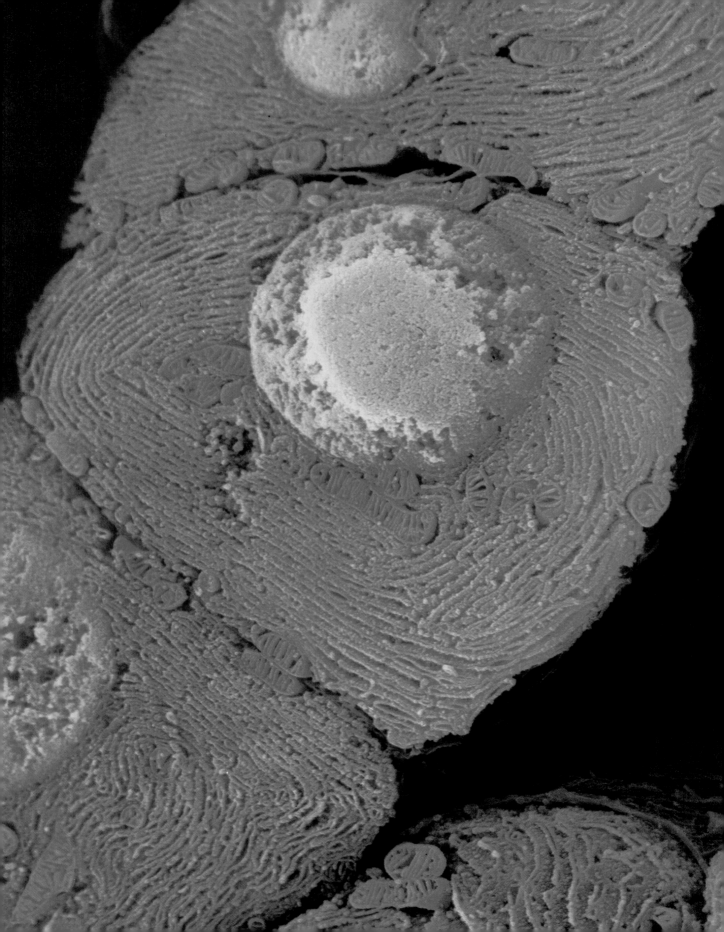

3 Cells

CHAPTER SECTIONS

3-1 Cell Structure and Function
3-2 Cell Activities

CHAPTER OBJECTIVES

After completing this chapter, you will be able to:

3-1 Describe the structure and function of the parts of a cell.

3-1 Compare a plant with an animal cell.

3-2 Describe the activities of a cell.

3-2 Distinguish between diffusion and osmosis.

3-2 Explain the importance of reproduction to a living organism.

3-2 Describe the processes of mitosis and meiosis.

When it first appeared on earth about 3.5 billion years ago, it was a tiny structure made up of tinier parts alive with activity. As the years passed, it changed a bit here and a bit there. New parts developed through unknown processes. And it became able to do increasingly different and fascinating jobs—it could build complex chemicals, it could release bursts of energy, and eventually it could even move by itself.

Millions of years later it would join not only with others of its kind, but with others not quite like it. Together they would form the most amazing inhabitants of the universe—living things with many harmonious parts, such as plants that grow from the soil and animals that race over it.

Today these tiny structures still exist. They are a bridge to the distant past. They are the building blocks of all living things. They are cells! Cells are fascinating and, in many ways, very mysterious objects. Scientists continue to probe the secrets of cells like explorers journeying through parts of an uncharted world.

Human skin cells magnified 10,000 times

3-1 Cell Structure and Function

You are about to take an imaginary journey. It will be quite an unusual trip because you will be traveling inside a living organism, visiting its tiny cells.

All living things are made up of one or more **cells,** which are the basic units of structure and function. Most cells are much too small to be seen without the aid of a microscope. In fact, most cells are smaller than the period at the end of this sentence. Yet believe it or not, within these tiny cells are even smaller structures. **The structures within the cells function in storing and releasing energy, building and repairing cell parts, getting rid of waste materials, responding to the environment, and increasing in number.**

There are many types of cells. For example, human cells include muscle cells, bone cells, and nerve cells. In plants, there are leaf cells, stem cells, and root cells. However, whether in an animal or a plant, most cells share certain similar characteristics. So hop aboard your imaginary ship and prepare to enter a

Figure 3-1 *A typical animal cell consists of many different structures, each having a characteristic shape and function. What are some of the functions carried out by cells?*

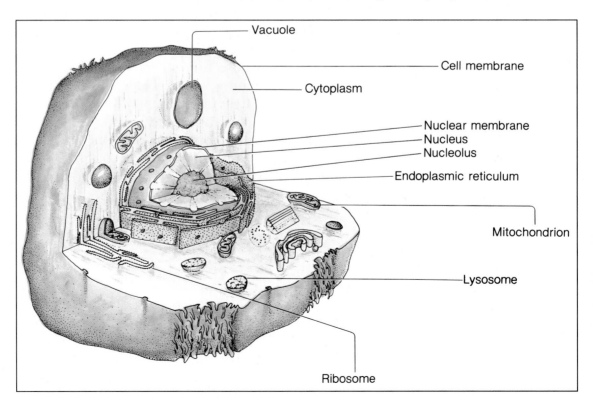

- Vacuole
- Cell membrane
- Cytoplasm
- Nuclear membrane
- Nucleus
- Nucleolus
- Endoplasmic reticulum
- Mitochondrion
- Lysosome
- Ribosome

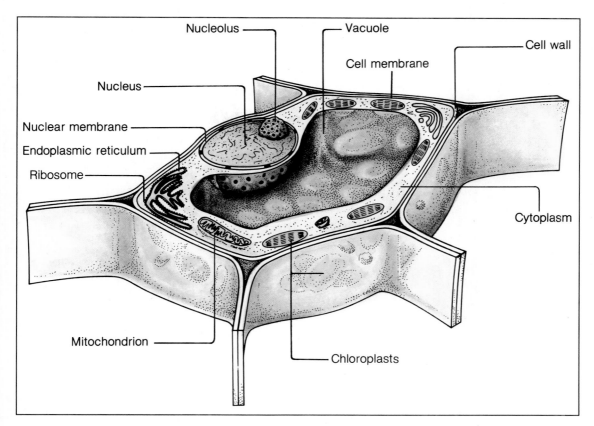

Nucleolus — Vacuole

Cell membrane

Cell wall

Nucleus —

Nuclear membrane —

Endoplasmic reticulum —

Ribosome —

Cytoplasm

Mitochondrion —

Chloroplasts

Figure 3-2 *A plant cell has many of the same structures as an animal cell. What structures do you see in this diagram that are not found in animal cells?*

typical plant cell. You will begin by sailing up through the trunk of an oak tree. Your destination is that box-shaped structure directly ahead. See Figure 3-2.

Cell Wall

Entering the cell of an oak tree is a bit difficult. First you must pass through the **cell wall.** Strong and stiff, the cell wall is made of cellulose, a nonliving material. Cellulose is a long chain of sugar molecules that the cell manufactures. Although the cell wall is hard, it does allow water, oxygen, carbon dioxide, and certain dissolved materials to pass through it. So sail on through.

The rigid cell wall is found only in plant cells. This structure helps give protection and support so the oak tree can grow tall. Think for a moment of grasses and flowers that support themselves upright. No doubt you can appreciate the important role the cell wall plays for the individual cell and for the entire plant.

Figure 3-3 *The cell wall gives support and protection to plant cells, enabling grasses, flowering plants, and trees to grow upright.*

Cell Membrane

Once past the cell wall, you prepare to enter the living material of the cell. Biologists call all the living material in *both* plant and animal cells **protoplasm.** Protoplasm is not a single structure or substance. It is a term used to describe all the living materials in a cell.

The first structure of protoplasm you encounter is a thin, flexible envelope called the **cell membrane.** In a plant cell, the cell membrane is just inside the cell wall. In an animal cell, the cell membrane forms the outer covering of the cell. Look again at Figures 3-1 and 3-2.

The cell membrane has several important jobs. You can discover one of its jobs on your own. Push down on your skin with your thumb. Your skin does not break, does it? Now lift your thumb. The skin bounces back to its original position. Your skin can do this because the cell membrane around each skin cell is elastic and flexible. It allows the cell to change shape under pressure. The flexible cell membrane also keeps the protoplasm of the cell separated from the environment outside the cell.

As your ship nears the edge of the cell membrane, you notice that there are tiny openings in the membrane. You steer toward an opening. Suddenly, your ship narrowly misses being struck by a chunk of floating material passing out of the cell. You have discovered another job of the cell membrane. This membrane helps control the movement of materials into and out of the cell.

Everything that the cell needs, from food to oxygen, enters the cell through this membrane. And harmful waste products exit through the cell membrane. In this way, the cell stays in smooth-running order, keeping conditions inside the cell the same even though conditions outside the cell may change. This ability of a cell to maintain a stable internal environment is called homeostasis. Now sail on to an important structure inside the living cell.

Nucleus

A large oval structure comes into view just ahead of you. This structure is the control center of the cell—the **nucleus** (NOO-klee-uhs), which acts as the

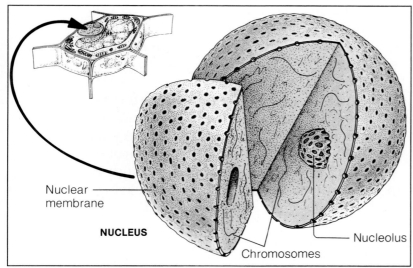

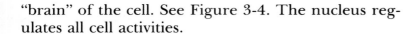

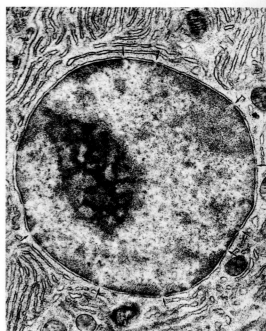

Figure 3-4 *This nucleus of a typical cell* (left) *shows the nuclear membrane, chromosomes, and nucleolus. In this photograph of the nucleus* (right), *the arrows point to tiny pores in the nuclear membrane.*

"brain" of the cell. See Figure 3-4. The nucleus regulates all cell activities.

NUCLEAR MEMBRANE   The thin membrane that separates the nucleus from the protoplasm of the cell is called the **nuclear membrane.** This membrane is similar to the cell membrane in that it allows materials to pass into and out of the nucleus. Small openings, or pores, are spaced regularly around the nuclear membrane. Each pore acts as a passageway into and out of the nucleus. Set your sights for that pore ahead and carefully glide into the nucleus.

CHROMOSOMES   Those thick, rodlike objects floating in the nucleus are called **chromosomes.** Steer very carefully to avoid colliding with and damaging the delicate chromosomes. For the chromosomes direct the activities of the cell and pass on the traits of the cell to new cells.

The large, complex molecules that make up the chromosomes are compounds called nucleic acids. You may recall from Chapter 2 that nucleic acids store the information that helps a cell make the proteins it needs. And proteins are necessary for life. Some proteins, for example, are used to form structural parts of the cell such as the cell membrane. Other proteins make up different enzymes and hormones used inside and outside the cell. Enzymes and hormones regulate cell activities.

The two nucleic acids that make up the chromosomes are DNA and RNA. You can think of these nucleic acids as the "blueprints" of life. Working together, DNA and RNA store the information and carry out the steps in the protein-making process—a process necessary to life. The DNA remains in the nucleus. But the RNA, carrying its protein-building instructions, leaves the nucleus through a nuclear pore. So hitch a ride on the RNA leaving the nucleus and continue your exploration of the cell.

NUCLEOLUS　As you prepare to leave the nucleus, you see a small, dense object float past. It is the **nucleolus** (noo-KLEE-uh-luhs), or "little nucleus." You are looking at a cell structure whose function remains something of a mystery. Biologists know that

Career: *Medical Artist*

Have you ever looked at a health book or a magazine about health that did not have diagrams? Probably not, because many concepts and objects related to health cannot be easily understood by reading only words. For example, cell structures and functions, body parts, and organism development can best be "described" through the use of drawings. Making such drawings is the job of a special group of artists.

Artists who create visual materials dealing with health and medicine are **medical artists.** Sometimes their work involves viewing a specimen through various kinds of microscopes in order to draw it. Or a medical artist may dissect and study the parts of animals and plants. Some medical artists work closely with surgeons or other kinds of doctors in order to pre-

pare accurate drawings of medical conditions.

Most medical artists are employed by publishers, medical, veterinary, or dental schools, or by hospitals with programs in teaching and research. To receive more information about this field, write to the Association of Medical Illustrators, Route 5, Box 311F, Midlothian, VA 23113.

the nucleolus is made up of RNA and protein. And they believe this tiny structure may play an important role in making proteins for the cell.

Endoplasmic Reticulum

Outside the nucleus, floating in a clear, thick fluid, your ship needs no propulsion. For here the jellylike material called **cytoplasm** is constantly moving. Cytoplasm is the term for all the protoplasm, or living material of the cell, *outside* the nucleus.

Steering will be a bit difficult here because many particles and tubelike structures are scattered throughout the cytoplasm. You cannot help noticing a maze of tubular passageways that leads out from the nuclear membrane. These clear tubes form the **endoplasmic reticulum** (en-doh-PLAZ-mik ri-TIK-yuh-luhm). See Figure 3-5.

The endoplasmic reticulum is involved in the manufacture and transport of proteins. You can see that it is well suited for its job. Its network of passageways spreads throughout the cell. Proteins made in one part of the cell can pass through the endoplasmic reticulum to other parts of the cell. Other materials can be transported to the outside of the cell through this system.

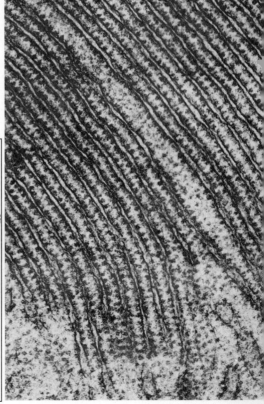

Figure 3-5 *The endoplasmic reticulum* (left) *manufactures and transports proteins. In this photograph of the endoplasmic reticulum* (right), *the dark dots lining the tubelike passageways are ribosomes.*

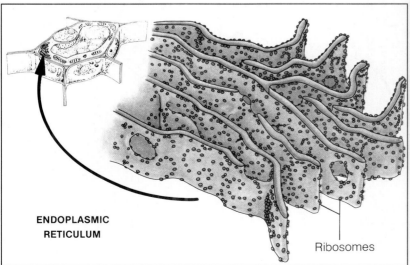

ENDOPLASMIC
RETICULUM

Ribosomes

Ribosomes

Look closely at the inner surface of one of the endoplasmic passageways. Attached to the surface are grainlike bodies called **ribosomes,** which are made up mainly of the nucleic acid RNA. Ribosomes are the protein-making sites of the cell. The RNA in the ribosomes, along with the RNA sent out from the nucleus, directs the production of proteins. Ribosomes are well positioned as they not only help make proteins, they "drop" them directly into the endoplasmic reticulum. From there the proteins go to any part of the cell that needs them.

Not all ribosomes are attached to the endoplasmic reticulum. Some float freely in the cytoplasm. Watch out! There go a few passing by. The cell you are in has many ribosomes. What might this tell you about its protein-making activity?

Mitochondria

As you pass by the ribosomes, you see other structures looming ahead. These structures are **mitochondria** (migh-toh-кon-dree-uh; singular: mitochondrion), which are the main source of energy for the cell. Somewhat larger than the ribosomes, these rod-shaped structures are often referred to as the "powerhouses" of the cell. See Figure 3-6.

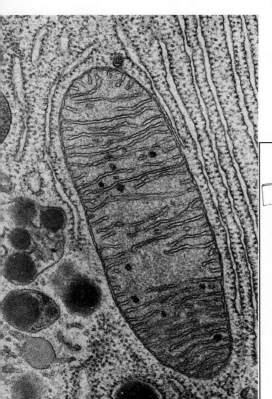

Figure 3-6 *The mitochondrion is the "powerhouse" of the cell.*

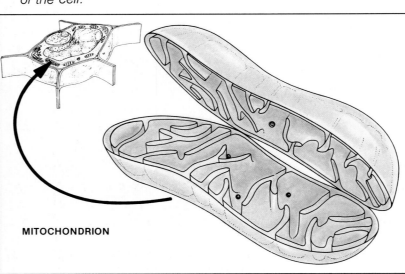

MITOCHONDRION

Inside the mitochondria, simple food substances such as sugars are broken down. Large amounts of energy are released during the breakdown of sugars. The mitochondria gather this energy and store it in special energy-rich molecules. These molecules are convenient energy packages that the cell uses to do all its work. The more active a cell is, the more mitochondria it has. Some cells, such as a human liver cell, contain more than 1000 mitochondria. Would you expect your muscle cells or your bone cells to have more mitochondria?

Because mitochondria have a small amount of their own DNA, some scientists believe that they were once tiny organisms that invaded living cells millions of years ago. The DNA molecules in the mitochondria were passed from one generation of cells to the next as simple organisms evolved into complex ones. Now all living cells contain mitochondria. No longer invaders, mitochondria are an essential part of living cells.

Vacuoles

That large, round, water-filled sac you see floating in the cytoplasm of this plant cell is called a **vacuole** (VA-kyoo-ohl). Both plant and animal cells have vacuoles. However, plant cells often have one very large vacuole while animal cells have a few small vacuoles.

Vacuoles act like storage tanks. Food, enzymes, and other materials needed by the cell are stored inside the vacuole sacs. Vacuoles also can store waste products. In plant cells, vacuoles are the main water-storage areas. When water vacuoles in plant cells are full, they swell and make the cell plump. This plumpness keeps a plant firm. During its lifetime, a plant cell may increase to 500 times its original size because of an increase in the amount of water in its expanding vacuoles.

Lysosomes

If you carefully swing your ship around the lake-like vacuole, you may be lucky enough to see a **lysosome.** Lucky because lysosomes are common in animal cells but not often observed in plant cells.

Activity

Word Clues

The definition of a word can often be determined by knowing the meaning of its prefix. Look up the prefix for each of the following words, and tell how it relates to the definition.

chloroplast
protoplasm
mitochondria
vacuole
chromosome
lysosome
cytoplasm

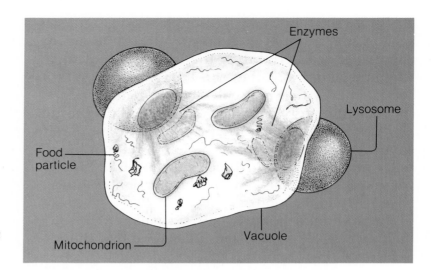

Figure 3-7 *Enzymes from a lysosome digest the contents of a vacuole.*

Activity

Plant and Animal Cells

1. To view a plant cell, remove a very thin transparent piece of tissue from an onion.

2. Place the onion tissue on a glass slide.

3. Add a drop of iodine stain to the tissue and cover with a cover slip.

4. Observe the onion under the low and high power of your microscope. Draw a diagram of one onion cell and label its parts.

5. To view an animal cell, gently scrape the inside of your cheek with a toothpick.

6. Gently tap the toothpick on the center of another glass slide.

7. Add a drop of methylene blue and cover with a cover slip.

8. Observe the cheek cells under the high and low power of your microscope. Draw a diagram of one cell and label its parts.

Compare the two cells.

Lysosomes are small, round structures involved with the digestive activities of the cell. See Figure 3-7. Lysosomes contain enzymes that break down large food molecules into smaller ones. Then these smaller food molecules are passed on to the mitochondria, where they are "burned" to provide energy.

Although lysosomes digest substances in the cytoplasm, you need not worry about your ship's safety! The membrane surrounding a lysosome keeps the enzymes from escaping and digesting the entire cell. However, lysosomes do digest whole cells when the cells are injured or dead. In an interesting process in the growth of a tadpole into a frog, lysosomes in the tadpole's tail cells digest the tail. Then this protoplasmic material is reused to make new body parts for the frog.

Chloroplasts

Your journey is just about over, and you will soon be leaving the cell. But first look around you. Floating in the cytoplasm are large, irregularly shaped structures that are easily sighted. They are green! These structures are **chloroplasts,** and they contain a green pigment called chlorophyll. Chlorophyll captures the energy of sunlight and uses it to make food for the plant cell.

Chloroplasts are found *only* in plant cells. However, the sea slug, an animal, often eats plants that

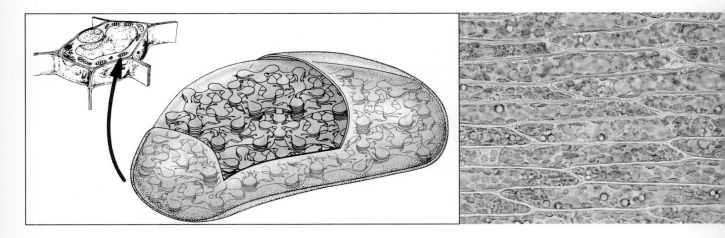

Figure 3-8 *Chloroplasts* (left), *the food-making sites, are found only in the cells of green plants* (right).

contain chloroplasts. After the sea slug digests the plant, some of the chloroplasts get into the cells of its digestive system. There the chloroplasts continue to make food just as they do in a plant. The process goes on for a week or so and provides the sea slug's cells with food for energy.

SECTION REVIEW

1. What does protoplasm mean?
2. What two nucleic acids are found in the nucleus?
3. Name the structures in the cytoplasm needed for the manufacture and transport of proteins.
4. Describe three differences between plant cells and animal cells.

3-2 Cell Activities

Each structure within a cell performs a vital activity. And the cell as a whole carries out the chemical processes necessary to life. **Life activities performed by cells include metabolism, diffusion, osmosis, and reproduction.** The tiny cell is like a miniature factory that produces many kinds of chemicals. Like any factory, a cell must have energy to do work. Working day and night, a cell traps, converts, stores, and uses energy.

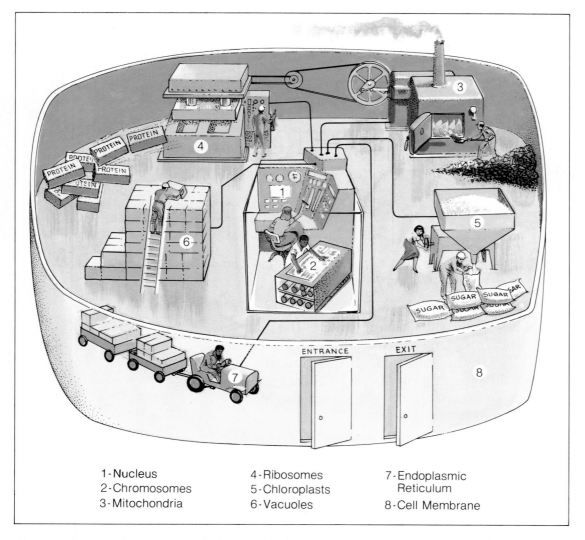

1-Nucleus	4-Ribosomes	7-Endoplasmic
2-Chromosomes	5-Chloroplasts	Reticulum
3-Mitochondria	6-Vacuoles	8-Cell Membrane

Figure 3-9 *A cell, such as this plant cell, is like a miniature factory that carries out all the activities necessary to life. What is the function of structure 7?*

Metabolism

Even while you sleep, you need energy to keep you alive. But where does this energy come from? Cells provide it. Although cells do not *make* energy, they do *change* energy from one form to another. Cells obtain energy from their environment and convert it into a usable form.

This conversion process is very complex. And it involves many chemical reactions. Some reactions break down molecules. Other reactions build new molecules. The sum of all the building-up and breaking-down activities that occur in a living cell is called **metabolism.**

Think for a moment of all the things cells do: grow, repair structures, absorb food, manufacture proteins, get rid of wastes, and reproduce. The energy for these activities is locked up in the molecules in food. As a result of metabolism, the stored energy in food is set free so it can be used to do work.

Diffusion

Remember how you sailed through the cell membrane to enter the cell? Well, the substances that get into and out of the cell do the same thing. Food molecules, oxygen, water, and other materials enter and leave the cell through openings in the cell membrane by a process called **diffusion.**

Why does diffusion occur? Molecules of all substances are in constant motion, continuously colliding with one another. This motion causes the molecules to spread out. The molecules move from an area where there are more of them to an area where there are fewer of them. See Figure 3-10.

If there are many food molecules outside the cell, for example, some diffuse through the membrane into the cell. At the same time, waste materials built up in the cell pass out of the cell by diffusion.

You can observe the process of diffusion for yourself. Drop some ink into a glass of water and watch what happens. The drop of ink spreads throughout the water, getting lighter in color as the ink molecules move through the liquid.

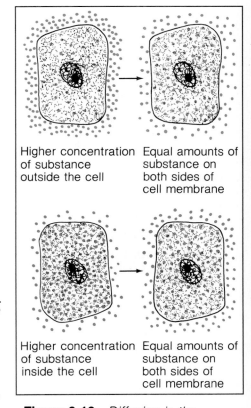

Higher concentration of substance outside the cell

Equal amounts of substance on both sides of cell membrane

Higher concentration of substance inside the cell

Equal amounts of substance on both sides of cell membrane

Figure 3-10 *Diffusion is the movement of molecules of a substance into a cell (top) or out of a cell (bottom). Substances move from places where they are more concentrated to places where they are less concentrated.*

Figure 3-11 *The cell membrane is selective, permitting oxygen and food molecules to enter and waste materials to leave.*

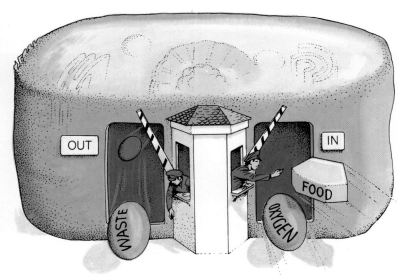

OUT

IN

FOOD

WASTE

OXYGEN

If substances can move into and out of the cell through the membrane, what keeps the protoplasm from oozing out? What keeps harmful materials from moving in? The cell membrane safeguards the contents of the cell because it is selective. That is, it permits only certain substances, mainly oxygen and food molecules, to diffuse into the cell. Only waste products such as carbon dioxide are allowed to diffuse out of the cell.

Osmosis

Water is the most important substance that passes through the cell membrane. In fact, about 80 percent of protoplasm is water. Water passes through the cell membrane by a special type of diffusion called **osmosis**. During osmosis, water molecules move from a place of greater concentration to a place of lesser concentration. This movement keeps the cell from drying out.

Suppose you put a cell in a glass of salt water. The concentration of water outside the cell is lower than the concentration of water inside the cell. So water leaves the cell, and the cell starts to shrink. If too much water leaves the cell, the cell dries up and dies.

Now, if the cell was put in a glass of fresh water instead of salt water, just the opposite occurs. Water enters the cell, and the cell swells. This happens because the concentration of water is lower inside the cell than outside the cell. As you might imagine, if too much water enters the cell, the cell bursts.

Figure 3-12 *Normal red blood cells* (left) *will shrink* (center) *if too much water leaves the cells. If too much water enters the cells, they will swell* (right).

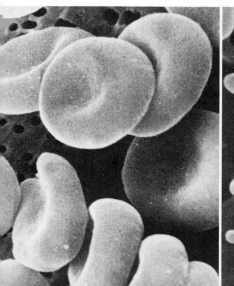 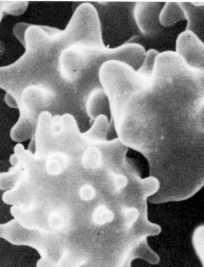 

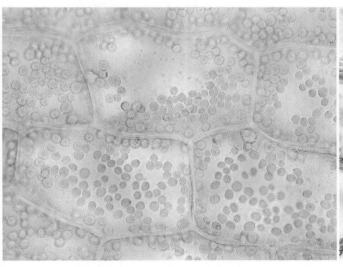
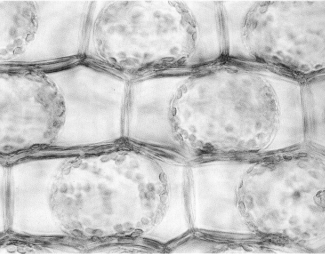

Reproduction

How many cells do you think you are made of? The number of cells in an organism depends on its size, and so no specific number can be given. But you may be surprised to learn that as an adult, you will consist of about 50 thousand billion cells! All of these cells come from just one original cell.

GROWTH AND DEVELOPMENT Body cells must undergo reproduction in order for the total number of cells to increase and for the organism to grow. These cells reproduce by dividing into two new cells. Each new cell, called a daughter cell, is identical to the other and to the parent cell. How does this process occur?

If a parent cell—a skin cell, leaf cell, or bone cell, for example—is to produce two identical daughter cells, then the exact contents of its nucleus must go into the nucleus of each new cell. In other words, the "blueprints" of life in the parent cell must be passed on to each daughter cell. Now, if the parent cell simply splits in half, each daughter cell would get only half the contents of the nucleus—only half the "blueprints." It would no longer be the same kind of cell—a skin cell, leaf cell, or bone cell.

Fortunately, this is not what happens. For just before a cell divides, all the material in the nucleus is duplicated, or copied. The duplication and division of the nucleus and of the chromosomes is called **mitosis** (migh-TOH-sis).

Figure 3-13 *In these normal plant leaf cells* (left), *the movement of too much water from the cell vacuoles causes the cell contents to shrink away from the cell wall* (right).

Activity

Making Cell Models

Make an original cell model using food products.

1. Dissolve some colorless gelatin in warm water.

2. Pour the gelatin in a rectangular pan (for a plant cell) or a round pan (for an animal cell).

3. Find edible materials that resemble cell structures. Place these materials in the gelatin before it begins to gel.

4. On a sheet of paper, identify each cell structure.

Figure 3-14 *During mitosis, each chromosome is duplicated before the nucleus divides. In this drawing, the magician represents a nucleus. And the balloons represent chromosomes.*

Figure 3-15 *In one stage of mitosis, the chromosomes in the nucleus are duplicated (left). In another stage, one of each pair of chromosomes moves to the opposite ends of the nucleus (center). Finally, the nucleus splits and two new cells with identical chromosomes are formed (right).*

Mitosis is a very complex process that occurs in several stages. During mitosis, each chromosome in the nucleus makes a copy of itself. See Figure 3-14. When the nuclear membrane disappears, one set of chromosomes moves to one end of the parent cell, and the other set of chromosomes moves to the opposite end. A new nuclear membrane forms around each set of chromosomes. The parent cell then divides into two. Each daughter cell contains an exact copy of the chromosomes of the parent cell. The complete "blueprint" of life is passed from one cell to another. The two new skin cells are exactly like the parent skin cell and so are able to do the same job. And the two new nerve cells are identical in form and function to their parent nerve cell.

Mitosis, then, is the process by which the cells of an organism reproduce to form exact copies of one another. Through mitosis, both plants and animals grow larger, repair damaged parts, and replace dead

cells. For example, the root tip of a plant contains many cells undergoing mitosis. The formation of new cells makes the root longer and allows it to push through the ground toward water.

PRODUCTION OF OFFSPRING Mitosis is a method to reproduce cells inside an organism. However, there is another kind of reproduction in which a new organism comes from two parents. This is called sexual reproduction. Sexual reproduction involves the joining of two special types of cells—the male sex cell and the female sex cell—in a process known as fertilization. The offspring of fertilization contains a *combination* of the chromosomes of the male sex cell and the female sex cell.

Sex cells reproduce by a special type of cell division called **meiosis** (migh-OH-sis). Meiosis is a form of cell division that *halves* the number of chromosomes in a male or female sex cell as it forms. When the sex cells later join, the offspring gets half its chromosomes from the male and the other half from the female. The offspring's cells now have the same number of chromosomes as the cells of the parents.

Activity

How Many Cells?

Suppose a cell splits in half every 10 minutes. How many cells will there be after 1½ hours?

Figure 3-16 *Sexual reproduction produces offspring that have a combination of the characteristics of the parents.*

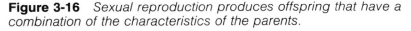

SECTION REVIEW

1. What is metabolism?
2. Describe the process of osmosis.
3. What process causes an organism to grow?

LABORATORY ACTIVITY

Things Look Different Under a Microscope

Purpose

In this activity, you will examine newspaper and magazine paper under a microscope.

Materials *(per group)*

Microscope
Microscope slide
Cover slip
Small pieces of newspaper print
Small pieces of colorful magazine
   photographs

Procedure

1. Obtain a small piece of newspaper print and place it on a clean microscope slide. Cover the slide with a cover slip.
2. Place the slide on the stage of the microscope. The newspaper should be facing up and be in the normal reading position. **CAUTION:** *Always use a cover slip to protect the objective lens from coming into contact with the material being observed.*
3. With the low-power objective in place, follow your teacher's directions for focusing on a letter.
4. While focusing on a letter, move the slide to the left. Which way does the letter seem to move? Now move the slide to the right. Which way does the letter seem to move this time?
5. While looking through the eyepiece, adjust the slide so that a letter is in the center of your field of view. Now, looking at the stage and objectives from the side, revolve the nosepiece until the high-power objective clicks into place. Using *only* the fine adjustment knob, bring the letter into focus. Describe what you see. Now follow the same

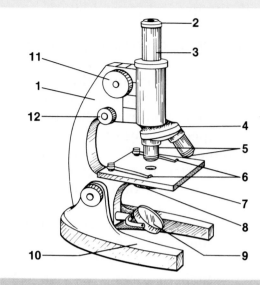

MICROSCOPE PARTS AND THEIR FUNCTIONS

1. **Arm**   Supports the body tube
2. **Eyepiece**   Contains the magnifying lens you look through
3. **Body tube**   Maintains the proper distance between the eyepiece and objective lenses
4. **Nosepiece**   Holds high- and low-power objective lenses and can be rotated to change magnification
5. **Objective lenses**   Low-power lens usually magnifies 10 times; high-power lens usually magnifies 40 times
6. **Stage clips**   Hold the slide in place
7. **Stage**   Supports the slide
8. **Diaphragm**   Regulates the amount of light let into the body tube
9. **Mirror**   Reflects the light upward through the diaphragm, the specimen, and the lenses
10. **Base**   Supports the microscope
11. **Coarse-adjustment knob**   Moves the body tube up and down for focusing
12. **Fine-adjustment knob**   Moves the body tube slightly to sharpen the image

steps using magazine paper.

Observations and Conclusions

1. What letter did you choose? How does this letter appear when viewed through the microscope? Focus on another letter. How does it appear? What conclusion can you draw about the way objects appear when viewed under the microscope?

SUMMARY

3-1 Cell Structure and Function

- The cell wall, found only in plant cells, is made of nonliving cellulose and gives protection and support to the cell.

- Protoplasm is all the living material of a cell.

- The cell membrane is a thin, flexible membrane that regulates the movement of materials into and out of the cell.

- The control center of the cell is the nucleus. It is surrounded by the nuclear membrane.

- Chromosomes found in the nucleus are made of nucleic acids, which are the "blueprints" of life.

- Cytoplasm is all the protoplasm outside the nucleus.

- The endoplasmic reticulum, a network of tubelike passageways, is the site of the manufacture and transport of proteins.

- Ribosomes, often attached to the endoplasmic reticulum, are the protein-making sites.

- Mitochondria are the "powerhouses" of the cell.

- Vacuoles store food, water, enzymes, and waste products.

- Lysosomes play a role in the digestive activities of the cell.

- Chloroplasts, found only in green plant cells, capture the energy of the sun and use it to make food for the cell.

3-2 Cell Activities

- The sum of all the activities that occur in a living cell is called metabolism.

- Food, oxygen, water, and other materials enter and leave the cell by a process called diffusion.

- Water passes through the cell membrane by a type of diffusion called osmosis.

- Mitosis is the duplication and division of the nucleus and of the chromosomes during cell division, which results in daughter cells identical to the parent cell.

- During the formation of the male and female sex cells, meiosis takes place and the chromosome number is halved.

VOCABULARY

Define each term in a complete sentence.

cell	cytoplasm	metabolism	nucleus
cell membrane	diffusion	mitochondria	osmosis
cell wall	endoplasmic reticulum	mitosis	protoplasm
chloroplast	lysosome	nuclear membrane	ribosome
chromosome	meiosis	nucleolus	vacuole

CONTENT REVIEW: MULTIPLE CHOICE

Choose the letter of the answer that best completes each statement.

1. The cell wall is made of a nonliving material called
   a. protoplasm.   b. nucleic acid.   c. cellulose.   d. chromosomes.

2. The cell membrane
   a. provides protection for the cell.
   b. keeps the cell's inner contents together.
   c. regulates the movement of materials into and out of the cell.
   d. does all of these.
3. The "brain" of the cell is its
   a. nucleus.   b. mitochondria.   c. ribosomes.   d. cytoplasm.
4. The rodlike structures that direct the activities of the cell and pass on traits to new cells are the
   a. chloroplasts.   b. chromosomes.   c. ribosomes.   d. lysosomes.
5. The network of passageways that transports proteins throughout the cell is known as the
   a. nuclear membrane.   b. endoplasmic reticulum.
   c. mitochondria.   d. vacuole.
6. Food, water, and wastes are stored in
   a. lysosomes.   b. chromosomes.   c. ribosomes.   d. vacuoles.
7. Food-making structures found in cells of green plants are called
   a. chloroplasts.   b. chromosomes.
   c. chromoplasts.   d. mitochondria.
8. Water usually moves through a cell membrane from an area of
   a. lesser concentration to greater concentration.
   b. equal concentration to equal concentration.
   c. greater concentration to lesser concentration.
   d. none of these.
9. The total number of cells in an organism increases as a result of
   a. respiration.   b. reproduction.   c. homeostasis.   d. diffusion.
10. Each daughter cell gets an exact copy of the chromosomes of the parent cell through the process of
   a. mitosis.   b. diffusion.   c. homeostasis.   d. osmosis.

CONTENT REVIEW: COMPLETION

Fill in the word or words that best complete each statement.

1. All the living material in a cell is called _____.
2. The ability of a cell to maintain a stable internal environment even if external conditions change is called _____.
3. _____ and _____ are two important nucleic acids.
4. Simple food substances are broken down and the energy they release is stored in structures called _____.
5. Food, enzymes, and other materials needed by cells are stored inside sacs called _____.
6. Structures involved in the digestive activities of the cell are called _____.
7. The passage of food, oxygen, water, and other materials in and out of a cell is called _____.
8. When only water enters or leaves a cell, the process is called _____.
9. During _____, the cells of an organism reproduce to form exact copies of one another.
10. During _____, the chromosome number in the male sex cell and in the female sex cell is halved.

Determine whether each statement is true or false. If it is true, write "true." If it is false, change the underlined word or words to make the statement true.

1. The outer covering of the <u>animal</u> cell is the cell wall.
2. The <u>cytoplasm</u> controls all cell activities.
3. Chromosomes are made of <u>nucleic acids</u>.
4. All the living material outside the nucleus is called <u>protoplasm</u>.
5. <u>Ribosomes</u> are the protein-making sites of the cell.
6. The green pigment found in special structures of a plant cell is called <u>chromatin</u>.
7. The sum of all the activities that occur in a living cell is called <u>metabolism</u>.
8. If a cell is placed in a glass of salt water, water will <u>enter</u> the cell.
9. The duplication and division of the nucleus and of the chromosomes is called <u>mitosis</u>.
10. The chromosome number in the male sex cell and in the female sex cell is halved during <u>fertilization</u>.

Use the skills you have developed in the chapter to complete each activity.

1. **Classifying organelles** On a sheet of paper, list the various activities of a cell. Then, next to each activity, give the organelle that is involved in that activity.
2. **Making inferences** If it were possible to implant chloroplasts in human cells, which cells would be the best sites? Explain.
3. **Relating facts** Your favorite plant has begun to wilt. You feel the soil in its pot and find that it is very dry. You water your plant and, about 20 minutes later, you discover that the plant is standing up straight again. How does this observation relate to osmosis?
4. **Interpreting graphs** At different temperatures, cells reproduce at different rates.

According to the accompanying graph, at what temperature does cell A reproduce most quickly? What happens to the rate of reproduction as the temperature increases between 10° C and 35° C? As the temperature increases between 35° C and 50° C?

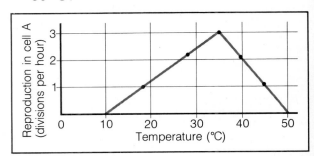

Discuss each of the following in a brief paragraph.

1. Explain how you can distinguish between a plant cell and an animal cell.
2. Describe five functions of a cell and name the structure involved in each function.
3. Why is it important that a cell membrane be selective in allowing materials into and out of the cell?
4. Compare the processes of mitosis and meiosis in terms of introducing new characteristics into the offspring.

4 Tissues, Organs, and Organ Systems

CHAPTER SECTIONS

4-1 A Division of Labor
4-2 Organization of Living Things

CHAPTER OBJECTIVES

After completing this chapter,
you will be able to:

4-1 Explain what is meant by division of labor in living things.

4-2 Describe the five levels of organization of living things.

4-2 Explain how the levels of organization of living things are dependent upon one another.

Poised high upon the edge of a jagged rock, the cheetah seems almost motionless. Yet every muscle is tensed and ready to spring into action.

Its nostrils quiver as the familiar scent of an antelope reaches its nose. The sleek animal's back arches, its ears prick up to catch even the faintest sound in the bushes below, and its tongue slowly and smoothly licks its lips.

In anticipation, the cheetah's heart pounds faster and its breathing quickens. A low, menacing sound escapes from its throat. Its paws curl more tightly around the rock as its limbs flex and tighten, flex and tighten. Its flanks ripple with excitement, and juices pour into its mouth as it prepares to descend upon its prey.

The unsuspecting antelope calmly grazes on the plain just below. A young antelope lies near, secure in the protection of its parent. Above them, the cheetah silently readies itself for attack. Every part of the animal—from the smallest cell to its entire body—is working together to ensure that the cheetah will eat well this night.

Cheetah in search of prey

Figure 4-1 *Multicellular organisms, such as this beetle and the green plant upon which it feeds, carry on a wide variety of complex activities.*

Figure 4-2 *Different parts of this bat's body work in harmony with each other as the bat prepares to attack. If the tree frog's body parts work well together, the frog may escape.*

4-1 A Division of Labor

Bacteria lead very simple lives. They do not walk, run, or listen to music. They do not see, smell, talk, or shake hands. They just grow, divide, and then grow some more. A cheetah, on the other hand, leads a life that is not that simple. Its life includes activities like roaming the plains, climbing trees, hunting for food, and playing with other cheetahs.

The whole body of a bacterium is made up of one cell. On its own, that single cell must do all the jobs that keep a bacterium alive. This accounts, in part, for the simple lives bacteria live. A cheetah, however, is multicellular—it is made of a great many cells. And these numerous cells are organized into the different parts of the cheetah's body, enabling the animal to carry out more complex activities than a single-celled bacterium can.

Some of the cheetah's body parts, such as muscle cells, are relatively small and simple. Other parts, like strands of muscle fibers, are larger and more complex. Still other parts, the cheetah's heart and circulatory system, for example, are even larger and more complex. However, all the different parts, whether small or large, interact with each other, perform their special functions, and keep the cheetah alive.

There is a **division of labor** within the body of the cheetah, as within most living things. **Division of labor means that the work of keeping the organism alive is divided among the various parts of its body.** Each part has a specific job to do. And as the part does its special job, it works in harmony with all the other parts to keep the organism healthy and active.

SECTION REVIEW

1. What is the basic difference between a bacterium and an organism such as the cheetah?
2. What is meant by the term "division of labor" in living things?

4-2 Organization of Living Things

The arrangement of specialized parts within a living thing can be referred to as levels of organization. **The five basic levels of organization, arranged from the smallest, least complex structure to the largest, most complex structure are cells, tissues, organs, organ systems, and organisms.**

Level One: Cells

In Chapter 3, you learned that all living things are made up of **cells.** These microscopic units of structure and function are the building blocks of life. Some living things, such as a bacterium, are made of only one cell. For these organisms, the single cell exists as a free-living organism. It does all the jobs that keep the organism alive.

In multicellular organisms, different cells perform specialized tasks. Muscle cells, for example, help the cheetah move through its environment, climb rocks, and spring to attack. Nerve cells receive and send messages throughout the cheetah's body. Every kind of cell, however, depends on other cells for its survival and for the survival of the entire organism. Those muscle cells move only when set into action by nerve cells. And both muscle cells and nerve cells rely on blood cells for oxygen.

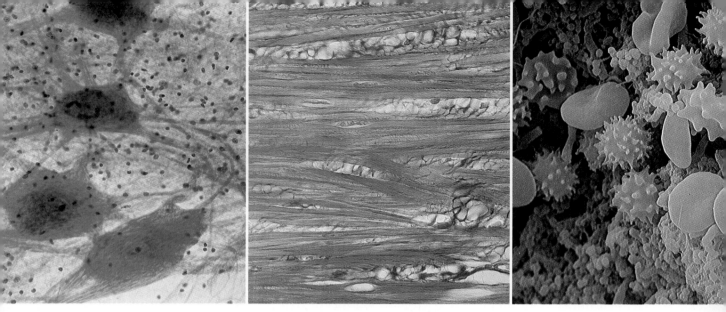

Figure 4-3 *Cells come in different shapes and sizes, as you can see from these nerve* (left), *muscle* (center), *and blood cells* (right).

Level Two: Tissues

In a multicellular organism, cells usually do not work alone. Cells that are similar in structure and function are joined together to form **tissues.** Tissues are the second level of organization.

Like the single cell of the bacterium, each tissue cell must carry on all the activities needed to keep that cell alive. But at the same time, tissues perform one or more specialized functions in an organism's body. In other words, tissues work for themselves as well as for the good of the entire living thing.

For example, bone cells in the cheetah form bone tissue, a strong, solid tissue that gives shape and support to the bodies of animals. Blood cells are part of blood tissue, a liquid tissue responsible for carrying food, oxygen, and wastes throughout the cheetah's body. Some muscle tissue helps move the cheetah's legs, neck, and other body parts. Another kind of muscle tissue enables its heart to pump blood. A third type of muscle tissue lines its stomach and helps the cheetah digest its meal.

Plants have tissues too. The leaves and stems of a plant are covered by a type of tissue called epidermis, which protects the plant and prevents it from losing water. Tissue known as xylem (ZIGH-luhm) conducts water and dissolved minerals up through

Figure 4-4 *The sundew plant has special hairlike tissues that produce a sticky fluid that traps insects.*

the stems to the leaves. And another special tissue called phloem (FLOH-em) brings food made in the leaves back down to the stems and roots.

Level Three: Organs

The cheetah is a clever hunter. Stalking about on its padded feet, it uses its keen senses of smell, sight, and hearing to locate its prey. Then, as its lungs fill with oxygen, it moves with incredible speed and strikes down its victim with a blow of its front paws.

The cheetah's eyes, ears, nose, and lungs are several of the **organs** that help the animal find food and stay alive. Organs are groups of different tissues working together. The cheetah's heart, for example, is an organ composed of nerve tissue, muscle tissue, and blood tissue. Each tissue does its special job. Nerve tissue signals the muscle tissue to contract. Muscle tissue contracts and causes the heart to pump the blood tissue. Blood tissue carries oxygen and wastes to and from every cell in the cheetah's heart— and eventually to cells throughout the entire body.

Figure 4-5 *Various organs in the cheetah's body work together so that the animal can run as fast as 115 kilometers per hour.*

Figure 4-6 *Each organ system is made up of groups of organs that work together. What is the function of the endocrine system?*

ORGAN SYSTEMS

System	Function
Skeletal	Protects and supports the body
Muscular	Supports the body and enables it to move
Skin	Protects the body
Digestive	Receives, transports, breaks down, and absorbs food throughout the body
Circulatory	Transports oxygen, wastes, and digested food throughout the body
Respiratory	Permits the exchange of gases in the body
Excretory	Removes liquid and solid wastes from the body
Endocrine	Regulates various body functions
Nervous	Conducts messages throughout the body to aid in coordination of body functions
Reproductive	Produces male and female sex cells

You are probably familiar with the names of many of the organs that make up your body. Your brain, stomach, kidneys, and skin are some examples. Can you name some others?

Plants have organs too. Roots, stems, and leaves are common plant organs. Like animal organs, plant organs are made up of groups of tissues performing the same function. For example, various tissues in the leaf help this organ make food for the plant.

Level Four: Systems

Like cells and tissues, organs seldom work alone. They "cooperate" with each other to form specific **systems.** A system, then, is a group of organs that work together to perform certain functions.

The cheetah is able to spot its prey because its sense organs—its eyes, ears, and nose—do their job. They receive messages in the form of sights, sounds, and smells. The cheetah's brain processes this information. And its spinal cord and nerves send out impulses to all parts of its body so that the animal is able to prepare to attack. Each of these organs, doing its individual job as well as working together with other organs, forms part of the cheetah's nervous system.

A living thing cannot survive unless all its systems are "go." For example, its digestive system must receive, carry, break down, and absorb food. Its excretory system must remove certain waste materials from its body. And its endocrine system must make chemical substances called hormones. Hormones speed up or slow down the activities of many organs. They also play a part in the growth and development of the organism.

The organs that make up a system vary in number and complexity from one kind of living thing to another. For example, a very simple animal called the hydra has a nervous system that is a simple net of nerves spread throughout the organism. More complex animals, such as the earthworm, have a more highly organized system of nerves and a primitive brain. The most highly developed animals, people, for example, have nervous systems consisting of a complex brain, a spinal cord, and nerves.

Figure 4-7 *The skin of the camel* (left), *part of its excretory system, helps it get rid of waste materials and excess heat. The circulatory system of the eucalyptus tree* (right) *brings water and other substances to the very top of the tree.*

Career: *Histologic Technician*

HELP WANTED: HISTOLOGIC TECHNICIAN Position involves preparation of tissue for microscopic study and detection of cell features that suggest disease or damage. Completion of a formal training program or an associate degree program in histotechnology required.

New drugs and chemical food additives are constantly being manufactured and introduced into the marketplace. Before these substances can be used, however, they must be carefully tested to ensure that they are safe for human use. The United States Food and Drug Administration requires these tests. Controlled amounts of a new drug or additive are given to research animals over a period of time. Scientists then study the tissues of the animals, looking for possible damage or disease.

People who prepare animal or plant tissue for microscopic study are called **histologic technicians** or histotechnologists. They prepare tissue by first treating it with special chemicals that prevent decomposition of the tissue. They then remove water from the tissue so that they can place it in liquid wax. The wax quickly hardens and gives support to the tissue

so that the tissue can be sliced into extremely thin sections with a very sharp knife. The sections are placed on microscope slides and are stained with various dyes that help to distinguish tissue structures. A specially trained technician or a doctor examines the slide.

Opportunities for histologic technicians exist in various fields of medicine, in marine biology, and in certain areas of industrial and university research. For further information, write to the National Society for Histotechnology, 5900 Princess Garden Parkway, Suite 805, Lanham, MD 20706.

Level Five: Organisms

Throughout this chapter, you have been reading the word "organism." Perhaps you have already determined what an **organism** is. An organism is an entire living thing that carries out *all* the basic life functions. You, like the cheetah, are an organism. A buttercup is an organism, as are a cactus, a caribou, and a whale. Even a one-celled bacterium is an organism. The organism is the highest level of organization of living things.

A complex organism is a combination of organ systems. Each system performs its particular function, but all the systems work together to keep the organism alive. Without the smooth operation of any one of its systems, a living thing could not survive.

The behavior of the cheetah you read about earlier is the result of many systems performing their specific functions and interacting with other systems. For example, when the cheetah's nervous system senses the antelope's presence, it signals the muscular system. The cheetah's spine arches, its tail goes

Figure 4-8 *The diagram below shows the levels of organization in an organism. What is the order of organization from least to most complex?*

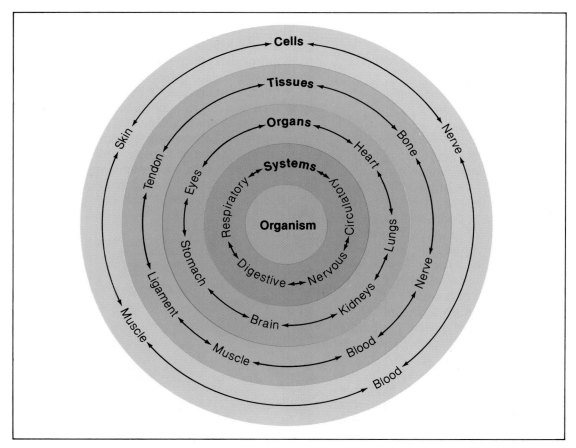

Figure 4-9 *Survival often depends on the cooperation of body parts—from simple cells to complex systems.*

straight back, and its hind legs extend forward. In this position, the cheetah is able to accelerate to speeds of 75 to 115 kilometers per hour. The nervous system also alerts organs of the endocrine system, which increase their production of hormones. As a result, the cheetah's heart rate increases and more oxygen than usual is delivered to the muscle cells. As you can see, no one process or one system is independent of the others.

Cells, tissues, organs, systems, organisms. By now one thing should be clear to you: Each level of organization interacts with every other level. And the smooth functioning of a complex organism is the result of all its various parts working together.

The antelope, of course, is also an organism. The parts of its body must work together as well. In fact, once the antelope spots the cheetah lying in wait, its body parts work fast and furiously to spare it an untimely death at the paws of the cheetah. Often the cheetah wins this deadly battle, but this time the antelope and its young escape into the bush—just as the cheetah is about to jump and pounce. Tonight, at least, the cheetah will go hungry.

SECTION REVIEW

1. List and define the five levels of organization of living things.
2. Give an example of two organ systems working together within an organism.

LABORATORY ACTIVITY

Have You Tasted These?

Purpose

In this activity, you will be introduced to some unusual foods that are derived from cells, tissues, and organs of various animals.

Materials *(per group)*

Dictionary or encyclopedia
Cookbooks

Procedure

1. Examine the following list of foods:

tripe	jerky
sweetbreads	suet
chitterlings	marrow
escargot	pâté de foie gras
sushi	caviar

   How many of these foods can you identify?
   How many of them have you eaten?

2. Using a dictionary, encyclopedia, or cook-book, look up the foods that no one in the class was able to identify. Name the animal that is the source of each of these foods. From what part of the animal is each of these foods derived?

Observations and Conclusions

1. Classify each of these foods using the levels of organization you learned in this chapter as categories: cells, tissues, organs, organ systems, organisms.
2. List other animal organs that are used as foods. How many of these have you tasted? How were these foods prepared?

CHAPTER REVIEW

4-1 A Division of Labor

■ In a one-celled organism, the single cell performs all the activities necessary to keep the organism alive.

■ In multicellular organisms, different parts of the body have specific jobs to do. This division of labor keeps the organism alive.

4-2 Organization of Living Things

■ The least complex level of organization of living things is the cell. The cell is the basic unit of structure and function of all organisms.

■ In multicellular organisms, different cells perform specialized tasks. Every kind of cell, however, depends on other cells for its survival and for the survival of the entire organism.

■ The five basic levels of organization—arranged from the smallest, least complex structure to the largest, most complex structure—are cells, tissues, organs, organ systems, and organisms.

■ Cells that are similar in structure and function are joined together to form tissue. For example, bone cells in a cheetah form bone tissue, a strong, solid tissue that gives shape and support to the body of the animal.

■ Plants as well as animals have tissue. For example, the leaves and stems of a plant are covered by a type of tissue called epidermis, which protects the plant and prevents it from losing water.

■ Groups of different tissues work together as organs. For example, the cheetah's heart is an organ composed of nerve tissue, muscle tissue, and blood tissue. Each tissue does its special job.

■ Roots, stems, and leaves are common organs in plants.

■ A group of different organs working together to perform certain functions is known as a system.

■ The organs that make up a system vary in number from one kind of living thing to another. The most highly developed animals, for example, have nervous systems consisting of a complex brain, a spinal cord, and nerves. However, a simple animal such as the hydra has a nervous system that is only a simple net of nerves spread throughout the organism.

■ An organism is an entire living thing that carries out all the life functions. Complex organisms are made up of systems. The organism is the highest level of organization of living things.

■ In a complex organism, each system performs its particular function, but all systems work together to keep the organism alive.

Define each term in a complete sentence.

cell	**organ**	**system**
division of labor	**organism**	**tissue**

Choose the letter of the answer that best completes each statement.

1. In a bacterium, the single cell carries on
   a. digestion only.　b. respiration and digestion only.　c. all life functions.　d. excretion only.

2. The concept of various body parts each doing a specific job is called
   a. division of labor.   b. reduction division.
   c. differentiation.   d. specialization.

3. The basic units of structure and function of all organisms are the
   a. bones.   b. systems.   c. cells.   d. tissues.

4. Multicellular organisms have
   a. one cell.   b. many cells.   c. solar cells.   d. no cells.

5. Cells that are similar in structure and function are joined together to form
   a. organs.   b. systems.   c. tissues.   d. organisms.

6. Xylem, phloem, and epidermis are examples of plant
   a. organs.   b. tissues.   c. cells.   d. systems.

7. Roots, stems, and leaves are examples of plant
   a. organs.   b. cells.   c. tissues.   d. bones.

8. The highest level of organization in living things is the
   a. cell.   b. organ.   c. organism.   d. system.

9. From the most complex to the least complex, the levels of organization of most living things are
   a. organism, systems, organs, tissues, cells.
   b. systems, cells, tissues, organs, organism.
   c. organism, systems, organs, cells, tissues.
   d. cells, tissues, organs, systems, organism.

10. In order for any multicellular organism to stay alive,
   a. each level of organization must perform its specific job.
   b. all levels of organization must interact with one another.
   c. neither of these.
   d. both of these.

CONTENT REVIEW: COMPLETION

Fill in the word or words that best complete each statement.

1. The least complex level of organization in a living thing is the basic unit of structure called the _____.

2. Messages are received and transmitted throughout a complex organism's body by _____ cells.

3. The type of tissue that helps an organism move is _____ tissue.

4. Xylem and phloem are examples of plant _____.

5. The type of tissue that carries oxygen and wastes to and from cells of the heart is _____ tissue.

6. Eyes, kidneys, and skin are examples of animal _____.

7. Roots, stems, and leaves are common plant _____.

8. A system is a group of _____ that work together to perform a certain activity.

9. Chemical substances called _____ are produced by the endocrine system and regulate the activities of many organs of the body.

10. A(n) _____ is an entire living thing made up of systems that carry out all the basic life functions.

Determine whether each statement is true or false. If it is true, write "true." If it is false, change the underlined word or words to make the statement true.

1. A bacterium is a <u>multicellular</u> organism.
2. In a complex organism, there is a <u>division of labor</u> among the different parts of the body.
3. There are <u>seven</u> basic levels of organization in living things.
4. The unit of structure and function of living things is the <u>nucleus</u>.
5. Groups of cells similar in structure and activity are called <u>tissues</u>.
6. Organs are made up of groups of different systems, each performing its particular job.
7. The heart, lungs, and eyes are examples of animal <u>organs</u>.
8. Leaves are important plant <u>tissues</u>.
9. Most organisms are composed of many <u>tissues</u>, each carrying out a specific life function.
10. An organism <u>can</u> survive without the smooth operation of any one of its basic systems.

Use the skills you have developed in the chapter to complete each activity.

1. **Classifying objects** To which level of organization does each of the following belong?
   a. xylem
   b. ear
   c. bacterium
   d. geranium
   e. skeleton
   f. muscle
   g. root
   h. bone
   i. cheetah
   j. blood

2. **Relating facts** Name the organ system to which each of the following organs belongs.
   a. heart
   b. eye
   c. lung
   d. stomach
   e. kidney
   f. brain
   g. skin
   h. nose

3. **Making diagrams** Draw a pyramid to illustrate the five basic levels of organization within an organism. The most complex level should be at the bottom of the pyramid, the least complex at the top.
4. **Relating cause and effect** Describe two changes in your environment that your nervous system might respond to. In each case, describe the response. Which organs are involved in each response?
5. **Applying concepts** Use the sequence of activities that you do from the time you wake up in the morning to the time you leave for school to explain how your body systems work together.

Discuss each of the following in a brief paragraph.

1. Explain the difference between a simple organism and a complex organism.
2. Identify five different organ systems. Then explain how each of these systems is necessary for the normal functioning of an entire organism.
3. Describe the five levels of organization in an organism and give two examples of each level.
4. Defend this statement: One-celled organisms are often more complex than the individual cells of multicellular organisms.

5 Interactions Among Living Things

CHAPTER SECTIONS

5-1 Living Things and Their Environment

5-2 Food and Energy in the Environment

5-3 Relationships in an Ecosystem

CHAPTER OBJECTIVES

After completing this chapter, you will be able to:

5-1 Describe the interdependence between living and nonliving things in an environment.

5-2 Explain the relationships that exist among producers, consumers, and decomposers in an ecosystem.

5-2 Describe a food chain, food web, and energy pyramid.

5-3 Explain why competition among organisms occurs in every ecosystem.

5-3 Compare the symbiotic relationships of commensalism, mutualism, and parasitism.

5-3 Predict how a disturbance in the balance in one part of an ecosystem can affect the entire ecosystem.

For more than 30 years, Great Gull Island in Long Island Sound, New York, has been an exciting outdoor laboratory for ornithologists, or people who study birds. The ornithologists have been studying two graceful sea birds—the common tern and the roseate tern.

Gradually, a dangerous inhabitant of the island began to take control and threaten the lives of the terns. This enemy was grass! Scientists know that terns need bare, sandy beaches on which to build nests and raise their young. By 1981, the beaches of Great Gull Island were covered with grass. Human efforts to remove it were useless. Were the terns doomed?

A hundred years ago, Great Gull Island had a large population of field mice called voles. These voles fed on the roots and stems of the island's grasses. But by 1981 voles had long been gone from the island. Could voles now be brought back to the island in an effort to save the terns?

Scientists captured 36 voles and set them loose on the island. Over the next three years, the tern population soared. So did the vole population at first. Then it suddenly shrank. The little voles had eaten up much of their food supply. Will the vole population bounce back? Will a natural balance of living things return to Great Gull Island? Scientists hope so, but only time will tell.

Vole on Great Gull Island

5-1 Living Things and Their Environment

Deep within the cool, dark waters of the earth's oceans lives an unusual variety of animals and other living things. Some animals glow like streetlights in the dark, attracting their prey with their light. Other animals swim very slowly, using huge eyes to find their way in a nighttime world. The only other living things that can survive in these waters are the fungi. Fungi do not need light to live.

On land, in a lush tropical rain forest, tall trees with clinging vines form a giant umbrella. This umbrella blocks the sun and casts a permanent shadow on the forest floor. In the treetops, brightly colored

Figure 5-1 *An environment includes all the living and nonliving things that interact with one another.*

Environment

Animals

Plants

Nonliving

parrots munch on seeds while monkeys chatter to one another. Snakes and lizards climb up and down the tree trunks in search of food. And long-nosed anteaters calmly make their way on the ground.

The deep sea and a rain forest are only two of many different **environments** found on the earth. An environment includes all the living and nonliving things with which an organism may interact. **All of the living and nonliving things in an environment are interdependent.** You can think of each kind of environment as being like a giant spider web. However, the threads of this web are not spun from silk. The threads of an environmental web are the plants, animals, soil, water, temperature, and light found there.

Consider for a moment what happens when an insect gets caught in a spider's web. As one thread of the web is disturbed, the shaking motion is transferred to all the threads that are part of the web. So a spider resting some distance from the trapped insect suddenly receives a signal that dinner is nearby!

In an environmental web, all the living and non-living things make up different threads. Some threads are delicate. Others are hardy. But all have one thing in common: Like a real spider web, changes in one thread may be transmitted to and have an effect on other threads in the environment.

In order to understand the changes that can occur in an environment, and how they can affect the environment, you must study the science called **ecology.** Ecology is the study of the relationships and interactions of living things with one another and with their environment. Scientists who study these interactions are called ecologists.

Figure 5-2 *Like the threads of a spider web, the various parts of an environment are interconnected. Changes in one part of the environment can affect other parts.*

Ecosystems

Living things inhabit many different environments. From the poles to the equator, life can be found underground, in air, in water, and on land. A group of organisms in an area that interact with each other, together with their nonliving environment, is often called an **ecosystem.** An ecosystem can be as tiny as a drop of pond water or a square meter of a garden. Or it can be as large as an ocean or an entire forest.

If, for example, you look at a drop of pond water through a microscope, you will see a world of living things. Tiny plants, such as diatoms and green algae, float through the water in this microscopic ecosystem. Rotifers and copepods, very small animals, chase after these plants and eat them.

In the forest ecosystem, other microscopic organisms can be found. Some live in the soil and feed off dead animals and plants. Much larger living organisms such as foxes roam through the forest looking for food, while birds fly above. The foxes eat earthworms, birds, fruits, and small animals such as mice. Fox families live in burrows, which are holes dug into the ground. The trees of the forest supply shelter for birds, which eat insects and earthworms. From this example you can see that the various threads or factors in an ecosystem are interdependent. In other words, the plants, animals, and nonliving parts of the ecosystem all interact with one another.

Figure 5-3 *These copepods are among the animals that live in pond water.*

Figure 5-4 *The deciduous forest is the ecosystem for many plants and animals that interact with one another.*

Communities

An ecosystem is composed of both living and nonliving things. The living part of any ecosystem—all the different organisms that live together in that area—is called a **community.** Fish, insects, frogs, and plants are members of a pond community. The insects, birds, small animals, and trees make up a community in a forest ecosystem. Are these living things interdependent? If you have ever observed pond life, you may know the answer to this question. Frogs eat insects, and fish eat tadpoles. Insects eat plants, as do some of the fish.

In a desert ecosystem's community, insects and birds feed on plants. Other animals, such as lizards, feed on insects and bird eggs. And larger animals eat lizards. Can you see a pattern to these communities? The plants are a source of food to plant-eating animals. And the rest of the organisms feed on the plant eaters and on other animals. So although not all the animals in these communities eat plants, they could not exist without them! Perhaps you are asking yourself what plants eat. Most plants make their own food, as you will soon learn in the next section.

Populations

You probably live in a community. And you know from your experience that your community is made up of many different kinds of living things: people, dogs, cats, birds, fish, roses, and daisies.

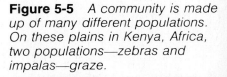

Figure 5-5 *A community is made up of many different populations. On these plains in Kenya, Africa, two populations—zebras and impalas—graze.*

Each kind of living thing makes up a **population** in the community. A population is a group of the *same* type of organism living together in the same area. For example, all the trout living in a lake are a population of trout. All the mesquite bushes surviving in the desert make up another population.

Different ecosystems support different populations of plants and animals. You might expect to see squirrels in a park near your home. The park is the squirrel's natural environment. But, certainly, you would be quite surprised to see a group of zebras grazing there! For the natural environment of zebras is the African plain.

In any ecosystem, the most successful organisms are those that are best adapted to their environment. Perhaps the finest example of an animal population that is well adapted to its environment is the tortoise of the Galapagos Islands. Located in the Pacific Ocean off the western coast of South America, the Galapagos Islands are the home of two different kinds of tortoises. On some of the islands, the tortoises have short necks and shells that hang over the backs of their necks. These shells act like stiff collars and prevent the tortoises from raising their heads. On other islands of the Galapagos, the tortoises have long necks and the part of the shells above their necks is high. These tortoises can raise their heads.

The tortoises with the short necks and low shells live on islands where food is close to the ground. So these tortoises do not have to raise their heads to find food. The tortoises with long necks and high shells live on islands where the only vegetation these animals can eat is high off the ground. So the tortoises must raise their heads high in order to reach food. In other words, each kind of tortoise is adapted to its own environment in ways that help it obtain food.

Habitats and Niches

Where would you look for deer in a forest? Would you look for them in the same places you would look for birds or snakes? Probably not. You would expect to find deer among the trees and bushes of the forest; the birds in the branches of the trees; and the snakes in the soil.

Figure 5-6 *The yellow crab spider is well adapted to its environment. Looking much like a yellow mustard flower, it easily attracts insects and then traps them.*

Figure 5-7 *The habitat of these condors is the high, barren peaks of the Andes Mountains of South America.*

The forest contains a community of living things. And each member of that community has a certain place where it lives. The place in which an organism lives is called its **habitat.** A burrow, a tree, or a cave is a habitat. A habitat provides food and shelter for an organism. Plants have habitats too. The beautiful orchid, for example, grows from the branches of tall trees in the rain forest. The branches of these trees are the orchid's habitat.

In addition to a habitat, each organism in a community plays a particular role. The organism has a **niche,** or "occupation." A niche is everything the organism does and everything the organism needs within its habitat. And an organism's niche can affect the lives of other organisms.

Beavers, for example, build dams across streams, creating small lakes. The waters of the stream no longer rush along, wearing down the stream banks. Plants can now grow alongside the lake. Fish, such as trout, can make their home in the calm waters of the lake, and songbirds can nest along the quiet banks. Meanwhile, the beaver lives in an underwater home that it makes from sticks and mud. So the beaver's niche not only makes a home for the beaver, it also makes a habitat in which other animals and plants can thrive.

Organisms in an ecosystem can share the same habitat without any problems, but they *cannot* occupy the same niche. This fact seems obvious since sharing the niche would mean competing for the same

Activity

Home Sweet Home

What does it take to build an animal home?

1. Choose one of the following animals and find out what kind of shelter it builds: beaver, trapdoor spider, mud dauber wasp, prairie dog, cliff swallow, termite.

2. On a sheet of paper, draw a picture of the animal's shelter and make a list of the materials needed to build it.

3. Build a model of your animal's shelter, using the same materials the animal would use whenever possible.

Predict what would happen if the materials that an animal uses to build its shelter were not available.

Figure 5-8 *The dam that this beaver is building will become its underwater home, as well as a habitat for other animals and plants.*

food and space. Here is an example of how similar organisms in a habitat occupy different niches.

Three types of birds are found on the Galapagos Islands. The three types of birds are the blue-footed booby, the red-footed booby, and the white booby. These three birds all feed on the same kind of fish in the nearby waters. However, the blue-footed booby feeds close to shore, while the red-footed booby flies further out to sea to catch its food. And the white booby dives for its meals in the water in between. Can you think of another example of organisms sharing habitats but not niches?

SECTION REVIEW

1. What is ecology?
2. What is the difference between a community and a population?
3. What is an organism's habitat? Its niche?

5-2 Food and Energy in the Environment

All living things need energy in order to live. They use energy to carry on all the basic life functions. For most living organisms, the immediate source of energy is the food they eat. But this food can be traced all the way back to green plants, which use the sun's energy. Thus, all the energy used by plants and animals comes directly or indirectly from the sun.

Green Plants: Food Factories

Green plants have one very important advantage over other living things. They can make their own food, while most other living things cannot. Plants make food by the process of **photosynthesis.** During photosynthesis the green parts of plants, especially the leaves, capture the energy of sunlight and use it to make glucose, a type of sugar. The glucose is formed when the plants chemically combine water and carbon dioxide. The reason green plants can carry on photosynthesis is that they contain the green pigment chlorophyll. It is the chlorophyll that captures the energy of sunlight. In addition to glucose, oxygen is also produced during photosynthesis. In fact, photosynthesis is an important source of oxygen on the earth. If it were not for green plants, animals would quickly use up all the oxygen available to them.

Because green plants use the energy of the sun directly to make their own food, they are called **autotrophs** (AWT-uh-trohfs), or "self-feeders." Plants use glucose to provide energy for carrying out life functions. But plants also combine the glucose with other chemicals to make starches, fats, and proteins. As you can see, photosynthesis is a very important process to green plants. But photosynthesis is also very important to animals. Can you guess why this process is so important?

Interactions Among Organisms

As you know, all organisms in an ecosystem are interdependent. **Organisms can be classified into three main groups based on how they obtain energy: producers, consumers, and decomposers.**

PRODUCERS Green plants make their own food and are thus the food **producers** of the ecosystem. Animals cannot make their own food. They must eat either plants or other animals that eat plants.

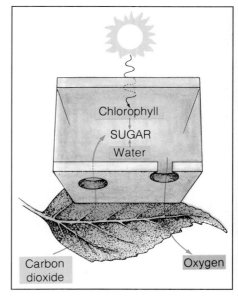

Figure 5-9 *The leaves of green plants are food factories that make glucose during photosynthesis.*

Figure 5-10 *Indian pipe plants lack chlorophyll and cannot make their own food. But a certain fungus that lives on nearby green plants forms a bridge to the Indian pipe plants. The fungus takes in glucose from the green plants. And the Indian pipes take the glucose from the fungus.*

CONSUMERS An organism that feeds directly or indirectly on producers is called a **consumer.** Consumers are also called **heterotrophs** (HET-uhr-uh-trohfs), or "other-feeders."

There are many kinds of consumers. Some organisms such as mice, insects, and rabbits are plant eaters. Snakes, frogs, and wolves are flesh eaters. They consume animals that are plant eaters or animals that feed on plant eaters.

In the northern parts of Norway, Sweden, and Finland, a plant called the reindeer moss carries on photosynthesis. Reindeer feed on the reindeer moss. And people who live in this area eat the reindeer. Can you identify the producers and consumers?

A special type of animal consumer feeds on the bodies of dead animals. These organisms are called **scavengers.** Jackals and vultures are examples of scavengers. So are crayfish and snails, who "clean up" lake waters by eating dead organisms.

DECOMPOSERS After plants and animals die, organisms called **decomposers** use the dead organic matter as a food source. Unlike scavengers, decom-

Figure 5-11 *Organisms are classified as producers, consumers, or decomposers, depending on how they get their food. Producers are autotrophs. Consumers and decomposers are heterotrophs.*

Producer   Consumer   Consumer

Decomposer

posers break down dead plants and animals into simpler substances. In the process, they return important materials to the soil and water. You may be familiar with the term "decay," which is often used to describe this process. Bacteria and mushrooms are examples of decomposers.

Figure 5-12 *The small stickleback fish, which feeds on water fleas, is about to become food for the larger pike fish (left). Spotted hyenas are often scavengers (right).*

Career: *Game Warden*

HELP WANTED: GAME WARDEN College degree in zoology, ecology, or wildlife management desired. Must be familiar with animal behavior and habitats within this state.

The crack of the rifle broke the peaceful quiet of the forest, turning the game warden's attention from the nest full of screeching young robins to more serious matters. This was not the hunting season so there was no reason for anyone to use a gun in the forest. The warden walked carefully to the spot from where the sound seemed to come, calling out "hello" so as not to be mistaken for a target.

This is a scene from the duties of the **game warden.** Each state has rules and regulations protecting its wildlife. The game warden's job is to enforce these rules. They may warn offenders, fine them, arrest them, and confiscate guns, equipment, and any illegally killed animals if necessary.

Game wardens have other duties, too. They keep accurate records of the wildlife in their areas. They are responsible for planning con-

trolled hunts. Wardens issue hunting permits and conduct safety programs to educate hunters. During emergency situations, they may take part in rescue operations.

If you are interested in this career, write to the National Park Service, U.S. Department of the Interior, 18th & C Streets, NW, Washington, DC 20240.

Figure 5-13 *In this Antarctic food chain, microscopic plants known as diatoms (top)* are the food of *zooplankton (top, center),* tiny *water animals. The zooplankton are then eaten by krill (bottom, center), shrimplike animals. Krill feed many creatures, including popeyed squid (bottom).* The right whale *(bottom, right)* feeds on both krill and squid.

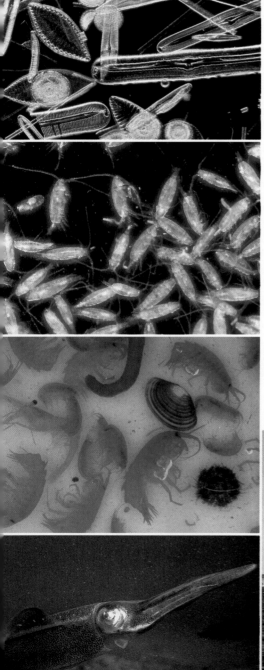

Decomposers are essential to the ecosystem for two reasons. They rid the environment of dead plant and animal matter. But even more important, decomposers return substances such as nitrogen, carbon, phosphorus, sulfur, and magnesium to the environment. These substances then are used by other plants to make food, and the cycle begins again. If the nutrients were not returned to the environment, organisms within that ecosystem could not survive for long.

Food Chains and Food Webs

Within an ecosystem, there are food and energy links between the different plants and animals living there. A **food chain** illustrates how groups of organisms within an ecosystem get their food and energy.

Green plants are autotrophs, or producers. So they are the first link in a food chain. Animals that eat the green plants are the second link. And animals that eat animals that eat plants are the third link.

Here are two examples of food chains. On land, a grasshopper eats a plant. A bird then eats the grasshopper. Finally, a snake eats the bird. In a freshwater pond, microscopic green plants are eaten by water fleas. In turn, the water fleas become the food of minnows, or small fish. Larger fish such as perch and bass feed on the minnows. If no animal eats the perch or bass, it will eventually die and become a source of food for a scavenger like the crayfish. As the perch or bass decays, important substances are returned to the lake water. The microscopic green plants use these substances to make their food. The

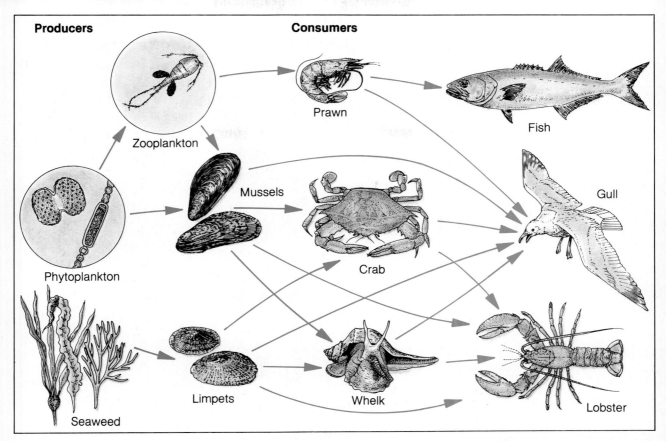

Producers

Zooplankton

Phytoplankton

Seaweed

Consumers

Prawn

Fish

Mussels

Crab

Gull

Limpets

Whelk

Lobster

Figure 5-14 *This ocean food web is a complex overlapping of many individual food chains. How many food chains can you find within the food web?*

food chain goes on and on. This food chain could have been extended beyond the perch or bass. Can you think of who the next consumer might be?

Food chains are good descriptions of how food energy is passed from one organism to another. But interactions among organisms often are more complex because most animals eat more than one type of food.

For example, in a saltwater environment, sea snails eat various types of seaweed. But seaweed is also eaten by other small fish. And these small fish may become food for larger fish, birds, and octopuses. There are several different food chains involved here, and they overlap to form a **food web.** A food web includes all the food chains in an ecosystem that are connected together. See Figure 5-14.

Feeding and Energy Levels

A feeding level is the location of a plant or an animal along a food chain. Because green plants produce their own food, they form the first feeding level. Consumers that eat plants form the second

Activity

Drawing a Food Web

Using the following plants and animals, draw the food web as you think it might exist: grass, mice, deer, mountain lions, vultures, bacteria.

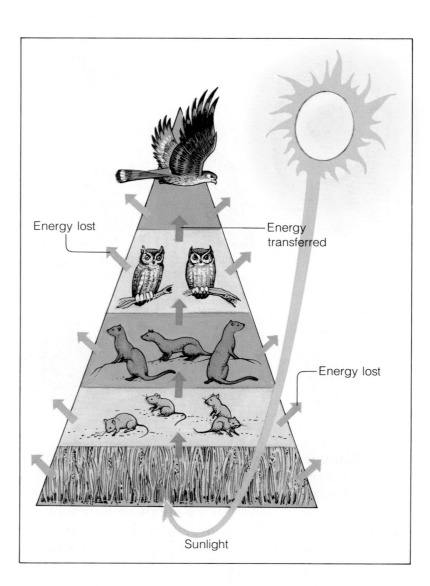

Energy lost

Energy transferred

Energy lost

Sunlight

Figure 5-15 *In this food chain, grasses and other plants make their own food by photosynthesis. Mice feed on the grasses and are consumed by weasels. In turn, owls feed on weasels. Owls also become a source of food for the hawks. At each point along the food chain, some energy is lost.*

feeding level. And consumers that eat animals that eat plants form a third feeding level.

At each feeding level, however, much of the energy in food is lost. Each organism at a particular feeding level uses up some of the energy locked in food to carry out its life activities. In addition, a great deal of energy is lost in the form of heat as it is transferred from one feeding level to another. What does this mean for living things at higher energy levels? There is less energy available to organisms at each higher level. The loss of energy as it moves through a food chain can be pictured as an energy pyramid. See Figure 5-15. The energy pyramid represents the decreasing amount of energy available at each feeding level.

Since the autotrophs, or producers such as green plants, support all other living organisms on the earth, they form the base of the energy pyramid. This first level is very broad. Each level above the first level is made up of consumers. And each successive level of consumers in the pyramid is narrower than the one beneath it. As energy moves through the pyramid, from the first feeding level up through all the other levels, much of it is lost.

SECTION REVIEW

1. What is photosynthesis?
2. What is the difference between autotrophs and heterotrophs?
3. What is a food chain? A food web?

5-3 Relationships in an Ecosystem

Whether an ecosystem is a huge patch of ocean bottom or just a dark corner of a forest floor, all the living and nonliving things in it must interact successfully in order for the ecosystem to survive. From

Figure 5-16 *Living things, such as this adult and young chameleon, must interact with other living and nonliving things in the ecosystem. If conditions are right and organisms can find food, water, and shelter, they will reproduce and increase their populations.*

Figure 5-17 *The snowshoe hare shares its habitat with moose. During the cold winter, the hare must successfully compete with the moose for food, or else the hare will die.*

their environment, all the living organisms must be able to obtain food, water, and shelter. Given the right conditions, the plant and animal populations can reproduce themselves and increase their number. However, if certain living and nonliving factors in the environment interfere with the growth of the population, the size of the population will be limited.

Competition

Ecosystems often cannot satisfy the needs of all the living things in a particular habitat. When there is only a limited amount of food, water, shelter, or even light in an environment, **competition** occurs. **Competition is a type of relationship in which organisms struggle with one another and their environment in order to obtain the materials they need to live.**

Most of the relationships among living things in an ecosystem are based on competition. The moose and the snowshoe hare, for example, share the same habitat and compete for the same food. Birch trees are the most important food source for these two animals. However, the small hares can hardly compete with the large, hungry moose. So the hares may face a shortage of food, and possibly death, during the cold winter.

Competition often has a positive effect on an ecosystem. Through natural competition, different populations of animals usually are prevented from growing so large that they disrupt the ecosystem. But sometimes outside forces can unbalance natural competition. For example, people interfered with such a natural plan when they introduced rabbits to Australia in 1788. The rabbits had few natural enemies, so the rabbit population grew very quickly. By the middle of the 1800s, these harmless-looking animals were stripping the grasslands bare of vegetation. Cattle herds that also grazed on this vegetation were threatened with starvation. Finally, a disease-causing virus was given to many of the rabbits by scientists. These rabbits died, and so the cattle were saved from starvation.

Plants, too, compete with one another for light, carbon dioxide, minerals, and water. In the forest, plants usually compete for light. Tall trees soak up plenty of sunlight. Smaller trees that also need sunlight may not survive in the shade of these big trees. However, shade can be an advantage to some trees. The red maple tree is hardier than the sugar maple tree, and it usually outnumbers the sugar maple tree in a forest. But the sugar maple tree can grow in the shade, and the red maple tree cannot. So if a young red maple tree and a young sugar maple tree are competing for space and food in the shade of a forest, the sugar maple tree will be more likely to survive.

Activity

Shady Survival

Suppose 140 trees are growing in a shaded area of a forest. Of those trees, 65 percent are sugar maples and 35 percent are red maples. How many trees of each kind are there?

Symbiotic Relationships

Instead of competing with one another, some plants and animals survive by "living together" and helping one another. Such a partnership is called **symbiosis** (sim-bee-OH-sis). Symbiosis is a relationship in which one organism lives on, near, or even inside another organism. **A symbiotic relationship may benefit either one partner or both partners in the relationship.** Some symbiotic relationships may sound rather strange to you. But no matter how odd they may seem, all symbiotic relationships have one thing in common. They provide the means by which one or both of the organisms can survive.

COMMENSALISM High in the branches of a tree, a large, fierce hawk called the osprey builds a big platform-shaped nest for its eggs. Smaller birds such as sparrows and wrens set up their homes beneath the osprey's nest. Because the osprey eats mostly fish,

Figure 5-18 *In an example of commensalism, small birds such as this sparrow* (left) *make their homes beneath the nests of large, fish-eating osprey* (right). *The presence of the fierce osprey provides protection for the little birds.*

these smaller birds are in no danger from the osprey. In fact, the little birds obtain protection from their enemies by living close to the fierce hawk.

Beautiful tropical orchids survive in dense jungles by growing high above the shade. There among the branches of trees, the flowers get a great deal of sunlight. The roots of these flowers are exposed, so they can take water right out of the air. The tree does not benefit from this relationship. It simply plays the role of "good neighbor."

Both of these symbiotic relationships are examples of **commensalism.** In commensalism, one organism in the partnership benefits. The other organism is neither helped nor harmed.

In another example of commensalism, whales make good neighbors for tiny, crusty-looking animals called barnacles. If you could swim alongside a whale, you would see these barnacles attached to the whale's sides. There the barnacles get a free ride through vast areas of the ocean, which greatly increases their chances of finding food. The whale, unharmed by the barnacles, simply ignores its tiny passengers!

MUTUALISM   Some relationships are necessary for the survival of both organisms. This type of symbiosis is called **mutualism** and is helpful to both organisms. Food and protection are two common reasons organisms share such a partnership.

Figure 5-19 *This furry ratel* (left) *works with the honey guide bird* (right) *so that both can find their favorite foods—honey and beeswax.*

In certain areas of Africa, a small bird known as the honey guide bird lives in a mutualistic relationship with a furry little animal called a ratel. The honey guide bird loves to eat beeswax, but it is too small to break into a bee's nest easily. The ratel likes honey, but it cannot always find a supply on its own. So the two animals work together. The honey guide locates a bee's nest and chirps loudly for the ratel. The ratel moves toward the sound. This chirping and following continues until the ratel reaches the bee's nest. With its sharp claws, the ratel rips the nest open and enjoys a fine feast. The honey guide bird then gets its chance to finish the beeswax.

Strange, undersea creatures called tubeworms create an unusual team with bacteria. At the bottom of the Pacific Ocean in an area near the Galapagos Islands, cracks in the ocean floor leak hot water. This water contains a foul-smelling substance called hydrogen sulfide. Nearby, tubeworms that are three meters long grow together in small bunches. The tubeworms, which lack intestines for digesting food, attach themselves to the ocean bottom, looking very much like rubbery flagpoles bending in the breeze. Each worm has a red, blood-filled organ sticking out of the top of its white tube. These red organs filter the hydrogen sulfide out of the water. Inside the tubeworms, bacteria use the hydrogen sulfide to carry on chemical reactions that release energy. The bacteria use this energy to make food for themselves. The tubeworms also can use the food made by the bacteria. They do not need to digest it, so the absence of intestines is not a problem. This strange relationship between tubeworms and bacteria allows these two organisms to survive deep in the inky darkness of the ocean bottom.

In some cases of mutualism, an animal will help feed another in return for protection. Large fish-eating birds called herons and ibises make their nests in the trees of the Florida swamps. At the base of these trees live poisonous snakes, who gather there to catch pieces of fish the birds may drop. At the same time these snakes are getting a free meal, they are providing protection for the herons and ibises. For the poisonous snakes keep away raccoons and other animals that would feast on the birds' eggs and baby chicks.

Figure 5-20 *Poisonous snakes live at the base of the tree in which this white ibis makes its nest. They keep raccoons and other animals away from the ibis's eggs and baby chicks.*

Figure 5-21 *The relationship between these water buffaloes and tickbirds is an example of mutualism. The tickbirds feed on tiny insects they pluck from the buffaloes's hides, and the buffaloes get a good cleaning.*

Figure 5-22 *The vinelike dodder plant is a parasite. It benefits by getting all its food from its host plant, which is harmed by the relationship.*

As you can see, mutualism can occur in just about any ecosystem. All that is necessary is the need for two organisms to cooperate with each other in order that they both may survive.

PARASITISM   So far you have seen that in a relationship between two organisms, both may benefit or just one may benefit. In the relationship called **parasitism,** however, one partner not only does *not* benefit but is actually harmed by the other organism. The organism that benefits is the parasite. The organism that the parasite lives off and harms is called the host. A parasite has special adaptations that help it to take advantage of its host.

The sea lamprey, a very primitive fish that lacks jaws, is a blood-sucking parasite. This strange-looking fish resembles a swimming tube that has fins on its back. The lamprey's round mouth acts as a suction cup by which the lamprey attaches itself to other fish. Even as the victim tries to shake the lamprey loose, the parasite's toothed tongue carves a hole in the fish and sucks out its blood. Small fish often die from loss of blood. However, a successful parasite does not usually kill its victim. Can you explain why?

Plants, as well as animals, can be parasites. The dodder plant lives by obtaining all of its food from host plants, such as clover and alfalfa. Wrapping its pale stem around the host plant, the dodder pushes its "suckers" onto its host. Then it releases itself completely from the soil and stays attached to the host plant for support and food.

Balance in the Ecosystem

An ecosystem is a finely balanced environment in which living things successfully interact in order to survive. **A disturbance in the balance in one part of an ecosystem can cause problems in another part of the ecosystem.** Such disturbances can be the result of nature or of human interference.

A natural disaster regularly strikes the giant panda, which lives in the bamboo forests of China and Tibet. The bamboo plants, which make up most of the panda's diet, produce seeds about once every 100 years. Then the bamboo plants die. It takes the new bamboo plants several years to grow large enough for the pandas to eat them. During this time, the pandas face a serious shortage of food. Many of them die.

Ecologists do not always have to study the death of living things in order to understand the importance of interdependence among organisms in an ecosystem. Sometimes such interdependence can be studied by observing the rebirth of an ecological system.

In May of 1980, Mount St. Helens, a volcano in the state of Washington, exploded. Thousands of trees, shrubs, flowers, and animals were destroyed by the eruption. Volcanic ash covered the soil as far away as 14 kilometers from the volcano. What had once been a beautiful, green forest soon looked like

Figure 5-23 *In May of 1980, the lush, green forests of Mount St. Helens* (top, left) *were destroyed by a volcanic eruption. Volcanic ash covered the soil* (top, right). *But within a month, life began to appear amid the fallen trees and ash* (center). *A year later, flowers began to bloom and birds and insects returned to the area* (bottom). *An ecosystem had been reborn.*

the barren surface of the moon. Within a month, however, life began to return to the area. Roots of the red-flowered fireweed bush and other plants that had survived pushed growing stems up through the ash. These plants attracted insects such as aphids, which feed on the juices of the fireweed. In turn, birds came into the area to feed on insects. Spiders crawled on the ash-covered surface. When these animals died, their bodies fertilized the ash, returning important nutrients to the soil. Hoofed animals such as elk wandered through the area, breaking up the ash cover and leaving holes through which more seeds could sprout.

Once plant and animal life started again, relationships among organisms were reestablished. What was once a bleak, lifeless landscape is now an area filled with colorful flowers, green shrubs, and growing trees. Scientists are carefully studying this area for clues to the secret of how living things can turn a barren land into a lively ecosystem inhabited by interdependent organisms.

People can often be the cause of the destruction of an ecological system. Mono Lake, in eastern California, is a beautiful saltwater lake fed by streams of melting snow from the Sierra Nevada Mountains. Two small islands within Mono Lake attract thou-

Figure 5-24 *The ecosystem of Mono Lake* (left), *once disturbed by human interference, is now returning to its delicate balance* (right).

sands of birds, especially sea gulls. More than 80 species of birds nest on these islands and feed on the lake's shrimp, flies, and algae. That is, until 1981. During the summer of that year, many baby sea gulls were found dead. How strange this seemed to be for an ecosystem that had long provided food, water, and shelter for the sea gull population. As people investigated the situation, they discovered that the ecosystem had been disturbed by actions taken far away from the lake many years before.

About 40 years ago, the city of Los Angeles began to use water from the major streams that feed into Mono Lake. Less and less water emptied into Mono Lake, and the lake began to dry up. Thousands of acres of dust formed where there was once water.

As the amount of water in the lake decreased, the concentration of salt dissolved in the water increased. The shrimp that sea gulls fed on could not survive in water so salty. As the shrimp died, less food was available for the sea gulls. Baby sea gulls starved to death.

To make matters worse, as the water level in Mono Lake dropped, a land bridge that connected the shore to the nesting islands formed. Coyotes crossed this bridge, killed many sea gulls, and invaded the gulls' nests.

Many people want to save Mono Lake. They realize that human actions have damaged the lake and disturbed an ecosystem. Without a water conservation plan, Mono Lake will continue to dry up. And the delicate balance between living and nonliving things in this ecosystem will be seriously altered.

Mono Lake illustrates how important it is to understand how an ecosystem operates and how it can be damaged by human activity. With this sort of knowledge, people can save the environment, and perhaps even improve it!

Activity

Changes in Populations

Isle Royale is a long, narrow island in Lake Superior, 25 kilometers from the shore of Canada. In the early 1900s, a few moose reached the island and within 20 years increased their population to more than 2000.

During the next 40 years, the moose population underwent several changes. Using books and other materials in the library, find out what changes occurred on Isle Royale and what caused the changes. Include answers to the following questions in your report.

1. What are limiting factors and in what ways do they affect a population?

2. How do birth and death rates affect a population?

3. What is the definition of a population cycle?

SECTION REVIEW

1. What is competition? Why does it occur?
2. Compare the relationships of commensalism, mutualism, and parasitism.
3. What are the two main causes of disturbances in the balance within an ecosystem?

LABORATORY ACTIVITY

A Little Off Balance

Purpose

In this activity, you will observe how the addition of lawn fertilizer can affect the balance of an aquatic ecosystem.

Materials *(per group)*

2 2-L wide-mouthed jars
Pond water
8 *Elodea* (or other aquatic plant)
Lawn fertilizer (or house plant food)
Teaspoon

Procedure

1. Label the jars A and B.
2. Fill each jar about three-fourths full with pond water.
3. Place four *Elodea* in each jar.
4. Add one-half teaspoon of lawn fertilizer to jar B.
5. Place the jars next to each other in a lighted area.
6. Observe the jars daily for three weeks. Record your observations.

Observations and Conclusions

1. Were there any differences between jars A and B? If so, when did you observe these differences?

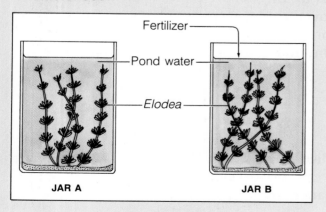

2. What was the control in this experiment? The variable?
3. Why did you place the jars next to each other? Why did you place them in the light?
4. What effect did the fertilizer have on the *Elodea*?
5. Lawn fertilizer contains nitrogen, phosphorus, and potassium. These nutrients are often present in sewage as well. Predict the effects of dumping untreated sewage into ponds and lakes.

CHAPTER REVIEW

5-1 Living Things and Their Environment

- Ecology is the study of the relationships and interactions of living things with one another and with their environment.

- An ecosystem is a group of organisms in an area that interact with each other, together with their nonliving environment.

- The living part of an ecosystem is called the community.

- A population is a group of the same type of organism living together in the same area.

- Different ecosystems support different living things.

- The place in a community in which an organism lives is its habitat. Its niche is its role in the community. Habitats can overlap, but organisms cannot share the same niche.

5-2 Food and Energy in the Environment

- Green plants are autotrophs because they make their own food by photosynthesis.

- Green plants are the producers in an ecosystem; heterotrophs are the consumers.

- Scavengers feed on dead animals.

- Decomposers are organisms that break down dead plants and animals into simpler substances during the decay process. As a result, important substances are returned to the soil and water.

- A food chain illustrates how groups of organisms within an ecosystem get their food and energy.

- Food chains often overlap or connect to form food webs.

- Each plant or animal in a food chain has a particular location called a feeding level.

- At each successive level in a food chain, energy is lost. The loss of energy as it moves through a food chain can be pictured as an energy pyramid.

5-3 Relationships in an Ecosystem

- Competition among organisms for food, water, and shelter exists in all ecosystems.

- Symbiosis is a relationship in which two organisms live together for the benefit of either one or both of the partners.

- In commensalism, one organism in the partnership benefits.

- A relationship in which both partners benefit is called mutualism.

- In parasitism, one organism benefits but only by harming the other organism.

- An ecosystem is a finely balanced environment in which living things successfully interact in order to survive.

- Disturbances in an ecosystem can be caused by nature or by human interference.

VOCABULARY

Define each term in a complete sentence.

autotroph	ecology	heterotroph	producer
commensalism	ecosystem	mutualism	scavenger
community	environment	niche	symbiosis
competition	food chain	parasitism	
consumer	food web	photosynthesis	
decomposer	habitat	population	

CONTENT REVIEW: MULTIPLE CHOICE

Choose the letter of the answer that best completes each statement.

1. The study of the relationships of living things and their environment is called
   a. commensalism.   b. parasitism.   c. ecology.   d. botany.
2. A forest is an example of a(n)
   a. ecosystem.   b. population.   c. food chain.   d. niche.
3. A group of the same type of organism living together in the same area is called a(n)
   a. ecosystem.   b. habitat.   c. niche.   d. population.
4. An organism's "occupation," or role, in an ecosystem is called its
   a. niche.   b. habitat.   c. community.   d. level.
5. Green plants make their own food by
   a. mutualism.   b. adaptation.   c. population.   d. photosynthesis.
6. In order to make food, green plants need
   a. water, carbon dioxide, and sunlight.
   b. oxygen, carbon dioxide, and sunlight.
   c. glucose, oxygen, and carbon dioxide.
   d. glucose, nitrogen, and phosphorus.
7. A whale is an example of a(n)
   a. producer.   b. autotroph.   c. consumer.   d. scavenger.
8. How organisms in an ecosystem get their food can be described by a(n)
   a. energy web.   b. food chain.
   c. population pyramid.   d. symbiotic relationship.
9. Two organisms living together for the benefit of both is an example of
   a. commensalism.   b. parasitism.
   c. decay.   d. mutualism.
10. The delicate balance of an ecosystem can be disturbed by
    a. nature.   b. human interference.
    c. both of these.   d. neither of these.

CONTENT REVIEW: COMPLETION

Fill in the word or words that best complete each statement.

1. A group of organisms and their nonliving environment is a(n) _____.
2. The place in a community in which an organism lives is called its _____.
3. The process by which a green plant makes its own food is called _____.
4. Organisms that feed on the bodies of dead animals are called _____.
5. Organisms known as _____ break down dead plants and animals.
6. When food chains overlap or are connected together, a(n) _____ is formed.
7. Energy loss through a food chain can be pictured as a(n) _____.
8. There is _____ among organisms for food, water, light, and shelter.
9. In _____ each animal benefits from the partnership.
10. An organism that lives off and harms its host is called a(n) _____.

CONTENT REVIEW: TRUE OR FALSE

Determine whether each statement is true or false. If it is true, write "true." If it is false, change the underlined word or words to make the statement true.

1. The study of the relationships of living things to one another and to their environment is called photosynthesis.
2. The living part of an ecosystem is called a community.
3. A tree, a cave, or a pile of leaves is an example of an organism's habitat.
4. Green plants can make food because they contain chlorophyll.
5. An organism that cannot make its own food is called a(n) autotroph.
6. Decomposers help return important substances to the environment.
7. Consumers, such as green plants, are the first link in a food chain.
8. Within a food chain, there is more energy available at each higher feeding level.
9. Most relationships among living things in an ecosystem are based on competition.
10. A type of symbiosis in which one organism benefits and the other organism is harmed is commensalism.

CONCEPT REVIEW: SKILL BUILDING

Use the skills you have developed in the chapter to complete each activity.

1. **Applying definitions** The African tick-bird lives on the back of the rhinoceros, where it picks bloodsucking ticks off the back of the huge animal. What type of symbiosis is this? Explain your answer.
2. **Making diagrams** Draw a food web that includes the following organisms: deer, snake, owl, mouse, grasshopper, wolf, hawk, rabbit, grass, frog, tree. Then identify each organism as a producer or a consumer.
3. **Making predictions** How could the spraying of an insecticide interfere with the balance in an ecosystem?
4. **Relating concepts** Lions, zebras, and grasses are three populations that live on the plains of Africa. How are these populations interdependent?
5. **Developing a model** Pretend you are in charge of building a city. What design features would you use to make the city part of the existing ecosystem?
6. **Applying concepts** Suppose a new predator was introduced into an island ecosystem, and it reproduced successfully. What could happen to the prey and to some of the predators on the island?

CONCEPT REVIEW: ESSAY

Discuss each of the following in a brief paragraph.

1. How is each of the following terms related to the others: environment, ecosystem, community, population, habitat, niche.
2. What is the difference between a food chain and a food web? Describe a food chain and a food web that include you.
3. Why are decomposers an important part of an ecosystem?
4. Compare three types of symbiosis and give an example of each.
5. What is the role of green plants in an ecosystem?

Adventures in Science

katharine payne & the "Language" of elephants

Sometimes Mrs. Payne follows the travels of an elephant herd in her land rover. Rumbling noises picked up by microphones near a water hole tell her that elephants are on the way.

Soon the elephants appear—roaring, trumpeting, snorting. Humans can easily hear these elephant sounds. However, Mrs. Payne, a biologist working for Cornell University, has found that elephants make some sounds that human ears cannot hear.

These newly discovered elephant sounds can travel over a much greater distance than an elephant's trumpet or roar. Mrs. Payne wondered whether elephants use these sounds to locate each other in the vast plains and forests of Africa. In 1986, Mrs. Payne went to Africa to find out.

A chance discovery in the fall of 1984 gave her the idea for her trip. While observing elephants in a zoo, Mrs. Payne felt the air around her throb, as if thunder were rolling in from some far-off place. "Only after a week," Mrs. Payne recalls, "did I think that these might actually be very low frequency sounds that I couldn't hear."

Later, she returned to the zoo with two other researchers from Cornell. Using sensitive recording equipment, they discovered that the elephants were indeed making sounds with a frequency too low for human ears to hear.

You may know that sounds have different frequencies. The sounds made by a flute have a very high frequency. The sounds made by a tuba have a very low frequency. Human ears can hear sounds over a wide range of frequencies. But they cannot hear sounds of a very high frequency, such as the squeaks made by a bat flying through the night air. And, Mrs. Payne found out, humans cannot hear the low-frequency sounds made by elephants. Suddenly, researchers had a clue to explain one long-standing mystery of elephant behavior.

Wild elephants constantly move from place to place in well-organized herds and family groups. But sometimes individual elephants become separated from their group as they wander over many kilometers of grassland or forest. Yet, without a signal that can be detected by humans, the separated elephants come together. "It's always been mysterious," says Mrs. Payne. "African elephant researchers have always said that there must be some kind of ESP between the animals. And there is. It's extrasensory as far as human beings are concerned, but ordinary as far as elephants are concerned."

Mrs. Payne and the Cornell team think that elephant calls are the key to elephant communication. Most of the elephants' calls are too low for human ears to hear. But these low-frequency calls can travel over great distances, and elephants have no trouble hearing them.

While in Africa, Mrs. Payne observed that elephants' foreheads flutter and their ears flap when they make low-frequency calls as well as calls humans can hear. The forehead flutterings most likely occur when sounds made by the elephants' vocal cords cause the animal's forehead to vibrate.

Some of the elephant calls bring calves running to their mothers. Other calls cause elephants to respond over a great distance. Sometimes the sounds can be heard by human observers, says Mrs. Payne, as "soft, puttering, furry rumbles." But, Mrs. Payne points out that the sounds humans can hear are only a small part of the calls made by elephants.

During the second part of Mrs. Payne's research, recorded calls will be played back to the elephants to see how they react. In the past, researchers have placed electronic collars on some wild elephants. The collars are used to keep track of the animals as they wander over great distances. Mrs. Payne would like to put microphones on some of the collared elephants so that the sounds they make as they move can be recorded. "Our ultimate hope is that our work may increase the elephant's chances of survival," says Mrs. Payne.

Elephants have few natural enemies. Why are they in danger of becoming extinct?

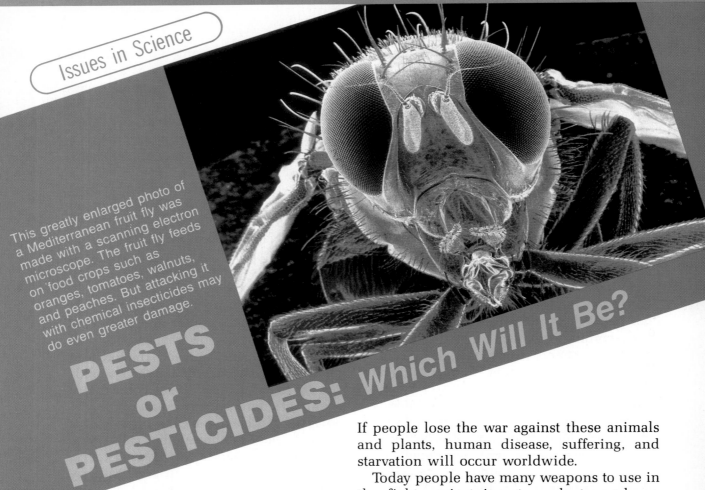

Issues in Science

This greatly enlarged photo of a Mediterranean fruit fly was made with a scanning electron microscope. The fruit fly feeds on food crops such as oranges, tomatoes, walnuts, and peaches. But attacking it with chemical insecticides may do even greater damage.

PESTS or PESTICIDES: Which Will It Be?

There is a war being fought right now that has been going on for thousands of years. It is a fight for survival against armies that far outnumber the earth's entire human population. It is the war people wage against insects, rats, mice, weeds, and fungi.

Some insects, rats, and mice carry deadly diseases such as malaria and typhoid fever. Throughout history, diseases carried by pests have killed hundreds of millions of people. These animals also threaten food supplies around the world.

Other threats to world food supplies are weeds and fungi. Weeds compete with crops for water and nutrients. Some fungi cause plant diseases that result in huge crop losses.

If people lose the war against these animals and plants, human disease, suffering, and starvation will occur worldwide.

Today people have many weapons to use in the fight against insects, rodents, and unwanted plants. During the past few decades, scientists have made or discovered many chemicals that kill pests. These chemicals, which are called pesticides, have helped increase food production by killing the pests that destroy crops and eat stored food. Pesticides have also saved many human lives by killing disease-carrying pests.

Unfortunately, people have not always used pesticides wisely. Farmers and others who use pesticides have accidentally killed useful animals and plants. Also, incorrect use of certain pesticides has made it harder to kill some pests. That is because many pests are now able to withstand assaults of deadly chemicals. In other words, the pests have become resistant to the pesticides.

In addition, pesticides are sometimes washed into rivers and streams, where they kill fish and other animals. Winds can spread pesticides over hundreds or thousands of miles. This pollutes areas far from where the chemical was used to kill pests. Pesticides have injured and killed people in all parts of the world.

So now we face a difficult problem. How can we save crops and kill disease-carrying insects without harming the environment?

The Other Side of Pesticides

There are now about 35,000 different pesticides on the market. Each year in the United States alone, about one-half billion kilograms of these chemicals are used by farmers, homeowners, and industry.

Specific pesticides called herbicides and fungicides have helped farmers to reduce crop losses due to weeds and fungi. Yet during the past 30 years, the amount of crops destroyed by insects has nearly doubled. This is true despite the fact that farmers have been using more powerful insecticides in greater quantities than ever before!

Incorrect use of pesticides may account for the alarming comeback of malaria in countries where it had been practically wiped out. More than 200 million people in Asia, Africa, and Latin America suffer from this disease, which is spread from person to person by mosquitoes. Perhaps because of overspraying of crops, mosquitoes are becoming resistant to insecticides that used to control them.

This begins when a few resistant insects survive after being sprayed with insecticide. These survivors then produce more mosquitoes that are resistant to the insecticide. In a short time, most of the population of insects in the sprayed area is resistant.

Insecticides can also kill the natural enemies of insect pests. For example, insecticides have killed ladybugs in some apple orchards. Now there are no more ladybugs in these orchards to keep apple-eating insects, such as mites, under control.

Because of the harmful effects of pesticides, some people believe that these chemicals are

One way to combat insect pests is to spray them from the air with chemical insecticides. But this method, called crop dusting, also affects living things other than pests.

too dangerous to use. But those in favor of using pesticides disagree. They say that pesticides would not be so dangerous if people knew how to use them properly.

For example, pesticides should not be sprayed in fields when the wind is blowing. When the wind is blowing, much of the pesticide is blown away. The pesticide then travels to pollute the air people breathe, the water they drink, and the rivers and lakes in which fish swim. People should also be taught to use only as much pesticide as they need for a particular job. This would reduce the over-spraying that can lead to resistant pests.

New Weapons

One way to lessen our dependence on pesticides is to understand how crops and insects interact with their environments. The study of how living things interact with their environments is called ecology. Ecology provides clues to how to control pests by changing the environment of either the pest or its victim.

Farmers use pesticides against such destructive insects as the tobacco hornworm. The hornworm attacks many kinds of crops, including these tomato plants. However, pesticides can also harm helpful insects, animals, and even people.

For example, a plant called barberry often carries a fungus that causes a disease called black stem rust. When barberry grows near wheat, the rust spreads from the barberry to the wheat. Some farmers have protected their wheat from black stem rust by destroying nearby barberry plants rather than by spraying fungicide.

Other diseases can be controlled by crop rotation. Periodically planting crops other than cabbage in a cabbage field is an example. This method prevents disease-causing organisms that attack only cabbage from building up in the soil.

Also, scientists might discover new chemicals that are harmful only to pests. For example, scientists at the University of Georgia discovered that the oil in orange peels kills fire ants, wasps, and fleas but is harmless to other animals.

Not all new types of pest control are so down-to-earth, however. By studying how the crop-eating desert locust interacts with its environment, scientists have been able to use satellites to fight this pest.

The desert locust is a flying insect related to the grasshopper. From time to time, millions of these locusts gather and sweep across Africa and India, eating every crop and blade of grass in their path. No weapons have been able to stop these insects once they take flight. But in recent years, satellites orbiting the earth have been taking pictures of areas in Africa and India where locusts might breed. Scientists can identify possible breeding areas by the amount of moisture they contain. If satellite photos show that an area is moist enough for locust eggs to survive there, scientists warn the people that may be threatened. The people can then concentrate their pesticide spraying in these areas.

The better we understand how living things interact with their environments, the more clues we will find for controlling pests without using large amounts of chemicals.

Ronda and her family lived in a space settlement on Pluto. One day, a strong radiation storm swept across the Purple Mountains of their planet. There had been many such storms on the planet in the year, 2101. The module in which Ronda and her family lived had been directly in the path of the storm. Somehow, radioactive dust penetrated the sealed glass that served as windows in the module. As a result, Ronda was blind. Radiation had destroyed the nerves that carried the electrical signals from Ronda's eyes to her brain. Her brain could no longer interpret what her eyes were "seeing."

Months after the storm, Ronda sat nervously in a plush armchair in the waiting room of Venus General Hospital. Today was the day the bandages would be removed from her eyes. Ronda was terrified that the operation to restore her sight might have been a failure. She did not want to rely on a seeing-eye robot for the rest of her life.

As the doctors removed the bandages, Ronda thought about the computer that had been implanted in her brain. No larger than a grain of rice, the computer was programmed to record all the images Ronda's eyes picked up and then translate them into messages her brain could understand. The computer was designed to work exactly like the eye nerves that had been destroyed.

The bandages fell from Ronda's eyes. She could see! The living computer inside her head had restored her sight.

Today scientists believe that living computers will be a reality in the not-so-distant

THE COMPUTER THAT LIVES!

Vacuum tubes like these made the first computers possible.

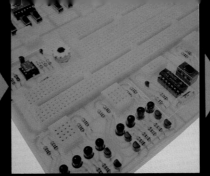
The computers of the 1950s used transistors instead of vacuum tubes.

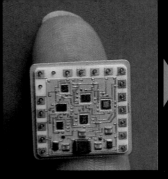
Today, thousands of transistors are packed onto a silicon chip.

future. Living computers, like the one in Ronda's brain, require no outside power source and never need to be replaced. To understand how living computers may be possible, let's look briefly at how computers have evolved since the 1800s.

The first computers, made up of clunky gears and wheels, were turned by hand. They had only the simplest ability to answer questions based on the information stored inside them. By 1950, computers were run by electricity and operated with switches instead of gears. Information was stored when thousands of switches turned on and off in certain ways. While a lot of information could be fed into electrical memory banks, the computers of the 1950s were still very crude. In fact, the typical 1950s computer took up an entire room and could do less than many video-arcade games of the 1980s.

Time Marches On

The computers of the 1980s contain thousands of switches and can be placed on a tabletop. The reason for the compactness of these computers is the silicon chip. Engineers can put hundreds of switches on a tiny piece of the chemical silicon. These tiny pieces of silicon, known as chips, are manufactured using laser beams and microscopes. It is these chips that record the information when, for example, you tell a computer your name.

But even with the silicon chip, modern computers cannot really think creatively or reason. And a computer has less sense than an ordinary garden snail. Experts feel that in order for computers to "graduate" to higher-level tasks, a whole new way must be developed of storing information in them. The key to developing a new system of information storage may lie in molecules of certain chemicals.

Why molecules? Scientists know that when some molecules are brought together, interesting changes take place. For example, electricity can jump from one molecule to another almost as if tiny switches were being shut on and off between them. Can we learn how to work these tiny switches? If so, then perhaps a whole new type of computer could be built!

This new computer might be able to hold more information in a single drop of liquid than today's computer could store in an entire roomful of chips. As you can imagine, the molecules in this computer of the future would have to be pretty special. And they would have to be produced in a new way.

Leave It to Bacteria

One of the most popular current ideas concerning how these molecules could be produced is: Let bacteria do it for us! Bacteria

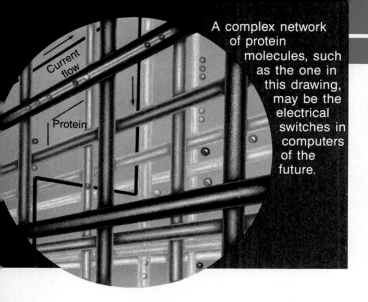

A complex network of protein molecules, such as the one in this drawing, may be the electrical switches in computers of the future.

Remember that bacteria need food to make molecules. Suppose that the computer in Ronda's brain was fed by her own blood, like all the other cells in her body. If this were the case, Ronda's computer would live as long as Ronda herself.

It may be many years before the living computer becomes a reality. Scientists must learn more about such things as how molecules react together, and how they can be programmed. But many scientists await the day when they can look at a computer and say, "It's alive."

are all around us. They constantly break down very complicated chemicals into molecules. Bacteria are at work in our bodies, in our food, and in our environment every minute of every day. Some scientists feel that bacteria could be "taught" to make special molecules. These molecules, when mixed together, could produce the flow of electricity needed to make a computer.

Of course, bacteria cannot be taught in the same sense that people can. Bacteria are not able to "learn." However, scientists can now *control* bacteria in many unusual ways. There are new techniques available that allow scientists to combine two different types of bacteria to produce a third, totally different type. In the future, bacteria may produce chemicals that have never been seen before.

In terms of a living computer, imagine that some bacteria have been taught to make special molecules. These bacteria could be grown in a special container and fed a particular substance to produce certain molecules. If the molecules could be told, or programmed, to do the right things, you would have a computer. And the computer would actually be alive because the bacteria live, grow, and produce molecules inside their container.

Think about the living computer implanted in Ronda's brain that allowed her to see again.

When nerves connecting the eye to the brain are destroyed, no electrical signals can be carried. A person cannot see. By implanting a computer the size of a grain of rice, the person's sight is restored. The computer is designed to work exactly like the eye nerves.

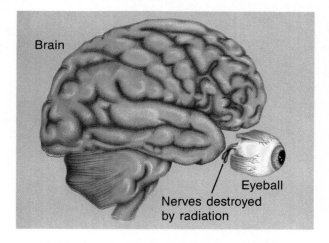

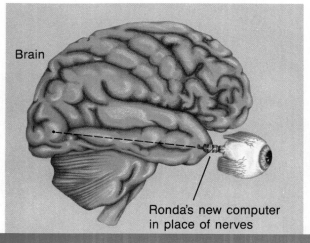

Classification of Living Things

Deer in pond ecosystem

On a small pond in northern Minnesota, tiny water-striding insects glide along the slate-blue surface, paying little attention to the deer standing near the pond. Beneath the water, a hungry pop-eyed minnow follows the rapid movement of the insects. The pleasant odors of pond grasses drift to the twitching nostrils of a cottontail rabbit standing beside the edge of the pond. Suddenly, without warning, the croak of a bullfrog breaks the calm silence.

Not far away, a camper with binoculars observes this tiny slice of nature. "There must be some kind of order to this," she thinks to herself. The woman tries to remember the ways in which living things are grouped. Then she smiles as she remembers a strange sentence: "Kings play cards on fat green stools." This sentence is a kind of code that reveals the way living things are grouped. See page 137 for the secret of the code.

CHAPTERS

6 Classification

7 Viruses, Bacteria, and Protists

8 Nonvascular Plants and Plantlike Organisms

9 Vascular Plants

10 Animals: Invertebrates

11 Animals: Vertebrates

12 Mammals

⑥ Classification

CHAPTER SECTIONS

6-1 History of Classification

6-2 Modern Classification Systems

6-3 The Five Kingdoms

CHAPTER OBJECTIVES

After completing this chapter, you will be able to:

6-1 Trace the history of classification systems.

6-1 Explain how binomial nomenclature is used to classify living things.

6-2 Identify the seven major classification groups.

6-3 Give some general characteristics of the plant, animal, protist, monera, and fungi kingdoms.

The people fishing from the boat could not believe their eyes. Lying in the boat's net was a fish none of them ever had seen before. It stretched more than 1.5 meters from the tip of its ugly nose to the end of its fan-shaped tail. Large steel-blue scales covered its body. A powerful lower jaw hung down from a frightening face. But most peculiar of all, its fins were attached to what appeared to be stubby legs!

The unusual fish, caught at the mouth of the Chalumna River in South Africa, was taken to a local museum. There M. Courtenay-Latimer, a South African museum curator, happened to see the fish. After searching through many books, she had found no description of the strange fish. However, she knew of someone who might be able to solve the riddle. That someone was Professor J. L. B. Smith, an African fish expert. So M. Courtenay-Latimer preserved and sent the fish to Professor Smith.

The scientist was shocked. He later wrote, "I would hardly have been more surprised if I met a dinosaur on the street." Professor Smith was looking at an animal thought to have become extinct more than 60 million years ago. Yet, in a flash, Professor Smith had been able to identify the fish as a coelacanth (SEE-luh-kanth). The discovery was exciting because coelacanths are thought to be closely related to fish that evolved into four-footed land animals.

What led Professor Smith to make his startling identification? A knowledge of biological classification, a special system that helps scientists to identify and name organisms.

Rare photograph of a coelacanth

Figure 6-1 *Thousands of years ago, people drew this painting on a cave wall in Spain. What message does the painting communicate?*

6-1 History of Classification

Thousands of years ago, people began to recognize that there were different groups of living things in the world. Some animals had claws and sharp teeth and roamed the land. Others had feathers and beaks and flew in the air. Still others had scales and fins and swam in the water.

People also made observations about plants. Not only did plants vary in shape, size, and color, but some were good to eat while others were poisonous. In a similar sense, some animals, such as those with sharp teeth, were very dangerous, while others, such as those with feathers, were relatively harmless.

Without knowing exactly what they were doing, these people developed simple systems of classification. **Classification is the grouping of living things according to similar characteristics.** Knowledge of these characteristics helped people to survive in their environment. For example, they quickly learned to fear the sharp-toothed animals and to hunt the feathered ones.

Perhaps these people painted pictures on the walls of caves to communicate this knowledge. See Figure 6-1. Today, similar but much more complex information is found in the drawings, photographs, and words in scientific books. This information is organized into the science of classification, which is called **taxonomy** (tak-SAH-nuh-mee). The scientists who work in this field are called taxonomists. The purpose of taxonomy is to group all the plants and animals on earth in an orderly system. This system helps to provide a better understanding of the relationships among living things. Meaningful names are given to newly discovered animals and plants based on taxonomy. Sometimes taxonomy even helps solve biological riddles of the past.

Early Classification Systems

In the fourth century B.C., the Greek philosopher Aristotle first proposed a system to classify life. He placed the animals into three groups. One group included all animals that flew, another group included those that swam, and a third group included those that walked.

Aristotle classified animals according to the way they moved. Although this system was useful, it caused problems. According to Aristotle, both a bird

Figure 6-2 *Because of its unusual characteristics and behavior, the giant panda* (right) *was once thought to be more closely related to the raccoon* (left) *than to the bear* (top right). *Today, giant pandas are classified as bears.*

and a bat would fall into the same flying group. Yet in some basic respects, birds and bats are very different. Birds, for example, are covered with feathers. Bats, on the other hand, are covered with hair.

Although the system devised by Aristotle would not satisfy today's taxonomists, it was the first attempt to develop a scientific and orderly system of classification. Aristotle's classification system was used for almost 2000 years.

In the seventeenth century, John Ray, an English biologist, set an enormous goal for himself. He decided to collect, name, and classify all the plants and animals in England. But unlike Aristotle, Ray based his system of classification on the internal anatomy of plants and animals. He examined how they behaved and what they looked like as well. Ray was the first person to scientifically use the term **species** (SPEE-sheez). A species is a group of organisms that are able to interbreed, or produce young.

John Ray achieved his goal. Moreover his work aided in the development of more complete and accurate classification systems.

Binomial Nomenclature

The eighteenth-century Swedish scientist Carolus Linnaeus spent the major part of his life developing a new system of classification. The system placed all living things into plant and animal groups according to similarities in form or structure.

Linnaeus also developed a simple system for naming organisms. Before Linnaeus developed his naming system, plants and animals had been identified by a series of Latin words. These words described the physical features of the organism. Sometimes five or six Latin words were used to describe a single organism!

Linnaeus devised a simpler naming system of **binomial nomenclature** (bigh-NOH-mee-uhl NOH-muhn-klay-cher). In this system, each plant and animal are given two names, a **genus** (plural: genera) name and a species name. For example, you could think of the genus name as your family name. The species name could be thought of as your first name. Like your family, a genus may consist of several closely related organisms or only one species.

1. What is taxonomy?
2. How did the classification systems of Aristotle and Ray differ?
3. What is meant by binomial nomenclature?

6-2 Modern Classification Systems

Today, 200 years after Linnaeus completed his work, scientists consider many additional factors when classifying organisms. Of course, scientists still examine large internal and external structures, but they also examine microscopic structures. Scientists even analyze the chemical makeup of an organism.

Although such a classification system may at first seem complicated, it is really quite simple. The modern system of classification does two jobs. First, it groups organisms according to their *basic* characteristics. Second, it gives a *unique name* to an organism that scientists all over the world can use and understand. For example, in North and South America

Figure 6-3 *Scientists often use skeletons of animals to help in classification. Notice how the similarity of forelimb structures of these animals helps to classify them as being part of the same group, in this case, mammals.*

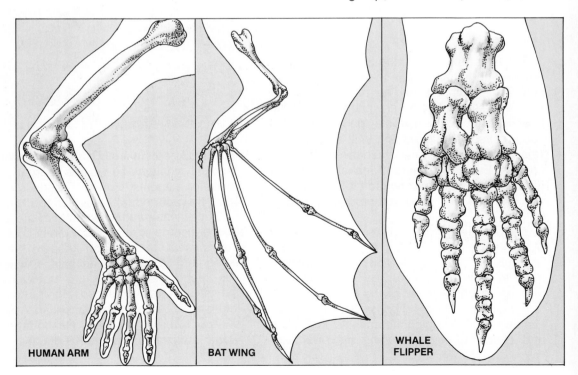

HUMAN ARM

BAT WING

WHALE FLIPPER

one large cat is called a mountain lion by some people, a cougar by others, and a puma by still others. If these people were to talk to one another about the animal, they might think they were talking about three different animals. But scientists throughout the world use only one name for this large cat, *Felis concolor*. This name easily identifies the cat to all scientists, no matter what language they speak.

Classification Groupings

All living things are classified into seven major groups: kingdom, phylum, class, order, family, genus, and species. The largest group is called a **kingdom.** All animals, for example, belong to the animal kingdom, and all plants belong to the plant kingdom. The second largest group is called a

Career: *Zoo Keeper*

HELP WANTED: ZOO KEEPER High school diploma required. Minimum one year experience as an apprentice zoo keeper needed. Must like animals and be tolerant of both animal and human behavior. Apply in person.

Today is a big day at the zoo. The arrival of a male and female giraffe is expected from Africa. For months, everyone has prepared for the new exhibit. Gardeners planted fruit trees bearing the giraffe's favorite food. In addition, zoo architects designed and built a new home, while tour guides learned the habits of the newcomers. Everyone wants to make sure the giraffes will be safe and comfortable. If all goes well, the pair will breed and produce young giraffes.

At first, the giraffes will be kept away from other animals. Once tests show they are strong and healthy, the **zoo keeper** will help move them to their new home. The zoo keeper will also be responsible for giving food and water to the giraffes. Other responsibilities of the zoo keeper include keeping the animals' area clean and observing and recording their behavior.

The zoo keeper usually is the first to notice any medical problems as well as to treat minor injuries or ailments. However, serious problems must be reported to the senior zoo keeper.

Of the many people working at the zoo, zoo keepers come into the most direct contact with the animals. In fact, zoo keepers sometimes bathe and groom the animals. Occasionally, zoo keepers answer visitors' questions about the inhabitants of the zoo. For further career information, write to the American Association of Zoo Keepers National Headquarters, 635 Gage Boulevard, Topeka, KS 66606.

Figure 6-4 *The variety of living things in a rain forest, such as this one in Uganda, Africa, is greater than in any other place on the surface of the earth. Here gorillas share their territory with countless different plants and animals.*

phylum (FIGH-luhm; plural: phyla). Each phylum is made up of **classes.** Within each class are **orders.** In turn, each order is divided into **families** that consist of many related genera. Each genus usually is divided into one or more species.

The words for an organism's genus and species make up its scientific name. The genus name is capitalized, but the species name begins with a small letter. For example, the genus and species name for a wolf is *Canis lupus*. These two names identify the organism. Although most of these names are in Latin, some are in Greek. Scientists estimate that there are at least three million and perhaps as many as ten million different species alive today. Many of them have yet to be identified and named.

Classifying an Organism

Figure 6-5 shows the classification groupings of several organisms. Each grouping indicates something about the organism's characteristics. For example, the lion belongs to the order Carnivora.

CLASSIFICATION OF FIVE DIFFERENT ORGANISMS

	Lion	Onion	Paramecium	Yogurt-making Bacterium	Edible Mushroom
Kingdom	Animalia	Plantae	Protista	Monera	Fungi
Phylum	Chordata	Tracheophyta	Ciliophora	Eubacteriacea	Basidiomycetes
Class	Mammalia	Angiospermae	Ciliatea	Schizomycetes	Homobasidiomycetes
Order	Carnivora	Liliales	Hymenostomatida	Eubacteriales	Agaricales
Family	Felidae	Liliaceae	Paramecidae	Lactobacillaceae	Agaricaceae
Genus	*Panthera*	*Allium*	*Paramecium*	*Lactobacillus*	*Agaricus*
Species	*leo*	*cepa*	*caudatum*	*bulgarius*	*campestris*

Figure 6-5 *The classification of five different organisms is shown in this chart. Which organism is a member of the family Liliaceae?*

"Carnivora" is the Latin word for flesh eater. Many other familiar organisms also belong to this order such as dogs, raccoons, and bears. Look at Figure 6-5 again and notice that the lion is in the family Felidae. This family contains not only the lion but other cats, including ordinary house cats.

This knowledge allows you to have a very good idea of how a lion acts and looks even if you have never seen one in person. You can do this because lions and house cats are in the same family. But lions and house cats are not in the same genus and species, which indicates they are somewhat different. For example, taxonomists include the lion in the genus *Panthera* along with other large cats. All cats in the genus *Panthera* roar; they do not purr. Other cats, including house cats, are in the genus *Felis.* They, of course, purr and do not roar. Finally, the species name for the lion is *leo.* In this case, the lion, *Panthera leo,* is the animal that you see jumping through hoops in the circus or lounging lazily in a cage at your local zoo. *Felis domesticus* is the scientific name for your playful pet cat.

SECTION REVIEW

1. What are the seven major classification groups?
2. What is the scientific name for an onion?

Kingdom Animalia			
Phylum Chordata			
Class Mammalia			
Order Carnivora			
Family Felidae			
Genus *Panthera*			
Species *leo*			

Figure 6-6 *Examine each row from top to bottom. What pattern do you discover?*

6-3 The Five Kingdoms

In Figure 6-5, you may have noticed that some organisms were not in the plant or animal kingdoms. The paramecium, for example, is usually placed in a kingdom called Protista. Scientists invented this kingdom to include organisms that did not seem to fit into either the plant or animal kingdoms. Later, two more kingdoms called Monera (muh-NIHR-uh) and Fungi (FUHN-jigh) were added to many modern classification systems. **Today, most scientists use a system of classification that includes five kingdoms. These five kingdoms are plants, animals, protists, monerans, and fungi.**

PLANTS Most plants are **multicellular,** or many-celled, organisms that contain specialized tissues and organs. A few plants are **unicellular,** or one-celled. Some algae are examples of unicellular plants. In general, plants are **autotrophs** (AWT-uh-trohfs). Autotrophs are organisms that can make their own food from simple substances. Most plants contain chlorophyll, a green pigment necessary for making food.

Figure 6-7 *The ability to move from place to place is one way scientists distinguish the wasp, a member of the animal kingdom, from the berry bush, a member of the plant kingdom.*

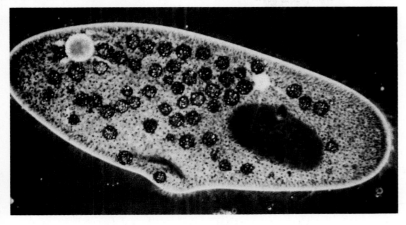

Figure 6–8 *The unicellular paramecium is a member of the Protista kingdom. This paramecium is magnified 200 times.*

ANIMALS Only multicellular organisms are in the animal kingdom. These organisms have tissues and most have organs and organ systems. Unlike plants, animals do not contain chlorophyll and are not able to make their own food. They depend upon autotrophs. These organisms are called **heterotrophs** (HET-uh-roh-trohfs).

PROTISTS The Protista kingdom includes most unicellular organisms. Microscopic protozoans such as paramecia are found in this kingdom.

MONERANS All of the earth's bacteria are found in the Monera kingdom. One kind of algae, the blue-green algae, are also in the Monera kingdom. Like protists, monerans are unicellular. However, the cells of monerans do not contain a well-defined nucleus. The nucleus is the control center of a cell.

FUNGI As you might expect, the world's wide variety of fungi make up the Fungi kingdom. The kinds of fungi you are probably most familiar with are mushrooms and molds. Fungi share many characteristics with plants. However, fungi do not contain the green pigment chlorophyll. So, unlike plants, fungi cannot make their own food.

SECTION REVIEW

1. In what kingdom are most protozoans found?
2. Define multicellular and unicellular.

LABORATORY ACTIVITY

Whose Shoe Is That?

Purpose

In this activity, you will develop a classification system for shoes.

> **Materials** *(per group of 6)*
> Students' shoes
> Pencil and paper

Procedure

1. At your teacher's direction, remove your right shoe and place it on a work table.
2. As a group, think of a characteristic that will divide all six shoes into two kingdoms. For example, you may first divide the shoes by the characteristic of color into the brown shoe kingdom and the nonbrown-shoe kingdom.
3. Place the shoes into two separate piles based on the characteristic your group has selected.
4. Next, working only with those shoes in one kingdom, divide that kingdom into two groups based on a new characteristic. The brown shoe kingdom, for example, may be divided into a shoelace group and a nonshoelace group.
5. Further divide these groups into subgroups. For example, the shoes in the shoelace group may be again separated into shoes with rubber soles and shoes without rubber soles.
6. Continue to divide the shoes by choosing new characteristics until you have only one shoe left in each group. Identify the person who owns this shoe.
7. Now repeat this process working with the nonbrown shoes.

Observations and Conclusions

1. Test your shoe classification system for accuracy by doing the following: Have a member of your group hold up a shoe. Starting with the kingdom, classify it according to the system you have just developed. The system should lead you to the correct person's name.

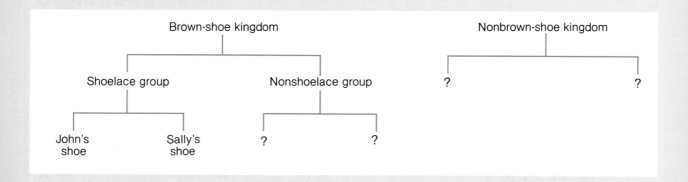

CHAPTER REVIEW

6-1 History of Classification

- Classification is the grouping of living things according to similar characteristics.

- The science of classification is known as taxonomy.

- Aristotle was the first person to develop a classification system for living things. His system was used for almost 2000 years.

- In the seventeenth century, John Ray, an English biologist, introduced a classification system that became the foundation of modern systems.

- In the eighteenth century, Carolus Linnaeus, a Swedish scientist, devised a system for naming organisms called binomial nomenclature. Linnaeus also developed a classification system based on the structural similarities of organisms.

6-2 Modern Classification Systems

- Today, most scientists use a system of classification that includes five kingdoms. These kingdoms are plants, animals, protists, and fungi.

- Organisms are classified into seven groups. In order of decreasing size, these groups are kingdom, phylum, class, order, family, genus, and species.

6-3 The Five Kingdoms

- A five-kingdom system of classification consists of plants, animals, protists, monerans, and fungi.

- Autotrophs are organisms that are able to make their own food.

- Heterotrophs are organisms that cannot make their own food.

Define each term in a complete sentence.

autotroph

binomial nomenclature

class

family

genus

heterotroph

kingdom

multicellular

order

phylum

species

taxonomy

unicellular

Choose the letter of the answer that best completes each statement.

1. The first person to propose a classification system was
   a. Ray.   b. Linnaeus.   c. Aristotle.   d. Haeckel.
2. A group of organisms that are able to interbreed, or produce young, is a
   a. species.   b. family.   c. genus.   d. kingdom.
3. What language is used most often to name organisms in modern classification systems?
   a. French   b. Latin   c. English   d. German

4. The largest classification group is the
   a. species.   b. order.   c. phylum.   d. kingdom.
5. A classification group that is smaller than an order is
   a. kingdom.   b. phylum.   c. family.   d. class.
6. A classification group that is larger than an order is
   a. genus.   b. species.   c. family.   d. class.
7. A genus can be divided into
   a. phyla.   b. orders.   c. species.   d. families.
8. The term "Protista" refers to a
   a. class.   b. kingdom.   c. genus.   d. species.
9. Which organism is a heterotroph?
   a. frog   b. maple tree   c. seaweed   d. spinach
10. The animal kingdom is made up of only
   a. autotrophs.   b. unicellular organisms.
   c. multicellular organisms.   d. families.

CONTENT REVIEW: COMPLETION

Fill in the word or words that best complete each statement.

1. The science of classification is known as
   _____.
2. In classification, the two-word naming system is known as _____.
3. The first word in a scientific name is the
   _____.
4. In classification, the largest group is called a(n) _____.
5. The smallest classification group is a(n)
   _____.

6. The second largest classification group is a(n) _____.
7. _____ is the Latin word for flesh eater.
8. A paramecium can be classified as a member of the _____ kingdom.
9. An organism that can make its own food is called a(n) _____.
10. An organism that cannot make its own food is called a(n) _____.

CONTENT REVIEW: TRUE OR FALSE

Determine whether each statement is true or false. If it is true, write "true." If it is false, change the underlined word or words to make the statement true.

1. Aristotle introduced the term "species."
2. In Linnaeus's classification system, the smallest group was the genus.
3. The correct classification order from largest to smallest groups is kingdom, phylum, class, order, family, species, genus.
4. The scientific name for a lion is *Panthera leo.*
5. *Felis* is the Latin word for flesh eater.

6. Multicellular organisms are composed of only one cell.
7. In a five-kingdom classification system, bacteria are classified as plants.
8. Green plants are heterotrophs.
9. Animal cells contain chlorophyll.
10. Heterotrophs are organisms that cannot make their own food.

CONCEPT REVIEW: SKILL BUILDING

Use the skills you have developed in the chapter to complete each activity.

1. **Making comparisons** Use the following words to classify the place in which you live: street, county, continent, city, number, country, house. Then compare each word with one of the seven groups used to classify organisms.

2. **Developing a model** Design a classification system for objects that might be found in your closet. Then draw a diagram that will illustrate your classification system.

3. **Making charts** Create a chart in which you classify each of the following into its correct kingdom:

   a. tulip
   b. wasp
   c. bread mold
   d. straw mushroom
   e. zebra
   f. blue-green alga
   g. oak tree
   h. bacterium
   i. toadstool
   j. paramecium

4. **Making generalizations** Explain why the common name for each of these organisms may be confusing:

   a. sea lion
   b. starfish
   c. horse chestnut
   d. sea horse
   e. jellyfish
   f. reindeer moss
   g. sea cucumber
   h. horseshoe crab

5. **Identifying relationships** Which two of the following three organisms are most closely related: *Morus nigra, Pinus nigra, Pinus strobus*? Explain your answer.

6. **Relating concepts** Explain why a cocker spaniel and a poodle can interbreed and produce young, while a fox and a wolf cannot.

7. **Relating cause and effect** How do you think the invention of the compound microscope affected the classification of living things?

8. **Applying concepts** Why is it that scientists do not classify animals by what they eat or where they live?

CONCEPT REVIEW: ESSAY

Discuss each of the following in a brief paragraph.

1. Explain why it is important for scientists to classify organisms.

2. What type of characteristics did Linnaeus use to develop his classification system of living things?

3. How is the classification system used by scientists today different from the classification system developed by Linnaeus? How is it similar?

4. Describe each of the kingdoms used in the five-kingdom classification system. Give an example of an organism in each kingdom.

5. How do an autotroph and a heterotroph differ? Give an example of each.

6. List the seven major groups in scientific classification in order from the largest to the smallest.

7 Viruses, Bacteria, and Protists

CHAPTER SECTIONS

7-1 Viruses

7-2 Bacteria

7-3 Protozoans

CHAPTER OBJECTIVES

After completing this chapter, you will be able to:

7-1 Describe the structure of virus.

7-2 Classify bacteria according to shape.

7-2 Describe the structure of a bacterial cell.

7-3 Define protozoan and describe the structure and behavior of three typical protozoans.

7-3 Describe a sporozoan.

In July of 1976, the city of Philadelphia was full of people wearing navy blue military caps. These people were members of the American Legion, a veterans' organization that was holding its yearly convention in what is known as "the city of brotherly love." However, before the month was out, Philadelphia might well have been called "the city of brotherly fear." For shortly after the close of the convention, a serious disease struck many of the legionnaires.

What caused the frightening illness, which was given the name "Legionnaires' Disease"? One possible cause was a microorganism, a living thing too small to be seen without the aid of instruments such as microscopes. But what particular microorganism? There were millions.

Dr. Joseph McDade of the Center for Disease Control at Atlanta, Georgia, was one of the medical detectives trying to solve the mystery of Legionnaires' Disease. If a microorganism was responsible for Legionnaires' Disease, McDade would find it. Early in 1977 he discovered the microorganism responsible.

The microorganism McDade identified was a new bacterium, a kind of germ. Fortunately, the new bacterium could be treated with an old kind of medicine called erythromycin, which adds another twist to this strange story. Erythromycin is made by bacteria. So the illness caused by one kind of bacteria was cured by a substance produced by another kind of bacteria.

Erythromycin crystals

7-1 Viruses

In 1892, a terrible disease swept through certain areas of Russia. Victims of the disease were not people or even animals. They were plants—tobacco plants. Because tobacco was a very important crop, many people were interested in discovering the cause and, perhaps, a cure for the disease. One of these people was a 28-year-old Russian botanist, or plant expert, named Dimitri Iwanowski.

By the late 1800s, scientists had discovered that many diseases of human beings, animals, and plants were caused by unicellular microorganisms called **bacteria** (singular: bacterium). These discoveries were made possible by hard work and the invention of powerful light microscopes. These microscopes made visible microorganisms never seen before. Based on these discoveries Iwanowski assumed the tobacco disease was also caused by bacteria. So he set out to devise an experiment to identify them.

Iwanowski's procedure was simple. He would gather some infected tobacco leaves, crush the leaves, and collect the juice. Then he would pass the juices through a filter whose holes were so small that bacteria could not slip through. Finally, Iwanowski would place the pure juices on healthy tobacco plants. He

Figure 7-1 *Tobacco mosaic disease causes healthy tobacco plant leaves* (left) *to become spotted* (right).

reasoned the plants would remain healthy and this would be proof that bacteria were the cause of the disease.

All this reasoning made very good sense. And Iwanowski performed his experiment perfectly. The only problem was that the healthy plants caught the disease. Iwanowski thought his experiment was a failure. He thought his filters were not well made and that cracks in them must have let through the disease-causing bacteria. However, Iwanowski was wrong. He had made a great discovery without recognizing it. The recognition came six years later from Delft, Holland, about 1600 kilometers to the east.

Viruses—Smaller than Bacteria

In 1898, the Dutch microbiologist Martinus Beijerinck, was also working on the devastating disease of tobacco plants. A microbiologist is a scientist who studies **microbiology,** or the science of microorganisms. Using the best microscopes, Beijerinck searched for bacteria in the diseased, spotted leaves of tobacco plants. He also searched in their filtered juices and in the material trapped by filters that should have contained bacteria. Like Iwanowski's, Beijerinck's experiments seemed to end in failure. He could find no bacteria. Nevertheless, the filtered juices from diseased plants continued to cause healthy plants to become infected.

These repeated observations led Beijerinck to draw a momentous conclusion that had escaped Iwanowski. The filtered juices from diseased plants caused infection, but the juices did not contain bacteria. Therefore, they contained something else that caused infection, a germ much smaller than bacteria. This germ was too small to be visible even under the lenses of the most powerful light microscope. Beijerinck named this germ a **virus,** which comes from the Latin word for poison.

Almost 40 years passed before Wendell Stanley, an American scientist, isolated the virus that caused the disease in tobacco leaves. He called it the tobacco mosaic virus. The word "mosaic" refers to the pattern of spots found on the leaves of diseased plants. See Figure 7-1.

Figure 7-2 *These rod-shaped objects are tobacco mosaic viruses.*

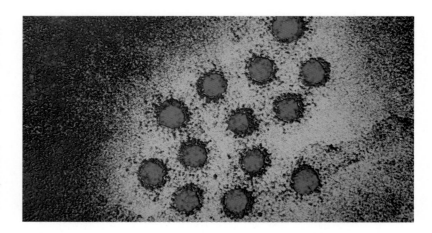

Figure 7-3 *These red spheres, magnified 70,000 times, are viruses that cause a type of liver disease called hepatitis A.*

Since the discovery of the tobacco mosaic virus, scientists have found that there are many different kinds of viruses. By studying many of these viruses, scientists have learned a great deal about the function and structure of viruses.

What Is a Virus?

Living things come in many shapes and sizes. However, all living things seem to have one thing in common. They all contain cells. Some organisms consist of only a single cell. Other organisms, such as yourself, are made up of many cells. Unlike these organisms, viruses are not cells and do not contain cells. Viruses are tiny particles that contain hereditary material.

Because viruses are not cells, they cannot perform the life functions of living cells. They cannot, for example, take in food or get rid of wastes. In fact, about the only similarity that viruses share with cells is that viruses are able to reproduce. However, viruses cannot reproduce on their own. They need the help of other living cells. For this reason, many scientists consider viruses an unusual form of life. Other scientists strongly disagree and do not classify viruses as living things. Thus, it might help if you think of viruses as being on the threshold of life.

Structure of Viruses

A virus has two basic parts, a core of hereditary material and an outer coat of protein. The hereditary material in the virus's core may be either **DNA,**

Activity

Building a Bacteriophage

You can better understand the structure of a bacteriophage by building your own model.

1. Use the diagram on page 151 and any of the following materials to build your own model bacteriophage: pipe cleaners, construction paper, screws, nuts, bolts, scissors, tape, glue, crayons, screw driver.

2. Make a drawing of your model and label the parts. Which part contains the hereditary material of the bacteriophage? Which part would the bacteriophage use to attach itself to a bacterial cell?

deoxyribonucleic acid, or **RNA,** *ribonucleic acid.* DNA and RNA are substances that control the production of new viruses.

Surrounding the DNA or RNA in the virus is a protein coat. The coat is much like the shell of a turtle. Like the turtle's shell, the protein coat encloses and offers some protection to the virus. In fact, the protein coat is so protective that some viruses survive after being dried and frozen for many years.

With the invention of the electron microscope in the 1930s, scientists were able to see and to study the shapes and sizes of certain viruses. Some viruses, such as those that cause the common cold, have 20 surfaces. Each of these surfaces is in the shape of a triangle that has equal sides. Other viruses look like small threads, while still others resemble small spheres. Some even resemble small spaceships. See Figure 7-5.

Reproduction of Viruses

In order to understand how a virus reproduces, causing disease, you can examine the activities of one kind of virus called a **bacteriophage** (bak-TEE-ree-uh-fayj). A bacteriophage is a virus that infects bacterial cells. The word "bacteriophage" means "bacteria eater."

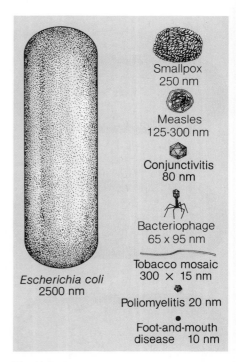

Figure 7-4 *Viruses vary in size from about 10 to 250 nanometers, or nm. A nanometer is equal to one millionth of a millimeter. Compare the sizes of the viruses on the right to the large bacterium on the left.*

Figure 7-5 *This drawing shows the structure of a bacteriophage, which attacks bacterial cells. The photograph is of the same virus magnified 190,000 times.*

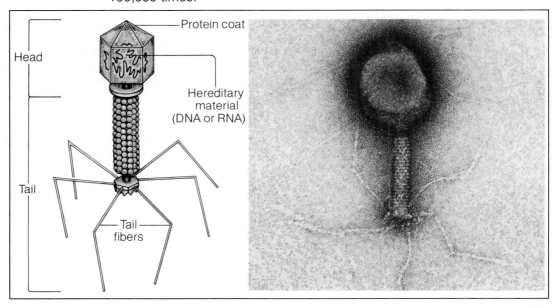

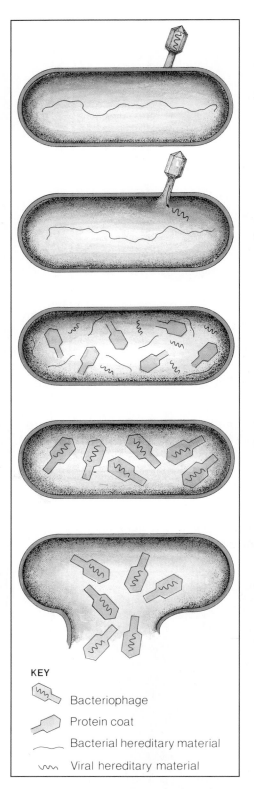

KEY

⌇ Bacteriophage

⬡ Protein coat

— Bacterial hereditary material

⌇ Viral hereditary material

Figure 7-6 *Viruses reproduce in cells. A virus attaches to the cell and injects its heredity material. The cell then makes more viruses, which burst from the cell.*

In Figure 7-6, you can see how a bacteriophage attaches its tail to the outside of a bacterial cell. The virus quickly injects its hereditary material directly into the living cell. The protein coat is left behind and discarded by the virus. Once inside the cell, the virus's hereditary material takes control of all of the bacterial cell's activities. As a result, the bacterial cell is no longer in control. The cell begins to produce new viruses rather than its own chemicals.

Soon the bacterial cell fills up with new viruses, perhaps as many as several hundred. Eventually, the bacterial cell bursts open. The new viruses are released and infect nearby bacterial cells. This process continues until all living bacterial cells have been infected by the virus.

The viruses that attack plants, animals, and people may vary in size and shape. However, all viruses act in much the same way as bacteriophages.

SECTION REVIEW

1. What was the first virus to be isolated?
2. Name the two parts of a virus.
3. What is a bacteriophage?

7-2 Bacteria

Unlike viruses, bacteria clearly are living organisms. At one time, scientists placed bacteria in the plant kingdom because, like plants, bacteria have **cell walls.** The cell wall is the outermost boundary of plant and bacterial cells. The cell wall helps the cells of these organisms to keep their shape. Today, most classification systems consider bacteria as monerans. You may recall from Chapter 6 that monerans are members of the Monera kingdom. Like all other monerans, bacteria are unicellular.

Bacteria are considered the simplest organisms. However, bacteria are more complex than they may appear. Each cell performs the same basic functions that more complex organisms, including you, perform.

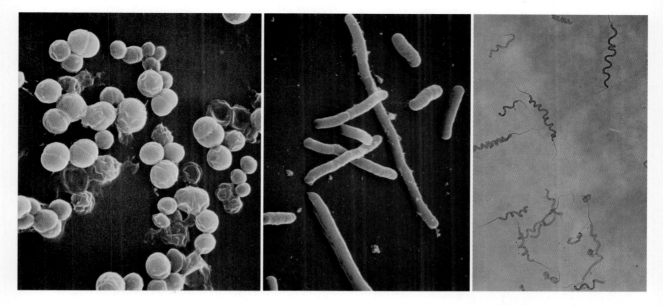

Figure 7-7 *Bacteria are grouped and named according to their three basic shapes. Spherical bacteria are called cocci* (left), *rodlike bacteria are called bacilli* (center), *and spiral-shaped bacteria are called spirilla* (right).

Bacteria are among the most numerous organisms on earth. Scientists estimate there are about 2.5 billion bacteria in a gram of garden soil. And the total number of bacteria living in your mouth is greater than the number of people who have ever lived.

Bacteria are classified according to shape as either cocci, bacilli, or spirilla. Bacteria that resemble spheres are called **cocci** (KAHK-sigh; singular: coccus). Bacteria that look like rods are called **bacilli** (buh-SIL-igh; singular: bacillus). And spiral-shaped bacteria are called **spirilla** (spigh-RIL-uh; singular: spirillum). See Figure 7-7.

Structure of Bacteria

All bacteria have a **cell membrane** on the inside of the cell wall. The cell membrane controls which substances enter and leave the bacterial cell. Unlike most other cells, the hereditary material of bacteria is not confined in a **nucleus** (NOO-klee-uhs; plural: nuclei). The nucleus is a spherical structure within a cell that directs all the activities of the cell. Instead, the hereditary material is spread throughout the **cytoplasm** in the cell. The cytoplasm is the jellylike material found inside the cell membrane.

Figure 7-8 *This drawing shows the typical structure of a bacterium.*

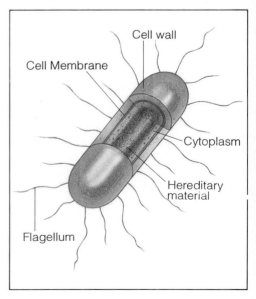

Cell wall

Cell Membrane

Cytoplasm

Hereditary material

Flagellum

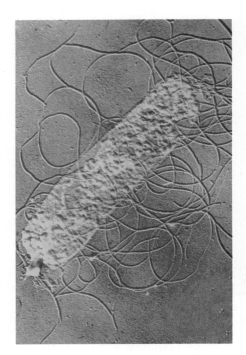

Figure 7-9 *The bacterium,* Proteus vulgaris, *uses its many whiplike flagella to move through water.*

Many bacteria are not able to move on their own. However, they can be carried from one place to another by air and water currents, clothing, and other objects. Other bacteria have special structures that help them move in watery surroundings. One type of structure is a **flagellum** (fla-JEL-um; plural: flagella). A flagellum is a long, thin, whiplike structure that propels the bacterial cell. Some bacteria may have many flagella.

Life Functions of Bacteria

Bacteria are in water, air, and the upper layers of soil. In fact, bacteria live almost everywhere, even in places where other living things cannot survive. For example, some bacteria were discovered living in volcanic vents at the bottom of the Pacific Ocean south of Baja, California. Temperatures here are as high as 250° C. Unlike most living things, some bacteria can thrive without oxygen. However, all bacteria need water or they eventually die.

Most bacteria are heterotrophs. These bacteria feed on other living things or on dead things. Bacteria that feed on living organisms are called **parasites** (PA-ruh-sights). These bacteria cause infections in

Figure 7-10 *Bacteria that live in Morning Glory Pool, a very hot spring in Yellowstone National Park, make up the blue-green growth.*

Figure 7-11 *Saprophytic bacteria of decay break down material in a dead tree and return important substances to the soil.*

people, animals, and plants. Bacteria that feed on dead things are called **saprophytes** (SA-pruh-fights). Why are saprophytes among the most important organisms found on earth?

Some bacteria are autotrophs. Like green plants, some of these food-making bacteria use the energy of sunlight to produce food. Other bacteria use the energy in substances such as sulfur and iron to make food.

Conditions may become unfavorable for bacteria. If the food, water, or air supply of bacteria becomes used up, some bacteria form microscopic **endospores.** An endospore is shaped like a ball or oval and is surrounded by a thick protective membrane. The protective membrane enables the endospores to survive long periods of boiling and disinfectant chemicals. When food, air, and water again become available, the endospores develop into active bacteria.

Most bacteria reproduce by **binary fission.** In binary fission a cell divides into two cells. Under the best conditions, most bacteria reproduce quickly. Some types can double in number every 20 minutes. At this rate, after about 24 hours the offspring of a single bacterium would have a mass greater than 2 million kilograms, or as much as 2000 small cars. In a few more days, their mass would be greater than that of the earth. Obviously, this does not happen.

Figure 7-12 *These bacteria are splitting in two, a process of reproduction called binary fission. Which of the three basic groups of bacteria are reproducing here?*

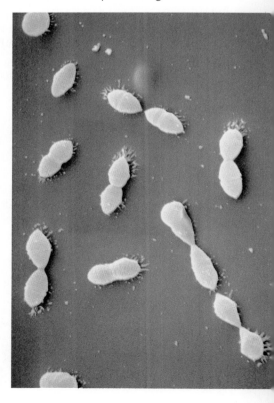

155

In the real world, the rate of reproduction slows down because the bacteria soon use up their food, water, and space. They also produce wastes that eventually poison them.

Helpful Bacteria

Most types of bacteria are not harmful and do not cause disease. For example, many food products, especially dairy products, are produced with the help of bacteria. Bacteria are needed to make cheeses, butter, yogurt, and sour cream. Some species of bacteria are used in the process of tanning leather.

Some helpful bacteria are used to fight other, harmful bacteria. These helpful bacteria, for example, can help produce **antibiotics.** Antibiotics destroy or weaken disease-causing bacteria. Scientists also have found a way to turn certain types of bacteria into "chemical factories." The DNA within these bacteria is changed. The bacteria then produce large

Career: *Bacteriologist*

> **HELP WANTED: BACTERIOLOGIST**
> College degree required; master's or Ph.D. desirable. Strong background in science necessary. Applicant should be creative and innovative. Position involves testing and research. Past experience as lab helper/technician an asset.

The specially equipped plane landed at the Atlanta airport. Within minutes, white-coated technicians rushed the test tube the plane was carrying to the Center for Disease Control. There, under strict laboratory conditions, the contents of the test tube were analyzed.

Through the powerful lens of the microscope, a tiny rod-shaped object became visible. Was it a living organism? The answer soon became obvious. Twenty minutes later a second rod-shaped object became visible under the lens of the microscope. The organism had reproduced.

Now a more important question had to be answered. Could this rod-shaped bacteria cause disease in human beings? Was it related to a type of bacteria that had caused diseases such as diphtheria, typhoid fever, and plague in the past? A **bacteriologist** would determine the type of bacteria it was and whether or not it was dangerous. In San Francisco, a sick patient and her doctor waited eagerly for the results.

Many bacteriologists specialize in identifying unknown microorganisms from the 2000 or so known types of bacteria. Others try to devise methods to combat harmful bacteria. Still others study how disease-causing bacteria may be spread in our environment. For further information on this career, write to the American Society of Microbiology, 1913 I Street N.W., Washington, DC 20006.

amounts of important substances such as insulin. Insulin helps to control the rate at which the human body breaks down sugar. People who do not produce enough of their own insulin can use the insulin produced by the bacteria.

Certain bacteria, called nitrogen-fixing bacteria, can make nitrogen compounds from nitrogen gas in the atmosphere. Nitrogen-fixing bacteria turn nitrogen gas, which plants cannot use for food, into nitrogen compounds that plants can use for food. These nitrogen-fixing bacteria often appear as lumps on the roots of plants such as alfalfa. See Figure 7-13. Nitrogen-fixing bacteria also help replace the nitrogen compounds in the soil. Without such nitrogen-fixing bacteria, most nitrogen compounds in the soil would be quickly used up and plants could no longer grow.

Harmful Bacteria

Although most bacteria are harmless, and some are helpful, a few can cause trouble. The trouble comes in a number of forms—food spoilage, diseases of people, diseases of farm animals and pets, and diseases of food crops. Fortunately, there are a number of defenses against attacks by harmful bacteria.

FOOD SPOILAGE Spoilage can be prevented or slowed down by heating, drying, salting, or smoking foods. Each one of these processes prevents or slows down the growth of bacteria. Milk, for example, is heated to 71° C for 15 seconds before it is placed in containers and shipped to the grocery or supermarket. This process, called pasteurization, destroys most of the bacteria that would cause the milk to spoil quickly. Heating and then canning foods such as vegetables, fruits, meat, and fish are also used to prevent bacterial growth. But if the foods are not sufficiently heated before canning, bacteria can grow inside the can and produce poisons called **toxins.**

HUMAN DISEASES These diseases caused by bacteria include strep throat, certain kinds of pneumonia, diphtheria, tuberculosis, and whooping cough. Some of these diseases can be prevented by an immunization shot. Others can be treated with antibiotics.

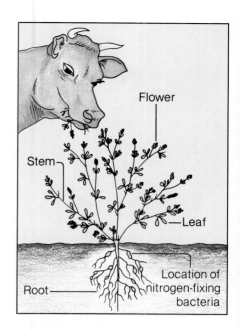

Figure 7-13 *Nitrogen-fixing bacteria on the roots of alfalfa plants convert nitrogen gas in the air to nitrogen compounds that enter the soil. These compounds are needed by plants for growth.*

ANIMAL DISEASES Bacteria cause diseases in animals. These diseases include anthrax, which attacks sheep, horses, cattle, and other large farm animals, and fowl cholera, which attacks chickens. Vaccinations can prevent both diseases.

PLANT DISEASES These diseases caused by bacteria include fire blight of apples and pears and soft rot of vegetables. There are many ways of treating plant diseases, including the use of antibiotics and various chemicals.

SECTION REVIEW

1. What are the three basic shapes of bacteria?
2. What are two ways in which bacteria are helpful? Harmful?

Figure 7-14 *Leaves on this pear tree have been attacked by a bacterial disease called fire blight.*

Figure 7-15 *The radolarian, a protozoan, is surrounded by a hard silicon shell.*

7-3 Protozoans

Two billion years ago, the earth was a strange and barren place. No animals roamed the land, swam in the sea, or flew in the air. No trees, shrubs, or grasses grew from the soil. From the air, the earth

looked gray, brown, and blue. But even though it looked lifeless, an unseen new form of life was taking hold in its blue waters. This form of life, the **protozoans,** represented a giant step in the parade of living things that would follow. **Protozoans are unicellular animal-like organisms.** The protozoans still inhabit the world's seas, lakes, rivers, and ponds.

Protozoans differ in many ways from the bacteria that first inhabited the earth. For one thing, protozoans do not have cell walls. They do contain a distinct cell nucleus, which contains hereditary material. Protozoans are, in fact, the first animal-like organisms to evolve on the earth. For this reason, they were given their name, which comes from the Greek words for "first animal." However, protozoans are not true animals and are classified in the Protista kingdom.

Activity

A Protozoan Population

The largest existing protozoan is *Pelomyxa palustrius*. It may grow to a length of up to 1.5 centimeters. If all the *Pelomyxa palustrius* in a 30-meter-long pond were placed end-to-end and equaled the pond's length, how many would be present in the pond?

Amoebas

Amoebas (uh-MEE-buhz) make up one of the simplest groups of protozoans. Although some amoebas are visible to the unaided eye, most are microscopic. Under the microscope, an amoeba looks like a blob of jelly.

The amoeba moves slowly in a watery environment by extending its cell membrane and cytoplasm. This extension is called a **pseudopod** (soo-duh-pahd), or "false foot." When the pseudopod is fully extended, it pulls the amoeba along with it.

Figure 7-16 *This drawing shows the structure of a typical amoeba. The photograph of the amoeba was magnified 160 times.*

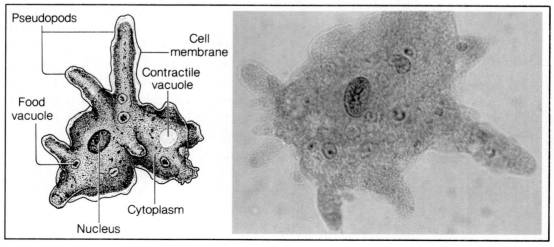

Activity

Harmful Microorganisms

Using reference materials in the library, prepare a report on the following diseases.

measles

smallpox

amoebic dysentery

poliomyelitis

pneumonia

tetanus

In your report, include information about how these diseases are transmitted to human beings. Also include what types of treatment are used to prevent or cure the diseases.

Figure 7-17 *The drawing shows the wavelike motion of a cilium.*

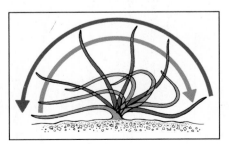

The amoeba also uses pseudopods to obtain food. As the amoeba nears a small piece of food, such as a smaller protozoan, the amoeba extends its pseudopod around the food. Soon the food particle is engulfed, or surrounded, by the pseudopod. A spherical **food vacuole** (VAK-yoo-ohl) in the pseudopod forms around the engulfed food particle. The food vacuole releases special digestive chemicals, called enzymes, in order to break down the captured food. The digested food can then be taken in and used by the amoeba. The waste products left behind in the food vacuole are eliminated through the cell membrane.

To supply itself with energy, the amoeba requires oxygen as well as food. Oxygen passes from the watery environment into the amoeba through the cell membrane. At the same time, waste products, such as carbon dioxide, pass out of the amoeba through the cell membrane. Excess water in the amoeba is pumped out through the cell membrane by a **contractile vacuole.**

Like bacteria, amoebas reproduce by binary fission. A parent cell divides into two new identical cells. Each of these new cells has the same amount and kind of hereditary material as the parent cell.

Amoebas respond simply to changes in their environments. They are sensitive to bright light and move to areas of dim light. Amoebas are also sensitive to certain chemicals, moving away from some and toward others.

Ciliates

The protist kingdom also includes the ciliates (SIHL-ee-ayts). These protozoans have **cilia** (SIHL-ee-uh; singular: cilium). Cilia are small hairlike projections on the outside of the cells. Sweeping through the water like tiny oars, the cilia enable these organisms to move, and help them to obtain food. In addition, the cilia function as sensors through which these organisms receive information about their environment.

One of the most familiar ciliates is the paramecium (pa-ruh-MEE-shi-uhm; plural: paramecia). A hard membrane covers the outer surface of the paramecium. This membrane gives the paramecium its

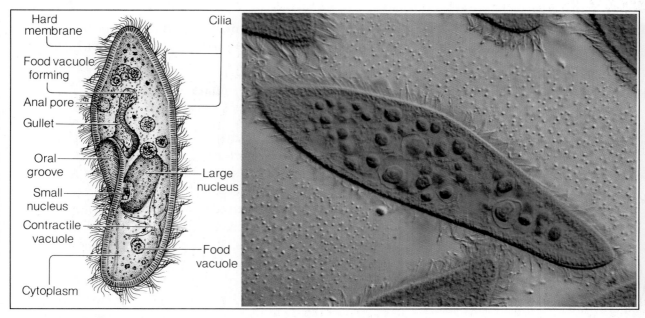

Figure 7-18 *This drawing shows the structure of a typical paramecium. The photograph of the paramecium was magnified 140 times.*

slipper shape. The cilia of the paramecium move food particles in the water into its **oral groove.** The oral groove is an indentation in the paramecium. Food goes from the oral groove into the **gullet.** The gullet is a funnel-shaped structure that ends at the food vacuole. The food vacuole distributes food particles as it moves through the organism. Undigested material is eliminated through the **anal pore.**

Located in the cytoplasm of paramecia are a small nucleus and a large nucleus. The small nucleus controls reproduction. The large nucleus controls all other life functions.

Reproduction in paramecia occurs in two ways. Like an amoeba, paramecia reproduce by binary fission. A paramecium may also share its hereditary material with another paramecium through a process called **conjugation** (kahn-joo-GAY-shuhn). During conjugation, two paramecia join together. Soon the larger nuclei disappear and the smaller nuclei divide in two. Then, one of the smaller nuclei from each pair passes into a special tube joining both paramecia. After exchanging the hereditary material, the two paramecia move away from each other. A new small nucleus and a new large nucleus form in each of the two paramecia. Conjugation is beneficial

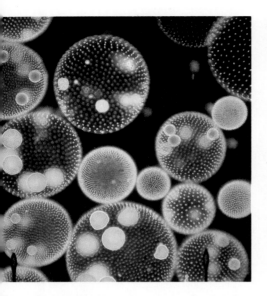

because it allows paramecia to share hereditary characteristics that may help the paramecia become better able to survive a changing environment.

Flagellates

The flagellates include protozoans that have flagella. Most of the flagellates, such as *Euglena,* are unicellular. However, some flagellates, such as *Volvox,* form colonies, or clusters of cells.

There are two groups of flagellates. One group contains the green substance chlorophyll. These flagellates are autotrophs. *Volvox* is an example of this type of flagellate.

The second group of flagellates do not contain chlorophyll. They are heterotrophs. Most of these flagellates are parasites. Some of them cause disease such as African sleeping sickness. This group of disease-causing flagellates is transmitted to people and animals by the tsetse fly.

Figure 7-19 Volvox *are flagellates that form colonies.* Volvox *are autotrophs because they contain the green substance chlorophyll, which enables them to make their own food.*

Figure 7-20 *This drawing shows the structure of the autotrophic flagellate called* Euglena. *The photograph is of a typical* Euglena.

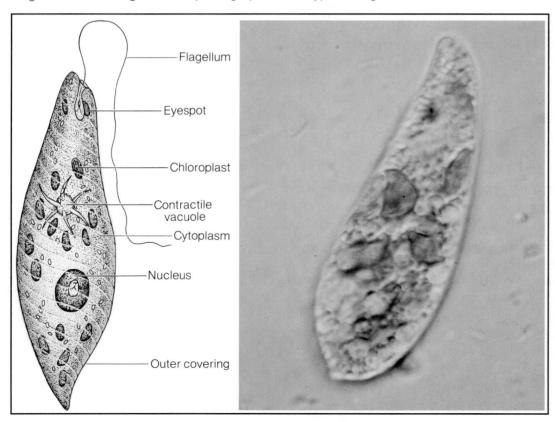

Flagellum

Eyespot

Chloroplast

Contractile vacuole

Cytoplasm

Nucleus

Outer covering

A flagellate that is both an autotroph and a heterotroph is *Euglena*. *Euglena* is an oval-shaped organism with one pointed end and one rounded end. The rounded end contains the flagellum. Also located in this area in the cytoplasm is the **eyespot.** The eyespot is a reddish structure that is sensitive to light. *Euglena* tends to move toward areas where there is enough light. *Euglena* uses light energy to make its own food.

Like the amoeba and paramecium, *Euglena* reproduces by binary fission. However, unlike most protozoans, *Euglena* splits in two lengthwise. This type of division produces two cells that are mirror images of each other.

Sporozoans

Sporozoans are protozoans that cannot move from place to place. These organisms are parasites whose foods are the cells and body fluids of animals.

Many of these sporozoans have complicated life cycles. During their life cycles, sporozoans form spores. Each spore contains hereditary material and a small amount of cytoplasm. Eventually, the sporozoans release these spores. Each spore can develop into a mature sporozoan.

Perhaps the most familiar type of sporozoan is the organism that causes the disease malaria. This sporozoan is carried by the *Anopheles* mosquito. When an infected mosquito bites a human being, the mosquito injects its saliva, and the spores enter the person's body. The infected person soon begins to experience chills and fever, which are two symptoms of malaria.

SECTION REVIEW

1. What is a pseudopod?
2. What are cilia?
3. How do amoebas, paramecia, and *Euglena* reproduce?
4. What is the function of the eyespot in *Euglena*?
5. How do sporozoans differ from other protozoans?

Activity

Capturing Food

How does a paramecium capture its food?

1. Place one drop of paramecia from a paramecium culture on a slide.
2. Add one drop of *Chlorella,* a green algae, to the slide.
3. To a second slide, add another drop of paramecia. Then, add a drop of India ink.
4. Observe the two slides under the low and high power of the microscope.

What happened to the *Chlorella?* What did the addition of India ink enable you to see? Describe the movement of the India ink into a paramecium.

LABORATORY ACTIVITY

Where Are Bacteria Found?

Purpose

In this activity, you will determine some common sources of bacteria.

> **Materials** *(per group)*
> 5 petri dishes with sterile nutrient agar
> Glass-marking pencil
> Pencil with eraser
> Soap and water

Procedure

1. Turn each petri dish bottom side up on the table. **Note:** *Be careful not to open the petri dish.*
2. With the glass-marking pencil, label the bottom of the petri dishes containing the sterile nutrient agar A to E. Turn the petri dishes right side up.
3. Remove the lid of dish A and lightly rub a pencil eraser across the petri dish. Close the dish immediately.
4. Remove the lid of dish B and leave it open to the air until the class period ends. Then close the lid.
5. Remove the lid of dish C and lightly rub your index finger over the surface of the agar. Then close the lid.
6. Wash your hands thoroughly. Remove the lid of dish D and lightly rub the same index finger over the surface of the agar. Then close the lid.
7. Do not open dish E.
8. Place all five dishes upside-down in a warm, dark place for three or four days.
9. After three or four days, examine each dish. **CAUTION:** *Do not open dishes.*
10. On a sheet of paper, construct a table similar to the one on this page. Then fill in the table.
11. Return the petri dishes to your teacher. Your teacher will properly dispose of the petri dishes.

Observations and Conclusions

1. How many colonies, or similar types of bacteria, appear to be growing on each petri dish? How can you distinguish between different bacterial colonies?

Petri Dish	Source	Description of Bacterial Colonies
A		
B		
C		
D		
E		

2. Which petri dish has the most bacterial growth? Which has the least?
3. Which petri dish was the control?
4. Did the dish that you touched with your unwashed finger contain more or less bacteria than the one that you touched with your washed finger? Explain.
5. Explain why the agar was sterilized before the investigation.
6. Design an experiment to show if a particular antibiotic will inhibit bacterial growth.
7. Suggest some methods that might stop the growth of bacteria.
8. What kinds of environmental conditions seem to influence where bacteria are found?

7-1 Viruses

- Viruses cannot carry out any life processes unless within a living cell.

- Viruses are tiny particles that contain a center of either DNA or RNA surrounded by a protein coat.

- Reproduction of viruses occurs only when the virus invades a living cell.

- Bacteriophages are viruses that infect bacterial cells.

- When a virus's hereditary material enters a living cell, the virus takes control of the cell. The cell begins to produce new viruses, which are released from the cell.

7-2 Bacteria

- Bacteria are simple unicellular monerans.

- Bacteria have three basic shapes: cocci, bacilli, or spirilla.

- Bacterial cells have a cell wall and a cell membrane surrounding the cytoplasm. The hereditary material of a bacterial cell is spread throughout the cytoplasm.

- Some bacteria have flagella, or whiplike structures, that enable them to move.

- Some bacteria called autotrophs use energy from the sun or chemicals to make food.

- Bacteria that must obtain their food from other organisms are called heterotrophs.

- Bacteria usually reproduce by binary fission, or splitting in two.

7-3 Protozoans

- Protozoans are unicellular animallike microorganisms. Their hereditary material is confined in a nucleus.

- Amoebas move and obtain food by the movement of their pseudopods. Amoebas reproduce by binary fission.

- Ciliates, such as paramecia, have small hairlike cilia used for obtaining food and for movement.

- Paramecia reproduce by binary fission and conjugation.

- Flagellates use whiplike flagella to move. There are two groups of flagellates. The members of one group contain chlorophyll and can make their own food. The second group of flagellates do not contain chlorophyll and cannot make their own food.

- Sporozoans cannot move from place to place. Sporozoans are parasites and have complex life cycles.

Define each term in a complete sentence.

anal pore	cilium	flagellum	pseudopod
antibiotic	coccus	food vacuole	RNA
bacillus	conjugation	gullet	saprophyte
bacteriophage	contractile vacuole	microbiology	spirillum
bacterium	cytoplasm	nucleus	toxin
binary fission	DNA	oral groove	virus
cell membrane	endospore	parasite	
cell wall	eyespot	protozoan	

CONTENT REVIEW: MULTIPLE CHOICE

Choose the letter of the answer that best completes each statement.

1. Viruses are
    a. shaped like spheres.   b. shaped like tadpoles.
    c. shaped like cylinders.   d. any of these shapes.

2. What is used to observe viruses?
    a. the unaided eye   b. an electron microscope
    c. a light microscope   d. all of these

3. The scientist who gave viruses their name was
    a. Martinus Beijerinck.   b. Wendell Stanley.
    c. Dimitri Iwanowski.   d. Anton van Leeuwenhoek.

4. The type of hereditary material in a virus may be
    a. DNA.   b. RNA.
    c. either DNA or RNA.   d. neither DNA nor RNA.

5. An organism that feeds on dead matter is called a(n)
    a. autotroph.   b. saprophyte.   c. parasite.   d. flagellum.

6. An amoeba moves by means of
    a. flagella.   b. cilia.   c. pseudopods.   d. conjugation.

7. Which organism reproduces by binary fission and conjugation?
    a. amoeba   b. paramecium   c. sporozoan   d. *Euglena*

8. *Euglena* is an example of a(n)
    a. flagellate.   b. ciliate.   c. sporozoan.   d. amoeba.

9. Which group of protozoans cannot move by themselves?
    a. amoebas   b. ciliates   c. flagellates   d. sporozoans

10. The most familiar type of sporozoan causes
    a. pneumonia.   b. tuberculosis.
    c. malaria.   d. African sleeping sickness.

CONTENT REVIEW: COMPLETION

Fill in the word or words that best complete each statement.

1. A virus that infects a bacterial cell is called a(n) _____.

2. The bacteria that look like rods are called _____.

3. Bacteria usually reproduce through _____.

4. Bacteria that make nitrogen compounds from nitrogen gas are called _____.

5. Some bacteria produce poisons called _____.

6. Paramecia have _____ that enable them to move.

7. The spherical structure in a cell that releases enzymes to digest food is the _____.

8. In paramecia, food particles are swept by cilia into an indented structure called a(n) _____.

9. A flagellate that is both an autotroph and a heterotroph is the _____.

10. The structure in *Euglena* that responds to changes in light is the _____.

CONTENT REVIEW: TRUE OR FALSE

Determine whether each statement is true or false. If it is true, write "true." If it is false, change the underlined word or words to make the statement true.

1. A virus is made up of hereditary material surrounded by a <u>protein coat</u>.
2. The outermost boundary of a bacterial cell is the <u>cell membrane</u>.
3. <u>Cilia</u> are long, thin, whiplike structures that are used to propel some microorganisms.
4. <u>Saprophytes</u> are organisms that feed on living organisms.
5. <u>Endospores</u> allow bacteria to survive unfavorable conditions.
6. <u>Protozoan</u> means false foot.
7. In a paramecium, the <u>oral groove</u> is the funnel-shaped structure that ends in a food vacuole.
8. The <u>contractile vacuole</u> pumps excess water out of an amoeba.
9. In a paramecium, undigested material is eliminated through an opening called the <u>anal pore</u>.
10. *Euglena* is an example of a <u>flagellate</u>.

CONCEPT REVIEW: SKILL BUILDING

Use the skills you have developed in the chapter to complete each activity.

1. **Interpreting a graph** The following graph shows the growth of bacteria. Describe what is happening at each of the numbered growth stages. Suggest a hypothesis to explain the growth pattern in stage 3 and in stage 4.

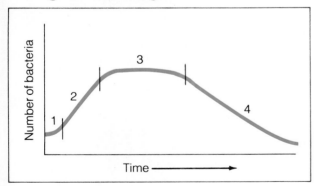

2. **Applying definitions** Suppose a biologist reported the discovery of a sporozoan that moves by means of pseudopods and has a thick cell wall made of cellulose. Could the report be true? Explain.
3. **Applying concepts** The growth of bacteria is slowed by cooler temperatures. How can you apply this information to control food spoilage?
4. **Designing an experiment** Penicillin is an antibiotic that kills some types of bacteria. Suppose you have five different bacteria cultures. Design an experiment to determine which of the cultures could be destroyed by penicillin. Include a control and a variable in your experiment.

CONCEPT REVIEW: ESSAY

Discuss each of the following in a brief paragraph.

1. Compare viruses to cells.
2. Explain why some bacteria are harmful.
3. What contributions did Dimitri Iwanowski and Martinus Beijerinck make to the study of viruses?
4. What is the difference between autotrophic and heterotrophic bacteria?
5. Compare the methods of movement in an amoeba, a paramecium, and a *Euglena*.
6. Describe how viruses reproduce.

8 Nonvascular Plants and Plantlike Organisms

CHAPTER SECTIONS

8-1 Algae
8-2 Fungi
8-3 Lichens and Slime Molds
8-4 Mosses and Liverworts

CHAPTER OBJECTIVES

After completing this chapter, you will be able to:

8-1 Define nonvascular plants.

8-1 Identify the characteristics of algae.

8-2 Identify the characteristics of fungi.

8-3 Describe lichens and slime molds.

8-4 Compare mosses and liverworts.

The sun blazes in a cloudless sky. Far to the east, a tall pillar of orange smoke billows from an erupting volcano. The air, almost empty of oxygen, blows swiftly over the ocean, whipping up waves that crash against a huge sand bar. But there is no one here to witness or record these happenings. No people sail on this ocean or wade in the protected tidal pool, which is dotted with countless peculiar pillows of rock. No fish swim below the ocean's surface, nor do any birds fly above it. This is the world of 2.5 billion years ago. Here, there are no signs of life—except for those strange rocky pillows. One day in the future scientists will recognize these softly rounded rocks as the first structures built by living things.

Scientists call these softly rounded rocks stromatolites, which comes from Greek words that roughly mean "mattress of stone." But what living thing could build these 2.5-billion-year-old stony mattresses? The answer is blue-green algae. Undisturbed in protected pools of very salty water, the blue-green algae grew even larger and larger. As they did so, they produced a rocky mineral called lime. The lime piled up—year after year, century after century—and built a seascape of gray-brown cushions. And in certain parts of the world, such as in Shark Bay on the northwest coast of Australia, the process still goes on.

Stromatolites in Shark Bay, Australia

8-1 Algae

In a northern California forest, a giant redwood tree over 200 years old stands through a violent rainstorm. Deep in the soil the tree's roots soak up water. Soon thin tubes in the tree's trunk will carry the water nearly 60 meters to the top of the tree. Without these tubes, the redwood could not bring water to its millions of living cells.

If you were walking through this forest, you would probably marvel at the height of the redwood tree. However, unless you looked closely, you might not notice a smaller plant growing on the bark near the bottom of the tree. Unlike the redwood, this plant cannot grow to majestic heights. It is one of the earth's **nonvascular** (nahn-VA-skyuh-ler) **plants.** Nonvascular plants do not have transportation tubes to carry water and food throughout the plant.

The plant living on the bark of the redwood tree is a type of **alga** (AL-guh; plural: algae—AL-jee). **Algae are nonvascular plants that contain chlorophyll.** Because algae have no way of transporting water and food over long distances, they must live close to a source of water.

Figure 8-1 *The green patches floating on the surface of this lake are colonies of threadlike algae.*

Nonvascular plants such as the algae are often called simple plants. Simple plants lack true stems, leaves, and roots. However, do not let the term "simple" fool you. Nonvascular plants have managed to survive for hundreds of millions of years while other forms of life have come into being and then died off. In fact, through their long history nonvascular plants have become well adapted to many different environments on the earth.

Where Algae Live

No doubt you enjoy a visit to the zoo. Walking past one of the cages, you might notice a greenish stump hanging from a large branch. You look more closely and you see that the stump is breathing. The stump is alive! Looking at the small plaque on the cage, you discover that the "stump" is an animal called the three-toed sloth. Interestingly, the hair of this and many other three-toed sloths is the home for certain green algae. Because the sloth is such a slow-moving animal, it is unable to escape if there is danger. The algae's green color helps the sloth to blend in with its surroundings until the danger has passed. In return, the sloth gives the algae a place to live.

Most algae, of course, do not live on sloths. Algae live in many different places. The majority of algae live in watery environments such as oceans, ponds, and lakes. Other algae grow in the soil, on the sides of houses, and at the base of trees. Certain species of algae thrive in the near-boiling water of hot springs such as those in Yellowstone National Park. Other algae grow in snow. Some even grow in the icy waters of such places as the Antarctic continent, in which lies the South Pole.

Structure of Algae

Some species of algae are unicellular, or one-celled, and can only be seen with a microscope. Quite often unicellular algae group together to form colonies. These colonies may even attach themselves to one another and form chains of algae.

Beaches often become littered with seaweed after a heavy storm. Seaweed is one type of multicellular

Figure 8-2 *Algae live in many different places. Some grow on the bark of trees* (top). *Others are at home in the hair of a three-toed sloth* (bottom).

Figure 8-3 *Several kinds of seaweeds, which are types of algae, washed up on a New England beach.*

algae. Multicellular algae can grow quite large. The giant kelp, for example, may stretch over 30 meters.

Whether unicellular or multicellular, all algae are autotrophs, or organisms that can make their own food. All algae contain **chlorophyll,** a green substance found in green plant cells. Chlorophyll is used in the process of **photosynthesis** (foh-tuh-SIN-thuh-sis). In photosynthesis, plants use the energy in sunlight to make their own food. Plants make food by combining carbon dioxide from the air with water and minerals from the soil. During the process of photosynthesis, oxygen is released from the plant.

Early in the earth's history there was very little oxygen in the atmosphere. In time, algae and other simple green plants, along with certain bacteria, released vast amounts of oxygen into the air. Eventually there was enough oxygen in the air to allow other forms of life to develop. If it were not for these simple green plants, no animals or people would now exist on the earth. And, as a matter of fact, if green plants were to suddenly vanish from the earth, oxygen in the air would soon become so rare that most living things would vanish.

Algae have several similarities and differences. Most algae reproduce by binary fission. Others have very complicated life cycles. Regardless of these differences, scientists have placed the algae into six groups. The groups are arranged according to the color of the algae.

Blue-Green Algae

In 1883, on the island of Krakatoa in Indonesia, a great volcano exploded. The sound of the explosion was heard by people thousands of kilometers away. In an instant, all living things on the island were destroyed, leaving behind only bare rock. Yet a few years later, one form of life had begun to grow on the barren island. This living thing was a blue-green alga.

Soon a layer of blue-green algae carpeted much of the island. The layer of algae eventually became so thick that plants were able to grow on top of it. Today, as they did before the volcanic eruption, many kinds of plants live and flourish on the island of Krakatoa.

Blue-green algae are considered to be the simplest of all algae. In fact, unlike all other algae, blue-green algae are not considered plants. They are placed in the Monera kingdom, along with bacteria. All blue-green algae need to live is sunlight, nitrogen and carbon dioxide gas from the air, and a few minerals in their water supply. It is likely that they were the first organisms to grow on land.

Blue-green algae are special for other reasons. Some blue-green algae can remove nitrogen gas from the air and combine the nitrogen with other substances to make nitrogen compounds. In this way, blue-green algae help provide the nitrogen compounds that plants need to live. Normally, farmers must use fertilizers to replace nitrogen compounds used by green plants. However, in places like Asia where blue-green algae live in the water, farmers can plant rice year after year without the need of fertilizers. The blue-green algae fertilize the rice paddies naturally.

Not all blue-green algae are blue-green in color. In some algae, the blue-green substance is masked by another substance. For example, one species of blue-green algae is actually red. It lives in the Red Sea, which accounts for the sea's name.

Figure 8-4 *Algae are found in many environments on the earth. These blue-green algae (left) are in a hot spring in Yellowstone National Park. Some blue-green algae (right) grow below the frozen surface of Lake Hoare in Antarctica.*

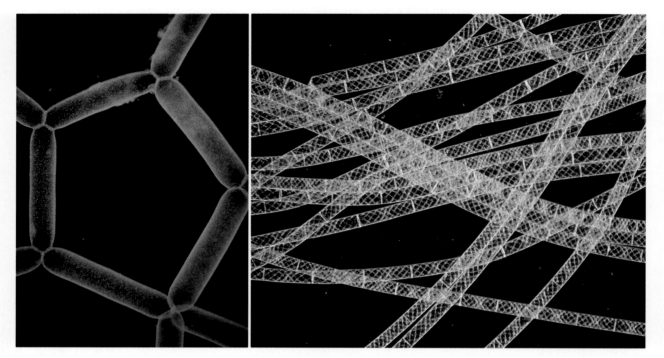

Figure 8-5 *The green alga* (left), *magnified 50 times, forms "water nets" on ponds.* Spirogyra (right) *is a green alga that forms filaments and is found in pools of fresh water.*

Green Algae

The year is 2001. Deep in space, a silvery ship is on its second year in a four-year journey to study the planets. On board, the two astronauts are about to finish dinner. Although they brought along enough food to last the entire journey, they could not carry enough oxygen to last several years. Are the astronauts doomed to suffocate in space? Of course not.

In a tiny room near the back of the ship lies a tub of water filled with green algae. The green algae use the carbon dioxide wastes exhaled by the astronauts to make food during photosynthesis. In return, the algae release their own waste, oxygen, for the astronauts to breathe. If you looked closely at the tub, you could see bubbles containing oxygen floating toward the surface. In this way, the astronauts and the green algae support each other's lives.

This scene is one that will not be played out for some time. However, scientists today are hard at work developing methods of growing green algae in closed environments. These methods will allow the algae to produce the oxygen future travelers will use in their explorations of space.

Right now you can find green algae only at home on the earth. Most green algae live in the water, but some plants may grow on the branches, stems, and leaves of trees. A few types of green algae may anchor themselves to rocks and pieces of wood.

Golden Algae

Every morning and evening you probably brush your teeth. Chances are that the last thing you would consider brushing with is algae. Yet a part of many toothpastes is made of golden algae. Do not let their name fool you, however. Golden algae all contain the green substance chlorophyll. Their golden color comes from a mixture of orange, yellow, and brown substances in their cells.

The most common, and certainly the most attractive, golden algae are the diatoms (DIGH-uh-tuhms). If you looked at diatoms through a microscope, they would resemble tiny glass boxes. See Figure 8-6. The appearance of diatoms is due to a glassy material in their cell walls. When diatoms die, their tough glasslike walls remain. In time, the walls collect in layers and form deposits of diatomaceous (digh-uh-tuh-MAY-shuhs) earth. Diatomaceous earth is a coarse, powdery material. For this reason, it is often added to toothpastes to help polish teeth. And, because

Figure 8-6 *Diatoms have cell walls made of silica, a glasslike substance. The diatoms* (left) *show their many different shapes. The single diatom* (right) *is magnified 3000 times.*

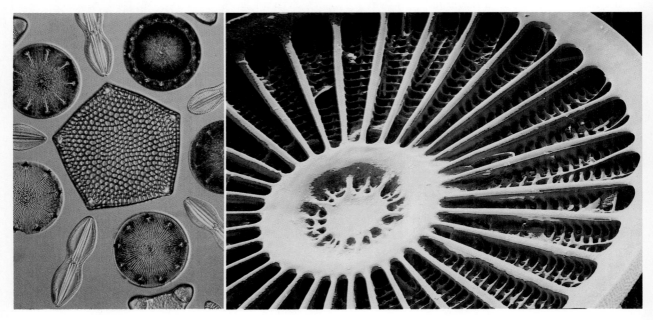

Some algae appear as green masses on the bark of trees.

1. Find such algae and re-move it from the tree along with some bark.

2. Place the algae in a dish containing a small amount of water. Cover the dish.

3. After a few days, scrape off some of the green material and place it on a glass slide containing a drop of water. Cover with a cover slip.

4. Examine the slide under the low and high powers of a microscope.

How does this alga compare with the photographs in Figure 8-5? Draw and label this alga under low and high power.

Figure 8-7 *The brown alga,* Sargassum, *provides a home for the* Sargassum filefish *and the* Sargassum crab. *The tiny grape-shaped structures are air bladders, which help to keep the alga afloat.*

diatomaceous earth reflects light, it is also added to the paint used to indicate separate traffic lanes on highways.

Brown Algae

For centuries, sailors whispered tales of a huge sea within a sea in the Atlantic Ocean southeast of Bermuda. This sea, the Sargasso Sea, the sailors said was filled with endless tangles of brown seaweed. The name of the sea comes from the brown *Sargassum* algae that grow in great amounts in this part of the Atlantic Ocean. Legend had it that ships trapped in this thick growth of seaweed would remain here forever, forming a fleet of dead ships guarded by skeletons. Today, some people believe that the sailors traveling with Christopher Columbus mutinied not out of fear of falling off the side of the earth, but out of fear of being trapped in the Sargasso Sea.

The legends about the Sargasso Sea are merely a product of people's strong imagination. However, the brown algae that float there are very real. The *Sargassum* lie on or near the ocean's surface. There they are able to receive enough sunlight to perform photosynthesis. They stay near the surface because they have **air bladders.** Air bladders are tiny grape-

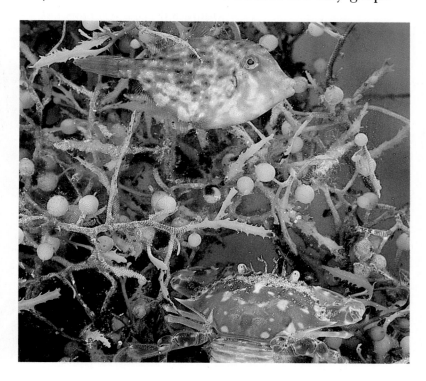

shaped structures. These air bladders act like inflatable life preservers.

Brown algae, such as *Sargassum*, are the largest and most complex of the algae. Most brown algae live in salt water and are called seaweeds or kelps. Some brown algae float freely while others remain attached to the sea floor.

Red Algae

Red algae, named for a red substance found in their cells, make up another large group of algae. Some red algae produce a jellylike material called agar (AH-guhr). Agar is a substance on which scientists grow bacteria.

Red algae can grow to be several meters long, but they never reach the size of brown algae such as *Sargassum*. Red algae usually grow attached to rocks on the ocean floor. Their red color allows them to absorb a part of sunlight that can penetrate deep into the ocean. For this reason, some species of red algae grow as far as 200 meters below the ocean's surface.

Fire Algae

In the winter and spring of 1974, the waters near the west coast of Florida suddenly turned brown and red. Soon thousands of dead fish washed up on shore. One young boy became very ill after eating clams taken from the area. This was not the first time a "red tide" had struck a Florida beach, or, for that matter, other beaches in the United States. Red tides have swept onto beaches in such places as New England and Los Angeles.

The red tide is not a tide at all. It is a large group of unicellular fire algae. Fire algae range in color from yellow-green to orange-brown. Some of these fire algae produce poisons. These poisons can injure or kill living things.

If you observed fire algae through a microscope, you would notice something interesting. Fire algae have cell walls that look like plates of armor. In addition, fire algae have two flagella that help propel them forward. So the algae might look like tiny submarines spinning through the water like tops.

Figure 8-8 *Unlike brown algae which float free, red algae usually are attached to rocks on the ocean floor. Red algae also are smaller and more delicate than brown algae.*

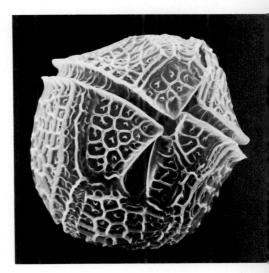

Figure 8-9 *Notice that the cell wall of this fire alga, magnified 5000 times, looks like armor plates. This particular fire alga can cause "red tides."*

Some fire algae have a characteristic that has amazed sailors since they first set sail on the world's oceans. These sailors often saw a strange glow at night in the water behind their ships. What the sailors did not know was that the glow was produced by fire algae. This glow is called **bioluminescence** (bigh-oh-loo-muh-NE-suhns), which means "having living light." The glow is similar to that produced by fireflies, or "lightning bugs."

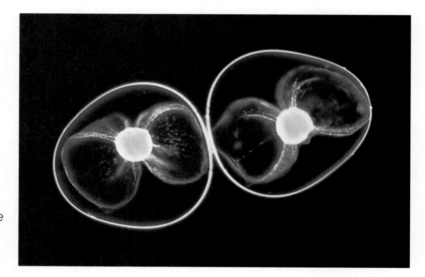

Figure 8-10 *These two fire algae cells produce a cold light, or a glow, called bioluminescence.*

SECTION REVIEW

1. What are nonvascular plants?
2. List six groups of algae.
3. What is bioluminescence?

8-2 Fungi

In 1927, scientists discovered a deadly elm tree disease in England. The disease, called Dutch elm disease, caused the leaves of the trees to wither. Eventually, the trees died. You would think that elm trees in the United States, separated from England by the Atlantic Ocean, would be safe. However, despite repeated warnings, wood of the English elm trees was shipped to this country to make furniture. By 1930, Dutch elm disease had struck trees in Ohio.

Figure 8-11 *The elm tree* (left) *has been attacked by a fungus that causes Dutch elm disease. This disease is carried by the bark beetle whose wormlike larvae* (right) *burrow through the bark of the tree.*

Today, Dutch elm disease has spread to almost every state in the country. The disease is carried from tree to tree by insects called bark beetles. However, as scientists learned, Dutch elm disease actually is caused by a type of **fungus,** (FUHNG-guhs; plural: fungi) carried by the beetles.

Fungi are nonvascular plantlike organisms that have no chlorophyll. Therefore, fungi cannot perform photosynthesis. Because fungi must obtain their food from living or once-living organisms, they are heterotrophs.

Fungi that live and grow on other living things are called parasites. The fungus that kills elm trees is an example of a parasite. Other parasitic fungi grow on and destroy crop plants, which people depend upon for food. Fungi can also attack people directly, as anyone who has ever suffered from the itching of athlete's foot can tell you. Animals, too, can be victims of fungi. Some fungi, for example, infect fishes, including those that are raised in home aquariums.

Other species of fungi get their food from once-living organisms. These fungi are called saprophytes. They, along with many types of bacteria, are the earth's "clean-up crew." These fungi decompose, or

Figure 8-12 *The four shelflike structures growing on this tree are shelf fungi. These fungi are parasites and get their food from the living tree.*

Figure 8-13 *Fungi have many shapes and can be very colorful. The
bird's nest* (top left), *morel* (top right), *scarlet cup* (bottom left), *and death
cup* (bottom right) *are different kinds of fungi.*

break down, dead plant and animal matter. These
broken-down products become the foods of other
living things. Without saprophytes, dead plants and
animals would soon litter and pollute the earth.

Structure of Fungi

Fungi have several types of structures. Most
members of the Fungi kingdom have threadlike
structures called **hyphae** (HIGH-fee; singular: hypha).
These hyphae produce special chemicals called enzymes. The enzymes digest or break down the cells
of living or dead organisms. The broken-down cells
and their chemicals are used by fungi as food. Fungi
absorb food through the walls of the hyphae.

Most fungi reproduce by means of spores. These
spores are contained in special **fruiting bodies.**

Fruiting bodies are structures that form from the closely packed hyphae. When the spores are released and land in moist areas, such as on the forest floor, they grow into new fungi.

Mushrooms

Have you ever ordered a pizza with all the trimmings? If so, you probably ate one type of fungi called the mushroom. All you may know about the mushrooms on pizza is that they taste good. But the pizza maker has to know a lot more because certain mushrooms are poisonous, and poisonous mushrooms on a pizza certainly would not improve sales.

Fortunately, the mushrooms on pizzas and stocked on grocery shelves come from special farms and are safe to eat. However, mushrooms that grow in the wild often are not safe to eat. One of the most poisonous wild mushrooms is the death cup. This well-named mushroom produces a poison that acts much like the venom of a rattlesnake. Since most people cannot tell the difference between poisonous and nonpoisonous mushrooms, wild mushrooms should never be picked or eaten.

The umbrella-shaped part of the mushroom you probably are most familiar with is the mushroom's **cap.** It is actually the mushroom's fruiting body, which contains spores. See Figure 8-14. The cap can be any color, depending on the species of mushroom. The cap is at the top of a **stalk,** a stemlike

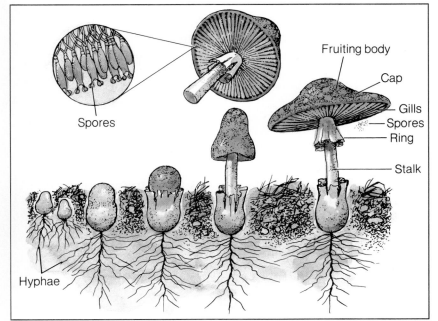

Spores

Fruiting body

Cap

Gills

Spores

Ring

Stalk

Hyphae

Figure 8-14 *As a mushroom develops, the fruiting body emerges from under the ground and releases spores. These spores then develop into new mushrooms.*

Figure 8-15 *When a water droplet hits this puff ball fungus, the fungus responds by releasing a cloud of spores.*

Figure 8-16 *Yeasts reproduce by budding, as shown in this photograph. The cells that result can form new yeast colonies.*

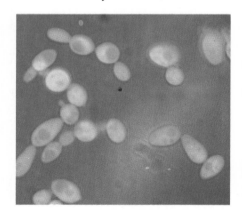

structure that has a ring near its top. If you were to turn the mushroom upside down, you would see its **gills.** The gills are the mushroom's spore factories.

Not all mushrooms resemble the types that you see in the grocery store. The puffball, for example, looks like a giant softball and can grow up to 60 centimeters in diameter. When a raindrop hits the puffball, a tiny puff of "smoke" is given off. The puff of smoke contains thousands of spores. See Figure 8-15.

Yeasts

Most people cannot help but stop and take a deep breath when they pass a bakery. There is something about the aroma of fresh bread that excites our senses. The next time you pass a bakery you might whisper a soft thank-you to another type of fungi, the yeasts.

Yeasts, like other fungi, have no chlorophyll. They obtain their energy through a process called **fermentation.** During fermentation, sugars and starches are changed into alcohol and carbon dioxide gas. At the same time, energy is released.

Bakers add yeast to bread dough. As the dough bakes, the yeast produces carbon dioxide. This causes the bread to rise. The carbon dioxide also produces millions of tiny bubbles in the bread, which you can see as holes in a slice of bread.

Although yeasts are unicellular, they can clump together to form chains of cells. Yeasts reproduce by forming spores or by **budding.** See Figure 8-16. During budding, a portion of the yeast cell pushes out of the cell wall and forms a tiny bud. In time, the bud forms a new yeast.

Molds

Centuries ago people treated infections in a rather curious way. They often placed decaying breads, cheeses, and fruits such as oranges on the infection. Although the people did not have a scientific reason to do this, every once in a while the infection was cured. What these people did not and could not know was that the cure was due to a type of fungus, called mold, which grows on certain foods.

In 1928, the Scottish scientist, Sir Alexander Fleming found out why this treatment worked. Fleming discovered that a substance produced by the mold *Penicillium* could kill certain bacteria that caused infections. Fleming named the substance penicillin. Since that time penicillin, an antibiotic, has saved millions of lives.

You have probably seen the common mold that grows on bread. This mold looks like tiny fluffs of cotton. Actually, these fluffs are groups of long hyphae that grow over the surface of bread. Shorter hyphae grow down into the bread and resemble tiny roots. The shorter hyphae release the enzymes that break down chemicals in the bread. The broken-down chemicals are food for the mold and are absorbed by the hyphae. See Figure 8-17.

Perhaps you have noticed tiny black spheres on bread mold. These spheres are spore cases, which produce spores. The spores are carried from one place to another through the air. When the spores land on food, they begin to develop into a new mold.

Figure 8-17 *Bread mold reproduces by producing spores. They are released from structures called spore cases. Long hyphae anchor the mold to bread. Short hyphae absorb food from bread.*

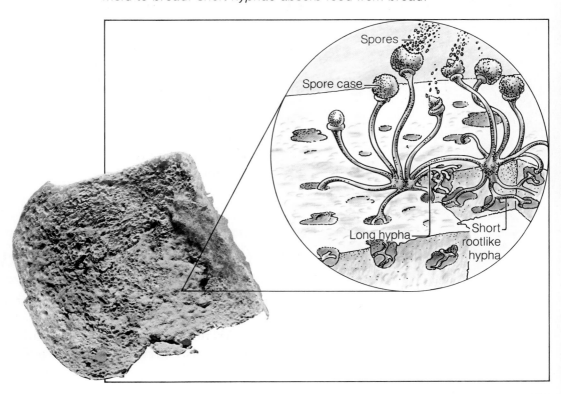

HELP WANTED: MUSHROOM GROW-ER Must know basics of mushroom growing and have an interest in botany. High school diploma needed. Business and marketing courses desirable.

People have been using mushrooms to flavor food for thousands of years. Usually the mushrooms were found growing wild in fields. It was not until the late 1800s that mushrooms were grown on a large scale in the United States for sale in the marketplace.

Mushroom growers must grow their crop indoors, where conditions can be controlled. The growers keep careful watch over the special devices that control temperature, humidity, and ventilation. In addition, mushroom growers must know how to identify and treat diseases of mushrooms.

Growers work in all stages of mushroom production. Because mushrooms live on dead or decayed matter, growers prepare mixtures of corn and hay. This mixture is placed in a shallow bed and then steam heated to destroy harmful insects, worms, and fungi. Then the hyphae, or cottony masses of material from which the mushrooms will develop is planted in the mixture of corn and hay and covered with a layer of soil.

Two to three months later, the mushrooms are picked just before the gills appear under the caps. The mushrooms are sent to large canning companies or supermarkets the same day they are picked. Some mushroom growers sell directly to consumers. If becoming a mushroom grower appeals to you, you can write to the American Mushroom Institute, P.O. Box 373, Kennett Square, PA 19348.

SECTION REVIEW

1. How are fungi different from algae?
2. What are hyphae?
3. How do yeast cells reproduce?
4. What is penicillin?

8-3 Lichens and Slime Molds

Suppose someone asked you what kind of organism can live in the hot, dry desert as well as the cold, wet Arctic. What if the person added that this organism can also survive on bare rocks, wooden poles, the sides of trees, and even the tops of mountains? You might reply that no one organism can survive in so many different environments. In a way, your response would be right. For although **lichens** (LIGH-kuhnz) can actually live in all of these environments, they are not one organism but two. **A lichen is made up of a fungus and an alga that live together.** Combined, these two organisms can live in many places that neither could survive in alone.

The fungus part of the lichen provides the alga with water and minerals that the fungus absorbs from whatever the lichen is growing on. The alga part of the lichen uses the minerals and water to make food for the fungus and itself. This type of relationship, in which two different organisms live together, is called **symbiosis** (sim-bigh-OH-sis).

Lichens are called pioneer plants because they are often the first plants to appear in rocky, barren areas. Lichens release acids that break down rock and cause it to crack. Dust and dead lichens fill the cracks, which eventually become fertile places for other organisms to grow. In time, the rocky area may become a lush, green forest.

Figure 8-18 *This green structure with the red top is a lichen. A lichen is made up of an alga and a fungus that live together.*

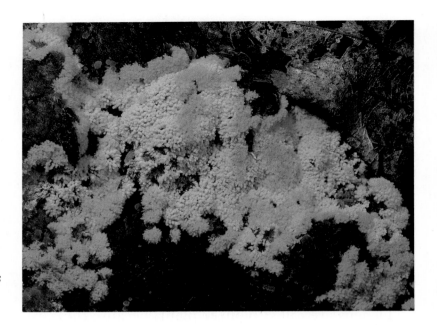

Figure 8-19 *The lavender bloblike organism growing on this dead leaf is a slime mold.*

While walking through a forest, you may have seen a bloblike organism growing in moist areas, on dead leaves, rotting logs, and other types of decaying material. This organism is called a **slime mold** because of its appearances during its life cycle. **The slime mold resembles a protozoan and a fungus during the two stages of its life cycle.**

In one of the slime mold's stages, it resembles a jellylike mass of protoplasm, engulfing and digesting food like a giant amoeba. In the other stage, the slime mold develops fruiting bodies like its cousin the mushroom. The fruiting bodies produce spores. The spores develop into new slime molds.

SECTION REVIEW

1. What is a lichen?
2. Describe a slime mold's life cycle.

8-4 Mosses and Liverworts

In a barren cold part of northern Europe, above the Arctic Circle, is the region of Lapland. Its rocky landscape has a few small trees and beds of lichens and **mosses.** The people who live in this icy place are

Figure 8-20 *The rounded structures at the top of these haircap mosses are capsules. Spores are produced within these capsules.*

Figure 8-21 *The small, flat, green plants growing on the rock are liverworts.*

called Lapps. For them, everything in their environment is important, including the mosses. Because the mosses are soft and keep in warmth, the Lapps use them to line their baby cradles.

Mosses are small green nonvascular plants that have stemlike and leaflike parts. They live almost everywhere in the world. They are found near or on the ground, close to sources of water. Mosses absorb water through rootlike structures called **rhizoids** (RIGH-zoids). Because mosses contain chlorophyll, they make their own food through photosynthesis. They live in damp and cool places such as the shaded surfaces of trees and rocks.

Although **liverworts** share characteristics with mosses, they are different plants. **Liverworts are small green nonvascular plants that have flat leaflike parts.** Each liverwort looks like a tiny green leaf, although it is not a real leaf. Some liverworts look like miniature livers, which explains how these simple plants got their name. Like mosses, liverworts grow in moist places and have rhizoids. Certain liverworts have a special way of reproducing. New plants grow from pieces broken off older plants.

SECTION REVIEW

1. What is the function of a rhizoid?
2. How are liverworts like mosses? Unlike mosses?

LABORATORY ACTIVITY

Examining a Slime Mold

Purpose

In this activity, you will observe the characteristics of a slime mold.

Materials *(per group)*

Petri dish containing agar
Filter paper containing slime mold
Crushed oatmeal flakes
Water   Forceps
Glass slide   Microscope
Masking tape   Medicine dropper
Cover slip   Dissecting needle

Procedure

1. With a forceps, place the small piece of filter paper containing the slime mold in the center of the petri dish.
2. Sprinkle some crushed oatmeal flakes next to the piece of filter paper.
3. Add two to three drops of water to the slime mold and oatmeal flakes.
4. Cover the petri dish. Seal the dish with masking tape.
5. Place the sealed petri dish in a cool, dark place.
6. Examine the petri dish each day for three days. Record your observations.
7. After three days, remove a small amount of the slime mold from the petri dish and place it on a glass slide.
8. Examine the slime mold under the low power of a microscope.
9. With a dissecting needle, puncture a branch of the slime mold. **CAUTION:** *Be careful when using a dissecting needle.* Observe the slime mold for a few minutes.

Observations and Conclusions

1. Describe the changes that took place in the slime mold during the three-day observation period.
2. What activity did you observe in the slime mold after placing it on the glass slide?
3. Describe what happened to the puncture that you made in the slime mold.
4. Why was oatmeal added to the petri dish?
5. Is the slime mold a heterotroph or an autotroph? Explain.
6. Based on your observations, describe the characteristics of a slime mold.
7. Describe an experiment to determine the response of the slime mold to certain substances, such as salt or sugar.

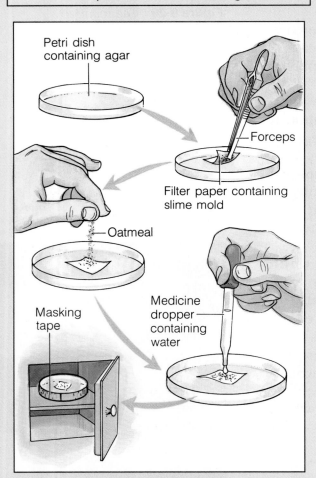

CHAPTER REVIEW

SUMMARY

8-1 Algae

■ Algae are nonvascular organisms that lack true stems, roots, and leaves.

■ Algae contain chlorophyll, a green substance needed for photosynthesis.

■ The majority of algae live in watery environments such as oceans, ponds, and lakes. Other algae grow in soil, on the sides of trees, or even near hot springs.

■ Some species of algae are unicellular, or one-celled. These algae often group together to form colonies.

■ Algae are placed into six groups according to their color. They are grouped as blue-green, green, golden, brown, red, and fire algae. All but the blue-green are plants.

8-2 Fungi

■ Fungi are nonvascular organisms that lack true stems, roots, and leaves.

■ Unlike algae, fungi do not contain chlorophyll and cannot perform photosynthesis.

■ Fungi are heterotrophs. They cannot make their own food. Some fungi are parasites, organisms that feed on other living things. Others are saprophytes, organisms that feed on once-living organisms.

■ Most members of the Fungi kingdom have threadlike structures called hyphae, which produce chemicals called enzymes.

■ Most fungi reproduce by means of spores, which are contained in special structures called fruiting bodies.

■ Yeasts obtain energy through a process called fermentation.

8-3 Lichens and Slime Molds

■ Lichens are made up of two organisms, a fungus and an alga, that live together. This type of relationship is called symbiosis.

■ Slime molds are found in moist areas on once-living leaves, rotting logs, and other types of decaying material.

8-4 Mosses and Liverworts

■ Mosses are nonvascular plants that have rootlike structures called rhizoids. Rhizoids help to absorb water from the soil.

■ Liverworts are smaller than mosses. Some liverworts reproduce when pieces of the plant break off older plants.

VOCABULARY

Define each term in a complete sentence.

air bladder	hypha
alga	lichen
bioluminescence	liverwort
budding	moss
cap	nonvascular plant
chlorophyll	photosynthesis
fermentation	rhizoid
fruiting body	slime mold
fungus	stalk
gill	symbiosis

CONTENT REVIEW: MULTIPLE CHOICE

Choose the letter of the answer that best completes each statement.

1. The green substance that is found in the cells of green plants and is needed for photosynthesis is
   a. diatomaceous earth.　b. hypha.　c. chlorophyll.　d. rhizoid.
2. Algae whose gritty, glasslike skeletons form a substance often used in toothpaste are
   a. blue-green algae.　b. green algae.
   c. golden algae.　d. red algae.
3. Tiny structures that enable brown algae to float near the surface of the water are called
   a. rhizoids.　b. hyphae.　c. fruiting bodies.　d. air bladders.
4. The structures that fire algae use to propel themselves through the water are called
   a. rhizoids.　b. cilia.　c. flagella.　d. pseudopodia.
5. Most fungi have threadlike structures called
   a. caps.　b. hyphae.　c. fruiting bodies.　d. stalks.
6. Yeasts change sugars into alcohol and carbon dioxide during a process known as
   a. budding.　b. fermentation.　c. symbiosis.　d. conjugation.
7. An important product produced by the *Penicillium* mold is
   a. chocolate milk.　b. toothpaste.　c. fertilizer.　d. an antibiotic.
8. The black, rounded structures in bread mold produce
   a. rhizoids.　b. spores.　c. fruiting bodies.　d. hyphae.
9. Mosses have rootlike structures that are called
   a. hyphae.　b. stalks.　c. caps.　d. rhizoids.
10. A small green nonvascular plant that has flat leaflike structures is known as a(n)
    a. mushroom.　b. alga.　c. liverwort.　d. fungus.

CONTENT REVIEW: COMPLETION

Fill in the word or words that best complete each statement.

1. All plants that lack true roots, stems, and leaves are _____.
2. The process by which green plants make their own food is _____.
3. An example of a golden alga is a(n) _____.
4. In most fungi, spores are contained in special _____.
5. The umbrella-shaped part of a mushroom is the _____.
6. In a mushroom, the cap is found at the top of a(n) _____.
7. A puffball is an example of a(n) _____.
8. Yeasts reproduce by forming spores or by _____.
9. A relationship in which two different organisms live together is _____.
10. A moss absorbs water from its environment with its rootlike _____.

CONTENT REVIEW: TRUE OR FALSE

Determine whether each statement is true or false. If it is true, write "true." If it is false, change the underlined word or words to make the statement true.

1. Most algae live in a <u>watery</u> environment.
2. Algae contain <u>chlorophyll</u>.
3. <u>Blue-green</u> algae are considered to be the most complex of all algae.
4. Diatoms are examples of <u>red</u> algae.
5. *Sargassum* is an example of a brown alga.
6. Some types of <u>brown</u> algae are capable of bioluminescence.
7. Dutch elm disease is caused by a <u>fungus</u>.
8. Fungi are <u>autotrophs</u>.
9. Yeasts are unicellular <u>algae</u>.
10. A <u>slime mold</u> is made up of an alga and a fungus.

CONCEPT REVIEW: SKILL BUILDING

Use the skills you have developed in the chapter to complete each activity.

1. **Making predictions** Would you expect to find more fungi in a sunny field or in a shady forest? Explain your answer.
2. **Relating facts** Why do most algae live in shallow water or float on the surface of the water?
3. **Applying concepts** A friend tells you that he has seen mosses that were two meters tall. Is your friend mistaken? Why or why not?
4. **Developing a hypothesis** Develop a hypothesis to explain why in many forests, mushrooms suddenly spring up out of the soil after a rainstorm.
5. **Designing an experiment** Design an experiment to show how light affects the growth of bread mold. Be sure to include a control in your experiment.
6. **Relating concepts** How would a forest be affected by the removal of all fungi?

7. **Interpreting a graph** The graph shows the results of a photosynthesis experiment in which algae were used.

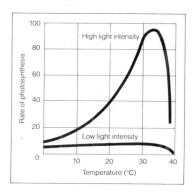

What do you think the purpose of the experiment was? What conclusion can you draw from the graph?

CONCEPT REVIEW: ESSAY

Discuss each of the following in a brief paragraph.

1. Explain why algae are classified as plants and fungi are not.
2. Describe three uses of algae.
3. Why are fungi called heterotrophs?
4. Describe the six groups of algae.
5. What is fermentation? Why are yeast cells used in baking bread?
6. Describe the structure of the mushroom and explain the function of each structure.

9 Vascular Plants

CHAPTER SECTIONS

9-1 Ferns

9-2 Seed Plants

9-3 Gymnosperms

9-4 Angiosperms

CHAPTER OBJECTIVES

After completing this chapter, you will be able to:

9-1 Compare vascular and nonvascular plants.

9-2 Identify the functions of roots, stems, and leaves in seed plants.

9-2 Explain the processes of photosynthesis and transpiration.

9-3 Describe the characteristics of gymnosperms.

9-4 Describe the characteristics of angiosperms.

9-4 Discuss the processes of pollination, fertilization, seed germination, and seed dispersal.

Life at the top of Mount Washington in New Hampshire is not easy. Winds often whip through the air at more than 160 kilometers an hour. Winter temperatures can dive to −40°C. Yet even in this harsh environment, living things can survive. As a matter of fact, one of the rarest plants in the world lives here. The tiny plant, less than 5 centimeters tall, is called the Robbins cinquefoil (SINK-foil). This plant is able to survive the wind and cold because it grows under patches of snow and ice. The snow and ice act as a blanket that protects the plant from low temperatures and from blowing away.

Today, there are fewer than 4000 Robbins cinquefoil plants in the world. However, it is not the cold environment that threatens them, but rather people. Hikers enjoying the pleasures of Mount Washington often walk near the plant. As they do, they kick away some of the soil around the plant. Without the soil, new seeds cannot grow, which endangers the future of the plant.

Can the Robbins cinquefoil be saved? The federal government has gone to great lengths to protect the plants. But, in the end, it will be up to people to save the Robbins cinquefoil. Through education and understanding, people will know next time to step around a tiny plant growing at the top of a tall mountain.

Robbins cinquefoil on Mount Washington

9-1 Ferns

Imagine walking through a rain forest, such as Washington State's Olympic National Park. As you enter, you immediately feel the cool dampness of the air. Tall trees, such as firs, spruces, and cedars, are everywhere. Mosses drape the branches and trunks of trees and hold moisture like a sponge.

As you continue your walk, you notice feathery green leaves above some moss plants. Many of these leaves belong to ferns. Unlike mosses, which are nonvascular plants, ferns are **vascular plants.** Vascular plants contain transporting tubes that carry material throughout the plant. Remember that mosses must live close to the ground. Mosses have no transporting tubes to carry water and nutrients to their parts.

Ferns are one of the oldest plants on the earth. They appeared more than 300 million years ago and soon became the most abundant type of plant. These ferns were as large as trees. Today, some ferns the size of trees are still found in tropical rain forests.

Most ferns disappeared as the earth's climate changed. All that remained of some ferns was dead

Figure 9-1 *The photograph on the left shows tree ferns as they appear today in a rain forest in Costa Rica. The photograph on the right shows a model of a fern forest during the Carboniferous period.*

plant material. This material later formed great coal deposits. Most living or once-living material contains carbon. Because coal is made up mostly of carbon, the geological period in which ferns were abundant is called the Carboniferous Period.

Structure of Ferns

Like all vascular plants, ferns have true leaves, stems, and roots. In fact, a fern's **fronds,** or leaves, are the part of the plant you usually notice. See Figure 9-2. For the most part, developing fern leaves are curled at the top and resemble the top of a violin. Because of their appearance, these developing leaves are called fiddleheads. As they mature, the fiddleheads uncurl until they reach their full size.

Following the leaves down toward the ground, you find the **rhizome** (RIGH-zohm), or stem of the fern. In some ferns, the rhizome looks like a large fuzzy, brown caterpillar with leaves. The rhizomes of many ferns grow along the surface of the soil. In other types of ferns, the rhizomes grow beneath the ground. Roots grow from the rhizomes and anchor the ferns to the ground. The roots also absorb water and minerals for the plant.

Transporting tubes travel throughout the fern's leaves, stems, and roots. These tubes carry materials throughout the plant. These special tubes allow the fern to grow taller than nonvascular plants.

Reproduction of Ferns

As the fern grows, it goes through two stages in its life cycle. If you were to look at both stages of the same plant, you would think that each was a different plant.

The fern uses a different type of reproduction in each stage. In the first stage of a fern's life cycle, small brown structures appear on the underside of the fronds. These structures are spore cases and contain spores. See Figure 9-3. Once the spore cases ripen, they open and release spores. Spores are carried through the air and eventually fall to the ground. If growth conditions are favorable, the spores begin to grow into new fern plants. The development of new organisms from spores is an

Figure 9-2 *The curled structures at the tops of these ferns are called fiddleheads because they resemble the tops of violins. Fiddleheads are the developing fronds, or leaves, of ferns.*

Figure 9-3 *The tiny brown spots on the underside of this fern frond are spore cases. Spore cases contain spores.*

example of **asexual reproduction.** Asexual reproduction is the formation of an organism from a single parent.

The next stage of a fern's life cycle begins as the spores grow into structures that do not resemble their parents. These structures look like tiny heart-shaped green plants. The plants develop special tissues that produce male and female sex cells. The male sex cell is called the sperm and the female sex cell is called the egg. Both are located on the plant. The sperm unites with the eggs by swimming across the plant through dew and rainwater.

The united sperm and egg grow into a new fern plant. This plant is similar in appearance to the plant with fronds that produced spores. The new fern plant was produced by **sexual reproduction.** In sexual reproduction, an organism develops from the uniting of two different sex cells.

Although the fern's life cycle seems complicated, it is successful. Ferns have survived, with little change, for millions of years.

SECTION REVIEW

1. How are vascular plants different from nonvascular plants?
2. What is a frond? A rhizome?
3. What is the difference between asexual and sexual reproduction?

Figure 9-4 *The sticklike structure growing out of the avocado fruit is a developing plant. This plant grew from the seed within the avocado.*

9-2 Seed Plants

If you wanted to plant a vegetable garden, you would begin by loosening the soil. Also you would have to make sure that your garden had a source of water. Only then would you plant your **seeds.** A seed contains a young plant, stored food, and a seed coat. With proper care, the seeds in your garden would begin to grow and, after a few months, produce adult plants loaded with vegetables.

Seed plants are vascular plants that produce seeds and have true roots, stems, and leaves. Seed plants also go through the same two reproductive

Figure 9-5 *This zucchini squash plant is an example of an angiosperm. Angiosperms produce seeds covered by a protective wall and flowers.*

stages as ferns. Seed plants are divided into two groups based on the structure of their seeds. The seeds of **gymnosperms** (JIM-nuh-spermz), *are not* covered by a protective wall. In **angiosperms** (AN-jee-uh-spermz), the seeds are covered by a protective wall.

Seed plants are among the most numerous plants on the earth. Also, they are the plants with which most people are familiar. The trees in the forest, the vegetables in a garden, and the cotton plant are all examples of seed plants. What other seed plants can you name?

Roots

Anyone who lives near trees no doubt has seen what a violent storm can do to them. The tremendous force of the storm's wind can pull a tree right out of the ground. A large hole marks the spot where the tree once was anchored to the ground. If you were to look carefully at the exposed base of the tree, you would notice small and large structures that resemble tentacles. These structures are the tree's roots, which anchor the plant in the ground. Roots also absorb water and minerals from the soil. In addition, the roots of some plants, such as those of the

Figure 9-6 *Although all roots absorb materials from the soil and anchor a plant to the soil, they do not all look the same. Notice the differences in the roots of the banyan trees* (left), *grasses* (top right) *and carrots* (bottom right).

Activity

Plant Transport

1. Fill a medium-sized jar one-fourth full of water. Then add a few drops of vegetable coloring and stir.

2. Place a freshly cut twig from a tree and a stalk of celery in the jar so that only the cut part of each is underwater.

3. After 24 hours, remove the twig and the stalk.

4. With a knife cut off the portion of each plant that was underwater. **CAUTION:** *Be very careful when using a knife.* Discard these portions.

5. Cut another small section across the bottom of each remaining portion. Examine.

How do the two sections differ? How are they alike? What structure transports the colored water up the plants?

---

carrot, store food for the plant. The roots of some plants, such as those of turnips, go straight down. Other plants, such as the grasses, have slender roots that spread out in many directions. See Figure 9-6.

Tiny root hairs cover the surface of many roots. Root hairs are microscopic extensions of single cells. The root hairs greatly increase the surface area of the root. They allow the plant to take in water and minerals from the soil. The minerals pass through the root hairs into tissue called **xylem** (ZIGH-luhm). The xylem tissue forms tubes that carry water and minerals from the roots up through the plant. The roots also contain another kind of tissue called **phloem** (FLOH-uhm). Phloem tissue forms tubes that carry food substances down from the plant's leaves.

Stems

Have you ever seen a group of maple trees with buckets attached to their trunks and wondered what was going on? Remember that the stem, or trunk, of the tree contains xylem and phloem tissue. Within these tissues, there flows a liquid called sap. The sap in the xylem tissue contains water and minerals, while the phloem tissue's sap contains sugary plant food. Usually, the sugary sap moves downward. At certain times of the year in some trees, such as the sugar maple, the sap moves both up and down. The sap is collected from sugar maple trees and used to produce the maple syrup that you pour over your breakfast pancakes!

Stems also contain a tissue called **cambium** (KAM-bee-uhm). Cambium is the growth tissue of the stem. New xylem and phloem cells are produced in the cambium, causing the wood in the stem to become

Figure 9-7 *Maple syrup comes from the sap of certain types of maple trees. This tree is being tapped for its sugary sap.*

Figure 9-8 *In a stem, the xylem transports water and other materials from the roots up to the leaves. The phloem conducts sap from the leaves down to the roots. Cambium is the growth tissue of the plant and produces new xylem and phloem cells.*

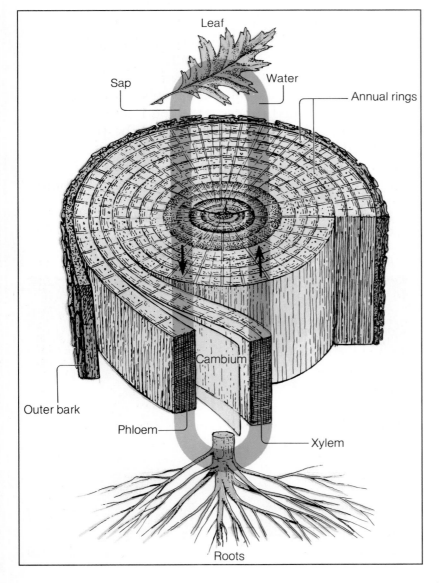

Leaf

Sap

Water

Annual rings

Cambium

Outer bark

Phloem

Xylem

Roots

Figure 9-9 *The age of a tree can be determined by counting the number of rings in its stem. Each ring represents one year's growth.*

Activity

Annual Rings

Find a sawed-off tree stump or a fallen tree. Count the number of annual rings to determine the age of the tree. Notice the widths of different rings. A wide ring is produced during a year of heavy rainfall, while a narrow ring is produced during a year of little rain. Closely examine one ring. Within each ring, you should be able to see a wide growth area and a narrow growth area. Which of these areas do you think took place in the spring? In the summer? Explain why.

thicker. Each year, as a new layer of xylem cells grows, it wraps itself around the layer before it. Because each layer is one year's growth of xylem cells, these layers are called **annual rings.** Scientists estimate the age of a tree by counting its annual rings.

Plant stems vary in size, shape, and function. The trunk, branches, and twigs of a tree are all stems. Some plants, such as the cabbage, have stems so short that you probably would not recognize them.

Stems provide the means for the transportation of water, minerals, and food. Another function of the stems is to support the other parts of the plant. In addition, the stems hold the leaves up in the air so that they can receive sunlight and make their own food.

Although most stems grow vertically and above the ground, some grow like roots. In some plants, such as the iris and lily of the valley, the stems grow horizontally and under the ground. Like those of ferns, these stems are called rhizomes. Other underground stems called tubers store food. The potato, for example, is a tuber. The "eyes" of the potato are buds. Each bud is capable of developing into a new potato plant. Certain spring plants, such as onions and tulips, produce a short, thick stem called a bulb.

Figure 9-10 *A potato is actually a special kind of stem called a tuber that grows under the ground. The fingerlike structures growing on the potato are actually new potato plants.*

Figure 9-11 *Stems are either herbaceous or woody. The soft, green herbaceous stems on the left are of a daisylike plant. On the right are the rigid woody stems of trees.*

Bulbs have thick leaves that contain food for the plant. When planted, the bulbs develop into new plants.

Stems may be placed into two groups based on their hardness. A **herbaceous** (her-BAY-shuhs) **stem** is green and soft. Sunflowers, eggplants, peas, beans, and tomatoes are examples of plants with herbaceous stems. Most plants that have herbaceous stems are annuals. An annual is a plant that completes its life cycle within one growing season. A plant's life cycle begins when the plant starts to grow from a seed and ends when the plant produces its own seeds. Wheat, rye, and tobacco plants are examples of annuals.

Unlike herbaceous stems, **woody stems** are rigid. These stems have large amounts of woody xylem tissue. Plants that have woody stems are called perennials (puh-REN-ee-uhls). A perennial is a plant that lives for more than two growing seasons. Included in the group of perennial plants are trees and woody shrubs. Plants that live for two growing seasons are called biennials (bigh-EN-ee-uhls). Biennials

Figure 9-12 *Leaves come in a wide variety of types and shapes. The tulip tree leaf* (left) *is a simple leaf, while the poison ivy leaf* (right) *is a compound leaf.*

may be either herbaceous or woody. Many garden vegetable plants, such as beets, celery, carrots, and cabbage, are biennials.

Leaves

Have you ever heard of the drug digitalis (di-ji-TAL-is)? It is given to people who have certain types of heart problems. This drug is not made in a laboratory. It is made from the dried leaves of a garden flower called the foxglove. The leaves are found growing along the stem of the plant.

Plant leaves vary greatly in shape and size. For example, leaves of the foxglove are long and oval-shaped. Pines, firs, and balsams have needle-shaped leaves. Other plants have flat, wide leaves. Most leaves have a stalk and a blade. The stalk connects the leaf to the stem, while the blade is the thin, flat part of the leaf. Most of the cells in which food making takes place are in the blade.

In addition, there are two types of leaves. Some leaves have only one blade and are called simple leaves. The silver maple leaf and apple leaf are examples of simple leaves. Leaves such as the black locust and buckeye have two or more blades. These are examples of compound leaves.

Whatever their shape, leaves are very important structures. Within the leaves, the sun's energy is trapped and used to produce food. This process is called **photosynthesis.** It is the largest and most important manufacturing process in the world.

Activity

Plant Responses

The growth response of a plant to a stimulus, or change in its surroundings, is called a tropism. If a tropism is positive, the plant grows toward the stimulus. If the tropism is negative, the plant grows away from the stimulus. Using reference materials in the library, look up information on the following tropisms:

phototropism

geotropism

hydrotropism

thigmotropism

chemotropism

Write a brief report in which you describe and give examples of each of these tropisms. Present your report to the class.

In photosynthesis, the sun's light energy is captured by chlorophyll, the green substance in plants. The sun's energy is used to combine water from the soil and carbon dioxide from the air. The food made by this combination is a sugar called glucose. Glucose is used by the plant for growth and to repair its parts. Glucose can be stored in special areas in the roots and stems. Photosynthesis also yields a waste product—oxygen! Of what value is this product of photosynthesis?

Photosynthesis is a complicated process, although an equation can be used to sum up what occurs. An equation is the scientist's shorthand for describing a reaction. This is the equation for photosynthesis.

$$\textbf{carbon dioxide + water} \xrightarrow[\text{chlorophyll}]{\text{sunlight}} \textbf{glucose + oxygen}$$

$$\textbf{6CO}_2 \textbf{ + 6H}_2\textbf{O} \xrightarrow[\text{chlorophyll}]{\text{sunlight}} \textbf{C}_6\textbf{H}_{12}\textbf{O}_6 \textbf{ + 6O}_2$$

In photosynthesis, carbon dioxide enters the leaves through **stomata** (STOH-muh-tuh; singular: stoma). Stomata are openings in the surface of the leaf. Although most plants have stomata on the lower surface of their leaves, some plants have stomata on the top surface of their leaves. Stomata also permit oxygen to pass out of the leaf into the air.

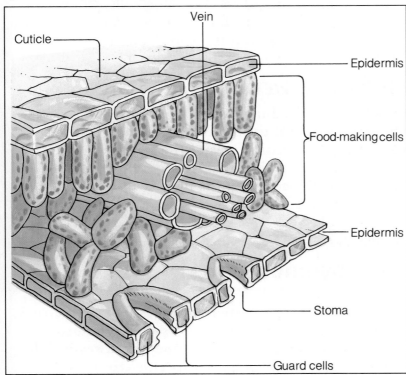

Figure 9-13 *This section of a leaf shows the tissues and structures found in various parts of the leaf.*

Figure 9-14 *Plants release excess moisture, which can be seen on the inside of the jar. The process by which plants release excess water through the leaves is called transpiration.*

Figure 9-15 *These palmlike trees are cycads, which grow in tropical areas. The cones at the top of the trees are the reproductive structures.*

The stomata also regulate water loss through the leaves of a plant. This regulating process is called **transpiration.** You might be surprised at the amount of water that a plant can give off. Scientists estimate that a single corn plant can give off more than 200 liters of water during a single growing season. This water is enough to fill a very large bathtub. Of course, this amount is not all the water a plant takes in during its growing season. Although the corn plant takes in much more water, the plant uses much of it to make glucose.

If you closely examined a leaf section, you would be able to see how a living food factory works. The outer protective layer of the leaf is called the **epidermis** (E-puh-DER-mis). The epidermis contains many stomata. Each stoma is surrounded by two sausage-shaped structures called **guard cells.** Guard cells regulate the opening and closing of the stomata. When the guard cells swell, the stoma opens and carbon dioxide enters the leaf. When the guard cells relax, the stoma closes. Most stomata are open during the day and closed at night.

Some leaves have a waxy cuticle (KYOO-ti-kuhl) that covers the epidermis. The cuticle prevents the loss of too much water from the leaf. Within the leaf are two thin layers of food-making cells, which contain chlorophyll. In addition, the leaf has small veins that contain xylem and phloem tissue.

SECTION REVIEW

1. What are the functions of the roots?
2. What is xylem tissue? Phloem tissue?
3. What are the functions of the stem?
4. Define annual, biennial, and perennial.
5. What is the equation for photosynthesis?

9-3 Gymnosperms

The word "gymnosperm" comes from two Greek words meaning uncovered and seed. **Gymnosperms are seed plants that produce uncovered seeds.** The three main groups of gymnosperms are conifers

(KAHN-uh-fuhrz), cycads (SIGH-kadz), and gingkoes (GING-kohz).

The cycads are tropical trees that look like small palm trees or ferns. Cycads have leaves that look like a feathery crown. In the center of the leaves is a large cone. The trees have either male or female cones. Inside the male cones are **pollen.** Inside the female cones are **ovules** (OH-vyoolz). Pollen contain male sex cells called sperm. Ovules contain female sex cells called eggs. The pollen is carried to the female cones by wind. After a male and female sex cell join, a seed forms. As the seeds mature, part of the cone dries up and releases the seeds, which fall to the ground. These seeds develop into new plants.

The second group of gymnosperms, gingkoes, contains only one species, which is commonly called the maidenhair tree. Gingkoes come from China and now grow on many streets in the United States. The gingko can grow as tall as 30 meters and has fan-shaped leaves. As with the cycads, male and female cones are found on separate gingko plants. After the female and male sex cells join, yellowish fruits form. These fruits on the female gingko have an awful odor. In fact, the odor is so bad that only male gingko trees are planted on city streets.

The largest group of gymnosperms is the conifers. The word "conifer" means cone-bearing. Like the gingkoes and cycads, they have cones that produce pollen or ovules. Conifers are woody plants that live in the termperate areas of the world.

Figure 9-16 *Gingko, or maidenhair, trees are often planted along city streets.*

Figure 9-17 *The conifers, or cone-bearing plants, grow in forests in many cool areas of the world.*

Figure 9-18 *These wild desert plants produce colorful structures called flowers, a characteristic of angiosperms. Flowers contain the male and female structures of the plant.*

Figure 9-19 *The seeds of a gymnosperm are not covered by a fleshy fruit, while those of an angiosperm are.*

Most conifers, such as pines, cedars, firs, spruces, and hemlocks, are called evergreens. Evergreens are trees that appear to keep their needles or leaves year round. Actually, evergreens lose leaves while adding new ones. The needles or leaves may remain on an evergreen tree for 2 to 12 years.

SECTION REVIEW

1. What are the three main groups of gymnosperms?
2. What are evergreens?

9-4 Angiosperms

Angiosperms are seed plants that produce covered seeds. They make up the largest group of plants in the world. Because they produce **flowers,** angiosperms are also called flowering plants. The flowers of angiosperms fill the earth with beautiful colors and pleasant smells. But more importantly, flowers are the structures that contain the reproductive organs of angiosperms.

Angiosperms differ in size and living environment. Plant sizes range from the tiny duckweed, a water plant less than 1 millimeter long, to a giant redwood tree 100 meters tall. Some angiosperms,

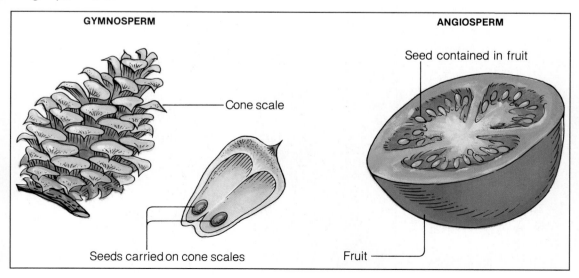

GYMNOSPERM

Cone scale

Seeds carried on cone scales

ANGIOSPERM

Seed contained in fruit

Fruit

such as the orchids, live in rain forests where the air and ground are moist. Others, such as the cacti, live in deserts where rain may fall only once a year.

Like gymnosperms, angiosperms form seeds and have leaves, stems, and roots. However, these two groups of plants differ from each other in several ways. The most obvious difference is that only angiosperms produce flowers.

Flowers

When a flower is still a bud, it is enclosed by leaflike structures called **sepals** (SEE-puhls). Sepals protect the flower. The sepals open and reveal the flower's **petals.** The colors and shapes of the petals attract insects, which play a vital role in the reproduction of flowering plants. See Figure 9-20.

The petals surround the reproductive organs. The **stamens** (STAY-muhns) are the male organs of the flower. In most flowers, each stamen has two parts. The filament is stalklike and supports the anther. The anther produces the pollen, which contains the sperm.

In the center of the flower are the **pistils.** The pistils are the female organs of the flower. Most flowers have two or more pistils. Some flowers, such as the sweet pea and clover, have only one pistil. The pistils of most flowers have three parts. At the base of the flower is the hollow ovary (OH-vuh-ree). The ovary contains egg cells. A slender tube, called the

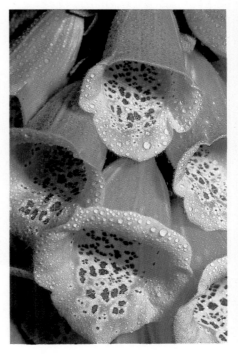

Figure 9-20 *The patterns inside the petals of this foxglove plant act as a "landing strip" for insects. These patterns help to guide insects to the male and female reproductive structures within the flower.*

Figure 9-21 *In the photograph, some of the petals have been removed to show the structures inside a flower. The drawing of the flower indicates the names of these structures.*

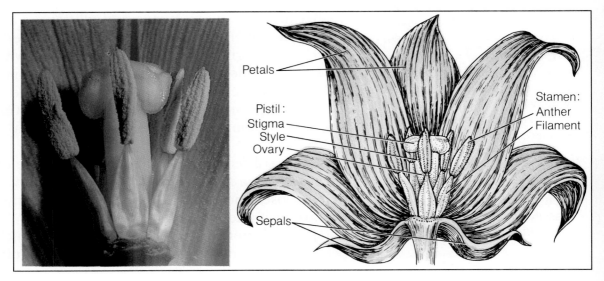

Figure 9-22 *Insects, such as this butterfly, help to transfer pollen from one flower to another.*

Activity

Perfect or Imperfect?

A perfect flower contains petals, sepals, stamens, and pistils. An imperfect flower is missing one or more of these structures.

1. Obtain either a gladiolus or a snapdragon flower and a flower from an ailanthus, or tree of heaven.

2. Examine the reproductive structures within each flower.

3. Draw each flower and label its structures.

How are the two flowers different? How are they similar? Classify each flower as perfect or imperfect.

style, connects the ovary to a sticky structure at the top of the pistil. This structure is called the stigma (STIG-muh).

In flowers, reproduction occurs in two stages. First, the pollen must be transferred to the stigma. This stage is called **pollination.** In *self*-pollination, pollen is transferred to the stigma of the same flower, or to the pistil of another flower on the same plant.

When pollen is transferred from the flower of one plant to the stigma of another plant, *cross*-pollination occurs. In this kind of pollination, pollen grains are carried from flower to flower by wind, insects, and birds. Usually, cross-pollinated plants have large sweet-smelling flowers. These features help to attract insects and birds.

Because the stigma surfaces of all flowers are sticky, the pollen grains cling to it. Once pollen reaches the stigma, a tube pushes its way down the style to an ovule in the ovary. The sperm from the pollen grain then travels down the tube to the ovule. When the sperm unites with an egg, **fertilization** occurs. Fertilization is the second stage in flower reproduction.

The fertilized egg becomes a seed and the ovary develops into a **fruit.** A fruit is the ripened ovary that encloses and protects the seed. Apples and cherries are examples of fruits.

If it were not for the activities of insects such as bees, moths, and butterflies, many flowering plants would not be able to reproduce. In some cases, only one species of insect can cross-pollinate a single species of plant. For example, in a species of Central American yucca plant, the stamens of the flowers can be reached only by a curved object. That object is the long noselike tube of a particular small moth.

The moth lands on a flower and gathers pollen from the stamen. After rolling the pollen into a ball, the moth flies off to another yucca flower. There the moth crawls deep into the flower, punches a hole in the flower's ovary, and lays its eggs inside the ovary. Then, for some reason not known to scientists, the moth creeps up to the top of the flower's stigma and pushes down the ball of pollen. This action pollinates the yucca. Without this special relationship, both the moth and the yucca would quickly vanish from the earth.

Career: *Nursery Manager*

HELP WANTED: NURSERY MANAGER Requires two- or four-year degree in horticulture. Business background in marketing and management desirable. Nursery or greenhouse experience helpful. Apply in person.

Nearly every community has a garden center that provides its customers with the plants and supplies they need for their homes and gardens. If you pass by a garden center in April, you see pots of tulips and daffodils on display. In July, petunias and other colorful flowers catch your eye. Piles of pumpkins appear in October, and rows of pine trees emerge in December. However, all these plants are not grown at the garden center. They are ordered and delivered by a nursery.

Nurseries are run under the direction of **nursery managers.** The managers supervise the growing of plants and flowers from seeds, seedlings, or cuttings until they are large enough to sell. Nursery managers make sure nursery workers properly fertilize, weed, transplant, and apply pesticides to the plants. In addition, nursery managers make sure that proper inventory records are kept and that the orders placed by garden centers are filled quickly.

Nursery managers also make many business decisions, such as choosing new equipment, deciding how much money to spend on the growing of various plants, and determining the kinds of plants to sell. Nursery managers also are involved in planning chemical use, in deciding which new plant varieties should be planted, and in directing the building of storage areas. If you enjoy owning a business that involves working with plants, write to the American Society for Horticultural Science, 701 North Saint Asaph Street, Alexandria, VA 22314.

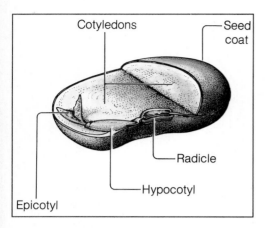

Figure 9-23 *This bean seed is an example of a dicot, which contains two cotyledons. Within the seed is an embryo plant, which is made up of the epicotyl, radicle, and hypocotyl.*

Figure 9-24 *The stage in a plant's development when a seed begins to grow is called germination. Notice how the roots and stem grow.*

Seeds

A seed is a tiny package that can develop into a new plant—if conditions are right. Surrounding the seed is a coating that develops from the ovule's wall. Like your winter coat, the seed coat protects what is inside it. Within the seed is a tiny embryo plant and the endosperm. The endosperm is a tissue that contains food the plant will need until it can make its own food.

If you were to remove the seed coat of a bean seed carefully, the seed would divide into two halves. These halves are called **cotyledons** (kaht-uh-LEE-duhnz). A cotyledon is the embryo plant's leaflike structure that stores food. Angiosperms have one or two cotyledons. Those angiosperms that have one cotyledon are called monocotyledons, or monocots. Grasses, orchids, and irises are examples of monocots. Angiosperms with two cotyledons, such as cacti, roses, and peas, are called dicotyledons, or dicots.

Most seeds remain dormant, or inactive, for a short time after being scattered. If there is enough moisture and oxygen, and the temperature is just right, most seeds go through a process called **germination** (jer-muh-NA-shuhn). Germination is the early growth stage of an embryo plant. Some people call this stage "sprouting."

When germination begins, part of the embryo below the cotyledon starts to grow down into the soil. This part of the embryo is called the hypocotyl (high-puh-COT-uhl) and will become the plant's stem. The upper part of the embryo is called the epicotyl (ep-uh-COT-uhl). The epicotyl becomes the leaves, while a part called the radicle gives rise to roots. See Figure 9-24.

Seed Dispersal

After seeds ripen, they usually are scattered far from where they were made. The scattering of seeds is called seed dispersal (di-SPER-suhl). Seeds are dispersed in many ways. Have you ever picked a dandelion puff and blown away all its tiny fluffy seeds? If you have, you have helped to scatter the seeds. Usually, the wind scatters dandelion seeds.

Figure 9-25 *Seeds are dispersed, or scattered, in many ways. Seeds of the milkweed (left) and red maple (center) are dispersed by the wind. The seeds of the burdock are carried by people's clothes or animal fur.*

Maple and elm seeds also travel on the wind with the help of their winglike structures. In addition, human beings and animals play a part in seed dispersal. For example, burdock seeds have spines that stick to people's clothing or animal fur. People or animals may pick up the seeds on a walk through a field or forest. At some other place, the seeds may fall off and eventually start a new plant.

The seeds of most water plants are scattered by floating in oceans, rivers, and streams. The coconut, which is the seed of the coconut palm, floats in water. This seed is carried from one piece of land to another by ocean currents.

Other seeds are scattered by a kind of natural explosion, which sends the seeds flying into the air. This is how the dwarf mistletoe disperses its seeds. The popping open of a dwarf mistletoe's seed case can shoot its seeds up to a distance of 15 meters.

SECTION REVIEW

1. What is a flower?
2. What is pollination? Fertilization?
3. What conditions are necessary for seed germination?

LABORATORY ACTIVITY

Geotropism

Purpose

In this activity, you will observe how gravity affects the growth of a seed.

Materials (per group)

4 corn seeds soaked in water for 24
   hours

Paper towels	Clay
Petri dish	Scissors
Masking tape	Water
Glass-marking pencil	Medicine dropper

Procedure

1. Arrange four soaked corn seeds in a petri dish. The pointed ends of the seeds should all point toward the center of the dish. One of the seeds should be at the 12 o'clock position of the circle, and the other seeds at 3, 6, and 9 o'clock.
2. Place a circle of paper towel over the seeds. Then pack the dish with enough pieces of paper towel so that the seeds will be held firmly in place when the other half of the petri dish is put on.
3. Moisten the paper towels with water. Cover the petri dish and seal the two halves together with a strip of masking tape.

4. With the glass-marking pencil, draw an arrow on the lid pointing toward 12 o'clock. Label the lid with your name and the date.
5. With pieces of clay, prop the dish up so that the arrow is pointing up. Place the dish in a completely dark place.
6. Predict what will happen to the seeds. Then observe the seeds each day for about one week. Make a sketch of them each day. Be sure to return the dish and seeds to their original position when you have finished.

Observations and Conclusions

1. Describe your observations. In which direction did the roots and the stems grow?
2. Explain your observations in terms of geotropism, or the effect of gravity on plant growth.
3. What would happen to the corn seeds if the dish was turned so that the arrow was pointing toward the bottom of the dish? To the right or left?
4. Why is it important that the petri dish remain in a stable position throughout the investigation?
5. Suppose you planted all your corn seeds in the soil upside down. In which direction would the stems grow? The roots?
6. Explain why the seeds were placed in the dark rather than near a sunny window.

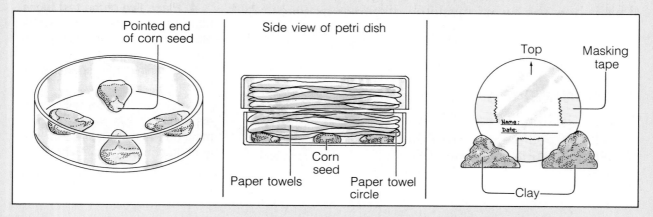

Pointed end of corn seed

Side view of petri dish

Top — Masking tape

Name:
Date:

Paper towels — Corn seed — Paper towel circle

Clay

CHAPTER REVIEW

SUMMARY

9-1 Ferns

■ Vascular plants contain tubes that carry material throughout the plant.

■ Ferns have true leaves, stems, and roots.

■ In asexual reproduction, new fern plants develop from spores.

■ In sexual reproduction, fern plants develop from the uniting of a sperm and an egg cell.

9-2 Seed Plants

■ A seed contains an embryo plant, stored food, and a seed coat.

■ Seed plants are divided into two groups: gymnosperms and angiosperms.

■ Roots are structures that anchor plants and absorb water and minerals.

■ In the roots, minerals and water travel up the plant through the xylem. Food substances travel down the plant through the phloem.

■ Stems support plant parts.

■ Herbaceous stems are soft and green, while woody stems are rigid.

■ During photosynthesis, the sun's energy is used to combine carbon dioxide from the air and water from the soil to produce glucose and oxygen.

■ In transpiration, the stomata regulate the amount of water lost through the plant leaves.

■ The leaf has an epidermis, two layers of food-making cells, and veins containing the xylem and phloem.

9-3 Gymnosperms

■ Gymnosperms produce uncovered seeds.

■ Cycads, gingkoes, and conifers are the three main groups of gymnosperms.

9-4 Angiosperms

■ Angiosperms, or flowering plants, produce seeds with a protective covering.

■ Flowers contain the male and female reproductive organs. The stamens produce sperm-containing pollen. The pistils contain the egg-producing ovary.

■ Fertilization occurs when the sperm unites with the egg in the ovary. The ovary then develops into a fruit that encloses the seed.

■ Seeds have one or two cotyledons. A cotyledon is the embryo plant's food storehouse.

VOCABULARY

Define each term in a complete sentence.

angiosperm	frond	phloem	sexual reproduction
annual ring	fruit	photosynthesis	stamen
asexual reproduction	germination	pistil	stoma
cambium	guard cell	pollen	transpiration
cotyledon	gymnosperm	pollination	vascular plant
epidermis	herbaceous stem	rhizome	woody stem
fertilization	ovule	seed	xylem
flower	petal	sepal	

CONTENT REVIEW: MULTIPLE CHOICE

Choose the letter of the answer that best completes each statement.

1. Vascular plants have
   a. true leaves and roots.   b. true roots and stems.
   c. true stems and leaves.   d. true roots, stems, and leaves.
2. Ferns produce spores during
   a. germination.   b. fertilization.
   c. sexual reproduction.   d. asexual reproduction.
3. Plant tissue that forms tubes that carry water and minerals up through the plant is called
   a. stoma.   b. cambium.   c. phloem.   d. xylem.
4. Which of these structures is *not* a stem?
   a. bulb   b. rhizome   c. frond   d. tuber
5. During photosynthesis, oxygen leaves the leaf of a plant through structures called
   a. stomata.   b. rhizoids.   c. guard cells.   d. rhizomes.
6. Gymnosperms
   a. produce flowers.   b. have seeds with no protective wall.
   c. have seeds with a protective wall.   d. are found only in deserts.
7. Which structure produces pollen?
   a. pistil   b. anther   c. ovary   d. style
8. The union of the sperm and the egg is called
   a. germination.   b. transpiration.   c. pollination.   d. fertilization.
9. Seeds can be scattered by
   a. wind.   b. water.   c. people.   d. all of these.
10. How many cotyledons does a monocot contain?
   a. one   b. two   c. three   d. four

CONTENT REVIEW: COMPLETION

Fill in the word or words that best complete each statement.

1. A group of vascular plants that were abundant during the Carboniferous Period were the _____.
2. Small brown structures on the underside of fern fronds produce _____.
3. _____ are fern structures that absorb water and minerals from the soil.
4. In the stem, new xylem and phloem cells are produced by the _____.
5. Leaves that have two or more blades are called _____.
6. The outer, protective cell layer of a leaf is the _____.
7. Conifers belong to a group of seed plants called _____.
8. During pollination, pollen grains cling to the sticky surface at the top of the pistil called the _____.
9. When conditions are just right, a seed may go through a process of growth called _____.
10. The seeds of the coconut palm are dispersed by _____.

Determine whether each statement is true or false. If it is true, write "true." If it is false, change the underlined word or words to make the statement true.

1. In <u>sexual</u> reproduction, an organism develops from the union of an egg and a sperm.
2. Seed plants absorb water and minerals through microscopic extensions of single cells called <u>guard cells</u>.
3. One year's <u>growth</u> of xylem cells produces a layer called an <u>epidermis</u>.
4. A <u>biennial</u> is a plant that lives for more than two growing seasons.
5. Glucose is the food made by a plant during <u>germination</u>.
6. The <u>cuticle</u> prevents the loss of too much <u>oxygen</u> from the leaf.
7. Conifers produce <u>flowers</u>.
8. Angiosperms produce <u>cones</u>.
9. When a sperm unites with an egg in a flower's ovary, <u>pollination</u> occurs.
10. A <u>fruit</u> is the ripened ovary that encloses and protects the seed.

Use the skills you have developed in the chapter to complete each activity.

1. **Relating concepts** In your friend's backyard, you find a plant that is 3 meters tall. Is it a vascular or a nonvascular plant? Explain your answer.
2. **Drawing diagrams** Based on what you learned in the chapter, draw a diagram of a simple and a compound leaf. Label the stalk and the blade in each leaf.
3. **Making predictions** Predict what would happen to the petals of a carnation if you placed the stem in a vase filled with colored water.
4. **Applying concepts** Most leaves are broad and flat. How are these characteristics helpful to a plant?
5. **Making inferences** Pesticides are chemicals designed to kill harmful insects. But sometimes these chemicals also kill helpful insects. What effect could this have on angiosperms?
6. **Developing a hypothesis** A scientist performed an experiment in which he covered the leaves of a plant with petroleum jelly. The plant died. Explain why.
7. **Relating facts** What is the advantage for a gymnosperm of having both male and female cones on the same tree?
8. **Designing an experiment** Design an experiment to determine whether or not water is needed for seed germination. Describe your experimental setup. Be sure to include a control.
9. **Relating cause and effect** Girdling is the complete removal of bark from a section of a tree. Explain why girdling can kill a tree.

Discuss each of the following in a brief paragraph.

1. Describe the two stages in the reproductive cycle of a fern.
2. Compare the functions of roots and stems.
3. Distinguish between herbaceous and woody stems.
4. Distinguish between gymnosperms and angiosperms.
5. Discuss the difference between self-pollination and cross-pollination.

10 Animals: Invertebrates

CHAPTER SECTIONS

10-1 Characteristics of Invertebrates

10-2 Sponges

10-3 Coelenterates

10-4 Worms

10-5 Mollusks

10-6 Spiny-Skinned Animals

10-7 Arthropods

10-8 Insects

CHAPTER OBJECTIVES

After completing this chapter, you will be able to:

10-1 Distinguish between vertebrates and invertebrates.

10-2 Describe the characteristics of sponges.

10-3 Describe the characteristics of coelenterates.

10-4 Compare flatworms, roundworms, and segmented worms.

10-5 Describe the characteristics of mollusks.

10-6 Describe the characteristics of spiny-skinned invertebrates.

10-7 Identify the characteristics of arthropods

10-8 Describe the anatomy and characteristics of insects.

A hard-working person is often described as being "busy as a bee." But, you may wonder, just how busy is a bee? Kirk Visscher, a scientist, wondered the same thing. Visscher is an *entomologist* (en-tuh-MAHL-uh-jist), a person who studies insects.

Visscher knew that one group of bees, worker bees, had the jobs of cleaning up the hive, feeding young bees, finding and processing pollen, and guarding the nest. However, while watching bees in a glass-enclosed colony, Visscher noticed that certain bees also seemed to have the responsibility of removing dead bees from the hive. While most worker bees ignored their dead companions, these undertaker bees grasped the dead bees in their jaws and flew hundreds of meters from the hive before dropping them off.

This special task of beehive undertaking interested Visscher. He wondered what proportion of worker bees acted as undertakers for the hive. To find out, the entomologist painted dots on the bees that removed the dead. He then determined that only about 2 percent of the worker bees actually did the undertaking. And, he discovered another interesting fact. The task of carrying away the dead was only a temporary one. After a few days, the undertakers moved on to other jobs.

Honeybee flying over a flower

10-1 Characteristics of Invertebrates

Animals! Just hearing the word brings a different image to almost everyone. Some people think of the fierce great cats in Africa. To others, the word brings to mind the friendly porpoise, certainly among the most intelligent of all animals. Of course, for a great many people the word "animal" reminds them of that cuddly puppy they had, or have, or have always wanted to get. All of these animals, no matter how different they may seem, have one thing in common. They are **vertebrates** (VER-tuh-brits). **Vertebrates are animals with a backbone.**

Figure 10-1 *There are many kinds of invertebrates, or animals without backbones. The skeleton butterfly* (top left), *hercules beetle* (top right), *giant clam* (bottom left), *and flame lobster* (bottom right) *are examples of invertebrates.*

On the other hand, almost nobody thinks of the earthworm crawling through the soil when the word "animals" is mentioned. Or the mosquito about to raise a bump on another victim. Or the jellyfish with its stinging cells always ready to poison a passing fish. And yet, these organisms are among a group of animals called **invertebrates** that make up more than 90 percent of all animal species. **Invertebrates are animals without a backbone.** They are found in just about every corner of the world.

All animals, including the invertebrates, are multicellular. Most have cells that perform specialized functions. Some cells, for example, are involved with the digestion of food. Other cells help circulate the digested food particles throughout the body. In many animals, these specialized cells are grouped together into tissues. Skin cells, for example, form skin tissue. Tissues that work together can be further organized into organs. For example, the lungs are organs made up of different tissues that work together to help you breathe. Finally, organs that work together often are grouped as organ systems. The mouth, stomach, and intestines all work together as part of the digestive system.

SECTION REVIEW

1. What are animals with backbones called?
2. What are animals without backbones called?

10-2 Sponges

Today, the sponge you use to wash the dishes or take a bath is probably made of synthetic material. In the past, however, people used natural, or real, sponges from the sea. A natural sponge is the dried remains of an animal that lives in the ocean, or as in a few cases, in fresh water. You might think a sponge, whether synthetic or natural, looks nothing like any animal you ever saw. In a way you would be right, for sponges seem to be totally unrelated to all other forms of animal life. For many years, in fact, sponges were classified as "plant-animals."

Activity

Observing a Sponge

How is a real sponge different from a synthetic sponge?

1. Obtain a natural sponge from your teacher.

2. Use a hand lens to examine the surface and the pores. Make a drawing of what you see.

3. Tear off a small piece of the sponge and place it on a glass microscope slide. Draw what you observe under the microscope. Spicules are hard, pointed structures that support the body of some sponges. Can you see any spicules? Draw what you observe.

4. Now repeat this activity with a synthetic kitchen sponge. How does it compare with a natural sponge?

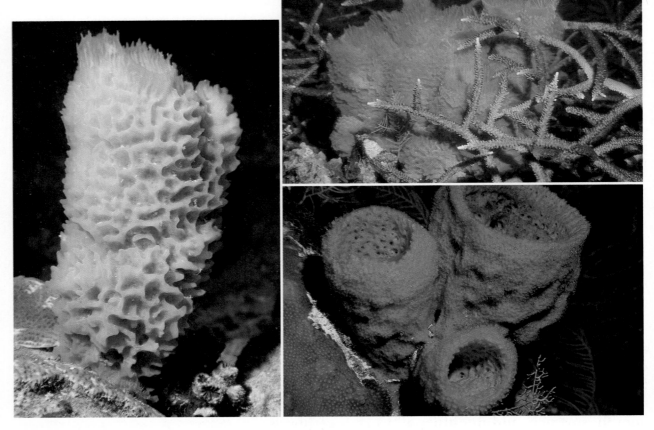

Figure 10-2 *Although there are different types of sponges, they all share the characteristic that their bodies contain many pores.*

Figure 10-3 *Notice the pores in this diagram of a sponge. What is the function of the pores?*

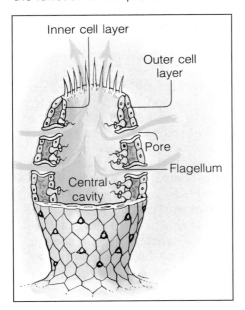

Inner cell layer
Outer cell layer
Pore
Flagellum
Central cavity

Sponges lead a very simple life. They grow attached to one spot on the ocean floor, usually in shallow water. A sponge stays in that one spot its entire life unless a strong wave or current washes it somewhere else. **The body of a sponge has a great many pores, or holes.** Moving ocean water carries food and oxygen through the **pores** into the sponge. The sponge's cells remove food and oxygen from the water and, at the same time, release waste products into the water. Because the pores of a sponge are small, most sponges live in clear water that is free of floating matter that could clog the pores.

Sponge cells are unusual in that they function on their own without any coordination between one another. In fact, some people think of sponges as a colony of cells living together. However, despite their independent functioning, sponge cells have a mysterious attraction to one another. This attraction can be demonstrated easily by passing a sponge through a fine filter so that it is broken into clumps of cells.

Within hours, these cells reform into the shape of the original sponge. No other animal species shares this amazing ability of sponge cells to reorganize themselves.

SECTION REVIEW

1. How do sponges obtain food?
2. How do sponges remove waste products?
3. Why do most sponges live in clear waters that are free of floating matter?

10-3 Coelenterates

In the shallow waters off the coast of Puerto Rico, a group of scientists drill into the sea floor. To an ordinary person, the scientists might appear to be hunting for oil and gas, or perhaps valuable minerals. However, these scientists are drilling through layers of coral in order to read a very special "diary"—a diary of the earth's past. The scientists have discovered that corals are extremely sensitive to environmental changes, including changes in temperature and the chemicals in sea water. These changes are recorded in the daily growth rings of coral. By studying the layers of coral that were laid down year after year for more than 500 million years, scientists hope to uncover evidence of past events. For example, many scientists believe the length of the earth's day has increased by several hours or more in the last few hundred million years. Scientists hope to find evidence for this increase in the coral growth rings.

Corals are among a group of animals called the coelenterates (si-LEN-tuh-rayts). Also included among the coelenterates are the jellyfish, the hydra, and the sea anemone (uh-NEM-uh-nee). **All coelenterates contain a central cavity with only one opening.** You can think of coelenterates as being cup-shaped animals with an open mouth. Tentacles with stinging cells called **nematocysts** (NEM-uh-toh-sists) surround the mouth of most coelenterates. Coelenterates use nematocysts to stun or kill other animals. It is no

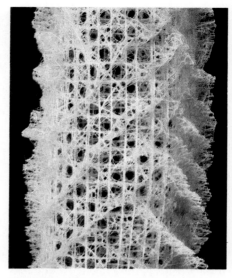

Figure 10-4 *Venus' flower baskets are sponges having glassy skeletons. These sponges have been on the earth at least 500 million years.*

Figure 10-5 *Meters below the surface of the ocean, these scientists use a coring machine to remove a sample of coral. Like trees, coral forms annual layers as it grows.*

Figure 10-6 *Jellyfish, like this Portuguese man-of-war, use their tentacles to capture prey. Nematocysts, or stinging cells, on the tentacles then paralyze the prey.*

surprise, then, that the stinging cells are near the mouth. For after capturing an animal with their tentacles, coelenterates pull it into their mouth and then into their central body cavity. Once the food is digested, coelenterates then release waste products back out, through their mouth.

Unlike the sponges, coelenterates contain groups of cells that perform special functions. That is, coelenterates have specialized tissues. Some coelenterates like the jellyfish move about in the water using muscle tissues. Others, like the corals, remain in one place.

Corals

In the warm waters off the coast of eastern Australia lies one of the largest structures ever built by living things—the 2000-kilometer-long Great Barrier Reef. However, the reef was not built by people. Instead, it was built by tiny corals.

Corals, like all coelenterates, are soft-bodied organisms. However, corals use minerals in the water to build a hard protective covering of limestone. When the coral dies, the hard outer covering is left behind. Year after year, for many millions of years, generations of corals live and die, each adding a layer of limestone. In time, a coral reef such as the Great Barrier Reef forms. The outer layer of the reef, then, contains living corals. But underneath this

Figure 10-7 *When these brightly colored corals die, their skeletons remain. Over the years, the skeletons pile up, creating a coral reef.*

Figure 10-8 *Surrounding the mouth of this delicate-looking coral are tentacles, which are used to trap food.*

"living stone" are the remains of corals that may have lived when dinosaurs walked the earth.

Corals live together in colonies that can grow into a wide variety of shapes and colors. Some corals look like antlers, others like fans swaying in the water, while still others look like underwater brains.

At first glance, a coral appears to be little more than a mouth surrounded by stinging tentacles. See Figure 10-8. However, there is more to a coral than meets the eye. Algae live inside the coral's body. The algae help make food for the coral. And since algae need sunlight to make food, corals must live in shallow waters where sunlight can reach them. This relationship between a coral animal and an alga plant is among the most unusual in nature.

Sea Anemones

Can you spot the clownfish swimming through the brightly colored plant in Figure 10-9? You might be surprised to discover that the "plant" is actually an animal—a type of coelenterate called a sea anemone. Sea anemones look like underwater flowers. However, the "petals" are really tentacles, and their brilliant coloring helps attract passing fish. When a fish passes over the anemone's stinging cells, the cells poison the fish. The tentacles then pull the fish into the anemone's mouth, and the stunned prey soon is digested.

The clownfish, however, is not harmed by the anemone. It swims safely through the anemone's

Figure 10-9 *The lavender-tipped "petals" in this photograph are actually the tentacles of a sea anemone. Notice the black and white clownfish swimming among the tentacles.*

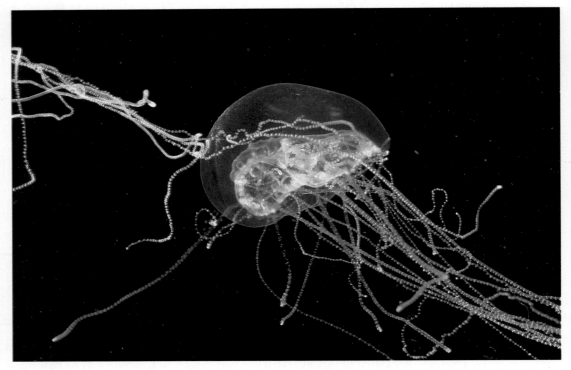

Figure 10-10 *Jellyfish move with a jetlike motion by contracting their muscle cells. The long tentacles are used to capture food.*

Activity

Observing Hydra

1. Use a medicine dropper to place a hydra in a small dish along with some of the water in which it lives.

2. Observe the hydra. Locate its mouth, body cavity, and tentacles. Draw a diagram in which you label these parts.

3. With a toothpick, gently touch the hydra in three different places. How does the animal respond to each touch?

4. Place some *Daphnia* in the dish. How does the hydra feed?

5. Add one drop of vinegar to the dish. How does the hydra react?

tentacles. In this way, the clownfish is protected from other fish that might try to attack it. At the same time, the clownfish serves as a kind of living bait for the anemone. Other fish see the clownfish, come closer, and are quickly trapped by the anemone. So the sea anemone and the clownfish live in harmony.

Jellyfish

If you ever swam in the ocean and saw a jellylike cup floating in the water, you probably knew enough to swim away. Most people quickly recognize this coelenterate, the jellyfish. While the jellyfish may look harmless, it can deliver a painful poison through its stinging cells. In fact, even when they are broken up into small pieces, the stinging cells remain active and can sting a passing swimmer who accidentally bumps into them. Of course, jellyfish do not have stinging cells merely to bother passing swimmers. Like the other coelenterates, jellyfish use the stinging cells to capture prey.

1. What are nematocysts?
2. Which of the coelenterates discussed have muscle tissue that can help move them about?
3. What type of coelenterate formed the Great Barrier Reef?

10-4 Worms

You might be surprised to find out that a group of invertebrates—the worms—is involved in the formation of many natural pearls. Natural pearls are formed inside oysters. When a particular type of worm gets into an oyster, the worm acts as an irritant. The oyster's response to the worm is to produce a hard material that surrounds the worm. That material is a pearl.

Most people think of a worm as a slimy, squiggly creature. And, in fact, many are. However, there are some worms that look nothing like the worms used to bait fishing hooks. See Figure 10-11. **Worms are classified into three groups: the flatworms, the roundworms, and the segmented worms.**

Figure 10-11 *Not all worms are slimy and squiggly. The plume worms* (left) *resemble feathered flowers, while the sea mouse* (right) *looks like a furry animal.*

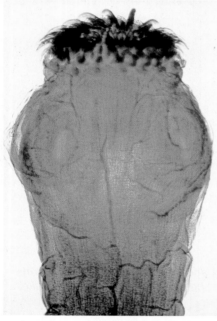

Figure 10-12 *The planarians* (top) *and the tapeworm* (bottom) *are examples of flatworms.*

Flatworms

You have probably never seen worms that look like those in Figure 10-12. These worms are flatworms. Flatworms, as you might expect, have flat bodies. A planarian is a kind of flatworm. Most planarians live in ponds and streams, often on the bottom of plants or on underwater rocks. Planarians feed on any dead plant or animal matter. However, when there is little food available, some planarians do a rather unusual thing. They break down their own organs and body parts for food. Later, when food is available again, the missing parts regrow. In fact, if a planarian is cut into pieces, each piece eventually grows into a new planarian!

Not all flatworms are found on dead matter. Some are parasites and grow on or in living things. Tapeworms, for example, look like long flat ribbons and live in the bodies of many animals, including human beings.

The head of a tapeworm has special hooks that it uses to attach itself to the tissues of the **host,** or animal in which it lives. The tapeworm then takes food and water from its host. However, the tapeworm gives its host nothing in return.

Tapeworms can grow quite large inside the host. One of the largest tapeworms can live in human beings and grow to be 18 meters long. However, size is not always a good indicator of danger. The most dangerous tapeworm known to humans is only about 8 millimeters long and enters the body through microscopic eggs in food.

Roundworms

You probably have been told time and time again never to eat pork unless it is well cooked. Did you know that the reason has to do with the *Trichina* (trick-EE-nuh) worm? This worm lives in the muscle tissue of pigs. If a piece of pork is cooked improperly, the worm may survive and enter a human's body. In the body, the worm lives in the muscle tissue. The disease it causes, called trichinosis (tri-kuh-NOH-sis), can be very painful and is difficult to cure.

Trichina is a kind of roundworm. All roundworms resemble strands of spaghetti with pointed ends.

Roundworms live on land or in water. Many roundworms are animal parasites, although some live on plant tissue. One roundworm, the hookworm, infects more than 600 million people in the world each year. The worms enter the body by burrowing through the skin. Eventually, they end up in the intestines where they live on the blood of the host.

Roundworms, like other worms, have both a head end and a tail end. In fact, worms were the first organisms to develop with distinct head and tail ends. Connecting the two ends is a tube called the digestive tube. Food enters the tube in the head end and waste products leave through the tail end. Although this system is not very complex, it is far more advanced than that of coelenterates. How do coelenterates take in food and release wastes?

Segmented Worms

The worm you probably are most familiar with is the common earthworm. The earthworm is a type of segmented worm. As you might expect, its body is divided up into numerous segments, usually at least 100. Earthworms, of course, live in the soil. But other segmented worms may live in salty oceans or the fresh waters of lakes and streams. Segmented worms also include sandworms and leeches.

If you ever felt an earthworm, you know it has a slimy outer layer. This layer, made up of slippery mucus, helps the earthworm glide through the soil.

Figure 10-13 *This drawing shows that segmented earthworms have a well-developed digestive system.*

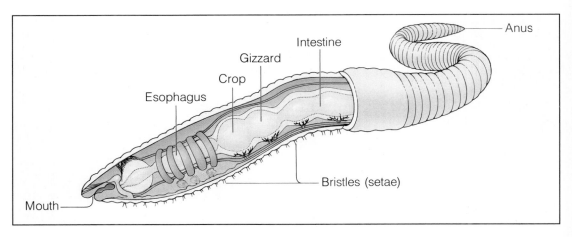

Small bristles, or setae, on the segments of an earthworm help it to pull itself along the ground.

Earthworms are good friends to have in the garden. As they pass through the soil, the earthworms feed on dead plant and animal matter. Earthworms create tiny passages as they move. Air enters these passages and improves the quality of the soil. Also, waste products released by earthworms help fertilize the soil.

Earthworms have a well-developed digestive system. After the earthworm eats the food, it passes through several structures before reaching the worm's **crop.** The crop is a saclike organ that stores food. From the crop, the food travels into the worm's muscular **gizzard.** The gizzard grinds up food and then passes it into the worm's intestine. Here, nutrients are removed and enter the worm's circulatory system.

The earthworm has a closed circulatory system. All of its body fluids are contained within small tubes. The fluids are pumped throughout the earthworm's body by a series of special vessels that act like a tiny "heart."

In the respiratory system of the earthworm, oxygen enters through the skin. The earthworm produces carbon dioxide gas, which leaves through the animal's skin. However, the skin must remain moist in order for gases to pass through. If an earthworm remains out in the heat of the sun, the skin dries out and the animal suffocates.

The earthworm's reproductive system has both male and female structures. In one part of the earthworm, sperm cells are produced. In another part,

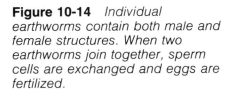

Figure 10-14 *Individual earthworms contain both male and female structures. When two earthworms join together, sperm cells are exchanged and eggs are fertilized.*

egg cells are made. However, despite the fact earthworms contain both types of reproductive cells, reproduction occurs through sexual reproduction. Earthworms mate at night when two worms join together and exchange sperm cells. The sperm of each worm unites with the eggs of the other worm. This process is called fertilization. Soon after, the worms move apart. Each worm then lays a number of fertilized eggs in a slimy shell or cocoon. Eventually, the young worms break out of the shell and crawl away.

Although earthworms have a simple nervous system, they are very sensitive to their environment. Earthworms seem to be able to both sense danger and warn other earthworms as well. They do so by releasing a kind of sweat that helps them glide away much faster and warns other worms in the area at the same time.

SECTION REVIEW

1. A planarian is an example of what type of worm?
2. Name two kinds of parasitic roundworms.
3. How do earthworms reproduce?

10-5 Mollusks

In 1873, two men and a young boy were fishing off the coast of Newfoundland in Canada when they spotted a dark object in the water. One of the men poked the object to see what it was. Suddenly, two large green eyes looked up at the men. Before they could move, the strange creature attacked their boat. A huge tentacle wrapped itself around the boat and began to pull it under. The two men were terrified, but the boy thought quickly and chopped through the tentacle with an axe. The water immediately turned jet black as the creature dove beneath the waves. Later, a part of the tentacle left in the boat was fed to hungry dogs on shore. Without knowing it, the boaters had destroyed one of the few parts of a giant squid ever recovered.

Although this story actually happened, most legends about giant squids are false. Giant squids do

Figure 10-15 *Giant squids can grow up to 17 meters in length. In this historical print, one of the few actual cases of a giant squid attacking people is shown.*

Figure 10-16 *Many types of mollusks are covered with a hard shell. Notice the different colors and patterns of these mollusk shells.*

not normally attack boats. They usually live in deep ocean waters far from people. In fact, until 1980, when an entire giant squid body was found washed onto a Massachusetts shore, few scientists had ever seen or been able to study the legendary giant squid. Today the remains of this squid are on view in the Smithsonian Institution in Washington, D.C.

Giant squids are included among a group of invertebrates called mollusks (MAHL-uhsks). If you enjoy seafood, you are probably more familiar with other mollusks such as clams, oysters, octopuses, and normal-sized squids. You would not find giant squids on any menu, by the way, even if they could be easily found. They are rumored to taste like ammonia!

The word "mollusk" comes from the Latin word meaning soft. **Mollusks have a soft, fleshy body, which in many species is covered with a hard shell.** See Figure 10-16.

The bodies of most kinds of mollusks having outer shells are similar. Most mollusks have a thick muscular foot. The foot of some mollusks opens and closes their shells. In other species, the foot is used for movement. Some mollusks even use their foot to bury themselves in the sand or mud.

The head region of a mollusk generally contains the mouth and sense organs such as the eyes. The rest of the body contains various organs involved in reproduction, circulation, digestion, and other important processes. Covering much of the body is a soft **mantle.** The mantle is the part of a mollusk that produces the material that makes up the hard shell.

Activity

Mollusks in the Supermarket

Visit your neighborhood supermarket to look for mollusks that are being sold. Make a chart of all the mollusks you find. Include in your chart the name of the mollusk, the part of the mollusk that is sold, and how it is packaged.

As the animal grows, the mantle enlarges the shell, providing more room for its occupant.

Mollusks are grouped according to certain characteristics. These characteristics include the presence of a shell, the type of shell, and the type of foot.

One-Shelled Mollusks

Many kinds of mollusks have only one shell and are called univalves. "Uni-" is the prefix that means one and "valve" is the word scientists use to mean shell. There are many kinds of univalves, which live in oceans, fresh waters, or on land. However, univalves that live on land still must have a moist environment to survive.

Univalves have an interesting feature in their mouth called a **radula.** The radula resembles a file used by carpenters to file wood. The radula files off bits of plant matter into small pieces that can be swallowed by the univalve. Some species of univalves can inject a poison through the radula that can be dangerous to people.

The land univalve you probably are most familiar with is the common garden snail. These snails move slowly along a trail of mucus that they produce. As they release this slippery mucus, they are able to travel easily over rough surfaces because their body does not actually touch the ground. As you can see in Figure 10-17, univalves such as the snail have two eyes located on the end of two stalks sticking out of their head.

Figure 10-17 *Snails, which are examples of univalves, have eyes on stalks sticking out of their heads and a radula that files off bits of food (left). Some snails go into a resting state when the weather becomes too hot (right).*

Figure 10-18 *Although this sea slug does not have a hard outer shell, it is a mollusk. Its shell, however, is internal.*

It may seem strange to you, but there is one kind of univalve that does not have any visible shell. It is the slug. See Figure 10-18. Many slugs, called sea slugs, live in ocean waters. However, some slugs live on land. Most people are familiar with the simple slugs they often find in moist areas.

Two-Shelled Mollusks

If you have been to the beach, you may have seen clam and mussel shells littering the shore. Clams and mussels are members of a group of mollusks called bivalves, or two-shelled mollusks. Bivalves move

Figure 10-19 *The bay scallop (right) is a bivalve, or two-shelled mollusk. The blue dots are its eyes. The chambered nautilus (left), a head-footed mollusk, has a shell that consists of many sections.*

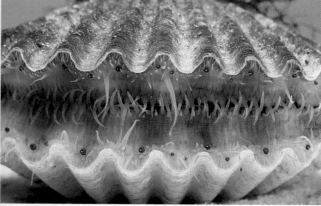

through the water by clapping their two shells together, which forces water out between the shells.
The force of the moving water propels the bivalve.

Bivalves do not have radula. Instead, they feed
on small organisms in the water. Bivalves are often
called filter feeders since they spend most of their
time straining the water for food.

Head-Footed Mollusks

The most highly developed mollusks are the
head-footed mollusks. These mollusks include the
octopus, the squid, and the nautilus. Most head-
footed mollusks do not have an outer shell, but do
have some part of a shell within their body. An exception is the chambered nautilus. The nautilus shell
consists of many chambers, or rooms. These chambers are small when the animal is young but increase
in size as the animal grows. The nautilus constructs a
new chamber as it grows. It lives in the outer chamber.

All head-footed mollusks have tentacles that are
used to capture food and for movement. However,
these mollusks differ in the number and type of tentacles they possess. The octopus, of course, has eight
tentacles. Squids have ten tentacles, although two of
them differ in shape from the other eight. These
two tentacles are shaped like paddles.

Octopuses, squids, and nautiluses use a water
propulsion system for movement. They force water
out of a tube in one direction, which pushes them
along in the opposite direction. Using this "jet" system, these animals can move away rapidly from
danger. Squids and octopuses can also produce a
purple dye. When they squirt this dye into the water,
it hides the animal and confuses predators. The
squid or octopus can then make good its escape. In
the example earlier in the chapter, the water turned
dark when the young boy chopped off the giant
squid's tentacle for this reason.

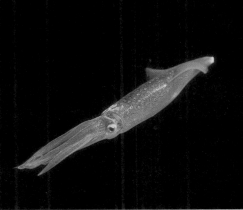

Figure 10-20 *Most head-footed
mollusks, such as the octopus*
(top) *and the squid* (bottom), *do
not have outer shells.*

SECTION REVIEW

1. List three groups of mollusks and give an example of each.
2. What is the main function of the mantle?
3. How does the radula help univalves eat?

Figure 10-21 *The spiny structures in this photograph are the arms of the crown-of-thorns sea star, a spiny-skinned animal. This animal feeds on the soft bodies of living corals.*

10-6 Spiny-Skinned Animals

Earlier you read about the Great Barrier Reef and how it took millions of years to build. Today, the living corals on the surface of the reef are in danger of being destroyed. If they are, the reef will grow no larger. What is damaging the corals? A kind of starfish called the crown-of-thorns sea star is responsible for the damage. See Figure 10-21. The crown-of-thorns eats the soft body parts of the living coral and leaves an empty shell behind.

The crown-of-thorns is a member of a group of animals commonly called the spiny-skinned animals. **Spiny-skinned animals are invertebrates that have a rough, spiny skin.**

Starfish

Starfish are *not* fish. But most *are* shaped like stars. They have five or more arms that extend from a central body. On the bottom of these arms are thousands of tube feet that resemble tiny suction cups. These tube feet not only help the animal to move about, but do much more. For example, when a starfish passes over a clam, one of its favorite foods, the tiny tube feet grasp the clam's shell. The

Figure 10-22 *This starfish is using its suctionlike tube feet to open a clam's shell.*

tube feet exert a tremendous force on the clam's shell, and eventually the shell opens. Then the starfish can eat a leisurely meal.

People who harvest clams from the ocean bottom have long been at war with starfish that destroy their clam beds. In the past, when starfish were captured near clam beds, they were cut into pieces and thrown back into the water. However, starfish have an amazing ability to regenerate, or grow back, missing body parts. So by cutting them up, all people did was make sure there would always be more and more starfish than before—exactly the opposite of what was wanted.

Other Spiny-Skinned Animals

Other spiny-skinned animals vary widely in appearance. Some, like the sea cucumber, resemble a vegetable. These animals usually are found lying on the bottom of the sea. Sea cucumbers lack arms. They slowly move along the sea's bottom with tube feet or by wiggling back and forth.

Sea lilies have many arms that look like flower petals. These animals grow on stalks attached to the sea bottom. Most sea lilies remain in one spot for their entire lives.

Sea urchins and sand dollars are round and lack arms. They may be flat like the sand dollar, or dome-shaped like the sea urchin. Some species have long poisonous spines used for protection.

Figure 10-23 *Like starfish, the sea urchin* (left) *and the sand dollar* (right) *are also spiny-skinned animals.*

SECTION REVIEW

1. What spiny-skinned animal is causing severe damage to the Great Barrier Reef?
2. What does it mean to regenerate?
3. Name three spiny-skinned animals other than the starfish.

10-7 Arthropods

The arthropods (AR-thruh-podz) are the most successful invertebrates on the earth. There are more species of arthropods than all the other animal species combined. Arthropods live in air, on land, and in water. Wherever you happen to live, you can be sure arthropods live there too. In fact, arthropods are our main competitors for food, and if left alone and unchecked, these invertebrates would eventually take over the world.

The name "arthropod" means jointed legs. **Jointed legs and an exoskeleton are the main characteristics of arthropods.** An **exoskeleton** is a rigid outer covering. In some ways, an exoskeleton is similar to the armor once worn by knights as protection in battle. However, there is a drawback to having an exoskeleton. It does not grow as the animal grows. So the arthropod's armor must be shed and replaced

Figure 10-24 *The rigid outer covering of this horseshoe crab is called an exoskeleton. An exoskeleton is characteristic of all arthropods.*

Figure 10-25 *Like all arthropods, these spider crabs have jointed legs and exoskeletons.*

Figure 10-26 *A hermit crab peers out from its borrowed shell atop a fire coral.*

from time to time. While the exoskeleton is being replaced, the arthropod is more vulnerable to attack from other animals.

Arthropods include a variety of animal groups. Among the many types of arthropods are crustaceans, centipedes and millipedes, arachnids, and insects.

Crustaceans

Do you see the two eyes peering out of the shell in Figure 10-26? These eyes belong to a hermit crab, a crab that uses discarded shells for its home. Crabs, along with lobsters, crayfish, and shrimp, are arthropods that are included among the crustaceans (kruh-STAY-shuhnz). All of these animals live in a watery environment. Crustaceans obtain their oxygen from the water through special structures called **gills.** Even the few land-dwelling crustaceans have gills and must live in damp areas to get oxygen.

The bodies of crustaceans are divided into segments. A pair of limbs or other body parts, such as claws, are attached to each segment. These limbs have many different functions, depending on the organism. The claws of some crabs, for example, are strong enough to enable them to open their favorite food, coconuts. Crabs use their claws to cut through the tough outer husk of a coconut to reach the tender flesh inside. Other limbs are adapted for walking. The female lobster even attaches clusters of eggs to the limbs beneath her tail. She carries the eggs in this way.

Activity

Symmetry

The body shapes of invertebrates show either radial symmetry, bilateral symmetry, or asymmetry. Visit the reference section of your library. Using a dictionary, look up the meaning of the word "symmetry." Then use a science dictionary or science encyclopedia to define "radial" and "bilateral" symmetry, as well as "asymmetry."

Make a list of the invertebrates discussed in this chapter. Indicate what type of symmetry is shown by each one.

Figure 10-27 *Centipedes have one pair of legs in a segment (top). Millipedes have two pairs (bottom). Centipedes are carnivores. The centipede shown here is injecting poison into its prey—an unlucky toad.*

Crustaceans are able to regrow certain parts of their body. A crab for example, can grow new claws. The stone crab lives in the waters off the coast of Florida. Its claws are considered to be particularly tasty. When a stone crab is caught, one of its claws is broken off and the crab is returned to the water. In about a year's time, the broken claw has regrown. If the crab is unlucky enough to be caught again, that claw may once again be removed.

Centipedes and Millipedes

Both centipedes and millipedes have been described as worms with legs. In fact, you probably think the main difference between centipedes and millipedes is the number of legs. Actually, both types of arthropods have many legs, and you cannot easily tell them apart by counting. Centipedes have one pair of legs in a segment, while millipedes have two pairs of legs in a segment. However, if you were a tiny earthworm crawling through the soil you would certainly know the difference between the two. Millipedes live on plants and simply would pass you by. Centipedes, however, are carnivorous and are active hunters. The centipede would use its well-developed claws to inject a poison into your body. So, for the earthworm, the difference between the two can mean the difference between life and death.

Arachnids

In Greek mythology, there is a legend of a young woman named Arachne who challenged the gods to a weaving contest. When the mortal Arachne won, the angered gods tore up her tapestry. Arachne hanged herself in sorrow. The gods, the legend goes, then changed her into a spider. Her tapestry became a spider's web. Today, spiders, along with scorpions, ticks, and mites, are all included in a group of arthropods called arachnids (uh-RACK-nidz). As you can guess, arachnids are named for the young Arachne.

The bodies of arachnids are divided into two main sections: a head-chest section and an abdominal section. Although arachnids vary in size and shape, they all have eight legs. So, if you ever find a small

Figure 10-28 *While underwater, the diving spider breathes air it stores in bubbles.*

"bug," one way you can tell if it is an arachnid is to count its legs.

Arachnids live in many environments. Most spiders, for example, live on land. However, one spider lives underwater inside a bubble of air it brings from the surface. Scorpions, for the most part, are found in dry desert areas. Ticks and mites, however, live on organisms. They may live on a plant and stay in one place, or they may live on an animal and go wherever the animal goes.

Spiders catch their prey in different ways. Many spiders make webs of fine, yet very strong, strands of silk. Special glands in the abdomens of spiders secrete this silk. Spiders' webs are often constructed in

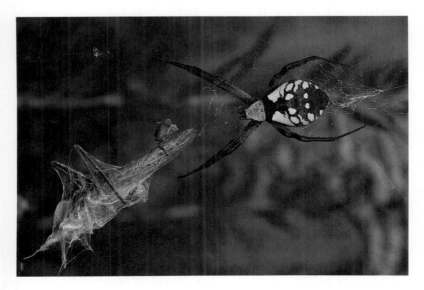

Figure 10-29 *Like many spiders, this spider traps its prey in a web.*

Figure 10-30 *The fishing spider* (left) *and the jumping spider* (right) *do not spin webs to catch their prey. These spiders hunt their prey.*

Figure 10-31 *The scorpion, an arachnid, is found in dry environments. Located at the tip of its tail is a stinger, which the scorpion uses to stab and poison its prey.*

complicated and beautiful patterns. You may be surprised to learn that the spider actually spins two different kinds of silk. Some strands of the silk are sticky. These strands catch and hold prey until the spider is able to kill it. Other strands are not sticky. These are the strands the spider uses when it walks around its web. Many spiders weave a new web every day. At night the spiders eat the strands of that day's web, recycling this material the following day when a new web is produced.

Some spiders hide and spring out to surprise their prey. The trapdoor spider lives in a hole in the ground covered by a door made of silk and hidden by dirt and pieces of plants. When an unsuspecting insect passes close to the trapdoor, the spider rushes out to catch it.

Once a spider catches its dinner, it uses a pair of fangs to inject venom, or poison, into its prey. Sometimes the venom kills the prey immediately. Other times it paralyzes the prey so that the spider can save living creatures trapped in its web for another day when it needs more food.

Scorpions are active mostly at night. They capture and hold their prey with their large front claws while they inject venom through the stinger in their tail. During the day, scorpions hide under logs, stones, or in holes in the ground. Campers have to be careful when they put their boots on in the morning because a scorpion may have mistaken a boot lying on the ground for a suitable place to hide to escape the heat of the day.

Ticks and mites live off the body fluids of animals and plants. Many ticks suck blood from larger animals. When they do this they may spread disease. Rocky Mountain spotted fever is spread to people through the bites of ticks. Some ticks and mites live on insects. Other mites live by sucking juices from plant stems and leaves. They may also spread disease.

SECTION REVIEW

1. What is an exoskeleton?
2. Through what structure do crustaceans take in oxygen from the water?
3. Describe the body of an arachnid.

10-8 Insects

By now you may have noticed that there is one group of arthropods, or animals with jointed legs, that has not been discussed. This group, of course, is the insects. However, it would be hard to overlook insects for too long since there are more kinds of insects than all other animal species combined. In fact, it has been estimated that there may be as many as

Figure 10-32 *Insects, like the may beetle* (left) *and the banded woollybear* (right), *vary greatly in appearance.*

300 million insects for every single person alive on the earth!

Along with birds and bats, certain insects are the only animals that can fly. Insects vary greatly in appearance. If you examine different insect species, for example, you would find that the mouth parts vary greatly. A mosquito's mouth resembles a tiny needle. It can push its needlelike mouth through an animal's skin and remove some of the animal's body fluids. Other insects have mouths that are adapted to eating parts of plants. If you have ever watched a caterpillar eating a leaf, you know how efficient these insects' mouths are.

Many insects compete directly with humans. Insects eat the plants we use for food. Others eat the clothes we wear. If you live in a house made of wood, you may be surprised to find that some species of insects, such as termites, may even be eating your house.

Insect Anatomy

Although both are arthropods, insects are different from arachnids. An arachnid's body is divided into two sections. **An insect's body is divided into three main sections: a head, a thorax, and an abdomen. And, an insect has three pairs of legs.**

Figure 10-33 *A rainbow grasshopper investigates a flower. Compare the photograph of the grasshopper with the diagram showing its structure.*

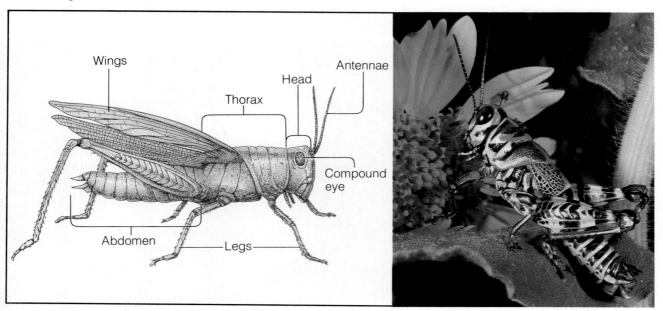

The grasshopper is a typical insect in many ways. See Figure 10-33 on page 242. In the grasshopper, the three pairs of legs are not identical. One pair of legs is much larger than the other two. This pair of legs enables the grasshopper to jump away if an enemy gets too close.

If you took a close look at the head of a grasshopper, you would find five eyes peering at you. The grasshopper has three simple eyes on the front of its head. These eyes can detect only light and dark. However, on the sides of its head are two compound eyes. Compound eyes contain many lenses. See Figure 10-34. These compound eyes can detect some colors, but they are best at detecting movement. The ability to detect movement is important to an animal such as a grasshopper that is hunted daily by other animals for food.

Most insects have wings. The grasshopper has two pairs of wings, and it can fly quite well for short distances. Some kinds of grasshoppers can fly great distances in search of food. Insect flight varies from the gentle fluttering flight of a butterfly to the speedy flight of the hawkmoth, an insect that can fly as fast as 50 kilometers per hour.

Insects have an open circulatory system. Their blood usually is not contained within a system of blood vessels, as it is in humans. The blood moves around the inside of the insect's body, bathing the internal organs. An insect's blood carries food. But the blood does not carry oxygen. Insects do not have a well-developed system for moving oxygen into the body and waste gases out. Instead, they have a system of tubes that pass through the exoskeleton and into the insect's body. Gases move into and out of the insect's body through these tubes.

Insect Growth and Development

Insects spend a great deal of time eating, and they grow rapidly. Like other arthropods, insects must shed their exoskeleton as they grow. As insects develop, they pass through several stages. Some species of insects change their appearance completely as they pass through the different stages. This change in appearance due to development is known as **metamorphosis** (met-uh-MAWR-fuh-sis).

Figure 10-34 *Insects, such as this fly, have compound eyes. Within these eyes are many lenses, which enable the insect to detect the slightest movement of an object.*

Activity

The Life of a Mealworm

Here is a way to observe metamorphosis for yourself.

1. Fill a clean liter jar about one-third full of bran cereal.

2. Place four mealworms in the jar.

3. Add a few slides of raw potato to the jar.

4. Shred some newspaper and place it loosely in the jar.

5. Cover the top of the jar with a layer of cheesecloth. Use a rubber band to hold the cheesecloth in place.

6. Observe the jar at least once a week. Record all changes that take place in the mealworms.

What is this insect called in its larval stage? In its adult stage? How long was the mealworms' life cycle?

Figure 10-35 *During metamorphosis, an insect goes through a series of changes. The monarch butterfly begins life as an egg* (top left), *then becomes a larva, also known as a caterpillar* (bottom left), *and finally wraps itself up into a cocoon* (right), *where it becomes a pupa.*

Figure 10-36 *In the last stage of metamorphosis, the monarch has wings and other parts of a typical adult insect. These monarch butterflies are wintering in a tree in southern California.*

During metamorphosis, an insect passes through four distinct stages. The first stage is the egg. When the egg hatches, a **larva** emerges. A caterpillar, for example, is the larva of an insect that will one day become a butterfly or a moth. The larva spends almost all of its time eating and can eat all the leaves of a plant in a short time.

Eventually, the caterpillar begins the next phase, the **pupa** (PYOO-puh) phase. In this phase, the caterpillar secretes a covering made of silk or another material. It wraps itself in this cocoon and appears to be sleeping. But inside the cocoon remarkable changes take place. The pupa changes into an adult insect with a completely different appearance. It is often difficult to believe that a beautiful butterfly was once a creeping caterpillar.

Insect Behavior

Most insects lead solitary lives. They live alone. In this way, they do not compete directly with other members of their species for available food. They come together only to mate and to produce fertilized eggs. Insects attract mates in different ways. One way involves the giving off of a special scent, which you might think of as a kind of perfume. These scents are called **pheromones** (FER-uh-mohnz), extremely powerful chemicals that cannot be smelled by a human. However, even a small amount of a pheromone can be noticed by a potential mate over great distances. Some pheromones produced by female insects can attract a male located more than 11 kilometers away.

Other insects, known as social insects, cannot survive alone. These insects form colonies or hives. Ants, termites, some wasp species, and bees are social insects. They survive as a society of individual insects that perform different jobs. Many of these colonies are highly organized.

A beehive is a marvel of organization. Worker bees, actually infertile females, perform all of the work needed to ensure the survival of the hive. For example, worker bees supply the hive with food. They make the honey and the combs to store it. They feed the queen bee, whose only function is to lay huge numbers of eggs. Worker bees keep the

Figure 10-37 *Insect behavior often helps other organisms. This moth flies from flower to flower. As it does, it helps pollinate the flowers.*

Figure 10-38 *This large mound of soil was built by termites. Termites, like bees, are social insects and work and live together in a colony.*

queen bee clean as well as do the housekeeping for the hive. They also protect the hive. Male bees, whose only function is to fertilize the queen, are unable to feed themselves and so also are dependent upon the workers.

Defense Mechanisms

Insects have many defense methods to ensure their survival. Wasps and bees have stingers that they use to defend them against their enemies. Other insects are masters of camouflage. These insects survive because their bodies are not easily seen by their enemies. Some insects, for example, resemble sticks and twigs. Other insects resemble leaves or the

Career: *Beekeeper*

HELP WANTED: BEEKEEPER No special education required. Courses in beekeeping, agriculture, and business helpful. Will train to harvest honey from honeycombs and clean, repair, and inspect beehives.

The worker bee hovered over the flower while sucking nectar with its long tongue into its stomach. In the bee's stomach, special chemicals mixed with the nectar. When its

stomach was full, it returned to its hive. At the hive it brought the nectar mixture back up through its mouth and placed it in a compartment or cell in the hive. As water evaporated from the mixture, the nectar changed to honey. Other bees placed a wax cap on the honey-filled cell. Honey stored in this way provides food for all the bees during the winter.

People who maintain hives of bees from which they collect honey and beeswax are called **beekeepers.** They sell the honey to bakeries for use in cookies and crackers or package it to sell in markets by the jar. The beeswax is sold for use in making candles, lipsticks, and polishes.

Beekeepers construct wooden boxes with removable frames as hives for the bees. The bees build honeycombs of wax on the frames, which contain many cells to receive the nectar mixtures. Bees are free to come and go so they can bring nectar from flowers back to the hive.

Anyone interested in beekeeping might begin by keeping a hive or two in a backyard or on a roof. Beginner colonies can usually be bought or rented from local beekeepers. For more information on a career working with fascinating insects, write to the New Jersey Beekeepers Association, 157 Five Point Road, Colts Neck, NJ 07722.

Figure 10-39 *Insects defend themselves in many ways. The wasp* (left) *uses its stinger, the assassin bug* (top right) *is camouflaged, the bombardier beetle* (center right) *sprays a foul-smelling chemical, and the eye spot coloring on this moth* (bottom right) *startles its predators.*

thorns of plants. Some insects have the ability to spray foul-smelling chemicals at an enemy. Other insects have markings that frighten birds and other animals that might eat them. In Figure 10-39, you can see two large "eyespots" on the wings of the moth. These spots startle predatory animals and may confuse a predator long enough for the insect to make an escape.

SECTION REVIEW

1. What are the three main sections of an insect's body?
2. What are the four stages of metamorphosis?
3. List three kinds of social insects.

LABORATORY ACTIVITY

Which Way Did That Isopod Go?

Purpose

In this activity, you will determine the type of environment isopods prefer.

Materials *(per group)*

Collecting jar	2 paper towels
10 isopods	Masking tape
Shoe box with a lid	Water
Aluminum foil	

Procedure

1. With your collecting jar, gather some isopods. These are usually found under loose bricks or logs. Observe the characteristics of the isopods.
2. Line a shoe box with aluminum foil.
3. Tape down two paper towels side by side in the bottom of the shoe box. Separate them with a strip of masking tape.
4. Moisten the paper towel on the left side of the box only.
5. Place the ten isopods on the masking tape. Put the lid back on the shoe box.
6. Predict what will happen when you open the lid. Wait five minutes. Meanwhile, make a data table.
7. After five minutes, open the lid and quickly count the number of isopods on the dry paper, on the masking tape, and on the moist paper. Record the results in your table.
8. Repeat the procedure two more times. Before each trial, be sure to place the isopods on the masking tape. Record your results in your data table.
9. After you have completed the three trials, find the average result for each column (dry, tape, moist). To do this, add up each column and divide by 3. Record your average results on a class chart.

Observations and Conclusions

1. How did the isopods react when you opened the lid of the box? How did this reaction compare with your prediction?
2. What was the variable in this experiment?
3. Were there other variables in the experiment that could have affected the outcome? If so, what were they?
4. What was the control in this experiment?
5. How did your results compare to the class results?
6. From the class results, what conclusions can you draw about the habitats isopods prefer?
7. To which group of invertebrates do isopods belong? What characteristics led you to your conclusion?
8. What was the purpose of the masking tape in the experiment?
9. Why did you go through the procedure three times?
10. Design another experiment in which you test the following hypothesis: Isopods prefer dark environments over light environments. Be sure to include a variable and a control in your design.

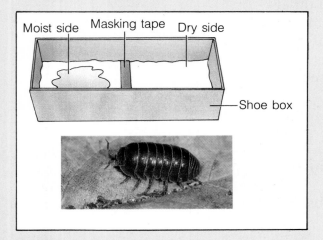

Moist side   Masking tape   Dry side

Shoe box

CHAPTER REVIEW

SUMMARY

10-1 Invertebrates

- Vertebrates have backbones, while invertebrates have no backbones.

- All animals are multicellular, and most have specialized cells.

10-2 Sponges

- The cells of sponges remove food and oxygen from ocean water as the water flows through pores. The out-flowing water carries away waste products.

10-3 Coelenterates

- Coelenterates have a cup-shaped body with one opening. Examples include corals, sea anemones, and jellyfish.

- Most coelenterates have stinging cells called nematocysts on their tentacles. Coelenterates sting and capture their prey, which is digested in the central body cavity. Waste products are released through the mouth.

10-4 Worms

- Flatworms have flat bodies and live in ponds and streams. Flatworms can regrow missing or cut-off parts. Examples of flatworms are planarians and tapeworms.

- Roundworms resemble strands of spaghetti. Food passes from the mouth end to tail end through a digestive tube. Trichinosis is a disease caused by eating pork containing roundworms.

- Segmented worms, such as earthworms, have segmented bodies and live in soil, salt water, or fresh water.

- Earthworms have a digestive system with a crop and gizzard, a closed circulatory system, a moist skin for gas exchange, a sexual reproductive system, and a simple nervous system.

10-5 Mollusks

- Mollusks have soft bodies covered by a shell-producing mantle. Their muscular foot opens and closes the shell and permits movement. Snails, clams, and squids are examples of mollusks.

10-6 Spiny-Skinned Animals

- Starfish have tiny tube feet for movement and can regenerate missing parts.

- The spiny-skinned animals also include sea cucumbers, sea lilies, sea urchins, and sand dollars.

10-7 Arthropods

- Arthropods are invertebrates that have jointed legs and an exoskeleton. The group includes crustaceans, centipedes and millipedes, arachnids, and insects.

10-8 Insects

- Insects have bodies divided into three parts, have three pairs of legs and an open circulatory system.

VOCABULARY

Define each term in a complete sentence.

crop	host	metamorphosis	pupa
exoskeleton	invertebrate	nematocyst	radula
gill	larva	pheromone	vertebrate
gizzard	mantle	pore	

CONTENT REVIEW: MULTIPLE CHOICE

Choose the letter of the answer that best completes each statement.

1. Tissues that work together are organized into
   a. cells.   b. organs.   c. organ systems.   d. tissue systems.
2. Which of these invertebrate groups is responsible for building the Great Barrier Reef?
   a. sponges   b. corals   c. sea anemones   d. jellyfish
3. Scientists hope to learn more about the earth's past by studying the daily growth rings of
   a. sponges.   b. corals.   c. segmented worms.   d. mollusks.
4. Tapeworms are examples of parasitic
   a. flatworms.   b. roundworms.   c. segmented worms.   d. earthworms.
5. Which of these is *not* a function of a mollusk's thick muscular foot?
   a. movement   b. production of a hard outer shell
   c. digging   d. opening and closing the shell
6. Which of these animals can regenerate lost body parts?
   a. crabs   b. planarians   c. starfish   d. all of these
7. In which group of invertebrates do the animals have jointed legs and exoskeletons?
   a. coelenterates   b. worms   c. mollusks   d. arthropods
8. Spiders belong to a group of invertebrates called
   a. coelenterates.   b. crustaceans.   c. arthropods.   d. insects.
9. In which stage of metamorphosis is a caterpillar?
   a. egg   b. larva   c. pupa   d. adult
10. The only function of the queen bee is to
    a. lay large numbers of eggs.   b. do the beehive housekeeping.
    c. protect the hive.   d. make the honey to store in combs.

CONTENT REVIEW: COMPLETION

Fill in the word or words that best complete each statement.

1. Animals that do not have backbones are called _____.
2. _____ are the stinging cells that are found around the mouth of most coelenterates.
3. The painful disease caused by eating raw pork containing certain roundworms is called _____.
4. The _____ is a roundworm that infects over 600 million people each year by burrowing through the skin.
5. Giant squids belong to a group of invertebrates called _____.
6. The _____ is the structure that files off tiny bits of plant matter in most mollusks.
7. The crown-of-thorns sea star is an example of a(n) _____.
8. The rigid outer covering of an arthropod is called a(n) _____.
9. The changing appearance of insects as they pass through different stages is called _____.
10. The special scents produced by insects to attract mates are called _____.

CONTENT REVIEW: TRUE OR FALSE

Determine whether each statement is true or false. If it is true, write "true." If it is false, change the underlined word or words to make the statement true.

1. All animals are <u>multicellular</u>.
2. Animals that do not have backbones are called <u>vertebrates</u>.
3. Certain <u>worms</u> get into oysters causing the oysters to produce pearls.
4. In an earthworm, the <u>crop</u> is the muscular organ that grinds up <u>food</u>.
5. The soft <u>radula</u> covering the body of a mollusk produces the material making up the mollusk's hard shell.
6. Sea cucumbers and sea lilies are examples of <u>spiny-skinned animals</u>.
7. In crustaceans, the structures that remove oxygen from water are called <u>pores</u>.
8. Spiders are examples of <u>crustaceans</u>.
9. Oxygen and waste gases pass out of the exoskeleton of an insect's body through <u>gills</u>.
10. In order to grow, insects must shed their <u>mantles</u>.

CONCEPT REVIEW: SKILL BUILDING

Use the skills you have developed in the chapter to complete each activity.

1. **Making predictions** Suppose the water in which a sponge lived became polluted with a lot of floating matter. How would the sponge be affected?
2. **Making charts** Construct a chart with three columns. In the first column, list each group of invertebrates you read about in the chapter. In the second column, list the characteristics of each group. In the third column, name two animals from each group.
3. **Making comparisons** Which group of invertebrates is more complex, the sponges or the coelenterates? Explain.
4. **Relating facts** Your friend said she found an insect with four legs and two body parts. Is this possible? Explain.
5. **Making inferences** Why is it unsafe to eat clams from polluted water?
6. **Making generalizations** Explain how insects are helpful to humans.
7. **Relating concepts** Describe a method that would prevent people from being infected by hookworms.
8. **Applying concepts** How might scientists use pheromones to control insect pests?
9. **Relating cause and effect** Explain why people with tapeworm infections eat a lot but still feel hungry and tired.
10. **Applying concepts** Insects are often described as the most successful group of animals. What characteristics of insects could account for this description?

CONCEPT REVIEW: ESSAY

Discuss each of the following in a brief paragraph.

1. Discuss the ways in which insects compete with human beings. Give two examples.
2. Describe the protective method each of the following uses against predators: sea anemone, earthworm, squid, insect.
3. Explain the process of metamorphosis.
4. List the different methods invertebrates use to get food. For each method, give examples of those invertebrates that use it.

11 Animals: Vertebrates

CHAPTER SECTIONS

11-1 Fish
11-2 Amphibians
11-3 Reptiles
11-4 Birds

CHAPTER OBJECTIVES

After completing this chapter, you will be able to:

11-1 Describe the characteristics of vertebrates.

11-1 List the three groups of fish and give an example of each.

11-2 Describe the characteristics of amphibians.

11-3 Describe the adaptations that allow reptiles to live their entire lives on land.

11-4 Describe the characteristics of birds.

11-4 List the four main categories of birds and their adaptations for flight.

A small fish swims past a rock. As it does, it notices a worm wriggling and moves closer to investigate. However, the fish is in for a deadly surprise. No, the worm is not at the end of a fishing line that leads to the surface. But it *is* being used as bait. In fact, the worm is attached to the rock, which is quietly watching the small fish. For the "rock" is not made of minerals; it is actually a fish called an anglerfish. And the "worm" is really an organ attached to the fish's head. In order to catch a meal, the anglerfish must wait patiently, as still as a rock.

The worm lures the fish closer. When the prey is near, the anglerfish takes a big gulp. The small fish ends up in the anglerfish's huge mouth.

To trap its prey, the anglerfish must remain very still and show unlimited patience. However, it can move quickly when it strikes. In fact, the strike of the anglerfish, one of the fastest in the animal kingdom, has been timed at less than 4/1000 of a second!

Anglerfish luring its prey

11-1 Fish

Around 500 million years ago, a tiny animal first appeared in the earth's oceans. This strange animal had no jaws. It did have fins, but they were not like the fins of modern fish. However, there was something very special about this animal—something that would group it with the many kinds of fish that were to come in later years. This early fish was the first animal with a backbone—the first vertebrate.

The main characteristic of all vertebrates, including fish, is a backbone, although you will read about some fish whose backbone is not made of bone at all! The bones that make up a vertebrate's backbone are called **vertebrae** (singular: vertebra). See Figure 11-1. The backbone is part of the vertebrate's internal skeleton, although, again, not all skeletons are made of bone. The skeleton provides support and helps give the body of a vertebrate its shape. One important advantage of an internal skeleton is that it increases in size as the animal grows. It does not have to be shed, as does the exoskeleton of an insect.

An important function of the backbone of a vertebrate is to protect the nerves of the spinal cord, which runs down through the center of the backbone. These spinal cord nerves connect the vertebrate's well-developed brain to nerves that carry information to and from every part of the body.

Figure 11-1 *Like all vertebrates, fish have a series of bones called vertebrae that make up their backbone.*

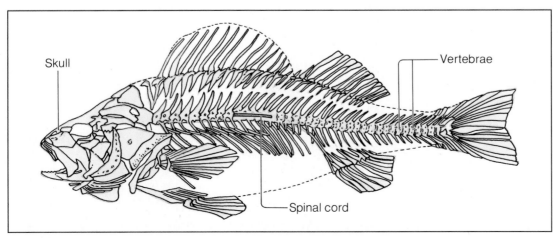

Figure 11-2 *Some fish, like these in the Coral Sea, travel in schools.*

Fish are the vertebrates that are best adapted to a life under water. Their smooth body, usually covered with scales, is streamlined, allowing them to glide through the water. Most fish have fins. Some fins keep a fish upright so that it does not roll over on its side. Other fins help the fish steer and stop. The side-to-side movement of the large tail fin propels the fish through the water. Rapid movement of its tail fin, for example, allows the pike to travel up to 12 times its body length in less than one second.

Like some invertebrates, fish take oxygen from the water through gills. As a fish swims, water passes through its gills. Oxygen passes from the water into blood vessels in the gills. Carbon dioxide wastes also pass out of the fish through the gills. Fish have well-developed digestive, circulatory, and nervous systems, as do the other vertebrates you will read about.

Fish live in all of the earth's waters, in both fresh and salt water. As you might expect, however, the same fish usually cannot live in both fresh and salt water. Also, while some fish, like the cod, may live in the cold waters of the Arctic, others, like the ferocious piranha, live in warm, tropical waters. If you take a tropical piranha and place it in arctic waters, it will soon die. Why? Fish are coldblooded. They have no internal control over their body temperature. So changes in their environment can affect their body temperature. If the change is severe, as from tropical to arctic waters, most fish will not survive. However,

Figure 11-3 *Like this emperor angelfish, most fish have fins and streamlined bodies that help them glide through the water.*

Figure 11-4 *Some fish, such as the potato cod* (right), *live only in cold water. Other fish, such as* Priacanthus (left), *live only in warm water. Notice the small "cleaner" fish near the tail of* Priacanthus.

Figure 11-5 *The lamprey, a jawless fish, attaches to other fish with its suction-cup mouth. Then the lamprey uses its teeth to drill a hole into the other fish.*

since the water temperature in an area remains relatively constant compared to the temperature on land, fish have little trouble maintaining a constant body temperature as long as they remain in their native waters. This results in a saving of energy, for fish do not have to use food energy to keep warm.

Fish are divided into three groups. The three groups of fish are the jawless fish, the cartilaginous fish, and the bony fish.

Jawless Fish

Jawless fish are the most primitive of all fish. They are so primitive, in fact, that they lack scales and fins as well as jaws. In Figure 11-5, you can see the most common jawless fish—the lamprey. The lamprey looks like a snake with a suction-cup mouth at one end. Even though the fish has no jaws, this suction-cup mouth is very efficient. Using its mouth, the lamprey attaches itself to the soft belly of some other fish, such as a trout. Then, with its teeth and rough tongue, the lamprey drills a hole into the fish and sucks out its blood and other body fluids. At one time, lampreys in the Great Lakes killed so many other fish that special poisons were used to kill lamprey young.

There is something else that makes jawless fish unusual. To find out what it is, take your ear between your fingers and move it back and forth a few times. Nothing breaks, does it? The reason is that your ear contains a flexible material called **cartilage** (KAHRT-uhl-ij). In fact, before you were born your entire skeleton was made of cartilage. In time, the cartilage was replaced by bone, except in some places like your ear and the tip of your nose. The entire skeleton of a jawless fish is made of cartilage. The skeleton is never replaced by bone tissue. As you might expect, such a fish is very flexible and can be bent so that its head touches its tail without causing any damage to the fish.

Cartilaginous Fish

A monstrous figure moves slowly toward a group of skin divers. However, the divers are too intent on their swimming to notice the 18-meter-long fish as it approaches. Then, suddenly, just as it reaches them one of the divers turns and sees the creature. It is a shark! The diver signals her companions. But they do not swim away in fear, even though they are confronted by the largest shark on earth—the whale

Figure 11-6 *In spite of their enormous size, whale sharks are harmless to people. Whale sharks only eat microscopic plants and animals.*

Figure 11-7 *The great white shark* (left) *and the horn shark* (right) *are examples of cartilaginous fish.*

Figure 11-8 *Rays, such as this blue-spotted lagoon ray, swim by beating their huge fins much the same way as a bird flaps its wings when flying.*

shark. Instead, they grab the shark's top fin and playfully hitch a short ride. The divers know that the whale shark has little interest in people. It eats only microscopic plants and animals.

Sharks are included in a group of fish called the cartilaginous (kahrt-uhl-AJ-uh-nuhs) fish. Like those of jawless fish, sharks' skeletons are made of cartilage. But unlike the jawless fish, sharks definitely have jaws. See Figure 11-7. In fact, sharks are probably the most successful predators on earth. And they have been so for hundreds of millions of years. When you think of sharks, you probably think of the great white shark, which has a reputation for eating people. Great white sharks, along with a few other types, have been known to attack people occasionally. But for the most part sharks let people alone and prefer to be let alone as well.

Also included among the cartilaginous fish are skates and rays. These fish have two large, broad fins that stick out from their sides. They beat these fins to move through the water, much as a bird beats its wings to fly through air. Rays and skates often lie on the ocean bottom, where they use their "wings" to cover their bodies with sand and hide. When an unsuspecting fish or invertebrate comes near, the hidden skate or ray is ready to attack. Some rays have a poisonous spine at the end of their long, thin tail. However, they use this for defense, not to catch prey. Other rays are able to produce small charges of electricity to stun and capture prey.

Bony Fish

Anyone who has eaten a flounder or a trout knows why such fish are called bony fish. Their skeleton is composed of hard bones, many of which are quite small and sharp. That is one reason that many restaurants serve fish with the bones removed. Some of the bony fish, including the tuna and herring you may eat, travel in groups called schools. Because of this schooling behavior, these fish can be caught in large numbers at one time by fishing boats.

One important characteristic of bony fish is their **swim bladder.** The swim bladder is a sac that the fish can empty or fill with air. The swim bladder acts in much the same way as a life preserver that keeps people afloat. However, by letting air in and out of the bladder, a fish can float at any level in the water. That is why a fish can sleep under water and not sink, even though it is not moving its fins.

There are many different kinds of bony fish. Some have made remarkable adaptations to life in the water. The electric eel, for example, can generate considerable amounts of electricity. This eel, found in South American streams, uses the electricity it produces to stun its prey. The remora, a saltwater fish, uses a sucker to attach itself to a shark or other marine animal. It feeds on bits of food the shark leaves behind. Some fish, such as the flounder, are

Activity

Observing a Fish

1. Obtain a preserved fish from your teacher and place it in a tray.

2. Observe the fish. Note its size, shape, and color. To which group does your fish belong?

3. Draw a diagram of the fish and label as many structures as you can.

4. Locate the fish's gill cover. Lift it up and examine the gills with a hand lens. If necessary, use a scissor to cut away the gill cover. **CAUTION:** *Be careful when using sharp instruments.* How many gills do you see?

5. Remove one of the scales from the fish.

6. Examine the scale under a microscope. Each year a new dark ring is added to the scale. How old is your fish?

Figure 11-9 *Fish are adapted in many different ways to a life under water. The stonefish (left) not only blends in with its surroundings, it also gives off a deadly poison through its spines. The deep sea fish (right) has large eyes, a huge mouth, fanglike teeth, and light-emitting organs that flash on and off.*

Figure 11-10 *The mudskipper is a "fish out of water." It can crawl along the mud of tropical swamps and breathe in air as well as in water.*

masters of camouflage. They are able to change color to match their surroundings. By changing to the same color as the ocean bottom, the flounder "hides" from predators.

Some fish that live in the dark ocean depths have developed light-producing organs that can flash on and off to attract prey. Other deep-sea fish have huge eyes to help them see in dim light.

You might think that all fish have one thing in common—a need to stay in water at all times. However, the mudskipper and the walking catfish have adaptations that allow them to come out of the water and spend some time on land. And the lungfish can bury itself in mud in order to survive a dry season during which the water of the stream or pond in which it lives evaporates.

SECTION REVIEW

1. What are vertebrae?
2. What material makes up the skeleton of lampreys and sharks?
3. What structure allows bony fish to float at any depth in the water, even when asleep?

11-2 Amphibians

In the forests of Colombia, South America, lives the Choco Indian tribe. Today, as they have done for centuries, these Indians hunt deer, monkeys, and even jaguar with poisoned arrows. To do so, the Indians must first capture a supply of a certain frog that lives in the area. They then collect a milky fluid from the frog's back. The tips of their arrows are dipped into this fluid, a poison so powerful that a few drops can kill several thousand mice. The common name for this frog is no surprise—it is called the arrow-poison frog.

The arrow-poison frog is included among a group of coldblooded animals called the amphibians. The word "amphibian" means double life. And most amphibians do live double lives. **Amphibians spend part of their lives in water and part on land.** All amphibians, for example, are born from eggs laid in water. And even those that spend their entire lives on land must return to the water to reproduce. Why? The eggs of amphibians lack a hard outer shell and would dry out if they were not deposited in the water.

There is yet another reason amphibians cannot stray too far from water—or at least from a moist area. Amphibians breathe through their skin, but the skin must remain damp for them to take in oxygen in this way.

Frogs and Toads

Have you ever wondered where frogs and toads go in the winter when the temperature drops? Frogs and toads, like all amphibians, are unable to move to warmer climates. But they can survive. Frogs often bury themselves beneath the muddy floor of a lake during the winter. Toads dig through dry ground below the frost line. Then these amphibians go into a winter sleep called **hibernation.** During hibernation, all body activities slow down so that the animal can live on food stored in its body. The small amount of oxygen needed during hibernation passes through the amphibian's skin as it sleeps. Once warmer weather comes, the frog or toad awakes. If you live in the country, you can usually tell when this

Figure 11-11 *This brilliantly colored frog is called an arrow-poison frog. The poisonous fluid in its skin can kill small animals.*

Figure 11-12 *Amphibians such as the tree frog* (left) *and toad* (right) *lead a "double life." They spend part of their lives in water and part of them on land.*

happens. The night is suddenly filled with the familiar peeps, squeaks, chirps, and grunts that male frogs and toads use to attract their mates.

Frogs and toads appear similar in shape. But if you touch them, you can tell one difference immediately. Frogs have a smooth, moist skin. Toads are drier and are usually covered with small wartlike bumps. In many toads, the bumps behind the eyes contain a poisonous liquid, which the toad releases when attacked. The attacking animal quickly becomes sick and may even die.

Neither frogs nor toads have tails as adults. However, strange as it may seem, they do have tails when they hatch from eggs in the water. In this stage of their lives they are called tadpoles or polliwogs. A tadpole has gills to breathe under water and feeds on plants. Eventually the tadpole begins to undergo remarkable changes. Its tail begins to disappear. Two pairs of legs take shape. At the same time, its gills begin to close. Inside the tadpole's body, lungs are forming. Soon the tadpole will be an adult toad or frog, ready for its life on land.

If there is one thing most people know about adult toads and frogs, it is that they are excellent jumpers. The main reason for this is that the hind legs of a frog or toad are much larger than the front legs. It is these powerful hind legs that allow the animals to jump so well and help them escape from

Figure 11-13 *All amphibians lay their eggs* (left) *in a watery environment. Each egg then hatches into a larval form called a tadpole* (right).

Figure 11-14 *The sticky tongue in a frog's mouth is well adapted for catching insects, such as this fly.*

enemies. The largest frog, the goliath frog of West Africa, can jump more than 3 meters with little effort! A frog's large hind legs are also useful in water, where they serve as paddles to propel the animal.

Unlike tadpoles, adult frogs and toads are carnivorous. They catch their prey with a most unusual tongue. The sticky tongue of a frog or toad is attached to the front of its mouth. To trap an insect or other prey, the frog or toad quickly flicks its tongue out of its mouth and catches the insect as it flies by.

Salamanders and Newts

An important ingredient of a witches' brew or magic potion was the eye of a newt. Well, there are no magic potions, but there really are newts. Newts, along with salamanders, are amphibians with tails. Like frogs and toads, these animals have two pairs of legs. However, their legs are not developed like those of a frog. Newts and salamanders cannot jump at all.

Since they are amphibians, salamanders and newts must live in moist areas. Some live in the water all their lives. Others may spend most of their life under a single tree stump. Like frogs and toads, salamanders and newts must lay their eggs in water.

Figure 11-15 *Like all amphibians, this spotted salamander must live in a moist area. Notice the mass of eggs below the salamander.*

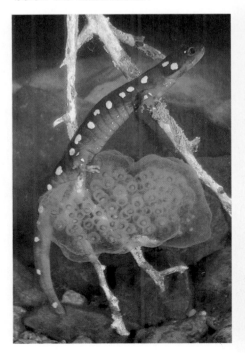

SECTION REVIEW

1. What does the term "amphibian" mean? How does it apply to amphibians?
2. How do frogs survive the cold winter months?
3. When do frogs and toads have tails and gills? When do they have legs and lungs?

11-3 Reptiles

On the barren, windswept shoreline of the Galapagos Islands in the Pacific Ocean, a group of iguanas (i-GWAH-nuhz) cling to the rocks. Wave after wave pounds against the rocks, but the iguanas do not let go. Then, without warning, the iguanas plunge into the cold sea in search of food. The iguanas did not suddenly become hungry. Instead, they basked on the rocks of the Galapagos until the sun warmed their bodies. Only then could these coldblooded animals enter the chilly waters. And once they become cold again in the water, they will have to return to the rocks to warm up.

The iguana, a kind of lizard, belongs to a group of animals called reptiles. **Reptiles are coldblooded vertebrates that have dry, scaly skin and lay eggs on land.** In addition to lizards, reptiles include snakes, turtles, and alligators. Although many rep-

Figure 11-16 *Sunning themselves on the shore of this Galapagos island, located off the west coast of South America, are marine iguanas. Marine iguanas are a type of reptile. A crab with red-tipped legs keeps them company.*

Figure 11-17 *Some reptiles, such as this gecko, must shed their skin as they grow.*

tiles live in or near water, as do amphibians, they do not have to go through a water-dwelling stage in their lives. And, because their scaly skin is resistant to drying out, reptiles do not have to live in a moist environment. In fact, many reptiles live in deserts. To grow larger, reptiles such as snakes and lizards periodically shed their skins. Snakes actually crawl out of their old skins through holes near their mouths. Lizards shed their skins in strips. Some of them then eat the pieces of old skin.

The eggs of reptiles have a leathery protective shell. This shell prevents the contents of the egg from drying out. So reptiles do not have to return to the water to lay their eggs. Since the eggs are enclosed within a shell, reptiles have developed a system of internal fertilization. The eggs are fertilized within the female's body before the shell forms around the egg.

Snakes and Lizards

Most people are naturally fearful of snakes. They mistakenly think that all snakes are dangerous. But most snakes are not poisonous and will not harm people. In fact, most snakes are helpful. They eat small animals like mice and rats. However, a good rule to follow is: When in doubt, leave a snake alone!

Those snakes which *are* poisonous have developed special glands that produce their **venom,** or poison. Snakes inject their venom into their prey

Activity

The Truth About Snakes

Many people hear the word snake and think of a slippery, poisonous animal. But snakes are not slippery. And most of them are not poisonous either.

Use reference books in the library to determine what proportion of the world's snakes actually are poisonous. In addition, find out about the ways in which snakes are helpful to people. Present your findings in a written report.

Figure 11-18 *The king cobra* (left) *is the largest poisonous snake in the world. The emerald tree boa* (right) *kills its prey by squeezing its victim's chest so tightly that it suffocates.*

through special teeth called fangs. Four kinds of poisonous snakes are found in the United States: rattlesnakes, copperheads, water moccasins, and coral snakes. Other poisonous snakes, like the king cobra, the largest poisonous snake in the world, are found on other continents.

Snakes have developed several remarkable ways of finding prey. Many snakes are able to detect the body heat produced by their prey. They have special pits on the sides of their head that are extremely sensitive to heat. Their tongue is also used as a sense organ. When a snake flicks its tongue in and out of its mouth, it is actually tasting the air, trying to detect those particles in the air that tell the snake that

Figure 11-19 *The Komodo dragons in this photograph are eating a goat. The largest lizards, Komodo dragons can grow to a length of 3 meters and weigh 113 kilograms.*

food is nearby. Snakes are deaf and have poor eyesight. But their other senses make up for these limitations.

A snake moves by wriggling its muscular body. The scales on its belly help the animal grip the ground and push itself forward. Many snakes, including the water moccasin, are quite at home in the water and can swim along at the surface or submerged.

Lizards differ from snakes in several ways. The most obvious difference is that lizards have legs. Lizards also have ears and can detect sounds. Most lizards are small and eat insects. However, one lizard, the Komodo dragon of Indonesia in Southeast Asia, is very large and looks like a prehistoric dinosaur. The Komodo dragon can swallow small pigs and chickens whole.

Lizards have developed various ways to trap prey. For example, the Gila (HEE-luh) monster, a lizard that lives in the American Southwest, poisons its prey. The Gila monster bites the prey, holds on tight, and rolls over on its side. Meanwhile, poison released from the lizard's lower jaw flows into the wound, aided only by the force of gravity. How does this differ from the way a snake poisons its prey?

Some lizards have developed special ways to protect themselves from becoming another animal's dinner. The chameleon is one of several kinds of lizard that can change color to match their surroundings. In this way, the chameleon hides from predators. Another lizard has an even stranger way of escaping.

Figure 11-20 *The Gila monster* (left) *lives in North American deserts and has a poisonous bite. The anole* (right) *is a lizard that is able to blend in with its surroundings. Can you find the anole in this photograph?*

If caught by its tail, it will quickly shed the tail. The tail remains behind, wriggling on the ground. This action confuses the predator, and the lizard scampers to safety. Later, the lizard's body regenerates the missing tail.

Turtles and Tortoises

Turtles and tortoises are two reptiles that look alike but have adapted to different environments. Turtles spend most of their time in the water. Their legs are shaped like paddles and are used for swimming. Turtles can swim quite well; however, on land they move slowly. Tortoises spend most of their time on land. They have solid, stumpy legs used for walking. Tortoises also have claws on their feet that are used for digging.

Covering most of the body of both turtles and tortoises are shells made of plates. Although the shells

---

Career: *Fish Farmer*

> **HELP WANTED: FISH FARMER** High school diploma desired. Courses in fish behavior, fish physiology, fish diseases, and business helpful. Job involves outdoor work.

In Mark Twain's *Huckleberry Finn,* Huck recalls fixing breakfast for his friend and himself. "I fetched meal and bacon and coffee and coffeepot and frying pan and sugar and tin cups. . . . I catched a good big catfish, too, and Jim cleaned him with his knife and fried him." In early America, when you sat down to a tasty fish dinner, it meant that somebody had had good luck fishing that day. Now, however, chances are that the fish you ate recently was raised and bred on a fish farm. **Fish farmers** throughout America raise catfish, salmon, trout, bass, and other types of fish to be sold at a profit to restaurants and markets.

At a fish farm, farmers begin by stripping eggs from female fish. They place them in moist pans, where they fertilize them with sperm cells from male fish. The fertilized eggs are then kept warm to ensure growth. When the fish hatch and grow to be as long as a person's finger, they are called fingerlings and are moved to rearing ponds until fully grown.

If fish farming interests you and you live in an area that will support some type of fish farming, you can learn more by writing to the Marine Resources Research Institute, South Carolina Wildlife and Marine Resources Department, P.O. Box 12559, Charleston, SC 29412.

Figure 11-21 *The Ridley turtle* (left) *and giant tortoise* (right) *are examples of reptiles with shells. Turtles spend most of their time in water, while tortoises spend most of their time on land.*

offer some protection, they are heavy and slow the animals down. The backbones of these reptiles are fused to their top shell. Turtles and tortoises have no teeth. They have beaks that are similar in structure to the beaks of birds. Many turtles and tortoises eat plants as well as animals.

Turtles and tortoises can live for a very long time. The Galapagos tortoise, for example, may live for as long as 200 years. When sailors first discovered these animals, they captured them and brought them back to their ships. The animals were kept alive and used as a source of fresh meat on long ocean voyages.

A sea turtle called the green turtle is among the most outstanding navigators in the animal kingdom. Soon after the turtle eggs hatch, perhaps on a beach in Brazil, the young turtles head for the ocean. There they wander for many years over thousands of square kilometers. Eventually, the turtles mature and mate. Now they are ready to lay their own eggs. Where do these turtles go? Back to the same beach where they were born!

That beach may be hundreds of kilometers away, across an ocean surface that has no road signs or other markings. Yet the turtles find their way home. How? No one knows. And here is another fascinating mystery. No matter how far they spread out

Figure 11-22 *How can you tell the difference between an alligator and a crocodile? An alligator has a broad snout* (left). *A crocodile has a narrower snout. When a crocodile closes its mouth, another basic difference can be seen. Some of its bottom teeth are visible* (right).

through the ocean, turtles born on a particular beach find one another in the ocean and return together to that beach. One scientist observed a huge group of green turtles in a line that stretched for more than 100 kilometers. Each turtle was almost exactly 200 meters ahead of the next!

Alligators and Crocodiles

To most people, alligators and crocodiles are very similar in appearance. Actually there are some differences. The snout of an alligator is broader than the snout of a crocodile, which is narrower and more pointed. When a crocodile's mouth is closed, some of its bottom teeth are visible. When an alligator closes its mouth, none of its teeth are visible. Most people, of course, do not feel the need to examine the mouth of either of these animals closely enough to tell them apart!

Alligators and crocodiles spend most of the time submerged in water with only their eyes and nostrils showing above the surface. Both kinds of animals eat meat. Their diet consists mainly of fish and other animals that venture too close to their large mouths.

Alligators and crocodiles have unusual reproductive behavior. The female alligator builds a nest of rotting plants in which to lay her eggs. The rotting plants give off heat as they decompose. This heat keeps the eggs warm and helps them to develop. The alligators inside the eggs make low chirping sounds when they are about to hatch. The sounds

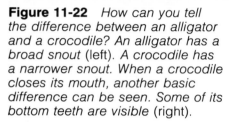

Activity

A Symbiotic Relationship

Look for information and write a short paragraph on the relationship between the Egyptian plover and the Nile crocodile.

are heard by the mother, who has remained nearby guarding her eggs. When she hears the hatchlings, she uncovers the eggs. The tiny alligators, looking like small copies of their parents, come out into the world. The female continues to care for the young for some time after they hatch. The male alligator also helps care for the young. This behavior is unlike the behavior of most reptiles, which usually leave their eggs after they are laid. Their young must care for themselves as soon as they hatch.

SECTION REVIEW

1. What is an important difference between the egg of an amphibian and the egg of a reptile?
2. How are the legs of a turtle different from the legs of a tortoise?

11-4   Birds

For many people, birds are the most fascinating and colorful animals on earth. Birds, along with bats and insects, are the only animals with the power of flight, although not all species of birds do fly.

The earliest known bird lived more than 150 million years ago, during a time when reptiles like the dinosaurs ruled the earth. In fact, this early bird had many of the characteristics of reptiles. For example, it had a long bony tail and sharp teeth. Modern birds have neither of these. However, there is no doubt that this early flying creature was a bird. For fossil evidence shows it had feathers, a characteristic that only birds have. If you look at a modern bird, you will notice another characteristic in common with reptiles. Birds have scales on their legs.

Birds are warmblooded vertebrates that have wings and a body covered with feathers. Warmblooded animals have the ability to maintain a constant body temperature despite the temperature of their environment. The penguins in Figure 11-23 are able to trap their own body heat under an insulating coat of feathers. Thus, the penguins can withstand very cold temperatures. However,

Figure 11-23 *Birds have feathers and are warmblooded. These penguins can withstand the cold of Antarctica because they are insulated by a coat of feathers.*

to maintain a high body temperature birds must consume a great deal of food for energy. For the penguins, that means eating a lot of fish.

Types of Birds

Birds can be divided into four main groups: perching birds, water birds, birds of prey, and flightless birds. The perching birds are perhaps the most familiar. These birds have feet that are adapted for perching. Their feet can easily grasp a branch. Cardinals, robins, and sparrows are perching birds. The beaks of some of these birds may be long and thin like the beak of the hummingbird. This beak enables hummingbirds to reach deep into flowers for nectar. Other perching birds have beaks that are adapted for cracking seeds or catching insects. The macaw, a kind of parrot, has a beak that is strong enough to crack open tough Brazil nuts. The woodpecker has a beak that can open the bark of trees where insects, the food of woodpeckers, live.

Water birds have feet that are adapted for swimming. Ducks and geese are water birds with feet that resemble paddles. These birds glide across the surface of the water looking for food. All water birds can fly as well as swim.

Birds of prey are superb fliers and also have keen eyesight. Soaring high in the air, they can spot prey on the ground or in the water far beneath them. Birds of prey eat small animals including fish, reptiles, and other birds. Some, such as a certain eagle, even eat small monkeys.

Birds of prey are able to fly very fast. The peregrine falcon has been clocked at more than 125 kilometers per hour while diving at its prey. Birds of prey have sharp claws called **talons** on their toes. Talons enable the bird to grasp and hold its prey. Some eagles have talons that are longer than the fangs of a lion. Birds of prey also have strong, curved beaks that are used to tear their prey into pieces small enough to be swallowed.

The flightless birds include the ostrich of Africa, the largest bird alive today; the rhea of South America; and the emu and cassowary of Australia. Also included in this group are penguins, flightless birds that are able to "fly" through the water. All of these

Figure 11-24 *Perching birds, such as this macaw, live on land and spend their lives in trees or other high places when they are not flying. Macaws are members of the parrot family.*

Figure 11-25 *The paddlelike feet of the wood duck* (top left) *enable it to swim in water. The bald eagle* (bottom left) *has keen eyesight, sharp bill, and talons, or curved claws, for grasping prey. A road runner* (right) *can run as fast as 24 kilometers per hour.*

birds have small wings relative to the size of their bodies. All flightless birds except penguins have strong leg muscles that enable the birds to run quickly. These birds also use their strong legs for defense, kicking viciously at any enemy foolish enough to challenge them.

Adaptations for Flight

Birds have light, hollow bones—certainly an advantage to any flying animal. Birds are also covered with feathers. They usually have large feathers on their wings. These feathers provide lift, much as an airplane's wings lift it off the ground.

The feathers on the wings and most of the bird's body feathers are called **contour feathers.** These feathers are the largest and most familiar feathers. They give birds their streamlined shape. Other feathers, called **down feathers,** are short and fuzzy

Figure 11-26 *Male peacocks are famous for their beautiful tail feathers. They display these feathers to attract females.*

and act as insulation. Most birds have down feathers on their breasts. Down feathers are also found covering young birds after they hatch, but before contour feathers have grown in.

Breeding Habits and Development

Many birds have interesting behaviors. Bird songs are used to establish a territory, an area where the bird lives. The song chases other birds of the same species away. Establishing a territory is important because it ensures that few birds will compete for food and living space in the same area.

The bright feathers of some male birds are used to attract females. However, brightly colored feathers also make the bird more obvious to predators. So many birds sport bright colors only during the breeding season.

Some birds attract a mate by constructing a large and colorful nesting site. Male bowerbirds use bits of colorful material to call attention to themselves and thereby attract a mate. The male penguin, on the other hand, does not construct a colorful structure. Instead, he presents his intended mate with a pebble. The pebble indicates that he is ready to breed and care for a youngster.

Most birds build nests. These nests can be little more than a space hollowed out in the ground, or they can be quite elaborate like the nest of the weaver, which is actually more like a crowded apartment house in a big city. All of these structures are designed to protect the eggs and the young birds as they develop.

Figure 11-27 *Birds are the most famous nest-builders. Weavers use their feet and bills to weave their enclosed nests of grass. These nests hang from tree branches.*

Unlike a reptile's egg, a bird's egg is encased within a hard, strong shell. The shell protects the developing bird and contains food for the bird. The shell, while seemingly quite solid, allows oxygen to pass into the egg and carbon dioxide to pass out.

Most birds incubate their eggs by sitting on them. This behavior keeps the eggs warm as the young develop. However, the penguin keeps its single egg warm by balancing it on the top of its feet and pressing down on the egg with its abdomen. The egg never rests on the cold ground.

Among birds, sometimes only one parent will incubate the eggs. In other species, both parents take turns incubating the eggs. After the eggs hatch, the young birds are quite helpless. They cannot fly to look for food. Their parents must bring them food and water until they are old enough to fly and take care of themselves.

Migration

Many birds **migrate,** or move to a new environment, during the course of a year. Some birds migrate over tremendous distances. For example, the American golden plover flies more than 25,000 kilometers when it migrates. Birds migrate for many reasons, but perhaps the most important reason is to follow seasonal food supplies.

Some birds fly south in the winter in search of food. The whooping crane, for example, flies south from its nesting area in Canada to winter on the Texas shore. Birds have developed extremely accurate mechanisms for migrating. Scientists have learned that some birds navigate, or find their way, by observing the sun and other stars. Other birds follow coastlines or other natural formations such as mountain ranges. Still other birds are believed to have magnetic centers in their brain. These centers act like a compass to help the bird find its way.

SECTION REVIEW

1. How do bird legs resemble lizard legs?
2. What are the four main categories of birds?
3. List three possible ways birds may navigate across great distances.

Figure 11-28 *Young birds are quite helpless. Their parents must bring them food and water until they are able to fly.*

Activity

Bird Watching

Many people find bird watching a relaxing, enjoyable activity. Obtain a field guide to birds from the library. See if you can borrow a pair of binoculars. Then, early in the morning, see how many kinds of birds you can identify in your neighborhood. Make a list of those you spot. Check your list in different seasons to see if it changes.

LABORATORY ACTIVITY

Classifying Vertebrate Bones in Owl Pellets

Purpose

In this activity, you will identify undigested bones of small vertebrates present in a pellet coughed up by an owl.

Materials (*per group*)

Owl pellet
Metal dissecting needle or small spatula
Magnifying glass
Small metric ruler
Pencil and paper

Procedure

1. Observe the outside of an owl pellet and record your observations.
2. Gently break the pellet into two pieces.
3. Using a metal dissecting needle or small spatula, separate any bones and fur from the pellet. Also remove all fur from any skulls found in the pellet.
4. Group similar bones together in a pile. For example, put all skull bones in one group. Observe the skulls. Record the length, number, shape, and color of their teeth.
5. Now try to fit together bones from the different piles to form complete skeletons.

Observations and Conclusions

1. On the basis of your observations of the skulls, use the chart to identify the kinds of animals eaten by the owl.
2. What are the functions of the different bones you found?

Shrew	Upper jaw has at least 18 teeth. Skull length is 23 mm or less. Teeth are brown.
House Mouse	Upper jaw has 2 biting teeth. Upper jaw extends past lower jaw. Skull length is 22 mm or less.
Meadow Vole	Upper jaw has 2 biting teeth. Upper jaw does not extend past lower jaw. Molar teeth are flat.
Mole	Upper jaw has at least 18 teeth. Skull length is 23 mm or more.
Rat	Upper jaw has 2 biting teeth. Upper jaw extends past lower jaw. Skull length is 22 mm or more.

CHAPTER REVIEW

SUMMARY

11-1 Fish

- All vertebrates, including fish, have a backbone made up of bones called vertebrae. The backbone is part of their internal skeleton.

- Jawless fish, such as the lamprey, are the most primitive fish.

- Like that of jawless fish, the skeleton of cartilaginous fish is made of flexible cartilage, rather than hard bone. Examples of cartilaginous fish are sharks, skates, and rays.

- Bony fish have a swim bladder that allows them to float at different levels in the water, even when asleep.

11-2 Amphibians

- The term "amphibian" means "double life." Amphibians spend part of their lives on land and part in water.

- The eggs of amphibians do not have hard shells. They must be laid in water or they will dry out.

- Frog and toad eggs hatch into tadpoles. Tadpoles have gills and a tail.

- As adults, frogs and toads develop lungs and legs. The powerful hind legs of these animals allow them to leap great distances.

- Like frogs and toads, salamanders and newts have two pairs of legs.

- Salamanders and newts are examples of amphibians with tails.

11-3 Reptiles

- The eggs of reptiles have leathery shells and will not dry out when laid on land.

- Most snakes are nonpoisonous. However, those snakes which are poisonous inject their venom through special teeth called fangs.

- Snakes and lizards are covered with a scaly skin. They must shed their skins to grow larger.

- Turtles are adapted for a life in the water. Tortoises are adapted for a life on land.

- Alligators have a broader snout than do crocodiles.

11-4 Birds

- Birds, along with bats and insects, are the only animals that can fly.

- The four main groups of birds are perching birds, water birds, birds of prey, and flightless birds.

- The beaks of many birds are adapted for the kinds of foods they eat.

- Contour feathers give birds their streamlined appearance. Down feathers act as insulation.

- Birds have many ways to attract a mate, including songs, brightly colored feathers, and unusual nests.

- Many birds migrate long distances in search of food and warm climates.

VOCABULARY

Define each term in a complete sentence.

cartilage	hibernation	swim bladder	venom
contour feather	migrate	talon	vertebra
down feather			

CONTENT REVIEW: MULTIPLE CHOICE

Choose the letter of the answer that best completes each statement.

1. All vertebrates have
   a. an exoskeleton.   b. an internal skeleton.
   c. scales.   d. a bony skeleton.
2. The fins of fish help them
   a. steer.   b. swim upright.
   c. move through the water.   d. all of these.
3. Cartilaginous fish do *not* include
   a. cod.   b. sharks.   c. rays.   d. skates.
4. Tadpoles are the early stage of
   a. reptiles.   b. frogs.   c. newts.   d. salamanders.
5. Amphibians with tails include
   a. frogs.   b. toads.   c. newts.   d. lizards.
6. During a frog's life, it breathes through its
   a. skin.   b. gills.   c. lungs.   d. all of these.
7. A snake *not* native to the U.S. is the
   a. coral snake.   b. cobra.   c. copperhead.   d. rattlesnake.
8. One kind of poisonous reptile is the
   a. turtle.   b. chameleon.   c. Gila monster.   d. crocodile.
9. Modern birds and reptiles have
   a. feathers.   b. teeth.   c. bony tail.   d. scales on legs.
10. Which are warmblooded?
    a. fish   b. birds   c. reptiles   d. amphibians

CONTENT REVIEW: COMPLETION

Fill in the word or words that best complete each statement.

1. The bones that make up a vertebrate's backbone are called _____.
2. The backbone helps protect the nerves of the _____.
3. Fish are able to float at different levels in the water because of a structure called the _____.
4. The term _____ means "double life."
5. During the cold winter, frogs can go into a winter sleep called _____.
6. The peeps and grunts of male frogs are used to attract _____.
7. The poison injected by certain snakes is called _____.
8. The sparrow is a kind of _____ bird.
9. _____ feathers act as insulation for birds.
10. Many birds _____ to warmer climates in the winter.

CONTENT REVIEW: TRUE OR FALSE

Determine whether each statement is true or false. If it is true, write "true." If it is false, change the underlined word or words to make the statement true.

1. <u>Jawless</u> fish have a hard, bony skeleton.
2. The lamprey is a kind of <u>bony</u> fish.

3. Most fish <u>can</u> live in both fresh and salt water.
4. Amphibians live in a <u>dry</u> environment.
5. The <u>front</u> legs of a <u>toad</u> are very powerful and help the toad jump.
6. The tongue of a frog is attached to the <u>front</u> of its mouth.
7. In reptiles, a system of <u>external</u> fertilization has developed.
8. <u>Tortoises</u> are well adapted to a life in the water.
9. Penguins are a kind of <u>flightless</u> bird.
10. <u>Contour</u> feathers provide insulation for birds.

CONCEPT REVIEW: SKILL BUILDING

Use the skills you have developed in the chapter to complete each activity.

1. **Applying definitions** Are you a warm-blooded or a coldblooded vertebrate? Explain your answer.
2. **Classifying vertebrates** In the woods, you discover a small four-legged, cold-blooded vertebrate. How can you tell whether it is an amphibian or a reptile?
3. **Relating facts** There are no frogs living in Antarctica. Explain why.
4. **Making inferences** The sturgeon, a bony fish, can lay up to 6 million eggs. Why do you think it is necessary for most fish to produce so many eggs?
5. **Relating concepts** The poisonous coral snake has alternating bands of black, bright red, and bright yellow. The harmless scarlet king snake has a very similar color pattern. Why is this distinctive pattern an advantage to the king snake?
6. **Developing a hypothesis** A fish has light coloring on its bottom surface and dark coloring on its top surface. Explain how this coloration could be an advantage to the fish.
7. **Applying concepts** Scientists think that amphibians may have developed from a fishlike ancestor. What characteristics of amphibians provide evidence for such a belief?
8. **Relating facts** When a raccoon catches a toad, it usually wipes the amphibian along the ground before eating it. Suggest a reason for this strange behavior.
9. **Designing an experiment** A scientist wants to know if turtles can detect sound. Design an experiment that she can use. Be sure to include a variable and a control in your experiment.

CONCEPT REVIEW: ESSAY

Discuss each of the following in a brief paragraph.

1. Describe the three types of fish.
2. Because the skins of alligators make excellent leather, these animals have been hunted almost to the point of extinction. Do you think such animals should be protected from hunters? Or do people have a right to hunt all animals, even if they are endangered?
3. Why are reptiles able to live in dry environments when amphibians are not?
4. What are the different mechanisms birds may use to navigate long distances?
5. Describe the life cycle of a frog.
6. What are two adaptations that enable birds to fly?
7. Vertebrates that reproduce by internal fertilization usually produce fewer eggs than do animals that reproduce by external fertilization. Explain why.

12 Mammals

CHAPTER SECTIONS

12-1 Characteristics of Mammals
12-2 Egg-Laying Mammals
12-3 Pouched Mammals
12-4 Placental Mammals

CHAPTER OBJECTIVES

*After completing this chapter,
you will be able to:*

12-1 List the main characteristics
of mammals.

12-2 Describe the characteristics
of egg-laying mammals.

12-3 Describe the characteristics
of pouched mammals

12-4 Describe the characteristics
of placental mammals.

12-4 Name ten groups of placental
mammals and give an exam-
ple of each.

Imagine yourself living in London at the end of the eighteenth century. In the newspaper, the headline "Explorers Discover Strange Creature in Australia" catches your eye. As you read on, you find out that when the first dried skins of the creature arrived at London's Natural History Museum, they were thought to be fakes. The creature had thick fur, webbed feet, and a beak like a duck's. No one had ever seen such a strange animal!

Years later, when English scientists examined the complete body of this creature, they discovered it was not a fake. The creature was real, no matter how strange it looked. But what was it? It had a bill like a bird's, feet like a frog's, and fur like a beaver's. Moreover, it laid eggs and fed its young milk. As hard as it might be for you to believe, scientists decided that the mysterious creature belonged to a certain group of animals called mammals, which includes lions, dogs, and people!

When it came time to decide what to call this weird animal, scientists searched for a name that would describe its strange features. First, the animal was called a platypus (PLAT-uh-puhs), which means "flat-footed." Soon after, scientists discovered that this name had already been given to a flat-footed beetle. Scientists made the name more descriptive and called it duck-billed platypus.

Duckbilled platypus

12-1 Characteristics of Mammals

A few hundred meters off the coast of California, a small group of animals playfully swim around one another. These whiskered animals are called sea otters. Sea otters spend most of their lives swimming in the ocean. While lying on its back, a sea otter can pound a closed shell against a rock balanced on its chest. The sea otter uses the rock to crack open the shell so that it can eat what is inside.

The sea otter seems rather intelligent. To prevent itself from being swept away by waves, the sea otter wraps itself in strands of giant seaweed growing offshore. The otter uses the seaweed much as an ocean liner uses giant ropes to hold itself close to a pier.

Sea otters belong to a group of vertebrates called mammals. There are about 4000 kinds of mammals on the earth. In addition to sea otters, duckbilled platypuses, lions, dogs, and people, this group also includes such animals as whales, bats, and elephants. Since scientists group together animals that have common characteristics, you might wonder what such different-looking animals could have in common.

Mammals have characteristics that set them apart from all other living things. **Mammals are warm-blooded vertebrates that have hair and feed their young with milk produced in mammary glands.** In fact, the word "mammal" comes from the term

Figure 12-1 *The sea otter spends most of its time lying on its back in the cold waters of the North Pacific Ocean. The otter uses the rock balanced on its chest to crack open clams.*

Figure 12-2 *As with most mammals, a thick coat of hair covers the body and provides warmth for llamas.*

mammary gland. Another special characteristic of mammals is that they give their young more care and protection than do other animals.

At one time during their lives, all mammals possess fur or hair. The fur or hair, if it is thick enough, acts as insulation and enables some mammals to survive in very cold parts of the world. Mammals also can survive in harsh climates because, like birds, mammals are warmblooded. The body temperature of mammals remains almost unchanged no matter how the temperature of their surroundings may change.

Mammals are believed to be the most intelligent animals on the earth. This intelligence comes from a brain that is better developed than that of any other group of animals. Human beings, for example, have the most well-developed brain of all mammals and are considered to be the most intelligent of living things.

As in reptiles and birds, fertilization in mammals is internal. But despite the characteristics that all mammals have in common, their young develop in different ways. This difference can be used to place mammals into three basic groups: egg-laying mammals, pouched mammals, and placental mammals.

SECTION REVIEW

1. List the main characteristics of mammals.
2. What substance is produced by mammary glands?

Activity

Pet Mammals

If you have a pet cat, dog, mouse, gerbil, guinea pig, horse, or pig, then your pet belongs to the class Mammalia. Make observations of your pet mammal for a few days. On a sheet of paper, make a list of your pet's behaviors. Next to each item, record what the behavior means to you. Do you think other animals of the same species behave the same way? How could you go about finding out if they do?

Vertebrates have well-developed body systems. However, these systems are not the same in all vertebrates. Choose one of the systems listed below. Use posterboard and colored pencils to draw and label how a particular system changes from fish to amphibians to reptiles to birds to mammals.

nervous system
digestive system
circulatory system
reproductive system
excretory system

12-2 Egg-Laying Mammals

A strange-looking animal called the spiny anteater lives in Australia. It has long claws, a tubelike nose, fur, and short, stiff spines like those of a porcupine. See Figure 12-3. What makes the spiny anteater even stranger is that although it is a mammal, it lays eggs! **Mammals that lay eggs are called monotremes.** The spiny anteater and the duckbilled platypus are the world's only **monotremes.**

Just after the female spiny anteater lays her eggs, she places them into a pouch on her abdomen. The eggs hatch in seven to ten days. The young spiny anteaters feed on milk produced by their mother's mammary glands. Milk production, you may recall, is characteristic of mammals.

The female platypus lays her one to three eggs in a burrow that she digs in the side of a stream bank. She stays with the eggs to keep them warm until they hatch. After the eggs hatch, the young platypuses feed on milk produced by their mother.

The unusual body parts of the spiny anteater help it gather its food, which consists of ants and termites. For example, its nose holds a sticky, wormlike

Figure 12-3 *This porcupinelike animal is actually a spiny anteater. Unlike all other kinds of mammals, the spiny anteater and the duckbilled platypus do not give birth to live young. Instead, they lay eggs that have a leathery shell.*

tongue that flips out to catch insects. When in danger, the spiny anteater uses its short powerful legs and curved claws to dig a hole in the ground and cover itself until only its spines are showing. These 6-centimeter-long spines scare almost any enemy!

Just as the spiny anteaters have special structures to search for and eat insects on land, the duckbilled platypus has special structures for hunting small animals under water. The platypus is a very good swimmer that has webbed paws and waterproof fur. When underwater, the platypus keeps its eyes closed and uses its soft bill to feel around for snails, mussels, worms, and sometimes small fishes.

SECTION REVIEW

1. What is another name for egg-laying mammals?
2. Name the two egg-laying mammals.

12-3 Pouched Mammals

Mammals with pouches are called marsupials. Most people think of a **marsupial** (mahr-soo-pee-uhl) as a kangaroo. But kangaroos are not the only marsupials. Some marsupials resemble weasels or

Figure 12-4 *The bandicoot* (left) *and wombat* (right) *are examples of marsupials, or pouched mammals. These mammals live in Australia or nearby islands.*

Figure 12-5 *The young of some marsupials, such as the koala, hitch rides on their mother's back.*

Figure 12-6 *The most familiar marsupial is the kangaroo. A baby kangaroo, called a joey, rests in its mother's pouch.*

teddy bears. There are also marsupials that look like rats and mice.

One of the cuddliest and cutest of marsupials is the koala (koh-AH-luh). See Figure 12-5. The koala's ears are big and round and are covered by thick fur. Unlike most marsupials, the opening of the koala's pouch faces its hind legs rather than its head. Eucalyptus leaves are about the only type of food that koalas eat. Oils from these leaves are an ingredient in cough drops. So you should not be surprised to learn that koalas actually smell like cough drops! Because koalas eat only plant material, they are called **herbivores** (HER-buh-vorz).

Kangaroos

"At best it resembles a jumping mouse but it is much larger." These words were spoken in 1770 by the famous English explorer James Cook. He was describing an animal never before seen by Europeans. He later gave the name "kangaroo" to this strange animal.

Kangaroos live in the forests and grasslands of Australia. They have short front legs but long, muscular hind legs and tails. The tail helps the kangaroo to keep its balance and to push itself forward.

When a kangaroo is born, it is only 2 centimeters long and cannot hear or see. Although the kangaroo is only partially developed at birth, its front legs enable it to crawl as much as 30 centimeters to its mother's pouch. How the newborn kangaroo finds its way is a mystery. It would be like a person being blindfolded and earplugged and placed in the center of a strange room the size of half a football field. The person would then be asked to find a single doorway on the first try. After the young kangaroo crawls into the pouch, it stays there for about nine months, feeding on its mother's milk.

Opossums

Have you ever heard the phrase "playing possum" and wondered what it meant? When in danger, opossums lie perfectly still, pretending to be dead. In some unknown way, this behavior helps to protect the opossum from its predators.

Figure 12-7 *The only marsupial that is native to North America is the opossum. Young opossums cling to their mother as she moves from place to place.*

The opossum is the only marsupial found in North America. It lives in trees, often hanging onto branches with its long tail. Opossums eat fruits, insects, and other small animals.

Female opossums may give birth to as many as 24 opossums at one time. Opossums are partially developed at birth and crawl along their mother's abdomen to her pouch. The newborn opossums are so tiny that all 24 of them could fit into a single teaspoon!

SECTION REVIEW

1. What is a marsupial? Give two examples.
2. What is an herbivore?
3. Name the only North American marsupial.

12-4   Placental Mammals

Figure 12-8 *Like all mammals, placental mammals feed their young with milk from mammary glands.*

Unlike those of egg-laying and pouched mammals, the young of placental mammals develop totally within the female. The females in this group of mammals have **placentas** (pluh-SEN-tuhz). The placenta is a structure through which the developing young receive food and oxygen while in the mother's body. The placenta also removes wastes from the developing young. After they give birth, female placental mammals, like all mammals, supply their young with milk from mammary glands.

There are more than 20 groups of placental mammals. They are grouped according to how they

Figure 12-9 *Mammals that give birth to well-developed young are called placental mammals. Grizzly bears are examples of placental mammals.*

eat, how they move about, or where they live. Of these groups, ten are discussed in the sections that follow.

Insect-Eating Mammals

What has a nose with 22 tentacles and spends half its time in water? If you have given up, the answer is the star-nosed mole. The star-nosed mole gets its name from the ring of 22 tentacles on the end of its nose. See Figure 12-10. No other mammal has this structure. Each tentacle has very sensitive feelers, which enable the mole to find insects to eat and to feel its way around. Even though these moles have eyes, they are too tiny to see anything. The star-nosed mole spends part of its day burrowing beneath the ground and the other part of the day in the water. Star-nosed moles are found in northeastern United States and eastern Canada.

In addition to moles, hedgehogs and shrews are also insect-eating mammals. Because they are covered with spines, hedgehogs look like walking cactuses. When threatened by predators, hedgehogs roll up into a ball with only their spines showing. This action makes the hedgehog's enemy a little less enthusiastic about disturbing the tiny animal.

One type of shrew is the smallest mammal in the world. This animal, called the pygmy shrew, weighs

Figure 12-10 *The star-nosed mole has 22 tentacles, or feelers, at the end of its nose. This tiny insect-eating mammal lives in moist or muddy soil in parts of eastern North America.*

only 1.5 to 2 grams—as an adult! Because shrews are so active, they must eat large amounts of food to maintain their energy. Shrews can eat twice their own weight in insects each day!

Flying Mammals

Bats look like mice and are the only flying mammals. In fact, the German word for bat is "Fledermaus," which means flying mouse. Bats are able to fly because they have skin stretched over their arms and fingers, which form wings. Other mammals such as the flying squirrels do not really fly. They simply glide to the ground after leaping from high places.

Although a bat's eyesight is poor, its hearing is excellent. While flying, bats give off high-pitched squeaks that people cannot hear. These squeaks bounce off nearby objects and return to the bat as

Figure 12-11 *Insect-eating mammals include the hedgehog* (left) *and shrew* (right). *The hedgehog curls up into a ball when threatened by predators. To keep healthy, shrews must eat twice their weight in insects each day.*

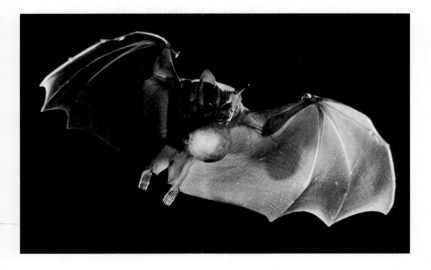

Figure 12-12 *Bats are the only flying mammals. This fruit-eating bat is carrying a fig in its mouth.*

Figure 12-13 *Although most mammals are herbivores, or plant eaters, some are carnivores, or flesh eaters. Flesh eaters have large pointed teeth called canines. Walruses have especially large canines, called tusks.*

Activity

The Fastest Runner

The cheetah is the fastest land animal and can run at speeds of up to 100 kilometers per hour. How far can it run in a second?

echoes. By listening to these echoes, the bat knows where objects are. Bats that hunt insects such as moths also use this method to find their prey.

There are two types of bats: fruit eaters and insect eaters. Fruit-eating bats are found in tropical areas, such as Africa, Australia, India, and the Orient. Insect-eating bats live almost everywhere.

Flesh-Eating Mammals

The ground is frozen solid with ice. Great icebergs move slowly in the sea. The shoreline is almost impossible to see through the ice and snow. The chilling wind makes the air feel colder than it already is. Yet, even in this brutal Arctic environment, there is life. In the distance, a group of walruses pull themselves out of the water onto a sheet of floating ice. As they stretch out on the ice, these large animals resemble sunbathers on a beach.

The frozen sheets of ice and freezing waters of the Arctic are home for the walruses. They are able to live in this freezing environment because they have a layer of fat, called blubber, under their skin that keeps body heat in. In addition to their large size, another very noticeable feature of walruses is their long ivory tusks. These tusks are really special teeth called **canines** (KAY-nighns) that point downward and may grow to 100 centimeters in length.

You also have canines; two in your top set of teeth and two on the bottom. To locate your upper canines, look at your top set of teeth in a mirror. Find your **incisors** (in-SIGH-zers). They are your four front teeth, which are used for biting. On one side of the incisors is a tooth that comes to a point. These teeth are your canines.

Unlike most flesh-eating mammals, walruses do not use their canines for tearing and shredding meat. Instead, the walruses use their tusks to defend themselves from polar bears. The walruses also use their tusks as hooks to help them when climbing onto ice.

All of the mammals in this group, including the walruses, are **carnivores** (KAR-ni-vorz), or flesh eaters. Carnivores are predators. Most carnivores, such as lions, wolves, and bears, have very muscular legs that help them to chase other animals. Carnivores

also have sharp claws on their toes to help them hold their prey. Most land-living carnivores include any members of the dog, cat, and bear families. Sea-living carnivores include otters, sea lions, and seals.

Figure 12-14 *Although most mammals run from a predator, this baboon battles a leopard face to face.*

Career: *Animal Technician*

> **HELP WANTED: ANIMAL TECHNICIAN** Completion of a two-year animal technology program required. Experience handling animals and knowledge of laboratory procedures desirable. Needed to assist veterinarian.

A veterinarian and assistant are called to a farm to treat a horse. The horse had difficulty chewing and swallowing and now is shaking violently. The veterinarian discovers that the horse was injured by a nail sticking out of a board in the horse's stall.

The vet's assistant prepares the medicine that will make the horse well. Then the vet injects the medicine into the horse. The assistant records the visit.

The vet's assistant is an **animal technician,** someone who has had training in assisting vets and working in laboratories and animal research. They work on farms, in kennels and pounds, in hospitals, and in laboratories.

Animal technicians must work under the supervision and instruction of a veterinarian. An animal technician's duties include record keeping, specimen collection, laboratory work, and

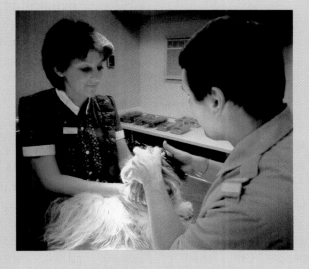

wound dressing. They also help with animals and equipment during surgery.

Patience, compassion, and a willingness to be involved with animal health care are important qualities for one interested in becoming an animal technician. To receive more information about this career, write to the American Veterinary Medical Association, 930 North Meacham Road, Schaumburg, IL 60196.

Figure 12-15 *The armor-plated armadillo* (left) *and two-toed sloth* (right) *are examples of toothless mammals.*

Activity

Useful Mammals

Visit your library to find out which mammals have benefited people. On a sheet of paper, make a list of these mammals. Beside each mammal, indicate how it benefited people. Discuss with your class whether the uses listed have been harmful, helpful, or had no effect upon the mammal. Was it necessary for people to use these mammals for their own survival?

"Toothless" Mammals

Although "true" anteaters belong to this group of mammals, they are the only members of the group that actually have no teeth. The other members, the armadillos and the sloths, have poorly developed teeth.

Unlike the spiny anteaters mentioned earlier in this chapter, the true anteater does not lay eggs. The young remain inside the female until they are fully developed. However, both types of anteaters have something in common—a long, sticky tongue that is used to catch insects.

The second group of "toothless" mammals are the armadillos. They live in the southern parts of the United States and in Central and South America. These mammals eat plants, insects, and small animals. The most striking feature of the armadillo is its protective, armorlike coat. In fact, the word "armadillo" comes from Spanish, meaning armored.

A type of armadillo called the nine-banded armadillo is the only "toothless" mammal found as far north as the United States. Its special feature is that the female always gives birth to identical quadruplets! This means that the four young are always the same sex and are exactly alike.

Sloths are the third type of "toothless" mammals. There are two kinds of sloths: the two-toed sloth and the three-toed sloth. They eat leaves and fruits and are extremely slow-moving creatures. Sloths spend most of their lives hanging upside down in trees. They can spend up to 19 hours a day resting in this position.

Trunk-Nosed Mammals

Holding its trunk high in the air, the elephant moves clumsily into the deep river. Little by little, the water seems to creep up the elephant's body. Will it drown? The answer comes a few seconds later as the huge animal actually begins to swim!

To an observer on the shore, nothing can be seen of the elephant except its trunk, through which the animal breathes in air. The trunk is the distinguishing feature of all elephants. And it is an amazingly complicated structure whose many kinds of movements are controlled by no fewer than 40,000 muscles!

Elephant trunks are powerful enough to tear large branches from trees. Yet the same trunk is capable of very delicate movements, such as picking up a single peanut thrown by a child at a zoo. These movements are made possible by the work of those 40,000 muscles and the brain that directs them.

Elephants are the largest land animals. There are two kinds of elephants: African and Asiatic. As their names suggest, African elephants live in Africa and Asiatic elephants in Asia, especially in India and

Figure 12-16 *Elephants are the only trunk-nosed mammals. The larger ears of the African elephant* (left) *distinguish it from the Asiatic elephant* (right).

Southeast Asia. Although there are a number of differences between the two kinds of elephants, the most obvious one is ear size. The ears of African elephants are much larger than those of their Asiatic cousins.

Hoofed Mammals

What do pigs, camels, horses, and rhinoceroses have in common? No much at first glance. They could not look more different. Yet look again—down where these animals meet the ground—and you see a common characteristic. The feet of these animals end in hoofs—two different kinds of hoofs.

One kind of hoof has an even number of toes and belongs to such mammals as pigs, camels, goats, cows, and the tallest of all mammals, the giraffes. The other kind of hoof has an odd number of toes and belongs to mammals such as horses, rhinoceroses, zebras, and tapirs.

Hoofed animals are among the most important "partners" of human beings and have been so for thousands of years. People eat their meat, drink their milk, wear their skins, ride on them, and use them to pull devices used in farming.

Figure 12-17 *Mammals with hoofs can be even-toed or odd-toed. A giraffe* (left) *has an even number of toes, while the rhinoceros* (top right) *and tapir* (bottom right) *have odd numbers of toes.*

Figure 12-18 *The most numerous of all mammals are the rodents. The harvest mouse (left) is the smallest rodent, while the capybara (right) is the largest.*

Gnawing Mammals

Hardly a day goes by that people in the country or even in cities do not see a gnawing mammal. There are more gnawing mammals than any others on earth. These mammals are commonly known as rodents.

Among the rodents are such animals as squirrels, beavers, chipmunks, rats, mice, and porcupines. As you might guess, what they have in common has something to do with the way they eat—by gnawing. The common characteristics are four special incisors that are used for gnawing. These teeth are chisel-like and constantly grow for as long as the animal lives. Because rodents gnaw or chew on hard objects such as wood, nuts, and grain, their teeth are worn down as the teeth grow. If this were not the case, a rodent's incisors would grow to be so long that the animal could not open its mouth wide enough to eat.

Some rodents, especially rats and mice, compete with human beings for food. They eat the seeds of plants and many other foods used by people. Rodents also spread serious diseases.

Rodentlike Mammals

Rabbits, hares, and pikas (PIGH-kuhz) belong to the group of rodentlike mammals. These mammals have gnawing teeth, similar to rodents. But unlike rodents, they have a small pair of grinding teeth behind their gnawing teeth. Another difference

Figure 12-19 *A pika is a close relative of the rabbit and hare, which are rodentlike mammals. Pikas live on the sides of mountains where they eat the sparse vegetation.*

Figure 12-20 *Two groups of mammals live in water. One group includes whales such as the baleen whale (left). The other group includes animals called manatees (right). The manatee in this photograph is nursing her calf.*

Activity

Migration of Mammals

Certain mammals migrate, or move, to places that offer better living conditions. Using posterboard and colored pencils, draw maps that trace the migration of the following mammals: North American bat, African zebra, American elk, and gray whale.

At the bottom of each map, give the reasons why each particular mammal migrates. Display these maps on a bulletin board at school.

between these two groups of mammals is that the rodentlike mammals move their jaws from side to side as they chew their food, while rodents move their jaws from front to back as they chew.

Water-Dwelling Mammals

"Thar she blows!" is the traditional cry of a sailor who spots the fountain of water that a whale sends skyward just before it dives. Sailors of the past recognized this sign of a whale, but they did not have the slightest idea that this sea animal was not a fish but a mammal.

Whales, along with dolphins, porpoises, dugongs, and manatees are intelligent. They have hair and feed their young with milk. They are all mammals—mammals that live in water most or all of the time but breathe air. They are also different from one another. Their differences have allowed scientists to place whales, dolphins, and porpoises in one group and manatees and dugongs in a second group.

Animals in the first group spend their entire lives in the ocean. They cannot survive on land. Animals in the second group live in shallower water, often in rivers and canals. They can move around on land but with great difficulty and only for short periods of time when they become stranded.

Primates

On a visit to your local zoo, you come upon a crowd of people standing and laughing in front of one of the cages. Hurrying over to see what the

excitement is about, you hear strange noises. Carefully you make your way to the front of the crowd. What has caused all the excitement and noise? Soon you see a family of chimpanzees entertaining the crowd by running and tumbling around their cage. The baby chimpanzee comes to the front of the cage and extends its hand to you. You are amazed to see how much the chimpanzee's hand looks like yours. It is no wonder they are similar. After all, the chimpanzee along with the gibbon (GIB-uhn), orangutan (oh-RANG-oo-tan), and gorilla are the closest mammals, in structure, to human beings. These mammals, along with baboons, monkeys, and human beings belong to the same group of mammals—the primates.

All primates have eyes that face forward, enabling the animal to see depth. The primates also have five fingers on each hand and five toes on each foot. The fingers are capable of very complicated movements, especially grasping objects.

Primates also have large brains and are the most intelligent of all mammals. There is evidence that chimpanzees can be taught to communicate with people by using a kind of sign language. Some scientists have reported that chimpanzees can *use* tools, such as the use of twigs to remove insects from a log. Human beings, on the other hand, are the only primates that can *make* their own tools.

Figure 12-21 *Chimpanzees* (top left), *gorillas* (top right), *and lemurs* (bottom right) *are all primates. Among the characteristics that primates share are eyes that face forward and hands and feet adapted for grasping.*

SECTION REVIEW

1. What is the placenta?
2. What are canines? Incisors?
3. Define carnivore.

LABORATORY ACTIVITY

Classifying and Comparing Mammals

Purpose

In this activity, you will classify different mammals and compare their characteristics.

Materials *(per group)*

Reference materials that provide information on the 14 major orders of mammals

Pictures of mammals of different orders, cut from magazines and old texts

14 sheets of white construction paper

Tape

TABLE 1

Identification Code	Characteristics	Predicted Order

TABLE 2

Identification Code	Name of Organism	Correct Order

Procedure

1. Using reference books, make a list of the fourteen major orders of mammals and their distinguishing characteristics.
2. Fold each of 14 sheets of construction paper in half along its width.
3. Tape the sides of each sheet, forming a pocket envelope. Do not tape the top of the paper.
4. Study the pictures of mammals provided by your teacher. Each picture should have an identification code.
5. Label each pocket envelope with the name of an order.
6. Place each picture in the envelope you think represents that animal's order.
7. Copy Table 1 on a sheet of paper. Place the identification code from each of your pictures in the proper space.
8. In the second column of the table, fill in the characteristics of each of the animals based on your study of the pictures.
9. Fill in the order in which you classified each of the mammals.
10. Copy Table 2 on the same sheet of paper as Table 1. Check with your teacher to find out the correct order and the name of each mammal. Fill in this information in Table 2. Compare the correct order with your predicted order.

Observations and Conclusions

1. How do the monotremes differ from the marsupials?
2. What distinguishes the marsupials from the other mammals?
3. Which orders of mammals appear most similar? Explain your answer.
4. List the characteristics that all mammals have in common.

CHAPTER REVIEW

SUMMARY

12-1 Characteristics of Mammals

- Mammals are warmblooded vertebrates that have hair or fur.

- Female mammals feed their young milk from mammary glands. Most mammals give their young more care and protection than do other animals.

- Mammals have well-developed brains.

- Mammals can be placed into three basic groups depending upon how their young develop. These groups are the egg-laying mammals, the pouched mammals, and the placental mammals.

12-2 Egg-Laying Mammals

- Like birds and reptiles, monotremes are mammals that lay eggs.

- The spiny anteater and duckbilled platypus are examples of egg-laying mammals.

12-3 Pouched Mammals

- Marsupials are pouched mammals.

- The young of the marsupials are born only partially developed. They further develop in the pouch of their mother.

- The koala, kangaroo, and opossum are examples of marsupials.

12-4 Placental Mammals

- In placental mammals, the placenta provides food for the developing young inside the females.

- There are more than 20 groups of placental mammals.

- Insect-eating mammals include moles, hedgehogs, and shrews.

- Bats are the only flying mammals.

- Flesh-eating mammals, or carnivores, include sea-living animals such as walruses. The land-living carnivores include any members of the dog, cat, and bear families.

- Armadillos, anteaters, and sloths are "toothless" mammals.

- The only members of the trunk-nosed mammal group are the elephants.

- Hoofed mammals are divided into those with an even number of toes on each hoof and those with an odd number of toes. Even-toed mammals include pigs, camels, goats, cows, and giraffes. Odd-toed mammals include horses, rhinoceroses, and tapirs.

- Gnawing mammals, such as beavers, chipmunks, rats, mice, and porcupines, have chisel-like incisors for chewing.

- Rabbits, hares, and pikas are examples of rodentlike mammals.

- Mammals such as whales, dolphins, porpoises, dugongs, and manatees are water-dwelling mammals.

- Human beings, monkeys, and apes are known as primates.

VOCABULARY

Define each term in a complete sentence.

canine
carnivore
herbivore
incisor

mammary gland
marsupial
monotreme
placenta

CONTENT REVIEW: MULTIPLE CHOICE

Choose the letter of the answer that best completes each statement.

1. All mammals have
   a. pouches.   b. well-developed brains.
   c. feathers.   d. fins.
2. The kangaroo is a(n)
   a. pouched mammal.   b. egg-laying mammal.
   c. placental mammal.   d. gnawing mammal.
3. The only North American marsupial is the
   a. kangaroo.   b. koala.   c. platypus.   d. opossum.
4. Young mammals that develop totally within the female belong to the group called
   a. egg-laying mammals.   b. pouched mammals.
   c. placental mammals.   d. marsupial mammals.
5. Which is an insect-eating mammal?
   a. whale   b. elephant   c. bear   d. mole
6. Teeth used for tearing and shredding food are
   a. carnivores.   b. canines.   c. incisors.   d. all of these.
7. A "toothless" mammal is the
   a. skunk.   b. mole.   c. armadillo.   d. camel.
8. The largest land animal is the
   a. blue whale.   b. rhinoceros.   c. elephant.   d. giraffe.
9. An example of a water-dwelling mammal is the
   a. spiny anteater.   b. dolphin.   c. shrew.   d. elephant.
10. Human beings belong to a group of mammals called the
    a. insect-eating mammals.   b. rodents.
    c. primates.   d. carnivores.

CONTENT REVIEW: COMPLETION

Fill in the word or words that best complete each statement.

1. Mammals are a group of _____ blooded vertebrates.
2. Female mammals feed their young with milk from _____.
3. An egg-laying mammal that is covered with spines is the _____.
4. The internal structure through which the developing young of some mammals receive their food is the _____.
5. Another name for flesh-eating mammals is _____.
6. The teeth that are used for biting are the _____.
7. Elephants are _____ mammals.
8. Gnawing mammals are also known as _____.
9. Rabbits are examples of _____ mammals.
10. Mammals that have five fingers on each hand and five toes on each foot are called _____.

Determine whether each statement is true or false. If it is true, write "true."
If it is false, change the underlined word or words to make the statement true.

1. Mammals are <u>invertebrates</u>.
2. In <u>coldblooded</u> animals, the body temperature remains about the same all the time.
3. The duckbilled platypus is an example of a <u>monotreme</u>.
4. Animals that eat only plants are called <u>herbivores</u>.
5. The <u>flying squirrels</u> are the only examples of flying mammals.
6. <u>Canines</u> are teeth that are used for biting.
7. Organisms upon which other organisms feed are called <u>predators</u>.
8. A <u>squirrel</u> is an example of a gnawing mammal.
9. Rhinoceroses are examples of <u>hoofed</u> mammals.
10. The <u>dolphin</u> has the most well-developed brain of all the mammals.

Use the skills you have developed in the chapter to complete each activity.

1. **Relating facts** Which group of mammals is most similar to birds? Explain your answer.
2. **Making charts** Prepare a chart with three columns. In the first column, list the ten groups of mammals that you learned about in this chapter. In the second column, list the characteristics of each group. And in the third column, list at least two examples of each group.
3. **Classifying animals** Although koalas are often called koala bears, they are not really bears. Explain this statement.
4. **Applying concepts** Why do whales usually come to the surface of the ocean several times an hour?
5. **Making inferences** Many species of hoofed mammals feed in large groups, or herds. What possible advantage could this behavior have for the survival of these mammals?
6. **Making generalizations** What is the relationship between how complex an animal is and the amount of care the animal gives to its young? Provide an example to support your answer.
7. **Designing an experiment** Design an experiment that will test the following hypothesis: Chimpanzees are able to understand the meaning of the spoken words for the numbers one through ten.

Discuss each of the following in a brief paragraph.

1. What are the three groups of mammals? How do they differ from one another?
2. What is the difference between an anteater and a spiny anteater?
3. Name two pouched mammals. Explain how their young develop.
4. What features make carnivores good predators?
5. List ten groups of placental mammals and give an example of each.

Jane Goodall
and the Chimps of Gombe Stream

Deep in the heart of the African jungle, Jane Goodall has been doing research among the wild animals. She is studying one of our closest living relatives, the chimpanzee.

Goodall has always wanted to study the animals in Africa. When she was a young girl, she was inspired by Rudyard Kipling's jungle tales. Ever since reading Kipling's vivid descriptions of the jungle and its inhabitants, Goodall has known where she wanted to spend her time.

For more than 20 years, Goodall has lived at Gombe Stream, Tanzania's Game Preserve on Lake Tanganyika. She is both an ethologist, a person who studies animal behavior, and a primatologist, a person who studies primates. She hopes that her studies will help scientists better understand prehistoric and present-day humans.

In 1960, she stepped off a small boat and came face to face with the majestic mountains of Africa. Over the years, she has learned to live with blistering heat and drenching rain. She has learned how to travel in a country with deep valleys, high mountains, and steep gorges. She has adjusted to living among threatening animals such as cobras and leopards.

But for the first few months after her arrival, Goodall was in despair. Until she discovered wild pig and baboon trails, she had to fight her way through dense underbrush to do her research. Although she could hear the loud calls of the chimps and the rustling of the leaves as the chimps moved, she rarely saw them. They would always run when they heard her approaching. After eight months, Goodall had not come within 500 yards of the chimps. She was about to give up!

Suddenly her luck changed. A chimp she had named David Greybeard came shyly to her camp one day. He continued coming to the camp every day. After two weeks of observing her camp, David Greybeard actually took a banana from Goodall's hand. The other chimps, after seeing their leader's bold move, gradually allowed Goodall to get close to them too.

At about the same time, Goodall began to make some amazing discoveries. One of the most important is that chimps use objects as tools. Once again, David Greybeard was the star of the show. Goodall saw David Greybeard and a female chimp she had named Flo strip the leaves from thin branches. They then went over to a termite mound. For protection, termites seal the tops of their tunnels. Chimps look for these protective coverings and peel them off. Goodall watched as David and Flo dipped their branches into the tunnels and pulled them out covered with termites. The chimps then ate the termites off the sticks, just as you might take a piece of meat from a fork. Goodall also noticed that the chimps would go out of their way to select sticks and carry them to termite nests that were far away.

Chimps often chew leaves, which they then use as "sponges" to soak up drinking water from places such as hollows in logs.

This behavior seems to show that the chimps not only are able to use tools, but can think about their use ahead of time.

In time, Goodall was able to observe other chimp behavior. She saw another male, Evered, strip the leaves off a small branch and stuff them into his mouth. He chewed them for a short time and took them out of his mouth. He then dipped them, like a sponge, into a fallen log to get water. Goodall observed that the other chimps also used leaves to get water. So she collected some leaves and chewed them in order to understand what the chimps were doing. She found that chewing the leaves before dipping them helped to increase their absorbency.

When Goodall is not at Gombe Stream, she and her son live in Palo Alto, California, where she does laboratory research. However, she much prefers studying in the wild. Even in California, she keeps in touch with what is happening at Gombe by corresponding with her assistants there. She has lived among the wild chimps for more than twenty years. If asked why she chooses to live her life this way, Goodall replies that it is her "inborn love of the place and the beasts."

Jane Goodall (left) and companion observe the behavior of an adult and a young chimp.

Bathed in early morning light, a herd of large, dark brown sambar deer grazes on a grassy hillside at the edge of a forest in southern Asia. Suddenly, one of the deer raises its head in alarm and sniffs the air. Soon the entire herd is wary and watchful—ready to flee in an instant.

Conservationists to the Rescue?

The reason for their alarm quickly becomes obvious. Emerging from the woods a mere 225 meters away, a tiger strides up the hillside. The big cat's powerful muscles ripple as it moves. For a moment, the tiger stops and turns its head toward the deer. Then it continues on its way. This morning, at least, the tiger is not hungry. The deer are left to graze in peace.

Tigers are a vanishing species. They have disappeared from many parts of Asia where they were once common. In an effort to save them, conservation groups such as the World Wildlife Fund have raised more than one million dollars. Some of the money has been spent on research into tiger behavior. And the rest of the money has been used to establish preserves in the wild where the cats are protected.

To some extent, the effort has been successful. India now has 11 preserves for tigers. In some of these protected areas, the cat population is increasing once more. Conservationists are hopeful that tigers can continue to live in the wild.

But not everyone wants tigers living in the wild. In areas near some of India's preserves, tigers have killed both animals and people. Some Indians living near preserves oppose the government's attempts to save the tiger. They feel the tiger is not a species that should be saved, but a threat that should be removed.

A Fight to the Finish

Each year, more plants and animals become endangered. As conservationists work to save them, questions often arise about whether all species of living things should be saved. And if not all, which ones should be saved?

The answers are not simple. Some situations involve human needs versus the needs of animals. Other situations require a decision about which species is worth more time, effort, and money. For example, should developers be prevented from building in the Pine Barrens forest of New Jersey if the construction endangers a type of moth that lives there? Or is it worth thousands of dollars to save a kind of sparrow that lives only in a small part of Florida near Cape Canaveral?

Facing the Facts

To do their job, conservationists have to face tough questions like these. Some leading conservationists are very practical about the issues. Norman Meyers, for example, is a well-known environmental scientist. He notes that by the end of the 1980s, one species an hour, counting insects and other invertebrates, will disappear.

"Sad to say," Meyers writes, "the question is not how to save *all* these species; we just do not have the resources to rescue more than a small fraction."

Meyers suggests that first the value of each species be determined. The decision would be based on economics, the environment, and the survival of people. Then, the most valuable species should receive help first.

For example, in the African country of Kenya, lions are a big tourist attraction. Tourism brings lots of money to the country. Therefore, lions may be worth saving.

A tropical plant called the periwinkle is the source of two drugs used to treat cancer. And the venom of the Malayan pit viper, a cousin of the rattlesnake, is used to stop blood clots that cause heart attacks. In Meyers' view, the periwinkle and the pit viper should be among the first to receive help.

Environmental scientists predict that by the end of the 1980s, one species an hour will disappear.

This California condor is one of several species of animals that faces possible extinction.

The Unknown Factor

It is clearly to our advantage to invest time and money in preserving such species of plants and animals. The trouble is, there are probably thousands of species that could be very valuable to people—only no one yet knows it!

Are we wiping out species that hold secrets to curing cancer or solving the energy crisis? Scientists and conservationists Paul and Anne Ehrlich of Stanford University think we might be. And they also see a further complication. When species disappear, the ecosystems, or environments, to which they belong are changed or even destroyed. All life on the earth depends on ecosystems. Ecosystems provide important services such as the maintenance of soils and the control of crop pests and transmitters of human disease. As the Ehrlichs write, "Humanity has no way of replacing these free services should they be lost . . . and civilization cannot persist without them."

The Ehrlichs cite yet another reason for saving as many species as possible—"plain old-fashioned compassion." For many conservationists, stopping the extinction of species is a moral issue.

Concern Around the World

The International Union for the Conservation of Nature and Natural Resources is a worldwide group associated with the United Nations. The union's position is that we are "morally obliged to our descendants and to other creatures" to act wisely when it comes to conserving plants and animals.

Most conservationists would agree that each time a species vanishes, the world is a bit poorer. Consider just the sheer beauty of many of the endangered plants and animals. The main reason for saving tigers and condors, for example, is that they are among the earth's most magnificent creatures.

Perhaps sadly, people tend to feel more concern for species that are pretty or striking than for those that are plain. The black rhinoceros of Africa and the Higgin's eye mussel of midwestern rivers are both in danger. The world knows about the threat to the rhinoceros. But few people know about the Higgin's eye, even though it is closer to extinction than the rhino.

How can conservationists decide which endangered species to help or, at least, to help first? Norman Meyers has an interesting approach. When many people are injured in a big disaster, physicians often first treat victims who are badly hurt but who will recover if treated promptly. Meyers suggests that the same approach be used for species in danger. First help those species that are in the greatest danger and that have a good chance of surviving extinction. Still, says Meyers, it will not be easy to decide which species to aid and which to ignore. Making these decisions, he adds, "will cause us many a sleepless night."

The Corn Is as High as a Satellite's Eye

Farms of the future will move into space, and crops will be far out, too.

The old man held his granddaughter's hand as the high-speed elevator zoomed 180 floors to the top of the Triple Towers. Out on the observation deck, the young girl stared in wonder at the huge city that fanned out to meet the horizon in all directions. Far below, crowds of little dots moved along in neat columns. "Look at all those people!" the girl exclaimed. "There must be millions of them."

The old man nodded. "Twenty-two million, to be exact," he said softly.

"But Grandpa, how do all these people keep from starving? I read that years ago people in cities all over the world couldn't get enough to eat. And there are even more people now than there were back then."

The old man frowned as he remembered his own youth. "Yes, that's true, Lisa," he said with a sigh. "Twenty percent of the world was going hungry when I was a young man in 1985. The farmers could use only a quarter of the earth's land for farming."

"Why couldn't they use more of the land, Grandpa?" Lisa asked.

"Well," he answered, "the rest was either sizzling hot deserts, barren mountains, or frozen tundras. Of the available farmlands, some had to be used for nonfood crops like cotton. Less food was available and more and more people were being born."

"Are people still starving, Grandpa?" Lisa asked in a worried voice.

"Well, dear, some are, but because of techniques that were developed during the late twentieth century, farmers can now produce more food."

"Oh, Grandpa, that sounds interesting. Will you tell me how more food is made?" Lisa asked.

"Of course I will, Lisa. Let's sit down on that bench and I will tell you all about it," the old man said with a smile.

Space Crops

"Look up there. What do you see?" the old man asked.

"Stars, Grandpa. Why?" the girl responded.

"Well, Lisa, much of the world's food is now being grown in space. We have space stations that contain rotating drums filled with plants. The rotation simulates the earth's gravity. The plants are bathed in fluorescent light, which simulates the sun. Crops that do not grow very tall or that grow in the ground, like lettuce, potatoes, radishes, and carrots, are grown in the drums," the old man stated proudly.

"Wow, that's neat, Grandpa. I never knew that salad came from outer space," Lisa said excitedly.

Laughing, the old man said, "Well, most of it does. We also have space stations where plants grow out of the sides of walls or are moved along conveyor belts through humid air."

Genetics Makes the Difference

"Is all our food grown in outer space, Grandpa?" asked Lisa with a curious look on her face.

"Why, of course not. Methods of growing plants on Earth have been improved too. When I was young, Lisa, twenty percent of the crops that were grown on Earth died off. Now, because of changes scientists have made in the genetic material of plants, very few crops die. The genetic changes have resulted in plants with increased resistance to temperature changes, diseases, herbicides, and harsh environments. Plants have been made resistant by several methods. Some plants were altered by a process called protoplast fusion," the old man said.

Short food plants such as lettuce can be grown out of the sides of revolving drums. Such devices could be used in orbiting space stations to grow food crops in the future.

Dwarf trees being grown right now may one day supply enough fruit to fill most of our needs.

"That sounds complicated," Lisa said.

"It's not really very complicated," he replied. "The plant cell walls are dissolved by enzymes. The part remaining is called a protoplast. This protoplast is then fused to another protoplast from a different strain of the same plant or from an entirely different plant. The cell wall is regrown around the fused protoplasts, and a new plant develops. We now have many varieties of such plants. And you might think it strange, but many are smaller than those that used to be grown."

"Smaller? But that doesn't make sense," Lisa protested.

"Well, the smaller plants can produce as much as or more than the big ones because they have been genetically changed to be highly productive," explained the old man. "Also, more of them can be grown in the same amount of space. Two examples of the smaller plants are dwarf rice plants and dwarf peach trees."

"Wow, that's neat. Tell me more," Lisa said.

"All right. We also have plants that can get the nitrogen they need directly from the air. Plants need nitrogen to build amino acids, proteins, and other cell chemicals. In the old days, most plants got their nitrogen from the soil. But this process was using up all the nitrogen in the soil, and the plants didn't grow well. So fertilizer had to be added to the soil. Soybeans, legumes, alfalfa, and clover have always been able to use nitrogen directly from the air with the help of nitrogen-fixing bacteria. Other plants that can use nitrogen directly from the air were developed by combining genes from these nitrogen-fixing bacteria with genes from plants that normally took their nitrogen from the soil. Now almost all the plants take their nitrogen directly from the endless supply in the air."

"I didn't know that. Are any other plants different from the plants you saw when you were young?" Lisa asked.

"Oh, yes," the old man declared. "Many of the crops are now considered to be high-yield. That means they can be harvested faster than they could before, so that more can be grown. By redesigning the plants genetically, scientists have shortened the plants' growing time."

"It seems that genetic changes have kept people from starving," Lisa said thoughtfully. " That and the growing of food in space or on land."

"That's true," said her grandfather. "But there's still a third place. Some of the crops are grown in the ocean. This leaves more room for crops that can be grown only on land."

"That's a neat story, Grandpa," Lisa exclaimed.

"It's not a story, Lisa. It's the truth. But scientists still have to keep working to improve crop production because the population continues to grow," the old man observed.

Matter

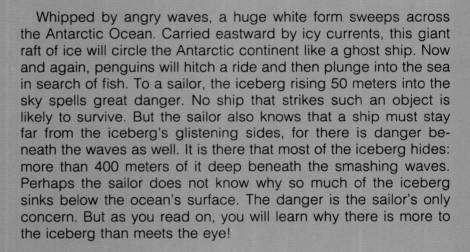

Whipped by angry waves, a huge white form sweeps across the Antarctic Ocean. Carried eastward by icy currents, this giant raft of ice will circle the Antarctic continent like a ghost ship. Now and again, penguins will hitch a ride and then plunge into the sea in search of fish. To a sailor, the iceberg rising 50 meters into the sky spells great danger. No ship that strikes such an object is likely to survive. But the sailor also knows that a ship must stay far from the iceberg's glistening sides, for there is danger beneath the waves as well. It is there that most of the iceberg hides: more than 400 meters of it deep beneath the smashing waves. Perhaps the sailor does not know why so much of the iceberg sinks below the ocean's surface. The danger is the sailor's only concern. But as you read on, you will learn why there is more to the iceberg than meets the eye!

CHAPTERS

13 General Properties of Matter

14 Physical and Chemical Changes

Adelie Penguins hitch a ride on an iceberg.

13 General Properties of Matter

CHAPTER SECTIONS

13-1 Matter

13-2 Mass

13-3 Weight

13-4 Volume

13-5 Density

CHAPTER OBJECTIVES

After completing this chapter, you will be able to:

13-1 Explain what is meant by the term matter.

13-1 Identify the general properties of matter.

13-2 Define mass.

13-2 Relate mass and inertia.

13-3 Define gravity and explain its relation to weight.

13-4 Explain what is meant by the term volume.

13-5 Provide a word definition and a mathematical formula for density.

As King Henry VIII of England watched proudly, his fighting ship the *Mary Rose* sailed slowly out of Portsmouth Harbor. The *Mary Rose* was among a fleet of English warships that set out on the morning of July 19, 1545, to battle an invading French fleet. In addition to a crew of 415 sailors, the ship carried 285 soldiers and a number of new, heavy bronze cannons.

But the *Mary Rose* never met the French ships. As the story goes, a sudden gust of wind sprang up, and in seconds the *Mary Rose* tipped over and sank to the bottom of the sea. Did this really happen? Or did the mighty ship actually sink at the hands of the French?

Partly to answer this question, teams of scuba divers began to search for the wreck of the *Mary Rose* in 1965. Some of the divers wore lead belts so that they could hover above the sandy ocean bottom in search of the *Mary Rose*.

In 1970, the divers found it. And with their discovery came the answer to its mysterious disappearance. The weight of the cannons had made the ship top-heavy. And when it tipped, water had flowed into the open spaces inside the ship, replacing the air. Without air inside it, the *Mary Rose* had sunk like a rock to the sea floor. It was as simple as that.

But perhaps there is still a mystery to solve. How can a diver wearing a lead belt hover in the sea, while a ship weighted with cannons and excess water plunges to the bottom? The solution to the mystery can be found as you read on.

Examining ruins of the Mary Rose

13-1 Matter

Stop what you are doing for a moment, and look around you. You are surrounded by a tremendous variety of materials. There are objects such as a desk, a chair, the book you are reading, and a pencil that you may be holding. Through the window you may see the sky and clouds. Observe your surroundings again. Then make a mental list of several of the objects you see. How would you describe them? Would you use such words as "large," "small," "red," "blue," "cold," "hot," "heavy," "light," "rough," "smooth"?

You see and touch hundreds of things each day. And although most of these things are probably very different from each other, they share one important quality. They are all forms of **matter.** Matter is what the world is made of. All materials consist of matter.

Through your senses of smell, sight, taste, and touch, you are familiar with matter. Some kinds of matter are easily recognized. Wood, water, salt, clay, glass, gold, plants, and animals are examples of matter that are easily observed. Oxygen, carbon dioxide, ammonia, and air are kinds of matter that are not as easily recognized. Are these different kinds of matter

Figure 13-1 *Many of the various forms of matter can be seen in this photograph. Can you identify at least five examples of matter?*

similar in some ways? Is salt anything like ammonia? Do water and glass have anything in common?

In order to answer these questions, you must know something about the **properties,** or characteristics, of matter. Properties describe an object. Color, odor, shape, texture, and hardness are properties of matter. They are very specific properties of matter, however. Specific properties make it easy to tell one kind of matter from another.

Some properties of matter are more general. Instead of describing the differences among forms of matter, general properties describe how all matter is the same. **General properties of matter include mass, weight, volume, and density.**

SECTION REVIEW

1. What is matter?
2. Name four general properties of matter.

13-2 Mass

The most important general property of matter is that it has **mass.** All of the objects you put on your mental list have mass. But what is mass?

Think of the materials you listed. They are all made up of a certain amount of matter. **Mass is the amount of matter in an object.** The mass of an object does not change unless some matter is either removed from the object or added to the object. Mass, then, does not change when you move an object from one location to another. You, for example, have the same mass whether you are on top of a mountain, at the bottom of a deep mine, or on the moon! Later in this chapter you will discover why this is a very important concept.

Suppose you were given the choice of pushing either an empty supermarket cart up a hill or a cart full of groceries up the hill. The full cart, of course, has more mass than the empty cart. And you know from experience that it will be easier for you to push the empty cart. Now suppose both carts are at the top of the hill and begin to roll down. Again, you

Figure 13-2 *Because of its large mass, a bowling ball is able to produce the results shown in this photograph. Would a hollow bowling ball or a tennis ball do the same?*

Figure 13-3 *It's not really magic, just a demonstration of inertia. As the table on which this dinner is set (left) is moved quickly, the objects are suspended in midair for an instant (right).*

Activity

Demonstrating Inertia

You can demonstrate that objects at rest tend to remain at rest by using a drinking glass, playing card, and coin.

1. Place the glass on a table.

2. Lay a flat playing card on top of the glass. Place the coin in the center of the card.

3. Using either a flicking motion or a pulling motion of your fingers, quickly remove the card so it flies out from under the coin. Can you remove the card fast enough so the coin lands in the glass? You might need to practice a few times.

How does this activity demonstrate inertia? What happens to the coin if you remove the card slowly? How does removing the card slowly demonstrate inertia?

know from experience that the full cart—the cart with more mass—will be harder to stop than the empty cart. In other words, it is harder to get a cart with more mass moving; and it is harder to get it to stop again.

Scientists use this idea to define mass in another way. Objects that have mass resist changes in their motion. For example, if an object is at rest, a force must be used to make it move. If you move it, you notice that it resists your push or pull. In the same way, if an object is moving and you stop it, you see that it resists this effort too. The property of a mass to resist changes in motion is called **inertia** (in-ER-shuh). **Mass is a measure of the inertia of an object.**

The more mass an object has, the greater its inertia. So the force that must be exerted to overcome its inertia is also greater. That is why you must push or pull harder to speed up and slow down a supermarket cart if it is loaded with groceries than if it is empty.

Mass is measured in units called grams, g, and kilograms, kg. One kilogram is equal to 1000 grams. The mass of small objects is usually expressed in grams. A nickel, for example, has a mass of about 5 grams. The mass of this book is about 1600 grams, or 1.6 kilograms.

SECTION REVIEW

1. What is mass?

2. What is inertia?

3. How are mass and inertia related?

13-3 Weight

In addition to mass giving an object inertia, mass is also the reason an object has **weight.** Weight is another general property of matter. In order to understand what weight is, you must know something about gravity.

You have probably noticed that a ball thrown up in the air soon falls to the ground. And you know that an apple that drops off a tree falls down, not up. The ball and the apple fall to earth because of the earth's force of attraction for these, and all other, objects. The force of attraction between objects is called **gravity.**

Gravitational force is not a property of the earth alone. All objects exert a gravitational attraction on other objects. Indeed, your two hands attract each other, and you are attracted to books, papers, and chairs. Why, then, are you not pulled toward these objects as you are toward the earth? In fact, you are! But the attractions in these cases are just too weak

Figure 13-4 *In his novel* From the Earth to the Moon, *author Jules Verne pictured this condition of weightlessness, or zero gravity, inside a spaceship* (left). *His prediction came true, as you can see from the orange-juice sphere and book floating in this astronaut's space capsule.*

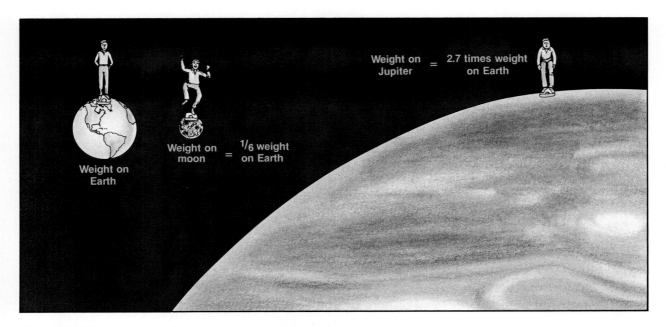

Weight on Jupiter = 2.7 times weight on Earth

Weight on moon = 1/6 weight on Earth

Weight on Earth

Figure 13-5 *Because of differences in the gravity of the earth, the moon, and Jupiter, this boy's weight changes from one place to another. His mass, however, stays the same.*

for you to notice them. The earth's gravity, however, is great because the earth is so massive. In fact, the greater the mass of an object, the greater its gravitational force. How do you think the gravity of Jupiter compares with that of the earth?

The pull of gravity on an object determines the object's weight. On the earth, your weight is a direct measure of the planet's force pulling you toward the surface. The pull of gravity between objects weakens as the distance between the centers of the objects becomes greater. So at a high altitude, on top of a tall mountain for example, you actually weigh less than on the surface of the earth. Again, this is because you are farther from the center of the earth when you are on top of a mountain. And when an object is sent into space far from the earth, the object is said to be weightless. However—and this is a very important point—the object *does not* become massless. Mass, remember, does not change when location changes. So no matter what happens to the force of gravity, mass stays the same. Only weight changes.

SECTION REVIEW

1. What is gravity?
2. What is weight?
3. What is the basic difference between mass and weight?

Activity

A Quick Weight Change

An inhabitant of Planet X weighs 243 "jupes" on his home planet. The gravity of Planet X is 2.7 times greater than that of the earth. How many "jupes" will he weigh on the earth? On the moon?

13-4 Volume

Did you have this book on your mental list of examples of matter? Let's use the book to help discover another general property of matter. Suppose you could wrap a piece of paper around the entire book and then remove the book. How would you describe what is left inside the paper? You probably would use the word "space." For an important property of matter is that it takes up space. And when the book is occupying its space, nothing else can be in that same space. You might go ahead and prove this to yourself.

The amount of space an object takes up is called its volume. The units used to express **volume** are liters, L; milliliters, mL; and cubic centimeters, cm^3. One liter is equal to 1000 milliliters. How many milliliters are there in 2.5 liters?

SECTION REVIEW

1. What is volume?
2. In what units is volume commonly measured?

Career: *Scuba Diver*

HELP WANTED: SCUBA DIVER To perform tasks under water for limited periods of time. Requires scuba diver certification with advanced scuba training.

On a warm, muggy day in August, a salvage diving crew finally raised a 29-meter-long sailing vessel off the bottom of the Los Angeles harbor. The vessel had been at the bottom of the harbor for a year after mysteriously sinking. The crew consisted of specially trained **scuba divers** who earn their livings by completing underwater tasks with the use of scuba gear.

The tasks of scuba divers differ from job to job. Their work may include inspecting dams, pipelines, and cables. Or it may involve recovering sunken objects, or doing underwater repair and construction. They may work from a

boat, off a dock, or from the shore.

Scuba divers must wear wet suits to protect them from the cold temperatures of deep water. They must also wear air tanks. Anyone interested in scuba diving as a career can obtain more information by writing to NASDS Headquarters, P.O. Box 17067, Long Beach, CA 90807.

Describing Properties

Collect at least six different kinds of objects as samples of matter. You might include rocks, pieces of wood or metal, and objects made by people. Identify each sample by its general properties and its special properties. Now write a sentence that describes each sample. Be sure to use the following words in your descriptions.

color

density

hardness

mass

matter

property

shape

volume

weight

13-5 Density

Suppose you were asked to determine which is heavier, wood or lead. Could you answer this question right away? How would you go about it? Perhaps you would suggest comparing the masses of both on a balance. You are on the right track, but there is one problem with this solution. What size pieces of lead and wood should you use? After all, a small chip of lead does not have a greater mass than a baseball bat made of wood!

You probably realize now that in order to compare the masses of two objects, you need to use equal volumes of each. In other words, you need to compare the way masses of objects are related to their volumes. When you do, you soon discover that a piece of lead has a greater mass than a piece of wood of the *same* size. A cubic centimeter of lead, for example, is heavier than a cubic centimeter of wood. An object's mass per unit volume is called its **density.**

All matter has density. And the density of a specific kind of matter is a property that helps to identify it and distinguish it from other kinds of matter.

Figure 13-6 *Salt water has a higher density than fresh water, so it's easy to float in the great Salt Lake, Utah.*

Since density is mass per unit volume, the formula used to calculate the density of an object is

$$\text{density} = \frac{\text{mass}}{\text{volume}}$$

Density is often expressed in grams per milliliter or grams per cubic centimeter. The density of wood is about 0.8 g/cm³. This means that any piece of wood 1 cubic centimeter in volume has a mass of about 0.8 gram. The density of lead is 11.3 g/cm³. So a piece of lead has a mass about 14 times that of a piece of wood of the same size.

The density of water is 1 g/mL. Wood floats in water because its density is less than the density of water. What happens to a piece of lead when it is put in water?

From the fact that ice floats, you now know that it too is less dense than liquid water. Actually, the density of ice is about 89 percent that of cold water. What this means is that only about 11 percent of a block of ice stays above the surface of the water. The

DENSITIES OF SOME COMMON SUBSTANCES

Substance	Density (g/cm³)
Air	0.0013
Aluminum	2.7
Gasoline	0.68
Gold	19.3
Ice	0.9
Steel	7.8
Water (liquid)	1.0

Figure 13-7 *According to this chart, which substances will float on water?*

Figure 13-8 *Although this iceberg may appear harmless to passing ships, it is really quite dangerous. Only the tip of the iceberg is visible. Nearly 90 percent of it lurks beneath the water's surface!*

Archimedes and the Crown

The famous Greek mathematician and scientist Archimedes was once faced with a most difficult task. He had to determine whether a crown received by King Hieron was made of gold or a mixture of gold and silver. And he had to accomplish this task without damaging the crown!

Pretend that you are Archimedes' assistant and describe an experiment that would help determine whether the crown is made of gold or a mixture of gold and silver. Hint: The concept of density is useful.

rest is below the surface. This fact is what makes icebergs, like the one pictured on page 321, so dangerous. What is visible is only the "tip" of the iceberg. The rest of it lurks silently below the water's surface!

Can you now solve the mystery posed at the beginning of this chapter? An object floats in water if its density is less than 1 g/mL. In order for the scuba diver to sink in the water, the diver's overall density has to be greater than 1 g/mL. So the diver wears a lead belt to increase mass.

Now, the density of water increases as the water gets colder. So below the surface, the density of water is greater than 1 g/mL. At a certain depth, the scuba diver's density becomes equal to the water's density. The diver will not sink further.

With its large volume partly filled with air, the *Mary Rose* was less dense than water, and so it floated. The air was able to balance the added mass of the cannons. However, when its volume was filled with water, the added mass of the cannons made the *Mary Rose*'s overall density greater than that of the surrounding water at any depth. Down, down went the *Mary Rose*!

Figure 13-9 *The objects and liquids in this container have different densities. So some float while others sink.*

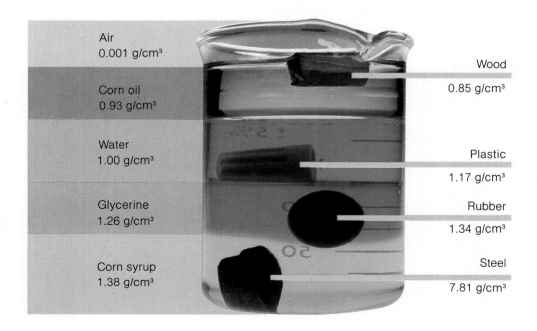

Air 0.001 g/cm³	
Corn oil 0.93 g/cm³	Wood 0.85 g/cm³
Water 1.00 g/cm³	Plastic 1.17 g/cm³
Glycerine 1.26 g/cm³	Rubber 1.34 g/cm³
Corn syrup 1.38 g/cm³	Steel 7.81 g/cm³

Figure 13-10 *It is the density of an object, not its size, that determines whether it will float or sink in water. This large ocean liner (above) has an overall density less than 1 g/mL, so it floats in water. The density of this coin (left) is greater than 1 g/mL, and so it sinks.*

SECTION REVIEW

1. What is density?
2. What determines whether an object floats or sinks in water?

LABORATORY ACTIVITY

Inertia

Purpose

In this activity, you will define mass in terms of the behavior of objects, showing that the more resistance to change of position, or inertia, an object has, the more mass it has.

Materials (*per group*)

Several objects of various masses that will fit into shoe boxes

Smooth table surface

Household broom

Several shoe boxes of similar size

Metric ruler

Procedure

1. Place one object in each shoe box and replace the shoe box's lid.
2. Set the box so that it hangs over the edge of the table by 8 cm.
3. Stand the broom directly behind the table. Put your foot on the straw to hold it in place. The handle should be pointing up in the air directly behind the box.
4. Now slowly bring the handle back away from the box.
5. When you release the handle, it should spring forward, striking the middle of the end of the box.
6. Measure how far the box travels across the table owing to the force of the broom.
7. Repeat the procedure with each of the boxes.

Observations and Conclusions

At this point, you will have noticed that when the same force—the impact of the broom handle—is delivered, the distance that the box and its contents move varies from box to box.

1. What part of the definition of inertia applies to your observations about the movements of the boxes?
2. Why do you think some boxes moved farther than others?
3. Open the boxes and examine the contents. What do you notice about the objects that moved the farthest from resting position? What do you notice about the objects that moved the least from resting position?
4. Mass can be determined on a balance, but do you now see another way to compare masses?

CHAPTER REVIEW

SUMMARY

13-1 Matter

- All objects are made up of matter.

- A quality or characteristic that describes an object is called a property.

- General properties tell how all matter is the same. Specific properties describe the differences among forms of matter.

13-2 Mass

- One property of matter is that it has mass. Mass is the amount of matter an object contains.

- The property of a mass to resist changes in motion is called inertia. Mass is a measure of the inertia of an object.

- Mass is commonly measured in grams and kilograms.

13-3 Weight

- The force of attraction between objects is called gravity.

- The pull of gravity on an object determines the object's weight.

- The pull of gravity between objects weakens as the distance between the centers of the objects becomes greater.

- The weight of an object can vary, but its mass remains unchanged.

13-4 Volume

- The amount of space an object takes up is called its volume.

- Volume is expressed in liters, milliliters, and cubic centimeters.

13-5 Density

- The density of an object is its mass per unit volume.

- The density of a specific kind of matter is a property that helps identify it.

- Objects with a density less than 1 gram per milliliter, which is the density of water, will float in water. Objects with a density greater than 1 gram per milliliter will sink.

VOCABULARY

Define each term in a complete sentence.

density

gravity

inertia

mass

matter

property

volume

weight

CONTENT REVIEW: MULTIPLE CHOICE

Choose the letter of the answer that best completes each statement.

1. Air, water, glass, and clay are examples of
   a. energy.   b. matter.   c. volume.   d. properties.
2. Characteristics that tell how all matter is the same are called
   a. specific properties.   b. universal differences.
   c. density numbers.   d. general properties.

3. The amount of matter an object possesses is called its
   a. mass.   b. volume.   c. density.   d. weight.

4. In describing mass, it is correct to say that
   a. mass changes with altitude.   b. mass changes with location.
   c. mass remains unchanged.   d. mass changes with weight.

5. An object's resistance to a change in motion is called its
   a. density.   b. inertia.   c. mass.   d. volume.

6. The force of attraction between objects is
   a. inertia.   b. weight.   c. density.   d. gravity.

7. As an object gets farther away from the earth,
   a. its weight increases.   b. its weight decreases.
   c. its mass decreases.   d. its weight remains the same.

8. The amount of space an object takes up is called its
   a. volume.   b. density.   c. weight.   d. graduated cylinder.

9. The formula for finding density is
   a. volume/mass.   b. volume × mass.
   c. mass/volume.   d. mass/weight.

10. General properties of matter include
   a. mass, shape, and density.   b. mass and volume.
   c. weight, volume, and color.   d. volume and density.

CONTENT REVIEW: COMPLETION

Fill in the word or words that best complete each statement.

1. A quality or characteristic that describes an object is called a(n) _____.

2. The amount of matter an object has is called its _____.

3. One kilogram is equal to _____ grams.

4. The force that pulls objects toward the earth is called _____.

5. The earth's pull on an object determines the object's _____.

6. As an object gets farther from the center of the earth, its weight _____.

7. In order to compare the masses of two objects, you must use equal _____.

8. An object's mass per unit volume is called its _____.

9. An object with a mass of 10 g and a volume of 5 mL will _____ in water.

10. An ice cube floats in water because it is _____ dense than water.

CONTENT REVIEW: TRUE OR FALSE

Determine whether each statement is true or false. If it is true, write "true." If it is false, change the underlined word or words to make the statement true.

1. All objects are made up of <u>matter</u>.

2. <u>Volume</u> is a measure of the resistance of an object to change in its motion.

3. An object at rest tends to remain at rest because of <u>inertia</u>.

4. One liter is equal to <u>100</u> milliliters.

5. The mass of a small object is usually measured in <u>liters</u>.
6. The earth's force of attraction for all objects is called <u>mass</u>.
7. As the pull of gravity decreases, an object's weight <u>decreases</u>.
8. The amount of space an object takes up is called its <u>volume</u> and is measured in liters and milliliters.
9. As an object's weight decreases, its mass <u>increases</u>.
10. An object's mass per unit volume is called its <u>density</u>.

CONCEPT REVIEW: SKILL BUILDING

Use the skills you have developed in the chapter to complete each activity.

1. **Making comparisons**   You are given two samples of pure copper, one with a mass of 20 grams and the other with a mass of 100 grams. Compare the two samples in terms of (a) volume, (b) weight, and (c) density.
2. **Making calculations**   If the density of a certain plastic used to make a bracelet is 0.78 g/cm³, what mass would a bracelet of 4 cm³ have? Would this bracelet sink or float in water?
3. **Designing an experiment**   Air is matter, although it is less easily recognized than other kinds of matter. Using the general properties of matter, suggest two situations in which you could illustrate that air is matter.
4. **Applying concepts**   "I have to lose weight" might be the reaction of a person who discovers that clothes fit too tightly. From a scientific point of view, discuss whether a weight loss will make the clothes fit better. What would be a more accurate way of stating the situation?
5. **Relating concepts**   Explain why fish are able to survive in lakes during very cold winter months when the lakes freeze.
6. **Making inferences**   Suppose you are an astronaut floating in space, far from any other object. What is your weight in space? What is your mass? Would you be willing to remove your space boot and with your bare foot kick a large boulder that comes hurtling past you? Explain your answer.

CONCEPT REVIEW: ESSAY

Discuss each of the following in a brief paragraph.

1. Aluminum is used to make airplanes. Cast iron is used to make heavy machines. How do the densities of these metals make them useful for these purposes?
2. The common metal iron pyrite is often called "fool's gold" because it can be mistaken for gold. How would you go about determining whether a particular sample is iron pyrite or gold?
3. Each year some college students have a contest to build and race concrete boats. What advice would you give the students to make sure their boats float?

14 Physical and Chemical Changes

CHAPTER SECTIONS

14-1 Physical Properties and Changes

14-2 The Phases of Matter

14-3 Phase Changes

14-4 Chemical Properties and Changes

CHAPTER OBJECTIVES

After completing this chapter, you will be able to:

14-1 Distinguish between a physical property and a physical change.

14-2 Classify matter according to phase.

14-2 State Boyle's and Charles's laws.

14-3 Identify the various phase changes.

14-3 Relate phase changes to changes in heat energy.

14-4 Distinguish between a chemical property and a chemical change.

All day long, the temperature had been steadily dropping. Only a few people working in the orange grove could remember a day as cold in that area of Florida. The branches of the orange trees were heavy with fruit that was not yet ripe enough for picking. If the temperature fell much lower, the juice in the oranges would freeze. The entire crop of fruit would be ruined.

Something had to be done quickly in order to save the orange crop. So workers lighted small fires in the groves. But they soon realized that this heat would not be enough to save the oranges. Suddenly, some of the workers carried large hoses into the grove. Racing against time and temperature, the workers sprayed the trees with water. As the temperature dropped, this water would freeze and turn into ice. Strange as it may seem, ice was being used to keep the oranges warm!

When the sun rose the next day and temperatures began to climb, the glistening ice that had covered the fruit trees melted away. The fruit was undamaged—cold but not frozen. The orange crop had been saved.

Was this some sort of magic? In a sense, yes. But it was magic that anyone who knows science can do. And as you read further, you will learn how freezing water can sometimes do a better job of keeping things warm than fire can.

Keeping oranges warm with ice!

14-1 Physical Properties and Changes

How would you describe a copper penny? Or a wooden stick? Well, after reading Chapter 13, you would probably say both the penny and the stick are matter. And because they are matter, they have mass, weight, volume, and density. You are using general properties of matter to tell how the penny and the stick are alike.

What else could you say about them? You might say a copper penny is reddish-brown, round, hard to scratch, and dense enough to sink in water. In contrast, a wooden stick is brown, long and narrow, easy to scratch, and floats in water. Now you are using specific properties of matter to distinguish the penny from the wooden stick. Properties such as color, shape, hardness, and density are called **physical properties.**

Now suppose you take the wooden stick and break it into pieces. Are the pieces still wood? To answer that question, you must determine whether the pieces are still the same kind of matter. In this example, they are. You changed the shape of the wood, but it is still wood. In other words, the wood that makes up the stick has not changed into another substance. **Changes in which physical properties of**

Figure 14-1 *Various types of matter, each having its characteristic properties, can be seen in this photograph. Can you identify three types and some of their properties? Remember, invisible gases are matter!*

a substance are altered, but the substance remains the same kind of matter, are physical changes.

Breaking an object into pieces is one example of a **physical change.** Another example is dissolving a substance. You can easily dissolve a cube of sugar in a glass of warm water. The sugar disappears from sight, and the liquid remains clear. You might be tempted to think that somehow the sugar has changed its identity—that it is no longer sugar. But the sugar is still there, as you can tell by the sweet taste of the liquid. Taste, then, is another physical property of matter. Although the sugar has lost its white color and its original shape, it is still the same kind of matter. It still has its physical property of sweet taste. This physical property makes it easy to identify. However, scientists rarely use taste to identify substances. Why do you think this is so?

SECTION REVIEW

1. Give three examples of physical properties.
2. Give an example of a physical change.

Figure 14-2 *Even after this karate expert breaks the three boards, the wood remains the same kind of substance. Breaking an object into pieces is a physical change.*

Figure 14-3 *Three familiar phases of the substance water are visible in this photograph. Can you identify them?*

14-2 The Phases of Matter

Ice, liquid water, steam. Perhaps these three materials seem very different to you. Certainly you can use them in very different ways. You can cool a drink with ice, wash a car with liquid water, and cook vegetables in steam. And because they all look and feel different, you usually do not mix them up.

Ice, liquid water, and steam, however, are all made up of exactly the same substance in different states. These states are called **phases.** Phase is an important physical property of matter. **Matter can exist in four phases—solid, liquid, gas, and plasma.** Ice, liquid water, and steam are phases of water.

Solids

Cubes of ice, cubes of sugar, metal coins, wooden sticks, rocks, and diamonds are several examples of **solids.** And although they look very different, as sol-

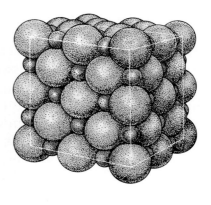

Figure 14-4 *The white cubic crystals in this photograph (left) are sodium chloride, or table salt. They are growing on crystals of calcium sulfate, or gypsum. Crystals have a regular arrangement of particles, as shown in the drawing of the structure of sodium chloride (right).*

ids they share two basic characteristics. All solids have a definite shape and a definite volume.

All the tiny particles in a solid are packed very close together, so it keeps its shape. The particles cannot move far out of their places and, in most solids, the particles cannot flow over or around each other. In many solids, the particles are arranged in a regular, repeating pattern. Such a regular arrangement of particles is called a **crystal** (KRIS-tuhl). Solids made up of crystals are called **crystalline solids.** Common table salt is a good example of a crystalline solid. See Figure 14-4.

Crystals often have beautiful shapes that result from the arrangement of the particles within them. Snowflakes are crystals of water in the solid phase. If you look at them closely, you will see that all the

Figure 14-5 *Snowflakes (left) are six-sided crystals of water in the solid phase. The repeating pattern of the particles in ice can be seen in this computer-generated drawing (right) of a portion of the crystal.*

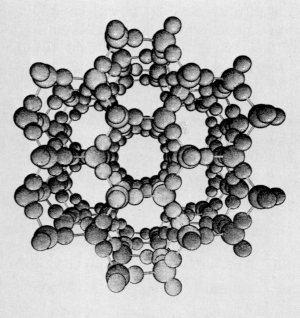

flakes have six sides. However, what is so amazing is that no two snowflakes in the world are exactly alike!

Have you ever played with sealing wax or silicone rubber? Both of these materials are solids. Yet from your experience, you may know that they do not keep their shapes permanently, as do crystalline solids. Left out on a table top for a long period of time, both of these solids will lose their shape and flatten out into a "puddle." Such solids that do not keep a definite shape are called **amorphous** (uh-MOR-fuhs) **solids.** Unlike crystals, the particles within amorphous solids are not arranged in a rigid way. So these particles can slowly flow around one another.

Some scientists think of amorphous solids as slow-moving liquids. Tar, candle wax, and glass are examples. Are you surprised to learn that glass actually flows? You might be able to see this for yourself if you can look at windowpanes in very old houses. Such windowpanes are thicker at the bottom than at the top because the glass has flowed slowly downward. Given enough centuries, the glass might flow completely out of its frame! Glass is sometimes described as a supercooled liquid. It is formed when a material in the liquid phase is cooled to a rigid condition, but no crystals form.

Liquids

When you put water into a glass, it takes on the same shape as the glass. But when you pour that water onto a table or floor, it takes on a different shape. This behavior is a property of another phase of matter—the **liquid** phase.

Liquids have no definite shape. They take the shape of the container into which they are placed. So liquid water in a square container is square. And liquid water in a round container is round. Liquids can take on different shapes because the particles in them can flow easily around one another, even though they are close together.

Although liquids do not have a definite shape, they do have a definite volume. For example, pouring one liter of water into a two-liter bottle does not fill the bottle. The water does not spread out to fill the entire volume of the bottle. What happens if you try to pour two liters of water into a one-liter bottle?

Figure 14-6 *Amorphous solids like this sealing wax lose their shape under certain conditions.*

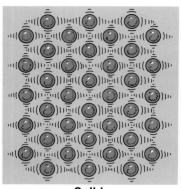 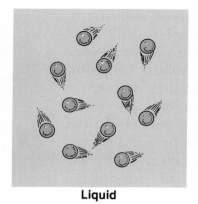 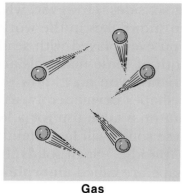

| Solid | Liquid | Gas |

Figure 14-7 *The arrangement and movement of particles vary in a solid, a liquid, and a gas.*

Gases

Have you ever pumped air into a bicycle tire or blown up a balloon? If so, you may have observed an important property of another phase of matter—the **gas** phase. Gases have no definite volume. They always fill their container, regardless of the size or shape of the container.

When air is pumped into a bicycle tire or a balloon, a large amount of gas is being squeezed into a small volume. Fortunately, the particles in a gas can be pushed close together.

Just the opposite can also happen. A small amount of gas can spread out to fill a large volume. The smell of an apple pie baking in the oven comes to you because gases from the pie spread out to

Figure 14-8 *A gas has no definite volume and will expand to fill its container. If allowed to, the gas will expand without limit, which is what has happened to the gas in Donald Duck's left hand. A hole in that part of the balloon has enabled the gas to escape into the air.*

every part of the room. In fact, if allowed to, gases will expand without limit. If not for the pull of gravity, all the gases making up the earth's atmosphere would do just that!

Like liquids, gases have no definite shape. They take the shape of their container. The particles that make up a gas are not arranged in any set pattern. So it is very easy for gas particles to move around, either spreading apart or moving close together.

The Behavior of Gases

The world inside a container of gas particles is not as quiet as it may seem to you. Although you cannot see the particles of gas, they are in constant motion. Whizzing around at speeds of about 500 meters per second, these bulletlike particles are constantly hitting one another. In fact, each particle undergoes about 10 billion collisions per second! Added to that are the collisions the particles make with the walls of the container. The effect of all these collisions is an outward pressure, or push, by the gas. The pressure is what makes the gas expand to fill its container. What do you think happens to a container when the pressure of the gas becomes too great?

BOYLE'S LAW Imagine you are holding an inflated balloon. If you press lightly on the outside of the balloon, you can feel the air inside pushing back. Now if you squeeze part of the balloon, what do you feel? You probably feel the air pressing against the walls of the balloon with even greater force.

This increase in pressure is due to a decrease in volume. By squeezing the balloon, you reduce the space the gas particles can occupy. As the particles are pushed a bit closer together, they collide with one another and the walls of the balloon even more. So the pressure from the moving gas particles increases. The relationship between volume and pressure is called **Boyle's Law:** The volume of a fixed amount of a gas varies *inversely* with the pressure of the gas. In other words, as one increases, the other decreases. If the volume increases, the pressure decreases. If the volume decreases, the pressure increases.

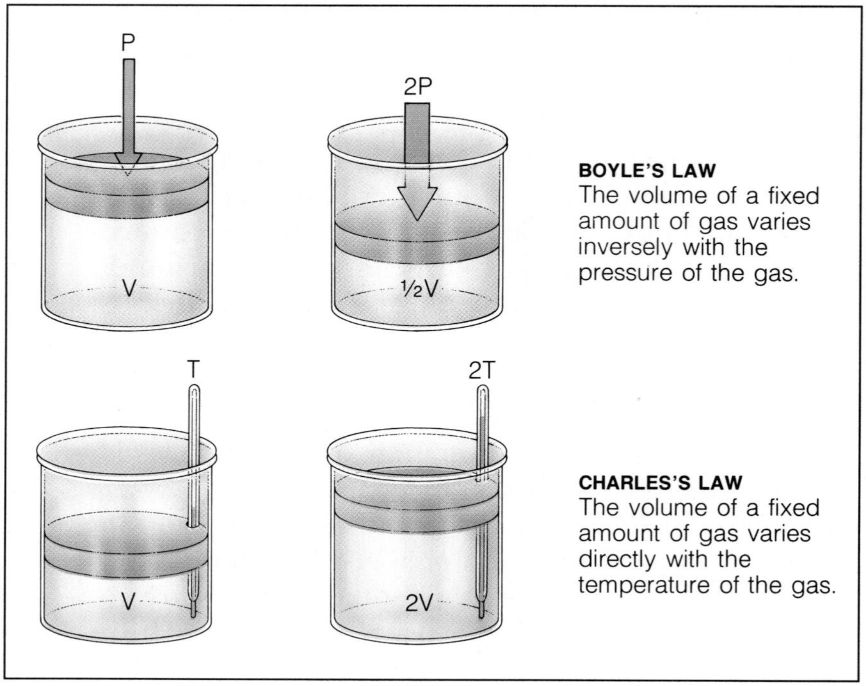

Figure 14-9 *You can see in this illustration that if the pressure of a fixed amount of gas increases, the volume of the gas decreases (top). This inverse proportion between pressure and volume is called Boyle's Law. According to Charles's Law, if the temperature of a fixed amount of gas increases, the volume of the gas increases (bottom). The relationship between temperature and volume is a direct proportion.*

BOYLE'S LAW
The volume of a fixed amount of gas varies inversely with the pressure of the gas.

CHARLES'S LAW
The volume of a fixed amount of gas varies directly with the temperature of the gas.

Activity

Charles's Law

1. Inflate a balloon, making sure it is not so large that it will break easily. Tie the end of the balloon so that air inside cannot escape.

2. Measure and record the diameter of the balloon.

3. Put the balloon in an oven set at a low temperature—not more than 150° F (65° C). Leave the balloon in the oven for about 15 minutes.

4. Remove the balloon and quickly measure its diameter.

5. Now place the balloon in a refrigerator for 15 minutes.

6. Remove the balloon and measure and record its diameter. What happens to its size at the different temperatures? Do your observations agree with Charles's Law?

CHARLES'S LAW Imagine you have that inflated balloon again. This time you heat it very gently. What do you think happens to its volume? As the temperature increases, the gas particles absorb more heat energy. They speed up and move further away from one another. So the increase in temperature results in an increase in volume. If the temperature had decreased, then the volume would have decreased. This relationship between temperature and volume of a gas is called **Charles's Law:** The volume of a fixed amount of gas varies *directly* with the temperature of the gas. What do you think happens as the temperature of a gas drops? Try to support your answer by putting an inflated balloon in your freezer.

Boyle's Law and Charles's Law together are called the Gas Laws. **The Gas Laws describe the behavior of gases with changes in pressure, temperature, and volume.**

Plasma

The fourth phase of matter is quite rare on the earth. It is called the **plasma** phase. Matter in the plasma phase is very high in energy. In fact, the particles contain so much energy that they are dangerous to living things. Luckily, plasma is not found naturally on the earth. It is, however, common in stars, such as the sun. Plasma can only be made on the earth by using equipment that produces very high energy. But the plasma cannot be contained by the walls of ordinary matter, which it would immediately destroy. Instead, magnetic fields produced by powerful magnets keep the high-energy particles in a plasma from escaping. One day, producing plasmas on the earth may meet most of our energy needs.

SECTION REVIEW

1. What are the four phases of matter?
2. How is a crystalline solid different from an amorphous solid?
3. State Boyle's Law and Charles's Law.

14-3 Phase Changes

Ice, liquid water, and steam are all the same substance. What, then, causes the particles of a substance to be in one particular phase rather than another? The answer has to do with energy—energy that can cause the particles to move faster and farther apart.

A solid substance tends to have less energy than that same substance in the liquid phase. A gas usually has more energy than the liquid phase of the same substance. So ice has less energy than liquid water, and steam has more energy than both ice and liquid water. The greater energy content of steam is what makes a burn caused by steam more serious than a burn caused by hot water!

Because energy content is responsible for the different phases of matter, substances can be made to change phase by adding or taking away energy. And the easiest way to do this is to heat or cool the substance, allowing heat energy to flow into or out of it. This idea should sound familiar to you since you frequently increase or decrease heat energy to produce phase changes in water. You put

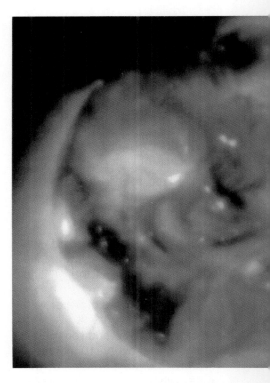

Figure 14-10 *These eruptions on the sun are examples of the high-energy plasma phase of matter.*

Figure 14-11 *When heat is applied, ice changes to liquid water and then to water vapor.*

In this activity, you will discover an important relationship between the melting and freezing points of water.

1. Place several ice cubes, a little water, and a thermometer in a glass and wait several minutes before observing.

2. Observe and record the temperature as the ice melts. This temperature is the melting point of ice.

3. Place a glass of water with a thermometer in it in the freezer. Observe and record the temperature every 10 minutes. Record the temperature of the water when it begins to freeze. This temperature is the freezing point of water.

How does the melting point of ice compare with the freezing point of water?

liquid water in the freezer to remove heat and make ice. On a hot stove you add heat to make liquid water turn to steam. **The phase changes in matter are melting, freezing, vaporization, condensation, and sublimation.**

Changes of phase are examples of physical changes. In a physical change, a substance changes from one form to another, but it remains the same *kind* of substance. No new or different *kinds* of matter are formed, even though physical properties may change.

Solid-Liquid Phase Changes

What happens to your popsicle on a very hot day if you do not eat it fast enough? Right—it begins to melt. **Melting** is the change of a solid to a liquid. Melting occurs when a substance absorbs heat energy. The rigid crystal structure of the particles breaks down, and the particles are free to flow around one another.

The temperature at which a solid changes to a liquid is called the **melting point.** Most substances have a characteristic melting point. It is a physical property that helps to identify the substance. The melting point of ice is 0° C. The melting point of table salt is 801° C, while that of a diamond is 3700° C.

Figure 14-12 *As some solids absorb heat energy, they begin to melt, or change to the liquid phase.*

The opposite phase change, that of a liquid to a solid, is called **freezing.** Freezing occurs when a substance loses heat energy. The temperature at which a substance changes from a liquid to a solid is called the **freezing point.** Strangely enough, the freezing point of a substance is equal to its melting point. So water both melts and freezes at 0° C.

Substances called alcohols have freezing points much lower than 0° C. These substances are used in automobile antifreeze because they can be cooled to low winter temperatures without freezing. One such substance, ethylene glycol, when mixed with water can lower the freezing point of the mixture to −49° C.

The fact that freezing involves a loss of heat energy explains the "magic" worked by the orange growers you read about at the beginning of this chapter. The liquid water sprayed onto the trees released heat energy as it froze. Some of this heat energy was released into the oranges, preventing them from freezing and being destroyed.

Liquid-Gas Phase Changes

Have you ever left a glass of water out overnight? If so, perhaps you noticed that the level of the water was lower the next morning. Some of the liquid changed phase and became a gas. The gas then escaped into the air.

The change of a substance from a liquid to a gas is called **vaporization** (vay-puhr-uh-ZAY-shuhn). During

Figure 14-14 *How did the mist hanging over this forest form?*

Figure 14-15 *During both evaporation and boiling, particles of a liquid absorb heat energy and change from the liquid phase to the gas phase.*

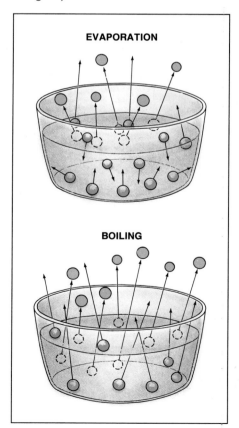

this process, particles in a liquid absorb enough heat energy to escape from the liquid phase. If vaporization takes place at the surface of the liquid, the process is called **evaporation** (ee-vap-uhr-AY-shuhn). So some of the water in the glass left out overnight evaporated.

Evaporation is often thought of as a cooling process. Does this sound strange to you? Think for a moment of perspiration on the surface of your skin. As this water evaporates, it absorbs and carries away heat energy from your body. In this way, your body is cooled. Can you explain why it is important to sweat on a hot day?

Vaporization does not occur *only* at the surface of a liquid. If enough energy is supplied, particles inside the liquid can change to gas. These particles travel to the surface of the liquid and then into the air. This process is called **boiling.** The temperature at which a liquid boils is called its **boiling point.** The boiling point of water at the earth's surface under normal conditions is 100° C. The boiling point of table salt is 1413° C, and that of a diamond is 4200° C!

The boiling point of a liquid is related to the pressure of the air above it. Since the gas particles must escape from the surface of the liquid, they need to have enough "push" to equal the "push" of the air pressing down. So the lower the air pressure, the more easily the bubbles of gas can form within the liquid and then escape. Lowering the air pressure lowers the boiling point.

At high altitudes, air pressure is much lower and so the boiling point is reduced. If you could go many kilometers above the earth's surface, the pressure of the air would be so low that you could boil water at ordinary room temperature! However, this boiling water would be cool! Certainly you would not be able to cook anything in this water. For it is the heat in boiling water that cooks food, not simply the boiling process.

Gases can change phase too. If a substance in the gas phase loses heat energy, it changes into a liquid. Scientists call this change **condensation** (kahn-den-SAY-shuhn). You have probably noticed that cold objects, such as glasses of iced drinks, tend to become wet on the outside. Water vapor present in the surrounding air loses heat energy when it comes in contact with the cold glass. The water vapor condenses and becomes liquid drops on the glass.

Solid-Gas Phase Changes

If you live in an area where winters are very cold, you may have noticed something unusual about fallen snow. Even when the temperature stays below the melting point of the water that makes up the snow, the fallen snow slowly disappears. What happens to it? The snow undergoes **sublimation** (suhb-luh-MAY-shuhn). When a solid sublimes, its surface

Figure 14-16 *When water vapor in the air cools and condenses, water droplets form. If the droplets become large enough, they fall as rain. Rain can vary from a drizzle to a heavy downpour.*

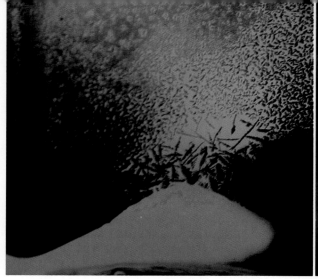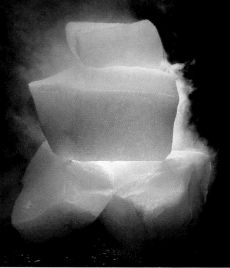

Figure 14-17 *Certain substances such as iodine* (left) *and dry ice* (right) *sublime, or go from the solid phase directly to the gas phase.*

Activity

An Almost Ruined Day

Using the following words, write a 250-word story about a day on which your birthday party was almost a disaster.

boiling	melting
freezing	phase
crystal	physical change
evaporation	solid
liquid	sublimation

particles escape *directly* into the gas phase. They do not pass through the liquid phase.

A substance called dry ice is often used to keep other substances, such as ice cream, very cold. Dry ice is solid carbon dioxide. At ordinary pressures, it cannot exist in the liquid phase. So as it absorbs heat energy, it sublimes directly to the gas phase. By absorbing and carrying off heat energy as it sublimes, dry ice keeps materials that are near it cold and dry. Just think what would happen to an ice cream cake if it were packed in regular ice rather than dry ice!

SECTION REVIEW

1. Define melting and freezing.
2. Explain the difference between evaporation and condensation.
3. What is sublimation?

14-4 Chemical Properties and Changes

At the beginning of this chapter, you learned that you could easily tell a copper penny from a wooden stick by its physical properties. It was easy to see the differences in color, shape, hardness, and density. But now suppose you have to distinguish between two gases—oxygen and hydrogen. Both are colorless, odorless, and tasteless. Since they are gases, they have no definite shape or volume. And although each has a specific density, you cannot drop them into water to see what happens! So in this case, physical properties are not very helpful in identifying the gases.

Fortunately, physical properties are not the only way to identify a substance. Both oxygen and hydrogen can turn into other substances and take on new identities. And the way in which they do this can be useful in determining the gas. The properties that describe how a substance changes into other new substances are called **chemical properties.**

If you collected some hydrogen in a test tube and put a glowing wooden stick in it, you would hear a loud pop. The pop results when hydrogen combines with oxygen in the air. The hydrogen is burning. The ability to burn is called **flammability** (flam-uh-BIL-uh-tee). It is a chemical property. A new kind of

Career: *Firefighter*

HELP WANTED: FIREFIGHTER High school diploma required. Must pass written test and physical examinations. Minimum age 18. Needed for firefighting team.

It was a dry October day when the field caught fire. Responding to the alarm sounded at their fire station, the men and women quickly jumped onto the trucks and raced to the burning field. Their first task was to keep the fire from spreading. The team began by clearing a strip of land a short distance from the approaching flames. They then set another fire between the cleared strip and the raging flames. This would keep the fire contained to a small area. Finally the fire was put out with water.

The brave individuals who often risk their lives in the line of duty are **firefighters.** It is their job to protect people and property from the thousands of fires that occur each year. In doing their job, they are sometimes exposed to explosive, flammable, or poisonous materials.

The duties of firefighters include driving emergency vehicles, hooking up hoses and pumps, setting up ladders, and rescuing victims. Some firefighters are trained to conduct fire safety checks in buildings and homes, while others investigate false alarms and suspicious fires. If you are interested in this career, write to the Department of Fire Protection and Safety Technology, Oklahoma State University, 303 Campus Fire Station, Stillwater, OK 74078.

Figure 14-18 *Burning is a chemical change in which oxygen combines with another substance and produces heat and light.*

matter forms as the hydrogen burns. This substance is water—a combination of hydrogen and oxygen.

Oxygen is not a flammable gas. So you can distinguish it from hydrogen through the chemical property of flammability. However, although oxygen does not burn, it does support the burning of other substances. A glowing wooden splint placed in a test tube of oxygen will continue to burn until the oxygen is used up. This ability to support burning is another example of a chemical property.

The changes that substances undergo when they turn into other substances are called **chemical changes.** Chemical changes are closely related to chemical properties, but they are not the same. **A chemical property describes a substance's ability**

Figure 14-19 *Rusting is a chemical change in which iron slowly combines with oxygen to form rust, or iron oxide.*

to change into a different substance; a chemical change is the process by which the substance changes. For example, the ability of a substance to burn is a chemical property. However, the process of burning is a chemical change. Figures 14-18 through 14-20 show several chemical changes.

Another name for a chemical change is a **chemical reaction.** Chemical reactions often involve chemically combining different substances. For example, during the burning of coal, oxygen combines chemically with carbon—the substance that makes up most of the coal. This combining reaction produces a new substance—carbon dioxide. The carbon and oxygen have changed chemically. They no longer exist in their original forms.

The ability to use and control chemical reactions is an important skill. For chemical reactions produce a range of products from glass to pottery glaze to medicines. Your life is made easier and more enjoyable because of the products of chemical reactions: synthetic fibers such as nylon, plastics, soaps, building materials, even foods you eat. The next time you eat cheese or a slice of bread, remember that you are eating the product of a chemical reaction!

SECTION REVIEW

1. Give two examples of chemical properties.
2. Give an example of a chemical change.

Activity

Physical and Chemical Changes

1. In a dry beaker, mix a teaspoon of citric acid crystals with a tablespoon of baking soda. Observe what happens.

2. Fill another beaker halfway with water. Pour the citric acid-baking soda mixture into the water. Observe what takes place.

What type of change took place in the first step of the procedure? In the second step? Did the water have an important role in the procedure? If so, what do you think was its purpose? Why are some substances marked "Store in a dry place only"?

LABORATORY ACTIVITY

Conservation of Mass

Purpose

In this activity, you will prove that changes in the appearance of substances, whether chemical or physical, do not change the masses of the substances.

Materials (per group)

1 large test tube and stopper
1 small test tube
3 beakers
Balance
Potassium thiocyanate, KSCN
Ferric nitrate, $Fe(NO_3)_3$
Flask with stopper or peanut butter jar with screw cap
Several chunks of rock salt
Water

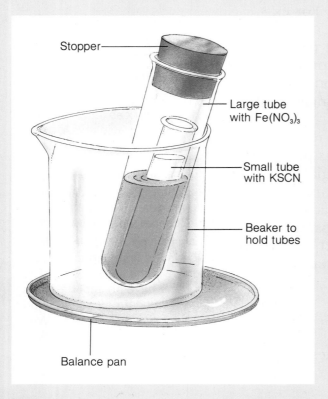

Stopper

Large tube with $Fe(NO_3)_3$

Small tube with KSCN

Beaker to hold tubes

Balance pan

Procedure

A. Chemical Change

1. Fill a large beaker with 100 mL of water. Then add 1.0 gram of KSCN to the beaker.
2. Fill another beaker with 100 mL of water. To this beaker add 2.4 grams of $Fe(NO_3)_3$. **CAUTION:** *KSCN and $Fe(NO_3)_3$ are poisonous if swallowed.*
3. Fill half of the small test tube with the KSCN solution. Carefully put the small test tube into the large test tube.
4. Now put the $Fe(NO_3)_3$ solution in the large test tube so that it comes to a height no higher than the height of the solution in the small test tube. Put the stopper into the large test tube. Then place the test tubes into a beaker.
5. Determine the combined mass of the beaker and the test tubes.
6. Invert the large test tube to observe the reaction. A dark red material, $Fe(SCN)_3$, forms.
7. Redetermine the mass of the total system.

B. Physical Change

1. Pour enough water into the glass container to make it half full. Add a few pieces of rock salt to the water and seal the container.
2. Use the balance to determine the mass of the container and its contents.
3. After some of the salt has dissolved, determine the mass of the container and contents again.

Observations and Conclusions

1. Did the mass of the total system in procedure A change after you inverted the test tube?
2. In procedure B, was there a change in the mass of the container, water, and salt after some of the salt had dissolved?

CHAPTER REVIEW

SUMMARY

14-1 Physical Properties and Changes

- Examples of physical properties of matter include color, shape, hardness, and density.

- Changes in which physical properties of a substance are altered but the substance remains the same kind of matter are called physical changes.

14-2 The Phases of Matter

- Matter can exist in any of four phases: solid, liquid, gas, and plasma.

- A solid has a definite shape and volume.

- A crystal is the regular, repeating pattern in which particles of a solid are arranged.

- Amorphous solids do not keep a definite shape because they do not form crystals.

- A liquid has a definite volume but not a definite shape. It takes the shape of its container.

- A gas has no definite volume or shape.

- Boyle's Law states that the volume of a fixed amount of gas varies inversely with the pressure. Charles's Law states that the volume of a fixed amount of gas varies directly with the temperature.

- Matter in the plasma state is very high in energy.

14-3 Phase Changes

- Phase changes are accompanied by either a loss or gain of heat energy.

- Melting is the change of a solid to a liquid at a temperature called the melting point. Freezing is the change of a liquid to a solid at the freezing point.

- Vaporization is the change of a liquid to a gas. Vaporization at the surface of a liquid is called evaporation. Vaporization throughout the liquid is called boiling.

- The boiling point of a liquid is related to the air pressure above the liquid.

- The change of a gas to a liquid is called condensation.

- Sublimation is the change of a solid directly to a gas.

14-4 Chemical Properties and Changes

- Chemical properties describe how a substance changes into other new substances.

- Flammability, the ability to burn, is a chemical property.

- When a substance undergoes a chemical change, or chemical reaction, it turns into a new and different substance.

VOCABULARY

Define each term in a complete sentence.

amorphous solid	chemical reaction	freezing point	physical change
boiling	condensation	gas	physical property
boiling point	crystal	liquid	plasma
Boyle's Law	crystalline solid	melting	solid
Charles's Law	evaporation	melting point	sublimation
chemical change	flammability	phase	vaporization
chemical property	freezing		

CONTENT REVIEW: MULTIPLE CHOICE

Choose the letter of the answer that best completes each statement.

1. Color, odor, and density are
a. chemical properties.   b. general properties.
c. physical properties.   d. solid properties.

2. The phase of matter characterized by definite shape and definite volume is
a. solid.   b. liquid.   c. gas.   d. plasma.

3. A regular pattern of particles is found in
a. molecules.   b. crystals.   c. compressions.   d. plasmas.

4. It is true that liquids have
a. definite shape and definite volume.
b. no definite shape but definite volume.
c. no definite shape and volume.
d. definite shape but no definite volume.

5. As the volume of a fixed amount of a gas decreases, the pressure of the gas
a. decreases.   b. remains the same.
c. first increases and then decreases.   d. increases.

6. As the temperature of a gas increases,
a. the volume decreases.   b. the volume remains the same.
c. the volume increases and decreases.   d. the volume increases.

7. The state of matter made up of very high-energy particles is
a. liquid.   b. plasma.   c. gas.   d. solid.

8. A solid changes to a liquid by
a. evaporation.   b. freezing.   c. melting.   d. sublimation.

9. Vaporization taking place at the surface of a liquid is called
a. boiling.   b. evaporation.   c. sublimation.   d. condensation.

10. Flammability is an example of a
a. chemical property.   b. physical property.
c. chemical change.   d. physical change.

CONTENT REVIEW: COMPLETION

Fill in the word or words that best complete each statement.

1. The phase of matter that has a definite volume but no definite shape is the _____ phase.

2. Solids that do not have a definite shape are called _____ solids.

3. If the volume of a certain amount of gas increases, the pressure _____.

4. High-energy particles that make up most of the matter on the sun are called the _____ phase of matter.

5. The temperature at which a solid changes to a liquid is called the _____.

6. The boiling point of water at the earth's surface is _____.

7. As air pressure decreases, the boiling point of water _____.

8. The process by which a gas changes into a liquid is called _____.

9. The process by which a solid changes directly to a gas is _____.

10. Another name for a chemical change is a chemical _____.

CONTENT REVIEW: TRUE OR FALSE

Determine whether each statement is true or false. If it is true, write "true." If it is false, change the underlined word or words to make the statement true.

1. Hardness, shape, taste, and melting point are <u>chemical</u> properties of matter.
2. Particles that make up a <u>solid</u> are packed very close together.
3. Common table salt, which has a regular, repeating arrangement of particles, is called <u>amorphous</u>.
4. The particles of matter are spread farthest apart in a <u>liquid</u>.
5. The pressure a gas exerts on the walls of its container is due to <u>collisions</u> of the particles of the gas with each other and with the walls of the container.
6. The relationship between the temperature of a gas and the volume it occupies is described by <u>Boyle's Law</u>.
7. A liquid will freeze when it <u>absorbs</u> heat energy.
8. The process by which a liquid changes to a gas is called <u>vaporization</u>.
9. Drops of water on the outside of a cold glass are water vapor that has <u>sublimed</u> into a liquid.
10. New substances having different properties are formed as a result of <u>physical</u> changes.

CONCEPT REVIEW: SKILL BUILDING

Use the skills you have developed in this chapter to complete each activity.

1. **Applying concepts** Explain the following statements:
   a. Frozen stringbeans have to be cooked for a longer time in Denver, Colorado, because of the city's high altitude.
   b. After traveling several kilometers on your bike, you notice that the tires feel hot and the pressure gauge indicates an increase in pressure.
2. **Classifying properties** Identify the following properties as either physical or chemical: (a) taste (b) combustibility (c) color (d) odor (e) flammability (f) ability to dissolve.
3. **Classifying changes** Identify the following changes as either physical or chemical: (a) burning coal (b) baking brownies (c) boiling water (d) digesting food (e) dissolving sugar (f) melting butter (g) exploding TNT (h) tarnishing silver.
4. **Relating cause and effect** Using the Gas Laws, predict what will happen to the volume of a gas if (a) the pressure triples (b) the temperature is halved (c) the pressure is decreased by a factor of five (d) the pressure is halved and the temperature is doubled.
5. **Making inferences** Explain why the temperature remains constant during a phase change even though the substance is absorbing heat.

CONCEPT REVIEW: ESSAY

Discuss each of the following in a brief paragraph.

1. What is a chemical reaction?
2. Compare the solid, liquid, and gas phases of matter in terms of shape, volume, and arrangement and movement of particles.
3. Explain how wet clothes hung on a clothesline on a very cold day dry.
4. Explain how evaporation and boiling are similar. Different.

Adventures in Science

W. LINCOLN HAWKINS

He Solved the Puzzle of the Aging Wires

Lincoln Hawkins examines a model of his "miracle" molecule. The molecule is that of a plastic used to protect wires from the weather.

When "Linc" Hawkins was twelve, his father and mother came home to find their son hard at work on a strange project. Linc was drawing plans for building a perpetual-motion machine. Such a machine never stops working. Linc thought that by laying out a series of tilted ramps, he would be able to keep a steel ball bearing rolling forever. What Linc did not realize was that friction and gravity would slow the ball down no matter how he tilted the ramps. But that did not stop Linc from trying to build his machine. After a few years of trying, however, Linc gave up the project. By then he had come to realize that the laws of physics make the invention of a perpetual-motion machine impossible.

Linc's impossible perpetual-motion machine was to be only the first in a series of challenges that awaited him. Although his first efforts had not been successful, they had convinced Linc that his future lay in science and engineering. Several years later, he attended Rensselaer Polytechnic Institute, from which he received a degree in chemical engineering.

Unfortunately for Linc, getting a degree was a lot easier than getting a job! For Linc graduated while the nation was experiencing the Great Depression of the 1930s. There were just no jobs available in engineering. But Linc Hawkins was not ready to call it quits. He went back to school and managed to earn a Master of Science degree from Howard University. A few years later, he received a higher degree, a Ph.D. from McGill University. And still he was not finished with his education. He continued his studies at Columbia University in New York. But was all this education leading anywhere?

Linc Hawkin's first break finally came in 1942. He was hired by the Bell System's Laboratories in New Jersey. There he worked on many chemical problems. But he did not find the problems challenging enough. So Linc convinced his supervisor to let him work with plastics. In this area, Linc believed, his training in chemistry and chemical engineering might be put to better use.

At this time, scientists were beginning to consider the use of plastics as insulators for electrical cables, including telephone cables. Insulators protect the cables. They keep the electricity in the wires. Up until then, lead had been used for this purpose. But lead was expensive, heavy, and in short supply.

Plastics known as polyethylenes, however, were lighter than lead. They were also inexpensive, flexible, strong, and water resistant. Some scientists felt that polyethylenes would make very good insulating coatings for electrical cables. But there was a problem. Tests showed that polyethylenes would wear out quickly when used outdoors. Exposure to light, heat, and moisture sometimes caused them to stiffen and crack. Was there a way to protect polyethylene against the weather?

This is where Linc Hawkins came in. He began to investigate how plastics become "old." And he also performed experiments to find ways of keeping the plastics "young." In other words, Hawkins was looking for a way to protect plastics from light, heat, and exposure to air. Each of these factors speeded up the aging of a plastic.

Hawkins soon realized that the key to keeping plastics young was to mix them with special chemicals. But which chemicals? The answer seemed simple. To keep a plastic safe from light, the plastic should be mixed with a chemical that did not break down when bathed in bright light for a long time. To protect a plastic against heat, the plastic should be mixed with a chemical that stood up to heat. And to keep a plastic from falling apart in air, the plastic should be mixed with a chemical that withstood long-time exposure to air.

Was there a single chemical with all these properties? And, if there were such a chemical, could it be mixed successfully with a plastic? Hawkins knew that such a single, miracle chemical probably did not exist. But

Hawkins and an assistant prepare to test wires coated with protective plastic.

there were different chemicals that were each strong in one way but not in others. So Hawkins began a search for a *combination* of chemicals. If he could find the right combination, he would be on the way to making the almost-perfect insulator.

Days stretched into weeks, weeks into months, and months into years as Hawkins worked on his problem. Little by little he began to solve it. First he found a chemical that could protect plastics against oxygen in the air. Then he found a chemical that could protect plastics against light. And finally he found a chemical that helped plastics stand up to heat.

Today, these chemicals and others like them make up the plastic that covers billions of kilometers of electrical wires. So the next time you pick up the telephone, stop and think how W. Lincoln Hawkin's career has made it easier for your call to reach its destination. And how ability, education, and hard work, even under the most difficult circumstances, can achieve great things.

This geothermal plant in Iceland helps bring heat and electricity to about 75 percent of homes in the country.

Can the Energy of Volcanoes Be Harnessed?

For many years, people living in different parts of the world have used heat from within the earth as a source of energy. They have done this in many ways. For example, when underground water comes in contact with hot rocks, the water's temperature can rise to above its boiling point.

The water then begins to turn to steam. This causes a tremendous buildup of pressure. The pressure forces steam and hot water to come rushing out through weak spots in the earth's crust. This spouting, steaming water is called a hot spring.

Water from these natural hot springs has been used by people as a source of heat. In cases where the water does not come up naturally, wells have been drilled near hot springs. These wells bring underground steam and boiling water to the surface where they can be put to use.

Heat energy from deep within the earth is called *geothermal* energy. One of the most important uses of geothermal energy is producing electricity. Since 1904, steam from deep underground has been used to run machines that generate electricity. This has been done in Italy, New Zealand, and California. In a year, these power plants can produce the same amount of energy that is in 13 million barrels of oil. That's enough to meet the electricity needs of a city the size of San Francisco! And the energy is there for the taking.

Up until now, most geothermal energy has come only from underground places near natural hot springs. But some engineers say that we could drill into underground hot spots far from hot springs.

If the hot spot turns out to be dry, cold water from the surface could be pumped down into the hot rocks. There the water would turn into steam. The steam would rush to the surface. And it could be used to generate electricity.

But several things could make this hard to do. Rocks hot enough to do the job might be much deeper underground than expected. Drilling very deep could cost a lot of money. Also, the steam rising from deep in the earth might cool on the way up. As a result, it would not provide enough pressure to run

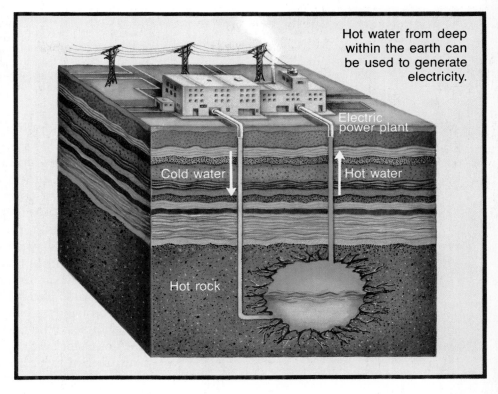

Hot water from deep within the earth can be used to generate electricity.

Electric power plant

Cold water

Hot water

Hot rock

machines that produce electricity. Another problem might be that the deep rocks might have so many cracks and holes that drilling would cause them to break up. Then the ground would collapse, destroying an expensive well and perhaps triggering an earthquake!

Taming a Volcano

Another way to use the earth's underground energy is to get it from an active volcano. This may seem like a crazy idea. After all, volcanoes are among the most powerful and "wild" natural furnaces on Earth. How can they be tamed? For one thing, the molten, or melted, rock of a volcano is often close to the surface of the earth. So there is no need to drill deep wells to get at the heat. Using the heat of volcanic rock is exactly what is done at the Eldfell volcano in Iceland.

Hot lava spurts freely from the ground in Iceland. However, in other parts of the country heat energy from inside the earth is trapped and used to warm homes and produce electricity. But there are risks in "taming" the earth's heat.

There spiral-shaped pipes are put into an area of hardening lava. Lava is molten rock that has reached the earth's surface. Water is then pumped through the pipes. The water is heated and then used to heat homes and do other jobs.

But there is a price to pay for getting heat from volcanoes. The pipes have to be made of a material that can withstand high temperatures. Unfortunately, making such pipes is very expensive. In addition, the water flowing through the pipes might not get hot enough to turn into high-pressure steam.

Of course, pipes don't have to be used. Water could be pumped directly into the cracks of a volcano crater. The steam, gases, and vapors that escape from the cracks could be passed through ordinary pipes to drive machines that produce electricity. But as one scientist said, "fooling around with a volcano involves risks."

Drilling holes and sending water into the cracks of a volcano could touch off a small but dangerous explosion. And a powerful volcanic eruption might be set off!

Does the need for energy make taking risks with volcanoes worthwhile? Many people say yes. They point out that electricity is not the only thing we could get by taming a volcano. For example, water heated up by a volcano could be used to heat homes, buildings, and greenhouses. But that is not all. Both steam and hot water could be used by industry to do a number of jobs. In addition, large amounts of valuable chemicals, particularly sulfur, are present in volcanic steam and hot water. Maybe these chemicals could be obtained from volcanoes. This would be a real bonus, point out many scientists.

Long ago, the people of Iceland learned to harness and use the energy from deep within the earth. Since then, Icelanders have used geothermal energy to improve their quality of living. Miles of greenhouses, warmed by the earth's own heat, provide large crops of fruits and vegetables for Icelanders. About 75 percent of their homes are heated by geothermal energy. Without this source of energy, Iceland would have to import millions of additional gallons of oil each year. Now the people are starting to use the earth's heat for fish farming, industry, and the generation of electricity. In time, Iceland may run entirely on geothermal power.

Is the greatest source of this power locked in volcanoes? Should we try to get at it? What do you think?

WIRED TO THE SUN

THE HOUSE OF THE FUTURE WILL RUN ON ENERGY FROM THE SUN, MAKE ITS OWN ELECTRICITY, AND EVEN SELL SOME OF IT TO THE ELECTRIC COMPANY.

It looks like an ordinary house, nestled among several others just like it. The lights are on in the kitchen. Good—dinner will be ready soon. Let's see . . . what was it you ordered for supper before you left the house this morning? Oh yes, a menu featuring your favorite Italian dishes. Mmm . . .

POWER PANELS

The thought of collapsing into a comfortable chair in a cool room makes you walk even faster. Not such a good idea on a day that saw the temperature reach 35 °C—for the sixth time in a row. The only advantage to this heat wave is that it will enable you to sell back lots of electricity to the power company. Yes indeed, those 64 solar panels rising up from the southern side of the roof really do their job. They produce enough electricity to run most of the major appliances in the house. The panels, covering a roof area of 5.5 square meters, are made up of *photovoltaic cells*. These cells change the energy in sunlight directly into electricity.

Now, of course, when there is no strong sunlight—like during the night and on cloudy days—the photovoltaic cells don't work. But you need not worry. At those times, your house is automatically switched to a local electric company's cables. You use its electricity and pay its prices. But so far this summer, the photovoltaic cells have produced more energy than the house needs. Some of the energy has been stored in the hot-water heater. The remainder has been sold back to the electric power company. The electricity is actually sent from the roof through cables to a nearby company station. Just think about it: The electricity you sell back is used to power one of those old-fashioned houses!

COMPUTER COMFORT

As you climb the stairs to the airlock entry, you happily notice that the outside window shutters have been automatically rolled down. These shutters reflect sunlight on hot days and help hold heat in the house on cold days. Shutters inside the windows have also been automatically lowered. Keeping direct sunlight out of the house on a day like today is very important.

Punching your code in the door keypad, you walk into the airlock entry. The airlock keeps hot air from entering the house in summer. In winter, it keeps the cold air out. The burglar-alarm system now shuts itself off. It feels a bit too cool in the house, so you signal the air-conditioning system to quit working so hard by punching a code into the thermostat.

As you pass from room to room, doors open automatically and lights switch on and off. The heat and motion sensors built into the floors, walls, and ceilings keep track of your path. And sure enough, as you enter the family room, your favorite music goes on.

With dinner cooking in the oven, which automatically went on when you walked in,

Each one of the 64 solar panels in the roof of this house is made up of photovoltaic cells. These cells capture the energy of the sun and change it directly into electricity.

you can sit down for awhile and relax. The dusting and vacuuming have all been done by the computer-driven robots. The kitchen computer keeps track of what food items you are getting low on. It will "call in" a list of groceries to the supermarket later.

So you're now free to sit and think about just how comfortable your home life is. The main computer of your house-management system takes care of almost everything—from controlling heating and cooling systems to providing news and sports information and educational courses. It opens locks, gives fire-alarm protection, cooks meals, turns lights on and off. It remembers when to turn certain appliances on or turn them off. It even takes readings of the dust level on the solar panels and lets you know when they need washing! Maybe someday soon, the computer will take care of cleaning the photovoltaic cells too!

SOLAR SERVICE

One amazing thing about your house is how well it uses energy. That's because it has several special features. These features are designed to get the most out of the sun's natural heating ability in winter. At the same time, they are designed not to add heat to the house in summer. How can this be done?

Both the trombe wall and the wall containing phasechange salts can be seen in this view of the house. These solar features, designed to get the most out of the sun's natural heating ability, are for winter use only.

The large, rounded shape in the front of the house is the airlock entry, which keeps hot air out of the house in summer and cold air in winter. The automatic shutters that reflect sunlight away in summer can be seen covering the upstairs windows.

That black wall covered with glass along the south side of the house is called a *trombe wall*. Its job is to collect the sun's rays. When these rays pass through the glass, they strike the trombe wall and are absorbed. The wall is painted black to make sure as much of the sun's energy as possible is absorbed. Dark colors absorb sunlight best. The wall heats up as it absorbs energy. Because the wall is very thick, a great deal of heat is stored. At night or on a cloudy day, that heat is slowly released into the house. The glass covering is about 15 centimeters from the wall and creates an air space. This space prevents the heat from escaping to the outside.

The trombe wall is a wintertime-only feature. During the summer months, the wall is shaded.

Phasechange salts are another amazing solar feature. Along the south side of the house, tubes no longer than 76 centimeters are built into the wall. These tubes are painted black on the outside to absorb the greatest amount of solar energy. Inside the tubes are special calcium compounds, which are solids at temperatures below 27.2° C, their melting point. During the day, the sun's radiation is absorbed by the salts. The salts melt if their temperature goes above 27.2° C. But during the time they melt and stay liquid, they store the sun's heat energy. Then at night, when the temperature drops below the melting point, the salts turn back to the solid phase. This phase change releases the stored heat to the house. However, like the trombe wall, the salt-containing tubes must be shaded during the summer months.

Well, these solar features have come a long way since they were first introduced back in the 1970s. Since then, they have been modified and improved. So now in 1997, they help keep your house warm as toast in winter and cool as a cucumber in summer. That thought reminds you your computer is calling — dinner is ready!

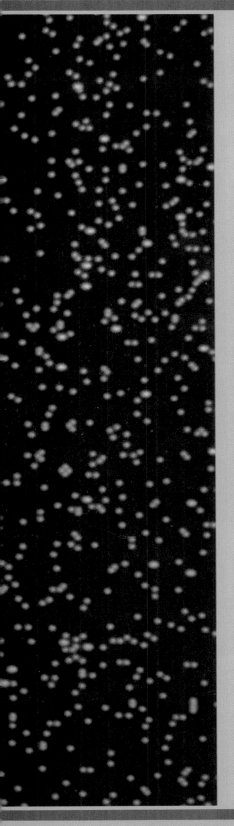

Structure of Matter

Probing ever further into space, scientists have discovered more and more distant objects. Somewhere out there is the most distant object in the universe, a sphere of tightly packed particles shooting out incredible bursts of energy. This object is a quasar. Located perhaps 20 billion light-years from the earth, this quasar has existed for 20 billion years. And its light has been traveling for that long a time. Perhaps by viewing the light from this quasar, scientists can witness the very beginning of the universe. For in that flash of light is evidence of the birth of all the matter in space—galaxies, stars, planets, rocks, molecules, atoms, and even the atoms' tiniest parts. These small particles, set loose billions of years ago, hold many secrets about the world around you.

CHAPTERS

15 Atoms and Molecules

16 Elements and Compounds

17 Mixtures and Solutions

Computer-generated image of Quasar 3C 273

15 Atoms and Molecules

CHAPTER SECTIONS

15-1 An Atomic Model of Matter
15-2 Structure of the Atom
15-3 The Molecule

CHAPTER OBJECTIVES

*After completing this chapter,
you will be able to:*

15-1 Discuss an early idea about
the nature of matter.

15-1 Describe the models of the
atom developed by Thomson
and Rutherford.

15-2 Classify three subatomic particles according to their
location, charge, and mass.

15-2 Define the terms atomic number, isotope, mass number,
and atomic mass.

15-2 Describe the arrangement of
electrons according to modern atomic theory.

15-3 Explain what a molecule is.

Beads of mercury gleam on a sheet of cloth. Some beads are small, others are large. But they are all still mercury, a pure substance. If you were to take the smallest bead of mercury and slice it in half once, twice, three times, even a thousand times, you would still be left with mercury—or would you?

Is there some incredibly tiny bead of mercury that if sliced one more time would no longer be mercury? It was just this kind of question that sparked the imagination and curiosity of early scientists. They hypothesized and argued as the years passed—for more than two thousand years, in fact.

Then, slowly, clues were found. Experiments were performed. New ideas were hatched. And finally an answer was developed. In many ways it was a very simple answer. To find it out, let's begin at the beginning.

Silvery beads of liquid mercury

15-1   An Atomic Model of Matter

Can matter be divided into smaller and smaller pieces forever? This was one of the questions that puzzled Greek philosophers more than 2400 years ago. For they were trying to figure out what matter was made of. Some of their ideas were rather strange and were certainly incorrect. Yet others were steps along the trail that would finally lead to the truth.

Early Ideas About the Atom

The search for a description of matter began with the Greek philosopher Democritus (de-MOK-rih-tuhs). He believed that an object could not be cut into smaller and smaller pieces forever. Eventually, the smallest possible piece would be obtained. And that piece could not be divided any further. It was indivisible. Democritus called this smallest piece of matter an **atom.** The word "atom" comes from the Greek word *atomos* meaning "indivisible."

What were these atoms? Democritus had no way of knowing. But he guessed they were small, hard particles that were all made of the *same* material but came in different shapes and sizes. Also, these atoms were infinite in number, always moving, and capable of joining together. Although Democritus was on the right trail, his theory of atoms was ignored and forgotten. In fact, it would be another 2100 years before others traveled down that trail.

Figure 15-1 *Ancient Greeks believed that all the matter on the earth was made of different combinations of four basic elements—fire, air, water, and earth (right). Alchemists, or early chemists, hoped to find a way to change ordinary metals into gold (left).*

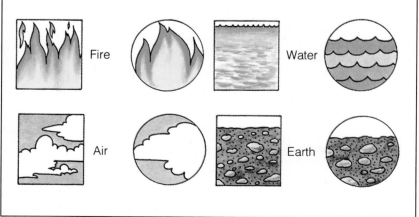

Fire   Water

Air   Earth

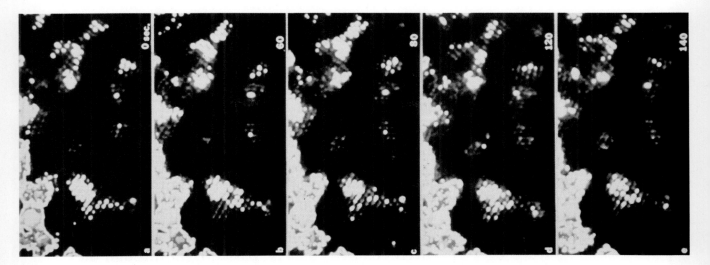

Modern Ideas About the Atom

In the early 1800s, the English chemist John Dalton did a number of experiments that led to an interesting conclusion. Dalton discovered that gases combined as if they were made of individual particles. These particles were the atoms of Democritus. For the first time, a theory of atomic structure was based on chemical experiments. Dalton had taken an important step along the atomic trail. But like Democritus, Dalton believed that atoms were "uncuttable." Was he right?

In 1897, the English scientist J. J. Thomson was studying the passage of an electric current through a gas. The gas gave off rays that Thomson showed were made of negatively charged particles. But the gas was known to be made of uncharged atoms. So where had the negatively charged particles come from? From within the atom, Thomson reasoned. A particle smaller than the atom had to exist. The atom was divisible! Thomson called the negatively charged particles "corpuscles." Today they are known as **electrons.**

Thomson's discovery of electrons presented him with a new problem to solve. If the atom as a whole was uncharged, yet it contained negatively charged particles, what balanced the negative charge? Thomson reasoned that the atom must also contain a positive charge. But try as he might, he was unable to find this positive charge.

So Thomson proposed a model of the atom that is sometimes called the "plum pudding" model. Thomson's proposed atomic model can be seen in Figure 15-3.

Figure 15-2 *Magnified more than 5 million times, the atoms that Democritus and other scientists labored to describe are clearly visible as blue, yellow, and red spots in these photographs of uranium atoms.*

Activity

A Mental Model

Scientists have developed an atomic model based on many experiments. Because scientists cannot see the subatomic particles, they must rely on observing how atoms behave under certain conditions. In this activity, you will develop a mental model of something you cannot see.

Place three to five small items in a shoe box. Seal the box. Exchange boxes with a friend or classmate. Using a variety of tests on the box, describe what you think is inside it. You can shake, turn, weigh, and smell the box. You can also hold a magnet near it. But do not open the box or damage it.

After you have developed a mental model of the contents, open the box and see how close your model is to the actual contents.

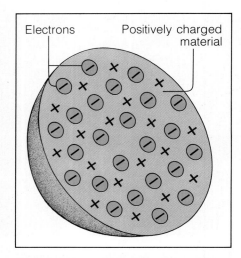

Figure 15-3 *Thomson's model of the atom pictured a "pudding" of positively charged material throughout which were scattered negatively charged electrons.*

According to Thomson's atomic model, the atom was made of a puddinglike positively charged material throughout which negatively charged electrons were scattered, like plums in a pudding. Thomson's model was far from correct, but it was an important step toward understanding the atom.

In 1908, the British physicist Ernest Rutherford was hard at work on an experiment that seemed to have little to do with the mysteries of the atom. Rutherford was doing experiments in which he fired tiny, positively charged particles at thin sheets of gold. Rutherford discovered that most of these positively charged "bullets" passed right through the gold atoms without changing course at all. This could only mean that the gold atoms in the sheet were mostly empty space! The atoms were not a pudding filled with a positively charged material, as Thomson had thought.

Some of the "bullets," however, did bounce away from the gold sheet as if they had hit something solid. What could this mean? Rutherford knew that positive charges repel other positive charges. So he proposed that an atom had a small, positively charged center that repelled his positively charged "bullets." He called this center of the atom the **nucleus** (NOO-klee-uhs; plural: nuclei, NOO-klee-igh).

In Rutherford's model, the atom looked like a tiny solar system in which electrons circled the nucleus in the same way that the planets circle the sun. Useful in many ways, this model did not explain the arrangement of the electrons.

Figure 15-4 *In Rutherford's experiment (left), most of the positively charged particles passed right through the gold sheet. A few were slightly deflected, while a very few bounced back. From these observations, Rutherford developed his model of the atom (right) as an object that was mostly space but had a dense, positively charged nucleus.*

EXPERIMENTAL SETUP

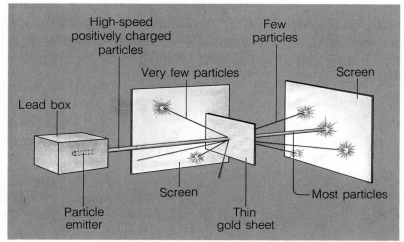

MODEL

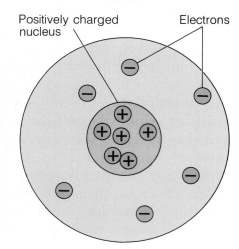

It would be the job of future scientists to improve upon Rutherford's atomic model. And it would not be a simple task! For the diameter of the atom is only one ten-billionth of a meter. Examining its structure is like finding one particular grain of sand among all the grains of the earth.

SECTION REVIEW

1. What atomic particle did J. J. Thomson discover?
2. What is the center of the atom called? Who discovered it?

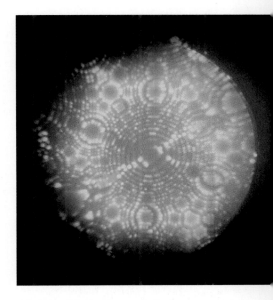

Figure 15-5 *A crystal of tungsten, magnified 3,000,000 times, shows a regular arrangement of atoms.*

15-2 Structure of the Atom

When Thomson performed his experiments, he was hoping to find a single particle smaller than the atom. Certainly Thomson would be surprised to learn that today about 200 different kinds of such particles are known to exist! Because these particles are smaller than an atom, they are called **subatomic particles**.

The three main subatomic particles are the proton, neutron, and electron. As you read about these particles, note the location, mass, and charge of each. In this way, you will better understand the modern atomic theory. Let's begin with the nucleus, or center, of the atom.

Figure 15-6 *When subatomic particles collide, new and unusual particles may be produced. By studying the tracks made by these particles in a bubble chamber, scientists can learn more about the nature and interactions of subatomic particles.*

The Nucleus

The nucleus is the "heart" of the atom, the core in which 99.9 percent of the mass of the atom is located. Yet the nucleus is about a hundred thousand times smaller than the entire atom! In fact, the size of the nucleus compared to the entire atom is like the size of a bee compared to a football stadium!

PROTONS Those positively charged "bullets" that Rutherford fired at the gold sheets bounced back because of the **protons** in the nucleus of the gold atoms. Protons are positively charged particles found in the nucleus.

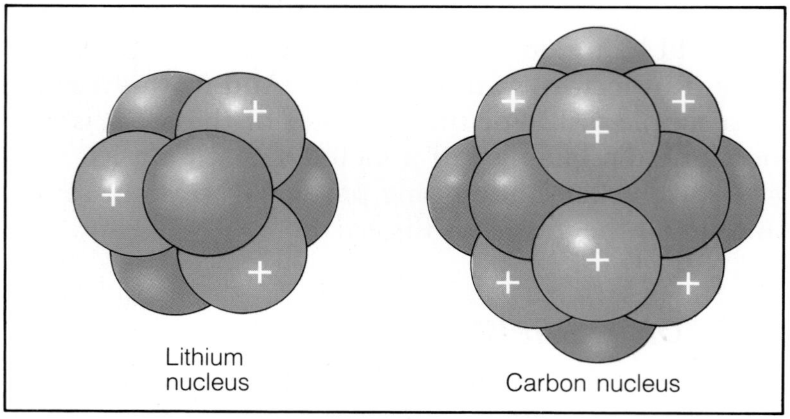

Figure 15-7 *A lithium nucleus contains 3 protons and 4 neutrons. A carbon nucleus contains 6 protons and 6 neutrons.*

Lithium nucleus

Carbon nucleus

Because the masses of subatomic particles are so small, scientists use a special unit to measure them. They call this unit an **atomic mass unit**, or amu. The mass of a proton is 1 amu. To get a better idea of how small a proton is, imagine the number 6 followed by 23 zeros. It would take that many protons to equal a mass of 1 gram!

NEUTRONS Sharing the nucleus with the protons are the electrically neutral **neutrons**. Neutrons have no charge. They do have mass, however. Each neutron has a mass of 1 amu.

Atomic Number

You read before that atoms of different substances are different. What is it that accounts for this difference? The answer lies in the nucleus. For it is the number of protons in a nucleus that determines what the substance is. For example, a carbon atom has 6 protons in its nucleus. Carbon is a dark solid. There are 7 protons in the nucleus of a nitrogen atom. That is only 1 more than carbon. Yet nitrogen is a colorless gas.

The number of protons in the nucleus is called the **atomic number**. It identifies the kind of atom. All hydrogen atoms—and *only* hydrogen atoms—have 1 proton and an atomic number of 1. Helium atoms have an atomic number of 2. So there are 2 protons in the nucleus of every helium atom. Oxygen has an atomic number of 8, and 8 protons in the nucleus of each atom. How many protons does uranium, atomic number 92, have?

Isotopes

The atomic number of a substance never changes. This means that there is always the same number of protons in the nucleus of every atom of that substance. But the number of neutrons is not so constant! Atoms of the same substance can have different numbers of neutrons.

Atoms that have the same number of protons but different numbers of neutrons are called **isotopes** (IGH-suh-tohps). Look at Figure 15-9. You will see three different isotopes of hydrogen. Notice that the number of protons does *not* change. Remember that the atomic number, or number of protons, identifies a substance. No matter how many neutrons there are in the nucleus, 1 proton always means the atom is hydrogen.

Figure 15-8 *The number of protons in an atom's nucleus determines what the atom is. Neon atoms, which make up the gas often used in colored lights (left), have 10 protons. Helium atoms, which make up a colorless, odorless gas often used in balloons (right), have 2 protons.*

Figure 15-9 *The three isotopes of hydrogen. Notice that the number of protons remains the same; the number of neutrons changes.*

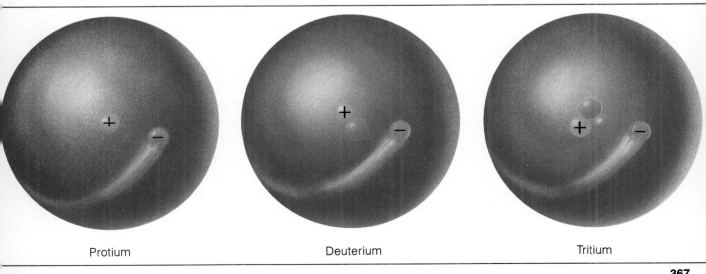

Protium   Deuterium   Tritium

COMMON ELEMENTS

Name		Atomic Number	Mass Number
Hydrogen	H	1	1
Helium	He	2	4
Carbon	C	6	12
Nitrogen	N	7	14
Oxygen	O	8	16
Fluorine	F	9	19
Sodium	Na	11	23
Aluminum	Al	13	27
Sulfur	S	16	32
Chlorine	Cl	17	35
Calcium	Ca	20	40
Iron	Fe	26	56
Copper	Cu	29	64
Zinc	Zn	30	65
Silver	Ag	47	108
Gold	Au	79	197
Mercury	Hg	80	201
Lead	Pb	82	207

Mass Number and Atomic Mass

All atoms have a **mass number.** The mass number of an atom is the sum of the protons and neutrons in its nucleus. The mass number of the carbon isotope with 6 neutrons is 6 (protons) + 6 (neutrons), or 12. The mass number of the carbon isotope with 8 neutrons is 6 (protons) + 8 (neutrons), or 14. To distinguish one isotope from another, the mass number is given with the element's name.

Two common isotopes of the element uranium are uranium-235 and uranium-238. The atomic number, or number of protons, of uranium is 92. Since the mass number is equal to the number of protons plus the number of neutrons, the number of neutrons can easily be determined. The number of neutrons is determined by subtracting the atomic number from the mass number. How many neutrons are there in each uranium isotope?

Any sample of an element as it occurs in nature will contain a mixture of isotopes. As a result, the **atomic mass** of the element will be the average of the masses of all the atoms in the sample. The atomic mass of an element refers to the average mass of all the isotopes of that element as they occur in nature. For this reason, the atomic mass of an element is not usually a whole number. The atomic mass of carbon is 12.011. This number indicates that in any sample of carbon there are more atoms of carbon-12 than there are of carbon-14.

The Electrons

If you think protons and neutrons are small, picture this. Whirling around outside the nucleus are particles that are about 1/2000 the mass of either a proton or a neutron! These particles are electrons. Electrons have a negative charge and a mass of 1/1836 amu. In an atom, the number of negatively charged electrons is usually equal to the number of positively charged protons. So the total charge on the atom is zero. The atom is neutral.

Rutherford pictured electrons moving around the nucleus like planets orbiting the sun. But as scientists learned more about the atom, they had to reject this

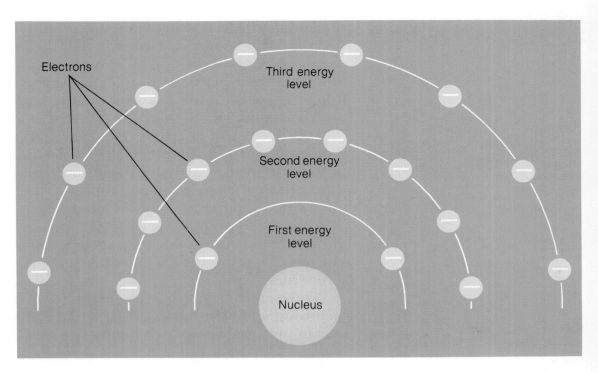

Electrons

Third energy level

Second energy level

First energy level

Nucleus

Figure 15-11 **Figure 15-11** *Each energy level in an atom can hold only a certain number of electrons. How many electrons are there in the first, second, and third energy levels shown here?*

theory. Their experiments showed that electrons do not move in fixed orbits. In fact, the *exact* location of an electron cannot be known. Only the probability, or likelihood, of finding an electron at a particular place in an atom can be determined.

In fact, the entire space in which electrons are found is what scientists think of as the atom itself. Sometimes this space is called the **electron cloud.** But do not think of the atom as a solid center surrounded by a fuzzy, blurry cloud. For the electron cloud is a *space* in which electrons are likely to be found. It is somewhat like the area around a beehive in which the bees move. Sometimes the electrons are near the nucleus. Sometimes they are farther away from it. In a hydrogen atom, one electron "fills" the cloud. It fills the cloud in the sense that it can be found almost anywhere within the space.

Although the electrons whirl about the nucleus billions of times in one second, they do not do this in a random way. For each electron seems to be locked into a certain area in the electron cloud. The location of an electron in the cloud depends upon how much energy the electron has.

According to modern atomic theory, electrons are arranged in **energy levels.** Energy levels represent

Activity

Electron Arrangement

Determine the electron arrangement for each of the following elements given their atomic numbers.

sodium 11	lithium 3
nitrogen 7	neon 10
chlorine 17	argon 18

the *most likely* location in the electron cloud in which electrons can be found. Electrons with the lowest energy are found in the energy level closest to the nucleus. Those electrons with higher energy are found in energy levels farther from the nucleus.

Each energy level within an atom can hold only a certain number of electrons. The energy level closest to the nucleus—the lowest energy level—can hold at most 2 electrons. The second and third energy levels can each hold 8 electrons. See Figure 15-11. The properties of different kinds of atoms depend on how many electrons are in the various energy levels of the atoms. In fact, the electron arrangement in the electron cloud is what gives the atom its chemical properties.

Is the atom "cuttable"? The existence of protons, neutrons, and electrons proves it is. And these particles in turn can be separated into even smaller particles. It is now believed that a new kind of particle makes up all the other known particles in the nucleus. This particle is called the **quark** (kwahrk). There are a number of different kinds of quarks. All nuclear particles are thought to be combinations of three quarks. According to current theory, quarks have properties called "flavor" and "color." There are six different flavors and three different colors.

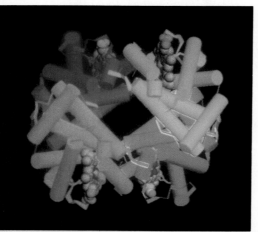

Figure 15-12 *Not all molecules are as simple as water. Here you see computer images of the more complex molecules of a body fluid* (top) *and a virus* (bottom).

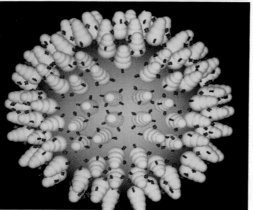

SECTION REVIEW

1. What two particles are found in the nucleus?
2. Define atomic number; isotopes; atomic mass.
3. Where are the electrons in an atom found?

15-3 The Molecule

Most atoms have a very important property. They can combine chemically with each other to produce new and different structures called **molecules** (MAH-luh-kyoolz). A molecule is made up of two or more atoms chemically bonded.

A molecule is the smallest particle of a substance that has all the properties of that substance. Suppose a sample of water was divided up into

HELP WANTED: SCIENCE TEACHER
To teach physical science to junior high school students. Science program includes laboratory and field activities. Teaching certification in science required. Must be available to guide students in after-school activities such as science club.

Saturday afternoon provided ideal weather for some backyard gardening. But the teacher's mind was back in the classroom rather than on the sprouting bean plants. This week the unit on chemistry was to begin. Many students would have trouble understanding what could not be seen with the unaided eye. The teacher thought about the best way to begin the lesson.

Science teachers spend much of their time developing lesson plans for different topics. They create interesting ways to present information to their students. Activities such as lectures, demonstrations, laboratory work, and field trips are often used.

Science teachers have other duties as well. They must correct homework and test papers, make up tests and quizzes, record pupil attendance and progress, and issue reports to parents. They also attend meetings, conferences, and workshops. If you are interested in this career, you can learn more by writing to the American Federation of Teachers, 1012 Fourteenth Street N.W., Washington, DC 20005.

smaller and smaller samples. Eventually a particle that could not be further divided without losing its properties would be reached. This particle is the water molecule. It is made up of two atoms of hydrogen and one atom of oxygen chemically bonded.

Some atoms form bonds with other atoms very easily. Other atoms hardly ever form bonds. What accounts for the differences in bonding ability? The answer can be found in the arrangement of the electrons in an atom. The bonding ability of an atom is a chemical property. And it is the electron arrangement in the electron cloud that gives an atom its chemical properties.

Figure 15-13 *This is the first photograph ever taken of atoms and their bonds. The bright round objects are single atoms. The fuzzy areas between atoms represent bonds.*

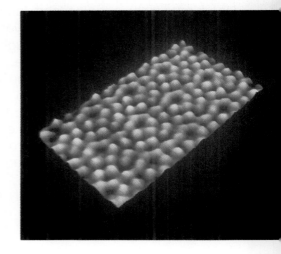

SECTION REVIEW

1. What is a molecule?
2. Give one example of a molecule.

LABORATORY ACTIVITY

Flame Tests

Purpose

In this activity, you will observe the colors produced by excited atoms of different substances. When some substances are heated in a flame, their electrons are raised to higher energy levels by heat energy. When these electrons fall back into the lower energy levels, energy is released. The released energy produces a color characteristic of that substance.

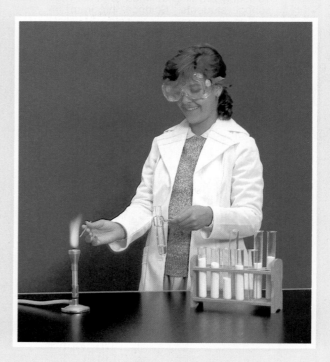

Materials (*per group*)

Bunsen burner
7 test tubes and test tube rack
Test tube clamp
Safety goggles
Wire loop with wooden handle
Hydrochloric acid, 6M HCl
.5M solutions of the nitrates of sodium, barium, calcium, lithium, potassium, strontium
Graduated cylinder
Test tube brush
Distilled water
Lab coat
Rubber gloves

Procedure

1. Put on safety goggles and lab coat. For steps 2 and 3 wear rubber gloves.
2. To clean each test tube thoroughly, hold it with the test tube clamp, place a few milliliters of 6M HCl into it and gently brush. Rinse the test tubes with tap water and then distilled water. **CAUTION:** *HCl burns. Avoid contact with skin, eyes, and clothes. If any should fall on you, immediately wash the area with water and then notify your teacher.*
3. Clean the wire loop by carefully dipping it first into some 6M HCl acid in a test tube

and then holding it in the colorless flame of the Bunsen burner. Repeat until the wire adds no color to the flame. **CAUTION:** *Be careful when lighting and using the Bunsen burner.*

4. Pour 4 mL of the sodium nitrate solution into a clean test tube. Dip the tip of the clean wire loop into the solution, and then hold it in the flame just above the wire. Note: Heat only the tip of the wire.
5. Clean the wire loop as in Step 3.
6. Repeat Step 4, using in turn 4 mL of the solutions of the nitrates of barium, calcium, lithium, potassium, strontium. Clean the wire thoroughly after each test. Record the color of the flame for each substance.

Observations and Conclusions

1. How might scientists use a flame test to study unknown substances?

CHAPTER REVIEW

VOCABULARY

Define each term in a complete sentence.

atom	**electron**	**mass number**	**proton**
atomic mass	**electron cloud**	**molecule**	**quark**
atomic mass unit	**energy level**	**neutron**	**subatomic particle**
atomic number	**isotope**	**nucleus**	

CONTENT REVIEW: MULTIPLE CHOICE

Choose the letter of the answer that best completes each statement.

1. The name Democritus gave to the smallest possible piece of matter is
   a. molecule.   b. atom.   c. electron.   d. proton.
2. The scientist J. J. Thomson discovered the
   a. proton.   b. electron.   c. neutron.   d. nucleus.
3. The small, heavy center of an atom is the
   a. neutron.   b. proton.   c. electron cloud.   d. nucleus.
4. Ernest Rutherford's atomic model pictured a
   a. negatively charged center with positively charged particles close to it.
   b. positively charged material with negatively charged particles in it.
   c. positively charged center with negatively charged particles around it.
   d. positively charged center only.

5. Particles smaller than the atom are
   a. molecules.   b. elements.
   c. compounds.   d. subatomic particles.
6. The nucleus of an atom contains
   a. protons and neutrons.   b. protons and electrons.
   c. neutrons and electrons.   d. protons, neutrons, and electrons.
7. The number of protons in an atom is called its
   a. mass number.   b. isotope number.
   c. quark number.   d. atomic number.
8. An isotope of oxygen, atomic number 8, could have
   a. 8 protons and 10 neutrons.   b. 10 protons and 10 neutrons.
   c. 10 protons and 8 electrons.   d. 6 protons and 8 neutrons.
9. All nuclear particles are thought to be made up of a combination of three
   a. electrons.   b. isotopes.   c. molecules.   d. quarks.
10. Two or more atoms chemically bonded together form a(n)
    a. quark.   b. isotope.   c. molecule.   d. nucleus.

CONTENT REVIEW: COMPLETION

Fill in the word or words that best complete each statement.

1. The smallest particle of matter is a(n) _____.

2. The negatively charged particles that Thomson called "corpuscles" are today known as _____.

3. Rutherford is credited with the discovery of the _____, or the center of the atom.

4. The particles in an atom that have a positive charge and a mass of 1 amu are the _____.

5. An atom with an atomic number of 18 has _____ protons in its nucleus.

6. Atoms that have the same number of protons but different numbers of neutrons are called _____.

7. The subatomic particle that has a negative charge and a mass almost equal to zero is the _____.

8. The negative particles in an atom are arranged in _____, which represent the most likely places of finding them based on their energy content.

9. The particle that is now thought to make up all other nuclear particles is called the _____.

10. When two or more atoms combine chemically, they form a(n) _____.

CONTENT REVIEW: TRUE OR FALSE

Determine whether each statement is true or false. If it is true, write "true." If it is false, change the underlined word or words to make the statement true.

1. The idea that matter was made up of indivisible particles called atoms was proposed by Democritus.

2. In the early 1800s, Aristotle developed a theory of atomic structure that was based on chemical experiments.

3. In Thomson's experiment, the gas in the tube gave off rays that were made of negatively charged particles called neutrons.

4. Rutherford's experiments detected the presence of a positively charged center in the atom.

5. Most of the mass of the atom is located in the electron cloud.
6. Subatomic particles with a mass of 1 amu and no electric charge are called protons.
7. Chlorine has an atomic number of 17. It has 17 protons in its nucleus.
8. Atoms having the same number of protons but different numbers of neutrons are called isomers.
9. Electrons having the least amount of energy are found farthest from the nucleus.
10. Two atoms of hydrogen and one atom of oxygen chemically bonded together form a water molecule.

CONCEPT REVIEW: SKILL BUILDING

Use the skills you have developed in the chapter to complete each activity.

1. **Making calculations** You can calculate the atomic number of element X by doing the following arithmetic:
   a. Multiply the atomic number of hydrogen by the number of electrons in mercury, atomic number 80.
   b. Divide this number by the number of neutrons in helium, atomic number 2, mass number 4.
   c. Add the number of protons in potassium, atomic number 19.
   d. Add the mass number of the most common isotope of carbon.
   e. Subtract the number of neutrons in sulfur, atomic number 16, mass number 32.
   f. Divide by the number of electrons in boron, atomic number 5, mass number 11.
   Which of the following elements is X: fluorine, atomic number 9; neon, atomic number 10; sodium, atomic number 11?

2. **Developing a model** You are trying to locate a friend on a sunny Saturday afternoon. Although you cannot say with absolute certainty where your friend is, you can estimate the chances of finding your friend in various places. Your estimates are based on past experiences. Construct a table listing at least seven possible locations for your friend. Next to each location, give the probability, or likelihood, of finding your friend in that location in percent. Remember that your total probability should equal 100 percent. Would a change in the weather affect your results? How about a change in the day of the week? How does this activity relate to an electron's location in an atom?

3. **Identifying relationships** Sodium has only one naturally occurring isotope. Explain how the atomic mass of this isotope compares with the mass number.

4. **Making inferences** Why are models useful in the study of atomic theory?

CONCEPT REVIEW: ESSAY

Discuss each of the following in a brief paragraph.

1. Describe the electron configuration of each element based on atomic number: sulfur, 16; fluorine, 9; argon, 18; lithium, 3.

2. A certain element contains 82 percent of an isotope of mass number J and 18 percent of an isotope of mass number K. Is the atomic mass of this element closer to J or to K? Explain your answer.

3. Why must scientists consider the concept of probability in describing the location of electrons?

4. Classify the three main subatomic particles according to location, charge, and atomic mass.

5. What is the atomic number of an element? What is its significance?

16 Elements and Compounds

CHAPTER SECTIONS

16-1 Elements

16-2 Compounds

CHAPTER OBJECTIVES

After completing this chapter, you will be able to:

16-1 Define an element and give several examples of elements.

16-1 Give the chemical symbols for ten common elements.

16-2 Distinguish between an element and a compound.

16-2 Describe what information a chemical formula provides.

16-2 Explain how a balanced chemical equation describes a chemical reaction.

A reddish stain on a scrap of fabric . . . some bits of dust gathered in the creases of a man's clothing . . . a seemingly unimportant clump of mud upon the floor . . . a few grains of tobacco let fall at the scene of a murder. . . . What could all these details mean? To detective Sherlock Holmes, the creation of British novelist Arthur Conan Doyle, they were clues to some of the most mysterious crimes imaginable. By paying close attention to the evidence, Holmes was able to solve many of the most perplexing crimes. And in so doing, he amazed not only the London police but also his own assistant, Dr. Watson.

Holmes's success had a simple, solid basis: logical thinking combined with a knowledge of chemistry. Using this knowledge, he was able to classify and analyze various substances that were clues to the mysteries. Holmes was a master at using scientific principles to solve crimes.

Criminology, of course, is not the only area in which scientific principles are applied. The whole world is a place of mystery, filled with puzzles and wonders that await the investigation of young detectives like you. But before you set out on your adventure, you will need to know how chemical substances are classified. And soon you will share the feelings of Holmes, who exclaimed at moments of discovery, "By Jove, Watson, I've got it!"

Detective Sherlock Holmes gathering clues

Figure 16-1 *The gold in this rock (left) is an example of a pure substance. Gold has long been used in jewelry and coins. These gold bars (right), called bullion, are part of a nation's money reserves.*

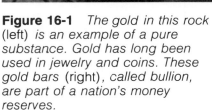

Activity

Getting to Know the Elements

Choose two elements that are commonly found in your surroundings. Mount a sample of each element on poster paper. Then illustrate the element's uses by cutting out and pasting pictures that show the various uses.

16-1 Elements

Suppose you were given a list of 100 different objects—objects common to your world. And you had to sort them out into different groups. How might you do it? Perhaps you would group them according to their color. Or their shape and size. Or their texture. Maybe you would sort them by their uses.

Well, scientists have faced just such a problem with the classification of matter. And by applying the concepts of atoms and molecules, they have been able to sort all forms of matter into logical groups. So a great deal of the work has already been done for you!

But before you discover what scientists have done, you should recall what you have learned about atoms and molecules. An atom is a tiny building block of matter. And a molecule, which is made up of two or more atoms chemically bonded, is the smallest particle of a substance that has all the properties of that substance.

The Simplest Pure Substances

The first thing scientists did was to divide matter into two groups: materials made up of parts that are all alike and materials made up of parts that are not alike. For example, in a sample of water, all the parts making up the water are exactly alike. These parts are water molecules. Scientists call such a material a **pure substance**. A pure substance contains only one *kind* of molecule. The oxygen you breathe is another example of a pure substance. All the molecules in the gas are exactly the same.

Now suppose you are looking at a sample of a rock called granite, like the one in Figure 16-2. You might notice that scattered throughout the granite are different-colored particles. These particles are the minerals quartz, feldspar, and mica. So granite is not made up of only one kind of molecule. It is not a pure substance. You will learn exactly what granite is in Chapter 17.

Let's go back to oxygen for a moment. Every molecule of oxygen is made up of two atoms of oxygen bonded together. So each oxygen molecule contains only one *kind* of atom—the oxygen atom. **A pure substance made up of only one kind of atom is called an element.** Oxygen is an **element.** So is hydrogen. Carbon, aluminum, iron, mercury, silver, and uranium are also elements.

Elements are the simplest type of pure substance. They cannot be changed into simpler substances by heating or by any chemical process. Suppose you melt a piece of iron by adding heat energy to it. You may think that you have changed the iron into a

Figure 16-2 *Granite, which is not a pure substance, is made up of the minerals quartz, feldspar, and mica.*

Figure 16-3 *The beautiful colors of fireworks* (left) *are produced by the rapid burning of elements such as magnesium, phosphorus, sulfur, barium, and strontium. The element silicon is used to make computer chips* (right).

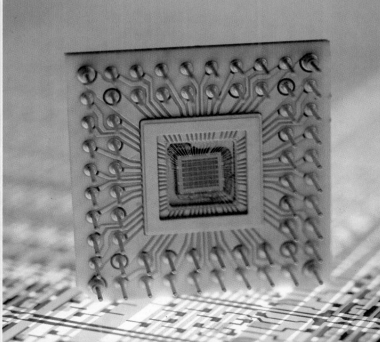

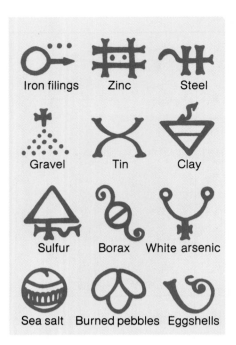

Iron filings   Zinc   Steel

Gravel   Tin   Clay

Sulfur   Borax   White arsenic

Sea salt   Burned pebbles   Eggshells

Figure 16-4 *These were the symbols used by the alchemists.*

simpler substance. But the liquid you now have still contains only iron atoms. True, the iron has changed phase—from solid to liquid. But it is still iron. No new or simpler substance has been formed.

Chemical Symbols

For many years, scientists had to spell out the full names of elements when writing about them. As you can imagine, this practice was time-consuming. Then in 1813, a system of representing the elements with symbols was introduced. After all, why couldn't chemists do what mathematicians and musicians did?

Chemical symbols are a shorthand way of representing the elements. Each symbol consists of one or two letters, usually taken from the element's name. The symbol for the element oxygen is O. The symbol for hydrogen is H; for carbon, C. The symbol for aluminum is Al; and for chlorine, Cl. You should note that when two letters are used in a symbol, the

COMMON ELEMENTS

Name	Symbol	Name	Symbol	Name	Symbol
Aluminum	Al	Helium	He	Oxygen	O
Bromine	Br	Hydrogen	H	Potassium	K
Calcium	Ca	Iodine	I	Silver	Ag
Carbon	C	Iron	Fe	Sodium	Na
Chlorine	Cl	Lead	Pb	Sulfur	S
Copper	Cu	Magnesium	Mg	Tin	Sn
Fluorine	F	Mercury	Hg	Uranium	U
Gold	Au	Nitrogen	N	Zinc	Zn

Figure 16-5 *This table shows the chemical symbols for some of the most common elements. What is the symbol for potassium? For lead?*

first letter is *always* capitalized, but the second letter is *never* capitalized. Do you know why two letters are sometimes needed for a symbol? Hint: Scientists have already identified more than 108 elements!

What do you think the symbol for gold is? Is it G? Is it Go? The symbol for gold is Au. Does that surprise you? Gold is not spelled with an "a" or a "u." But the reason for the symbol is really not so strange. The Latin name for gold is *aurum*. Scientists often use the Latin name of an element to create its symbol. Here are some other examples. The symbol for silver is Ag, from the Latin word *argentum*. The Latin word for iron is *ferrum*. So the symbol for this element is Fe. Mercury's symbol is Hg, from the Latin name *hydrargyrum*. The table in Figure 16-5 lists some common elements and their symbols.

SECTION REVIEW

1. What type of pure substance is made up of only one kind of atom?
2. What is the shorthand way of representing the elements?
3. What is the chemical symbol for: bromine; nitrogen; iron; calcium; oxygen; sodium?

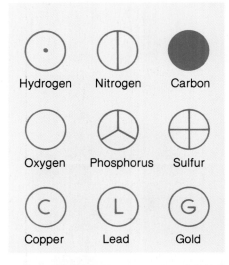

Figure 16-6 *These symbols were part of Dalton's system for representing the elements.*

Figure 16-7 *Sodium is a highly reactive element that must be stored in oil (top). Chlorine is a yellow-green, poisonous gas (center). The compound formed when these two elements chemically combine is sodium chloride, or common table salt (bottom).*

16-2 Compounds

Let's go back to the sample of water again. Water is a pure substance. It contains only *one kind of molecule.* That molecule is made up of two hydrogen atoms chemically bonded to one oxygen atom. So each molecule of water contains *more than one kind of atom.* Pure substances such as water are known as **compounds.** Compounds are made up of molecules that contain more than one kind of atom. **Compounds are two or more elements chemically combined.** Sugar is a compound. Each sugar molecule is made up of atoms of carbon, hydrogen, and oxygen. Baking soda is a compound you may be familiar with. Carbon dioxide, ammonia, and TNT are compounds. Can you name some other compounds?

Unlike elements, compounds can be broken down into simpler substances. Heating is one way of separating some compounds into their elements. For example, the ore known as chalcocite is the compound copper sulfide. When heated to a high temperature, this ore breaks down into the elements copper and sulfur.

Sometimes the elements in a compound are so strongly bonded that heating cannot separate them. So some other form of energy must be used. Often electric energy is used to break down a compound. For example, by passing an electric current through water, this compound can be broken down into the two different elements, hydrogen and oxygen, that make it up.

The properties of the elements that make up a compound are often very different from the properties of the compound itself. Would you want to flavor your French fried potatoes with a poisonous gas and a highly active metal? Probably not! Yet, in a way, this is exactly what you are doing when you sprinkle salt on your potatoes. Chlorine is a yellow-green gas that is poisonous. Sodium is a silvery metal that explodes if placed in water. But when chemically combined, these elements produce a harmless white compound—sodium chloride—that has a tasty flavor!

Chemical Formulas

When you began to read, you probably started by learning the alphabet. Well, you can think of chemical symbols as the letters of a chemical alphabet. Just as you learned to put letters together to make words, chemical symbols can be put together to make chemical "words." Combinations of chemical symbols are called **chemical formulas.** These formulas are a shorthand for the names of chemical substances.

Most chemical formulas represent compounds. For example, ammonia is a compound made up of the elements nitrogen and hydrogen. A molecule of ammonia has the formula NH_3. Sometimes, however, the formula represents a molecule of an element. For example, the symbol for the element oxygen is O. But oxygen occurs naturally as a molecule containing 2 atoms of oxygen bonded together. So the formula for a molecule of oxygen is O_2. Some other gases that exist only as pairs of atoms are hydrogen, H_2, nitrogen, N_2, fluorine, F_2, and chlorine, Cl_2. Remember, the *symbols* for the elements just listed are the letters only. The *formulas* are the letters with the small number 2 at the lower right.

Carbon dioxide is a compound of the elements carbon and oxygen. Its formula is CO_2. By looking at the formula, you can tell that every molecule is made up of 1 atom of carbon, C, and 2 atoms of oxygen, O. Water has the formula H_2O. How many hydrogen atoms and oxygen atoms are there in a molecule of water?

When writing a chemical formula, you use the symbol of each element in the compound. You also use small numbers called **subscripts.** Subscripts are placed to the lower right of the symbols. A subscript gives the number of atoms of the element in the compound. When there is only 1 atom of an element, the subscript 1 is *not* written. It is understood to be 1.

Can you now see the advantages of using chemical formulas? Not only does a formula save space, but it tells a lot about the compound. It tells you the elements that make up the compound. And it tells you how many atoms of each element combine to form the compound.

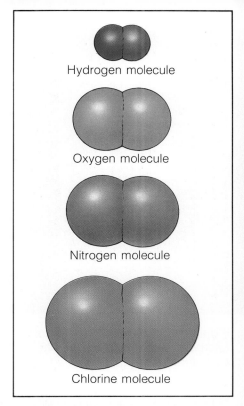

Figure 16-8 *Hydrogen, oxygen, nitrogen, and chlorine exist as pairs of atoms chemically bonded to form molecules.*

Figure 16-9 *A carbon dioxide molecule, CO_2, is made up of two atoms of oxygen bonded to one atom of carbon. A water molecule, H_2O, consists of two hydrogen atoms bonded to one oxygen atom.*

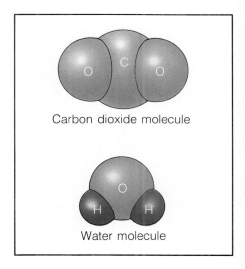

Figure 16-10 *The changing colors of autumn leaves* (left) *are caused by chemical reactions. Several chemical reactions are involved in the manufacture of plastic fibers* (right).

Figure 16-11 *The formation of a carbon dioxide molecule involves the chemical bonding of one carbon atom to one oxygen molecule.*

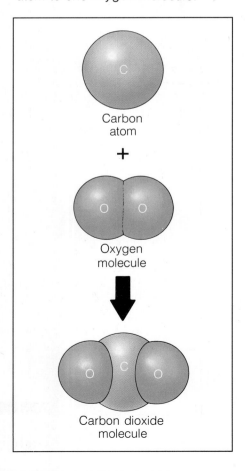

Carbon
atom

+

Oxygen
molecule

Carbon dioxide
molecule

Chemical Equations

If symbols are "letters" and formulas are "words," chemical "sentences" can be written. But what are chemical "sentences"? They are a way of describing a chemical process, or **chemical reaction.** In a chemical reaction, substances are changed into other substances through a rearrangement or new combination of their atoms. New chemical substances with new properties are formed.

Have you ever seen charcoal burning in a barbecue grill? If so, you were watching a chemical reaction. The carbon atoms in the charcoal were combining with the oxygen molecules in the air to form the gas carbon dioxide. This reaction could be written:

carbon atoms plus oxygen molecules
produce carbon dioxide molecules

But using symbols and formulas, this reaction can be written in a simpler way:

$$C + O_2 \rightarrow CO_2$$

The symbol C represents a carbon atom. The formula O_2 represents a molecule of oxygen. And the formula CO_2 represents a molecule of carbon dioxide. The arrow is read "yields," which is another way of saying "produces." This description of a chemical reaction using symbols and formulas is called a **chemical equation.**

Here is the chemical equation for the formation of water from the elements hydrogen and oxygen:

$$H_2 + O_2 \rightarrow H_2O$$

Look closely at this equation. It tells you what elements are combining and what product is formed. But there is something wrong. Do you know what it is?

Look at the number of oxygen atoms on each side of the equation. Are they the same? On the left side of the equation, there are 2 oxygen atoms. On the right side, there is only 1 oxygen atom. Could 1 oxygen atom have disappeared? Scientists know that atoms are *never* created or destroyed in a chemical reaction. Atoms can only be rearranged. So there must be the same number of atoms of each element on each side of an equation. The equation must be balanced.

$$2H_2 + O_2 \rightarrow 2H_2O$$

Now count the atoms of each element on each side of the equation. You will find they are the same: 4 atoms of hydrogen on the left and on the right, and 2 atoms of oxygen on the left and on the right. The equation is correctly balanced.

An equation can be balanced by placing the appropriate number in front of the chemical formula. This number is called a **coefficient** (koh-uh-FI-shuhnt). The equation now tells you that 2 molecules of hydrogen combine with 1 molecule of oxygen to produce 2 molecules of water.

A balanced chemical equation is "evidence" of a chemical reaction. Using your knowledge of elements, compounds, symbols, and formulas, you can now solve the mysteries of chemical reactions. Like Sherlock Holmes, you too can say, "I've got it!"

SECTION REVIEW

1. What is a compound? How is it different from an element?
2. What does a formula indicate about a compound?
3. Why must a chemical equation be balanced?

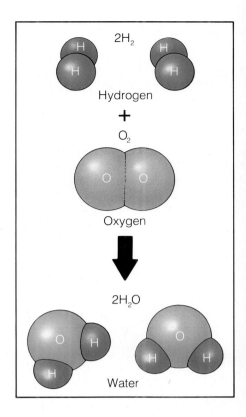

Figure 16-12 *When two molecules of hydrogen chemically combine with one molecule of oxygen, two molecules of water are formed.*

Activity

Naming and Counting Atoms

The chemical formula for baking soda is $NaHCO_3$. The chemical formula for table sugar is $C_{12}H_{22}O_{11}$. What elements make up each of these compounds, and how many atoms of each element are there?

LABORATORY ACTIVITY

Marshmallow Molecules

Purpose

In this activity, you will make model molecules and use them to learn why coefficients are necessary to balance chemical equations.

Materials *(per group)*

Toothpicks
Food coloring: red, yellow, green, blue,
    purple (red/blue), orange (yellow/red)
25 large marshmallows

Procedure

A. *Making Marshmallow Atoms*

1. Set 25 marshmallows out overnight so that they dry out.
2. Prepare marshmallow atoms by applying food coloring as follows:
    N (nitrogen)—red (2)
    H (hydrogen)—blue (6)
    Cu (copper)—green (4)
    O (oxygen)—white (8)
    C (carbon)—yellow (1)
    K (potassium)—orange (2)
    Cl (chlorine)—purple (2)
3. Allow the marshmallows to dry for a few hours.

B. *Assembling the Marshmallow Molecules*

1. Using two red marshmallows and a toothpick, make a molecule of N_2. Then make a molecule of H_2 using blue marshmallows.
2. Ammonia, NH_3, is used in cleaning solutions and fertilizers. A molecule of ammonia contains 1 nitrogen atom and 3 hydrogen atoms. Using the marshmallow molecules that you made in step 1, produce an ammonia molecule of nitrogen and hydrogen. You may use as many nitrogen and hydrogen molecules as you need to make ammonia molecules as long as you do not

leave any atoms over. Note: Hydrogen and nitrogen must start out as molecules consisting of two atoms each. Now balance the equation that produces ammonia:

$$\_\_ N_2 + \_\_ H_2 \rightarrow \_\_ NH_3$$

3. Using two green marshmallows for copper and one white one for oxygen, prepare copper oxide, Cu_2O. Using a yellow marshmallow for carbon, manipulate the molecules to represent and balance this equation, which produces metallic copper:

$$\_\_ Cu_2O + \_\_ C \rightarrow \_\_ Cu + \_\_ CO_2$$

4. Using orange for potassium, purple for chlorine, and white for oxygen, assemble $KClO_3$.
5. The decomposition of $KClO_3$ is a way to produce O_2. Take apart your $KClO_3$ to make KCl and O_2. You may need more than one molecule of $KClO_3$ to do this.

Observations and Conclusions

1. How many molecules of N_2 and H_2 are needed to produce two molecules of NH_3?
2. How many molecules of copper are produced from two molecules of Cu_2O?
3. How many molecules of O_2 are produced from two molecules of $KClO_3$?

CHAPTER REVIEW

SUMMARY

16-1 Elements

■ A pure substance is made up of parts that are all alike.

■ Elements are the simplest type of pure substance because they are made up of only one kind of atom. They cannot be broken down into simpler substances by chemical means.

■ Examples of elements include oxygen, carbon, aluminum, iron, mercury, silver, uranium, magnesium, and silicon.

■ Chemical symbols made up of one or two letters are used to represent the elements. When two letters are used in a symbol, the first letter is always capitalized, but the second letter is never capitalized.

16-2 Compounds

■ Pure substances that contain more than one kind of atom are called compounds.

■ Compounds are two or more elements chemically combined. Compounds can be broken down into simpler substances. The elements in a compound are most often separated by heating and by electricity.

■ The properties of the elements that make up a compound are often very different from the properties of the compound itself.

■ Combinations of chemical symbols, used to represent substances, are called formulas.

■ Most chemical formulas represent compounds. Sometimes, however, a formula represents a molecule of an element. This is true for substances that exist only as pairs of atoms, such as oxygen, nitrogen, hydrogen, chlorine, and fluorine.

■ Subscripts indicate the number of atoms of an element present in a compound.

■ A chemical reaction is described by a chemical equation.

■ In a chemical equation, the same number of atoms of each element must appear on each side of the equation. Therefore, a chemical equation must be balanced. Coefficients are used to balance an equation.

■ A balanced chemical equation indicates what substances are combining, what products are formed, and how many atoms and molecules are involved in the reaction.

VOCABULARY

Define each term in a complete sentence.

chemical equation	**chemical symbol**	**compound**	**pure substance**
chemical formula	**coefficient**	**element**	**subscript**
chemical reaction			

CONTENT REVIEW: MULTIPLE CHOICE

Choose the letter of the answer that best completes each statement.

1. A material made up of parts that are all alike is called a(n)
   a. atom.   b. pure substance.   c. mixture.   d. granite.
2. The simplest form of matter made up of only one kind of atom is a(n)
   a. element.   b. mixture.   c. compound.   d. molecule.
3. Oxygen, iron, and silver are examples of
   a. particles.   b. formulas.   c. compounds.   d. elements.

4. One or two letters used to represent the name of an element are called a chemical
   a. symbol. b. formula. c. compound. d. equation.
5. Two or more elements chemically combined form a(n)
   a. mixture. b. atom. c. symbol. d. compound.
6. Two methods of separating a compound into its elements are
   a. heating and filtering. b. heating and electric current.
   c. electric current and magnetizing. d. filtering and magnetizing.
7. A shorthand way of representing a chemical substance as a combination of symbols is a(n)
   a. equation. b. reaction. c. formula. d. atom.
8. Numbers that indicate the number of atoms of an element in a certain compound are called
   a. coefficients. b. subscripts. c. fractions. d. superscripts.
9. The process by which substances are changed into other substances as a result of rearranging atoms is called a(n)
   a. chemical equation. b. chemical symbol.
   c. chemical reaction. d. chemical formula.
10. A chemical equation can be balanced by using numbers called
   a. subscripts. b. coefficients. c. superscripts. d. fractions.

CONTENT REVIEW: COMPLETION

Fill in the word or words that best complete each statement.

1. A material that contains only one kind of molecule is called a(n) _____.

2. Oxygen, which is made up of only one kind of atom, is called a(n) _____.

3. Chemical _____ are used to represent elements.

4. A(n) _____ is a pure substance made up of more than one kind of atom.

5. Carbon dioxide and water are examples of _____.

6. Two forms of energy often used to break down a compound into simpler substances are electricity and _____.

7. Molecules of gases such as chlorine and oxygen occur naturally as _____ atoms of the element bonded together.

8. Chemical _____ are used to represent compounds.

9. A chemical process in which substances are changed into other substances is called a chemical _____.

10. In order to balance the equation $MgO \rightarrow Mg + O_2$, the number _____ must be placed in front of MgO and Mg.

CONTENT REVIEW: TRUE OR FALSE

Determine whether each statement is true or false. If it is true, write "true." If it is false, change the underlined word or words to make the statement true.

1. The tiny building blocks of matter are called <u>atoms</u>.

2. Two or more atoms chemically bonded make a <u>mixture</u>.

3. A substance made up of parts that are all alike is called a <u>complex</u> substance.

4. Silver, gold, and <u>carbon</u> are examples of <u>compounds</u>.

5. Elements <u>cannot</u> be changed into simpler substances by heating them.

6. Ca and Fe are examples of <u>formulas</u> of chemical substances.

7. Two or more elements chemically combined form a <u>compound</u>.

8. One molecule of nitrogen, N_2, is made up of <u>one</u> atom of nitrogen.

9. Small numbers placed at the lower right of a chemical symbol in a formula are called <u>superscripts</u>.

10. The description of a chemical reaction using symbols and formulas is called a <u>chemical equation</u>.

CONCEPT REVIEW: SKILL BUILDING

Use the skills you have developed in the chapter to complete each activity.

1. Classifying data Develop a classification system for the months of the year. State the property or properties you used to develop your system. Make your system as useful and specific as possible. Do *not* use the four seasons.

2. Making inferences The language of chemistry is a universal language.. Scientists all over the world use the same representations for chemical substances. Explain why the system of symbols and formulas you learned about is so important to this idea.

3. Relating concepts Why is it more useful to classify matter according to makeup than according to phase?

4. Making calculations Calculate how many atoms of each element are present in the following compounds:

$NaHCO_3$ $Mg(OH)_2$

$C_2H_4O_2$ $3H_3PO_4$

5. Making generalizations What three things does a chemical equation indicate about a chemical reaction?

6. Designing an experiment Describe an experiment to demonstrate that water is a compound, not an element, and that salt water is not a pure substance.

7. Applying facts Balance the following equations:

a. $Mg + O_2 \rightarrow MgO$
b. $NaCl \rightarrow Na + Cl_2$
c. $CH_4 + O_2 \rightarrow CO_2 + H_2O$
d. $H_2 + O_2 \rightarrow H_2O$

8. Applying concepts The equation below is not balanced. Explain why it would be incorrect to balance it by changing H_2O to H_2O_2. Hint: The name for H_2O_2 is hydrogen peroxide.

$$H_2 + O_2 \rightarrow H_2O$$

CONCEPT REVIEW: ESSAY

Discuss each of the following in a brief paragraph.

1. Explain what happens to atoms in a chemical reaction.

2. What is a molecule? How is a molecule of an element or a compound represented?

3. What is an atom? How do atoms of the same element compare? Atoms of different elements?

4. Write the chemical symbols for aluminum, calcium, iron, sulfur, sodium, and helium.

5. Why are elements and compounds considered pure substances? Do you think breakfast cereal with bananas and milk would be a pure substance? How about iron filings mixed with powdered sulfur? Explain your answers.

6. Explain the following statement: "A balanced chemical equation is evidence of a chemical reaction."

17 Mixtures and Solutions

CHAPTER SECTIONS

17-1 Properties of Mixtures
17-2 Types of Mixtures
17-3 Solutions

CHAPTER OBJECTIVES

After completing this chapter,
you will be able to:

17-1 Describe a mixture.

17-1 Identify three important properties of a mixture.

17-2 Distinguish between heterogeneous mixtures and homogeneous mixtures.

17-2 Describe a suspension and a colloid.

17-3 Define the terms solute, solvent, and solution.

Hold the ketchup! Extra mustard, a dab of mayonnaise, sliced onion, pickle relish, and cheese! Don't forget the lettuce, but no tomato, please!

Is this the way you order your hamburger? Or do you prefer it plain? In either case, you are getting a combination of many ingredients. Substances such as fats, oils, proteins, and minerals are in the hamburger. Flour, salt, water, and other ingredients are mixed together in the bun. If you order a milkshake, you are drinking a blend of milk, sugar, ice cream, various flavorings, and air.

Making a list of all the chemical substances found in your burger and shake might surprise you. For your list would probably contain thousands of entries! After reading this chapter, why not try it?

A dazzling combination of chemical substances

Figure 17-1 *Granite is a mixture that contains crystals of the minerals quartz, feldspar, and mica.*

17-1 Properties of Mixtures

In Chapter 16, you learned that pure substances are made up of a single kind of particle. So it follows that any amount of a pure substance—a gram, a kilogram, or a ton—has the same properties as any other amount. You also learned that elements are the simplest type of pure substance. Compounds, which are chemical combinations of two or more elements, are also pure substances.

Do you remember the picture of a piece of granite? See Figure 17-1. Granite contains particles of different minerals. Looking closely at the rock in the photograph, you can see crystals of quartz, feldspar, and mica. Granite, then, is *not* made up of a single kind of particle. Such a material is called a **mixture.**

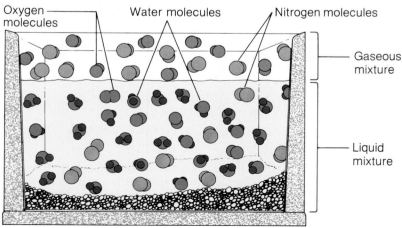

Figure 17-2 *There are two different mixtures in this photo of a fish tank (top). The air above the water is a gaseous mixture made up mostly of oxygen and nitrogen molecules. The liquid mixture contains water molecules, nitrogen molecules, and oxygen molecules (bottom).*

Makeup of Mixtures

A mixture consists of two or more pure substances that are mixed together but not chemically combined. Beach sand is a mixture, as is soil. Salad dressing, concrete, and sea water are other examples of mixtures. The pure substances that make up a mixture can be elements or compounds. For example, in a mixture of sugar and water, there are molecules of the compound sugar, $C_{12}H_{22}O_{11}$, and molecules of the compound water, H_2O. In the mixture known as air, there are molecules of the elements oxygen, O_2, and nitrogen, N_2. There are also other pure substances, such as molecules of the compound carbon dioxide, CO_2.

Because the substances in a mixture are not chemically combined, they keep their separate identities and most of their own properties. Think of the mixture of sugar and water you just read about. The water is still a colorless liquid. And the sugar, although dissolved in the water, still keeps its property of sweetness. Your sense of taste tells you this is so. The same molecules of water and sugar are present after the mixing as before it. No new chemical substances have been formed. Substances in a mixture may change in physical appearance, as when they dissolve. But they do not change in chemical composition.

If you eat cereal for breakfast, you are probably making a mixture. That is what you produce when you pour milk over the cereal. And if you put berries or raisins into your cereal, you make an even more complex mixture. But you do not use exactly the same amount of cereal, milk, and fruit each time. This illustrates another property of mixtures.

The substances that make up a mixture can be present in any amount. The amounts are not fixed. So you can make a mixture of a lot of cereal, a little milk, and loads of fruit. Or, if you prefer, a little cereal with lots of milk and fruit! This property illustrates an important difference between mixtures and compounds. Do you know what this difference is? You might remember that when elements combine chemically to form a compound, they do so in exact amounts. For example, 2 hydrogen atoms always combine with 1 oxygen atom—no more, no less—to form a molecule of water.

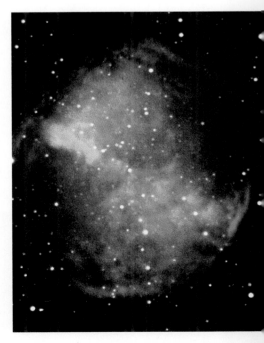

Figure 17-3 *A nebula, a cloud of gases and dust in space, is a mixture. Here you see the Dumbbell Nebula, which gets its name from its shape.*

Figure 17-4 *By combining powdered iron (top) with powdered sulfur (center), an iron-sulfur mixture is formed. What physical property of iron is being used to separate the mixture (bottom)?*

Separation of Mixtures

Look at the photographs in Figure 17-4. A mixture has been made by combining powdered iron with powdered sulfur. Iron is black and sulfur is yellow. The resulting mixture has a grayish color, although particles of iron and sulfur are clearly visible. This mixture illustrates the two properties of mixtures you have just learned: The substances in a mixture retain their original properties. And the substances can be present in varying amounts. Look again at the figure to discover another property.

Iron is attracted by a magnet. Sulfur is not. The powdered iron can be separated from the powdered sulfur by holding a strong magnet near this mixture. If the two elements were chemically combined in a compound, they could not be separated with a magnet. This happens to be the case for a compound called iron sulfide, FeS.

You can use a number of methods to separate substances in a mixture. The method you choose will depend on the type of mixture. See Figure 17-5. You should note that all the methods of separating mixtures are based on physical properties. No chemical reactions are involved.

SECTION REVIEW

1. Explain why a mixture is a physical combination of substances.
2. Describe three properties of a mixture.
3. List three ways to separate a mixture.

Figure 17-5 *Salt water is a mixture of various salts and water. When the water evaporates, which is a physical change, it leaves behind deposits of salt (right). Heavy pieces of gold can be separated from rock, sand, and dirt by shaking the mixture in a pan of water (left). The gold will settle to the bottom of the pan.*

17-2 Types of Mixtures

Does it surprise you to learn that both concrete and stainless steel are mixtures? Concrete is a mixture of pieces of rock, sand, and cement. Stainless steel is a mixture of the elements chromium and iron. But in looking at each of these mixtures, you might describe the stainless steel as "better mixed" than the concrete because you cannot see individual bits of chromium and iron in the steel. **Mixtures are classified according to how "well mixed" they are as either homogeneous or heterogeneous.**

Heterogeneous Mixtures

Looking closely at a piece of broken concrete, you will see particles of rock mixed in with sand and cement. You will also see that no two parts of the concrete piece appear exactly the same.

A mixture such as concrete or sand is said to be **heterogeneous** (het-uhr-uh-JEEN-ee-uhs). This means that no two parts of the mixture are identical. A heterogeneous mixture is the least "well mixed" of mixtures. The particles that make up the mixture are large enough to be seen. For this reason, they are easy to recognize and to separate from the mixture. A mixture of different-sized buttons or of different types of coins is an example of a heterogeneous mixture. Can you think of some other examples?

Not all heterogeneous mixtures contain solid particles. Shake up some pebbles or sand in water to make a solid-liquid mixture. This mixture is easily separated just by letting it stand. Oil and vinegar make up a liquid-liquid heterogeneous mixture. When the mixture is well shaken, large drops of oil spread throughout the vinegar. This mixture, too, will separate when allowed to stand. Both these mixtures contain particles that are mixed together but not dissolved. Such mixtures are called **suspensions.**

Homogeneous Mixtures

When the particles of a mixture are very small, are not easily recognized, and do not settle when the

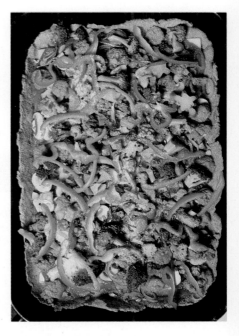

Figure 17-6 *Pizza is a heterogeneous mixture in which the parts are easy to recognize and to separate from the mixture.*

Figure 17-7 *This suspension of soil and water is a solid-liquid mixture. Notice how the particles separate when the mixture is allowed to stand.*

Figure 17-8 *Gelatin is a colloid containing liquid particles mixed in a solid, while whipped cream contains gas particles in a liquid* (left). *Fog is a type of colloid in which liquid particles are mixed in a gas* (right).

Figure 17-9 *Colloids include many commonly used materials, such as milk, toothpaste, liquid glue, jelly, and plastics. What type of colloid is mayonnaise? Butter?*

TYPES OF COLLOIDS

Name	Example
Fog (liquid in gas)	Clouds
Smoke (solid in gas)	Smoke
Foam (gas in liquid)	Whipped cream
Emulsion (liquid in liquid)	Mayonnaise
Sol (solid in liquid)	Paint
Gel (liquid in solid)	Butter

mixture is allowed to stand, the mixture is "well mixed." As a result, different parts seem to be identical. This type of mixture is said to be **homogeneous** (ho-muh-JEEN-ee-uhs). The stainless steel you read about is a homogeneous mixture.

Although you may not be aware of it, many of the materials you use and eat each day are homogeneous mixtures. Milk, whipped cream, toothpaste, mayonnaise, and suntan lotion are just a few examples. In these homogeneous mixtures, the particles are mixed together but not dissolved. As a group, these mixtures are called **colloids** (KAHL-oyds). The particles in a colloid are larger than ordinary molecules but too small to be easily seen through a microscope. In fact, it is the large size of the particles that often makes a colloid appear cloudy. Have you ever wondered why milk has a white, cloudy appearance? The colloidal particles in milk are just large enough to scatter light in all directions. The result of this scattering is the cloudy white color you see.

Colloidal particles, however, are too small to settle when the mixture is allowed to stand. There are several different types of colloids, as you can see in the table in Figure 17-9.

SECTION REVIEW

1. Based on how "well mixed" they are, what are the two types of mixtures?
2. What is the name given to mixtures such as milk and mayonnaise?

17-3 Solutions

When you are thirsty, you might drink a glass of lemonade. But did you know that you were drinking a homogeneous mixture called a **solution?** A solution is the "best mixed" of all mixtures. In fact, the substances making up the solution are not just mixed together. They are dissolved in one another.

Properties of Solutions

By picturing a glass of lemonade, you can discover several important properties of a solution. First of all, how was the lemonade made? Lemon juice and sugar were probably added to water. They dissolved in the water. **In a solution, the substance that is dissolved is called the solute and the substance that does the dissolving is called the solvent.** So the lemon juice and the sugar are **solutes** (SAHL-yoots). The water is the **solvent** (SAHL-vunt).

Looking at the glass of lemonade, you will notice that the particles are not large enough to be seen.

Activity

Expressing Solubility

Solubility can be described in several different ways. Using books in the library, find out what each of the following words means. Give an example of each term.

dilute
concentrated
unsaturated
saturated
supersaturated

Career: *Perfumer*

HELP WANTED: PERFUMER To create fragrances for cosmetic company. High school diploma required. On-the-job training provided.

Perhaps you have noticed that the second-hand car your neighbor just bought smells brand new. Or that your friend's new plastic wallet smells like real leather. Companies known as fragrance houses create scents to make products more attractive.

Most of the scents made by fragrance houses are used in soaps, detergents, perfumes, and other grooming items. The people who create the fragrances are **perfumers.** They combine many ingredients, including oils of flowers, to make a desired fragrance.

There are more than 3000 natural and synthetic ingredients used in making fragrances. In

a process that can take up to two years, perfumers mix solutions of ingredients, check to make sure the ingredients are properly balanced, and test the fragrances. For more information on this career, write to the Fragrance Foundation, 116 East Nineteenth Street, New York, NY 10003.

TYPES OF SOLUTIONS

Solute	Solvent	Example
Gas	Gas	Air (oxygen in nitrogen)
Gas	Liquid	Soda water (carbon dioxide in water)
Gas	Solid	Charcoal gas mask (poisonous gases on carbon)
Liquid	Gas	Humid air (water in air)
Liquid	Liquid	Antifreeze (ethylene glycol in water)
Liquid	Solid	Dental filling (mercury in silver)
Solid	Gas	Soot in air (carbon in air)
Solid	Liquid	Ocean water (salt in water)
Solid	Solid	Gold jewelry (copper in gold)

Figure 17-10 *Nine different types of solutions can be made from the three phases of matter. What are solutions of solids dissolved in solids called?*

Activity

Water Dissolves Most Substances

You can find out what substances will dissolve in water by performing the following activity. Fill seven glasses with water. Into each glass of water, add a small amount of one of the substances listed below. Stir and let stand for several minutes. Observe what happens. Make a chart of your observations. Include your conclusions about what substances dissolve in water.

sugar
starch
salt
flour
cooking oil
baking soda
cleaning powder

The particles in a solution are individual atoms or molecules. For this reason, most solutions cannot be easily separated by simple physical means. Unlike many colloids, liquid solutions appear clear and transparent. The particles in a liquid solution are too small to scatter light.

Tasting the lemonade illustrates another property of a solution. Every part of the solution tastes the same. This might lead you to believe that one property of a solution is that its particles are evenly spread out. And you would be right!

There are nine possible types of solutions, as you will see in Figure 17-10. Many liquid solutions contain water as the solvent. Ocean water is basically a water solution containing many salts. Body fluids are also water solutions. Because water can dissolve many substances, it is called the "universal solvent."

Solubility

A substance that dissolves in water is said to be **soluble** (SAHL-yuh-bul). Salt and sugar are soluble substances. Mercury and oil do not dissolve in water. They are **insoluble.**

The amount of solute that will completely dissolve in a given amount of solvent *at a specific temperature* is called **solubility.** What is the relationship between temperature and the solubility of solid solutes? In general, as the temperature of a solvent

increases, the solubility of the solute increases. What about gaseous solutes? An increase in the temperature of the solvent usually decreases the solubility of a gaseous solute. This explains why soda that warms up goes flat. The "fizz" of soda is due to bubbles of carbon dioxide dissolved in the solution.

Some substances are not very soluble in water. But they do dissolve easily in other solvents. For example, one of the reasons you use soap to wash dirt and grease from your skin or clothing is that the soap dissolves these substances, while water alone does not. Soap is made up of long molecules, with one end dissolving in water and the other end serving as a solvent for grease. The soap dissolves the grease and then, along with the grease, is washed away by the water.

Not all solutions are liquid, as the table in Figure 17-10 indicates. Metal solutions called **alloys** are examples of solids dissolved in solids. Gold jewelry is actually a solid solution of gold and copper. Brass is an alloy of copper and zinc. Sterling silver contains small amounts of copper in solution with silver. And the stainless steel you read about before is an alloy of chromium and iron. You may find it interesting to learn about the makeup of other alloys such as pewter, bronze, and solder.

SECTION REVIEW

1. What is a solute? A solvent?
2. What condition can increase or decrease the solubility of a substance?

Figure 17-11 *In the process of making steel, a solution of scrap steel and iron is made in a blast furnace (left). Near the end of the process, alloying substances are dissolved in the steel. In a water-purification plant, air dissolves in water as the water flows from sprinklers (right). The air-water solution now contains an increased amount of oxygen.*

Activity

Solubility of a Gas in a Liquid

You can determine what conditions affect the solubility of a gas in a liquid.

1. Remove the cap from a bottle of soda.

2. Immediately fit the opening of a balloon over the top of the bottle. Shake the bottle several times. Note any changes in the balloon.

3. Heat the bottle of soda very gently by placing it in a pan of hot water. Note any further changes in the balloon.

What two conditions of solubility are being tested here? What general statement about the solubility of a gas in a liquid can you now make?

LABORATORY ACTIVITY

Examination of Freezing-Point Depression

Purpose

In this activity, you will observe the effects of various dissolved substances on the freezing point of water.

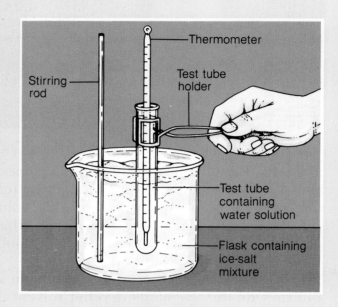

Thermometer

Stirring rod

Test tube holder

Test tube containing water solution

Flask containing ice-salt mixture

Materials *(per group)*

Water
Glucose
Sucrose
  (table sugar)
Sodium chloride
Test tube holder
Test tube rack
7 large test tubes and stoppers
Thermometer ($-10°$ to $100 °C$)

Glass-marking pencil
Coarse salt
Crushed ice
Glass stirring rod
500-mL beaker
Triple-beam balance
Graduated cylinder

Procedure

1. Label seven large test tubes with the numbers 1 through 7.
2. Place 10 mL of tap water in each of the test tubes.
3. Use the balance to pour out the following amounts of glucose ($C_6H_{12}O_6$), sucrose ($C_{12}H_{22}O_{11}$), and sodium chloride (NaCl).
   1. control
   2. 1.8 g glucose
   3. 3.6 g glucose
   4. 3.4 g sucrose
   5. 6.8 g sucrose
   6. 0.6 g NaCl
   7. 1.2 g NaCl
4. Add the measured substances to the corresponding numbered test tubes. Cover each test tube with a stopper. Shake until the substance is completely dissolved in the water.
5. Set up a low-temperature bath by mixing together 150 mL crushed ice, 100 mL coarse salt, and 100 mL water in a 500-mL beaker. Stir with a glass stirring rod for a

few minutes. If all the ice should melt at any time during the activity, simply add more.

6. Place a thermometer in test tube 1. Using the test tube holder, lower the tube into the ice-salt bath until it is submerged at least up to the level of the liquid it contains. Stirring gently with the thermometer, record the temperature at which the water begins to freeze. Remove the tube and thermometer. Wipe the thermometer clean.
7. Repeat step 6 for tubes 2 through 7.

Observations and Conclusions

1. What effect does the presence of a dissolved substance have on the freezing point of water?
2. What effect does doubling the amount of a given dissolved substance have on the freezing-point?
3. Tubes 2 and 4 contained roughly equal numbers of molecules of dissolved substances. Does the kind of substance have much effect on freezing-point?

CHAPTER REVIEW

17-1 Properties of Mixtures

■ Mixtures are made up of different substances mixed together but not chemically combined. They can be separated by ordinary physical means.

■ Substances in a mixture keep their properties and are present in varying amounts.

17-2 Types of Mixtures

■ No two parts of a heterogeneous mixture are identical. The particles are large enough to be seen, and they settle when the mixture is allowed to stand.

■ Homogeneous mixtures, which contain very small particles, have parts that seem to be identical.

■ Colloids are homogeneous mixtures of very small particles. Colloids often appear cloudy.

17-3 Solutions

■ A solution consists of a solute dissolved in a solvent. The particles of each are individual atoms or molecules.

■ Solutions are transparent. They cannot be easily separated by simple physical means.

■ Soluble substances dissolve in water. Insoluble substances do not.

■ The amount of solute that completely dissolves in a given amount of solvent is called solubility.

■ The solubility of a solute depends upon the temperature of the solvent. The solubility of a solid in a liquid usually increases as the temperature of the solvent increases. The solubility of a gas in a liquid decreases as the temperature of the solvent increases.

■ Alloys are solid solutions.

VOCABULARY

Define each term in a complete sentence.

alloy	**homogeneous mixture**	**solubility**	**solution**
colloid	**insoluble**	**soluble**	**solvent**
heterogeneous mixture	**mixture**	**solute**	**suspension**

CONTENT REVIEW: MULTIPLE CHOICE

Choose the letter of the answer that best completes each statement.

1. Which of the following substances is *not* a pure substance?
   a. oxygen   b. sugar   c. salt water   d. carbon dioxide

2. The particles in a mixture
   a. are always too small to be seen.
   b. are identical throughout the mixture.
   c. are chemically combined.
   d. are not identical throughout the mixture.

3. In a mixture, substances are present in
   a. varying amounts.   b. fixed amounts.
   c. a ratio of 2 to 1.   d. the liquid phase only.

4. Ways of separating a mixture depend on
  a. chemical properties.   b. physical properties.
  c. chemical reactions.   d. nuclear reactions.

5. A mixture in which no two parts are identical is a
  a. homogeneous mixture.   b. heterogeneous mixture.
  c. solution.   d. solvent.

6. A mixture that contains large particles that settle when the mixture is allowed to stand is called a
  a. suspension.   b. solution.   c. colloid.   d. solvent.

7. Homogeneous mixtures such as milk, toothpaste, and mayonnaise are examples of
  a. suspensions.   b. solutions.   c. colloids.   d. solvents.

8. In a solution, the substance that is dissolved is called the
  a. solvent.   b. gel.   c. solute.   d. emulsion.

9. In a saltwater solution, the water is the
  a. solute.   b. solvent.   c. alloy.   d. colloid.

10. Metal solutions of solids in solids are
  a. salts.   b. colloids.   c. alloys.   d. suspensions.

CONTENT REVIEW: COMPLETION

Fill in the word or words that best complete each statement.

1. Two or more pure substances mixed together but not chemically combined form a(n) _____.

2. Methods of separating mixtures are based on the _____ properties of the substances in the mixture.

3. Oil mixed with vinegar is an example of a mixture called a(n) _____.

4. Mixtures whose particles are very small and whose different parts seem to be identical are said to be _____.

5. A mixture that often appears cloudy, does not separate when allowed to stand, and contains very small particles is a(n)

6. Mayonnaise is a colloid known as a(n) _____.

7. A(n) _____ is the substance that does the dissolving in a solution.

8. _____ is the extent to which a substance dissolves in another substance at a given temperature.

9. Substances that do not dissolve in water are said to be _____.

10. Stainless steel, sterling silver, and brass are examples of solid solutions called _____.

CONTENT REVIEW: TRUE OR FALSE

Determine whether each statement is true or false. If it is true, write "true." If it is false, change the underlined word or words to make the statement true.

1. The rock granite is a <u>compound</u>.

2. In forming a mixture, substances <u>lose</u> their original properties.

3. The substances that make up a mixture are present in <u>varying</u> amounts.

4. Separating mixtures is based on the <u>chemical</u> properties of the substances.

5. A mixture whose particles are very small and whose parts are identical throughout is said to be <u>heterogeneous</u>.

6. A <u>suspension</u> will separate when allowed to stand.

7. In a solution of sugar water, the sugar is the <u>solute</u>.

8. The universal solvent is <u>alcohol</u>.

9. A gas is usually <u>more</u> soluble in warm water than in cold.

10. Brass, a solution of copper and zinc, is an example of an <u>alloy</u>.

CONCEPT REVIEW: SKILL BUILDING

Use the skills you have developed in the chapter to complete each activity.

1. Classifying matter Classify the following materials as either homogeneous or heterogeneous mixtures: sausage pizza, chocolate chip cookies, air inside a balloon, glass of water.

2. Relating facts You have learned that mixtures have three important properties. Using the example of breakfast cereal with milk and blueberries, how can you illustrate each of these properties?

3. Relating concepts Explain why a solution is classified as a mixture instead of as a compound.

4. Applying concepts Describe a method of separating the following mixtures:

    a. sugar and water

    b. powdered iron and powdered aluminum

    c. wood and gold

    d. nickels and dimes

5. Applying definitions Most milk sold in stores is homogenized. What do you think this means?

6. Identifying cause and effect The caps are removed from a warm bottle and a cold bottle of carbonated beverage. The soda in the cold bottle bubbles slightly. The soda in the warm bottle bubbles rapidly.

    a. What condition affecting solubility is present here?

    b. Which bottle is the variable? The control?

    c. Give an explanation for what happens.

7. Making generalizations Why can heterogeneous mixtures be separated by filtering but solutions cannot?

8. Making inferences Explain whether you believe there exists a true "universal solvent," capable of dissolving all other substances. Include a description of the kind of container you would put such a solvent in.

9. Making predictions Describe what would happen if you were to drop two lumps of sugar into a cup of hot tea; a cup of cold tea.

10. Making comparisons How is a solution different from a suspension and a colloid? What simple procedure could you perform to distinguish among the three mixtures?

CONCEPT REVIEW: ESSAY

Discuss each of the following in a brief paragraph.

1. What two physical properties determine whether a mixture is a suspension or a colloid?

2. What is a solution? What are its two parts?

3. Describe three properties of a solution.

4. What is solubility? What factor affects the solubility of a solute?

5. Describe three types of colloids.

6. Describe three properties of a mixture.

Adventures in Science

SHIRLEY ANN JACKSON:
HELPING OTHERS THROUGH SCIENCE

Imagine what it would be like to catch a glimpse of the universe as it was forming—to look back in time nearly 20 billion years! Of course, no one can really see the beginning of time. But physicists such as Shirley Ann Jackson believe that learning about the universe as it was in the past will help us understand the universe as it is now and as it will be in the future.

By unraveling some of the mysteries of the universe, Dr. Jackson hopes to fulfill a basic ambition: to enrich the lives of others and make the world a better place in which to live. This contribution, Dr. Jackson believes, can be achieved through science.

Jackson was born and raised in Washington, D.C. After graduating from high school as valedictorian, she attended the Massachusetts Institute of Technology, M.I.T. There, her role as a leader in physics began to take root. Jackson became the first American black woman to receive a doctorate degree from M.I.T. She also achieved the distinction of being the first American black woman to receive a Ph.D. in physics in the United States.

After graduate school, Jackson began work as a research associate in high-energy physics at the Fermi National Accelerator Laboratory in Batavia, Illinois. This branch of physics studies the characteristics of subatomic particles—such as protons and electrons—as they interact at high energies.

Using devices at Fermilab called particle accelerators, physicists accelerate subatomic particles to speeds that approach the speed of light. The particles collide and produce new subatomic particles. By analyzing these subatomic particles, physicists are able to learn more about the structure of atoms and the nature of matter.

The experiments in which Jackson participated at Fermilab helped to prove the existence of certain subatomic particles whose identity had only been theorized. This information is important in understanding the nuclear reactions that are taking place at the center of the sun and other stars.

Jackson's research is not limited to the world of subatomic particles alone. Her work also includes the study of semiconductors—materials that conduct electricity better than insulators but not as well as metal conductors. Semiconductors have made possible the development of transistor radios, televisions, and computers.

Jackson's current work in physics at Bell Laboratories in Murray Hill, New Jersey, has brought her from the beginnings of the universe to the future of communication. This talented physicist is presently doing research in the area of optoelectronic materials. This branch of electronics—which deals with solid-state devices that produce, regulate, transmit, and detect electromagnetic radiation—is changing the way telephones, computers, radios, and televisions are made and used.

Shirley Ann Jackson, in her office at Bell Laboratories, is presently doing research in the field of optoelectronic materials used in communication devices.

Looking back on her past, Jackson feels fortunate to have been given so many opportunities at such a young age. And she is optimistic about the future. "Research is exciting," she says. Motivated by her research, Shirley Ann Jackson is happy to be performing a service to the public in the way she knows best—as a dedicated and determined scientist.

◄ This particle-accelerator generator at Fermilab is familiar equipment to Shirley Ann Jackson.

Issues in Science

WASTING TIME:
The Nuclear Clock
Ticks Down

Today, nuclear power plants are producing more than energy. They are producing a potentially deadly form of garbage: nuclear wastes!

By the year 2000, there will be enough nuclear garbage to fill a giant box about 40 meters on each side. Such a "box" would not be much larger than a 13-story building on a square city block. If there will be no more waste than this, what's the grave danger? Why all the fuss? The answer, in a single word, is radiation!

Invisible Danger

Radiation is invisible energy. And nuclear radiation is *powerful* invisible energy. It is so powerful, in fact, that even small doses over a period of time can permanently harm, or even kill, living things.

Substances such as uranium and plutonium are common fuels for nuclear power plants. Like other fuels, these substances leave behind waste materials when they are used. But these wastes are not at all like the ashes that are the waste products of burning wood. Ashes are harmless. Nuclear wastes are extremely hazardous. The deadly radiation they give off can penetrate most ordinary substances. And this radiation can last for hundreds of thousands of years. So the disposal of nuclear wastes, even the smallest amount, is a giant problem.

Obviously, nuclear wastes cannot be disposed of like ordinary garbage. And they cannot be kept in giant containers, either. So how and where can they be safely stored? Scientists and engineers are trying to answer this question. But they cannot take forever to find a solution. For the wastes are piling up. Over the next few years, special tanks located near nuclear power plants will serve as temporary storehouses. But what is needed is a permanent home for these hazardous materials.

Space-Bound Garbage

If we cannot find a place on earth to get rid of nuclear garbage, why not send it into space? Rockets loaded with nuclear wastes could be launched into orbit between the earth and Venus. Traveling at the right speeds, the rockets could stay in orbit for a million years or more without bumping into either planet. By that time, the nuclear wastes would have become harmless.

Critics of this idea point to its cost and potential danger. An accident during rocket launch could harm thousands of people. These critics believe that the solution is not in the stars but on earth. Only where can these nuclear burying grounds be found?

Down-to-Earth Alternatives

The Antarctic ice sheet is more than 2500 meters thick in some places. Could nuclear wastes be buried under this huge, frozen blanket? No, according to some critics of this idea. Not enough is known about the behavior of ice sheets. And what is known is not comforting. For example, ice sheets move rapidly about every 10,000 years. Their movement might allow the wastes to get loose. In addition, nuclear wastes produce a tremendous amount of heat—enough heat, in fact, to melt the ice. Where the ice melted, nuclear radiation might leak out into the oceans and air.

If not under the Antarctic ice sheet, then how about a nuclear cemetery under the ocean floor? Thick, smooth rock layers have been building up there for millions of years. Nuclear wastes deposited in these rock layers would probably remain there almost forever.

But as with other proposals, there are problems with this idea. At present, the technology to do the job does not exist. And not enough is known about the various forces to which such rock is exposed. For example, the force of hot currents might pull the stored nuclear wastes out of the rock.

Rock Candidates

With ice sheet cemeteries and underwater graveyards all but impossible, one idea still remains. That idea is to put nuclear wastes in "rooms" dug out of underground rock.

In order to determine the best place to bury nuclear wastes, scientists must know all they can about the rock. Here are the properties scientists have determined are best: The rock must be strong, heat-resistant, and waterproof. The rock must be at least 6100 meters deep. And the ground where the rock exists must be very dry and free of earthquakes.

As you can see from the map, such rock formations exist in the United States. Scientists are now studying many of these formations. They plan to choose the best location and build a nuclear-waste garbage dump there between the years 1998 and 2006. There are four kinds of rocks that scientists believe will be the best.

Basalt is a volcanic rock that is strong and waterproof. It does not lose its strength when heated. However, basalt formations usually contain seams. Some scientists believe that water, which might carry nuclear wastes, could flow along these seams.

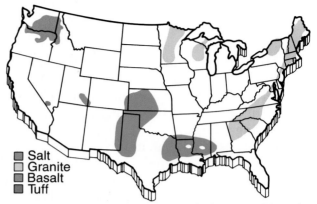

- Salt
- Granite
- Basalt
- Tuff

Various underground sites are being considered for the storage of nuclear waste material. There are a number of different kinds of rock in which wastes could be put. The map shows where some of these types of rock are located.

Storage of nuclear wastes requires a complex network of facilities. Here you see an artist's concept of the surface and underground features of a disposal site mined out of rock.

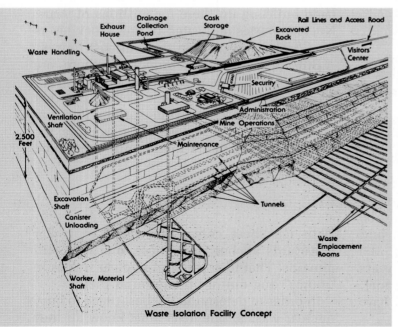

Waste Isolation Facility Concept

Tuff is another volcanic rock that has some of the properties of basalt. It is being studied in Nevada, where there is little underground water. Scientists point out that there is still much to be learned about tuff.

Granite is a very hard rock that resists heating. But water is found in many granite formations. And in addition, granite is very difficult to drill through. So building a nuclear-waste "room" in granite might be a very tough and costly job.

Salt is found in huge underground deposits. Although salt looks solid, it is really a flowing material. Scientists point out that this property of salt helps to seal cracks in salt formations. Unfortunately, salt is often not dry. And when heated, the salt will dissolve in the water and produce a saltwater solution called brine. The brine could carry nuclear wastes out of the salt formation.

So far, scientists have been unable to find the perfect graveyard for nuclear wastes. But the search goes on. Unfortunately, in the meantime the wastes pile up.

THE RIGHT STUFF—

Plastics

Cars, buildings, and appliances of the twenty-first century will be lighter, safer, and stronger than anything we have today.

Standing apart from a group of her classmates, Jennifer bounced her glass ball on the sidewalk. She was not paying attention to the other members of her class or to what her teacher, Ms. Parker, was saying.

As the sparkling ball bounced, Jennifer was barely aware of the sidewalk changing color to reduce the glare of sunlight. She did not notice a young woman hurrying along the street, carrying an auto engine in one hand and groceries in the other. She did not look up as cars sped by towing boats and houses by plastic threads.

Jennifer and her Design for Living class were on a field trip to a brand new "house of the future." The house had just been completed that year—2086. It certainly made the students' homes seem old-fashioned.

For days before the field trip, Ms. Parker had talked about the house of the future. She had described how safety, security, cleaning, maintenance, entertainment, home education, and communications systems in the house were completely controlled by a central computer. She had showed the students how the combination of a waste-recycling unit, solar cells, and wind turbines met all of the house's energy needs. Ms. Parker had spent a long time talking about the new materials that made such a house possible. She had drawn pictures of organic and inorganic molecules on the classroom computer screen.

Even with all this preparation, Jennifer did not care about the house. She was interested only in the designs of the past. Jennifer's real love was for twentieth-century antiques. In her opinion, the appliances, furnishings, and materials of 2086 were boring and ugly.

"*Jennifer!*" Ms. Parker's voice cut through the group.

Jennifer scooped up the bouncing ball and thrust it into her shoulder bag.

"Yes, Ms. Parker?"

"Please come forward and give us the benefit of your views on home design."

As Jennifer moved to the front of the group, she knew she was on the spot. The class was already aware of Jennifer's "good-old-days" views, which contrasted with Ms. Parker's enthusiasm for modern materials and designs.

Nervously, Jennifer started to talk. "Plastics, silicones, polymers . . . I don't think the scientists of the late twentieth-century did us a favor by developing all this phony stuff. I wish we could go back to using wood, steel, aluminum, copper, and real glass. Remember those beautiful steel-and-chrome cars and the polished wood furniture in the design museum?"

"Yes," Ms. Parker agreed, "many things produced in the last century were beautiful and well made. It's easy to admire them in museums. But I don't think we'd find them convenient to live with every day."

"I would," Jennifer insisted.

"All right," responded Ms. Parker. "Let's hop into a mental time machine and find out. What age should we go back to?"

"How about the 1980s?" Jeremy suggested.

"Perfect," said Ms. Parker. "The 1980s were just the beginning of the great materials revolution. Great changes in industry, electronics, and materials development began at that time. By the way, Jennifer, you'd better leave your bouncing ball behind. They didn't have elastic glass in the 1980s. Light-sensitive building materials that change color to reduce glare were also unheard of. However, the research to produce these materials was already under way."

A Trip Back in Time

The house of the future was forgotten as Ms. Parker and the class moved to a nearby park to talk about materials of the past.

Ms. Parker began by asking the students, "What would be the first thing you'd notice in the world of the 1980s?"

"Heaviness. The great weight of almost everything," Jeremy volunteered.

"Go on," Ms. Parker said.

"Appliances like refrigerators, stoves, washing machines, and air conditioners were still made of metal at that time. They were so heavy that it was almost impossible for a single person to lift one of them. And a lot of everyday things were much heavier than they are now. Many food items in supermarkets still came in metal cans and glass bottles. A bagful of those containers could weigh a lot. It wasn't until the 1990s that lightweight, tough plastic containers had completely replaced them."

A Safer Future

Turning to another student, Ms. Parker asked: "Carlee, what would you notice most about life in the 1980s?"

"That it wasn't safe," Carlee responded.

"Why?"

Carlee thought for a moment and then said, "I guess what I was thinking of was the danger of riding in a 1984 car. I've seen pictures of how those old metal cars hurt people in accidents. Sometimes the heavy metal engines and batteries in the front end were pushed back to where people were sitting. Sharp pieces of broken metal and glass were all over

This plastic automobile engine weighs much less than an all-metal engine. Plastic engines have already been used to power race cars, and it may not be long before they are used in passenger cars.

Cars of the future may be made entirely of plastics and powered by solar batteries. Such a car would be lightweight, durable, and clean and inexpensive to operate.

the scene of an accident. Cars could blow up or catch fire."

"That can't happen now," Marian said. "Our cars, including the engines, are made of superplastics and silicones inside and out. These materials are very light and strong, and they bounce. Even if a laser brake system fails, no one can get seriously hurt."

"Cars not only are lighter and safer now," Jeremy added, "they require less energy to run. The changeover from metal to plastic engines in the 1990s led to great energy savings. And, the changeover since then to solar battery-powered cars has meant even greater savings. If we'd kept on using heavy metal cars, the world might have run out of oil and other materials by now."

"You're quite right, Jeremy," Ms. Parker agreed. "Let's sum up what's happened since the 1980s. A great materials revolution started at that time. Chemists discovered how to produce polymers, very long chains and loops of carbon, oxygen, hydrogen, and nitrogen atoms.

"Around the same time, other scientists created a new family of polymers. Silicon atoms were used instead of carbon atoms, so the materials were called silicones. The result of all this chemistry was a new range of super strong, light, cheap plastics.

> *The result of all this chemistry was a new range of super strong, light, cheap plastics.*

"The new materials can be made into anything that was once made with metal, wood, glass, or ceramic. In fact, we can do many things with combinations of the new materials that we couldn't do with the old materials, like making a transparent bouncing ball." Ms. Parker smiled at Jennifer.

Jennifer smiled back, still not convinced of the advantages of living in 2086.

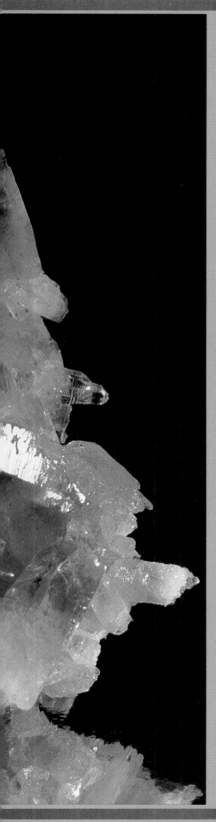

Amethyst uncut

Composition of the Earth

Imagine a place 160 kilometers below the surface of the earth. You are taking a journey deep into the earth in an unbelievably strong bubble—a kind of underground diving capsule. Rivers of orange, glowing rock ooze past your observation window. The temperature gauge on your instrument panel indicates that the outside temperature is a rock-melting 1500° C. You hammer your fist on the pressure gauge. Can it be right? It reads 70,000 kilograms per square centimeter.

Your instruments are accurate. They are giving you a picture of the inside of your planet—the birthplace of rocks and minerals. One day, perhaps millions of years into the future, the molten rocks around you will reach the earth's surface. If conditions are right, unusual and beautiful crystals could form in these rocks as they cool. And what was once formless, glowing ooze may become the rarest rocks on the earth—gemstones!

CHAPTERS

18   **Minerals**

19   **Rocks**

20   **Soils**

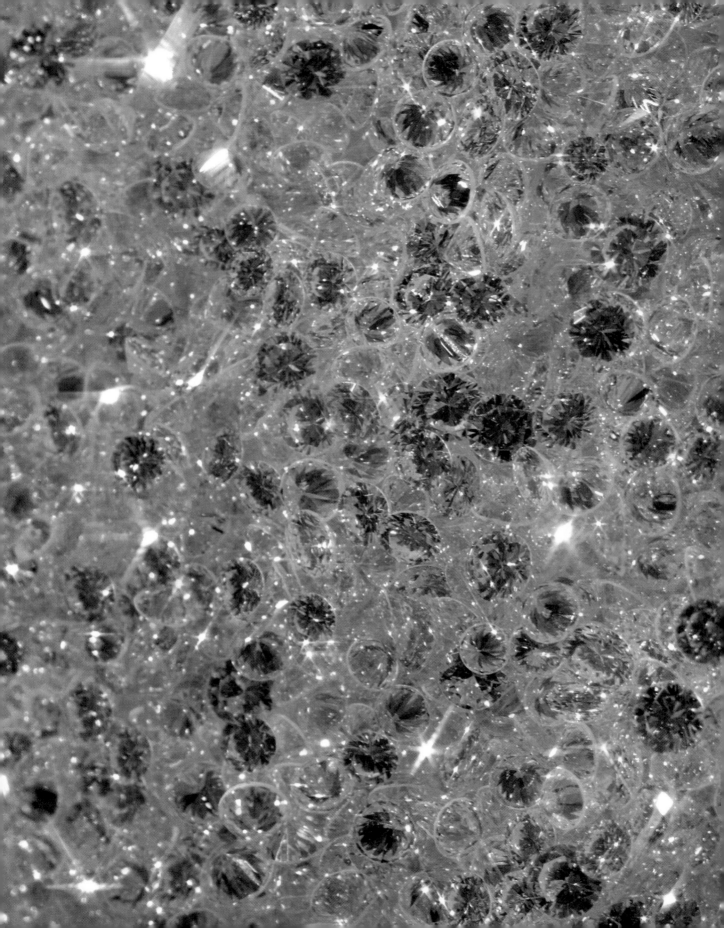

18 Minerals

CHAPTER SECTIONS

18-1 What Is a Mineral?
18-2 Uses of Minerals

CHAPTER OBJECTIVES

After completing this chapter, you will be able to:

18-1 Define the term mineral.

18-1 Describe the properties of minerals.

18-1 Identify minerals by their physical properties.

18-2 Describe some uses of minerals.

18-2 Compare metals and nonmetals.

18-2 Compare ores and gems.

Throughout history, diamonds have been prized as a symbol of great wealth and power. Many of the world's largest diamonds decorate the crowns and jewelry of royalty. Take, for example, the Orloff diamond—if you can find it!

The story goes that this diamond was once in the eye of an idol in a Buddhist shrine in India. In the 1700s the diamond was stolen by a French soldier, who sold it to a British sea captain. After many thefts and some violent crimes, including murder, the diamond found its way to Russia. It was bought by Count Gregory Orloff from an Armenian merchant for about four million dollars. The Count gave it to Catherine II, Empress of Russia. Later, the diamond disappeared during the Russian Revolution.

Other diamonds also have disappeared before their owners' eyes—not through magic, but through ignorance. Early diamond hunters in South America thought they had a simple test for diamonds. They knew that diamonds are the hardest natural substance known. When the hunters found a stone that looked like a diamond, they hit it with a hammer. Usually, the stone shattered into bits and pieces. To the hunters, the shattering just proved the object was worthless. Actually, the stone may have been a diamond.

What the hunters did not know was that diamonds are brittle. Tap a diamond with a knife edge at exactly the right angle and it breaks cleanly and beautifully along an absolutely straight line. Tap it at the wrong angle and the diamond shatters.

Why do diamonds and other precious stones behave in this way? The answer is just a part of the fascinating story of minerals.

Diamonds—one of the most precious minerals

18-1 What Is a Mineral?

The substance you just read about—diamond—is a mineral. A **mineral** is a naturally occurring substance formed in the earth. A mineral may be made of a single element, such as copper, gold, or sulfur. Or a mineral may be made of two or more elements chemically combined to form a compound. For example, the mineral halite is the compound sodium chloride, which is made of the elements sodium and chlorine.

In order for a substance to be called a mineral, it must have five special properties. The first property of a mineral is that it is an **inorganic** substance. Inorganic substances are not formed from living things or the remains of living things. Calcite, a compound made of calcium, carbon, and oxygen, is a mineral. It is formed underground from water containing these dissolved elements. Coal and oil, although found underground, are not minerals because they are formed from decayed plant and animal life.

The second property of a mineral is that it occurs naturally in the earth. Steel and cement are manufactured substances. So they are not minerals. But gold, silver, and asbestos, all of which occur naturally, are minerals.

The third property of a mineral is that it is always a solid. The minerals you just read about—halite, calcite, gold, silver, and asbestos—are solids.

The fourth property of a mineral is that, whether it is made of a single element or a compound, it has a definite chemical composition. The mineral silver is made of only silver atoms. The mineral quartz is made entirely of a compound formed from the elements silicon and oxygen. So even though a sample of quartz may contain billions of atoms, its atoms can only be silicon and oxygen joined in a definite way.

The fifth property of a mineral is that its atoms are arranged in a definite pattern repeated over and over again. This repeating pattern of atoms forms a solid called a **crystal.** A crystal has flat sides, or faces, that meet in sharp edges and corners. All minerals have a characteristic crystal shape.

Figure 18-1 *Chalk* (top), *aragonite* (center), *and pearl* (bottom) *are all made of calcium carbonate or limestone. But only aragonite is a mineral. Why?*

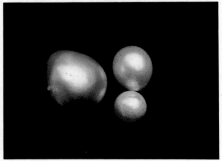

There are more than 2000 different kinds of minerals. But all minerals have the five special properties you just read about. Using these five properties, you can now define a mineral in a more scientific way. **A mineral is a naturally occurring, inorganic solid that has a definite chemical composition and crystal shape.**

Formation and Identification of Minerals

Almost all minerals come from the material deep inside the earth. This material is hot liquid rock called **magma.** When magma cools, mineral crystals are formed. How magma cools and where it cools determine the size of the mineral crystals.

When magma cools slowly beneath the earth's crust, large crystals form. When magma cools rapidly beneath the earth's crust, small crystals form. Sometimes the magma reaches the surface of the earth and cools so quickly that crystals do not form at all.

Crystals may also form from a mineral dissolved in a liquid. When the liquid evaporates, or changes to a gas, it leaves behind the mineral as crystals. Here too, the size of the crystals depends on the speed of evaporation.

Because there are so many different kinds of minerals, it is not an easy task to tell one from another. However, minerals have certain physical properties that can be used to identify them.

Figure 18-2 *Crystals are found in many different shapes, such as six-sided cubes of fluorite* (top right), *radiating crystals of wavelite* (top left), *and needlelike structures of croccolite* (bottom).

Figure 18-3 *A geode is a rock whose hollow interior is lined with mineral crystals, usually quartz, formed by evaporation.*

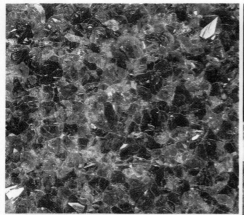

Figure 18-4 *The color of a mineral is not always a reliable way to identify it. Here you see the mineral quartz in three different varieties:* citrine quartz *(top left),* smoky quartz *(top right), and* amethyst *(bottom).* Note that each variety has a characteristic color.

Color

The color of a mineral is an easily observed physical property. But color can be used to identify only those few minerals that always have their own characteristic color. The mineral malachite is always green. The mineral azurite is always blue. No other minerals look quite the same as these.

Many minerals, however, come in a variety of colors. The mineral quartz is usually colorless. But it may be purple, yellow, or pink. You would not want to rely on color alone to identify such minerals.

Color is not always a reliable way to identify minerals for another reason. The color of most minerals changes. For example, minerals such as silver and copper turn color when they tarnish. Tarnish forms when the surface of a mineral reacts chemically with oxygen in the air. Rain, heat, cold, and pollution can also change the color of a mineral.

Luster

The **luster** of a mineral describes the way a mineral reflects light from its surface. Certain minerals reflect light the way highly polished metal does. Such minerals, which include silver, copper, gold, and graphite, have a metallic luster. The mineral in Figure 18-5 has a metallic luster.

Figure 18-5 *These crystals of pyrite have a metallic luster. How would you describe this luster?*

Figure 18-6 *Some minerals have a nonmetallic luster. Tourmaline has a glassy luster (top left). Diamond has a brilliant luster (top center). Malachite is described as having a silky luster (top right), while mica has a pearly luster (center). Serpentine looks as if it is covered by a thin layer of oil. It has a greasy luster (bottom).*

Minerals that do not reflect much light often appear dull. Such minerals have a nonmetallic luster. Their appearance is often described as glassy, pearly, silky, greasy, or brilliant. Quartz and tourmaline have a glassy luster. They appear transparent or partly transparent. Mica has a pearly luster. Malachite has a silky luster. Serpentine looks as if it is covered with a thin layer of oil. It has a greasy luster. Diamond has a brilliant luster. As the rays of light are reflected from diamond, they break up into sparkles and flashes of color.

Hardness

The ability of a mineral to resist being scratched is known as its **hardness.** Hardness is one of the most useful properties for identifying minerals. Friedrich Mohs, a German mineralogist, worked out a scale of hardness for minerals. He used ten common minerals and arranged them in order of increasing hardness. The number 1 is assigned to the softest mineral, talc. Diamond, the hardest of the ten minerals, is given the number 10. Each mineral will scratch any mineral with a lower number and will be scratched by any mineral with a higher number. Figure 18-7 shows the minerals of the **Mohs hardness scale** with their assigned numbers.

MOHS HARDNESS SCALE

Mineral	Hardness
Talc	1
Gypsum	2
Calcite	3
Fluorite	4
Apatite	5
Feldspar	6
Quartz	7
Topaz	8
Corundum	9
Diamond	10

Figure 18-7 *The Mohs hardness scale is a list of ten minerals that represent different degrees of hardness. Each mineral on the scale is harder than the minerals it scratches and softer than the minerals that scratch it. Which mineral is the hardest? The softest?*

To determine the hardness of an unknown mineral, the mineral is rubbed against the surface of each mineral in the hardness scale. If the unknown mineral is scratched by the known mineral, it is softer than the known mineral. If the unknown mineral scratches the known mineral, it is harder than that mineral. If two minerals do not scratch each other, they have the same hardness.

Suppose that you have a mineral sample that is scratched by fluorite, number 4, but not by calcite, number 3. The sample, however, scratches gypsum, number 2. Using the Mohs scale, what mineral could your sample be made of? You are right if you say calcite or any mineral that has a hardness of 3.

It is not always possible to have the minerals of the Mohs hardness scale with you. In such cases, a field scale is convenient to use. Although a field scale is not as exact as the Mohs scale, the materials it uses are easily obtained. Figure 18-8 shows a field hardness scale.

Streak

The color of the powder left by a mineral when it is rubbed against a hard, rough surface is called its

Figure 18-8 *A field hardness scale can be used when the minerals from the Mohs scale are not available. What mineral sample could be scratched by a penny but not by a fingernail?*

FIELD HARDNESS SCALE

Hardness	Common Tests
1	Easily scratched with fingernail
2	Scratched by fingernail (2.5)
3	Scratched by a penny (3)
4	Scratched easily by a knife, but will not scratch glass
5	Difficult to scratch with a knife; barely scratches glass (5.5)
6	Scratched by a steel file (6.5); easily scratches glass
7	Scratches a steel file and glass

Figure 18-9 *Talc is a mineral that leaves a white streak* (left). *Graphite is a mineral that leaves a gray-black shiny streak* (right). *Graphite mixed with clay is the "lead" used in pencils.*

streak. Streak color can be an excellent clue to identifying minerals that have a characteristic streak color and are fairly soft. Even though the color of a mineral may vary, its streak is always the same. Yet this streak color is often different from the color of the mineral itself. See Figure 18-9.

Streak color is determined by rubbing the mineral sample across a piece of unglazed porcelain. The back of a piece of bathroom tile or a streak plate is good to use. A streak plate has a hardness slightly less than 7. So a streak test is useful only with minerals whose hardness is less than 7. Harder minerals do not leave a streak.

Many minerals have white or colorless streaks. Talc, gypsum, and quartz are examples. Streak is not a useful physical property in identifying minerals such as these. Some other physical property must be used.

Density

Every mineral has a property called density. Density is the amount of matter in a given space. Density can also be expressed as mass per unit volume. The density of a mineral is always the same, no matter what the size of the sample is. Because each mineral has a characteristic density, one mineral can easily be compared with any other mineral.

Activity

Mineral Hardness

You can become familiar with the field hardness scale by doing this activity.

1. Obtain five different mineral samples, a penny, a penknife, a piece of glass, and a steel file.

2. Test the minerals to find their hardness according to the scale in Figure 18-8. Most minerals will probably fall between 3 and 7 on the scale.

3. Inside a shallow box, draw a chart listing the minerals by name in order of increasing hardness. Attach the minerals to the chart next to their names.

You can compare the densities of two minerals of about the same size by picking them up and hefting them. The denser mineral feels heavier.

Crystal Shape

Most minerals form crystals, or solids that have a definite geometric shape. The shape of a crystal results from the way the atoms or molecules of a mineral come together as the mineral is forming. Each mineral has its own pattern of atoms or molecules. So each mineral has its own crystal shape.

There are six basic shapes of crystals, or crystal systems. Each shape has a number of faces, or flat surfaces, that meet at certain angles to form sharp edges and corners. See Figure 18-10.

Cleavage and Fracture

The way a mineral breaks is called **cleavage** or **fracture.** When a mineral breaks along smooth, definite surfaces, cleavage occurs. Cleavage is a characteristic property of a mineral. Halite, for example, always cleaves in three directions. It breaks into small cubes. Mica cleaves along one surface, making layer after layer of very thin sheets.

When a mineral breaks unevenly, fracture occurs. The fracture surfaces are usually rough or jagged. Like cleavage, fracture is a property that helps identify a mineral.

Figure 18-10 *Garnet, corundum, sulfur, crocoite, anatase, and kyanite illustrate the six basic crystal systems, which are due to the way the atoms in a crystal bond.*

CRYSTAL SYSTEMS

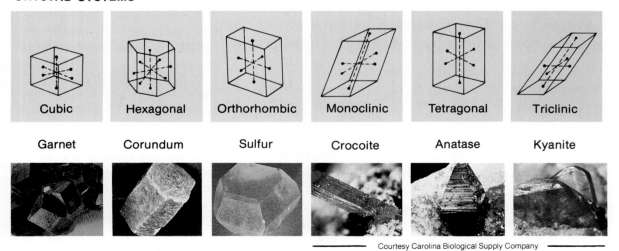

Cubic	Hexagonal	Orthorhombic	Monoclinic	Tetragonal	Triclinic
Garnet	Corundum	Sulfur	Crocoite	Anatase	Kyanite

Courtesy Carolina Biological Supply Company

Special Properties

Some minerals can be identified by special properties. Magnetite, a mineral made of iron and oxygen, is naturally magnetic. Fluorite, made of calcium and fluorine, glows when put under ultraviolet light. Halite, common table salt, has a special taste. Sulfur has a distinct smell. Calcite fizzes when hydrochloric acid is added to it. And jade has a bell-like ring when tapped.

Figure 18-11 *Many minerals break into different shapes. Galena cleaves into cubes* (left). *Hematite cleaves into thin sheets* (center). *Asbestos fractures into fibers* (right).

Career: *Gem Cutter*

HELP WANTED: GEM CUTTER Technical school coursework in gem cutting and jewelry making required. High school graduate preferred. Experience helpful but on-the-job training available.

Among the most valuable treasures obtained from the earth are gems. These hard, beautiful stones include diamonds, rubies, and emeralds. However, rough gems do not look very much like the stones used in jewelry. To become sparkling gems they must be cut and polished. This work is done by **gem cutters.**

Gem cutting requires a great deal of patience and concentration. It also requires a great deal of skill. If a gem cutter makes a mistake, a stone that could have had a value of hundreds of thousands of dollars may suddenly be worthless.

People who want to become gem cutters begin as apprentices. They learn their trade through on-the-job training. At first, apprentices only cut inexpensive stones. As they become more skillful, they work on more valuable stones.

You can learn more about gem cutting by writing to the Gemological Institute of America, 1660 Stewart Street, Santa Monica, CA 90400.

CHARACTERISTICS OF COMMON MINERALS

Mineral	Color	Luster/ Hardness	Cleavage or Fracture	Uses
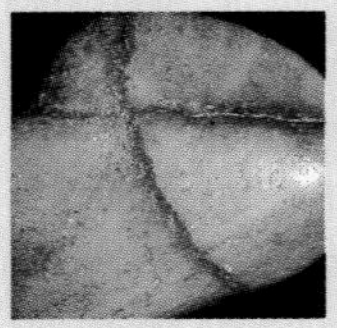 Jade	White or green or greyish green	Glassy to silky 6.5-7	Fracture	To make jewelry, vases, and figurines
 Calcite	White or colorless	Glassy 3	Perfect cleavage or fracture	In medicine and toothpaste; also found in marble and limestone, which are used as building material
 Graphite	Black to iron grey	Metallic 1	Perfect cleavage	In pencils and as a lubricant in machinery, clocks, and locks
 Malachite	Bright green	Silky 3.5-4	Perfect to fair cleavage or fracture	In jewelry and for table tops
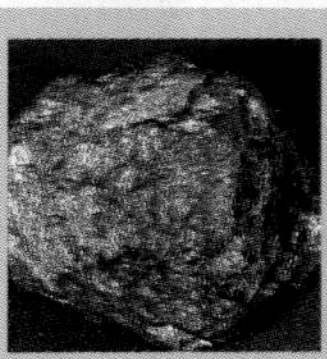 Silver	Silver white	Metallic 3	Fracture	In electrical equipment, photographic chemicals, and jewelry

Figure 18-12 *This table gives characteristics of some common minerals. Which mineral is easily scratched with a fingernail?*

1. What is a mineral?
2. List seven physical properties of minerals.
3. What is the difference between the cleavage and fracture of minerals?

18-2 Uses of Minerals

Throughout history, people have used minerals. At first, minerals were used just as they came from the earth. Later, people learned to combine and process the earth's minerals. **Today many of the earth's minerals are used to meet the everyday needs of people.** Minerals are raw materials for a wide variety of products from dyes to dishes and from table salt to televisions.

Ores

Minerals from which metals and nonmetals can be removed in usable amounts are called **ores.** **Metals** are elements that have certain special properties. Metals have shiny surfaces and are able to conduct electricity and heat. Metals also have the property of **malleability** (mal-ee-uh-BIL-uh-tee). Malleability is the ability of a substance to be hammered into thin sheets without breaking. Another property of metals is **ductility** (duhk-TIL-uh-tee). Ductility is the ability of a substance to be pulled into thin strands without breaking. Iron, lead, aluminum, copper, silver, and gold are metals.

Most metals are found combined with other substances, or impurities, in ores. After the ores are removed from the earth by mining, the metals must be removed from the ores. During a process called smelting, the ore is heated in such a way that the metal can be separated from it. For example, iron can be obtained from the ores limonite and hematite. Lead can be processed from the ore galena. And aluminum comes from the ore bauxite.

Metals are very useful. Probably the most useful metal is iron, which is used in making steel. Lead is a metal used in pipes. Copper is a metal used in pipes,

COMMON MINERALS AND THEIR USES

Minerals	Uses
Alum	Used in cosmetics, dyes, and water purification
Bauxite	Source of aluminum
Corundum	Used to make emery boards and to grind and polish metals
Feldspar	Used to make pottery, china, and glass
Halite	Table salt
Hematite	Source of iron
Quartz	Used in radios, television, and radar instruments
Sulfur	Used to make matches, medicine, rubber, and gunpowder

Figure 18-13 *According to this chart of common minerals and their uses, what mineral is the source of iron? Of aluminum?*

Figure 18-14 *The mineral aluminum can be obtained from the ore bauxite.*

Activity

Mineral Deposits

This activity will help you find out where some of the major mineral deposits in the world are located.

1. From the library, find a map of the world. Draw or trace the map on a piece of paper. Label Africa, Asia, Europe, North America, South America, Australia, and Antarctica.

2. Find out where uranium, sulfur, aluminum, iron, halite, and gold deposits are located.

3. Using a symbol to represent each mineral, show the locations of these deposits on the map.

4. Make a key by writing the name of each mineral next to its symbol. Make your map colorful and descriptive.

pennies, and electrical wire. Aluminum is a metal used in the production of cans, foil, lightweight motors, and airplanes. Silver and gold are metals used in fillings for teeth. Silver and gold are also used in decorative objects such as jewelry.

Nonmetals are minerals that are not shiny, are poor conductors of electricity and heat, and are not malleable or ductile. Sulfur, asbestos, and halite are nonmetals.

Some nonmetals are removed from the earth in usable form. Other nonmetals must be processed to separate them from the ores in which they are found. For example, halite can be found in large deposits in usable form. But asbestos must be separated from other minerals, such as serpentine.

Nonmetals are also useful. Sulfur is one of the most useful nonmetals. It is used to make matches, medicines, and fertilizers. It is also used in iron and steel production.

Gems

Some minerals are called **gems.** Gems are rare minerals. They are also beautiful and durable, or lasting. Not very many minerals have all of these qualities. The rarest and most valuable gems are called precious stones. Diamonds and emeralds are precious stones. Other gems are called semiprecious stones. Semiprecious stones are not as rare or valuable as precious stones. Amethysts, zircons, garnets, turquoises, and opals are semiprecious stones. They are all beautiful and durable. But they are more common than precious stones.

SOME CHARACTERISTICS OF GEMS

	Uncut	Cut	Color
Amethyst		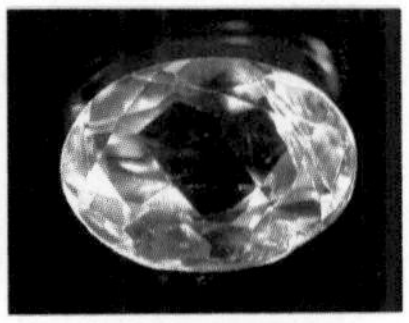	Purple, blue-violet
Aquamarine		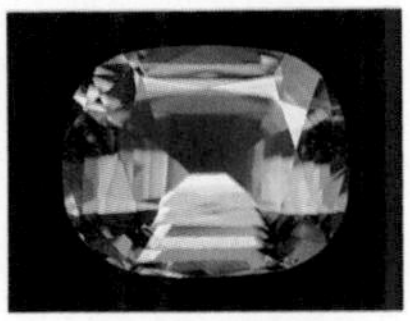	Blue-green, pale blue
Diamond			Yellow, brown, green, blue, violet, black, colorless
Emerald		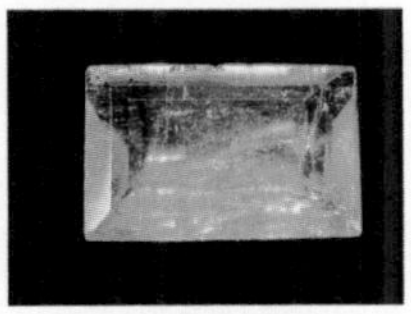	Green
Ruby			Red, blue-red
Topaz	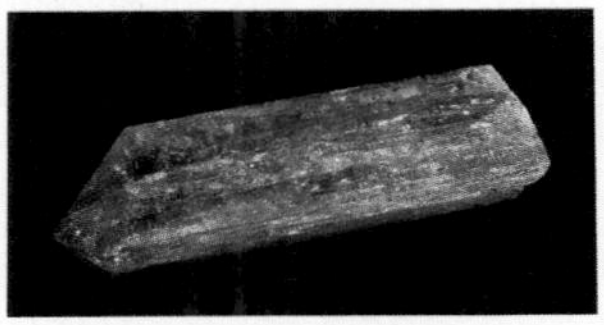		Yellow, brown, pale blue, pink, red, white
Tourmaline			Black, brown, pink, red, green, blue, colorless

SECTION REVIEW

1. What is an ore? A gem?
2. What is malleability? Ductility?
3. List some examples of precious and semiprecious stones.

Figure 18-15 *Very few minerals have the qualities that make them gems: beauty, rarity, and durability. Some gems in their uncut and cut forms are shown. Green is the characteristic color of what gem?*

LABORATORY ACTIVITY

Forming Mineral Crystals

Purpose

In this activity, you will grow different types of crystals.

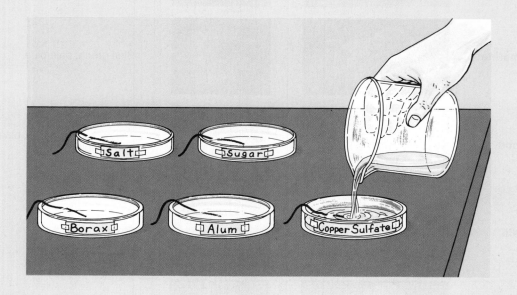

Materials (per group)

Table salt
Table sugar
Borax
Alum
Copper sulfate
250-mL beaker
Dental floss
Stirring rod
5 petri dishes
Magnifying glass or hand lens
Marking pencil

Procedure

1. Using a beaker and stirring rod, dissolve 25 grams of table salt in 200 milliliters of hot water.
2. Fill a petri dish with this solution. Use a marking pencil to label the dish.

3. Place a piece of dental floss in the solution and let it hang over the edge of the dish.
4. Repeat steps 1 to 3 four times, using sugar, borax, alum, and copper sulfate instead of salt.
5. Allow the solutions to evaporate slowly for a day or two. Note which crystals form quickly and which form slowly.
6. With a hand lens or magnifying glass, observe the crystals formed in the dish and along the dental floss. Note the difference in the crystal forms. Each substance has its own distinct crystal shape.

Observations and Conclusions

1. Write a brief statement describing the results of this activity.
2. Describe the appearance of each of the different crystals that you grew.
3. Draw a chart showing how long it took each of your crystals to grow.

CHAPTER REVIEW

SUMMARY

18-1 What Is a Mineral?

■ A mineral is a naturally occurring, inorganic solid that has a definite chemical composition and crystal shape.

■ Almost all minerals come from magma, the hot liquid rock deep inside the earth. The rate of cooling of magma determines the size of the mineral crystals.

■ When magma cools slowly beneath the earth's crust, large crystals form. When magma cools rapidly beneath the earth's crust, small crystals form.

■ Crystals also form when a mineral that is dissolved in a liquid is left behind as the liquid evaporates.

■ The following physical properties are used to identify minerals: color, luster, hardness, streak, density, crystal shape, and cleavage and fracture.

■ The luster of a mineral describes the way a mineral reflects light from its surface. Minerals have a metallic or nonmetallic luster.

■ The ability of a mineral to resist being scratched is known as its hardness.

■ The color of the powder left by a mineral when it is rubbed against a hard, rough surface is called its streak.

■ Hefting is a way of comparing the densities, or mass per unit volume, of two minerals.

■ The shape of a crystal results from the way the atoms or molecules of a mineral come together as the mineral is forming.

■ There are six basic shapes of crystals, or crystal systems.

■ The way a mineral breaks is called cleavage or fracture.

18-2 Uses of Minerals

■ Ores are minerals from which metals and nonmetals can be removed in usable amounts.

■ The ability of a substance to be hammered into thin sheets without breaking is called malleability.

■ Ductility is the ability of a substance to be pulled into thin strands without breaking.

■ Metals and nonmetals are elements that have properties useful to people.

■ Gems are rare minerals that are beautiful and durable.

VOCABULARY

Define each term in a complete sentence.

cleavage	gem	magma	Mohs hardness scale
crystal	hardness	malleability	nonmetal
ductility	inorganic	metal	ore
fracture	luster	mineral	streak

CONTENT REVIEW: MULTIPLE CHOICE

Choose the letter of the answer that best completes each statement.

1. Minerals are
   a. solid.   b. found in the earth.   c. inorganic.   d. all of these.

2. Hot liquid rock deep inside the earth is called
   a. magma.   b. plasma.   c. plastic.   d. mantle.
3. The physical property of a mineral that can be changed by rain, heat, cold, and pollution is
   a. ductility.   b. cleavage.   c. streak.   d. color.
4. The way in which a mineral reflects light from its surface is called
   a. streak.   b. luster.   c. fracture.   d. malleability.
5. The ability of a mineral to resist scratching is called
   a. ductility.   b. malleability.   c. hardness.   d. durability.
6. The softest mineral is
   a. fluorite.   b. talc.   c. diamond.   d. calcite.
7. The mass per unit volume of a mineral is called its
   a. ductility.   b. malleability.   c. streak.   d. density.
8. The breaking of a mineral along smooth, definite surfaces is called
   a. cleavage.   b. fracture.   c. splintering.   d. none of these.
9. The ability of a substance to be hammered into thin sheets is called
   a. ductility.   b. malleability.   c. hardness.   d. durability.
10. Elements that have shiny surfaces and are able to conduct electricity and heat are called
   a. metals.   b. nonmetals.   c. ores.   d. geodes.

CONTENT REVIEW: COMPLETION

Fill in the word or words that best complete each statement.

1. A solid in which the atoms are arranged in a definite and repeating pattern is called a(n) _____.
2. Hot liquid rock beneath the earth's surface is called _____.
3. When magma cools slowly beneath the earth's crust, the size of the crystals formed is _____.
4. Minerals that reflect light the way highly polished metal does are described as having a(n) _____ luster.
5. A commonly used scale that rates the hardness of minerals from 1 to 10 is called the _____.
6. The color of the powder left by a mineral when it is rubbed against a hard surface is called its _____.
7. The property of a mineral that can be expressed as mass per unit volume is called _____.
8. Minerals from which metals and nonmetals can be removed in usable amounts are called _____.
9. The ability of a substance to be pulled into thin strands without breaking is called _____.
10. Gems such as diamonds and emeralds are called _____.

CONTENT REVIEW: TRUE OR FALSE

Determine whether each statement is true or false. If it is true, write "true." If it is false, change the underlined word or words to make the statement true.

1. Substances not formed from living things or the remains of living things are called <u>organic</u>.
2. The repeating pattern of atoms in a solid forms a <u>crystal</u>.
3. Hot liquid <u>rock</u> is called <u>plasma</u>.

4. The faster magma cools, the <u>larger</u> the size of the mineral crystals <u>that</u> are formed.
5. The <u>chemical</u> properties of minerals are used to identify them.
6. The <u>hardness</u> of a mineral describes how the mineral reflects light from its surface.
7. The <u>Dalton</u> hardness scale gives the relative degrees of hardness of minerals.
8. When a mineral breaks along smooth, definite surfaces, <u>fracture</u> occurs.
9. Minerals from which metals and nonmetals can be removed in usable amounts are called <u>ores</u>.
10. Minerals <u>that</u> are rare, beautiful, and durable are called <u>nonmetals</u>.

CONCEPT REVIEW: SKILL BUILDING

Use the skills you have developed in the chapter to complete each activity.

1. **Making comparisons** Using the five special properties of a mineral, compare a mineral with a nonmineral.
2. **Relating facts** The black, glassy rock obsidian has no mineral crystals. Obsidian comes from volcanoes. How does obsidian's formation account for the absence of crystals?
3. **Applying concepts** You are using the following physical properties to distinguish among several different minerals: color, luster, and hardness.
   a. Which physical property is the least helpful? Why?
   b. Which physical property is the most helpful? Why?
   c. What property can you use to distinguish galena from graphite?
   d. What two properties can you use to distinguish talc from galena?
4. **Developing a classification scheme** Across the top of a piece of paper, print the numbers 1 through 20. On the next line, separate the odd numbers into one-digit and two-digit numbers. Do the same with the even numbers.
   Look carefully at the numbers you have written. Some numbers are made from only straight lines. Other numbers are made from only curved lines. Still others are made from both straight and curved lines. Classify each number in the one-digit and two-digit groups according to the following three headings: straight lines, curved lines, straight and curved lines.
   Explain how classification systems are useful in relating similar things.
5. **Applying concepts** Explain the following statement. You can determine the identity of a mineral by showing what it cannot be. Use specific properties of a mineral in your explanation.
6. **Drawing a conclusion** Charcoal, graphite, and diamonds are all made of carbon. Yet they are not considered types of the same mineral. Rubies, sapphires, and corundum are all made of aluminum oxide. They are considered types of the same mineral. Explain why this is so.

CONCEPT REVIEW: ESSAY

Discuss each of the following in a brief paragraph.

1. Describe six properties used to identify minerals. Which properties of a mineral can be tested without damaging the sample?
2. Compare metals and nonmetals.
3. Describe what your life would be like without minerals.
4. Why is density more useful than heft in identifying a mineral?

19 Rocks

CHAPTER SECTIONS

19-1 Rocks of Liquid and Fire: Igneous Rocks

19-2 Rocks in Layers: Sedimentary Rocks

19-3 Rocks That Change: Metamorphic Rocks

19-4 The Rock Cycle

CHAPTER OBJECTIVES

After completing this chapter, you will be able to:

19-1 Explain how igneous rocks are formed.

19-1 Compare extrusive and intrusive igneous rocks.

19-2 Explain how sedimentary rocks are formed.

19-2 Classify various types of sedimentary rocks.

19-3 Explain how metamorphic rocks are formed.

19-4 Describe the rock cycle.

On the Giant's Causeway, row after row of black, six-sided rock pillars rise from the shore. The thousands of rocky pillars form huge platforms that look like stepping stones for giants. And according to legend, that is how the Giant's Causeway got its name. As the legend goes, giants built the rocks so they could cross the sea from the northern coast of Ireland to Scotland.

If such giants had existed, they might have discovered another unusual rock formation south of Scotland. On the southeastern coast of England, white cliffs tower 114 meters above the town of Dover. These cliffs form a wall of bright, gleaming stone. But if you were to examine the stone through a microscope, you would discover countless tiny, beautiful shells. From these white cliffs, it is said, comes one of the ancient names for England—Albion, the "White Land."

These are but two examples of different and amazing forms of rock. There are many others. Each has its own history—a history hidden in the earth's past. This history is full of action and change. And although the next rock you see is not likely to move before your eyes, it got to be where it is by great movements on and within the earth—movements that built the Giant's Causeway and the white cliffs of Dover.

The Giant's Causeway

Figure 19-1 *This photograph shows hot, molten lava erupting from a volcano on Hawaii.*

Figure 19-2 *A pattern of roughly six-sided rock columns forms where mud flats dry out. This pattern is similar to the skin of solid rock that shrunk and split to form the Giant's Causeway.*

19-1 Rocks of Liquid and Fire: Igneous Rocks

The strange six-sided rocks of the Giant's Causeway were forged in fire. But not by giants, and not in an ordinary fire.

Deep within the earth it is so hot that some of the minerals that make up rocks melt and flow like liquid. The liquid rock is less dense than solid rock, so the liquid rock tends to rise—just as bubbles rise through water. This hot, molten rock deep inside the earth is called **magma.**

Sometimes the magma reaches the surface. It may erupt from a volcano. Or it may seep through weak spots in the ground. Magma that has reached the earth's surface is called **lava.**

At the site of the Giant's Causeway, melted rock seeped toward the surface, forming large pools of melted rock material. As the rock cooled and solidified, it shrank and cracked. The cracks formed a six-sided pattern. You can see a pattern something like this where mud flats dry out in places like the Painted Desert in Arizona. As the lower levels of the pool of melted rock material cooled and hardened, the pattern of cracks spread downward. Each pool broke up into rows of six-sided rock columns.

The rocks of the Giant's Causeway are basalt. They belong to one group of rocks called **igneous** (IG-nee-us) **rocks.** The word "igneous" comes from the Latin word "ignis," meaning coming from fire. **All rocks formed from the cooling and hardening of magma are igneous rocks.**

Extrusive Rocks

Basalt is only one kind of igneous rock. It is a kind known as **extrusive** (ek-STROO-siv) **rock.** Extrusive rocks form from melted rock or lava that cools and hardens at or near the earth's surface. Some extrusive rocks originally were pushed slowly onto the earth's surface, much as toothpaste is pushed out of a tube. Other extrusive rocks formed as melted rock material erupted rapidly from places such as volcanoes.

Obsidian is another kind of extrusive rock. Because it is glassy-looking, it is often referred to as volcanic glass. It is usually dark in color and forms from molten material that cools very rapidly on the earth's surface. Rapid cooling is the key to making all kinds of glass.

Sometimes igneous rocks form so quickly that bubbles of volcanic gases are trapped in them. Rocks formed in this way contain many holes and tiny needlelike slivers of volcanic glass. Pumice (PUH-mis) is an example of this kind of rock. Because pumice is filled with bubbles, it is a rock that actually floats on water! The particles of volcanic glass in pumice make it a good polishing agent. Have you had your teeth cleaned at a dentist's office? The gritty stuff in the cleaning powder was probably crushed pumice.

Figure 19-3 *These photographs show that basaltic rock can have very different shapes. Devil's Postpile National Monument (left) is a spectacular mass of blue-gray basalt columns. Shiprock (right) is the remains of the basaltic inner core of a volcano.*

Figure 19-4 *This obsidian dome is an example of an extrusive rock that cools rapidly on the earth's surface.*

Intrusive Rocks

Another kind of igneous rock is granite, one of the earth's most common types of rock. Chemically, granite is similar to obsidian. However, granite is usually white or gray, rather than black. Also granite contains large crystals, while obsidian contains none.

Rocks that form from melted rock or magma that cools and hardens deep below the earth's surface are called **intrusive** (in-TROO-siv) **rocks.** They intrude, or push between surrounding rocks, while in a molten state. Huge masses of granite form within the earth

Figure 19-5 *This batholith is a huge body of igneous rock containing granite that formed underground and was eroded at the earth's surface.*

Figure 19-6 *The igneous rock scoria cools so quickly that gas is trapped in it, producing hundreds of holes.*

in this way. In some places, the masses are more than a thousand kilometers long and 200 kilometers wide. Scientists call these gigantic masses of rock batholiths (BA-thuh-liths), or deep stones. Batholiths form the stony base of the earth's great mountains.

Why do obsidian and granite look so different? The reason is because granite forms from molten rock that cools and hardens *within* the earth instead of at the earth's surface. As a result, granite cools and hardens much more slowly than the molten rock that becomes obsidian. Why? Think of a pot of soup on a stove. Exposed to air, it cools quickly. With the lid on the pot, the soup cools much more slowly. Granite forms "with the lid on." Obsidian forms "with the lid off."

The amount of time it takes liquid rock to cool and harden affects the texture of the rock. Texture refers to the size and type of crystals, or grains, that make up that rock. The slower the rate of cooling, the larger the crystals. The faster the rate of cooling, the smaller the crystals.

Most extrusive igneous rocks, such as basalt, have small crystals and are fine-grained because they cool and harden very quickly at the earth's surface.

Most intrusive igneous rocks, such as granite, have large crystals and are coarse-grained because they cool and harden very slowly beneath the earth's surface. Sometimes, magma cools and hardens so quickly that crystals do not form at all. Obsidian, or volcanic glass, is an extrusive rock that did not have time to form crystals.

SECTION REVIEW

1. What is the difference between magma and lava?
2. What is the difference between extrusive and intrusive rocks? Give an example of each.
3. What determines the size and type of crystals in rocks?

19-2 Rocks in Layers: Sedimentary Rocks

The rocks in the limestone cliff in Arizona, shown in Figure 19-7, appear to be stacked very neatly. One layer is piled on top of another. The layers are almost as straight as if they had been drawn using a ruler. Layered rocks like these are called **sedimentary** (sed-uh-MEN-tuh-ree) **rocks.**

How did this layering happen? The answers are in the rocks themselves. The rocks of this cliff are made up largely of the same material as the white cliffs of Dover—the shells of small sea creatures.

Figure 19-7 *The sedimentary rocks of the limestone cliffs in Arizona* (left) *and New Zealand* (right) *are stacked neatly like piles of pancakes.*

Figure 19-8 *Sedimentary limestone rock contains the shells of once-living marine animals.*

Figure 19-9 *Conglomerates are made up of rock particles of different sizes, as well as sand and mud.*

Some 250 million years ago, this part of Arizona was believed to be at the bottom of a shallow sea. The sea stretched from what is now western Texas north to Canada. The sea was rich in life. Sharks and many kinds of fish swam in the waters. Most abundant of all were sea creatures that had shells. As these animals died, their remains settled to the sea floor. Steadily, more and more shells fell to the bottom. This process continued for millions of years.

Meanwhile, tropical forests of fernlike trees grew. Ancestors of the dinosaurs waddled on the shores of the sea. Rain and wind washed soil into rivers. The rivers flowed down to the sea, carrying muddy soil, pebbles, and rocks. These, too, built up in layers on the sea bottom.

Bones, shells, mud, and pebbles all settled to the sea floor as sediment. The sediment piled up in layers many hundreds of meters thick. Lower layers were pressed together, or compacted, more and more tightly under the weight of the layers above. Larger rock fragments became cemented together by dissolved minerals. **As a result of compaction and cementation, the sediments hardened into strata, or layers, of rock called sedimentary rock.**

Sedimentary rocks usually are formed in water. Most of the earth was under water at some time in the past. That is true now too—70 percent of the earth is covered by oceans. Consequently, sedimentary rocks are common all over the world. Sedimentary rocks often are rich in fossils—the remains or traces of animals or plants that lived in prehistoric times and were trapped in the layers of sediment.

Clastic Rocks

Conglomerates, sandstones, and shales are all examples of **clastic rocks.** They are sedimentary rocks made up of rock fragments mixed with sand, clay, and mud cemented together.

CONGLOMERATES Pebbles and other rocks of different sizes often cement together gradually by sand, mud, and clay to form a single large rock. It is an odd-looking rock. The sand, mud, and clay form the cement surrounding the pebbles. You can see in Figure 19-9 why the scientists who first studied this kind

of rock called it "puddingstone." Later, scientists gave it another name—conglomerate rock. The name means the same thing. Conglomerate rock translates as "rock-made-up-of-many-things-put-together."

SANDSTONE The layered rocks of sandstone, shown in Figure 19-10, are located in Bryce Canyon National Park, Utah. As their name implies, they form from sand grains cemented together. This sandstone is colored red due to traces of iron. Sandstone is very resistant to wear and decay and is often used as a building stone.

SHALE Mud and clay that has hardened into layers of rock is called shale. Shales often form in quiet waters such as swamps and bogs. Small particles of clay and mud make up shales. These particles could only settle to the bottom in quiet waters. In fast-moving rivers, these small particles would be swept along by the currents.

Organic Rocks

Not all sedimentary rocks are made from pieces of rock. There are two other kinds of sedimentary rock. Some sedimentary rocks, such as limestone, may be built up from the remains of living things. Such rocks are called **organic rocks.** The name for

Figure 19-10 *The unusual sandstone formations in Bryce Canyon, Utah were formed from cliffs made of layers of red sedimentary rocks.*

Figure 19-11 *This large deposit of shale is made up of small particles of clay and mud.*

Figure 19-12 *As the water in Mono Lake, California dries up, it leaves behind unusual shaped formations of rock salt.*

these rocks comes from the word "organism," meaning living thing. Shells of animals such as clams and oysters sink to the ocean bottom and eventually form limestone. Limestone may also contain mud and sand. The hard outer coverings of corals are cemented together to become limestone reefs. Chalk is another organic sedimentary rock. It is made up of small pieces of animal shells and crystals of limestone cemented together.

Chemical Rocks

Some sedimentary rocks are formed when a sea or lake dries up leaving large amounts of minerals that were dissolved in the water. These minerals may collect into large formations called **chemical rocks.** Examples of this type of sedimentary rock include rock salt and gypsum (JIP-sum).

SECTION REVIEW

1. What are clastic rocks made of? What are two examples?
2. What are organic rocks made of? What are two examples?
3. How are chemical rocks made? What are two examples?

Activity

Coral Conversions

The largest coral reef is the Great Barrier Reef, which parallels the northeastern coast of Australia for a distance of about 2000 kilometers. How many meters long is the Coral Reef? How many centimeters? Compare this distance to the distance across the United States which is 4517 km from east to west.

19-3 Rocks That Change: Metamorphic Rocks

There is a very simple chemical test to determine if a rock is limestone. Add some strong vinegar to limestone and the rock will fizz and begin to dissolve. If you add strong vinegar to a bit of marble, the marble will also fizz and begin to dissolve. Why? Marble is chemically the same as limestone. However, the resemblance ends there.

Marble does not look like chalk, a kind of limestone. Chalk is soft and powdery, which is one reason you can use it to write on a chalkboard. But you cannot write with a piece of marble. Why? The reason is because marble is much harder and not powdery like chalk. Marble can be smoothed and polished until it gleams. And, unlike chalk, you will find no trace of fossil shells in marble.

Yet all marble was once limestone, including organic limestone made of fossil shells. Any kind of limestone may become buried deep within the earth. Under very high temperatures and tremendous pressures, the limestone changed. For millions of years the limestone was bent, folded, twisted, squeezed, and changed by forces in the earth. A different kind of rock finally formed. In this case, the new rock was marble.

Activity

Rock Quarries

Quarrying is a method of taking solid blocks or smaller pieces of rock from the earth and preparing them for various uses. Using reference materials in the library, write a report about quarrying stone and include the answers to the following questions:

1. What kinds of rocks are usually taken from quarries?

2. Describe three methods used to remove rocks from a quarry.

3. What are some of the uses of rock material taken from quarries?

4. Where are some large rock quarries located in the United States?

Figure 19-13 *The igneous rock granite can be changed by heat and pressure into the metamorphic rock gneiss. How would you describe the appearance of gneiss?*

Figure 19-14 *The sedimentary rock shale can be changed by heat and pressure into the metamorphic rock slate. What type of texture does slate have?*

Rocks made in this way are called **metamorphic** (met-uh-MAWR-fik) **rocks.** These rocks are usually the hardest and densest rocks. The word "metamorphic" means a rock that has been changed.

Metamorphic rocks can be formed from igneous rocks, sedimentary rocks, and other metamorphic rocks that are exposed to tremendous heat, great pressure, and chemical reactions. Slate is a metamorphic rock made from clay or from shale, a sedimentary rock. Shale is porous. But under high temperatures and pressures, shale turns to slate, which is waterproof. Slate is used to make roofs, pathways, and chalkboards.

Figure 19-15 *The sedimentary rock sandstone can be changed by heat and pressure into the metamorphic rock quartzite. What differences can you see in the rocks?*

Another example of metamorphic rock is quartzite (KWORT-zight). This rock is formed from the sedimentary rock sandstone. Under high temperature and pressure, the sand grains change shape and are packed closer together. The result is that quartzite is harder than sandstone.

SECTION REVIEW

1. What are the two physical conditions needed for metamorphic rocks to form?
2. Metamorphic rock was once what kind of rock?
3. Name two metamorphic rocks. Name the rock from which each is formed.

Activity

A Rock Walk

Write a 500-word essay describing a walk through a rocky area. Make sure you use the following terms: igneous rock, sedimentary rock, metamorphic rock.

CAREER: *Geochronologist*

HELP WANTED: GEOCHRONOLOGIST Bachelor's degree in geology or related field required. Graduate study or coursework in geochronology a plus. Training will be provided during fieldwork and laboratory research.

For a very long time scientists could only guess at the age of the earth and the rocks upon it. Scientists tried determining age by estimating the time it took for the ocean to gain its present saltiness. They also made guesses on the time it takes for sediments to deposit, and then they measured the thickness of all the sedimentary rocks. Unfortunately, the scientists came up with age estimates of the earth ranging from 3 million to 1600 million years with no precise answer.

In the early 1900s, scientists began determining the age of rocks by using the half-life of radioactive minerals. Today scientists who specialize in the study of geologic time are called **geochronologists.** They figure out the age of rocks and landforms by the radioactive decay of certain elements such as carbon and uranium. They test igneous, metamorphic, and sedimentary rocks that range in age from being just recently formed to being almost as old as the earth itself, about 4.6 billion years.

Geochronologists work to learn more about how the earth came to be as it is. Through the study of sediments and fossils, they try to provide pictures of the earth throughout its history. These scientists have contributed to knowledge about the development of life from the first single-celled organisms to prehistoric human beings.

Some qualities that lead to a career in geochronology are natural curiosity, problem-solving ability, and enjoyment of the outdoors. Physical stamina is also required to do the fieldwork. More information may be obtained by writing to the American Geological Institute, 5205 Leesburg Pike, Falls Church, VA 22041.

19-4   The Rock Cycle

Rocks go through many changes. Igneous and sedimentary rocks can change to metamorphic rocks. Metamorphic rocks, too, may be remelted and become igneous rocks again. **The continuous changing of rocks from one kind to another over long periods of time is called the rock cycle.**

Figure 19-16   *This diagram of the rock cycle shows the many ways that rocks are changed. What changes sedimentary rocks to metamorphic?*

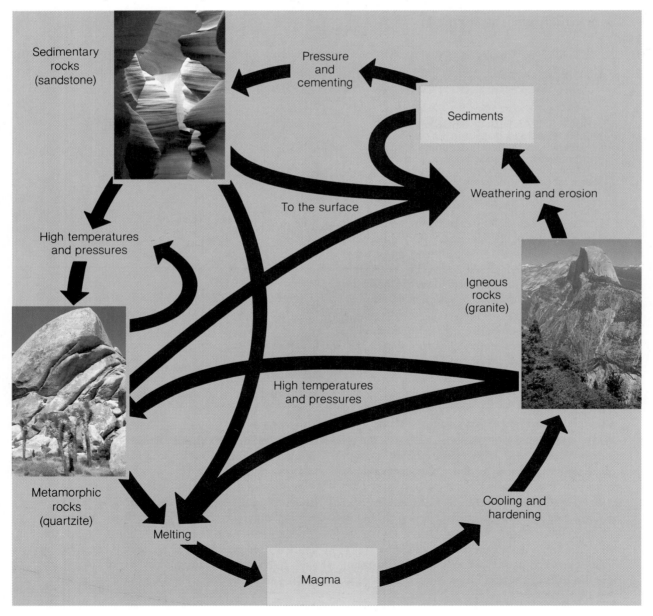

Let's follow a rock on its ages-long journey through the **rock cycle.** See Figure 19-16. A huge dome of granite, an igneous rock, lies exposed to the wind and the rain, the cold of winter, and the heat of summer. Millions upon millions of years ago, this mass of granite was seething molten rock within the earth. It pushed upward against the solid rock above it, forming a dome. The dome hardened into solid rock underground. Slowly, the rock and soil that covered the dome were washed and ground away by wind and rain. Now the harder granite stands alone on the earth's surface.

But though the granite is hard, it also eventually will be worn down under the steady force of wind, water, and temperature changes. Bits of granite will flake off. Dragged along in rushing streams, these sediments may be reduced to powder. Much of this powder will be sand grains, which are made up mainly of the mineral quartz. The quartz will mix with water and other minerals, such as aluminum. The small particles that form are called clay. Some of this clay, as you will see in the next chapter, will become part of the soil.

But these sediments may take another path. They may be deposited on the sea floor. Under high pressure, the sediments may be cemented together in layers to form a sedimentary rock such as sandstone. These rocks may become buried deep under the earth's surface.

High pressure and high temperature may then change the sandstone into quartzite, a metamorphic rock. The quartzite may be exposed at the earth's surface and eventually become eroded to sediments again. Or the quartzite may become molten deep inside the earth. The magma that forms may cool and harden back into granite again. So the rock cycle goes on and on.

SECTION REVIEW

1. What are the three main groups of rocks? Give one example from each group of rocks.
2. How do wind, temperature, and water cause changes in rocks?
3. What is the rock cycle? What two factors in this cycle may change sandstone to quartzite?

LABORATORY ACTIVITY

Making a Sedimentary Rock

Purpose

In this activity, you will make your own sedimentary rock.

Materials *(per group)*

25 g alum
Sand
Metric ruler
Plastic butter or margarine container
100-mL graduated cylinder
Stirring rod
250-mL beaker
Triple-beam balance

Procedure

1. Use a stirring rod to dissolve 25 g of alum in 100 mL of warm water.
2. Fill the bottom of a plastic container to a depth of 2 cm with sand.
3. Pour the alum solution onto the sand in the container. Stir the mixture so that the alum solution is evenly distributed throughout the sand.
4. Pour off and throw away any excess solution. Gently tap the plastic container to help the sand grains settle together.
5. Place the container in a location where it can cool slowly and evaporate to dryness. This usually takes about a day.
6. Gently twist the sides of the container to free its contents. You have created a sedimentary rock.

Observations and Conclusions

1. Describe your rock in terms of color, density, and overall appearance.
2. How is your rock similar to a piece of real sandstone?
3. How is your rock different from a piece of real sandstone?

CHAPTER REVIEW

SUMMARY

19-1 Rocks of Liquid and Fire: Igneous Rocks

■ Deep within the earth it is so hot that rock-forming minerals exist only in a liquid form known as magma.

■ If magma reaches the surface of the earth, it is known as lava.

■ Igneous rocks formed from the cooling of molten rock at or near the earth's surface are called extrusive rocks. Examples include basalt, obsidian, and pumice.

■ Igneous rocks formed from the cooling of molten rock deep beneath the earth's surface are called intrusive rocks. Granite is an example.

19-2 Rocks in Layers: Sedimentary Rocks

■ The hardening of layers of sediment results in the formation of sedimentary rocks. These rocks usually are formed in water.

■ Clastic sedimentary rocks are formed by the cementing together of rock fragments. Conglomerates, sandstones, and shales are examples of clastic rocks.

■ Organic sedimentary rocks are formed from the cementing together of the remains of living things. Chalk is an example.

■ Chemical sedimentary rocks are formed as large amounts of minerals—once dissolved in water—harden together.

19-3 Rocks That Change: Metamorphic Rocks

■ Rocks that underwent high temperatures and high pressures without melting lost their original features and are called metamorphic rocks. Marble and slate are examples.

19-4 The Rock Cycle

■ The continuous changing of rocks from one kind to another is called the rock cycle.

VOCABULARY

Define each term in a complete sentence.

chemical rock	**intrusive rock**	**organic rock**
clastic rock	**lava**	**rock cycle**
extrusive rock	**magma**	**sedimentary rock**
igneous rock	**metamorphic rock**	

CONTENT REVIEW: MULTIPLE CHOICE

Choose the letter of the answer that best completes each statement.

1. Molten rocks that cool at the earth's surface are
   a. igneous rocks.   b. extrusive rocks.
   c. volcanic glass.   d. all of these.
2. A kind of igneous rock that has cooled so quickly that gas bubbles remain trapped inside is called
   a. basalt.   b. pumice.   c. obsidian.   d. granite.
3. Which of these is an example of an intrusive rock?
   a. granite   b. obsidian   c. magma   d. pumice

4. The amount of time it takes molten rock to cool and harden mainly affects the rock's
a. color.   b. mass.   c. texture.   d. all of these.

5. Which of these igneous rocks cooled most slowly?
a. obsidian   b. granite   c. pumice   d. volcanic rock

6. Which sedimentary rock is formed from the cementing together of sand grains?
a. granite   b. shale   c. limestone   d. sandstone

7. Which of these is an example of a clastic rock?
a. basalt   b. shale   c. chalk   d. obsidian

8. Organic rocks are formed from
a. the cooling of magma.
b. the cementing together of sand and clay.
c. the remains of living things.
d. all of these.

9. Which of these is an example of a metamorphic rock?
a. pumice   b. shale   c. chalk   d. marble

10. In the rock cycle, weathering and erosion can change which rocks into sediments?
a. igneous   b. sedimentary   c. metamorphic   d. all of these

CONTENT REVIEW: COMPLETION

Fill in the word or words that best complete each statement.

1. Molten rock that reaches the earth's surface is called _____.

2. _____ is often called volcanic glass.

3. Gigantic masses of granite called _____ form the bases of the earth's mountain ranges.

4. An example of a rock formed by the cementing together of rock fragments is _____.

5. _____ is a sedimentary rock formed from the hardening of layers of mud and clay.

6. Limestone is _____ sedimentary rock formed from the shells of ocean animals.

7. Limestone reefs form from the hard outer coverings of _____ that become cemented together.

8. Sedimentary rocks that form from large amounts of minerals that were once dissolved in water are called _____ rocks.

9. _____ is a metamorphic rock formed from clay or shale.

10. The continuous changing of rocks from one kind to another over long periods of time is called the _____.

CONTENT REVIEW: TRUE OR FALSE

Determine whether each statement is true or false. If it is true, write "true." If it is false, change the underlined word or words to make the statement true.

1. Hot, molten rock deep inside the earth is called <u>lava</u>.

2. Granite and obsidian are igneous rocks of <u>similar</u> chemical composition.

3. Molten rocks that cool and harden beneath the earth's surface are extrusive rocks.
4. Due to rapid cooling, the crystals of extrusive rocks are smaller than those of intrusive rocks.
5. Sedimentary rocks may be rich in fossils.
6. A conglomerate is an example of a(n) chemical rock.
7. Chalk is a sedimentary rock made of small pieces of animal shells and limestone.
8. Strong vinegar will react chemically with most sandstone.
9. Metamorphic rocks can change into igneous rocks.
10. Under high temperature and high pressure, sandstone, a sedimentary rock, may change into quartzite, a metamorphic rock.

CONCEPT REVIEW: SKILL BUILDING

Use the skills you have developed in the chapter to complete each activity.

1. **Applying facts** Obsidian and diorite are both igneous rocks. However, they have different appearances. Obsidian is dark and glassy. Diorite is light-colored and coarse-grained. How do you account for the differences in these two rocks?
2. **Identifying patterns** Describe how and where sedimentary rocks form. Explain why scientists study sedimentary rocks to learn about prehistoric life.
3. **Classifying rocks** What information would you use to determine whether a rock sample is shale or slate?
4. **Relating cause and effect** Explain why fossils are present in sedimentary rocks but are not usually in metamorphic or igneous rocks.
5. **Sequencing events** Describe what may happen to a huge outcrop of quartzite as it goes through the rock cycle.
6. **Making diagrams** Obtain samples of sedimentary, metamorphic, and igneous rocks. Using Figure 19-16 on page 444, illustrate the rock cycle with the rocks you have collected.
7. **Making inferences** Suppose you find a metamorphic rock that breaks in layers. How do you think this rock formed? Hint: The minerals in the rock have different densities.

CONCEPT REVIEW: ESSAY

Discuss each of the following in a brief paragraph.

1. Clastic rocks, organic rocks, and chemical rocks are all examples of sedimentary rocks. Describe the differences among these three types and list one example of each.
2. How does an igneous rock become part of a sedimentary rock?
3. Explain why 75 percent of the rocks on the earth's surface are sedimentary rocks.
4. Relate the cooling rate of magma to the crystal size in igneous rocks.
5. Compare extrusive and intrusive igneous rocks. Give an example of each.
6. How can the shell of a snail become part of a sedimentary rock?
7. What three factors are responsible for the formation of metamorphic rocks from other rocks?

20 Soils

CHAPTER SECTIONS

20-1 Soil

20-2 Tropical Rain Forest Soil

20-3 Temperate Forest Soil

20-4 Prairie Grassland Soil

20-5 Desert Soil

20-6 Tundra Soil

CHAPTER OBJECTIVES

After completing this chapter, you will be able to:

20-1 Describe the different soil layers.

20-1 Identify the environmental factors that cause weathering.

20-2 Relate leaching to soil formation in tropical rain forests.

20-3 Explain why temperate forest soil does not provide enough minerals for widespread plant growth.

20-4 Explain how prairie grassland soil came to be so fertile.

20-5 Explain why little humus forms in desert soil.

20-6 Explain why tundra soil is different from most types of soil.

To the first settlers from Europe, much of North America looked like one vast forest. It stretched westward as far as the settlers could see.

Or so it seemed. The first settlers cleared some forest and built their towns along the Atlantic coast of the new continent. As more settlers arrived and families grew, the settlers slowly pushed westward. By the 1800s, they reached the edge of the forest—the Midwest.

It was like standing between two worlds. Behind the settlers, to the east, lay the forest—shaded, cool and damp. Under a thin layer of leaves, the soil was white and ashlike. To the west, in brilliant sunshine, a sea of grass rippled in the wind. Beneath the grass, though the settlers did not know it yet, lay some of the best farming soil in the world.

Beyond the western edges of the great grasslands, the grass grew scarcer and died away into desert land with cactus plants and shrubs. Here much of the soil was barren powdery rock.

The pioneers that settled on this new continent did not know why soils were different in forests, grasslands, and deserts. They may have guessed that factors in the environment were important. And they would have been right.

The prairie grasslands

20-1 Soil

Some people think of "soil" as being another word for dirt. And when people say something is "dirt cheap," they mean it is practically worthless. But soil is precious and vital to life on the earth. Without soil, most plants could not grow on the land. Without plants, no animals would survive. The earth's surface might look as barren as the moon.

Soil Layers

You can find out a lot about how a house is built by looking at what holds it up and what holds it together—its structure. But usually you cannot see much of the structure without taking the house apart. The framework of a house is hidden in the walls and floors. The foundation is underground.

The structure of soil is much the same. Soil is a covering over most of the earth's land surface. This soil covering can range in thickness from a few millimeters to a few meters. However, all you usually see of the soil covering is the very top.

Like a house with several floors, soil has different layers. **The three layers of soil are the topsoil, subsoil, and parent rock.** The uppermost layer is made up of **topsoil.** Topsoil is a mixture of small grains of rock and the decayed matter of plants and animals. How did this mixture come about? You can see its beginnings on the forest floor. Year after year a carpet of wood, pine needles, leaves, and bits of twigs is laid down. A rich variety of animals lives on and under this carpet, including worms, snails, insects, and mice.

Year after year, the remains of plant and animal life decay to become a part of the topsoil. The decayed matter combines with rocky soil particles to form a rich, dark soil called **humus.** Humus supplies essential chemicals for growing plants. Because humus is spongy, it stores water. In fact, humus can hold up to 600 times its own weight in water. Humus soil also contains many air spaces, or pores. When mixed with rock grains, humus forms a soil that allows air and water to reach plant roots.

Figure 20-1 *The two main ingredients of soil are pieces of rock and organic material, which is material that was once living or was formed by living organisms. How can you tell that the soil in the top photograph is low in organic material and the soil in the bottom photograph is high?*

Topsoil (containing humus)

Subsoil

Weathered parent rock

Unweathered parent rock

Figure 20-2 *Soil has different layers, as shown in an artist's view* (left) *and in a photograph* (right).

The thickness of the topsoil may be anywhere from a few centimeters to a meter or more. Beneath it is the **subsoil** level. This level is made up of larger bits of rock and has little or no humus.

As you dig down further into the soil, the rock particles become larger and more numerous. Finally you reach solid rock, which is called the **parent rock.** Most minerals and other rocky particles in the soil first originated from this parent rock. But how could tiny rock particles come from solid parent rock?

Soil and the Environment

If you place a rock on the ground and strike it with a hammer, the rock will break into pieces. Smash these pieces and they become even smaller. Continue smashing the pieces and they may even become part of the soil. Billions of years ago, before soil formed, the land surfaces of the earth were solid rock—parent rock. Naturally, there were no giant hammers crushing the parent rock into soil. But in a way environmental factors such as wind, water, heat,

Activity

Humus

1. Obtain some topsoil from a forest or grassy area or from a gardener who uses compost to enrich the soil.

2. Carefully sort through the soil or compost. Using a magnifying glass, separate the small particles of soil from the particles of decaying plants and animals.

What type of soil particles are in your topsoil? What does the soil look like?

Figure 20-3 *This photograph shows the longest natural bridge in the world. Made of sandstone, it was formed by the process of weathering.*

Activity

Studying Soil Layers

Using a shovel, dig down about 0.5 meter and obtain a soil sample from your neighborhood. Be sure not to disturb the soil sample or ground too much or you will not be able to see the different soil layers. From your observations, answer the following questions.

1. How deep is the topsoil layer? What color is this layer?

2. How deep is the subsoil layer? What color is this layer?

3. How do the soils in the two layers differ?

4. Did you find the layer of weathered parent rock? Describe this soil layer.

and cold acted much like a hammer. The process by which rocks are broken down by the environment is called **weathering.** Weathering helped produce soil when the earth was young, and weathering still is producing soil today.

How can weathering produce soil? There are many ways. Water, for example, may seep into cracks in the rock. In cold weather, the water freezes. As water freezes, it expands to take up more space than liquid water. The ice pushes against both sides of the cracks and splits the rock into smaller pieces. Small plants, such as lichens, may grow on these rocks. These plants produce acids that break down the rocks into even smaller pieces. Eventually, weathering breaks down parent rocks into mineral particles. Remains of plants and animals get mixed in with these mineral particles and soil is formed.

Running water can also break down rocks into smaller soil particles. Whipping winds can do the same. Environmental factors such as these not only help produce soil, they also distribute the soil—often far from the region where it formed. On the steep slope of a mountainside, for example, strong winds and heavy rains can break down rock, which may eventually become a part of the soil. But as fast as the soil forms, floods can sweep it away. The soil may eventually be deposited many kilometers away on a flat plain, forming the rich soil important to farmers.

But to say that soil is created in this way is only part of the story. There are many kinds of soil. Different soils are shaped by different environmental factors, including the weather, the land, and the organisms that live where the soil was formed. At the same time, the kind of soil in a place has an important influence on the kinds of things that can live in that place. For example, plants such as rhododendrons and azaleas grow best in soils containing large amounts of iron. Other plants have special needs for various elements in the soil.

SECTION REVIEW

1. Describe the three layers of soil.
2. What environmental factors cause weathering?

20-2 Tropical Rain Forest Soil

There are three major areas in the world where tropical rain forests grow: the Amazon area of South America, parts of Africa, and parts of Southeast Asia. This green belt of tropical rain forests is near the equator, where there is much rain and the temperatures are warm year round.

If you were to walk through a tropical rain forest, you might be amazed by the many different kinds of plants and animals. All around you tall trees, some 60 meters or more in height, soar toward the sky to capture sunlight. And soar they must, for the forest

Figure 20-4 *A tropical rain forest has many kinds of trees that grow very close together.*

Figure 20-5 *Some plants grow piggyback on the trunks and limbs of trees in a tropical rain forest.*

Figure 20-6 *Many interesting animals, such as these colorful macaws* (left) *and this large orangutan* (right), *live in a tropical rain forest.*

floor is dim and shadowy. Even at noon only scattered flecks of sunlight shine through the ceiling of trees and reach the forest floor.

You might wander for over a kilometer without seeing the same kind of tree twice! From some trees hang strange vines that weave their way around the tree trunks, forming coils and loops of living matter. Other vines snake through the air, waving in the warm tropical breeze. Colorful plants such as orchids grow on the bark of some trees. Surprisingly, you have little trouble walking on the forest floor. Very few plants block your way because they cannot grow where the light is so dim.

The tropical rain forest is a biologist's delight. Animals of all kinds, ranging from huge tarantulas that capture small birds for prey to brightly feathered parrots munching on nuts, live in the forest. Some animals, such as hunting leopards, glide through the shadows of the forest floor in search of food. Others, such as lizards and snakes, climb up and down tree trunks. Still others, including over 150 species of bats, fly through the air. In fact, scientists estimate that two-thirds of all plant and animal species make their home in tropical rain forests.

As you continue on your walk, you notice that many plants have leaves with unusually long pointed ends. These ends, called "drip tips," function like rain gutters. They allow water to quickly drip off the leaves of these plants. Drip tips are a big advantage in a tropical rain forest in which rainfall averages more than 200 centimeters per year. If the rain

could not quickly flow off the leaves, the plants might become covered with mold and die.

The heavy rainfall in the tropical rain forest plays a role in soil formation. Heavy rains can wash minerals important for plant growth downward into the soil. This process of washing minerals out of the topsoil is called **leaching.** Leaching is important in the formation of soils. **Normally, leaching can spread important minerals throughout the subsoil where roots can easily reach them. But in the tropics, where there is often too much rain for this to happen, the minerals are leached so far into the ground that they are lost to the plants.**

If leaching removes important minerals from the rain forest soil, why are so many different kinds of plants able to survive? The answer is right above you—all you need do is look up to see the forest's main source of minerals. Leaves, flowers, and other plant parts constantly fall to the forest floor. Added to these remains are the bodies of dead animals. Since the forest is hot and damp all year long, these remains decay very quickly and form a rich supply of food for the plants. Although rain constantly washes away this thin layer of humus, it is constantly replaced by a new layer. Also, the root systems of rain forest plants are so efficient that almost all the decaying matter is absorbed by living plants.

Figure 20-7 *Many tropical rain forest trees have extensive surface root systems that are so efficient they can recycle nearly all the nutrients from decaying plants.*

SECTION REVIEW

1. What is leaching? Why is leaching important in the formation of soils?
2. Tropical soil has a thin layer of humus. Why?

20-3 Temperate Forest Soil

"The American forests have generally one very interesting quality, that of being entirely free from underwood. This is owing to the extraordinary height and spreading tops of the trees; which thus prevent the sun from penetrating to the ground."

So wrote a traveler in Pennsylvania in 1806. Today only small areas of these temperate forests still exist in the United States. But they still take up a lot of ground. Temperate forests include such trees as beech, maple, oak, hemlock, wild cherry, and dogwood, as well as a variety of evergreens.

The traveler's description of the temperate forest sounds something like that of the tropical rain forest. Of course, there are important differences. The climate of the tropical forest is hot and damp. The climate of the temperate forest ranges from cold and fairly dry in the north to warm and damp further south. There are four different seasons in all temperate forests. In the cold seasons, particularly in the northern forests, most decay of plant and animal remains stops. As you might expect, little humus is produced in the cold weather and few minerals are added to the soil. However, even in warm weather, the temperate forest floor cannot support a wide variety of plant life. Why?

Career: *Soil Conservationist*

HELP WANTED: SOIL CONSERVATIONIST Bachelor's degree in soil conservation or natural resource sciences such as agronomy, forestry, or agriculture necessary.

The rain poured down hard and fast. Most of the valuable topsoil washed into the stream that ran across the farm. Enough soil filled the stream to cause flooding and destruction of the crops beside it. To obtain help, the farmer contacted the area's soil conservation service. A **soil conservationist** was immediately sent to inspect the situation.

Soil conservationists advise farmers and ranchers how best to water livestock or to prevent overgrazing. Other concerns include water conservation, sound land use, and environmental improvement. Soil conservationists prepare plans using soil conservation practices such as crop rotation, reforestation, terracing, and permanent vegetation. Usually in planning a soil program, soil conservationists work closely with government workers, farmers, ranchers, foresters, and urban planners.

Anyone who is interested in conserving and protecting our natural resources and who enjoys working with people might consider a career in soil conservation. In rural areas, positions arise in banks, insurance firms, and mortgage companies. Public utility, lumber, and paper companies also employ soil conservationists. Government positions are also available, such as in the Department of the Interior. For more information about this career, write to the United States Department of Agriculture, Soil Conservation Service, Room 5218—South, Fourteenth Street and Independence Avenue S.W., Washington, DC 20250.

Figure 20-8 *Trees in a temperate forest grow many leaves during the summer* (left). *But these leaves do not grow during the winter. In the winter, organic decay and plant growth stop* (right).

In temperate forests, there is no heavy year-round rainfall. However, although the forest floor is matted with leaves and evergreen needles, rainwater often leaches out important minerals. **Unlike tropical rain forest soil, little decay of dead plant matter occurs in temperate forest soil before leaching carries minerals deep into the subsoil.** So little humus forms in temperate forest soil.

Because the trees in temperate forests have deep roots, they can reach important minerals that have leached into the subsoil. However, smaller plants with shorter root systems cannot get to these minerals needed for plant growth. The lack of smaller plants is particularly true in northern temperate forests where almost all the plants are evergreen trees. The carpet of evergreen needles is especially poor in many important minerals. In more southern temperate forests, the leafy floor is richer in minerals and the warmer weather allows more decay to proceed at a faster pace. Why is this soil more fertile than soil in the most northern temperate forests?

SECTION REVIEW

1. Would you expect the rate of decay of dead plant and animal matter to be faster in a tropical rain forest or in a temperate forest? Why?
2. List three trees, other than evergreens, that grow in temperate forests in the United States.

Activity

Leaching

In a 500-word essay describe how leaching affects each of the following soil types: tropical soil, temperate forest soil, prairie grassland soil, desert soil, and tundra.

459

Figure 20-9 *Darrel Coble (far right) was three years old in April 1936 when he and his family fled this dust storm in Oklahoma. During the 1930s, prairie grassland soils became useless for growing crops.*

20-4 Prairie Grassland Soil

To the first settlers, the great prairie grasslands of the midwestern United States appeared as a vast sea of grasses. It stretched from the eastern forest region to the Rocky Mountains.

At first, the settlers felt that these prairie grasslands were useless for growing crops. The settlers were used to planting crops in cleared forest land. They had never seen anything like this land and believed that where trees did not grow in large numbers, the ground could not be good for crops.

In time, the settlers discovered that the soil of these regions was some of the richest in the world. Today the Canadian and United States prairie grasslands are considered the "breadbaskets of the world," for here is where great oceans of wheat are grown. Wheat is the grain from which bread is made. There are similar regions in Argentina and the Ukraine region of the Soviet Union. Together, these regions produce nearly all of the grain crops grown in the world. Grain crops include corn, wheat, barley, and rye.

The soils of North America's prairie grassland were not always so fertile. Millions of years ago most of the land west of the Rocky Mountains slowly turned to desert. As the soil dried up and crumbled to dust, winds carried it eastward and deposited the

Figure 20-10 *On the same land in Oklahoma 42 years later, Darrel Coble and his two sons walk through fertile fields of wheat. Changes in climate greatly influence soil and plant changes.*

soil over the prairie. Soon grasses began to grow in the newly laid soil. Year after year, thick mats of grass roots and stems decayed, building a deep layer of humus. Since the prairie, unlike the forests, was exposed to lots of sun and high winds, rainfall quickly evaporated. This prevented important minerals in the humus from leaching out of the topsoil. **Today prairie grassland soil is rich in humus, dark brown to black in color, and very fertile.**

SECTION REVIEW

1. Why are the Canadian and United States prairies called the "breadbaskets of the world"?
2. Why is there less leaching in prairie soil than in forest soil?

20-5 Desert Soil

You probably imagine deserts as being very hot, dusty places. And, in fact, many deserts are quite hot—at least during the day. However, the main characteristic of all deserts is not heat but a lack of water. This lack of water is a problem for many plants and animals that make their home in the desert. But it also means there is very little leaching of

Figure 20-11 *In the spring, desert flowers bloom in a spectacular display. But the flowers soon vanish so the plants can complete their life cycles before the start of the hot, dry summer.*

Figure 20-12 *These barrellike cacti act like living accordions by swelling up to store water and then contracting slowly as the water supply decreases. Cacti also have a waxy coating that keeps the stored water from evaporating.*

minerals from the desert soil. So you might expect desert soil to be rich in minerals—and it is.

Despite the minerals in the desert soil, there is little or no humus in the soil. Why? Desert plants often have root systems that spread out in a wide area around the plant. In this way, plants can take in as much water as possible whenever an infrequent rain shower occurs. However, because of their widespread root systems, there are often large spaces between desert plants. With so few plants in any one area, there is not a constant "rain" of plant matter onto the desert floor. **What little plant matter does fall to the desert floor decays so slowly in the dry desert heat that very little humus or topsoil can form.** How, then, do you think scientists might be able to grow plants and food crops in a desert?

SECTION REVIEW

1. What is the main characteristic of all deserts?
2. Why is there little leaching in the desert?

20-6 Tundra Soil

Beyond the edge of the northern evergreen forests and in much of northern Alaska lies the arctic tundra. Tundra also is found in other arctic regions in the world. In the tundra, the climate is very cold most of the year, and strong winds blow constantly.

There is little or no topsoil in the tundra and much of the soil just below the surface is permanently frozen. This frozen soil is called **permafrost.** As you might expect, few plants can grow in the harsh tundra, particularly during the long winter. Those plants that do grow are small plants, mainly reindeer moss, lichens, and dwarf trees. When these plants die, they decay very slowly due to the cold weather. So little humus forms in the tundra.

Unlike most soils, tundra soil does not have different levels. There is a constant mixing of the soil due to freezing and thawing. In summer, a thin layer at the top of the soil thaws. It stays wet because the water cannot go through the permanently frozen layers beneath. During this time, small lakes and marshes form on the tundra. Ducks of all kinds flock to the tundra lakes during the short summer months. When winter does return and the ground soil again freezes, the ducks and many other tundra animals will have already migrated to warmer areas farther south.

Figure 20-13 *Another kind of soil is mountain soil. Soil on the slopes of mountains is made up of jagged pieces of weathered parent rock and very small amounts of clay and sand. There usually is no topsoil in these regions.*

Figure 20-14 *Many small plants such as grasses, lichens, and reindeer moss grow on the tundra during summer (left). But during the winter the ground is snow-covered, and animals such as these caribou must keep traveling in search of food (right).*

SECTION REVIEW

1. What is permafrost?
2. Tundra soil has no distinct layers. Why?

LABORATORY ACTIVITY

Determining Rates of Weathering

Purpose

In this activity, you will find out what effect particle size has on the speed, or rate, at which a rock reacts with its surroundings.

```
Materials (per group)

1 antacid or          Paper
  seltzer tablet      Pen or pencil
4 100-mL beakers      Water
Graduated cylinder
```

Procedure

1. Break an antacid tablet in two.
2. Place one of the halves on a piece of paper, and fold the paper so that it covers the tablet.
3. With one end of your pencil or pen, gently tap the half tablet under the paper several times in order to break it into smaller pieces. Be careful not to crush the material to powder.
4. Place the other half of the tablet in one beaker. Place the crushed, smaller pieces in a second beaker.
5. Add 10 mL of water to each of the remaining beakers.
6. At the same time, pour the water from these two beakers into the beakers containing the seltzer tablets.
7. Observe both reactions until they end. Then record your observations. Be sure to describe the reactions you observed in both beakers and the time it took for the reactions to end.

Observations and Conclusions

1. What difference in reaction rates did you observe in the two beakers?
2. When you broke the tablet into very small pieces, you increased the surface area of that part of the tablet. State the relationship between surface area and reaction rate in a chemical change.
3. Your observations in this activity can be used to make a general statement about weathering processes that occur in the natural environment. Draw a graph showing the relationship between the particle size of a substance and the rate at which it weathers.

464

CHAPTER REVIEW

20-1 Soil

- Soil is the thin layer of minerals, decayed plant and animal matter, water, and air that covers the earth's surface.

- Topsoil, the uppermost soil layer, is made up of small rock grains, remains of dead organisms, and humus.

- Subsoil, the soil layer beneath the topsoil, contains larger rock grains and little or no humus.

- Parent rock is the solid rock that lies beneath the subsoil.

- The environmental factors that affect soils include climate, mineral content of parent rock, and different types of plants and animals.

20-2 Tropical Rain Forest Soil

- Tropical soils are found in the rain forests of South America, Africa, and Asia.

- Huge amounts of rain keep the forest floor damp, which increases the decay of plant and animal matter.

- The washing of minerals downward out of the topsoil is called leaching. In tropical soils, leaching quickly washes minerals out of reach of plant roots.

- Decayed remains become part of the thin humus layer. The humus layer repeatedly washes away and reforms.

- Root systems of rain forest plants are so efficient that they absorb almost all of the decaying matter from plants and animals.

20-3 Temperate Forest Soil

- Unlike tropical rain forests, temperate forests have four seasons. In winter, most decay of plant and animal matter stops.

- The process of leaching removes many minerals from temperate forest soils.

- Southern temperate forests have more fertile soil than northern temperate forests.

20-4 Prairie Grassland Soil

- Prairie grassland soils are found in the grassland areas of the midwestern United States and in similar regions of the world.

- Prairie grassland soils are very fertile, rich in humus, and dark in color.

20-5 Desert Soil

- Desert soils are found in very dry regions.

- Because there is little rain, there is little leaching and therefore little washing away of minerals.

- Because there are very few plants and animals as a result of the lack of water, there is little humus and little topsoil.

20-6 Tundra Soil

- Tundra soil is found in the arctic regions of the world.

- Tundra topsoil is very thin. The permanently frozen subsoil is known as permafrost.

- Few plants grow in tundra topsoil, and it is very cold. So there is little organic decay.

Define each term in a complete sentence.

humus	**permafrost**	**weathering**
leaching	**subsoil**	
parent rock	**topsoil**	

CONTENT REVIEW: MULTIPLE CHOICE

Choose the letter of the answer that best completes each statement.

1. Soil contains
   a. rock particles.   b. decayed plant and animal matter.
   c. air.   d. all of these.
2. The color of the humus layer of the topsoil is normally
   a. reddish.   b. reddish-yellow.   c. whitish.   d. black or brown.
3. The mixture of decayed plant and animal matter that combines with rocky particles to form a fertile soil is called
   a. permafrost.   b. subsoil.   c. humus.   d. leaching.
4. Which of these is most closely related to parent rock?
   a. topsoil   b. subsoil   c. humus   d. decayed plants
5. Climate is an important factor because it affects the kinds and amounts of
   a. plants.   b. animals.   c. soil.   d. all of these.
6. Which of these environmental factors can contribute to soil formation?
   a. wind   b. heat and cold
   c. running water   d. all of these
7. In which type of soil is the humus layer constantly replaced?
   a. tropical soil   b. forest soil   c. desert soil   d. tundra soil
8. Which area has the most fertile soil?
   a. tropical rain forests   b. forests
   c. prairie grasslands   d. deserts
9. The minerals and humus needed by plants remain in prairie grassland soils because there is little
   a. leaching.   b. subsoil.   c. sun and wind.   d. permafrost.
10. The soil of very dry regions with little water and little leaching is called
    a. tropical soil.   b. forest soil.
    c. desert soil.   d. tundra soil.

CONTENT REVIEW: COMPLETION

Fill in the word or words that best complete each statement.

1. Topsoil can range in thickness from a few _____ to a few meters.
2. Material that results from the decay of dead plants and animals is known as _____.
3. The uppermost layer of soil is called _____.
4. The breakdown of parent rock by environmental factors is called _____.
5. The leaves of many tropical rain forest plants have _____ that help to draw off water.
6. The washing of minerals out of the topsoil is called _____.
7. Heavy rainfalls cause many minerals to leach from the _____ layer in a tropical rain forest.
8. The topsoil of prairie grassland soil is dark in color because it contains a lot of _____.
9. The type of soil characteristic of the Arctic is called _____.
10. The permanently frozen subsoil of the Arctic is called _____.

Determine whether each statement is true or false. If it is true, write "true." If it is false, change the underlined word or words to make the statement true.

1. The uppermost layer of soil is <u>subsoil</u>.
2. Humus is used by <u>animals</u> as food.
3. Humus soil contains <u>few</u> air spaces.
4. The process in which rock is broken down into soil is called <u>weathering</u>.
5. If the leaves of plants in tropical rain forests do not dry quickly, <u>molds</u> may grow on them and kill the leaves.
6. Tropical rain forests are located near the earth's <u>poles</u>.
7. Rapid decaying and forming of humus occurs in <u>tropical</u> soils.
8. A mat of evergreen needles is <u>rich</u> in minerals needed for plant growth.
9. Plants and animals of the desert areas can survive because they are able to save and store <u>water</u>.
10. Constant mixing of the soil due to freezing and thawing prevents <u>tundra</u> soils from having different soil levels.

Use the skills you have developed in the chapter to complete each activity.

1. **Making comparisons** Soil is vital to life. Compare what the earth is like with soil to what it would be like without soil.
2. **Applying concepts** Many scientists consider the Antarctic among the world's largest deserts. Explain how such a cold place can be a desert.
3. **Making inferences** What environmental factors of weathering have more impact on soil formation in cold, dry regions? In hot, humid regions? Explain your answers.
4. **Relating concepts** How is the weathering of rocks helpful to life on the earth?
5. **Analyzing data** In an experiment to measure soil's ability to hold water, particle size and amount of humus were tested. The results are shown below.

   Construct a graph that represents the relationship between the amount of water retained and the size of the soil particles. Your graph should have two lines. Label each line appropriately as either "Without Humus" or With Humus."

   Based on your graph, describe a type of soil that would supply water for plant roots during a period of little rainfall.

	Small Particles		**Medium Particles**		**Large Particles**	
	With humus	*Without humus*	*With humus*	*Without humus*	*With humus*	*Without humus*
Water retained by soil	50.0 mL	20.8 mL	44.6 mL	13.6 mL	39.8 mL	10.2 mL

Discuss each of the following in a brief paragraph.

1. Describe the five different soil types.
2. How is soil formed?
3. What is humus? How is it formed?
4. Describe the process of leaching and explain why leaching is important in the formation of soil.

Maria Reiche Solving the

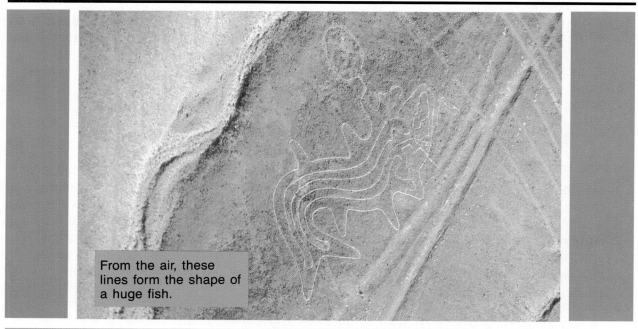

From the air, these lines form the shape of a huge fish.

Mysteries of the Nazca Lines

One of the driest spots on the earth is the Nazca Desert of Peru. Here, huge drawings of animals have been scratched into the earth's surface. These drawings are so large that they can be recognized only from the air.

The figure of a monkey capers across 80 meters of flat, dusty landscape. Nearby, a gigantic bird spreads its wings over more than 270 meters of desert soil. These are just two of about 30 huge mysterious drawings that, from the ground, look simply like furrows in the dirt.

The drawings are called the Nazca Lines, after the desert on which they are drawn. They were made many centuries ago by Peruvian Indians who left behind almost nothing else of their culture. But why did the ancient Peruvians make the drawings? This question remains unanswered.

Many scientists, as well as interested visitors, have tried to unlock the secret of the Nazca Lines. But the efforts of one woman stand out. Her name is Maria Reiche, a woman on a lifelong quest to solve the mystery of the lines. Maria Reiche is an 80-year-old mathematician and geographer. For more than 20 years she has lived in the desert studying the Nazca Lines and making careful measurements.

Speaking of her search for the answer to the mystery of the Nazca Lines, Maria Reiche says, "We have to penetrate into the minds of the Indians who drew these lines and find the way they worked to find the answer."

Reiche came to Peru from Germany in the 1930s. Her fascination with the desert drawings began in 1940, when she met an American archeologist named Paul Kosok. Kosok was in Peru studying ancient systems of watering crop lands. He had charted one of the winding desert markings thinking that it might be part of such a watering system. Instead, he found that the line formed the huge figure of a bird. It was the first drawing to be discovered. Reiche has since devoted herself to the drawings.

From her many years in the desert, Reiche discovered how the ancient Peruvians carved the lines in the soil. They created the 7- to 8-centimeter deep furrows by removing the surface of brown stones to reveal the yellow soil beneath. The yellow soil—a mixture of

Maria Reiche seeks to unlock the secrets of mysterious lines carved into the ground of the Nazca Desert of Peru.

sand, clay, and calcite—contrasts sharply with the stones.

The Indians could not have chosen a better spot for their artwork. The Nazca Desert receives less than one-quarter of a centimeter of rain each year. It is the dryness that has preserved the lines for the one or two thousand years since they were made. A cushion of warm air hovers over the desert surface and helps protect the drawings from being covered by blowing sand.

A Recent Breakthrough

Some scientists, including Reiche, believe that the drawings had something to do with religious ceremonies. But Reiche feels that religious ceremony was not their only function. She has been trying to prove that the lines were a kind of calendar that was used to chart the movement of the sun, moon, and stars. Many ancient civilizations had such calendars and used them to set dates for planting, harvesting, and festivals.

To test her hypothesis, Reiche must find a relationship between the lines and the positions of the sun and moon at special times of the year. Such times are the solstices, which mark the beginning of summer and winter, and the equinoxes, which mark the beginning of spring and fall.

In the early morning, before the desert heat becomes too intense, Maria Reiche can be seen shuffling across the desert. Even before the sun has risen, she is noting the position of the lines in relation to the sunrise. In this way, she has found that some of the straight lines in the figures were solstice lines. They pointed to where the sun rose and set on June 21 and December 21 hundreds of years ago.

Still, many scientists are not convinced that the Nazca Lines were drawn as a calendar. Although Reiche has proven to her own satisfaction that some lines mark ancient solstices and equinoxes, too many lines seemingly point to nothing at all. Also, scientists argue, the animal drawings remain a mystery.

Maria Reiche is not about to give up, however. The lines, she says, "can't be senseless. There is too much work in them."

DIVING FOR NATURAL TREASURES:

A Risky Business?

Edith Widder, with the Wasp diving suit in the background, prepares for a dive in California's Santa Barbara Channel.

Six hundred meters below the ocean's surface, Edith Widder looks out on a fascinating world. The powerful beam from her lamp illuminates oddly shaped fish. Glowing masses of plankton, or microscopic plants and animals, float within reach of her outstretched arms.

Edith Widder is one of five pioneer scientists who participated in a program of deep-ocean exploration conducted by the University of California at Santa Barbara in the summer of 1984. The program had two purposes. One was to study the strange and beautiful animals that live in the ocean depths. The other was to test a diving suit called the Wasp. As its name suggests, this special new suit makes the wearer look like a wasp, with a big head and a tapered body.

The scientists made a series of dives down to 600 meters in the deep Santa Barbara Channel off the coast of California. Despite the crushing water pressure, each scientist was able to spend long periods of time moving around on the ocean floor. Few divers have ever ventured to such a depth before. Those that have were not able to stay down for long. In fact, most deep-ocean exploration has been done by scientists in submarines and diving bells or by tanklike robots.

The Santa Barbara Channel dives have opened up a whole new way to explore the ocean depths. The Wasp provides deep-ocean protection and life support while giving the wearer remarkable freedom of movement. Some people have dubbed it the "body submarine" because it combines the best features of a submarine and a diving suit. Such a combination is vital for future exploration of the ocean depths and for future use of the ocean's wealth.

BURIED TREASURE

The treasures that lie beneath the waves are many and varied. People eat some of these treasures, such as fish, sea animals, and sea plants. Scientists have also discovered that many ocean plants and animals are a source of valuable medicines. Vast oil fields lie beneath the ocean floor. Some are being tapped now. Many more lie waiting to be tapped in the future. Large deposits of hard minerals have been discovered on the ocean floor as well. These minerals include manganese, tungsten, vanadium, nickel, cobalt, tin, titanium, silver, platinum, and gold.

Some of the minerals can be found just below the surface of the ocean floor. Others are a bit deeper in the sediment layers and would have to be mined. But perhaps the most interesting minerals are those that are just sitting on the ocean floor waiting to be scooped up. Trillions of tons of these

Trillions of tons of valuable metal ores lie on the ocean floor. These potato-sized rocks hold magnesium.

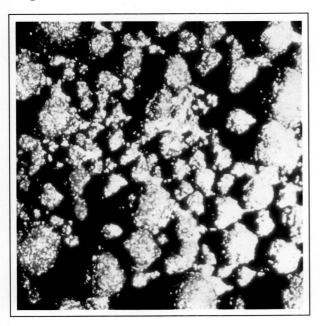

minerals in the form of potato-sized lumps, or nodules, cover the ocean bottom in many places.

A number of American companies have designed equipment to gather these nodules from the ocean floor. One craft, a tractorlike robot, would roam the ocean floor scooping up minerals. The craft would then wash and crush them and pipe them to the surface for further processing.

QUESTIONS RISE TO THE SURFACE

The harvesting of minerals raises some difficult questions. Will ocean mining pollute the water? Will mining in one area hurt

Before the Wasp was invented, deep ocean exploration had to be done in vehicles such as the one shown in this photo.

fishing in nearby areas? Will mining wipe out rare fish and other sea life?

Studies such as the one conducted in the Santa Barbara Channel may help to answer these questions. Divers wearing the Wasp would be able to keep a close watch on mining and drilling operations on the ocean floor. This kind of monitoring might reduce the chances of oil leaks and other such accidents. Deep-ocean divers could also keep track of the effects of mining and drilling operations on marine life.

International political questions also arise. Who has the right to mine the ocean depths? Where should this mining be allowed? Who should set the rules? And who should benefit from ocean mining?

These questions are difficult to answer. Since 1959, representatives from many nations have been meeting to try to create a Law of the Sea. This law would regulate ocean mining, oil drilling, fishing, energy usage, dumping of wastes, exploration, and research. Finally, in 1982, 119 nations signed a Law of the Sea treaty. But the United States was not one of them.

THE LAW OF THE SEA

Under provisions of the treaty, each coastal nation is given an exclusive economic zone 200 nautical miles from its shore. Within that zone, a nation controls all natural resources, dumping, economic use, and scientific research. Where economic zones of different nations overlap, the nations must work out agreements.

Outside of the economic zones, no single nation controls the ocean floor. The International Seabed Authority administers this vast ocean floor region, called the International Seabed Area. The Authority sets the rules for mining in the International Seabed Area. And further, all mining technology must be shared with the Authority.

The United States could not accept these provisions and, therefore, did not sign the Law of the Sea treaty. On March 10, 1983, the United States declared its own economic zone extending 200 nautical miles off the coasts of the United States and all its territories. Since then, a number of American companies have announced that they plan to drill for oil and mine hard minerals in the zone.

Conflict over the zone has already arisen. And it is likely that many disputes will come up when people start mining the sea floor for its mineral wealth.

Offshore oil rigs are already tapping vast oil reserves that lie beneath the ocean floor. Divers wearing the Wasp may be able to repair cracks in the rig and prevent underwater oil leaks.

Futures in Science

WANTED!
SPACE PIONEERS

KANSAS CITY STAR: JANUARY 12, 2021

WANTED: Moon Miners and Engineers to provide new space colony with building materials. We're looking for people who can turn moon rocks and lunar topsoil into usable metals such as aluminum, magnesium, and titanium. These metals will be used to make tools and to build support structures for the colony. We also want workers who can extract silicon from the moon's silicates. Silicon is needed to make solar cells and computer chips. Glass that will be used for windows in space colony homes also comes from lunar silicates. And iron and carbon mined from the moon need to be turned into steel.

In addition, we're looking for lunar gold miners to search the moon's surface for deposits of gold, as well as nickel and platinum. And oxygen, which will be used for both life-support systems and rocket fuel, needs to be extracted from moon rocks.

Terry had answered the advertisement. Now, in the year 2024, she was hard at work at Moon Mine Alpha.

Terry expertly plunged the heavy shovel of her bulldozer into the soil to pick up another load of valuable material. When she raised the shovel, it was filled with moon rocks and lunar dust. Terry dumped her cargo into her lunar hauler. "My last truckload of the day," she thought, jumping down from the bulldozer. "Now I can go watch the mass driver in action."

Terry swung into the driver's seat of the lunar hauler. Soon she was bumping along the moon highway, a dusty path her hauler and others like it had carved out of the lunar topsoil over the past few months.

A typical lunar colony with all the comforts of home!

surface of the sphere. Here 10,000 people or more will live and work inside an earthlike environment powered by the sun. The Space Colony will be constructed of materials mined almost entirely on the moon.

Resources in Space

As many scientists see it, our growing needs for raw materials, energy, and jumping-off places for journeys to the planets and stars make us look into space. Where else is there a free, continuous supply of solar energy, uninterrupted by darkness or weather? Where else does weightlessness, which will aid in the construction of huge structures, exist? Where else is there an untapped source of minerals?

A wealth of energy and materials is available in space. Let's start with the moon, a mere 356,000 kilometers away. This natural satellite could be an important source of aluminum, iron, silicon, and oxygen. A permanent base established on the moon could supply all the resources needed to support space settlement and exploration. Although these resources are abundant on the earth, bringing millions of tons of materials into space is out of the question!

The moon could become a gigantic "supply station" in the sky. Metals and lunar soil could be mined to build huge structures inside of which comfortable, earthlike homes would be

Fifteen minutes later, she spotted the huge piece of machinery known as the mass driver. She saw the "flying buckets" of the mass driver suspended magnetically above special tracks. The buckets, filled with packages of lunar rocks, soon would be sent speeding along above these tracks by powerful magnetic forces. When the buckets reached high enough speed, they would fling their contents into space at 2.4 kilometers per second. At this speed, an object can escape the moon's gravity. Hundreds or thousands of kilometers away, a mass catcher would be waiting to grab the lunar cargo. The lunar materials would then be turned into fuel or building materials for a new space colony. Surely the mass driver, developed in the 1970s at the Massachusetts Institute of Technology, had proved to be a valuable tool for space colonization.

What will this space colony be like? Stationed nearly 400,000 kilometers from the earth, a huge sphere more than 1.5 kilometers in diameter will rotate in space. The rotation will create artificial gravity on the inner

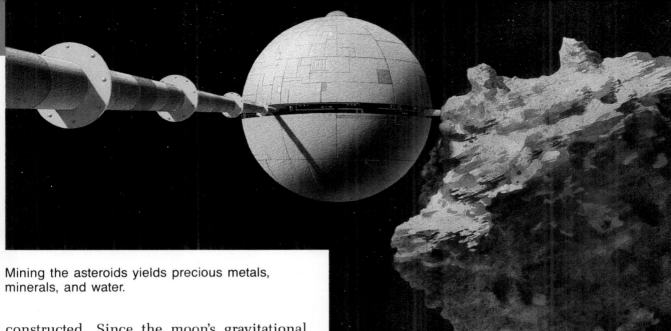

Mining the asteroids yields precious metals, minerals, and water.

constructed. Since the moon's gravitational force is one sixth the strength of the earth's, it would be cheaper and easier to build such space factories and colonies on the moon. These buildings could become part of the permanent moon base.

Almost half of the moon is made up of oxygen. This oxygen could be used to make rocket fuel. Liquid hydrogen mixed with liquid oxygen is a basic rocket fuel. Rockets bound for the outer plants could be launched more easily from the moon than from Earth, where the pull of gravity is six times greater.

A New Frontier

The moon is not the only source of natural materials in near space. Asteroids are also vast treasure houses of minerals. They contain metals such as nickel, iron, cobalt, magnesium, and aluminum. Phosphorus, carbon, and sulfur are also present on asteroids. And they may contain the precious metals gold, silver, and platinum. Asteroids are also important sources of water. One small asteroid can perhaps yield between one and ten billion tons of water.

"Hey, Terry, how's it going?" The voice belonged to Bill, one of the workers who ran the mass driver.

"Oh, I still like being a moon miner," Terry answered, "but a few years from now, I hope to be mining the asteroids instead. It should be a challenge trying to capture a small asteroid or land on a big one."

"I hope you like traveling, Terry," Bill said with a worried look. "The trip could take months or years."

"It would be worth it," said Terry as she waved to Bill and headed to her two-room apartment under the plastic dome of Hadleyville.

Turning on her TV set to watch live coverage from Earth of the 2024 Summer Olympics, Terry first tuned in the *Moon Miner's Daily Herald,* a TV "newspaper." Suddenly, an advertisement caught her eye.

WANTED: *Asteroid Miners and Engineers to capture small asteroids and collect samples from larger asteroids. Workers must be willing to spend long periods of time far from home. Travel to the asteroid belt, which lies between the orbits of Mars and Jupiter about 160 to 300 million kilometers away, is required.*

"Why not?" Terry thought as she began to type out a reply on her computer keyboard.

Structure of the Earth

Rising from the ocean floor up through the clouds, Hawaii's Mauna Kea from bottom to top is the tallest mountain in the world. Its 10,203-meter height is greater than that of Mount Everest by 1355 meters. Although the skiers who glide down the mountain's gentle slopes may not know it, Mauna Kea is the product of violent forces trapped deep beneath the earth's surface. For Mauna Kea is a volcano, one of many that have molded the Hawaiian Islands. The great eruptions of such volcanoes around the world have done more than change the earth's surface. Clouds of dust and gases shooting into the sky from these thundering mountains have dramatically changed the earth's atmosphere—sometimes for a short while, sometimes permanently.

CHAPTERS

21 **Internal Structure of the Earth**

22 **Surface Features of the Earth**

23 **Structure of the Atmosphere**

Hawaii's Mauna Kea

21 Internal Structure of the Earth

CHAPTER SECTIONS

21-1 The Earth's Core and Earthquake Waves

21-2 Exploring the Earth's Mantle

21-3 The Earth's Crust and Floating Continents

CHAPTER OBJECTIVES

After completing this chapter, you will be able to:

21-1 Relate seismic wave movements to the composition of the earth's core.

21-1 Describe the characteristics of the inner core and the outer core.

21-2 Describe the properties and composition of the mantle.

21-2 Define the term Moho.

21-2 Explain how mantle rocks form new ocean floor.

21-3 Describe the earth's crust.

21-3 Explain how continents can float.

Would you like to visit the center of the earth? It is not far away—no farther than the distance from New York City to Berlin, Germany. That comes to about 6450 kilometers.

But in some ways, the earth's center is harder to reach than planets that are millions of kilometers away. Scientists are sending probes into outer space that are traveling beyond the solar system. But no mechanical probe into inner space that scientists are able to build today can survive the enormous heat and pressure at the earth's center.

Yet there *are* probes that can reach the center of the earth and return to tell their story. As long ago as 1906, the Irish geologist Richard Dixon Oldham said that such a probe "enables us to see into the earth . . . as if we could drive a tunnel through it."

Oldham was a geologist who studied earthquakes. Great earthquakes topple buildings, shake the ground, and can change the shape of entire mountains. They also send shock waves through the earth. These shock waves penetrate the depths of the earth and return to the surface. Detected by special instruments, the shock waves can be used by scientists to "see" into the inside of the earth.

These shock waves were the probes that Oldham spoke of. Let's take a look at what they let Oldham, and the scientists who followed him, see!

Descending into the earth

21-1 The Earth's Core and Earthquake Waves

In Tokyo, Japan, at a little past two in the morning, a strong earthquake occurs more than a hundred kilometers beneath the ground. The date is April 18, 1889. The earthquake is so deep that few people are aware of it and little damage is done. However, in Tokyo, a special instrument called a **seismograph** (SIGHZ-muh-graf) records a strange message from the earthquake. The message is written as a pattern of squiggly lines.

In Potsdam, Germany, on the other side of the world, it is just past seven on the evening of April 17. There the seismograph is quiet—but not for long. One hour and four minutes after the earthquake in Tokyo, the Potsdam seismograph makes a pattern of squiggles like those in Figure 21-1.

Scientists quickly realized that the message recorded in Potsdam was really due to shock waves from the earthquake in Tokyo. And these waves had traveled through the earth's **core,** or center region, to reach Potsdam! This was the first time one of these messages from an earthquake was recorded by a seismograph on the opposite side of the world.

Figure 21-1 *A seismograph (left) detects and records earthquake waves, or seismic waves. A typical pattern of seismic waves is shown (right).*

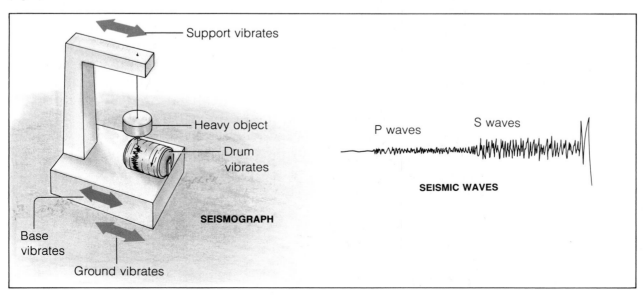

Figure 21-2 *A powerful earthquake in Alaska ripped a hole in the ground near this house.*

Here was a chance, scientists believed, to look deep inside the earth. A worldwide network of seismograph stations was set up to record future earthquakes. But how can earthquake waves provide a picture of the earth's interior? To find out, let's take a look at how these waves are produced.

Kinds of Earthquake Waves

Major earthquakes begin with a massive breaking and sliding of rocks underground. Shock waves called **seismic** (SIGHZ-mik) **waves** travel in every direction from the underground point of origin of the breakage. The point beneath the earth's surface where the rocks break and move is called the **focus** of the earthquake. Some seismic waves pass through the earth and come to the surface at points far from the earthquake's focus. Seismographs detect and record these waves, measure their strength, and record their time of arrival.

All earthquakes produce at least two kinds of shock waves at the same time. **Primary waves,** or **P waves,** result from a back-and-forth vibration of

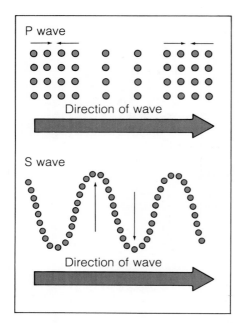

Figure 21-3 *P waves push together and pull apart rock particles in the direction of the wave movement. The slower S waves move rock particles from side to side at right angles to the wave movement.*

rock particles. These particles vibrate in the same direction as the path of the wave. See Figure 21-3. P waves move rapidly and can travel through both solids and liquids. **Secondary waves, or S waves,** result from an up-and-down or side-to-side vibration of rock particles. These particles vibrate at right angles to the path of the wave. See Figure 21-3. S waves are slower than P waves and can pass only through solids. **After observing the speeds of P waves and S waves, scientists have concluded that the earth's core, or center, is actually made of two very different layers.**

The Mystery of the Shadow Zones

By 1900, a worldwide network of seismographs was in place. And very soon, scientists noticed a regular but mysterious pattern to the P and S waves produced by earthquakes.

Suppose, for example, an earthquake strikes under the North Pole. Seismograph stations around the northern part of the earth record both P and S waves, but from northern Canada to southern Mexico there is a **shadow zone.** See Figure 21-4. In a

Figure 21-4 *There are no earthquake waves in a shadow zone. Something inside the earth blocks S waves and concentrates P waves on the other side of the world.*

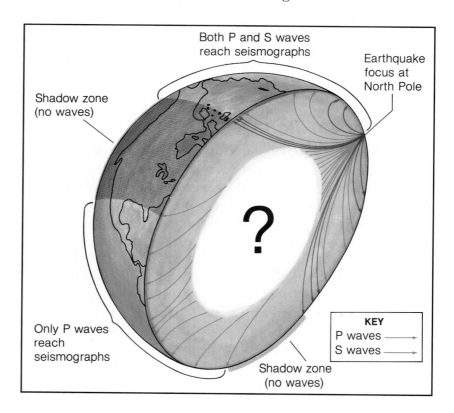

shadow zone, no earthquake waves are detected by seismographs. Why are there shadow zones? At first scientists could not solve this mystery.

Adding to the mystery is the fact that south of the shadow zone, very strong P waves *are* detected. But *no* S waves are found in this area. The P waves are strongest around the South Pole—the one place on the earth directly opposite the North Pole! Scientists needed to find out how this information was related to the mystery of the shadow zones.

Scientists discovered that the pattern is the same for every earthquake. Both P and S waves are detected up to a little more than a quarter of the way around the world from the focus of the earthquake. Beyond that lies a shadow zone. Then a strong concentration of P waves appears on the opposite side of the earth from the focus. S waves do not appear.

Scientists reached two conclusions. The first conclusion was that something inside the earth was blocking S waves and preventing them from getting through to the other side of the earth. The second conclusion was that something inside the earth was concentrating P waves on the other side of the world. The mystery had to be solved.

Seeing the Earth's Core

What did this pattern of shadow zones and concentration of P waves mean? Scientists found out that this pattern is a message from the depths of the earth that actually answers two questions. The answers to these questions are coded into the wiggly lines that record earthquake waves.

THE FIRST QUESTION What happened to the missing S waves? These waves disappear at the edge of the shadow zone and are not found on the opposite side of the world.

Scientists believed that something was deflecting the S waves. And since S waves pass through solids but not liquids, that something must be liquid. The earth's core, scientists concluded, is at least partly liquid. Using data from seismographs, the geologist Richard Dixon Oldham was able to map the boundary of the earth's liquid core at about 2900 kilometers beneath the earth's surface.

Figure 21-5 *This photograph shows a seismologist at the National Earthquake Information Service in Colorado. Each drum records the results from a different seismograph station.*

As you see in Figure 21-4, the earth's core deflects S waves, forming a shadow zone where no S waves appear. This deflection of S waves also explains why there are no S waves on the opposite side of the world from the earthquake's focus. Part of the mystery of the shadow zones had been solved.

THE SECOND QUESTION   Why is there a high concentration of P waves on the opposite side of the world from the earthquake's focus? The answer was decoded from earthquake waves by Inge Lehmann, who was chief of the Royal Danish Seismological Department from 1928 to 1953.

To see how she did it, let's look at a straw resting in a glass of water. See Figure 21-6. The straw seems to be broken right at the surface of the water—the boundary between air and water. Actually, the straw only makes visible what happens to light waves as they cross such a boundary—they bend because their speed changes. This bending of light causes the straight straw to appear broken.

Lehmann discovered that what is true of light waves is also true of earthquake waves speeding through the earth. The earthquake's shock waves bend at boundaries between different substances—boundaries that mark changes in the inner structure of the earth. Lehmann suggested that the earth's core is made up of two parts, a liquid outer core and a solid inner core. The answer to the mystery of the S waves had already shown that the liquid outer core boundary begins 2900 kilometers beneath the earth's surface. She suggested that the inner core is like a solid ball within the outer core. Lehmann estimated the radius, or distance from the edge to the center, of the inner core to be about 1200 kilometers.

Now Lehmann could explain why P waves are concentrated on the side of the world opposite the earthquake's focus. The waves would be bent four times—when entering the outer core, when entering the inner core, when leaving the inner core, and when leaving the outer core. The result of all this bending is that the waves are concentrated around the area opposite the earthquake's focus. See Figure 21-7. As you can see, P waves are also bent away from the shadow zones. The mystery of the shadow zones had been solved.

Figure 21-6   *The bending of light makes this straw appear broken. Earthquake waves, like light waves, change speed and bend when they enter a different substance.*

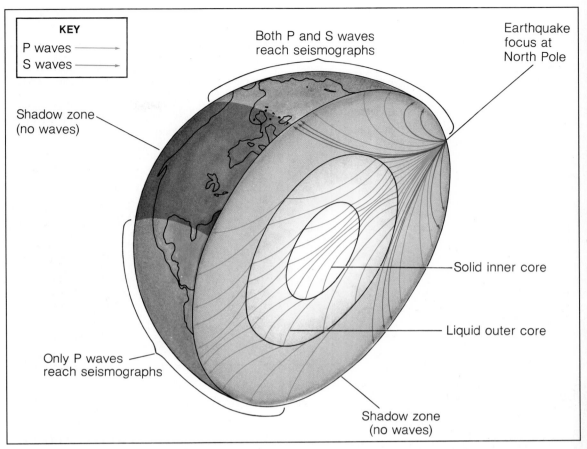

Figure 21-7 *Inge Lehmann solved the mystery of the shadow zones when she explained how P waves bend and change speeds as they move through the earth's outer and inner cores.*

Lehmann wrote about her discovery in 1936. Since then, other scientists using more sensitive instruments have developed an even clearer picture of the earth's core.

Lehmann's estimate of the size of the inner core remains amazingly accurate. Scientists now calculate that the radius of the inner core is about 1300 kilometers. An outer core about 2250 kilometers thick surrounds the inner core. The outside boundary of the outer core begins about 2900 kilometers beneath the earth's surface. Add these three numbers together and you get the approximate distance from the earth's surface to the actual center of the earth—6450 kilometers.

From studies of earthquake waves, scientists have learned much more about the earth's core. For example, they have learned that the hot outer core is probably a region of constantly churning liquid,

Activity

How Many Earths?

The distance from the earth's surface to the center of the earth is about 6450 kilometers. The average distance from the earth to the sun is 150 million kilometers. How many earths lined up in a row are needed to reach the sun?

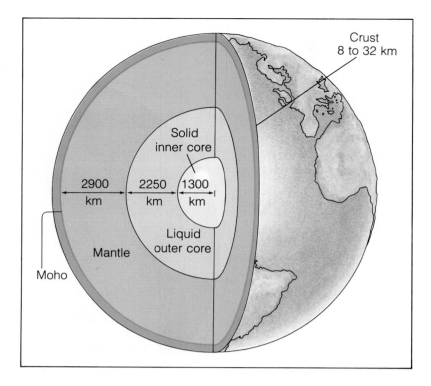

Figure 21-8 *The earth is made up of different layers. This drawing shows the distances you would have to travel through these layers from the surface to the earth's center.*

Crust
8 to 32 km

Solid
inner core

2900
km

2250
km

1300
km

Liquid
outer core

Mantle

Moho

mostly iron and nickel. The very hot inner core is made up mostly of solid iron and nickel under tremendous pressure. Temperatures probably range from about 2200° C in the upper part of the outer core to about 5000° C in the inner core.

SECTION REVIEW

1. Name and describe two kinds of earthquake waves.
2. What is a shadow zone?
3. What is the outer core made of? What is the inner core made of?

Activity

Model of the Earth's Interior

1. Obtain a Styrofoam ball 15 cm or more in diameter.
2. Carefully cut out a wedge from the ball so that the ball looks similar to Figure 21-8.
3. Draw lines on the inside of the ball and of the wedge to represent the four layers of the earth.
4. Label and color each layer on the ball and wedge.

21-2 Exploring the Earth's Mantle

The distance from the edge of the liquid outer core to the earth's surface is about 2900 kilometers. Most of this distance makes up the earth's **mantle.** Exactly what is the mantle? How is it different from the earth's core? Part of that question was answered in 1909. On October 8, an earthquake shook Croatia, which is now part of the country of Yugoslavia. In

Zagreb, the capital of Croatia, Yugoslavian geologist and seismologist Andrija Mohorovicic (moh-hoh-ROH-vuh-chich) studied seismograph records from many stations.

Mohorovicic noticed something odd about the seismograph recordings. Stations within about 160 kilometers of the earthquake's center showed a pattern of squiggles that indicated a strong earthquake followed by a weak one. But at stations more than 160 kilometers away from the earthquake the pattern of squiggles indicated a weak earthquake followed by a strong one. The second message was the reverse of the first message. But both messages had been sent out by the same earthquake at the same time! Here was a mystery to be solved.

Mohorovicic thought he must be misreading the messages. He knew there was only one earthquake. The stronger signals came from shock waves that had traveled a shorter distance. The weaker signals from the same earthquake came from shock waves that had traveled a longer distance and had lost some strength along the way. That seemed to explain the first set of messages from seismographs within 160 kilometers of the earthquake. The weaker waves traveled a longer distance and came in second. See Figure 21-9.

Figure 21-9 *The stronger earthquake waves arrive before the weaker waves at a seismograph station less than 160 kilometers from the earthquake's focus.*

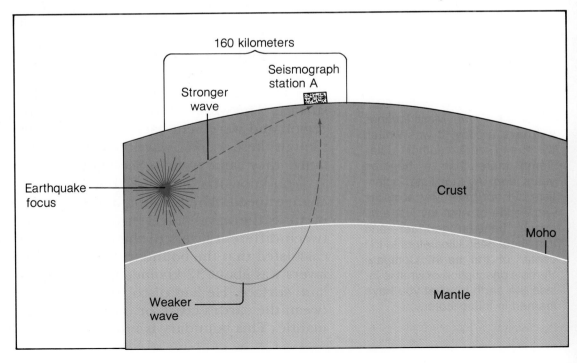

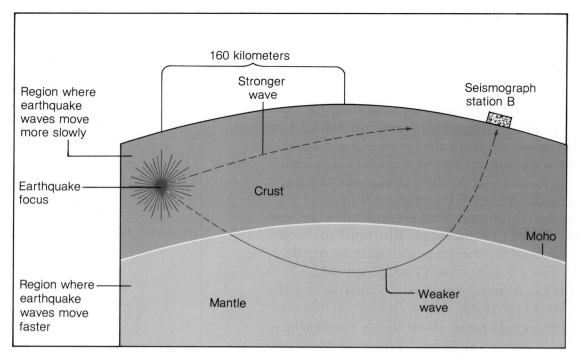

160 kilometers

Stronger wave

Region where earthquake waves move more slowly

Seismograph station B

Earthquake focus

Crust

Moho

Region where earthquake waves move faster

Mantle

Weaker wave

Figure 21-10 *The weaker earthquake waves arrive before the stronger waves at a seismograph station more than 160 kilometers from the earthquake's focus.*

But what about those stations farther from the earthquake's center than 160 kilometers? There the weaker waves came in first, although they had traveled farther than the stronger signals. Mohorovicic reasoned that there could be only one answer. Something had speeded up the weaker waves so that they outraced the stronger waves to the station. Mohorovicic calculated that the stronger waves traveled near the surface of the earth. The weaker waves had traveled through a deeper region well beneath the earth's surface. In this region, Mohorovicic thought, the earth's structure must be different than on the surface. The weaker waves speeded up in this lower region and were bent back toward the surface. Although these weaker waves traveled a longer distance, they came in first. See Figure 21-10.

You know that earthquake waves bend. They also change speed. The bending and the change in speed occur as the waves travel through the boundary between different layers of the earth. Mohorovicic calculated that the boundary between the different layers was about 32 kilometers beneath the earth's land surface. He had discovered the boundary between the earth's crust, or outermost layer, and the mantle. This boundary is now called the **Moho.**

Doorway into the Mantle

Over many years, scientists discovered that the Moho extends around the world. Beneath it, the mantle goes down about 2900 kilometers into the earth until it reaches the edge of the outer core.

The distance from the earth's surface to the Moho varies. It is a long distance from the surface of the land to the Moho. In comparison, it is a very short distance from the ocean floor to the Moho. In fact, on the floor of the Atlantic Ocean, scientists have found a doorway into the mantle.

In the 1950s, scientists mapped the floor of the Atlantic Ocean. Ships sailed back and forth, bouncing thousands of sound signals over the entire bottom of the Atlantic Ocean. From these sound signals, Marie Tharp, a draftswoman working for the Lamont-Doherty Geological Observatory in New York, made the first map of the Atlantic Ocean's bottom. Her map showed a great crack, or rift, in the crust that ran down the middle of a massive underwater mountain range in the Atlantic Ocean. This crack and the area on either side of it are called the **Mid-Atlantic Rift Valley.** Later, scientists found that the Mid-Atlantic Rift Valley is part of a much larger system of rift valleys and mountain ranges—a system called the **Mid-Ocean Ridge** that extends for about 74,000 kilometers under all the world's oceans.

Partially molten, or melted, rock from the mantle flows upward through a rift valley. It spreads outward on both sides of the valley. As it spreads, the partially molten rock cools quickly and hardens into solid rock. This rock becomes a new part of the ocean floor. Because it was "frozen" in the act of flowing, the solid rock shows a pattern of twisted ridges. See Figure 21-11.

This rock came from the earth's mantle. Now, for the first time, scientists could hold a piece of the mantle in their hands. **After studying rock samples, scientists have determined that the mantle is made mostly of the elements silicon, oxygen, iron, and magnesium.** So the unknown substance of the mantle is made up of the same ordinary materials found in rocks on the earth's surface.

But the mantle rocks were not acting like ordinary rocks. Are these rocks liquid? Evidence from

Figure 21-11 *Partially molten rock has been "frozen" while flowing from a rift valley in the ocean floor. Notice the ridges that formed when the rock hardened.*

Figure 21-12 *A research vessel travels through a rift valley of the Mid-Atlantic Ridge System. The partially molten rock near the rift's center will eventually become new ocean floor.*

earthquake waves suggests that the temperature in the upper part of the mantle is about 900 to 1000°C. This is more than hot enough to melt the mantle rocks completely. However, these rocks are not completely melted.

Are these rocks solid? Scientists found that S waves can travel through the mantle. And you know that S waves travel through solids but not liquids. But how can solid rock flow? How could a rock act like a solid and like a liquid at the same time? Here was another mystery to be solved.

Flexible Rocks and Conveyor Belts

Scientists found that the answer to this mystery is pressure. Pressure is the amount of force over a certain area. Mantle rocks are under great pressure from the weight of all the rocks above them. Under great pressure, the solid rocks flow very slowly. The mantle rocks do not melt under this great pressure but become a flexible solid that flows slowly like a gooey liquid—like very thick molasses. S waves can travel through this thick liquid.

But why does mantle rock flow steadily upward through the rift valleys? The answer is that the great heat from the earth's core sets up churning motions in the solid-liquid rocks of the mantle. They are much like the churning motions you can see in a pot of boiling soup on a stove. In this case, the soup acts like rocks in the mantle, and the stove provides heat as does the earth's core. The hottest soup, nearest the heat from the stove, rises to the top of the pot. There the soup cools and sinks back to the bottom of the pot. This soup is reheated and again moves upward to the surface.

Scientists reason that material in the mantle must move in the same way. These churning motions keep molten rock pouring out of the rift valleys. This molten rock becomes a new part of the ocean floor. As the flow out of a rift valley goes on, the older parts of the ocean floor are pushed farther away from the rift valley on either side.

Think of a conveyor belt like the ones that move groceries at supermarket counters. Then imagine a

Figure 21-13 *The continents and ocean floor ride on plates that may move like "conveyor belts."*

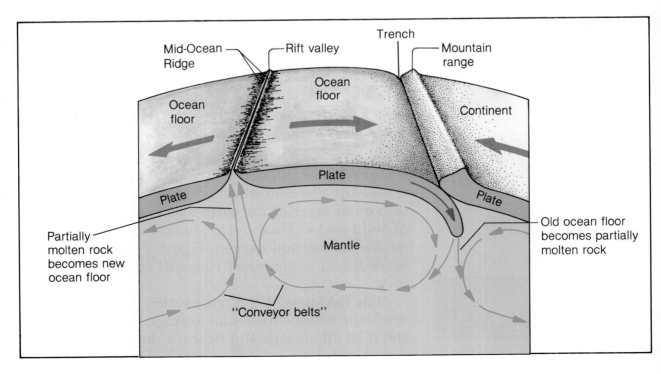

second conveyor belt at the end of the first one. The second belt is moving in the opposite direction. It is as if two such "belts" made of partially molten rock are rolling up out of a rift valley and spreading in opposite directions. See Figure 21-13.

These belts move much more slowly than conveyor belts at the supermarket. They add new floor to the ocean at the rate of only a few centimeters a year. But over millions of years, this adds up to hundreds of kilometers. Over such a length of time, the Atlantic Ocean has become hundreds of kilometers wider.

If you think about it, that is like saying that the continents, or large landmasses, on either side of the Atlantic have moved farther apart. In fact, scientists now have good evidence that all the continents on the earth's surface are slowly moving. And this is part of the story of the earth's crust.

Figure 21-14 *The elements that make up the earth's crust are listed in this chart. What two elements are the most abundant?*

ELEMENTS IN THE EARTH'S CRUST

Element	Percentage in Crust
Oxygen	46.60
Silicon	27.72
Aluminum	8.13
Iron	5.00
Calcium	3.63
Sodium	2.83
Potassium	2.59
Magnesium	2.09
Titanium	0.40
Hydrogen	0.14
Total	99.13

SECTION REVIEW

1. What two changes happen to earthquake waves when they enter a different substance?
2. Where did scientists find a doorway into the mantle?
3. What causes mantle rock to become a flexible solid that flows like thick molasses?

21-3 The Earth's Crust and Floating Continents

You now have traveled 6450 kilometers from the center of the earth's core to the earth's surface, or **crust**—the place on which you live. **The crust is the thin outer layer of the earth and is made up mainly of solid rocks.** These rocks contain mostly two elements—silicon and oxygen. Figure 21-14 provides a list of the most abundant elements in the crust of the earth.

The thickness of the crust varies. The crust beneath the continents has an average thickness of about 32 kilometers. But beneath the ocean floor,

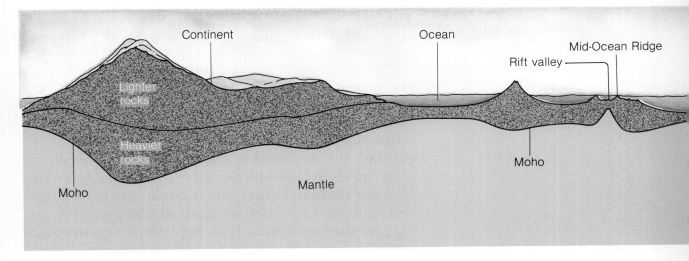

Figure 21-15 *The earth's crust has two layers. The upper layer is made of lighter rocks and is found only under the continents. The lower layer is made of heavier rocks. It is found both under the continents and under the oceans, where it forms the ocean floor.*

the crust has an average thickness of only about 8 kilometers. You learned earlier that new ocean floor is being added on either side of the rift valleys. If this is so, then why doesn't the ocean floor pile up higher and higher?

Let's go back to our picture of the supermarket conveyor belts. Although the belts come up to the counter in one place, they also go back under the counter at another. The "belts" that move the continents are like this too.

At a rift valley, the molten rock flows up from inside the earth, forming new crust. At other places, called trenches, older crust moves back down into the mantle to again form part of its solid-liquid rock. See Figure 21-13. After many millions of years the slowly moving mantle rocks once again emerge at a rift valley—just as the supermarket conveyor belt travels part of the time *under* the counter and then comes up again.

The trenches and rift valleys of the earth divide the crust into about 20 floating parts like the pieces of a jigsaw puzzle. Scientists call these parts plates. Plates usually move away from rift valleys and toward trenches. Each plate is like a package riding on the upper, visible part of a supermarket conveyor belt. The motion of these belts moves the continents

Activity

The Earth's Crust

Use sand, gravel, clay soil, water, and an empty aquarium to construct a model of a cross section of the earth's crust. Your model should look similar to Figure 21-15. Line the "ocean" with clear plastic before adding water to your model.

and ocean floor, which rest on the upper part of the plates. The plates float on the solid-liquid rocks of the earth's mantle. You can also think of the continents and ocean floor as floating ships slowly riding on the plates.

Balance is the key to the floating continents, as it is to floating ships. When a ship takes on cargo, it rides deeper in the water. When the cargo is unloaded, the ship rises in the water. Continents also rise higher or sink deeper into the mantle. Over the last ten thousand years, for example, parts of northern Europe have risen as much as 250 meters—higher than a 60-story building. Why? Ten thousand years ago, this land was covered with sheets of ice

Career: *Cave Guide*

HELP WANTED: CAVE GUIDES To conduct and instruct groups of all ages and backgrounds through local natural caves. High school or college students preferred. Courses or interest in geology or public speaking desirable. Summer or part-time work available.

There are more than 50,000 naturally formed caves in the United States. Caves are found at or near the surface of the earth's crust. The deepest cave in the world extends only about 1.5 kilometers into the crust. New caves are discovered, explored, surveyed, and named each year. One cave in Texas, for example, was discovered by highway engineers while building an interstate roadway. Visitors to this cave are shown special formations such as "icicles" made of stone. Fossils of extinct animals have also been discovered in this cave.

Workers who lead groups of visitors safely through a cave are the **cave guides.** Cave guides lecture about a cave's size, history, and how it was formed. They point out features of special interest and answer questions. They are concerned with cave conservation, preservation, and safety.

Each cave is different, so guides must spend time learning about their particular cave before they begin work. Visitors on cave tours walk or ride in vehicles such as jeeps. In caves with underground lakes or rivers, visitors may travel by boat. Besides explaining geologic formations to visitors, guides discuss topics such as underground waterfalls, fossils, Indian artifacts, cave life, and the constant temperature maintained in caves.

If you are interested in experience as a cave guide or would like to know more about the caves in your area, write to the National Caves Association, Route 9, Box 106, McMinnville, TN 37110.

Figure 21-16 *The plate that carries Egypt* (right) *is separating from the plate that carries Saudi Arabia* (left). *The Red Sea has become wider as a result of this separation.*

several kilometers thick. This ice was like a cargo of additional material. As the ice melted, the continent rose like a lightened ship.

You now have come to the end of the journey from the center of the earth to the surface. That familiar land on which you live and walk, with its rocks and water and soil is just the top of the earth's crust. And the crust is afloat, sinking and rising on the mantle and powered by heat from the very center of the earth.

SECTION REVIEW

1. What is the average thickness of the crust beneath the continents? Beneath the ocean floor?
2. How is new crust formed?
3. Approximately how many floating plates make up the crust?

Activity

Mohorovicic's Discovery

The boundary between the crust and the mantle is called the Moho after Andrija Mohorovicic. Write a 300 word essay explaining how Mohorovicic discovered this boundary. Your essay should emphasize all of the following vocabulary words:

crust	focus
mantle	Moho
P waves	S waves
seismograph	

LABORATORY ACTIVITY

Building an Active Geyser

Purpose

In this activity, you will build a model geyser and observe it in action.

Materials *(per group)*

250-mL beaker
Bunsen burner
Glass funnel
Tripod
Wire gauze
Safety goggles
Water

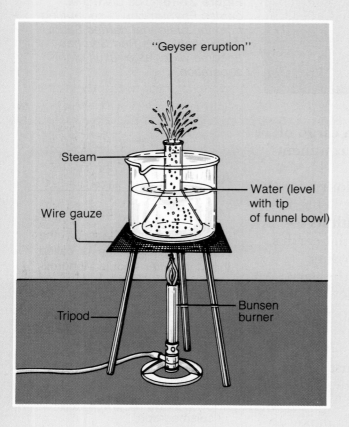

Procedure

1. Place a glass funnel upside-down in a beaker.
2. Add water until the bowl of the funnel is covered.
3. Place the beaker, water, and funnel on a piece of wire gauze resting on a tripod.
4. Put the Bunsen burner beneath the tripod and light it. **CAUTION:** *Be very careful in lighting the burner. Avoid putting your face or hands near the setup when the geyser becomes active. Be sure to wear your safety goggles.*
5. Allow time for the water to boil. Notice the bubbles of steam that push the hot water up the funnel stem. As the steam bubbles expand, you should be able to observe water spurting from the funnel stem, much as water acts in a coffee percolator.

Observations and Conclusions

1. Describe the behavior of your model geyser while it was erupting.
2. A Bunsen burner provided the heat source for your model geyser. What is the source of energy that heats the water in a real geyser?
3. According to your observations of the model geyser, what is the relationship between geyser activity and available heat energy?
4. If a natural geyser stopped erupting, what might have been the cause?
5. "Old Faithful" is a well-known geyser in Yellowstone National Park. It erupts on a very regular basis, just about every 66 minutes! What do you think must be true of the heat source and water supply that keep this geyser operating?

CHAPTER REVIEW

SUMMARY

21-1 The Earth's Core and Earthquake Waves

■ Seismographs detect and record the shock waves from earthquakes.

■ Shock waves, or seismic waves, originate at the focus of an earthquake and travel in every direction.

■ Earthquakes produce at least two kinds of waves: primary or P waves and secondary or S waves.

■ Primary waves vibrate in the direction of the path of an earthquake wave. They travel through both solids and liquids.

■ Secondary waves vibrate at right angles to the path of an earthquake wave. They travel only through solids.

■ Shadow zones are areas on the surface of the earth where seismographs cannot detect earthquake waves.

■ The earth's solid inner core has a radius of about 1300 kilometers.

21-2 Exploring the Earth's Mantle

■ The earth's mantle is about 2900 kilometers thick and surrounds the earth's outer core.

■ By knowing that earthquake waves bend and travel at different speeds through different substances, Andrija Mohorovicic was able to calculate how far below the earth's surface the boundary is located that separates the mantle from the crust. This boundary was named the Moho in his honor.

■ The Mid-Atlantic Rift Valley is a crack that runs down the middle of an underwater mountain range in the Atlantic Ocean. The Mid-Ocean Ridge is part of a mountain range system that extends under all the world's oceans.

■ Mantle rock is a flexible solid that flows like a thick gooey liquid.

■ It is believed that heat from the earth's core sets up churning motions that cause mantle rock to move. You can think of this motion as being like very slow conveyor belts in the mantle that bring molten rock up through rift valleys to form new ocean floor.

21-3 The Earth's Crust and Floating Continents

■ The crust is the thin, outermost layer of the earth.

■ At rift valleys, mantle rocks form new crust. At trenches, old crust becomes mantle rock.

■ The crust is divided into about 20 pieces called plates. The continents and ocean floor ride on the upper part of the plates.

■ Plates usually move away from rift valleys and toward trenches.

■ Floating continents rise higher or sink deeper into the mantle depending on the amount of material the continents have.

VOCABULARY

Define each term in a complete sentence.

core	Mid-Atlantic Rift Valley	secondary waves (S waves)
crust	Mid-Ocean Ridge	seismic waves
focus	Moho	seismograph
mantle	primary waves (P waves)	shadow zone

CONTENT REVIEW: MULTIPLE CHOICE

Choose the letter of the answer that best completes each statement.

1. Seismographs
   a. detect earthquake waves.   b. record earthquake waves.
   c. measure the strength of earthquake waves.   d. do all of these.
2. Primary waves are earthquake waves that can travel through
   a. liquids.   b. solids.   c. liquids and solids.   d. none of these.
3. Areas in which seismographs cannot detect earthquake waves are called
   a. Mohos.   b. shadow zones.   c. rifts.   d. seismozones.
4. The distance in kilometers from the earth's surface to the earth's center is
   a. 1300.   b. 2900.   c. 5000.   d. 6450.
5. Geologists now know that the earth's core is
   a. a solid center surrounded by a liquid.
   b. a liquid center surrounded by a solid.
   c. completely solid.
   d. completely liquid.
6. The distance from the earth's surface to the Moho
   a. is 2900 kilometers.   b. is longer than the radius of the earth's core.
   c. is 1300 kilometers.   d. varies between 8 and 32 kilometers.
7. The crack in the Atlantic Ocean crust through which mantle rock flows to
   form new ocean floor is called the
   a. Moho.   b. Mid-Atlantic Rift Valley.
   c. Mid-Ocean Ridge.   d. Mid-Atlantic Trench.
8. Rocks on the earth's surface are made mostly of
   a. iron and silicon.   b. oxygen and magnesium.
   c. iron and magnesium.   d. oxygen and silicon.
9. Which is the thinnest layer of the earth?
   a. mantle   b. crust   c. outer core   d. inner core
10. The earth's crust
   a. is least thick beneath the ocean floor.   b. is least thick beneath the continents.
   c. is equally thick around the world.   d. is none of these.

CONTENT REVIEW: COMPLETION

Fill in the word or words that best complete each statement.

1. A(n) _____ is an instrument that records shock waves from an earthquake.
2. The center region of the earth is known as the _____.
3. The underground point of origin, or center, of an earthquake is the _____.
4. Earthquake waves that travel through solids and are blocked by liquids are called _____.

5. The _____ is the region between the earth's outer core and the earth's crust.
6. Mantle rocks flow like a thick liquid because of the great _____ from the weight of all the rocks above them.
7. The mountain range system that runs under the world's oceans is called the _____.

8. The _____ is the boundary between the earth's crust and the mantle.
9. The thin, solid outer layer of the earth is called the _____.

10. About 74 percent of the earth's crust is made of the elements _____ and oxygen.

CONTENT REVIEW: TRUE OR FALSE

Determine whether each statement is true or false. If it is true, write "true." If it is false, change the underlined word or words to make the statement true.

1. Earthquakes produce <u>both</u> primary and secondary shock waves.
2. There are no <u>P waves</u> in the shadow zones because they are deflected by the earth's core.
3. Each time earthquake waves enter and leave the earth's outer and inner cores, they <u>bend</u>.
4. The boundary between the earth's mantle and <u>outer core</u> is called the Moho.
5. Earthquake waves change <u>speeds</u> as they travel through different substances.
6. Scientists are able to analyze mantle rock because mantle material flows up through <u>rift valleys</u>.
7. The temperature of the mantle <u>is not</u> hot enough to melt rocks.
8. Older crust moves back into the mantle through <u>trenches</u>.
9. The crust is <u>thicker</u> beneath the ocean floor than beneath the continents.
10. Continents and ocean floors ride on about 20 floating parts called <u>ridges</u>.

CONCEPT REVIEW: SKILL BUILDING

Use the skills you have developed in the chapter to complete each activity.

1. **Applying concepts** Suppose a mild earthquake occured in Washington, D.C., at 9:00 A.M. Earthquake waves were felt 8040 kilometers away in Moscow, U.S.S.R. According to seismographic readings, P waves arrived in Moscow at about 9:11 (Washington time). Did the S waves arrive before or after 9:11? Explain your answer.
2. **Relating facts** The temperature of the inner core reaches about 5000° C. The temperature of the outer core begins at about 2200° C. Yet the outer core is liquid while the inner core is solid. Explain how this can be so.
3. **Making graphs** Use the data in Figure 21-14 to construct a graph. Plot each element in the earth's crust on the horizontal axis. Plot the percentage of each element on the vertical axis. What general conclusions can you draw from your graph?

CONCEPT REVIEW: ESSAY

Discuss each of the following in a brief paragraph.

1. Compare S waves and P waves.
2. Explain how the movement of mantle rock is like a pot of soup boiling on a stove.
3. Compare the rising and sinking of floating ships to floating continents.
4. What is the importance of P waves and S waves in learning about the structure of the earth's interior?
5. What is the Moho? How does it affect earthquake waves?

22 Surface Features of the Earth

CHAPTER SECTIONS

22-1 The Earth's Surface: Landmasses

22-2 The Earth's Surface: Water

CHAPTER OBJECTIVES

After completing this chapter, you will be able to:

22-1 Describe the three major kinds of landscapes.

22-1 Explain how mountains are formed.

22-1 Compare plateaus and plains.

22-2 Identify the major sources of salt water and fresh water.

22-2 Explain how the water cycle works.

On February 20, 1943, a Mexican farmer, Dionisio Pulido, went to work as usual in his cornfield. But his cornfield had changed overnight. He stared in disbelief at a 24-meter-long crack in his land. Hot rocks and ash oozed from the crack. Pulido ran to the nearby village of Paricutín to tell what he had seen.

Pulido had witnessed a dramatic change in the earth's surface—the birth of a volcano! The volcano, called Paricutín after Pulido's village, grew rapidly. It was about 10 meters high by the next morning, and about 168 meters high after the first week. The volcano was about 335 meters high after the first year. By then, great amounts of ash had covered the land around for about 50 square kilometers. On February 25, 1952, Paricutín reached its final height of about 410 meters above the surrounding land.

Nine years and 12 days after its birth, Paricutín became inactive. During its active years it had thrown out about 3.6 billion tons of lava, rocks, and ash. Pulido had lost his cornfield, and about 4500 people in two villages had lost their homes. The surface of the land was completely different.

Volcanoes like Paricutín are among the great forces that shape and reshape the earth's surface. More slowly, folding of the earth's crust forms huge mountain ranges. And even more slowly, the mountains are worn down. The flow of water also changes the shape of the land. This process has been going on for billions of years. It is still going on today.

Paricutín erupting

22-1 The Earth's Surface: Landmasses

Nearly all the visible land on our planet rests on seven great landmasses—the continents. There are many different surface features on these continents. For example, Asia holds the highest place on earth—Mount Everest, the crown of the mighty Himalaya mountain range. Everest's peak is 8848 meters above sea level. Mount Everest is in Nepal, a small country north of India. Thousands of kilometers to the west, but still within Asia, lies the lowest place on earth's land surface—the shore of the Dead Sea in Israel, 392 meters below sea level.

Asia, the largest continent, stretches from the frozen Arctic tundra in the north to the steaming tropical rain forests and rice paddies of places such as Vietnam and Cambodia in the south. Asia also stretches from the parched Arabian Desert in the west to rich farmlands on the Pacific coasts of China and the Soviet Union.

But even within the smallest continent, Australia, the land takes many shapes. Along the western coast, the land is low and flat. Looking eastward, you can see what appears to be a long line of mountains. As you approach them, you realize that they are not

Figure 22-1 *Mount Everest* (left) *is the highest place on the earth's surface, and the shore of the Dead Sea* (right) *is the lowest place.*

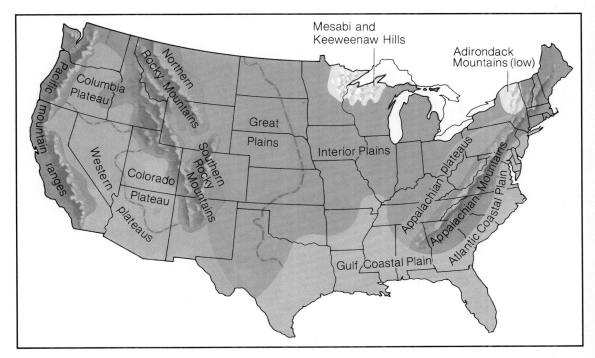

Figure 22-2 *This map shows the major landscape regions of the continental United States. What type of landscape region covers most of the United States?*

Labels on map: Mesabi and Keeweenaw Hills; Adirondack Mountains (low); Pacific mountain ranges; Columbia Plateau; Northern Rocky Mountains; Great Plains; Interior Plains; Appalachian plateaus; Appalachian Mountains; Western plateaus; Colorado Plateau; Southern Rocky Mountains; Atlantic Coastal Plain; Gulf Coastal Plain

mountains but steep cliffs. A climber reaching the tops of these cliffs finds a great area of roughly level land. This highland region covers most of western Australia. It is like an enormous table whose edges are cliffs. In fact, such highlands are often called tablelands.

Mountains, highlands, and lowlands are different kinds of physical features on the earth's land surface. Such areas that have certain physical features are called landscapes. **There are three main types of landscape regions on the earth's surface: mountains, plains, and plateaus.** Each type has different characteristics. Figure 22-2 shows the major landscape regions of the United States. In which landscape region do you live?

Mountains

You are walking through a region of tall, jagged peaks, long slopes, and high, narrow ridges. You can see deep valleys, forests, and small, rushing streams. Where are you? The region you are visiting is an example of a typical **mountain landscape.**

What is the difference between a mountain and a hill? Most geologists agree that a mountainous area rises at least 610 meters above the surrounding land.

Figure 22-3 *Some of the world's mountains are described below.*

SOME OF THE WORLD'S MOST FAMOUS MOUNTAINS

Name	Height Above Sea Level (meters)	Location	Interesting Facts
Aconcagua	6959	Andes in Argentina	Highest mountain in the Western Hemisphere
Cotopaxi	5897	Andes in Ecuador	Highest active volcano in the world
Elbert	4399	Colorado	Highest mountain of Rockies
Everest	8848	Himalayas on Nepal-Tibet border	Highest mountain in the world
K2	8611	Kashmir	Second highest mountain in the world
Kanchenjunga	8598	Himalayas on Nepal-India border	Third highest mountain in the world
Kilimanjaro	5895	Tanzania	Highest mountain in Africa
Logan	5950	Yukon	Highest mountain in Canada
Mauna Kea	4205	On volcanic island in Hawaii	Highest island mountain in the world
Mauna Loa	4169	On volcanic island in Hawaii	Famous volcanic mountain
McKinley	6194	Alaska	Highest mountain in North America
Mitchell	2037	North Carolina	Highest mountain in the Appalachians
Mont Blanc	4807	France	Highest mountain in the Alps
Mount St. Helens	2549	Cascades in Washington	Recent active volcano in the United States
Pikes Peak	4301	Colorado	Most famous of the Rocky Mountains
Rainier	4392	Cascades in Washington	Highest mountain in Washington
Vesuvius	1277	Italy	Only active volcano on the mainland of Europe
Whitney	4418	Sierra Nevadas in California	Highest mountain in California

But the actual height of a mountain is given as its height above sea level. For example, Pikes Peak in Colorado rises about 2700 meters above the surrounding land. But its actual height above sea level is 4301 meters.

The height of a mountain on an island is also measured from sea level. For example, Hawaii's Mauna Kea is listed in Figure 22-3 as 4205 meters above sea level. Actually, Mauna Kea is the world's tallest mountain, rising 10,203 meters from the sea floor to its peak.

Most of the world's mountains have been built up by the slow folding and wrinkling of the earth's crust. See Figure 22-4. These mountains include the Appalachians of the eastern United States, the Himalayas of Asia, the Andes of South America, the Rockies of the western United States, the Urals and Caucasus of the Soviet Union, and the Alps of Europe.

You can make a model of this kind of folding with a large piece of cloth. Lay it flat on a table. Put your hands on opposite ends of the cloth and push them slowly together. Wave-shaped wrinkles form in the cloth, making miniature mountains and valleys. You may notice that the wrinkles tend to form parallel rows at right angles to the direction of your push. If you flew over the Alps of Europe, you would see a large-scale version of your cloth model. There are row after parallel row of snow-capped, jagged peaks with steep, narrow valleys in between.

Mountains are built very slowly. It is thought that the Rocky Mountains began to form about 65 million years ago. It took about 10 million years for these mountains to reach their maximum height. It will take much longer for them to wear down. But wear down they will. Someday, many millions of years in the future, the majestic sharp-peaked Rockies will be worn down by the action of wind and moving water. On that day, the Rockies will be little more than low rounded hills.

Some mountains are formed when the earth's crust breaks into huge blocks. See Figure 22-4. The Sierra Nevada Mountains of northern and central California were formed in this way.

Sometimes the crust cracks, and lava and ashes come through the cracks and pile up, layer on layer.

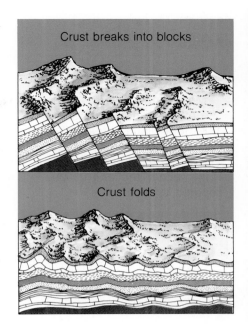

Crust breaks into blocks

Crust folds

Figure 22-4 *Mountains may form when the earth's crust breaks into great blocks that are then tilted or lifted (top). Folded mountains form when layers of the earth's crust wrinkle into wavelike folds (bottom).*

Figure 22-5 *The Alps are an example of folded mountains. These mountains show parallel rows of snow-capped, jagged peaks with steep, narrow valleys in between.*

Activity

Earth's Mountains

Mountains cover about one fifth of the earth's land surface. The total land area on the earth's surface is about 148,300,000 square kilometers. How much of the land surface is covered by mountains?

Such pile-ups may form volcanic mountains, such as the Cascade Mountains of Washington and Oregon. Many individual mountains are volcanoes. For example, Paricutín in Mexico, Vesuvius in Italy, and Kilimanjaro in Africa are all volcanoes.

Most mountains are part of a group of mountains. A group of mountains is called a **mountain range.** Examples of mountain ranges are the Alps, Andes, Himalayas, Rockies, and Appalachians.

Most mountain ranges are part of a larger group of mountains called a **mountain belt.** The Rocky Mountains, for example, are just one part of a huge chain of mountains that extends along the Pacific Coast of North and South America from Alaska to the southern tip of South America. This chain is one of the two major mountain belts on the earth's surface. Figure 22-6 shows the pattern of these two mountain belts. One is called the circum-Pacific belt. This belt roughly circles the Pacific Ocean. The other belt is the Eurasian-Melanesian belt, which extends across northern Africa, southern Europe, and southern Asia. The two belts meet in Indonesia.

The great mountain belts on the continents are rivaled by the undersea mountains of the worldwide Mid-Ocean Ridge system discussed in Chapter 21. This system extends through the Atlantic, Pacific, Indian, and Antarctic oceans. On either side of the rift valleys of the Mid-Ocean Ridge system are belts of

Figure 22-6 *Most of the mountains on the earth's surface are located in the two major mountain belts shown on this map. Which major mountain belt runs through the United States?*

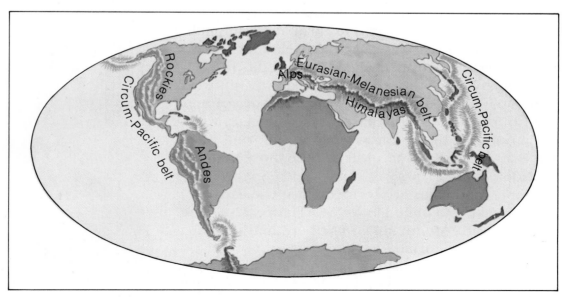

Figure 22-7 *In this photograph of the Colorado Plateau and Grand Canyon, a barren, dry landscape is revealed.*

high undersea mountains. These mountains were built by volcanic action. Many of the mountains are still active volcanoes.

Plateaus

Now you are walking through a different landscape. You are in a highland area dotted with enormous flat-topped hills. This region is dry, almost a desert. But the same kind of landscape at another place on the earth may be damp and covered with forests. No matter whether it is dry or wet, warm or cold, this type of region is a **plateau landscape,** or simply a plateau.

A plateau begins as flat land that is gradually lifted by movements of the earth's crust. A plateau is usually more than 600 meters above sea level. Some plateaus reach heights of more than 1500 meters.

The plateau upon which you are standing lies west of the Rocky Mountains, among some of the wildest and most beautiful scenery on the earth. It is the Colorado Plateau, which includes the Grand Canyon. The Colorado Plateau is roughly centered on the point where the boundaries of Colorado, New Mexico, Arizona, and Utah meet.

Plateaus usually form near mountain ranges. In fact, the Colorado Plateau began rising as the Rocky Mountains were forming some 65 million years ago.

Figure 22-8 *Here you can see the forests and rounded slopes of the Appalachian Plateau.*

Activity

Continental Sizes

Find out how the continents compare in size.

1. From a globe, trace the outline of each of the seven continents. Cut out the outlines. Trace each cutout on a piece of graph paper. Shade in the outlined continents.

2. Consider each square on the graph paper as an area unit of 1. Calculate the area units for each of the seven continents to the nearest whole unit. For example, suppose a continent covers all of 45 units, about one-half of 20 units, and about one-fourth of 16 units. The total area units the continent covers will be 45 + 10 + 4, or 59.

List the continents from largest to smallest.

But a plateau forms without the sideways folding and buckling of the crust that forms mountains. So its top stays more or less flat. In its youth, the Colorado Plateau was a single broad structure, towering 1500 meters and more above the surrounding land, but lower than the Rockies to the east.

Today, however, the Colorado Plateau is made of many plateaus. As you look around, you see an awesome landscape of huge flat-topped tables of rock. They are separated by steep clifflike canyon walls. Along the cliffsides, layers of brightly colored rock glow in the sun. The canyon walls are often terraced—almost as if a giant hand had carved a series of ledges there to make convenient steps.

Actually, the carving was done by the Colorado River and its branches over millions of years. They sliced deeper and deeper into the rock, cutting it up into separate plateaus. The steps of the terraces are layers of more water-resistant rock. The streams cut around this rock.

The Colorado River has carved the mighty Grand Canyon out of the hard rocks of the Colorado Plateau. It is a huge canyon about 2 kilometers deep, up to 29 kilometers wide, and 349 kilometers long. Today, the Colorado River continues to carve out more of this canyon.

By contrast, the Appalachian Plateau, west of the Blue Ridge Mountains, has more rounded slopes and forests. The Appalachian Plateau gets lots of rain. This plateau is many millions of years older than the

Colorado Plateau. So there has been much more time for rain, streams, and wind to smooth and round its slopes.

Plains

Now you are visiting another of the major landscape types. Here the land is mostly flat and of about equal height, like plateaus. But, unlike plateaus, this landscape is lower than the surrounding land. You are in a lowland area that is not far above sea level. You see broad rivers or streams, and the vegetation is mainly grass. The region you are visiting is a **plains landscape.**

The two major types of plains areas are determined by location and height above sea level. They are either along a coast or farther inland. Let's visit these two types of plains in the United States.

COASTAL PLAINS Low, flat regions called **coastal plains** spread gently upward from the Atlantic and Gulf coasts of the United States. These plains extend along the Atlantic coast from Cape Cod, Massachusetts, to Florida and from the Gulf coast of Florida to Texas. They average about 150 meters above sea level.

Many crops can be grown in coastal plain soil. Why? The reason is that the soil is very rich in substances needed for plant growth. In the United States, citrus crops, cotton, tobacco, and many different kinds of vegetables can be grown on the rich coastal plains.

Where does the rich soil come from? The soil is brought to the coastal plains by rivers. Rivers can break down rocks into sand and mud.

Rivers flow from high mountains and plateaus down to low-lying plains and out to sea. These rivers move fastest at the start of their journey. A fast-moving river is a powerful tool for wearing down rock. Because it is fast-moving, it can carry a large load of sand and mud.

As the river hits the gentler slopes of the lowlands, it slows down. And the more slowly it flows, the more sand and mud drops out of the flow. So, year after year, the rivers help to wear down the highlands and build up the lowland plains.

Figure 22-9 *In this plains landscape, the flat lowlands are not far above sea level. Such landscapes may include broad rivers or streams. The natural vegetation is mainly grass.*

Figure 22-10 *The flat land of the inland plains has very fertile soil that is good for growing crops such as wheat and corn.*

Activity

Surface Features

Suppose you take a trip across the earth's land surface. You will see many different kinds of features. Write a 200 word essay about what you see using the following vocabulary terms: mountain landscape, mountain range, plateau landscape, coastal plains, and inland plains. Your essay should describe the major similarities and differences between these features.

There is another reason that the coastal plains have rich soil. Long ago, shallow oceans covered these areas. As the shallow seas disappeared, they left behind rich deposits of soil that formed the coastal plains.

But not all coastal plains are available for farming. Some of the most fertile soil in coastal plains is not usable because it is found in swamps and marshes. This land is below river level and sometimes even below sea level. So the land usually floods with water.

INLAND PLAINS The central part of the United States is divided into two very large **inland plains**—the Interior Plains and the Great Plains. See Figure 22-2. Inland plains average about 450 meters above sea level. How were these plains formed? Over millions of years, mountains and hills were worn down by wind, rivers, and glaciers, leaving plains that have become the heartland of the United States farming country.

Why are these plains considered among the world's best for farming? There are three reasons. Many parts of these plains receive very rich soil deposits from such rivers as the Mississippi, Ohio, Missouri, Arkansas, and Red. More than half the material that built up the 65 million-year-old Rocky Mountains has been spread over these plains by rivers. Another reason is that plenty of rain falls on much of the plains during the growing season. A third reason is that these northern and western plains are much higher above sea level than are the coastal plains. So flooding, which could carry away rich soil, tends not to occur there.

Even where there is less water and rainfall, as in the western part of the Interior Plains and in the Great Plains, crops such as corn and wheat cover the land. Only within the "rain shadow" of the Rockies does farmland give way to semidesert and desert. Within a rain shadow, the mountains cut off the rains moving in from the west.

Water is very important to all living things. As you read in this section, too much or too little water can affect the growth of crops and the value of land to farmers. The next section will discuss the other major surface feature of the earth—water.

Career: *Surveyor*

In ancient Egypt, farmers placed boundary stones around their land to mark off property lines. But the annual flooding of the Nile River moved the stones or washed them away. So the Egyptians, who were excellent mathematicians, learned to survey their land. Thus they could replace any lost boundary markers accurately.

Today boundaries and areas of property on the earth's surface are determined by scientists called **surveyors.** They use an instrument called a transit to measure and plot angles and distances. Surveyors can measure the exact location of points and elevations on the earth's surface. The results of their survey are recorded, the data are checked, and sketches, maps, and reports are prepared. This information is used for construction projects, mapmaking, land division, mining, and deciding property ownership.

Surveyors must make very precise measurements. Their maps and land descriptions are recorded in the courthouse for anyone to check. A state licensing exam is taken after several years of work experience.

A person interested in surveying must have good judgment, enjoy problem solving, be able to communicate, and be attentive to detail. For more information, write to the American Congress on Surveying and Mapping, 210 Little Falls Street, Falls Church, VA 22046.

SECTION REVIEW

1. What are the three main types of landscapes on the earth's surface?
2. What are three ways that mountains can form?
3. What are the two major types of plains?

22-2 The Earth's Surface: Water

The earth is a watery planet. Oceans cover about 70 percent of its surface. And about 97 percent of all the water on our world is in the oceans. This is salt water. Every hundred kilograms of sea water contains about 3.5 kilograms of ordinary salt, as well as a number of other salts dissolved in the water.

Figure 22-11 *Oceans cover most of the earth's surface.*

Where do these salts come from and how do they get into sea water? Ocean salts are found in undersea volcanoes, in rivers, and along shores. Ocean water dissolves salts in volcanic rocks. Rivers dissolve salts in rocks and soil on land. The rivers then carry these salts to the oceans. As waves constantly pound on shores, the erosion from waves helps to dissolve the salts in rocks.

What about the other 3 percent of the earth's water? Most of it is locked up in the ice packs of the Arctic Ocean, and in the great sheets of ice that cover a large part of the continent of Antarctica. This is fresh water. The rest of the fresh water is in the ground and in lakes, ponds, streams, and rivers. Fresh water does not contain salt, though it does have small amounts of other dissolved minerals. Fresh water is drinking water. It is essential for all plants and animals that live on land.

Where does fresh water come from? The answer is part of the story of the water cycle. **In the water cycle, water circulates continually between the atmosphere and the surface of the earth.**

The Water Cycle

There is an old saying that every drop of water from the ocean rains five times before it returns to the ocean. Although this is not a very scientific statement, it does have a kind of scientific basis. Here is the reason.

512

Every day, the heat of the sun causes water on the earth's surface to change to a gas. This process is called **evaporation** (i-va-puh-RA-shun). Enormous amounts of water are evaporated from the oceans. Water also evaporates from fresh-water sources on land. See Figure 22-12.

When water evaporates, it gets into the air as an invisible gas—water vapor. There is always some water vapor in the air, even over the driest deserts.

Air can hold only a certain amount of water vapor. Warm air can hold more water vapor than can cold air. As warm air, loaded with water vapor, rises, it cools. The cooler air can no longer hold all of its water vapor. Some of the water vapor changes back into a liquid. This process is called **condensation** (kahn-den-SAY-shun). Next, clouds form. They are made up of billions of tiny water droplets so light that they can float in the air. Sooner or later, this water falls to the earth as rain, sleet, hail, or snow. This process is called **precipitation** (pree-sip-uh-TAY-shun). The water that falls is fresh water because when ocean water evaporates, dissolved solids are left behind. The cycle then begins again.

Figure 22-12 *The water cycle is made up of the processes of evaporation, condensation, and precipitation.*

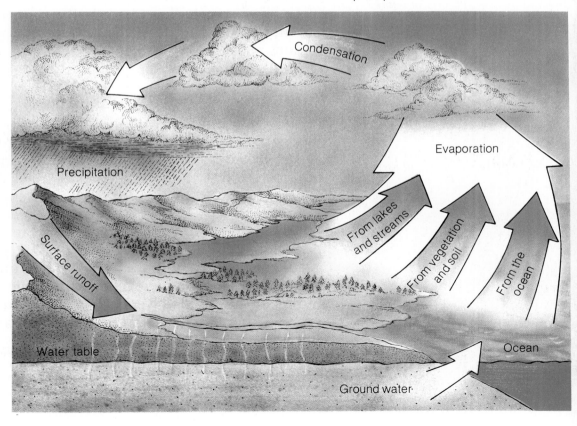

Figure 22-13 *Air on the western sides of mountains contains much moisture. The wet conditions allow many kinds of vegetation to grow (left). Air on the eastern sides of mountains contains much less moisture, and dry, desert conditions result (right).*

Figure 22-14 *The grooves in these mountains show how running water can cut deeply into mountains over millions of years.*

In some places, high mountain ranges generally prevent moisture from reaching the land, producing a desert climate. For example, moisture-laden air from the Pacific flows eastward over the California coast. Plenty of rain falls on the farms of the Great Central Valley in California. The air reaches the Sierra Nevada Mountains inland and is forced to rise. As it rises it cools. Lots of rain falls on the western slopes of the mountains. But by the time the air crosses the Sierras, it no longer contains enough moisture. So little rain falls on the desert lands east of the Sierras, including Death Valley. For the same reason, the eastern side of the Rockies is mostly desert land.

Running Water

Some of the water that falls to the earth evaporates again. But about a third of the water remains on the surface. It begins moving downhill and flows into rivers and streams. The water entering a river or stream is called surface runoff. In the spring, melting snow and ice add to the surface runoff.

From high mountains and steep plateau cliffs, water flows downward. It collects in basins, grooves, and channels worn in the rock by earlier runoffs. Streams like these come together to become the sources of the world's rivers. The rivers return to the oceans. Water evaporates from the oceans, and the cycle repeats endlessly.

Some rain water soaks into the ground. The ground takes on water like a sponge. This water is called **ground water.** About 0.6 percent of the earth's fresh water is in ground water. Even in the driest deserts, there is water underground. There is a place under the desert sands where the ground is soaked with water. Water fills spaces between the grains of soil. Eventually, ground water flows underground to the oceans. This water can then become part of the water cycle again.

The top level to which ground water rises when underground is called the **water table.** In the desert, the water table may be hundreds of meters underground. In places with more rainfall, the water table lies nearer the surface. There, water seeps up from the water table, keeping the roots of plants moist and supplying water for wells. See Figure 22-16. In some places, such as coastal plains, the land lies slightly below the level of the water table. Such land is usually swampy or marshy. When there is a long period without rain—a drought—the water table sinks deeper into the ground. Ponds begin to dry up. Wells go dry, the shallowest wells first.

On the other hand, after unusually heavy rains through much of the year, the water table may rise toward the surface. Normally dry ground becomes muddy. Puddles form everywhere. The ground is waterlogged right up to its top. Plants may be killed because their roots cannot get enough air.

Standing Water

Unlike rivers and streams, the water in lakes and ponds usually stays in one location. Both can be important sources of water. Moosehead Lake, in Maine, for example, is a natural source of fresh water. It is 56 kilometers long and 3 to 16 kilometers wide. The pine-forested shores of the lake can hold enormous amounts of water from rains and melting snow. This water is released slowly to the lake, making flooding less likely. During times of drought, the lake holds a huge supply of water in reserve.

Frozen Water

Aside from the oceans, the most enormous store of water on the earth lies in the ice sheets around the North and South poles. About 2 percent of the

Figure 22-15 *An oasis can form in a desert when ground water rises to the surface.*

Figure 22-16 *These diagrams show the changes in a water table after a long period of rain and after a long period without rain.*

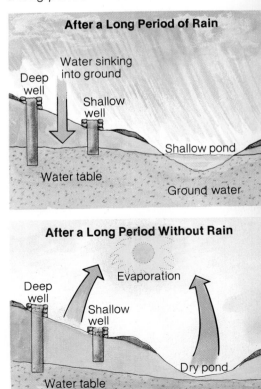

After a Long Period of Rain

Deep well

Water sinking into ground

Shallow well

Shallow pond

Water table

Ground water

After a Long Period Without Rain

Deep well

Shallow well

Evaporation

Dry pond

Water table

Ground water

Activity

Drought and the Water Table

1. Fill the bottom of a deep, clear baking dish about halfway with sand.

2. Slowly add enough water so that the sand becomes saturated and about 1 cm of water is visible above the surface of the sand.

3. Add more sand on top of the water in *only one-half* of the baking dish. You can now see how the water table looks above and below the "earth's" surface after a period of rain.

4. Observe the water level above and below the sand's surface during the next few days.

What changes do you notice in the water level?

earth's fresh water is frozen in ice sheets. If all this ice melted, the oceans would rise about 50 meters above their present level. New York, New Orleans, Houston, and Seattle would be under water. Memphis, Tennessee, now 560 kilometers from the sea, would become a major seaport. In Washington, D.C., the top floors of the Capitol Building and the tip of the Washington Monument would be above water. But the Pentagon would be completely covered.

The very thick ice sheets that cover most of the polar regions are called **continental glaciers.** Glaciers are huge, slow-moving masses of ice. During the Ice Ages, when the earth's climate was much colder, the ice piled up several kilometers thick around both poles. The pressure of the piled-up ice caused it to flow outward away from the poles. At times, these glaciers covered a third of all the land on the earth.

Valley glaciers are long, narrow glaciers. They move downhill between the steep sides of mountain valleys. Usually they follow channels worn by running water in the past.

As the glacier slides downward, it tears rock fragments from the mountainside. These fragments become frozen in the glacier. They cut deep grooves in the valley walls. Finer bits of rock sandpaper the walls, smoothing them. Glaciers often turn a steep, V-shaped valley into a U-shaped valley with smooth sides. There are many such valleys in the Alps.

Figure 22-17 *This valley glacier is slowly moving downhill between the steep sides of a mountain valley.*

Figure 22-18 *Glaciers cut valleys into U-shapes* (left), *and rivers cut valleys into V-shapes* (right).

Great chunks of ice break off from the edges of the Arctic and Antarctic ice sheets. These masses of free-floating ice are called **icebergs.** They can be a major hazard to ships. In 1912, the ocean liner *Titanic* sank after smashing into an iceberg in the North Atlantic Ocean. Today, sea lanes are patrolled constantly by ships and planes on the lookout for icebergs.

Around the Great Lakes are masses of boulders, rocks, and sand, heaped up into ridges and hills. They are deposits left by glaciers that covered this area thousands of years ago. As the climate grew warmer, the glaciers melted and dropped their cargo of rocks in piles. These piles mark the farthest advance of the glaciers.

You now have explored the earth's interior and the earth's surface. In the next chapter, you will explore the earth's atmosphere.

SECTION REVIEW

1. What percentage of the earth's water is fresh water? Where is most of it found?
2. Describe the water cycle.
3. What is the water table?
4. What is the difference between a valley glacier and a continental glacier?

LABORATORY ACTIVITY

Examining Differences Between Fresh and Salt Water

Purpose

In this activity, you will examine some of the differences in the physical characteristics of salt water and fresh water.

Materials *(per group)*

1 plastic drinking straw
Small piece of clay
4 to 6 steel BBs or ball bearings
250-mL beaker
Fresh water
Pencil
Metric ruler
3 samples of liquids

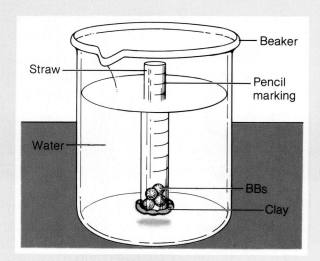

Procedure

1. Cut a straw in half and plug one end with a small piece of clay.
2. With a pencil, make a series of marks ½ cm apart along the entire length of the straw.
3. Add water to the beaker or glass container until it is about three-quarters full.
4. Carefully drop two or three BBs into the open end of the straw and let them roll down to the clay at the bottom.
5. With the clay end down, gently place the straw into the water. It should float. Add as many BBs as are necessary to cause your straw hydrometer to float very low in the water. Only two or three pencil lines on the hydrometer should show above the water's surface. Note exactly the level at which it floats. Your hydrometer is now ready to be used to compare densities of liquids. The higher it floats, the more dense (salty) the liquid will be.
6. Examine the three beakers containing sample fluids that have been provided by your teacher. They are labeled A, B, and C.

Each sample has had different amounts of salt added. As a result, each will have a different density.

7. Gently place your hydrometer into the fluid of the first container. Carefully note and record the level at which it floats. Repeat the procedure for each of the two remaining samples.

Observations and Conclusions

1. List the order of the samples tested, from the one that was least dense to the one that was most dense. Include the sample of fresh water in your list.
2. How would the hydrometer float in a fluid that was less dense than the fresh water?
3. How would the hydrometer float in a fluid that was more dense than any of those tested?
4. How would the level of any floating object in fresh water compare to the floating level of that same object in salt water?
5. What do you think happens to the density of sea water at the surface of the ocean whenever it rains for a long period of time?

CHAPTER REVIEW

SUMMARY

22-1 The Earth's Surface: Landmasses

■ Mountains, plateaus, and plains are the three main types of landscapes on the earth.

■ Most mountains have been formed by the slow folding and wrinkling of the earth's crust.

■ Some mountains are formed when the earth's crust breaks into huge blocks. Volcanic material also can form mountains.

■ Mountains are usually parts of larger groups called ranges and belts.

■ Plateau landscapes are usually areas of flat land of about equal height that are more than 600 meters above sea level and are higher than the surrounding land.

■ Plains landscapes are areas of flat land of about equal height that are lower than the surrounding land. Plains are lowland areas that are usually not far above sea level.

■ Coastal plains are low, flat regions that extend along coasts and usually average about 150 meters above sea level. Rich soil is brought to the coastal plains by rivers. Flooding is a problem in these low-lying plains.

■ Inland plains are low, flat regions that average about 450 meters above sea level. Rich soil is brought to such plains by rivers.

22-2 The Earth's Surface: Water

■ About 97 percent of the water on the earth is in the oceans. This ocean water is salt water. The other 3 percent is fresh water found in glaciers, ground water, lakes, and rivers.

■ The water cycle is a continual process. It involves the processes of evaporation, condensation, and precipitation.

■ Fresh water from streams, rivers, and ground water eventually returns to the oceans.

■ A water table is the top level to which ground water rises.

■ Fresh water from lakes and ponds usually stays in one location. About 2 percent of all fresh water is frozen in glaciers.

VOCABULARY

Define each term in a complete sentence.

coastal plains	ground water	mountain landscape	precipitation
condensation	iceberg	mountain range	valley glacier
continental glacier	inland plain	plains landscape	water table
evaporation	mountain belt	plateau landscape	

CONTENT REVIEW: MULTIPLE CHOICE

Choose the letter of the answer that best completes each statement.

1. The highest place on the earth's surface is
   a. Mauna Kea in Hawaii.　　b. Pikes Peak in Colorado.
   c. Mount Everest in Nepal.　　d. Vesuvius in Italy.
2. Most of the world's mountains have been built up by
   a. river deposits.　　b. folding and blocking of the earth's crust.
   c. earthquakes.　　d. all of these.

3. A mountain belt is a
   a. group of volcanic mountains.
   b. group of underwater mountains.
   c. group of mountains such as the Appalachians.
   d. group of mountain ranges.

4. Plateaus
   a. have jagged peaks.
   b. are sometimes called highlands.
   c. are lower than the surrounding land.
   d. are always found in dry, desert areas.

5. On the earth's surface flooding is a major problem for
   a. inland plains.   b. coastal plains.
   c. plateaus.   d. mountains.

6. Some of the best farmland is found
   a. in marshes.   b. on mountain slopes.
   c. on inland plains.   d. on plateaus.

7. An example of standing water is
   a. rivers.   b. lakes.   c. glaciers.   d. streams.

8. The process by which the sun's heat causes water on the earth's surface to change to a gas is called
   a. precipitation.   b. evaporation.
   c. condensation.   d. the water cycle.

9. Fresh water is not found in
   a. lakes.   b. ground water.   c. glaciers.   d. oceans.

10. Long, narrow masses of ice that move downhill along the sides of mountains are called
   a. icebergs.   b. valley glaciers.
   c. polar ice sheets.   d. continental glaciers.

CONTENT REVIEW: COMPLETION

Fill in the word or words that best complete each statement.

1. There are seven large landmasses on the earth called _____.

2. Most mountain ranges are part of a larger group of mountains that is called a(n) _____.

3. A(n) _____ is a major landscape feature that forms when a flat land surface is uplifted by movements from within the earth's crust.

4. Lowland areas that are not far above sea level are called _____.

5. The process in the water cycle by which the sun changes surface water to water vapor is called _____.

6. The process in the water cycle by which water vapor changes to liquid water is called _____.

7. The process in the water cycle by which water falls to the earth as rain, sleet, hail, or snow is _____.

8. The top level at which ground water is found is called the _____.

9. The thick ice sheets that cover most of the earth's polar regions are known as _____.

10. Most of the _____ water on the earth is found frozen in ice sheets.

CONTENT REVIEW: TRUE OR FALSE

Determine whether each statement is true of false. If it is true, write "true." If it is false, change the underlined word or words to make the statement true.

1. Three main types of landscapes on the earth's surface are mountains, <u>hills</u>, and plains.
2. Most of the world's mountains were built by the slow <u>folding and wrinkling</u> of the earth's crust.
3. There are two major mountain <u>ranges</u> on the earth's surface.
4. <u>Plains</u> are highland areas that look like enormous tabletops.
5. Rivers bring rich soil to <u>plateau</u> regions.
6. Coastal plains are <u>higher</u> above sea level than inland plains.
7. About <u>97 percent</u> of all the water on the earth's surface is salt water.
8. <u>Evaporation</u> is a process in the water cycle by which water vapor changes into liquid water.
9. Rivers and streams are examples of <u>standing</u> water.
10. Most fresh water is frozen in <u>glaciers</u>.

CONCEPT REVIEW: SKILL BUILDING

Use the skills you have developed in the chapter to complete each activity.

1. **Making generalizations** Why is it important to find new sources of fresh water and to conserve the sources now available?
2. **Making calculations** An average person needs about 2.5 liters of water a day to live. How much water will each person need in a year? How much water will your class need in a day to live? In a year?
3. **Making predictions** What would you predict might happen to the water table if a large industry using a well were built in the area?
4. **Applying concepts** Sometimes dangerous chemicals that have been dumped on land are found in drinking water. Explain how this is possible.
5. **Making inferences** Most of the earth's ice is found in or around Antarctica. Suppose the temperature of the South Pole were to rise high enough to melt all of Antarctica's ice. Which landscape region would be most affected? Why?
6. **Relating concepts** The water you drink today may have once been part of the Atlantic Ocean. Explain this statement.
7. **Designing an experiment** Clouds are not salty. The salt from the oceans is left behind when the water evaporates. Devise an experiment to illustrate this fact. Describe the problem, materials, procedure, expected observations, and conclusions of your experiment.

CONCEPT REVIEW: ESSAY

Discuss each of the following in a brief paragraph.

1. Briefly describe the three major kinds of landscapes.
2. Discuss three reasons why the inland plains of the United States are among the best farming land in the world.
3. Describe three ways in which mountains are formed.
4. Compare inland plains and coastal plains.
5. Describe the processes of the water cycle and explain how it is a continual process.

23 Structure of the Atmosphere

CHAPTER SECTIONS

23-1 The Layers of the Atmosphere

23-2 The Magnetosphere

CHAPTER OBJECTIVES

After completing this chapter, you will be able to:

23-1 Describe the layers of the atmosphere.

23-1 Explain the relationship between temperature and the layers of the atmosphere.

23-1 Relate the density of air at various altitudes to temperature and pressure.

23-2 Describe the magnetosphere.

23-2 Identify the probable causes of the magnetosphere.

"I caught my breath as I looked out. The scene as we topped 100,000 feet was utterly magnificent. For long moments, we drank in the beauty of earth, sea, and sky. Our horizon lay some 400 miles away. A narrow lower segment of the sky appeared bright and whitish-blue. I recognized it as the troposphere, the layer of the atmosphere closest to the earth. Above came another layer, a much richer, deeper, cleaner blue. Above that and over our heads, the blue darkened to a blue-black towards the void of space." That was the view from the pressurized cabin of a balloon soaring over the Gulf of Mexico.

Today, research balloons commonly explore the lower parts of the atmosphere. Rockets go up even farther, crossing that vague boundary where the last bit of earth's air fades into outer space. And down below, people travel through the lowest parts of the atmosphere—by foot, in elevators and cable cars, and in airplanes. These trips are not often scientific or mysterious. Yet there are mysteries in the air and scientists to solve them.

For example, a flight up through the clouds is often bumpy. But, above the clouds, the flight is smooth. There seems to be an invisible wall above which clouds and bumpy weather cannot rise. What is this wall? You will find the answer to this question and learn more about the atmosphere as you read the following pages.

Clouds in the lower atmosphere

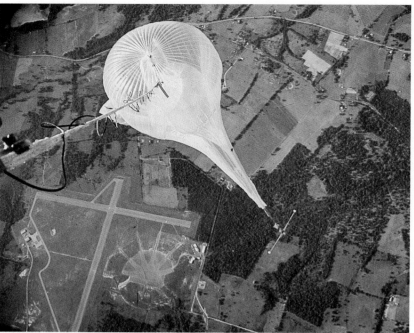

Figure 23-1 *In the last century, scientists studied the atmosphere from wicker baskets attached to balloons* (left). *Today, scientists use high-altitude balloons carrying instruments to study the atmosphere* (right).

23-1 The Layers of the Atmosphere

In the nineteenth century, some weather scientists began exploring the atmosphere. Their ships of exploration were wicker baskets! Baskets? Yes, that's right. The scientists soared into the sky in huge baskets hanging from hydrogen-filled balloons.

James Glaisher, an English scientist, was one of these early explorers. On a warm day in September 1862, he and another scientist, Henry Coxwell, began a balloon trip. They soon found themselves in serious danger.

Twenty-five minutes after leaving the ground, they reached an altitude of 4800 meters. They were nearly as high as the tallest mountain in Europe, Mont Blanc. The temperature had dropped to −11° C. Ice coated the basket and the rigging of the balloon. The explorers could have returned to the ground by slowly releasing hydrogen gas and deflating the balloon. They decided to go on instead.

The temperature continued to drop as they rose. At 5000 meters it was −12.5° C. At 10,000 meters it was −45° C. Finally they reached 11,000 meters, well over 2000 meters higher than the top of Mount Everest. Though warmly dressed and in bright sunshine, the two men were numbed with cold. It was −52° C.

And something else was wrong. The scientists could move only very slowly. It was almost as if they were paralyzed. The bright sun turned dim as their eyesight failed. Glaisher lost consciousness. Coxwell tried to open the gas valves to get them down. But the valve cord was tangled up with the ropes that held the basket under the balloon. Although frostbitten, Coxwell somehow climbed up the ropes. He was surrounded by long icicles hanging from the balloon.

At last he was able to untangle the valve cord. His hands were completely numb. He climbed back down into the basket by clinging to the ropes with his elbows. Coxwell knew they would both soon die if he could not bring the balloon down. He grabbed the valve cord with his teeth and tugged the valve open. They were on their way to safety.

The two explorers lived to tell their story—and to make other balloon flights. Some other daring scientists were not so lucky. But around the world, scientists continued to explore the atmosphere in balloons. Everywhere, the picture of the atmosphere was the same. The temperature, scientists discovered, drops at an average rate of 6.5° C per kilometer of altitude.

The air also gets "thinner," or less dense, with increasing altitude. It becomes more spread out. So there is less of it in a given space at a higher altitude. This is why Glaisher and Coxwell moved so slowly and why Glaisher became unconscious. They did not have enough oxygen to breathe. In fact, at 11,000 meters, they had to take about four breaths to get the same amount of oxygen that is in one breath at the surface of the earth.

What causes air to be less dense at higher altitudes? Suppose you take a couple of handfuls of cotton and squeeze them into a small ball. Obviously, the ball has the same amount of cotton in it that once filled up both your hands. But it is squeezed into a much smaller space.

In much the same way, the air around you is pressed together by the weight of all the air above it.

Figure 23-2 *Air becomes colder as altitude increases. That is why climbers need heavy clothing on a high mountain. Air also contains less oxygen at higher altitudes, so pilots must wear oxygen masks.*

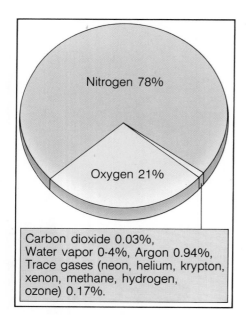

Nitrogen 78%

Oxygen 21%

Carbon dioxide 0.03%,
Water vapor 0-4%, Argon 0.94%,
Trace gases (neon, helium, krypton,
xenon, methane, hydrogen,
ozone) 0.17%.

Figure 23-3 *The atmosphere is a mixture of many gases. Which two gases make up most of the earth's atmosphere?*

Figure 23-4 *According to this chart, how does air pressure change as you go higher into the atmosphere?*

AIR PRESSURE AND ALTITUDE

Altitude (meters)	Air Pressure (g/cm²)
Sea level	1034
3000	717
6000	450
9000	302
12,000	190
15,000	112

This pressing force due to the weight of the air above you is called **air pressure.** Air pressure at sea level is about 1000 grams on each square centimeter. The air pressure on your body is around 12 tons. That would be enough to flatten you into a very thin pancake—except that there is also air inside your body under the same pressure, balancing the outside pressure.

As you go upward into the atmosphere, whether by climbing a mountain or flying in an airplane or even riding in an elevator, the air pressure decreases. See Figure 23-4. That's because there is less air above you, so there is less weight and less air pressure. The air pressure inside your body decreases too, but a little more slowly. That is why you sometimes sense the change in pressure in your ears.

Air is like a spring. Under pressure, it is squeezed into a smaller space. When the pressure is lower, the air expands, taking up more space. This not only explains why the air is thinner at higher altitudes. It also explains why the air gets colder there.

Think of the stream of air coming out of a tire when you open the valve. The tire may be warm, and the day may be warm—but the air stream is cold. The air in the tire is under higher pressure than the air around it. When you open the valve, air rushes out and expands. When air expands, it cools.

As air rises from the earth's surface, it expands because the air pressure becomes less and less. The higher it rises, the more it expands. And the more it expands, the colder it gets up to a certain height.

Air is always rising from the earth's surface. As you know, the earth's surface is heated by the sun. So air near the surface is warmed by that heat. Warm air is less dense than cold air. So the warm air heated at the surface floats up through the colder air above it. Cold air sinks to take its place.

So in the lower atmosphere, the air is constantly in motion. These churning motions or currents caused by heat are like the currents in the earth's mantle that you read about in Chapter 21.

Scientists who study the earth's atmosphere have divided it into four layers. **The four layers of the atmosphere are classified according to temperature changes into the troposphere, the stratosphere, the mesosphere, and the thermosphere.**

Figure 23-5 *In this photograph, you can see fog covering the Golden Gate Bridge in San Francisco. Fog is simply low-lying clouds that form when water vapor in cool, moist air condenses near the earth's surface.*

The Troposphere

The lowest layer of the atmosphere is called the **troposphere** (TRAH-puh-sfeer). This name means "turning over." Turning gives you the idea of constant change, and that is what the troposphere is all about. Almost all of the earth's weather takes place in the troposphere. Ninety-nine percent of the clouds, water vapor, dust, and pollution in the atmosphere is located in the troposphere. Many airplane flights take advantage of the air currents characteristic of this layer. These currents also keep the air in the

Activity

Air Pressure

Air exerts a pressure of about 1000 grams per square centimeter at sea level. Use the following steps to demonstrate the effects of air pressure.

1. Obtain a glass juice or milk bottle, a hard-boiled egg with the shell removed, scrap paper, a match, and a pencil.

2. Stuff most of the paper into the bottle.

3. Have *your teacher* light the rest of the paper and push it into the bottle with a pencil.

4. Immediately place the egg on the mouth of the open bottle. **CAUTION:** *Be careful when working near any flame.* What happens to the egg? Why?

Figure 23-6 *Winds and thunderstorms occur in the troposphere.*

527

Temperature Changes in the Troposphere

1. At three times during both the day and evening, use an outdoor thermometer to measure air temperature 1 cm above the ground and 1.25 m above the ground. You may have to leave the thermometer in place for a few minutes.

2. On a chart, record the time of day and the temperature for both locations.

3. On a piece of graph paper, plot time versus temperature for each thermometer location. Label both graphs.

In which area did temperature change more rapidly? By a greater amount over the entire time period? Why?

troposphere well mixed. And, most important, the troposphere is the layer in which you live.

The most important single fact about the troposphere is that it gets steadily colder from bottom to top. This is what makes the churning of its air possible. Suppose the troposphere were nearly the same temperature throughout. Then there would be no rising of warm air, no settling of cold air—no currents at all.

For a long time, scientists thought that the atmosphere just kept getting colder all the way up to the edge of space. By 1902, a French scientist, Léon Philippe Teisserenc de Bort, had shown this was not so. He had checked the temperatures instruments recorded from 236 balloon flights. The balloons rose from altitudes between about 9.5 kilometers and 14.5 kilometers. The instruments showed that at an altitude of about 12 kilometers, the temperature stopped falling. There seemed to be a "roof" over the troposphere!

The troposphere actually is like a sloping roof. On the average, the troposphere's roof is lowest at the poles and slopes upward toward the equator.

Figure 23-7 *Rainbows* (left) *and clouds* (right) *are caused by weather conditions in the troposphere.*

Over the United States, which is about halfway between the poles and the equator, the roof of the troposphere is 11 kilometers up. The temperature of the roof of the troposphere over the United States is about −55° C. About 76 percent of the earth's air is found in the troposphere.

The Stratosphere

The layer of the earth's atmosphere above the troposphere is called the **stratosphere** (STRAT-uh-sfeer). The stratosphere extends from about 16 kilometers to about 48 kilometers above the earth's surface. About 24 percent of the air lies in the stratosphere.

From about 12 kilometers high in the troposphere layer up to about 24 kilometers in the stratosphere layer, the temperature usually stays the same. The temperature remains about −55° C. Above that height, the air in the stratosphere actually warms up slowly with increasing height. At the top of the stratosphere, the temperature normally reaches between −2° C and 0° C.

Why doesn't the stratosphere get colder with the increasing height? Because **ozone** is present. Ozone is a high-energy form of oxygen. It has a sharp smell, something like the smell given off by sparking electric wires. Oxygen in the stratosphere reacts with sunlight to form ozone. The ozone forms a layer in the stratosphere. This ozone layer absorbs powerful ultraviolet rays from the sun. These rays warm the stratosphere. The ozone layer also acts as a screen, shielding the earth's surface from these harmful ultraviolet rays. Without this shield, most living things on the earth would be killed. The ozone layer ends at the top of the stratosphere.

In the troposphere, air rises when there are layers of colder air above it. This does not happen in the stratosphere. The temperature is constant or rises with increasing height. So there are no currents. There are no storms. This is why airliners fly in the stratosphere when they can.

Another reason for flying in the stratosphere is the **jet stream.** The jet stream is a narrow, fast-moving current of air that forms along the troposphere-stratosphere boundary.

Figure 23-8 *Jets fly in the stratosphere to avoid the storms and strong winds of the troposphere.*

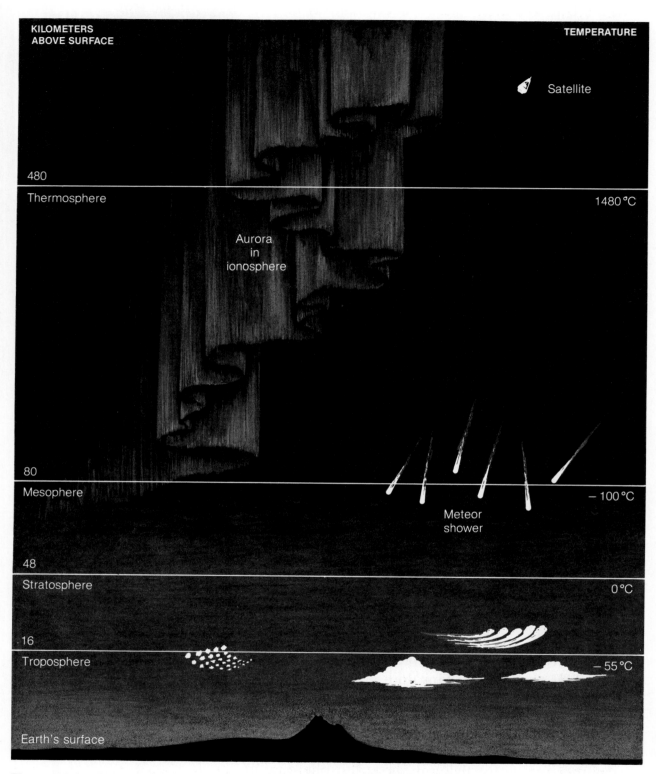

Figure 23-9 *The layers of the earth's atmosphere, from lowest to highest altitude, are the troposphere, the stratosphere, the mesosphere, and the thermosphere. How do scientists classify the layers of the atmosphere?*

In 1922, a weather balloon was sent aloft at Hampshire, England. It crossed the boundary between the troposphere and the stratosphere. Suddenly, it started sailing eastward at great speed. It came down four hours later in Leipzig, Germany, 900 kilometers east of its starting point. The balloon had been carried by a jet stream blowing at more than 200 kilometers an hour.

A jet stream usually forms where cold air from the poles meets warmer air from the equator. So there are two major jet streams that circle the earth. One jet stream is roughly halfway between the North Pole and the equator. The other is roughly halfway between the South Pole and the equator. Each usually blows in an easterly direction at more than 105

Career: *Physical Meteorologist*

HELP WANTED: PHYSICAL METEOROLOGIST Bachelor's degree in meteorology required. Master's degree preferred. Courses in air pollution and hydrology helpful. Apply to National Weather Service.

As you read these words, it is possible that somewhere in the world a volcano is "blowing its top." Almost countless tons of rock, dust, and gases are exploding into the earth's atmosphere. Wind will carry this volcanic "junk" around the world—perhaps to the sky above

your head. At the same time, factories near your home and cars on your street will puff more dust and gases into the atmosphere. Not so strangely, all of this material can affect the weather where you live. How? That is a question that **physical meteorologists** try to answer.

These scientists study the effects of gases and other particles in the air on weather and on other important things that affect the lives of people. The work of physical meteorologists can aid in the fight against air and water pollution.

Physical meteorologists study both the electrical and the chemical properties of the atmosphere. They observe the processes that produce winds and those that produce clouds, rain, snow, and hail. They do research to learn how the atmosphere affects light, sound, and radio waves. Meteorologists work for the government, universities, airlines, aerospace companies, and the radio and television industry.

If you are a curious person who enjoys detailed work in a laboratory and outdoors, physical meteorology may be a career for you. High school courses in physics, chemistry, and mathematics are very helpful. To learn more, write to the American Meteorological Society, 45 Beacon Street, Boston, MA 02108.

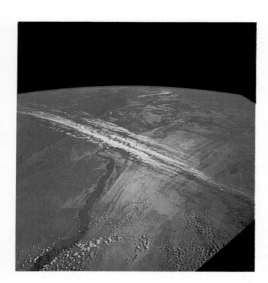

Figure 23-10 *A jet stream forms where cold air from the poles meets warmer air from the equator. This high-altitude jet stream is moving over the Nile Valley and the Red Sea.*

kilometers per hour. However, speeds may exceed 320 kilometers per hour. Airplanes flying eastward use the jet stream to make a faster trip and to save fuel. Airplanes traveling westward climb above the jet stream to avoid a head wind that would slow them down. There, of course, they do not get a push from the jet stream. That's why an airline flight schedule will show a shorter time for a flight from San Francisco to New York than a return flight, for example.

Jet streams also can steer large storms. You may have seen a television weather forecaster showing a jet stream on a map of the United States. Usually the jet stream is shown as a sort of twisted, moving belt snaking its way east across the country. As the jet stream changes its path, usually from day to day, the track of big storms changes with it.

The Mesosphere

The layer of the earth's atmosphere above the stratosphere is called the **mesosphere** (MES-uh-sfeer). This layer extends from about 48 kilometers above the earth to about 80 kilometers high. The air in the mesosphere is many thousands of times less dense than the air at sea level. Here again, the temperature begins to drop. At the top of the mesosphere, the temperature has dropped to about −100° C. This is the coldest part of the atmosphere.

Why does the temperature drop? Because there is no more ozone. Above the stratosphere, there is not enough oxygen left to form an ozone layer.

With very little air in the mesosphere, you might think that nothing ever happens there. But something does happen and you may see it when you look up into the sky at night. For it is in the mesosphere that most **meteoroids** (MEET-ee-uh-roidz) burn up. A meteoroid is a chunk of rocklike matter from outer space.

At speeds of 160,000 kilometers an hour or more, a meteoroid may strike the atmosphere. As it rubs against the air, the meteoroid is quickly heated and glows white hot.

This is what happens to the heat shield of a spacecraft as it reenters the atmosphere. But meteoroids do not have heat shields to protect them. If

Figure 23-11 *A heat shield protects the Space Shuttle from burning up in the earth's atmosphere.*

you are looking at the sky at night, you may see a streak of light, or **meteor** (MEE-tee-er). That streak of light is a meteoroid burning up in the mesosphere.

The Thermosphere

The upper layer of the atmosphere is called the **thermosphere** (THER-muh-sfeer). This layer extends upward from about 80 kilometers to between 480 kilometers and 600 kilometers. At the top of the thermosphere is the beginning of space. But there is no sharp line where one ends and the other begins. As you travel near the top of the thermosphere, you are in the neighborhood of that invisible boundary.

"Thermosphere" means "heat sphere" or "warm layer." And in the thermosphere the temperature rises to more than 1480° C. But don't be fooled about the high temperatures in the thermosphere. This is a very different kind of heat. On the earth's surface, such temperatures would melt many metals. However, a thermometer placed in the thermosphere would register far below zero!

Figure 23-12 *Most artificial satellites orbit above the thermosphere layer of the atmosphere.*

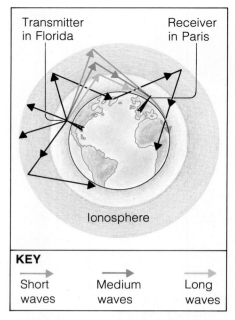

KEY

→ Short waves   → Medium waves   → Long waves

Figure 23-13 *Radio waves are bounced off the ionosphere to transmit radio messages overseas or across continents. There are three types of waves and each travels to a different height in the ionosphere.*

Figure 23-14 *Weather satellites orbit the earth in the upper part of the thermosphere. They transmit information used by scientists to track weather patterns. This photograph was taken by a weather satellite.*

Why? Temperature is a measure of how fast particles in air move. The faster the air particles travel, the higher the temperature. On the earth, particles in the air are packed so tightly together that a particle travels a very short distance before hitting another particle—about 0.06 microns. A micron is a millionth of a meter. In the thermosphere, however, the particles are few and far between. About 99.999 percent of the earth's atmosphere lies below the thermosphere. So the particles travel a long distance before they hit other particles.

A thermometer on the earth's surface is bombarded by countless billions of air particles. But in the thermosphere, few particles ever strike the thermometer. These particles are moving very fast and are far apart. They are very hot, but there would not be enough of them to warm a thermometer. However, special instruments can measure the temperature of particles in the thermosphere.

The particles are moving very fast because they are absorbing energy from the sun and outer space. This energy causes many of the particles to become charged with electricity. These charged particles are called **ions.**

Ions are found mainly in the lower part of the thermosphere and extend up for several hundred kilometers. This part of the thermosphere is a kind of sphere within a sphere. Scientists call it the **ionosphere** (igh-AHN-uh-sfeer).

There are a number of layers of ions in the ionosphere. They act like a mirror, reflecting radio waves back to the earth. Radio waves, like light waves, travel in straight lines. But when reflected by the ionosphere, they can travel long distances around the earth. These radio waves can be received thousands of kilometers from their source.

Sometimes streams of fast-moving ions from the sun streak through the ionosphere. They collide with other particles in the air, which causes them to glow. This is much the same thing that happens in a neon sign. A stream of electrically charged particles is passed through a small amount of neon gas in the sign. The neon glows brightly.

These sky glows are called the northern and southern lights or **auroras** (aw-RAW-ruhz). They are most brilliant in the polar regions. Why? As you will

Figure 23-15 *Auroras are bright bands of light in the upper atmosphere caused by electrically charged particles.*

Activity

Listening to the Radio

To find out from how far away radio waves can be received during the day and night, try the following: Listen to an AM radio during the day and late at night. Record the number of stations you can receive during the day and at night. Record what city these stations are broadcasting from. Plot the location of these stations on a map.

Answer the following questions:

1. Which of the radio stations you were able to receive during the day was the farthest away? At night?

2. How many kilometers away is the farthest station you heard during the day? During the night?

3. On the average, the ionosphere at night is higher above the earth's surface. What happens to radio signals when the ionosphere is higher?

see in the next section, the earth is like a giant magnet. The ends of this magnet are in the polar regions. Electrically charged particles are attracted toward the ends of this magnet.

SECTION REVIEW

1. In what layer does weather take place?
2. List two reasons that airplanes fly in the stratosphere.
3. Which is the coldest layer of the atmosphere?
4. In what layer are ions and auroras found?

23-2   The Magnetosphere

Place a pane of thin glass over a bar magnet. Sprinkle some iron filings over the top of the glass. Tap it gently. The tapping moves the filings and

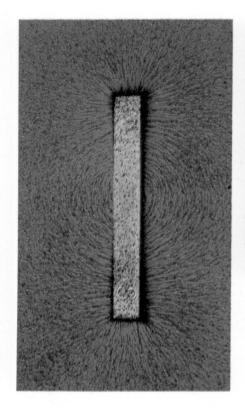

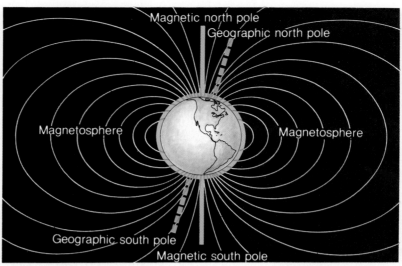

Figure 23-16 *The earth acts like a giant bar magnet* (right) *whose lines of force produce the same pattern as a small bar magnet* (left).

they form a pattern around the magnet, as shown in Figure 23-16.

The pattern of the iron filings shows you the invisible lines of force that are between the north and south poles of a bar magnet. The earth acts like a giant bar magnet whose lines of force produce the same pattern.

You can see in Figure 23-16 that the magnetic poles of the earth are in a different location from the geographic poles. The magnetic north pole is near Bathurst Island in northern Canada, about 1600 kilometers from the geographic north pole. The magnetic south pole is in Wilkes Land, a part of Antarctica, about 2570 kilometers from the geographic south pole.

The magnetic field around the earth extends beyond the earth's atmosphere. This field is called the **magnetosphere** (mag-NEE-toh-sfeer). The magnetosphere begins at an altitude of about 1000 kilometers and extends out into space about 64,000 kilometers on the side of the earth facing the sun. This magnetic field extends even farther out into space on the other side of the earth. Why? The difference is caused by streams of electrically charged ions from the sun. These ions form a kind of solar wind. This wind pushes the magnetosphere farther into space on the side of the earth away from the sun.

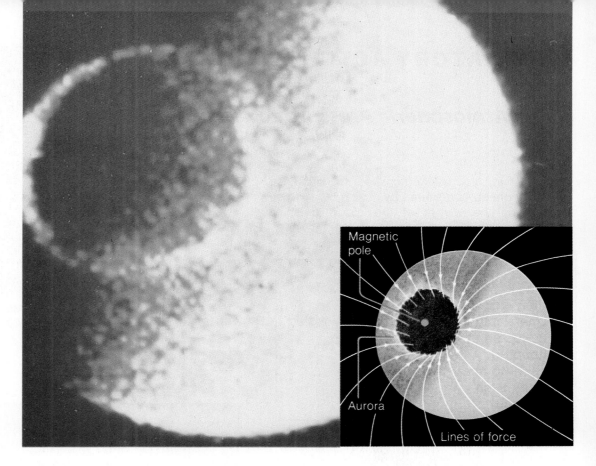

Labels on figure:
Magnetic pole
Aurora
Lines of force

What causes the earth's magnetic field? **Most scientists believe that the magnetosphere probably is caused by a combination of the earth's rotation and electric currents in the earth's core.** As the earth spins, these currents produce the magnetosphere.

By studying the magnetic direction of iron particles found in Earth's rocks, scientists such as Allan Cox and Richard Doell of the U.S. Geological Survey have discovered that Earth's magnetic poles have reversed many times. When poles reverse, magnetic north becomes magnetic south, and magnetic south becomes magnetic north. It is estimated that the magnetic poles have reversed 171 times in the last 76 million years. How? Scientists do not yet know the answer.

Figure 23-17 *An entire aurora was photographed for the first time by a satellite approximately 22,000 kilometers above the earth's magnetic north pole on September 15, 1981. An artist's drawing shows the magnetic lines of force that give the aurora its shape (lower right).*

SECTION REVIEW

1. What is the magnetosphere?
2. What may cause the earth's magnetic field?
3. How do scientists know that magnetic poles have reversed?

LABORATORY ACTIVITY

Using Atmospheric Pressure to Crush a Can

Purpose

In this activity, you will demonstrate the presence of atmospheric pressure by using the force caused by the weight of the air to crush a metal can.

Materials *(per group)*

Safety goggles
A metal can that can be securely sealed
Graduated cylinder
Tripod
Bunsen burner
Oven mitten
Wire gauze

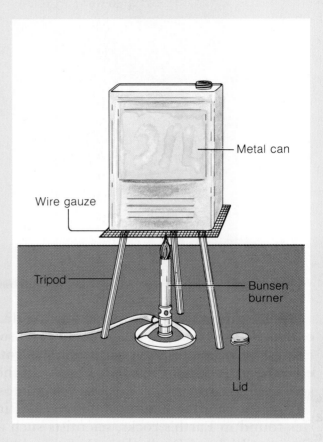

Metal can

Wire gauze

Tripod

Bunsen burner

Lid

Procedure

1. Put on your safety goggles and wear them during the entire activity.
2. Add 200 mL of water to a metal can. Place the unsealed can on a tripod. Position a Bunsen burner under the can and light it. **CAUTION:** *Be careful when lighting the Bunsen burner.*
3. Heat the water to boiling and allow it to boil for a few minutes after you have seen condensed water droplets leaving the opening of the can. Heating the liquid water will cause it to change to water vapor, which will force the air out of the can.
4. Turn off the Bunsen burner. Using the oven mitten, hold the heated can and carefully place the top on the can. Be sure it is on securely. **CAUTION:** *Be very careful; the can will be extremely hot.*

5. At the sink, carefully pour cold water over the hot can to cool it.

Observations and Conclusions

1. What happened when the heated can was sealed and allowed to cool? Why?
2. Describe a procedure to restore the can to its original state.

CHAPTER REVIEW

SUMMARY

23-1 The Layers of the Atmosphere

- Air pressure will decrease as altitude increases.

- Warm air is less dense than cold air, and so it rises.

- The atmosphere is divided into four layers based on temperature changes.

- The troposphere contains most of the earth's air. It is the weather layer. The temperature in the troposphere decreases with increasing altitude but then levels off.

- The stratosphere contains ozone, which absorbs ultraviolet rays from the sun. This accounts for the gradual warming within the stratosphere.

- The jet stream is the narrow, fast-moving current of air found between the troposphere and the stratosphere.

- The mesosphere is the coldest part of the atmosphere.

- Meteoroids, chunks of rocklike matter from outer space, are found in the mesosphere. A meteoroid burning up in the mesosphere is called a meteor.

- The thermosphere, the outer limit of the atmosphere, is heated by the sun's energy. It contains electrically charged particles called ions in an area called the ionosphere. A stream of these ions causes auroras.

23-2 The Magnetosphere

- The earth acts like a giant bar magnet surrounded by a magnetic field called the magnetosphere. This magnetic field is probably the result of the combination of the earth's rotation and electric currents in its core.

VOCABULARY

Define each term in a complete sentence.

air pressure　　　　　　　　**meteor**
aurora　　　　　　　　　　　**meteoroid**
ion　　　　　　　　　　　　　**ozone**
ionosphere　　　　　　　　　**stratosphere**
jet stream　　　　　　　　　**thermosphere**
magnetosphere　　　　　　　**troposphere**
mesosphere

CONTENT REVIEW: MULTIPLE CHOICE

Choose the letter of the answer that best completes each statement.

1. The force pressing down on the earth's surface due to the weight of the air is called air
a. density.　　b. mass.　　c. temperature.　　d. pressure.

2. Generally, as air rises it expands, and its temperature as recorded by an ordinary thermometer
a. decreases.　　b. increases.
c. remains the same.　　d. first increases, then decreases.

3. The division of the earth's atmosphere into four layers is based on
  a. surface pressure.   b. wind currents.
  c. temperature.   d. density.
4. The weather layer of the atmosphere is the
  a. troposphere.   b. stratosphere.
  c. mesosphere.   d. thermosphere.
5. As the altitude increases within the troposphere, the temperature
  a. increases continuously.
  b. increases and then decreases.
  c. decreases and then increases.
  d. decreases and then levels off.
6. The layer of the atmosphere that extends from about 16 kilometers to about
  48 kilometers above the earth's surface is called the
  a. mesosphere.   b. stratosphere.
  c. troposphere.   d. thermosphere.
7. A high-energy form of oxygen produced when oxygen reacts with sunlight is
  a. hydrogen.   b. helium.   c. water vapor.   d. ozone.
8. The coldest layer of the atmosphere is the
  a. mesosphere.   b. stratosphere.   c. ionosphere.   d. troposphere.
9. The upper layer of the atmosphere is the
  a. mesosphere.   b. thermosphere.
  c. stratosphere.   d. troposphere.
10. Scientists believe that the earth's magnetic field is caused by
  a. a combination of the earth's revolution and rotation.
  b. a combination of the earth's revolution and electric currents in its core.
  c. a combination of the earth's rotation and electric currents in its core.
  d. a combination of the magnetic poles and geographic poles.

CONTENT REVIEW: COMPLETION

Fill in the word or words that best complete each statement.

1. Within the atmosphere, as the altitude decreases, the air pressure _____.
2. Clouds, dust, and pollution are characteristics of the layer of the atmosphere called the _____.
3. Because there are no air currents or storms, pilots prefer to fly in the layer of the atmosphere called the _____.
4. The _____ layer in the stratosphere shields the earth from harmful ultraviolet rays.
5. The narrow, fast-moving current of air that forms at the boundary of the troposphere and the stratosphere is known as the _____.

6. The layer of the atmosphere characterized by the lowest ordinary temperatures and very little oxygen is the _____.
7. Chunks of rocklike matter from outer space are called _____.
8. Electrically charged particles found in the thermosphere are _____.
9. The glowing of the sky due to a stream of electrically charged particles is called a(n) _____.
10. The area beyond the earth's atmosphere that is a magnetic field is known as the _____.

CONTENT REVIEW: TRUE OR FALSE

Determine whether each statement is true or false. If it is true, write "true." If it is false, change the underlined word or words to make the statement true.

1. Warm air is <u>less</u> dense than cold air.
2. Most of the air is in the <u>stratosphere</u>.
3. Sunlight and oxygen <u>react</u> in the stratosphere to form the gas <u>peroxide</u>.
4. The coldest part of the <u>atmosphere</u> is the <u>mesosphere</u>.
5. <u>A</u> meteoroid burning up in the mesosphere is called a <u>northern light</u>.
6. The part of the <u>thermosphere</u> in which charged particles can be used to transmit radio waves is the <u>mesosphere</u>.
7. Magnetic lines of force are the strongest at the <u>poles</u> of a magnet.
8. The earth's magnetic poles <u>are not</u> in the same place as the earth's geographic poles.
9. The magnetic field around the earth extends farthest into space on the side of the earth facing <u>toward</u> the sun.
10. Most scientists believe that the earth's <u>revolution</u> is partly responsible for its magnetic field.

CONCEPT REVIEW: SKILL BUILDING

Use the skills you have developed in the chapter to complete each activity.

1. **Making comparisons** Compare the earth to a magnet.
2. **Making calculations** Figure 23-9 shows the layers of the earth's atmosphere and the altitudes at which they begin and end. Use this information to calculate the average thickness of each layer.
3. **Relating concepts** In the 1968 Summer Olympic Games held in Mexico City, Mexico, long jumper Bob Beamon set a world record of 8.90 meters. The altitude of Mexico City is 2309 meters. Relate this to the density of air and the resistance the air offers a jumper. Then explain Beamon's extraordinary jump.
4. **Applying concepts** Airline guides give flying time from Seattle, Washington, to New York, New York, as 5 hours, 5 minutes. The reverse trip from New York to Seattle takes 5 hours, 35 minutes. Explain this difference in travel time.
5. **Making graphs** Compare the temperatures found in the four main layers of the atmosphere by drawing a line graph of the data. Plot the altitude of the layers on the X-axis and the temperatures on the Y-axis. Use the average winter or summer temperature in your area as the beginning of the troposphere. Then explain why your graph is *not* a straight line.

CONCEPT REVIEW: ESSAY

Discuss each of the following in a brief paragraph.

1. Why do auroras appear near magnetic poles?
2. How might life on the earth be affected if the ozone layer were destroyed by the use of certain chemicals?
3. Describe the temperature changes in the four main layers of the atmosphere.
4. What is the magnetosphere? What are its possible causes?
5. Explain why air pressure decreases with altitude. What effect does this decrease have on air temperature?
6. Describe the ionosphere. Explain why it is important in transmitting radio waves.

William Haxby Maps the Invisible Ocean Floor

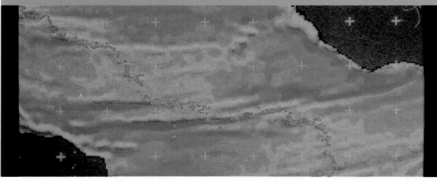

William Haxby's undersea maps provided a view of the ocean floor never before seen by people. In this photo, parts of Africa and South America are shown in gray. Red dots show locations of underwater earthquakes. Dark blue indicates areas of the ocean that have a greater depth than light-colored areas.

Vast canyons and craggy mountains make the ocean floor as mysterious as the surface of a far-off planet. It may be centuries before the bottom of the world's seas are fully explored. Yet using information from a space satellite, a 33-year-old scientist has created a startling map of the undersea landscape. This map is almost as detailed as if the water had been drained out of the seas and a man had walked over the land, making a map as he went.

That man is William Haxby of the Lamont Geological Observatory in Palisades, New York. Haxby fed readings from the satellite *Seasat* into a computer. Using computer graphics, he produced a three-dimensional map in vivid colors. This map provided a view of the ocean floor never before seen by people. Cracks in the sea bottom, underwater volcanoes, and other features of the ocean floor popped up on Haxby's map. These features provided new evidence about some of the most important earth science theories.

One of these theories, continental drift, suggests that all continents were once part of a single, large landmass. This landmass gradually broke up into the fragments now called continents. And the continents drifted to their present positions. Another theory, called plate tectonics, states that the earth's crust is made up of a number of very large plates. Heat and motion deep within the earth cause the plates to move. The movement of plates triggers earthquakes, thrusts up mountain ranges, and cuts deep ridges.

Haxby's map shows many signs of plate movement along the sea floor. One deep crack under the Indian Ocean may have been made when India drifted away from Antarctica and headed for Asia millions of years ago. Geologists believe a twisting ridge on the ocean floor off the southern tip of Africa was also formed millions of years ago, when Africa, South America, and Antarctica separated. The ridge, concealed under layers of sediment, was detected by Haxby's computer.

Mapping the Ocean Floor

Haxby started his mapping project, which took 18 months, in 1981. His work was based on *Seasat's* measurements of height differences on the sea's surface. Even if there were no waves or wind, Haxby points out that the surface of the ocean would not be perfectly flat. The height of the sea's surface varies by dozens of meters from one place to another. The reason for the variations in the sea's surface is the gravitational pull of structures on the bottom. Structures with large mass, such as undersea mountains, pull on the water with more force than those with less mass, such as canyons. The stronger the pull, the more water is attracted to a place above the structure. "As a result," says Haxby, "water piles up and there is a bump in the sea over a big object." So the sea surface imitates the sea bottom.

Measurements of differences in the sea's surface were recorded on *Seasat* by an instrument called an altimeter. It measured distances between the satellite and the surface of the sea to within a few centimeters. The satellite sent out 1000 electronic pulses a second. The altimeter measured the time it took for the pulses to hit the sea's surface and bounce back. Launched in 1978 for a five-year orbit, *Seasat* became silent after three months due to a short circuit in its electrical system. But the eight billion readings it had radioed back to tracking stations on the earth were enough for Haxby to start his computer work.

Tall and slender, Haxby has been interested in geology since his boyhood, when he was a "rockhound." At the University of Minnesota, he became interested in continental drift and plate tectonics. He eventually did graduate work in geophysics, leading to a doctoral degree from Cornell University. When he first began computer analysis of the satellite information, however, he did not intend to map the

William Haxby is an expert on continental drift and plate tectonics. His maps of the sea floor have helped scientists all over the world solve riddles about the earth.

entire ocean bottom. All he wanted to do was chart some small areas by matching sea surface heights with the gravitational forces that created them. This would enable him to figure out the mass of objects on the sea floor. His first maps were so detailed, however, that Haxby decided to go further.

Colorful Results

Sitting at his computer, often working late into the night, Haxby gradually expanded his map to include all of the ocean floor. He assigned different colors—ranging from blue to pink—to various sea levels. More than 250 different color intensities helped him create his three-dimensional map. Ridges, mountains, trenches, and canyons stand out by color. The detail—Haxby can pinpoint objects as small as 30 kilometers across—and colors reveal structures that are not on other large maps of the sea bottom. In fact, the images produced by Haxby's computer look so real that people looking at the images feel as if they are standing on the bottom of the sea. And around the globe, scientists now use Haxby's maps to help solve riddles about the earth.

Lakes affect the land around them. Runoff from a lake feeds surrounding trees and plants. More plant life attracts birds and animals to the area. But artificial lakes, if not well planned, can harm the environment.

Should People Build Lakes ?

The Benefits May Be Obvious, But What Are the Drawbacks?

Although it was a tiring trip, I looked forward to seeing my friend Jeff again. But I didn't look forward to leaving the air-conditioned comfort of the bus.

All around me, the landscape was dry, dusty, and sun-baked. There were few trees. I knew the temperature outside must be about 38° C.

Moments later, as we pulled into town, I spotted Jeff's car. And there was Jeff, looking tanned and happy.

I was neither tanned nor happy by the time we reached Jeff's house about four miles out of town. In fact, I was hot, dusty, and sweaty. So, Jeff's suggestion that we go for a swim at a nearby lake was very welcome. The suggestion was also surprising.

"I don't remember any lakes in this area," I remarked.

Jeff replied, "It's brand new. It was built since the last time you were here."

I had always thought that lakes were created only by nature way back when the earth was young. Then I realized that Jeff's artificial lake was probably no more than a muddy pond.

Did I get a pleasant surprise when we arrived at the lake! A great expanse of beautiful, clean water sparkled before us. It was surrounded by green grass, bushes, and young trees. There were sandy beaches at several spots along the winding shore. People were swimming and fishing in the clear water. A few boats bobbed on the lake's surface.

Lakes Influence Climate

"This is great," I said. "Even the air here feels fresher and cooler."

"Lakes influence local climate and vegetation," Jeff responded. "Water vapor rising from the lake surface makes the air moist and cool. Wait until you come back in a few years. The trees will be taller and the greenery will have spread. It will be a brand new ecosystem."

"But where does the water for this new lake come from?" I asked.

"The water for this lake comes from an underground spring," Jeff replied. "It's part of the groundwater system. There's lots of water down there."

"Do all artificial lakes get their water from underground springs?"

"Oh, no! Most of these lakes are created by damming rivers or streams. A few have their water piped in. If necessary, we could pipe water all the way down from Canada."

Over the following two weeks, I became very fond of Jeff's lake. In a dry, hot, dusty world, it was a delightful change. I was convinced that it would be a good idea to build lakes in all the dry regions of the country.

Life and Death of Lakes

By the time I got home, I was fascinated by the subject of lakes. But as I learned more and more about lakes, I realized that artificial lakes could have serious drawbacks as well as benefits. The drawbacks are caused by the very nature of lakes.

For example, all lakes eventually die. But artificial lakes tend to have much shorter life spans than natural lakes.

Lakes die in various ways. For one thing, water evaporates from the surface. If the loss of water through evaporation is greater than the incoming flow of water, the level of the lake will go down rapidly.

Artificial lakes tend to have shorter lives than do natural lakes. In each case, old age often turns a lake into a swamp.

Lake Meade in Nevada is an artificial lake that is a recreation spot for many people.

This is a problem especially in hot, dry areas. So unless the flow of water from the underground spring into Jeff's lake is greater than the evaporation from its surface, that lake might disappear in just a few years.

Evaporation is not the only thing that kills a lake. Water flowing into a lake is likely to carry with it large quantities of soil, sand, salts, and minerals. This material settles on the bottom of a lake to form a layer of sediment. It may be joined by leaves, branches, and other decaying vegetation.

Layer by layer, the sediment builds up. And if this process is combined with evaporation, a once clear lake might quickly turn into a muddy swamp.

This is more likely to happen to an artificial lake than to a natural lake. The reason is that artificial lakes are usually shallow and built in areas where water is scarce to begin with. Also, soil and sand are usually more easily washed into a lake in those areas.

A number of lakes that were built for resort communities over the past 30 years have turned into swamps. Others have become bitter or salty as a result of the seepage of fertilizers from surrounding farms and from the fall of acid rain—rain polluted by smoke and gases from industry.

A big drawback of creating lakes that might soon die is that water that could be used for other purposes is wasted. Also, taking great amounts of water from the ground may injure the earth. In Arizona, for example, so much water has been pumped out of the ground that great cracks have opened in the earth's surface. As ground water is removed, empty spaces form deep under ground. These spaces can collapse, creating depressions called sinkholes that can swallow homes and people.

In order for a lake to survive over a long period, it should be deep. Its water output should not exceed its input. And the water in the lake should be able to circulate. Care should be taken to prevent the buildup of soil, sand, salts, acids, fertilizers, and other pollutants. If these things are not considered, it might be better not to build any lakes at all. What do you think?

the longest winter

The team of Survivors shivered as the bouncing raft made its way across the river. An icy July wind whipped up the water all around the raft. The shore to which the Survivors were heading was covered with a thick coat of new snow. Although it was noon, the day was strangely dark.

Jonah, the Team Leader, peered into the strange darkness ahead. Members of the team lowered long poles into the water and pushed the raft toward the shore.

"There," Jonah said, pointing to a good landing spot. "Head for that flat beach."

Within seconds, the team members were ashore. Soon after, they had built a fire and cooked a meal of canned foods. And then they had settled down for Jonah's afternoon "story" about the past.

"Well, my friends," Jonah began, "this day makes me think of a frightening story that began long, long ago. If I remember correctly, the time was winter, 1983. The football season was in full swing. The holidays were approaching. Everything was kind of normal and happy. Of course, people were worried about such things as taxes and war. But that wasn't too unusual for those days. Then something happened that scared a lot of people. A group of some of the finest scientists in the United States made a report.

The scientists—there were 20 of them—had been trying to figure out what might happen if there were a nuclear war. And the report described what they had discovered."

Jonah paused and looked up at the dark sky as if searching for the July sun. But all he could see was an unbroken gray cloud that seemed to stretch forever. Jonah sighed and went on.

"To get an idea of what the scientists concluded, you must first know some basic facts about this planet of ours. Our atmosphere is very special. For one thing, as one of the scientists said, our atmosphere normally 'acts as a window for sunlight, but as a blanket for heat'."

"What does that cause," one of the Survivors asked as she tugged a blanket tightly around her shoulders.

"Normally, it causes the earth to stay warm. You see, the light from the sun is a form of energy. When this energy hits the earth, a new kind of energy is produced. It is called heat. Our atmosphere normally traps a lot of this heat. The heat keeps us warm. It keeps our oceans and lakes from freezing. And it makes plant and animal life possible on the earth. Now what do you think would happen if the 'window for sunlight' had a shade pulled down over it?"

A young Survivor, busily rubbing his hands together to keep them warm, answered. "The light from the sun would not reach the earth. So heat energy would not be produced. And the earth would cool down."

"Right," said Jonah. "And that's exactly what the scientists said could happen if there were a nuclear war. The scientists figured out that such a war would set millions of fires. Tons of black, sooty smoke would rise into the atmosphere. This smoke, they said, would have a mass of more than 100 million tons!

"The particles of soot would rise very high into the atmosphere, the scientists calculated. As high, maybe, as 20 kilometers. There the winds of the atmosphere would spread the soot over the entire earth.

"Now there's something very special about these two things—the soot and the height to which it would rise. Experiments showed that small particles of black soot absorb sunlight better than other kinds of particles. But that's not all. Researchers also found that the higher in the air particles are found, the longer they are going to stay there."

"That means that the soot closes the

'windows for sunlight.' And if the soot is high in the air, the 'window' stays closed for a long time," said one of the Survivors.

"Sadly, that's true," Jonah replied in a whisper. "Using the very best computers of the time, the scientists figured out that about 95 percent of the sun's light would not reach the ground. In their report, the scientists said that in some places the brightness at noon 'could be as low as that of a moonlit night'."

"Just like it is now," another Survivor said softly.

Jonah sighed. Telling this story wasn't easy, he thought to himself.

"So what would happen then?" asked another Survivor.

"Again, the computer came up with some answers. And they were chilling. Temperatures over land areas like North America, Europe, and Asia would suddenly drop about 40°C! That means that the average temperature in these places would be about −25°C."

"Why that's way below the freezing point of water!" exclaimed a Survivor.

"I'm afraid so," said Jonah. "And these freezing temperatures would last for months, said the scientists. The scientists called it a 'nuclear winter.' And the winter would cover the whole world."

"But that would kill off all sorts of plants, and animals that live on plants," the Survivor continued. "Why there would be no trees, no grass, no cows and sheep that feed on grass, no corn or wheat, no food for us."

"How about fish in lakes and streams?" another Survivor asked.

"Frozen solid," said Jonah about these waters. "Life in the water would die out."

"But wouldn't living things survive in the oceans and on the coasts of oceans? After all, ocean water holds a lot of heat for a long time. It might keep the land nearby warm enough to grow crops," suggested a Survivor.

"The scientists thought of that too," replied Jonah. "But the very cold air over the land meeting the warm air over the sea would cause terrible storms. Farming in areas struck by constant hurricanes would be impossible."

Jonah stopped speaking. Again he looked up at the sky, searching for a ray of sunshine. But there was none to be seen. The Survivors sat very quietly. Finally, one of them spoke.

"If that had happened, Jonah, the whole world would have looked and felt like this day. Everywhere it would be winter in July— not just here in Argentina and other southern countries. And we would be real survivors instead of members of an outdoor club."

"That's right," said Jonah, who now smiled. "But leaders of our country and of the other countries of the world saw to it that there was no nuclear war. So we still have our trees, and our grass, our forests, our animals . . . and our wilderness to explore. So let's pack up our gear and be on our way. We've got a long hike ahead of us."

For Further Reading

If you have an interest in a specific area of General Science or simply want to know more about the topics you are studying, one of the following books may open the door to an exciting learning adventure.

Chapter 1: Exploring Living Things

National Geographic Society. *Hidden Worlds.* Washington, DC: National Geographic Society.

Smith, N. F. *How Fast Do Your Oysters Grow? Investigate and Discover Through Science Projects.* New York: Messner.

Chapter 2: The Nature of Life

Adler, I. *How Life Began.* New York: John Day.

Silver, D. *Life on Earth.* New York: Random House.

Chapter 3: Cells

Cobb, V. *Cells: The Basic Structure of Life.* New York: Watts.

Silverstein, A., and V. B. Silverstein. *Cells: Building Blocks of Life.* Englewood Cliffs, NJ: Prentice-Hall.

Chapter 4: Tissues, Organs, and Organ Systems

Kelly, P. M. *The Mighty Human Cell.* New York: John Day.

Milne, L., and M. Milne. *The How and Why of Growing.* New York: Atheneum.

Chapter 5: Interactions Among Living Things

Carson, R. *The Edge of the Sea.* Boston: Houghton Mifflin.

Mabey, R. *Oak & Company.* New York: Greenwillow.

Chapter 6: Classification

Simon, S. *Strange Creatures.* New York: Four Winds/Scholastic.

Venino, S. *Amazing Animal Groups.* Washington, DC: National Geographic Society.

Chapter 7: Viruses, Bacteria, and Protists

Asimov, I. *How Did We Find Out About Germs?* New York: Walker.

Curtis, H. *The Marvelous Animals: An Introduction to the Protozoa.* New York: Natural History Press.

Chapter 8: Nonvascular Plants and Plantlike Organisms

Johnson, S. A. *Mushrooms.* Minneapolis: Lerner.

Shuttleworth, F. S., and H. S. Zim. *Non-Flowering Plants.* New York: Golden Press.

Chapter 9: Vascular Plants

Bauman, R. P. *Plants as Pets.* New York: Dodd, Mead.

Varnard, P. *Don't Tickle the Elephant Tree: Sensitive Plants.* New York: Messner.

Chapter 10: Animals: Invertebrates

Dallinger, J. *Grasshoppers.* Minneapolis: Lerner.

Johnson, S. A. *Snails.* Minneapolis: Lerner.

Chapter 11: Animals: Vertebrates

Rowland-Entwistle, T. *Illustrated Facts and Records Book of Animals.* New York: Arco.

Sadoway, M. *Owls: Hunters of the Night.* Minneapolis: Lerner.

Chapter 12: Mammals

Boitani, L. *Simon and Schuster's Guide to Mammals.* New York: Simon & Schuster.

Patent, D. *Whales: Giants of the Deep.* New York: Holiday House.

Chapter 13: General Properties of Matter

Asimov, I. *A Short History of Chemistry.* Garden City, NY: Anchor Books.

Lapp, R. E., and the editors of Time–Life Books. *Matter.* New York: Time–Life Books, Inc.

Chapter 14: Physical and Chemical Changes

Adler, I., *The Wonders of Physics: An Introduction to the Physical World.* New York: Golden Press.

Cobb, V. *Gobs of Goo.* New York: Lippincott.

Chapter 15: Atoms and Molecules

Asimov, I. *How Did We Find Out About Atoms?* New York: Walker.

Frisch, O. J. *Working With Atoms.* New York: Basic Books.

Chapter 16: Elements and Compounds

Drummond, A. H. *Molecules in the Service of Man.* Philadelphia: Lippincott.

Hyde, M. O. *Molecules Today and Tomorrow.* New York: McGraw-Hill.

Chapter 17: Mixtures and Solutions

Dickinson, E. *Colloids in Foods.* New York: Elsevier.

Stone, A. H. *The Chemistry of a Lemon.* Englewood Cliffs, NJ: Prentice-Hall.

Chapter 18: Minerals

Gilbert, M. *The Science Hobby Book of Rocks and Minerals.* Minneapolis: Lerner.

O'Neil, P., and the editors of Time–Life Books. *Planet Earth: Gemstones.* Alexandria, VA: Time–Life Books, Inc.

Chapter 19: Rocks

Gallant, R. A., and C. J. Schubeth. *Discovering Rocks and Minerals: A Nature and Science Guide to Their Collection and Identification.* New York: Natural History Press.

Shepherd, W. *Wealth from the Ground.* New York: John Day.

Chapter 20: Soils

Graham, A., and F. Graham. *The Changing Desert.* New York: Scribner's.

Shimer, J. A. *The Changing Earth: An Introduction to Geology.* New York: Barnes & Noble.

Chapter 21: Internal Structure of the Earth

Adler, I., and R. Adler. *The Earth's Crust.* New York: John Day.

Matthews, W. H. *Introducing the Earth.* New York: Dodd, Mead.

Chapter 22: Surface Features of the Earth

Bauer, E. *Wonders of the Earth.* New York: Watts.

Jacobs, L., Jr. *The Shapes of Our Land.* New York: Putnam.

Chapter 23: Structure of the Atmosphere

Chandler, T. J. *The Air Around Us: Man Looks at His Atmosphere.* New York: Natural History Press.

Weiss, M. *Storms: From the Inside Out.* New York: Julian Messner.

Appendix A THE METRIC SYSTEM

The metric system of measurement is used by scientists throughout the world. It is based on units of ten. Each unit is ten times larger or ten times smaller than the next unit. The most commonly used units of the metric system are given below. After you have finished reading about the metric system, try to put it to use. How tall are you in metrics? What is your mass? What is your body temperature in degrees Celsius?

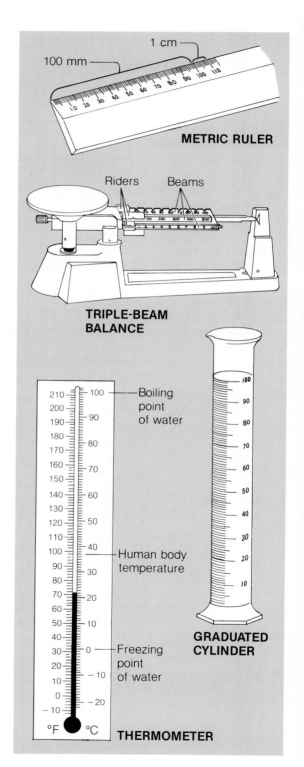

METRIC RULER

TRIPLE-BEAM BALANCE

Riders Beams

GRADUATED CYLINDER

THERMOMETER

Boiling point of water

Human body temperature

Freezing point of water

COMMONLY USED METRIC UNITS

Length   The distance from one point to another

meter (m)

(a meter is slightly longer than a yard)

1 meter = 1000 millimeters (mm)

1 meter = 100 centimeters (cm)

1000 meters = 1 kilometer (km)

Volume   The amount of space an object takes up

liter (L)

(a liter is slightly larger than a quart)

1 liter = 1000 milliliters (mL)

Mass   The amount of matter in an object

gram (g)

(a gram has a mass equal to about one paper clip)

1000 grams = 1 kilogram (kg)

Temperature   The measure of hotness or coldness

degrees Celsius (°C)   0°C = freezing point of water

100°C = boiling point of water

METRIC–ENGLISH EQUIVALENTS

2.54 centimeters (cm) = 1 inch (in.)
1 meter (m) = 39.37 inches (in.)
1 kilometer (km) = 0.62 miles (mi)
1 liter (L) = 1.06 quarts (qt)
250 milliliters (mL) = 1 cup (c)
1 kilogram (kg) = 2.2 pounds (lb)
28.3 grams (g) = 1 ounce (oz)
°C = 5/9 x (°F – 32)

Appendix B THE LABORATORY BALANCE

The laboratory balance is an important tool in scientific investigations. You can use the balance to determine the mass of materials that you study or experiment with in the laboratory.

Different kinds of balances are used in the laboratory. One kind of balance is the double-pan balance. Another kind of balance is the triple-beam balance. The balance that you may use in your science class is probably similar to one of the balances illustrated in this appendix. To use the balance properly, you should learn the name, function, and location of each part of the balance you are using.

THE DOUBLE-PAN BALANCE

The double-pan balance shown in this appendix has two beams. Some double-pan balances have only one beam. The beams are calibrated, or marked, in grams. The upper beam is divided into 10 major units of one gram each. Each of these units is further divided into units of 1/10 of a gram. The lower beam is divided into 20 units, and each unit is equal to 10 grams. The lower beam can be used to find the masses of objects up to 200 grams. Each beam has a rider that is moved to the right along the beam. The rider indicates the grams used to balance the object in the left pan.

Before you begin using the balance, you should be sure that both riders are pointing to zero grams on their beams and that the pans are empty. The balance should be on a flat, level surface. The pointer should be at the zero point. If your pointer does not read zero, slowly turn the adjustment knob until it does.

The following procedure can be used to find the mass of an object with a double-pan balance:

1. Place the object whose mass is to be determined on the left pan.

2. Move the rider on the lower beam to the 10-gram notch.

3. If the pointer moves to the right of the zero point on the scale, the object has a mass less than 10 grams. Return the rider on the lower beam to zero. Slowly move the rider on the upper beam until the pointer is at zero. The reading on the beam is the mass of the object.

4. If the pointer did not move to the right of the zero, move the rider on the lower beam notch by notch until it does. Move the rider back one notch. Then move the rider on the upper beam until the pointer is at zero. The sum of the readings on both beams is the mass of the object.

5. If the two riders are moved completely to the right side of the beams and the pointer remains to the left of the zero point, the object has a mass greater than the total mass that the balance can measure.

The total mass that most double-pan balances can measure is 210 grams. If an object has a mass greater than 210 grams, return the riders to zero.

PARTS OF A BALANCE AND THEIR FUNCTIONS

DOUBLE-PAN BALANCE

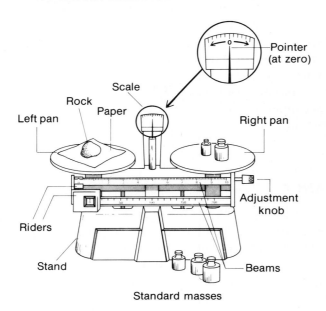

Standard masses

Scale Graduated instrument along which the pointer moves to show if the balance is balanced

Pointer Marker that indicates on the scale if the balance is balanced

Zero point Center line of the scale to which the pointer moves when the balance is balanced

Adjustment knob Knob used to balance the empty balance

Left pan Platform on which an object whose mass is to be determined is placed

Right pan Platform on which standard masses are placed

Beams Scales calibrated in grams

Riders Moveable markers that indicate the number of grams needed to balance an object

Stand Support for the balance

The following procedure can be used to find the mass of an object greater than 210 grams:

1. Place the standard masses on the right pan one at a time, starting with the largest, until the pointer remains to the right of the zero point.

2. Remove one of the large standard masses and replace it with a smaller one. Continue replacing the standard masses with smaller ones until the pointer remains to the left of the zero point. When the pointer remains to the left of the zero point, the mass of the object on the left pan is greater than the total mass of the standard masses on the right pan.

3. Move the rider on the lower beam and then the rider on the upper beam until the pointer stops at the zero point on the scale. The mass of the object is equal to the sum of the readings on the beams plus the mass of the standard masses.

THE TRIPLE-BEAM BALANCE

The triple-beam balance is a single-pan balance with three beams calibrated in grams. The back, or 100-gram, beam is divided into 10 units of 10 grams each. The middle, or 500-gram, beam is divided into 5 units of 100 grams each. The front, or 10-gram, beam is divided into 10 major units of 1 gram each. Each of these units is further divided into units of 1/10 of a gram.

TRIPLE-BEAM BALANCE

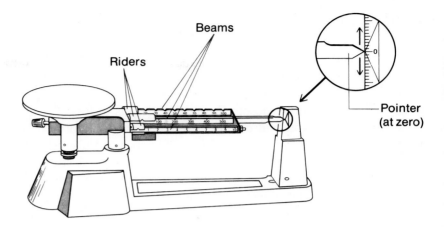

The following procedure can be used to find the mass of an object with a triple-beam balance:

1. Place the object whose mass is to be determined on the pan.

2. Move the rider on the middle beam notch by notch until the horizontal pointer drops below zero. Move the rider back one notch.

3. Move the rider on the front beam notch by notch until the pointer again drops below zero. Move the rider back one notch.

4. Slowly slide the rider along the back beam until the pointer stops at the zero point.

5. The mass of the object is equal to the sum of the readings on the three beams.

Appendix C THE MICROSCOPE

The microscope is an essential tool in the study of life science. It enables you to see things that are too small to be seen with the unaided eye. It also allows you to look more closely at the fine details of larger things.

The microscope you will use in your science class is probably similar to the one illustrated on the following page. This is a compound microscope. It is called compound because it has more than one lens. A simple microscope would only contain one lens. The lenses of the compound microscope are the parts that magnify the object being viewed.

Typically, a compound microscope has one lens in the eyepiece, the part you look through. The eyepiece lens usually has a magnification power of 10×. That is, if you were to look through the eyepiece alone, the object you were viewing would appear 10 times larger than it is.

The compound microscope may contain one or two other lenses. These two lenses are called the low- and high-power objective lenses. The low-power objective lens usually has a magnification of 10×. The high-power objective lens usually has a magnification of 40×. To figure out what the total magnification of your microscope is when using the eyepiece and an objective lens, multiply the powers of the lenses you are using. For example, eyepiece magnification (10×) multiplied by low-power objective lens magnification (10×) = 100× total magnification. What is the total magnification of your microscope using the eyepiece and the high-power objective lens?

To use the microscope properly, it is important to learn the name of each part, its function, and its location on your microscope. Keep the following procedures in mind when using the microscope:

1. Always carry the microscope with both hands. One hand should grasp the arm, and the other should support the base.

2. Place the microscope on the table with the arm toward you. The stage should be facing a light source.

3. Raise the body tube by turning the coarse adjustment knob.

4. Revolve the nosepiece so that the low-power objective lens (10×) is directly in line with the body tube. Click it into place. The low-power lens should be directly over the opening in the stage.

5. While looking through the eyepiece, adjust the diaphragm and the mirror so that the greatest amount of light is coming through the opening in the stage.

6. Place the slide to be viewed on the stage. Center the specimen to be viewed over the hole in the stage. Use the stage clips to hold the slide in position.

7. Look at the microscope from the side rather than through the eyepiece. In this way, you can watch as you use the coarse adjustment

MICROSCOPE PARTS AND THEIR FUNCTION

1. **Arm** Supports the body tube

2. **Eyepiece** Contains the magnifying lens you look through

3. **Body tube** Maintains the proper distance between the eyepiece and objective lenses

4. **Nosepiece** Holds high- and low-power objective lenses and can be rotated to change magnification

5. **Objective lenses** A low-power lens which usually provides 10X magnification, and a high-power lens which usually provides 40X magnification

6. **Stage clips** Hold the slide in place

7. **Stage** Supports the slide being viewed

8. **Diaphragm** Regulates the amount of light let into the body tube

9. **Mirror** Reflects the light upward through the diaphragm, the specimen, and the lenses

10. **Base** Supports the microscope

11. **Coarse adjustment knob** Moves the body tube up and down for focusing

12. **Fine adjustment knob** Moves the body tube slightly to sharpen the image

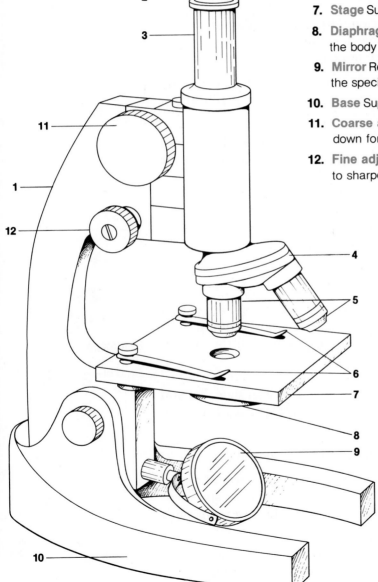

knob to lower the body tube until the low-power objective *almost* touches the slide. Do this slowly so you do not break the slide or damage the lens.

8. Now, looking through the eyepiece, observe the specimen. Use the coarse adjustment knob to *raise* the body tube, thus raising the low-power objective away from the slide. Continue to raise the body tube until the specimen comes into focus.

9. When viewing a specimen, be sure to keep both eyes open. Though this may seem strange at first, it is really much easier on your eyes. Keeping one eye closed may create a strain, and you might get a headache. Also, if you keep both eyes open, it is easier to draw diagrams of what you are observing. In this way, you do not have to turn your head away from the microscope as you draw.

10. To switch to the high-power objective lens (40 ×), look at the microscope from the side. Now, revolve the nosepiece so that the high-power objective lens clicks into place. Make sure the lens does not hit the slide.

11. Looking through the eyepiece, use only the fine adjustment knob to bring the specimen into focus. Why should you not use the coarse adjustment knob with the high-power objective?

12. Clean the microscope stage and lens when you are finished. To clean the lenses, use lens paper only. Other types of paper may scratch the lenses.

PREPARING A WET-MOUNT SLIDE

Most specimens to be observed with the compound microscope are placed on a slide in a liquid solution. This preparation is know as a wet-mount slide. To make a wet-mount slide, follow these directions along with the accompanying diagrams.

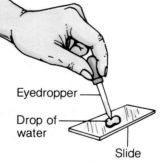

Eyedropper

Drop of water

Slide

1. Place the specimen to be observed in the middle of a clean slide. For you to observe any specimen with a compound microscope, the specimen must be thin enough for light to pass through it.

2. Using an eye dropper, place a drop of water on the specimen.

3. Place one side of a clean cover slip at the edge of the drop of water. Using a needle or probe, slowly lower the cover slip over the specimen and water. Try not to trap any air bubbles under the cover slip since these will interfere with your view of the specimen.

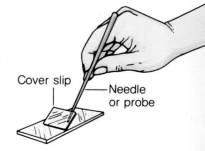

Cover slip

Needle or probe

4. Your wet-mount slide is now ready to be viewed with your microscope. Be sure you do not tilt the microscope when viewing a wet-mount slide. What do you think might happen if you did?

Glossary

air bladder: tiny grape-shaped structure that acts like an inflatable life-preserver in brown algae

air pressure: pressing force due to the weight of air

alga (AL-guh; plural: algae, AL-gee): member of the largest group of nonvascular plants

alloy: solid metal dissolved in another solid metal

amino acid: building block of protein

amorphous (uh-MOR-fuhs) **solid:** solid that does not keep a definite shape

anal pore: tiny opening through which a paramecium eliminates waste

angiosperm (AN-jee-oh-sperm): type of seed plant whose seeds are covered by a protective wall

annual ring: one year's growth of xylem cells

antibiotic: substance produced by helpful bacteria that destroys or weakens disease-causing bacteria

asexual reproduction: formation of an organism from a single parent

astronomy: study of planets, stars, and other objects beyond the earth

atom: tiny particle of matter consisting of a nucleus that contains protons and neutrons and an electron cloud that contains electrons

atomic mass: average of the masses of all the existing isotopes of an element

atomic mass unit (amu): unit used to measure the masses of subatomic particles; a proton has a mass of one amu

atomic number: number of protons in the nucleus of an atom; number that identifies the kind of atom

aurora (aw-RAW-ruh): bands of light in the upper atmosphere caused by electrically charged particles

autotroph (AWT-uh-trohf): organism that makes its own food from simple substances

bacillus (buh-SIL-uhs; plural: bacilli): rod-shaped bacterium

bacteriophage (bak-TEE-ree-uh-fayj): virus that infects bacterial cells

bacterium (plural: bacteria): unicellular microorganism

binary fission: reproductive process in which a cell divides into two cells

binomial nomenclature (bigh-NOH-mee-uhl NOH-muhn-klay-cher): naming system in which organisms are given two names: a genus and a species

bioluminescence (bigh-oh-loo-muh-NE-suhns): firefly-like glow produced by a kind of fire algae

boiling: process in which particles of a liquid change to gas, travel to the surface of the liquid, and then into the air

boiling point: temperature at which a liquid boils

botany: study of plants

Boyle's Law: law stating that the volume of a fixed amount of gas varies indirectly with the presure of the gas

budding: reproductive process in yeast, in which a new yeast cell is formed from a tiny bud

cambium (KAM-bee-uhm): growth tissue of the stem where xylem and phloem cells are produced

canine (KAY-nighn): pointed tooth next to the incisor

cap: fruiting body of a mushroom

carbohydrate: organic compound made up of the elements carbon, hydrogen, and oxygen, and a main source of energy for living things

carnivore: (KAR-ni-vor): flesh-eating animal

cartilage: flexible tissue that gives support and shape to body parts

catalyst: substance that speeds up or slows down chemical reactions, but is not itself changed by the reaction

cell: basic unit of structure and function in a living thing; building block of life

cell membrane: thin, flexible envelope of protoplasm that forms the outer covering of an animal cell and that is inside the cell wall of a plant cell; controls movement of materials into and out of the cell

cell wall: outermost boundary of plant and bacterial cells that is made of cellulose

Celsius: temperature scale used in the metric system at which water freezes at 0° and boils at 100°

Charles's Law: law stating that the volume of a fixed amount of gas varies directly with the temperature of the gas

chemical change: change a substance undergoes when it turns into another substance

chemical equation: description of a chemical reaction using symbols and formulas

chemical formula: combination of chemical symbols used as a shorthand for the names of chemical substances

chemical property: property that describes how a substance changes into another new substance

chemical reaction: process by which a substance is changed into another substance through a rearrangement or new combination of its atoms

chemical rock: sedimentary rock formed from large amounts of minerals when a body of water dries up

chemical symbol: shorthand way of representing the elements; usually consists of one or two letters, the first of which is always capitalized, but the second is never capitalized

chemistry: study of what substances are made of and how they change and combine

chlorophyll: green substance, needed for photosynthesis, found in green plant cells

chloroplast: large, irregularly shaped structure that contains the green pigment chlorophyll; food-making site in green plants

chromosome: thick, rodlike object found in the nucleus that directs the activities of the cell and passes on the traits of the cell to new cells

cilium (SIHL-ee-uhm; plural: cilia): small, hairlike projection on the outside of a cell

class: classification group between phylum and order

clastic rock: sedimentary rocks made up of rock fragments mixed with sand, clay, and mud

cleavage: breakage of a mineral along definite lines or smooth, flat surfaces

coastal plains: low, flat areas that average about 150 meters above sea level

coccus (KAHK-suhs; plural, cocci): sphere-shaped bacterium

coefficient (koh-uh-FI-shuhnt): number placed in front of a chemical formula in a chemical equation so that the equation is balanced

coldblooded: having a body temperature that can change somewhat with changes in the temperature of the environment

colloid (KAHL-oyd): homogeneous mixture in which the particles are mixed together but not dissolved

commensalism: symbiotic relationship in which one organism benefits and the other is neither helped nor harmed

community: the living part of an ecosystem; all the different organisms that live together in an area

competition: struggle among living things to get the proper amount of food, water, and energy from the environment

compound: substance made up of molecules that contain more than one kind of atom; two or more elements chemically combined

compound light microscope: microscope containing more than one lens that uses light to make an object look larger

condensation (kahn-den-SAY-shun): process in which a gas loses heat energy and changes into a liquid

conjugation (kahn-joo-GAY-shun): type of sexual reproduction in which hereditary material is exchanged

consumer: organism that feeds directly or indirectly on producers; heterotroph

continental glacier: very thick ice sheet that covers most of both polar regions

contour feather: largest bird feather needed for flight

control: experiment run exactly the same way as the experiment with the variable, but the variable is left out

core: center region of the earth

cotyledon (kaht-uh-LEE-duhn): leaflike structure of an embryo plant that stores food

crop: saclike organ that stores food in an earthworm

crust: thin outer layer on the earth's surface made up mainly of solid rocks

crystal (KRIS-tuhl): regular, repeating pattern of particles in a solid

crystalline solid: solid made up of crystals

cytoplasm: jellylike substance outside the nucleus

data: recorded observations and measurements

decomposer: organism that breaks down dead plants and animals into simpler substances

density: mass per unit volume, or how much mass is contained in a given volume of an object

diffusion: process by which food, oxygen, water, and other materials enter and leave a cell through openings in the cell membrane

digestion: process by which food is broken down into simpler substances

division of labor: division of the work that keeps an organism alive among the different parts of its body

DNA: (deoxyribonucleic acid) nucleic acid that stores the information needed to build proteins and carries genetic information about an organism

down feather: short, fuzzy bird feather that acts as insulation

ductility (duhk-TIHL-uh-tee): ability of a substance to be pulled into thin strands without breaking

ecology: study of the relationships and interactions of living things with one another and with their environment

ecosystem: group of organisms in an area that interact with one another and with their nonliving environment

electron: negatively charged particle that moves around the nucleus of an atom in a region called the electron cloud

electron cloud: space in which electrons are most likely to be found

electron microscope: microscope that uses a beam of electrons to magnify the image of an object

element (EL-uh-ment): pure substance made up of only one kind of atom that cannot be broken down into simpler substances by ordinary means

endoplasmic reticulum (en-doh-PLAZ-mik ri-TIK-yuh-luhm): maze of clear tubular passageways that leads out from the nuclear membrane; involved in the manufacture and transport of proteins

endospore: oval-shaped structure that protects a bacterium

energy level: most likely location in the electron cloud in which an electron can be found

environment: all the living and nonliving things with which an organism may interact

enzyme: special type of protein that regulates chemical activities within the body

epidermis (e-puh-DER-mis): outer protective layer of the leaf

evaporation (ee-va-puh-RA-shun): process in which a liquid changes into a gas by absorbing heat energy

excretion: process of getting rid of waste materials

exoskeleton: rigid, outer covering of an organism

extrusive (ek-STROO-sive) **rock:** igneous rock formed from melted rock or lava that cools and hardens at or near the earth's surface

eyespot: light-sensitive organ in lower organisms

family: classification group between order and genus

fat: energy-rich organic compound made up of carbon, hydrogen, and oxygen, that is solid at room temperature

fermentation: energy-releasing process in which sugars and starches are changed into alcohol and carbon dioxide

fertilization: joining of egg and sperm

flagellum (fla-JEL-um; plural, flagella): whiplike structure that propels some one-celled organisms

flammability (flam-uh-BIL-uh-tee): ability to burn

flower: structure containing the reproductive organs of the angiosperm

focus: underground center of an earthquake

food chain: illustration of how groups of organisms within an ecosystem get their food and energy

food web: all the food chains in an ecosystem

fracture: mineral breakage that forms an irregular surface that may be rough or jagged

freezing: change of a liquid to a solid

freezing point: temperature at which a liquid changes to a solid

frond: leaf of a fern plant

fruit: ripened ovary of an angiosperm

fruiting body: in a fungus, the spore-containing structure

fungus (FUHNG-guhs; plural: fungi): group of simple organisms that have no chlorophyll and must get food from other organisms

gas: phase in which matter has no definite shape or volume

gem: rare, very valuable, and beautiful mineral

genus (plural: genera): group of organisms that are closely related; classification group between family and species

germination (jer-muh-NA-shuhn): early growth stage of an embryo plant; also called sprouting

gill: structure through which fish and other aquatic animals breathe; in a mushroom, the spore-producing structure

gizzard: in an earthworm, the organ that grinds up food

glucose: simple sugar into which all carbohydrates are broken down in the body to produce energy

gravity: force of attraction between objects

ground water: water that has soaked into the ground

guard cell: sausage-shaped cell that regulates the opening and closing of stomata

gullet: funnel-shaped structure in the paramecium extending from the oral groove to the food vacuole

gymnosperm (JIM-nuh-sperm): type of seed plant whose seeds are not covered by a protective wall

habitat: place in which an organism lives

hardness: ability of a mineral to resist being scratched

herbaceous (her-BAY-shuhs) **stem:** green, soft stem

herbivore (HER-bi-vor): animal that eats only plants

heterogeneous (het-uhr-uh-JEEN-ee-uhs) **mixture:** mixture in which no two parts are identical

heterotroph (HET-uhr-u-trohf): organism that is not able to make its own food and thus feeds on other organisms

hibernation: winter sleep during which all body activities slow down

homeostasis (ho-mee-o-STAY-sis): ability of an organism to keep conditions inside its body the same even though conditions in its external environment change

homogeneous (ho-muh-JEEN-ee-uhs) mixture: mixture in which different parts seem to be identical

host: organism in which a parasite lives

humus: dark, rich soil made of decayed plant and animal matter combined with rocky soil particles

hypha (HIGH-fuh; plural: hyphae, HIGH-fee): threadlike structure in a fungus that produces digestive enzymes

hypothesis (high-PAH-thuh-sis): suggested solution to a scientific problem

iceberg: mass of free-floating ice that has broken off from the edges of the Arctic or Antarctic ice sheets

igneous (IG-nee-us) **rock:** rock formed from cooled and hardened magma or lava

incisor (in-SIGH-zer): one of the four front teeth used for biting

inertia (in-ER-shuh): property of a mass to resist changes in motion

ingestion: eating

inland plains: low, flat areas that average about 450 meters above sea level and are confined to the interior or central part of a country or region

inorganic: composed of material that is not and never was living

inorganic compound: compound that does not usually contain the element carbon

insoluble: cannot be dissolved in water

intrusive (in-TROO-siv) **rock:** rock that forms from melted rock or magma that cools and hardens deep below the earth's surface

invertebrate: animal without a backbone

ion: electrically charged particles

ionosphere (i-AH-nuh-sfeer): lower part of the thermosphere that contains ions

isotope (IGH-suh-tohp): atom of a substance that has the same number of protons but a different number of neutrons as another atom of the same substance

jet stream: narrow, fast-moving current of air that forms along the troposphere-stratosphere boundary

kilogram: basic unit of mass in the metric system

kingdom: largest classification grouping

larva: stage of insect that emerges from the egg

lava: magma that has reached the earth's surface

leaching: process in which rain washes minerals out of the top soil

lens: curved pieces of glass that bends light rays as they pass through it

lichen (LIGH-kuhn): organism made up of a fungus and an alga that live together

life span: maximum length of time a particular organism can be expected to live

liquid: phase in which matter has no definite shape but does have a definite volume

liter: basic unit of volume in the metric system

liverwort: nonvascular, green leaflike plant; similar to moss but smaller

luster: way a mineral reflects light

lysosome: small, round structure involved with the digestive activities of a cell

magma: hot, molten rock deep inside the earth

magnetosphere (mag-NEE-toh-sfeer): magnetic field of the earth

malleability (mal-ee-uh-BIHL-uh-tee): ability of a substance to be hammered into thin sheets without breaking

mammary gland: milk-producing gland in mammals

mantle: part of mollusk that produces material that makes up the hard shell; layer that extends from the edge of the liquid outer core to where the earth's crust begins

marsupial (mahr-SOO-ip-uhl): mammal that has a pouch

mass: amount of matter in an object

mass number: sum of the protons and the neutrons in the nucleus of an atom

matter: what all materials are made of

meiosis (migh-OH-sis): form of cell division that halves the number of chromosomes in a male and female sex cell as they form

melting: change of a solid to a liquid

melting point: temperature at which a solid changes to a liquid

mesosphere (MES-uh-sfeer): coldest layer of the atmosphere

metabolism (muh-TA-buh-li-zuhm): all chemical activities in an organims essential to life

metal: element that is a good conductor of heat and electricity, is shiny, has a high melting point, is ductile and malleable, and forms positive ions

metamorphic (met-uh-MAWR-fik) **rock:** rock changed by heat, pressure, or chemical action

metamorphosis (met-uh-MAWR-fuh-sis): change in appearance due to development

meteor (MEE-tee-er): bright trail or streak of light that results when a meteoroid burns up in the mesosphere

meteoroid (MEE-tu-uh-roid): chunk of rocklike matter from outer space

meter: basic unit of length in the metric system

metric system: universal system of measurement

microbiology: science of microorganisms

microscope: instrument that produces an enlarged image of an object

Mid-Atlantic Rift Valley: great crack, or rift, and the area on either side of it in the earth's crust that runs down the middle of a massive underwater mountain range in the Atlantic Ocean

Mid-Ocean Ridge: system of rift valleys and mountain ranges that extends for 74,000 kilometers under all the world's oceans

migrate: to move to a new environment during the course of a year

mineral: natural substance that forms in the earth

mitochondrion (plural: mitochondria): rod-shaped structure that is referred to as one of the powerhouses of a cell

mitosis (migh-TOH-sis): duplication and division of the nucleus and of the chromosomes during cell reproduction

mixture: two or more pure substances that are mixed but not chemically combined

Moho: boundary between earth's crust and mantle

Mohs (mohz) **hardness scale:** scale used to determine the hardness of a mineral

molecule (MAH-luh-kyool): smallest particle of a substance that has all the properties of that substance; made up to two or more atoms that are chemically bonded

monotreme (MAHN-uh-treem): egg-laying mammal

moss: nonvascular plant that contains chlorophyll

mountain belt: group of mountain ranges

mountain landscape: area of tall, jagged peaks, long slopes, and high, narrow ridges

mountain range: group of mountains

multicellular: having many cells

mutualism: symbiotic relationship in which both organisms benefit

nematocyst (NEM-uh-toh-sist): stinging cell around the mouth of a coelenterate

neutron: electrically neutral particle found in the nucleus of an atom

niche: everything an organism does and everything an organism needs within it habitat

nonmetal: element that is a poor conductor of heat and electricity, has a dull surface, low melting point, is brittle, breaks easily, and forms negative ions

nonvascular plant: plant that does not have transportation tubes to carry water and food

nuclear membrane: thin membrane that separates the nucleus from the protoplasm of the cell

nucleic acid: large organic compound that stores information that helps the body make the proteins it needs

nucleolus (noo-KLEE-uh-luhs): cell structure located in the nucleus and made up of RNA and protein; may play important role in making proteins for the cell

nucleus (NOO-klee-uhs; plural: nuclei, NOO-klee-igh): spherical cellular structure that directs all activities of the cell; positively charged center of an atom

oil: energy-rich organic compound made up of carbon, hydrogen, and oxygen that is liquid at room temperature

oral groove: mouthlike indentation in the paramecium

order: classification group between class and family

ore: rock from which metals and other minerals can be removed in usable amounts

organ: group of different tissues working together

organic compound: compound that contains the element carbon

organic rock: sedimentary rock built up from the remains of living things

organism: entire living thing that carries out all the basic life functions

osmosis: special type of diffusion by which water passes through the cell membrane

ovule (OH-vyool): structure that contains the female sex cells of a plant

ozone: high-energy form of oxygen that forms a layer mainly in the stratosphere

parasite (PA-ruh-sight): organism that feeds on other living organisms

parasitism: symbiotic relationship in which one organism benefits and the other is harmed

parent rock: solid rock found where soil is formed

permafrost: permanently frozen soil just below the surface

petal: colorful leaflike structure that surrounds the male and female reproductive organs in a flower

phase: state in which matter can exist; solid, liquid, gas, plasma are the phases of matter

pheromone (FER-uh-mohn): chemical substance given off by insects and other animals to attract a mate

phloem (FLOH-uhm): tubelike plant tissue that carries food down the plant

photosynthesis (foh-tuh-SIN-thuh-sis): process by which green plants make glucose for food by combining carbon dioxide and water by using the sun's energy

phylum (FY-luhm; plural: phyla): second largest classification group; between kingdom and class

physical change: change in which physical properties of a substance are altered, but the substance remains the same kind of matter

physical property: characteristic that distinguishes one type of matter from another and can be observed without changing the identity of the substance

physics: study of different forms of energy

pistil: female reproductive organ of the flower

placenta (pluh-SEN-tuh): structure through which developing young receive food and oxygen while in the mother

plains landscape: broad, flat lowland area divided into coastal or inland plains that are not far above sea level

plasma: phase in which matter is very high in energy and cannot be contained by the walls of ordinary matter; very rare on Earth

plateau landscape: broad, flat highland area usually more than 600 meters above sea level

pollen: particle containing the male sex cells of a plant

pollination: transfer of pollen to the stigma of a flower

population: group of the same type of organism living together in the same area

pore: opening on the outer surface of an animal through which materials enter and leave

precipitation (pree-sip-uh-TA-shun): water falling to the earth as rain, sleet, hail, or snow

primary waves (P waves): shock waves produced by a back-and-forth vibration of rock particles during an earthquake

producer: green plant that makes its own food; autotroph

property: quality or characteristic that describes an object

protein: organic compound made up of carbon, hydrogen, oxygen, nitrogen, and sometimes sulfur and phosphorus, necessary for the growth and repair of body structures

proton: positively charged particle found in the nucleus of an atom

protoplasm: all the living material found in both plant and animal cells

protozoan: unicellular animal-like organism

pseudopod: "false foot" in amoeba

pupa (PYOO-puh): stage in an insect's life cycle when it is wrapped in a cocoon

pure substance: substance that contains only one kind of molecule

quark (kwark): particle that makes up all subatomic nuclear particles

radula: filelike structure in the mouth of a univalve used to scrape food from an object

reproduction: process by which living things give rise to the same type of living thing

respiration: process by which living things take in oxygen and use it to produce energy

response: some action or movement of the organism brought on by a stimulus

rhizoid (RIGH-zoid): rootlike structure through which mosses absorb water

rhizome (RIGH-zohm): stem growing along or under the ground

ribosome: grainlike body made up of RNA and attached to the inner surface of an endoplasmic passageway; a protein-making site of the cell

RNA (ribonucleic acid): nucleic acid that "reads" the genetic information carried by DNA and guides the protein-making process

rock cycle: continuous changing of rocks from one kind to another

saprophyte (SA-pruh-fight): organism that feeds on dead things

scavenger: animal consumer that feeds on the bodies of dead animals

scientific method: basic steps that scientists follow in uncovering facts and solving scientific problems

secondary waves (S waves): shock waves produced by an up-and-down or side-to-side vibration of rock particles during an earthquake

sedimentary (sed-uh-MEN-tuh-ree) **rock:** rock formed in layers

seed: structure from which a plant grows; contains a young plant, stored food, and a seed coat

seismic (SIGHZ-mihk) **wave:** shock wave produced by an earthquake

seismograph (SIGHZ-muh-graf): instrument that records shock waves due to earthquakes

sepal (SEE-puhl): leaflike structure enclosing a flower when it is still a bud

sexual reproduction: formation of an organism from the uniting of two different sex cells

shadow zone: area in which no earthquake waves are detected by seismographs

slime mold: bloblike organism found on decaying material

solid: phase in which matter has a definite shape and volume

solubility: amount of solute that will completely dissolve in a given amount of solvent at a specific temperature

soluble (SAHL-yuh-bul): can be dissolved in water

solute (SAHL-yoot): in a solution, substance that is dissolved

solution: homogeneous mixture in which particles are dissolved in one another

solvent (SAHL-vunt): in a solution, substance that does the dissolving

species (SPEE-sheez): group of organisms that are able to interbreed, or produce young

spirillum (spigh-RIL-uhm); plural: spirilla): spiral-shaped bacterium

spontaneous generation: theory that states that life can spring from nonliving matter

stalk: in a mushroom, a stemlike structure with a ring near its top

stamen (STAH-muhn): male reproductive organ of the flower

stimulus: signal to which an organism reacts

stoma (STOH-muh; plural: stomata): opening in the surface of a leaf through which carbon dioxide enters and oxygen and water vapor pass out

stratosphere (STRAT-uh-sfeer): layer of the atmosphere where the ozone layer and jet streams are found

streak: color of a mineral in powder form

subatomic particle: particle that is smaller than an atom

sublimation (suhb-luh-MAY-shuhn): process in which the surface particles of a solid change directly into gas

subscript: number placed to the lower right of a chemical symbol to indicate the number of atoms of the element in the compound

subsoil: level beneath topsoil that is made up of larger bits of rock with little or no humus

suspension: heterogenious mixture containing particles that are mixed together but not dissolved

swim bladder: sac in a bony fish that enables the fish to rise or sink in water

symbiosis: (sim-bigh-OH-sis): relationship in which one organism lives on, near, or even inside another organism

system: group of organs that work together to perform certain functions

talon: sharp claw on the toe of birds of prey

taxonomy: (tak-SAH-nuh-mee): science of classification

thermosphere (THER-muh-sfeer): upper layer of the atmosphere where the ionosphere and auroras are found

tissue: group of cells similar in structure and joined together to perform a special function

topsoil: uppermost level of soil that is made of a mixture of small grains of rock and decayed matter of plants and animals

toxin: poison produced by bacteria

transpiration: process for regulating water loss through the leaves of a plant

troposphere: (TRAH-puh-sfeer): lowest layer of the atmosphere where all the earth's weather occurs

unicellular: having one cell

vacuole (VA-kyoo-ohl): large, round sac floating in the cytoplasm of a cell in which water, food, enzymes, and other materials are stored

valley glacier: long, narrow glacier that moves down hill between the steep sides of mountain valleys

vaporization (vay-puhr-uh-ZAY-shuhn): change of a liquid to a gas

variable: factor being tested in an experiment

vascular plant: plant that contains transporting tubes that carry material throughout the plant

venom: poison produced in special glands by snakes

vertebra (plural: vertebrae): one of the bones that make up a vertebrate's backbone

vertebrate (VER-tuh-brit): animal with a backbone

virus: tiny particle that contains hereditary material

volume: amount of space an object takes up

warmblooded: able to maintain a constant body temperature

water table: top level to which ground water rises when underground

weathering: process by which rocks are broken down by such factors as wind, water, heat, and cold

weight: measure of the force of attraction between objects due to gravity

woody stem: rigid stem containing woody xylem tissue

xylem (ZIGH-luhm): tubelike plant tissue that carries water and minerals through the plant

zoology: study of animals

Index

A

Abdomen, of insect, 242
Adaptations
  of birds, 272, 273–74
  of carnivores, 290
  of crustaceans, 237
  of fish, 259–60
  of insects, 246–47
  of lizards, 267–68
  of nonvascular plants, 171
  of primates, 297
  of reptiles, 265
  of snakes, 266
African elephant, 293–94
African sleeping sickness, 162
Agar, 177
Air, needed by living things, 46
Air bladders, 176
Air pressure, 526
Algae, 170–78
  blue-green, 172–73
  brown, 176–77
  classification of, 172
  and coral, 223
  fire, 177–78
  golden, 175–76
  green, 174–75
  habitats of, 171
  as lichens, 185
  red, 177
  reproduction in, 172
  structure of, 171–72
Alligators, 270–71
Alloys, 399
Amino acids, 50
Amoebas, 159–60
Amorphous solids, 333
Amphibians, 260–63
Amu, 336
Anal pore, 161
Angiosperms, 197, 206–11
Anglerfish, 253
Animals
  characteristics of, 218–19
  classification of, 141
  diseases of, 158
Annual plants, 201

Annual rings, 200
Anopheles mosquito, 163
Anteater, 292
Anther, 207
Anthrax, 158
Antibiotics, 156, 183
Ants, 245
Arachnids, 238–41
  anatomy of, 238
Aristotle, 133–34
Armadillos, 292
Arrow-poison frog, 260
Arthropods, 236–47
Asexual reproduction, 43, 187,
    196. *See also* Binary fission;
    Budding; Conjugation; Regen-
    eration; Reproduction;
    Spores.
Asiatic elephant, 293–94
Astronomy, 19
Atmosphere, 524–35
Atomic mass, 368
Atomic mass unit, 366
Atomic model of matter, 362–65
Atomic number, 366
Atoms, 362–71
  early ideas about, 362–63
  modern ideas about, 363–65
  structure of, 365–69
Auroras, 534–35
Autotrophs, 101, 104, 140, 141, 17

B

Baboons, 297
Bacilli, 153
Backbone, 218, 254, 269
Bacteria, 148, 152–58
  as autotrophs, 155
  classification of, 152–53
  harmful, 157–58
  helpful, 156–57
  life functions of, 154
  movement in, 154
  nitrogen-fixing, 157
  as parasites, 154–55
  reproduction in, 155–56
  shapes of, 153

  structure of, 153–54
  types of, 153
  in volcanic vents, 111, 154
Bacteriophages, 151–52
Bamboo, 113
Barnacles, 110
Basalt, 434
Batholiths, 436
Bats, 289–90
Beak, 269, 272
Bees, 217, 245–46
Behavior
  of birds, 274–75
  of cheetahs, 86–87
  of fish, 258, 259
  of insects, 245–46
  of rattlesnakes, 15
Beijerinck, Martinus, 149
Biennial plants, 201–202
Binary fission, 155
  in algae, 172
  in amoebas, 160
  in bacteria, 155
  in *Euglena*, 163
  in paramecia, 161
Binomial nomenclature, 134, 137,
    138
Bioluminescence, 178
Birds, 271–75
  adaptations for flight of,
    273–74
  breeding habits and develop-
    ment of, 274–75
  flightless, 273–74
  migration of, 275
  perching, 272
  of prey, 272
  types of, 272–73
  water, 272
Bivalves, 232–33
Blade, of leaf, 202
Blubber, 290
Boiling, 340
Boiling point, 340–41
Bonamo, Patricia, 28–29
Bonding, chemical, 370–71
Bony fish, 259–60
Botany, 19

Boyle's Law, 335, 336
Brain, 254, 282–83, 297
Budding, 182
Bulbs, 200–201

C

Calorie, 40
Cambium, 199
Camouflage, 246–47, 260, 267
Canine teeth, 290
Cap, mushroom, 181
Carbohydrate, 49
Carbon dioxide
    in photosynthesis, 203, 204
    as waste product, 46
Carboniferous Period, 195
Carnivores, 290–91
Cartilage, 257
Cartilaginous fish, 257–58
Catalysts, enzymes as, 51
CAT scanning (Computerized
        Axial Tomography), 27
Cell division, 71–72, 73
Cell membrane, 60, 61, 69–70,
        153, 159–60
Cells, 58–73, 81
    activities of, 58, 67–73, 82
    animal, 58, 60, 65, 72
    plant, 58, 59, 60, 65, 66–67,
        72–73
    reproduction of, 71–73
    structure and function of,
        58–67
    types of, 58, 80, 81
Cellulose, 59
Cell wall, 59, 152
Celsius scale, 24
Centipedes, 238
Chalk, 440, 441
Chambered nautilus, 233
Chameleon, 267
Charles's Law, 336
Chemical bonding, 370–71
Chemical changes, 344–45
Chemical equations, 384–85
Chemical formulas, 383–84
Chemical properties, 343–44, 371
Chemical reactions, 345, 384
Chemical rocks, 440
Chemical symbols, 380–81
Chemistry, 19
Chimpanzees, 297
Chlorophyll, 101, 140, 141, 170,
        172
    in algae, 172, 175
    in flagellates, 162
    in leaves, 203

in mosses, 187
Chloroplasts, 66–67
Chromosomes, 61–62, 71–73
Cilia, 160, 161
Ciliates, 160–62
Circulatory system
    of earthworm, 228
    of insect, 243
Clams, 230, 232, 234–35
Class, in biological classification,
        137
Classification, biological, 132–41
    characteristics used in, 135,
        137–38
    early systems of, 133–34
    five-kingdom system of, 140–41
    functions of modern, 135
    groupings in modern, 136–37
    history of, 132–34
    modern, 135–38
    systems of, 140–41
Clastic rock, 438–39
Cleavage of minerals, 422, 424
Closed circulatory system, 228
Clownfish, 223–24
Coastal plains, 509–10
Cocci, 153
Cocoon
    earthworm, 229
    insect, 245
Coefficients, 385
Coelacanth, 131
Coelenterates, 221–24, 227
Coldblooded animals, 48–49,
        255–56, 260–63, 264–71
Colloids, 396
Colonies
    of algae, 171
    of coral, 223
    of flagellates, 162
    of insects, 245
    of sponge cells, 220
    of yeasts, 182
Color of minerals, 418, 424, 427
Commensalism, 109–10
Communities, 97
Competition, among organisms,
        47, 108–109
Compound eyes, 243
Compound leaves, 202
Compound light microscopes, 26
Compounds, 48–51, 382–85
    inorganic, 49
    organic, 49–51
Computers, 27
Conclusion, stating a, 18
Condensation, 341
    in water cycle, 513
Cones, 205

Conglomerates, 438–39
Conifers, 204, 205–206
Conjugation, 161–62
Consumers, 102, 105–107
Continental glaciers, 516
Continents, 492–95, 502, 506
Contour feathers, 273
Contractile vacuole, 160
Control, experimental, 18
Copperhead, 266
Corals, 221, 222–23, 234
Coral snake, 266
Core, of earth, 480, 483–86
Cotyledon, 210
Crabs, 237–38
Crayfish, 237
Crocodiles, 270–71
Crop, of earthworm, 228
Cross-pollination, 208, 209
Crown-of-thorns sea star, 234
Crust, of earth, 492–95, 505–506,
        507
Crustaceans, 237–38
Crystalline solids, 332–33
Crystals, 332–33, 416, 422
Cuticle, of leaf, 204
Cycads, 205
Cytoplasm, 63–66, 153, 159, 161

D

Dalton, John, 363
Data, recording and analyzing, 18
Decay, of food, 103, 157
    bacteria and, 154–55
Decomposers, 102–104, 179–80
Deep sea
    animals of, 94–95
    fish of, 259–60
Defense mechanisms, insect,
        246–47
Democritus, 362–63
Density, 23–24, 320–22, 421–22
Deoxyribonucleic acid. See DNA.
Desert soil, 461–62
Development, growth and, 40–41,
        71–73
    of birds, 274–75
    of insects, 243–45
    of mammals, 283
Diamonds, 419, 426, 427
Diatomaceous earth, 175–76
Diatoms, 175–76
Dicots, 210
Diffusion, 69–70
Digestion, 39
    in amoeba, 160
    in cell, 66

in paramecium, 161
Digestive system, 84
  of earthworm, 228
Digitalis, 202
Diphtheria, 157
Discoveries, scientific, 28–29
Diseases
  animal, 158
  human, 157, 162, 295
  plant, 148–50, 158
Dispersal of seeds, 210
Division of labor, in living
  things, 80–81
DNA (deoxyribonucleic acid),
  51, 62
  in bacteria, 156
  in chromosomes, 62
  in mitochondria, 65
  in viruses, 150–51
Dodder plant, 112
Dolphins, 296
Down feathers, 273–74
Duckbilled platypus, 281, 284, 285
Ductility, 425
Dugongs, 296
Dutch elm disease, 178–79

E

Earth
  atmosphere, 524–35
  continents, 492–95
  core, 480, 483–86
  crust, 492–95
  magnetosphere, 535–37
  mantle, 486, 489–92
  surface, 502–17
Earthquakes, 480–88
  and earthquake waves, 481–82,
    487–88
  focus of, 481
  measuring, 480–81, 482, 483
Earth science, 19
Earthworm, 227–29
  anatomy of, 228
  reproduction in, 229
  role in soil, 228
Ecology, 95
Ecosystems, 95–96, 98
  balance in, 113–15
  desert, 97
  forest, 96
  pond, 96
  relationships in, 107–15
Egg cells
  of earthworm, 229
  of seed plants, 196, 205, 207
Egg-laying mammals, 284–85

Eggs
  of amphibians, 261, 262
  of birds, 274, 275
  of egg-laying mammals, 284
  of insects, 245
  of lobsters, 237
  of reptiles, 265, 269, 270–71
Electric eels, 259
Electric rays, 258
Electron cloud, 369
Electron microscopes, 26–27
Electrons, 363, 368–69
Elements, 48, 51, 378–81
Elephants, 293–94
Embryo, 210
Endocrine system, 84, 87
Endoplasmic reticulum, 63, 64
Endosperm, 210
Endospores, 155
Energy
  in food chains, 104–105
  food sources of, 49–51
  needed by living things, 44, 67,
    68, 99, 101
  and phases of matter, 337
  produced by living things,
    39–40, 101
Energy levels
  in atoms, 369–70
  in food chains, 105–107
Energy pyramids, in food chains,
  106–107
Environments, 95
  food and energy in, 100–107
  living things in, 94–100
Enzymes, 51, 61–62, 66
  in amoebas, 160
  in fungi, 180, 183
Epicotyl, 210
Epidermis, 82, 204
Euglena, 162–63
Evaporation, 340
  in water cycle, 513
Evergreens, 206
Excretion, 40
Excretory system, 84
Exoskeleton, 236, 243
Experimenting, 17–18
Extrusive rock, 434–35
Eyes
  insect, 243
  mollusk, 230
Eyespot, in *Euglena*, 163

F

Family, in biological
  classification, 137

Fangs, 266
Fats and oils, 49–50
Feathers, 271, 273–74, 275
Feeding levels, in food chains,
  105–107
Fermentation, 182
Ferns, 194–96
  reproduction in, 195–96
  structure of, 195
Fertilization, 73, 208, 229
  internal, 265
Fiddleheads, 195
Field hardness scale, 420
Filament, of flower, 207
Fins, 255
Fish, 254–60
  bony, 259–60
  cartilaginous, 257–58
  jawless, 256–57
Flagella, 154
  in algae, 177
  in bacteria, 154
  in flagellates, 162–63
Flagellates, 162–63
Flammability, 343–44
Flatworms, 226
Fleming, Alexander, 183
Flesh-eating mammals, 290–91
Flight
  in birds, 272–74
  in insects, 243
  in mammals, 289
Flightless birds, 272–73
Flounder, 259–60
Flowers, 206–209
  function of, 208
  structure of, 207
Flying mammals, 289–90
Focus, of earthquake, 481
Food, needed by living things, 45
Food chains, 104–107
Food poisoning, 157
Food spoilage, 157
Food vacuole, 160, 161
Food webs, 105
Foot, of mollusks, 230, 231
Forests
  bamboo, 113
  deciduous, 96
  temperate, 457–59
  tropical rain, 95, 194, 455–57
Fossils, 13, 28–29, 437–38,
  439–40, 441
Fracture of minerals, 422
Freezing, 339
Freezing point, 339
Frogs, 261–63
Fronds, 195
Fruiting bodies

in fungi, 180–81
in slime molds, 186
Fruits, 208
Fungi, 178–83
classification of, 141
as lichens, 185
reproduction in, 180–81, 182, 183
structure of, 180–81

G

Galapagos Islands, 98, 100, 111, 264
Galapagos tortoise, 269
Gases, 334–36
behavior of, 335–36
phase changes with liquids, 339–41
phase changes with solids, 341–42
Gas Laws, 335–36
Gems, 426, 427
Genus, in biological classification, 134, 137
Germination, 210
Giant squid, 229–30
Gibbon, 297
Gila monster, 267
Gills
of crustaceans, 237
of fish, 255
of tadpoles, 262
Gills, of mushrooms, 182
Gingkoes, 205
Gizzard, 228
Glaciers, 516–17
Glucose, 49, 101, 203
Gnawing mammals, 295
Gold, 416, 418, 425, 426
Gorilla, 297
Gram, 22, 316
Granite, 435–36, 445
Grasshopper, 242–43
Grasslands, 460–61
Gravity, 22–23, 317–18
Great Barrier Reef, 222, 234
Great Plains, 510
Great white shark, 258
Green plants, 101, 104, 105, 140, 172
Green turtle, 269–70
Grierson, James, 28–29
Ground water, 515
Growth
of arthropods, 236–37
of mollusks, 231
of trees, 199–200

Growth and development, 40–41, 71–73
of birds, 274–75
of insects, 243–45
of mammals, 283
Growth rings
of coral, 221
of trees, 200
Guard cells, 204
Gullet, 161
Gymnosperms, 197, 204–206

H

Habitats, 99–100
Halite, 416, 423
Hardness of minerals, 419–20
Hardness test for minerals, 420, 424
Hares, 295
Head, of insect, 242
Head-footed mollusks, 233
Hedgehogs, 288
Heft of minerals, 422
Herbaceous stems, 201, 202
Herbivores, 286
Heterogeneous mixtures, 395
Heterotrophs, 102, 141, 179
Hibernation, 261–62
Hives, insect, 245–46
Homeostasis, 47–48, 60
Homogeneous mixtures, 395–96
Honey guide bird, 111
Hoofed mammals, 294
Hookworm, 227
Hormones, 62, 84
Host, 226
Human beings, 283, 297
Human diseases, 157, 162, 295
Humus, 452, 459, 461, 462, 463
Hydra, 221
Hyphae, 180, 181, 183
Hypocotyl, 210
Hypothesis, forming of, 16–17

I

Icebergs, 517
Ice sheets, 515–17
Igneous rocks, 434–47
Iguanas, 264
Incisors, 290, 295
Incubation, 275
Inertia, 316
Information, gathering, 16
Ingestion, 39
Inland plains, 510
Inorganic compounds, 49
Inorganic substances, 416

Insect-eating mammals, 288–89
Insects, 241–47
anatomy of, 242–43
behavior of, 245–46
defense mechanisms of, 246–47
growth and development of, 243–45
role of in pollination, 207, 208–209
Insoluble, 398
Insulin produced by bacteria, 156–57
Interior Plains, 510
Internal fertilization, 265
Intestine, 228
Intrusive rocks, 435–37
Invertebrates, 218–47
characteristics of, 219
Ionosphere, 534
Ions, in atmosphere, 534, 536
Isotopes, 367
Iwanowski, Dimitri, 148–49

J

Jawless fish, 256–57
Jellyfish, 221, 222
Jet stream, 529–32

K

Kangaroos, 285, 286
Kelp, 172, 177
Kilogram, 22, 316
King cobra, 266
Kingdom, in biological classification, 136, 140
Koalas, 286
Komodo dragon, 267
Krakatoa, 172

L

Lampreys, 112, 256–57
Landmasses, 492–95, 502, 506
Landscapes, 503–510
Larva, 245
Lasers, 27
Latin
used in biological classification, 134, 137
used for chemical symbols, 381
Lava, 434
Leaching, 457
Leaves, 195, 196, 202–204, 207, 210
functions of, 202, 204
structure of, 202
types of, 202

Leeches, 227
Legionnaires' Disease, 147
Lehmann, Inge, 484–85
Length, 21–22
Lens, microscope, 26
Levels of organization, in living things, 81–87
Lichens, 184–85
Life science, 19
Life span, 41–42
Limestone, 222, 437–38, 439–40, 441
Linnaeus, Carolus, 134
Liquids, 333
    phase changes with gases, 339–41
    phase changes with solids, 338–39
Liter, 22, 319
Liverworts, 187
Living space, needed by living things, 46–47
Living things
    arising only from other living things, 37
    characteristics of, 36–43
    chemistry of, 48–51
    needs of, 44–48
    and their environment, 94–100
Lizards, 264, 265, 267–68
Lobsters, 237
Lungfish, 260
Lungs, 262
Luster of minerals, 418–19, 424
Lysosomes, 65–66

M

Magma, 417, 434
Magnetosphere, 535–37
Malaria, 163
Malleability, 425
Mammals, 282–97
    characteristics of, 282–83
    egg-laying, 284–85
    flesh-eating, 290–91
    flying, 289–90
    gnawing, 295
    hoofed, 294
    insect-eating, 288–89
    placental, 287–97
    pouched, 285–87
    primates, 296–97
    rodentlike, 295–96
    "toothless," 292–93
    trunk-nosed, 293–94
    water-dwelling, 296
Mammary glands, 282–83, 284, 287

Manatees, 296
Mantle, of earth, 486, 489–92
Mantle, of mollusks, 230–31
Marble, 441
Marsupials, 285–87
Mary Rose, 313, 322
Mass, 22, 315–16
    units of, 316
    and weight, 22–23
Mass number, 368
Matter, 314–15
    atomic model of, 362–65
    general properties of, 314–22
    phase changes of, 338–342
    phases of, 331–37
    specific (physical) properties of, 330
Mauna Kea, 477, 505
Megalosaurus, 13
Meiosis, 73
Melting, 338–39
Melting point, 338
Mesosphere, 532–33
Metabolism, 39–40
    in cell, 68–69
Metals, 425-426
Metamorphic rocks, 441–43
Metamorphosis, 243, 245
Meteoroids, 532
Meteors, 533
Meter, 21
Metric system, 20–24
    length, 21–22
    mass and weight, 22–24
    temperature, 24
    units, 20
    volume, 22
Mica, 419, 422
Microbiology, 149
Microscopes, 24–27
Mid-Atlantic Rift Valley, 489
Mid-Ocean Ridge, 489, 506
Migration, 275
Milk, 283, 284, 286, 287
Milliliter, 319
Millipedes, 238
Minerals, 415–27
    identifying, 417–24
    physical properties of, 417–22
    special properties of, 423
    uses of, 425–26
Mites, 238, 239, 241
Mitochondria, 64–65, 66
Mitosis, 71–73
Mixtures, 392–96
    heterogeneous, 395
    homogeneous, 395–96
    properties of, 392–94
    separation of, 395

types of, 395–96
Moho, 488, 489
Mohorovicic, Andrija, 487–88
Mohs hardness scale, 419–20
Molds, 182–83
Molecules, 370–71
Moles, 288
Mollusks, 229–33
    anatomy of, 230
    classification of, 231
Monerans, 173
    classification of, 141, 152
Monkeys, 297
Monocots, 210
Mono Lake, CA, 114–15
Monotreme, 284
Mosses, 186–87
Mountain belts, 506
Mountain landscapes, 503
Mountain ranges, 506, 507–508, 514
Mountains, 503, 505–507
    famous, 504
    formation of, 505
    volcanic, 506, 507
Mouth
    coelenterate, 221–22
    insect, 242
Movement, 38
    in amoebas, 159
    in amphibians, 262–63
    in bacteria, 154
    in ciliates, 160
    in fish, 255, 260
    in mollusks, 230, 231, 232–33
    in reptiles, 267, 268
    in slime molds, 186
    in snakes, 267
    in spiny-skinned animals, 234–35
Mudskipper, 260
Multicellular organisms, 81–87, 171–72, 219
    classification of, 140–41
Mushrooms, 181–82
Mussels, 232
Mutualism, 110–12

N

Nautiluses, 233
Navigation
    in birds, 275
    in turtles, 269
Nematocysts, 221–22
Nervous system, 84, 86, 87, of earthworm, 229
Neutrons, 366

Newts, 263
Niches, 99–100
Nitrogen-fixing algae, 173
Nitrogen-fixing bacteria, 157
NMR (Nuclear Magnetic
    Resonance), 28
Nonmetals, 426
Nonvascular plants, 170–87
Nuclear membrane, 61, 63, 72
Nucleic acids, 51, 61–62
Nucleolus, 62–63
Nucleus, of atom, 364, 365–66
Nucleus, of cell, 60–63, 71–72, 153
    in paramecia, 161
    in protozoans, 159

O

Obsidian, 435, 436, 437
Ocean floor, 489, 491–94
Oceans, 511–12
Octopus, 230, 233
Oils, fats and, 49–50
Oldham, Richard Dixon, 479, 483
One-celled organisms. *See*
    Unicellular organisms.
One-shelled mollusks, 231–32
Open circulatory system, 243
Opossums, 286–87
Oral groove, 161
Orangutan, 297
Order, in biological classification,
    137
Ores, 425–26
Organic compounds, 49–51
Organic rocks, 439–40
Organisms, 86–87
    classifying, 137–38, 140–41
    interactions among, 101–104
Organization of living things,
    81–87
Organs, 83–84, 219
Organ systems, 84, 219, 255
Osmosis, 70
Ovary, of flower, 207
Ovules, 205
Oxygen, 379
    in photosynthesis, 203
    used by living things 39–40, 46,
    101, 172, 237
Oysters, 225, 230
Ozone, 529

P

P waves, 481–84
Pandas, 113
Paramecia, 160–62

Parasites
    bacteria, 154–55
    flagellates, 162
    flatworms, 226
    fungi, 179
    lampreys, 256
    roundworms, 227
    sporozoans, 163
    ticks and mites, 241
Parasitism, 112
Parent rock, 453
Paricutín, 501
Pasteurization, 157
Pearls, formation of, 225
Penguins, 271–72, 273, 274, 275
Penicillin, 183
Perching birds, 272
Perennial plants, 201
Permafrost, 463
Petals, 207
Phases of matter, 331–37
    changes in, 337–42
Pheromones, 245
Phloem, 83, 198, 199, 204
Photosynthesis, 101, 172, 174,
    187, 202–203
    equation for, 203
    in leaves, 202–203
Phylum, in biological
    classification, 136
Physical changes, 330–31, 338
Physical properties, 330–31
    of minerals, 416–426
Physical science, 19
Physics, 19
Pikas, 295
Pioneer plants, 185
Pistils, 207
Placenta, 287
Placental mammals, 287–88
Plains, 509–510
Plains landscapes, 509
Planarians, 226
Plant diseases, 158
Plants, classification of, 140
Plasma, 336–37
Plateau landscapes, 507
Plateaus, 507–509
    formation of, 508
"Plum pudding" model of atom,
    363–64
Pneumonia, 157
Pollen, 205–207
Pollination, 208
Polliwogs, 262
Populations, 97–98
Pores
    of cell, 61, 62
    of sponges, 220

Porpoises, 296
Pouched mammals, 285–87
Prairie grassland soil, 460–61
Precious stones, 426, 427
Precipitation, 513
Primary earthquake waves
    (P waves), 481–84
Primates, 296–97
Problem, stating of, 15
Producers, 101, 104
Properties,
    of matter, 315
    of minerals, 416–426
Proteins, 50–51, 61–62, 63
Protists, 159
    classification of, 141
Protons, 365–66
Protoplasm, 60, 63, 70
Protozoans, 158–63
    classification of, 159
Pseudopods, 159–60
Puddingstone, 438–39
Puffball, 182
Pupa, 245
Pure substances, 378–80, 392

Q

Quarks, 370
Quartz, 416, 418, 419
Quartzite, 443

R

Rabbits, 295
Radicle, 210
Radula, 231
Rattlesnake, 266
Ray, John, 134
Rays, 258
Redi, Francesco, 37
"Red tide," 177
Reefs, coral, 222–23
Regeneration, 226, 235, 238, 268
Remora, 259
Reproduction, 43, 73
    in algae, 172
    in amoebas, 160
    asexual, 43, 187, 196
    in bacteria, 155–56
    of cells, 71–73
    in earthworms, 229
    in *Euglena*, 163
    in ferns, 195–96
    in fungi, 180–81, 182, 183
    in liverworts, 187
    in mosses, 187
    in paramecia, 161–62

in seed plants, 196, 205, 207–209
sexual, 196, 207–209, 229
in slime molds, 186
in viruses, 151–52
Reproductive system, earthworm, 228
Reptiles, 264–71
Respiration, 39–40
Respiratory system, earthworm, 228
Response, 42
Rhizoids, 187
Rhizomes
of ferns, 195
of seed plants, 200
Ribonucleic acid. *See* RNA.
Ribosomes, 64
Rift valleys, 489, 491, 493
RNA (ribonucleic acid), 51, 62, 63
in chromosomes, 62
in nucleolus, 62
in ribosomes, 64
in viruses, 151
Robbins cinquefoil, 193
Rock cycle, 444–45
Rocks, 434–45
chemical, 440
clastic, 438–39
extrusive, 434–45
igneous, 434–37
intrusive, 435–37
metamorphic, 441–43
organic, 439–40
sedimentary, 437–40
Rocky Mountain spotted fever, 241
Rodentlike mammals, 295–96
Rodents, 295
Root hairs, 198
Roots, 195, 196, 197–98, 207, 210
functions of, 197
structure of, 198
Roundworms, 226
Rutherford, Ernest, 364–65

S

S waves, 482–84
Safety in the laboratory, 28
St. Helens, Mount, 113–14
Salamanders, 263
Salt, 423
Sand dollar, 235
Sandstone, 439
Sandworms, 227
Sap, 199
Saprophytes, 155, 179–80
Sargasso Sea, 176

Sargassum, 176–77
Scanning electron
microscope, 26–27
Scavengers, 102, 104
Science, 14–29
branches of, 19
and discovery, 28–29
tools used in, 24–28
Scientific measurements, 20–24
length, 21–22
mass and weight, 22–24
temperature, 24
volume, 22
Scientific method, 15–18
Scientific name, 134, 137, 138
Scorpions, 238, 239, 240–41
Scratch test for minerals, 419–20
Sea anemones, 221, 223–24
Sea cucumbers, 235
Sea lilies, 235
Sea otters, 282
Sea slugs, 232
Sea stars, 234
Sea urchins, 235
Seaweed, 171–72, 176–77
Secondary earthquake waves
(S waves), 482–84
Sedimentary rocks, 437–440
Seed coat, 210
Seed dispersal, 210
Seed plants, 196–211
Seeds, 196, 197, 207, 210–11
Segmented worms, 227–29
Seismic waves, 481–84
Seismograph, 480, 481
Self-pollination, 208
SEM (scanning electron
microscope), 26–27
Semiprecious stones, 426
Sepals, 207
Sex cells, 73, 196, 205, 229
Sexual reproduction, 43, 73, 196,
207–208, 229
Shadow zones, 482–86
Shale, 439, 442
Sharks, 257–58, 259
Shells, of mollusks, 230, 231, 233
Shells, of turtles and tortoises,
268–69
Shrews, 288–89
Shrimp, 237
Simple eyes, 243
Simple leaves, 202
Simple plants. *See* Nonvascular
plants.
Skates, 258
Skeleton, 254
Slate, 442
Slime molds, 186

Sloths, 171, 292–93
Slugs, 232
Smelting, 425
Snails, 231
Snakes, 265–68
poisonous, 266
Social insects, 245–46
Soil, 452–63
of coastal plains, 509–510
desert, 461–62
and the environment, 453–55
of inland plains, 510
layers of, 452–53
prairie grassland, 460–61
temperate forest, 457–59
tropical rain forest, 455–57
tundra, 462–63
Solids, 331–33
amorphous, 333
crystalline, 332
phase changes with gases,
341–42
phase changes with liquids,
338–39
Solubility, 398–99
Soluble, 398
Solutes, 397
Solutions, 397–99
properties of, 397–98
types of, 398
Solvents, 397
Space, living, needed by living
things, 46–47
Special properties of minerals,
423, 425–26
Species, in biological
classification, 134, 137
Sperm cells, 196, 205, 207
of earthworm, 228
Spiders, 238–40
Spinal cord, 254
Spiny anteater, 284, 285
Spiny-skinned animals, 234–35
Spirilla, 153
Spoilage, food, 157
Sponges, 219–21
Spontaneous generation, 37
Spores
in ferns, 195–96
in fungi, 180–81, 182, 183
in mosses, 187
in slime molds, 186
in sporozoans, 163
Sporozoans, 163
Squid, 229–30, 233
Stalk, of leaf, 202
Stalk, of mushroom, 181–82
Stamens, 207
Stanley, Wendell, 149

Starch, 49
Starfish, 234–35
Star-nosed mole, 288
Stems, 195, 196, 198–202, 207, 210
  classification of, 201
  herbaceous, 201
  function of, 200
  types of, 200
  woody, 201–202
Stigma, 208
Stimulus, 42
Stomata, 203–204
Strata, 438
Stratosphere, 529–32
Streak test for minerals, 421
Strep throat, 157
Stromatolites, 169
Style, 208
Subatomic particles, 365
Sublimation, 341–42
Subscripts, 383
Subsoil, 453
Sugar, 49
Suspensions, 395
Swim bladder, 259
Symbiosis, 109–12, 185
Systems. *See* Organ systems.

T

Tadpoles, 262, 263
Talc, 419
Talons, 272
Tapeworms, 226
Taxonomy, 133, 137–38
  history of, 133–34
Teeth, 290, 292, 295
Temperate forest soil, 457–59
Temperature, 24
  proper, needed by living things,
    47–48
Tentacles
  of coelenterates, 221–22, 223
  of mollusks, 233
Termites, 245
Territory, 46–47, 274
Texture of rock, 436
Thermosphere, 533–35
Thomson, J. J., 363–64
Thorax, of insect, 242
Ticks, 238, 239, 241
Tissues, 82–83, 84, 219, 222
Toads, 261–63

Tobacco mosaic virus, 148–50
Tools
  making, 297
  of a scientist, 24–28
  using, 282, 297
"Toothless" mammals, 292–93
Topsoil, 452
Tortoises, 98, 268–69
Toxins, 157
Transpiration, 204
Trapdoor spider, 240
Trenches, in ocean floor, 493
Trichina, 226
Trichinosis, 226
Tropical rain forests, 94–95, 194
Tropical rain forest soil, 455–57
Troposphere, 527–29
Trunk-nosed mammals, 293–94
Tsetse fly, 162
Tube feet, 234–35
Tuberculosis, 157
Tubers, 200
Tubeworms, 111
Tundra soil, 462–63
Turtles, 268–70
Tusks, 290
Two-shelled mollusks, 232–33

U

Unicellular organisms, 80, 81,
    148, 152, 159, 162, 171, 182
  classification of, 140–41
Univalves, 231–32

V

Vacuoles, 65
  contractile, 160
  food, 160, 161
Valley glaciers, 516
Vaporization, 339–40
Variable, experimental, 17
Vascular plants, 194–211
Veins, of leaf, 204
Venom, 240, 265–66
Vertebrae, 254
Vertebrates, 218, 254–75, 282–97
  characteristics of, 254
Viruses, 148–52
  characteristics of, 150
  reproduction of, 151–52
  shapes and sizes of, 151

structure of, 150–51
Volcanic eruptions, 501
  effects of on life, 172, 113–14
Volcanic rock, 434, 435, 436, 437
Volcanic vents, organisms in, 111,
    154
Volcanoes, 501, 506, 507
Volume, 22, 319
  and pressure, 335
  and temperature, 336
Volvox, 162

W

Walking catfish, 260
Walruses, 290
Warmblooded animals, 48-49,
    271–75, 282–97
Wasps, 245, 246
Water, on earth's surface, 511–17
  frozen, 515–17
  needed by living things, 45–46
  running, 514–15
  standing, 515
Water birds, 272
Water cycle, 512–14
Water density, 321–22
Water-dwelling mammals, 296
Water moccasin, 266, 267
Water table, 515
Weathering, 454
Weight, 317–18
  mass and, 22–23
Whales, 296
Whale shark, 257–58
Whooping cough, 157
Woody stems, 201–202
Worms, 225–29

X

X-rays, 27
Xylem, 82–83, 198, 199, 200,
    201, 204

Y

Yeasts, 182

Z

Zoology, 19

Photograph Credits

1, Rick Smolan/Contact/*Woodfin Camp;* **2,** top, David O. Houston/*Bruce Coleman;* bottom left, Ed Cooper/*H. Armstrong Roberts;* bottom right, Wesley Frank/*Woodfin Camp;* **5,** top, NIH Science Source/*Photo Researchers;* bottom, T. Daniel/*Bruce Coleman;* **6,** top, Manfred Kage/*Peter Arnold;* bottom, Fred Bavendam/*Peter Arnold;* **7,** top, Taronga Zoo, Sydney-Tom McHugh/*Photo Researchers;* bottom, O.S. Pettingill/*Photo Researchers;* **8,** top, Werner Muller/*Peter Arnold;* bottom, Vulcain-Explorer/*Photo Researchers;* **9,** top, Steve Vidler/*Leo de Wys;* bottom, Margot Conte/© *Earth Scenes;* **14,** © Tom McHugh/*Photo Researchers;* **16,** Peter B. Kaplan; **17,** Peter B. Kaplan; **19,** top, *dpi;* bottom left, NASA; bottom right, Wally McNamee/*Woodfin Camp & Associates;* **21,** top left, Ken Karp; top right, Ken Karp; bottom left, Ken Karp; bottom right, Ken Karp; **22,** Jerry Wachter/*Focus on Sports;* **23,** NASA; **24,** Kim Taylor/*Bruce Coleman;* **25,** top, J.A.L. Cooke/*Animals Animals;* center, David Scharf/*Peter Arnold;* bottom, Manfred Kage/*Peter Arnold;* **26,** Dr. E.R. Degginger/*Bruce Coleman;* **27,** top, Howard Sochurek/*Woodfin Camp & Associates;* bottom, NIH/Science Source/*Photo Researchers;* **28,** left, Dan McCoy/*Rainbow;* right, Howard Sochurek/*Woodfin Camp & Associates;* **36,** top left, M.P. Kahl/*Bruce Coleman;* bottom left, Breck P. Kent; bottom right, Jen & Des Bartlett/*Bruce Coleman;* top right, Peter Ward/*Bruce Coleman;* **38,** right, Chris Newbert/*Bruce Coleman;* left, Wayne Lankinen/*Bruce Coleman;* **39,** T. Daniel/*Bruce Coleman;* **40,** left, Tom McHugh/*Photo Researchers;* right, Jen & Des Bartlett/*Bruce Coleman;* **41,** left, Harry Rogers/*dpi;* right, Harry Rogers/*dpi;* **42,** top left, John Shaw/*Bruce Coleman;* top right, Grant Heilman; bottom, Shelley Rotner/*OPC;* **43,** Runk/Schoenberger/*Grant Heilman;* **44,** top, R. Mariscal/*Bruce Coleman;* bottom left, Kjell B. Sandved/*Bruce Coleman;* bottom right, Bill Bridge/*dpi;* **45,** left, Miguel Castro/*Photo Researchers;* right, W. H. Hodge/*Peter Arnold;* **46,** David C. Fritts/*Animals Animals;* **47,** left, Manuel Rodriguez; right, Dr. E. R. Degginger; **49,** top, Dr. E. R. Degginger; bottom, Dr. E. R. Degginger; **50,** top, Barry L. Runk/*Grant Heilman;* bottom, Bill Stanton/*International Stock Photo;* **51,** Tripos Associates/*Peter Arnold;* **56,** Lennart Nilsson/The Incredible Machine/*The National Geographic Society;* **60,** Jack McConnell, *McConnell McNamara Assoc./dpi;* **61,** Fawcett/*Photo Researchers;* **62,** Ken Karp; **63,** Omikron/*Taurus Photos;* **64,** K. R. Porter/*Photo Researchers;* **67,** Manfred Kage/*Peter Arnold;* **70,** left, M. Sheetz/*University of Conn. Health Center/J. Cell. Biol.*; center, M. Sheetz/*Univ. of Conn. Health Center/J. Cell. Biol.*; right, M. Sheetz/*Univ. of Conn. Health Center/J. Cell. Biol.*; **71,** left, Runk/Schoenberger/*Grant Heilman;* right, Grant Heilman; **72,** Carolina Biological Supply Company; **73,** left, Sven Olaf Lindblad/*dpi;* right, Craig Aurness/*West Light;* **78,** Peter Davey/*Bruce Coleman;* **80,** top, © Hans Pfletschinger/*Peter Arnold;* bottom, Dr. Merlin D. Tuttle; **82,** top left, Manfred Kage/*Peter Arnold;* top center, Manfred Kage/*Peter Arnold;* top right, Manfred Kage/*Peter Arnold, Inc.*; bottom, © Hans Pfletschinger/*Peter Arnold;* **83,** G. Ziesler/*Peter Arnold;* **85,** left, Rod Allin/*Bruce Coleman;* right, Eric Crichton/*Bruce Coleman;* bottom, Wil Blanche/*dpi;* **87,** Charles G. Summers, Jr./*dpi;* **88,** Ken Karp; **92,** Raymond A. Mendez/*Animals Animals;* **95,** *dpi;* **96,** Kim Taylor/*Bruce Coleman;* **97,** J. Alex Langley/*dpi;* **98,** C. A. Morgan/*Peter Arnold;* **99,** Des and Jen Bartlett/*Bruce Coleman;* **100,** © Jonathan T. Wright/*Bruce Coleman;* **101,** Fred Bavendam/*Peter Arnold;* **103,** top left, Jane Burton/*Bruce Coleman;* top right, G. Ziesler/*Peter Arnold;* bottom, Lovett E. Williams, Jr./*dpi;* **104,** top left, Walker/*Photo Researchers;* second left, Michael Abbey/*Photo Researchers;* third left, © George Holton/*Photo Researchers;* bottom left, Chris Bry/*dpi;* bottom right, Jen & Des Bartlett/*Bruce Coleman;* **107,** R. Andrew Odum/*Peter Arnold;* **108,** Charlie Ott/*dpi;* **109,** left; Charlie Ott/*dpi;* right, J.M. Barr/*dpi;* **110,** left, Lee Lyon/*Bruce Coleman;* right, Peter Ward/*Bruce Coleman;* **111,** Leonard Lee Rue III/*dpi;* **112,** top, Mike Price/*Bruce Coleman;* bottom, Wilt Hodge/*Peter Arnold;* **113,** top left, John Bechteler/*Shostal;* top right, Kevin Schafer/*Tom Stack & Associates;* center right, Phil Degginger/*Bruce Coleman;* bottom right, Roger Werth/*Woodfin Camp and Associates;* **114,** left, John Gerlach/*Earth Scenes;* right, Liane Enkelis/*Mono Lake Committee;* **116,** Ken Karp; **120,** Laboratory of Ornithology/Photo: *Joyce Poole;* Jen & Des Bartlett/*Bruce Coleman;* **122,** David Scharf/*Peter Arnold;* **123,** Eric Kroll/*Taurus;* **124,** Michael Habicht/*Animals Animals;* **126,** left, Smithsonian Institution; center, Ken Karp/*OPC;* right, Joel Greenstein/*OPC;* **128,** Bryon Crader/*Tom Stack;* **130,** Peter Scoones/*Seaphoto/Colorific;* **132,** Mazonowicz/*Monkmeyer Press;* **133,** right, Robert C. Simpson/*Tom Stack;* left, John Pawloski/*Tom Stack;* top, © Boyd Norton/*Peter Arnold;* **136,** Dr. E.R. Degginger; **137,** G.B. Schaller/*Bruce Coleman;* **139,** first row, left to right, Phil Dotson/*dpi;* Jack Dermid, Charles G. Summers, Jr./*dpi;* Theodore Zywotko/*dpi;* second row, left to right, Dr. E. R. Degginger/*Bruce Coleman;* David M. Stone; Barbara K. Deans/*dpi;* third row, left to right, Jerry Frank/*dpi;* J. Alex Langley/*dpi;* fourth row, left to right, Phil Dotson/*dpi;* Phil Dotson/*dpi;* Francisco Erize/*Bruce Coleman;* fifth row, left to right, Lois and George Cox/*Bruce Coleman;* James Theologos/*Monkmeyer Press;* Mimi Forsyth/*Monkmeyer Press;* sixth row, left to right, Kenneth W. Fink/*Bruce Coleman;* Wil Blanche/*dpi;* Phil Dotson/*dpi;* bottom, Jon A. Hull/*Bruce Coleman;* **140,** Stephen Dalton/*Animals Animals;* **141,** Eric Grave/*Phototake;* **146,** Martin Rotker/*Taurus Photos;* **148,** left, Wendell Metzen/*Bruce Coleman;* right, *Grant Heilman;* **149,** Biology Media/*Photo Researchers;* **150,** E. H. Cook/*Photo Researchers;* **151,** Lee D. Simon/*Photo Researchers;* **153,** left, Manfred Kage/*Peter Arnold;* center, Manfred Kage/*Peter Arnold;* right, Dr. E. R. Degginger; **154,** top, *L. V. Bergman & Associates;* bottom, D. Jorgenson/*Tom Stack & Associates;* **155,** top, William E. Ferguson; botton, Manfred Kage/*Peter Arnold;* **156,** Martin M. Rotker/*Taurus Photos;* **158,** top, William E. Ferguson; botton, Manfred Kage/*Peter Arnold;* **159,** Jonathan D. Eisenback/*Phototake;* **161,** Michael Abbey/*Photo Researchers;* **162,** top, Manfred Kage/*Peter Arnold;* bottom, *L. V. Bergman & Associates;* **168,** Rick Smolan/*Contact/Woodfin Camp;* **170,** *Grant Heilman;* **171,** top, *Doug Wechsler;* bottom, *Bruce Coleman;* **172,** *Grant Heilman;* **173,** left, David C. Fritts/*Earth Scenes;* right, F. G. Love; **174,** left, L. S. Stepanowicz/*Photo Researchers;* right, Kim Taylor/*Bruce Coleman;* **175,** left, Dr. I. Metzner/*Peter Arnold;* right, Manfred Kage/*Peter Arnold;* **176,** Runk/Schoenberger/*Grant Heilman;* **177,** top, Breck P. Kent; bottom, Gordon Leedale/*Photo Researchers;* **178,** Oxford Scientific Films/*Animals Animals;* **179,** top left, Robert P. Carr/*Bruce Coleman;* top right, Heather Angel/*Biofotos;* bottom, Hal McKusick/*dpi;* **180,** top left; Manuel Rodriguez; top right, Cal Harbert/*dpi;* bottom left, John H. Gerard/*dpi;* bottom right, Manuel Rodriguez; **182,** top, Heather Angel/*Biofotos;* bottom, Eric V. Gravé/*Phototake;* **183,** Runk/Schoenberger/*Grant Heilman;* **184,** Cary Wolinsky/*Stock Boston;* **185,** Charles Ott/*dpi;* **186,** Dr. E. R. Degginger; **187,** top, David M. Stone; bottom, John H. Gerard/*dpi;* **188,** Ken Karp; **192,** Fred Bavendam/*Peter Arnold;* **194,** left, J. M. Barrs/*dpi;* right, *Field Museum of Natural History, Chicago;* **195,** top, Wendy Neefus/*Earth Scenes;* bottom, Adrienne T. Gibson/*Earth Scenes;* **196,** Jerome Wexler/*dpi;* **197,** Wendy Neefus/*Earth Scenes;* **198,** top left, Robert L. Dunne/*Bruce Coleman;* top right, Robert L. Dunne/*Bruce Coleman;* bottom right, Jerry Howard/*Photo Researchers;* **199,** Richard Kolar/*Earth Scenes;* **200,** top, *Ardea Photographs: London;* bottom, Manuel Rodriguez; **201,** left, *Peter Arnold;* right, Breck P. Kent/*Earth Scenes;* **202,** left, David M. Stone; right, *dpi;* **204,** top, Robert Weinreb/*Bruce Coleman;* bottom, W. H. Hodge/*Peter Arnold;* **205,** top, Norman O. Tomalin/*Bruce Coleman;* bottom, Charlie Ott/*dpi;* **206,** Darwin Van Campen/*dpi;* **207,** top, Manuel Rodriguez; bottom, Manuel Rodriguez; **208,** Patti Murray/*Animals Animals;* **209,** Elliott Varner Smith/*International Stock Photos;* **210,** Oxford Scientific Films/G. I. Bernard/*Earth Scenes;* **211,** left, Ann Hagen Griffith/*OPC;* center, Breck P. Kent/*Earth Scenes;* right, Marcia W. Griffen/*Earth Scenes;* **216,** Stephen Dalton/*Animals Animals;* **218,** top left, Stephen Dalton/*Animals Animals;* top right, Dr. E. R. Degginger/*Animals Animals;* bottom left, Tim Rock/*Animals Animals;* bottom right, Dr. E. R. Degginger/*Animals Animals;* **220,** left, Mike Schick/*Animals Animals;* top right, Carl Roessler/*Animals Animals;* bottom right, Carl Roessler/*Animals Animals;* **221,** top, Oxford Scientific Films/G. I. Bernard/*Animals Animals;* bottom, Steve Earley; **222,** top, Runk/Schoenberger/*Grant Heilman;* bottom left, Carl Roessler/*Animals Animals;* bottom right, Z. Leszczynski/*Animals Animals;* **223,** top, Jeff Rotman; bottom, Tim Rock/*Animals Animals;* **224,** Oxford Scientifc Films/*Animals Animals;* **225,** left, Phil Degginger/*Bruce Coleman;* right, G. I. Bernard/Oxford Scientific Films/*Animals Animals;* **226,** top, Runk/Schoenberger/*Grant Heilman;* bottom, *L. V. Bergman;* **228,** Hans Pfletschinger/*Peter Arnold;* **229,** *Culver Pictures;* **230,** Harry Hartman/*Bruce Coleman;* **231,** left, Hans Pfletschinger/*Peter Arnold;* right, Phil Degginger/*Bruce Coleman;* **232,** top, Bill Wood/*Bruce Coleman;* bottom left, Douglas Faulkner/*Photo Researchers;* bottom right, Jack Dermid; **233,** top, *Grant Heilman;* bottom, Steinhart Aquarium/Tom McHugh/*Photo Researchers;* **234,** top, Jeff Rotman; bottom, Z. Leszczynski/*Animals Animals;* **235,** left, Jeff Foott/*Bruce Coleman;* right, Phil Dotson/*dpi;* **236,** top, Fred Bavendam/*Peter Arnold;* bottom, Steinhart Aquarium/Tom McHugh/*Photo Researchers;* **237,** Jeff Rotman; **238,** top, Steve Martin/*Tom Stack;* bottom, Richard Kolar; **239,** top, W. Bayer/*Bruce Coleman;* bottom, John Shaw; **240,** top left, James H. Carmichael, Jr./*Bruce Coleman;* top right, John Shaw; bottom, M. P. L. Fogden/*Bruce Coleman;* **241,** left, Hans Pfletschinger/*Peter Arnold;* right, Runk/Schoenberger/*Grant Heilman;* **242,** Raymond A. Mendez/*Animals Animals;* **243,** Manuel Rodriguez; **244,** top and bottom left, John H. Gerard/*dpi;* top right, John H. Gerard/*dpi;* bottom, Verna R. Johnson/*dpi;* **245,** top, Stephen Dalton/*Animals Animals;* bottom, Phil Dotson/*dpi;* **246,** Leeanne Schmidt/*dpi;* **247,** left, Oxford Scientific Films/Stephen Dalton/*Animals Animals; bottom right, Jack Dermid; top right, Peter Ward/Bruce Coleman;* center right, Thomas Eisner/Daniel Aneshansley/*Discover* magazine; **255,** top, Carl Roessler/*Bruce Coleman;* bottom, Fred Bavendam/*Peter Arnold;* **256,** left, Roessler/*Animals Animals;* right, C. C. Lockwood/*Animals Animals;* bottom, Heather Angel/*Biofotos;* **257,** Valerie Taylor/*Ardea: London:* ***258,*** *top left, Valerie Taylor/Ardea: London;* top right, Bob Evans/*Peter Arnold;* bottom, Bill Wood/*Bruce Coleman;* **259,** left, Dr. E. R. Degginger; right, Oxford Scientific Films/*Animals Animals;* **260,** top, Andrew Gifford/*dpi;* bottom, Michael Fogden/*Bruce Coleman;* **261,** left, Brian Rogers/*Biofotos;* right, Hans Pfletschinger/*Peter Arnold;* **262,** left, John Shaw/*Bruce Coleman;* right, Robert L. Dunne/*Bruce Coleman;* **263,** top, Runk/Schoenberger/*Grant Heilman;* bottom, Dr. E. R. Degginger; **264,** Miguel Castro/*Photo Researchers;* **265,** Dr. E. R. Degginger; **266,** top left, E. Hanumantha Raa/*Photo Researchers;* top right, Kjell B. Sandved/*Photo Researchers;* bottom, Susan Pierres/*Peter Arnold;* **267,** left, Tom Brakefield/*Bruce Coleman;* right, John H. Pontier/*Animals Animals;* **268,** Phil Degginger; **269,** left, Carol Hughes/*Bruce Coleman;* right, G. Ziesler/*Peter Arnold;* **270,** left, Richard Kolar/*Animals Animals;* right, Marty Stouffer/© *Animals Animals;* **271,** Doug Allan/Oxford Scientific Films/*Animals Animals;* **272,** Dr. E. R. Degginger; **273,** top left, James R. Leard/*dpi;* bottom left, John E. Swedberg/*Bruce Coleman;* right, Panuska/*dpi;* **274,** top, John L. Pontier/*Animals Animals;* bottom, R. W. Young/*dpi;* **275,** Dr. E. R. Degginger/*Animals Animals;* **280,** Taronga Zoo, Sydney—Tom McHugh/*Photo Researchers;* **282,** F. Sohier/*Ardea: London;* **283,** Jerry Frank/*dpi;* **284,** Jen & Des Bartlett/*Bruce Coleman;* **285,** left, Jean-Paul Ferrero/*Ardea: London;* right, Ken Stepnell/*Taurus Photos;* **286,** top, Tom McHugh/*Photo Researchers;* bottom, Rob Chabot/*dpi;* **287,** top, Leonard Lee Rue III/*Photo Researchers;* bottom, Jen & Des Bartlett/*Bruce Coleman;* **288,** top, Erwin and Peggy Bauer/*Bruce Coleman;* bottom, John Serao/*Photo Researchers;* **289,** top left, Leonard Lee Rue III/*dpi;* top right, Stouffer Productions/*Animals Animals;* bottom, Dr. Melvin D. Tuttle; **290,** Al Giddings/*Bruce Coleman;* **291,** John Dominis/*Life* magazine © 1967, Time, Inc.; Barry L. Runk/*Grant Heilman;* **292,** left, Phil Dotson/*dpi;* right, Gunter Ziesler/*Peter Arnold;* **293,** left, J. Alex Langley/*dpi;* right, Leonard Lee Rue III/*dpi;* **294,** left, J. Alex Langley/*dpi;* top right, Dr. E.R. Degginger; bottom right, Norman Owen Tomalin/*Bruce Coleman;* **294,** top right, Dr. E.R. Degginger; **295,** top left, Stephen Dalton/*Photo Researchers;* top right, C. Robinson & J.A. Grant/*Bruce Coleman;* bottom, Charlie Ott/*dpi;* **296,** right, Jeff Foott/*Bruce Coleman;* left, M. Timothy O'Keefe/*Tom Stack & Associates;* **297,** top left, Halperin/*Animals Animals;* top right, Robert W. Hernandez/*Photo Researchers;* bottom, Norman O. Tomalin/*Bruce Coleman;* **303,** top, Wrangham/*Anthro Photo;* bottom, Wrangham/*Anthro Photo;* **306,** Jeff Foott/*Bruce Coleman;* **308,** Merle H. Jensen; **309,** Runk/Schoenberger/*Grant Heilman;* **310,** O.S. Pettingill, Jr./*Photo Researchers;* **312,** © William Curtsinger/*Photo Researchers;* **314,** © Porterfield/Chickering/*Photo Researchers;* **315,** Paul Kennedy/*Leo de Wys;* **316,** left, Loomis Dean/*Life* magazine © 1954, Time, Inc.; **317,** left, The Bettmann Archive; right, NASA; **319,** Ron Sefton/*dpi;* **320,** Margaret Durrance/*Photo Researchers;* **321,** © Tatarsky/*dpi;* **322,** Ken Karp; **323,** top, J. Alex Langley/*dpi;* bottom, Runk/Schoenberger/*Grant Heilman;* **324,** Ken Karp; **328,** Red Huber/*The Orlando Sentinel;* **330,** © Stan Pantovic/*Photo Researchers;* **331,** top, B. Benedict/*H.*